INTRODUCTION TO CHRISTIAN ETHICS

A READER

Edited by

Ronald P. Hamel and Kenneth R. Himes, OFM

PAULIST PRESS
New York and New Jersey

Library of Congress Cataloging-in-Publication Data

Introduction to Christian ethics : a reader / [edited] by Ronald P.
    Hamel & Kenneth R. Himes.
        p.   cm.
    Includes bibliographies.
    ISBN 0-8091-3065-3 : $12.95 (est.)
    1. Christian ethics—Catholic authors. 2. Catholic Church-
-Doctrines. I. Hamel. Ronald P., 1946– . II. Himes, Kenneth R.,
    1950– .
    BJ1249.I57   1989
    241′.042—dc20

89-3265
CIP

Published by Paulist Press
997 Macarthur Boulevard
Mahwah, New Jersey 07430

Printed and bound in the United States of America

Contents

Introduction 1

Part 1
SITUATING OURSELVES

Christian Ethics: Biblical and Historical Perspectives

1. The Bible and Christian Morality 9
   Seán Freyne

2. How Free and Creative Was and Is Moral Theology? 33
   Bernard Häring, CSsR

Shifts in Catholic Moral Theology

3. The Human Person in Contemporary Theology:
   From Human Nature to Authentic Subjectivity 49
   Michael J. Himes

4. New Patterns of Relationship:
   Beginnings of a Moral Revolution 63
   Margaret A. Farley, R.S.M.

5. Values, Victims, and Visions 80
   James Gaffney

Part 2
MORAL THEOLOGY: THE NATURE OF THE DISCIPLINE

Overview of the Discipline's Subject Matter

6. Method in Moral Theology:
   An Overview from an American Perspective 90
   Charles E. Curran

7. The Structure and Basis of the Moral Experience 106
    Enda McDonagh

The Role of Faith in Christian Ethics

8. The Criterion for Deciding What Is Christian 120
    Hans Küng

9. Can Ethics Be Christian? Some Conclusions 133
    James M. Gustafson

10. Does Religious Faith Add to Ethical Perception? 140
    Richard A. McCormick

Part 3
THE MORAL SELF
AND THE SORT OF PERSON ONE IS AND BECOMES

Moral Character

11. Toward an Ethics of Character 151
    Stanley Hauerwas

Spirituality and Moral Character

12. Spiritual Life and Moral Life 163
    James M. Gustafson

13. Liturgy and Ethics: Some New Beginnings 175
    Donald E. Saliers

Freedom and Fundamental Option

14. Basic Freedom and Morality 187
    Josef Fuchs, SJ

Sin and Conversion

15. Missing the Mark 199
    Bruce Vawter

16. Sin and Conversion 206
    Josef Fuchs, SJ

17. Social Sin and Conversion:
    A Theology of the Church's Social Involvement 217
    Peter Henriot, SJ

18. Christian Conversion: Developmental and
    Theological Reflections on Young Thomas Merton 227
    Walter E. Conn

19. Conversion and Christian Ethics 242
    James P. Hanigan

Conscience and Moral Development

20. Conscience: The Sanctuary of Creative
    Fidelity and Liberty 252
    Bernard Häring, CSsR

21. Visions of Maturity 281
    Carol Gilligan

22. Disciplines: Repentance, Prayer and Service 293
    Craig Dykstra

Part 4
MAKING MORAL CHOICES:
RESOURCES FOR REFLECTION

Scripture

23. What Are They Saying About Scripture and Ethics? 313
    William Spohn, SJ

24. The Use of the Bible in Christian Ethics 322
    Bruce Birch and Larry Rasmussen

The Church as Teacher and Dissent in the Church

25. The Dogmatic Constitution on the Church 333
    Vatican Council II

26. Doctrinal Authority for a Pilgrim Church 336
    Avery Dulles, SJ

27. Canon 752 352

28. Reflections on a Canon 353
    Ladislas Orsy, SJ

29. Bishops, Theologians and Morality 359
    Josef Ratzinger

30. The Search for Truth in a Catholic Context 373
    Richard A. McCormick, SJ

31. Norms of Licit Theological Dissent 381
    National Conference of Catholic Bishops

32. Public Dissent in the Church 383
    Charles E. Curran

33. Conscience Formation and the Teaching of the Church 397
    William E. May

Reason and Natural Law

34. Can Moral Theology Ignore Natural Law? 407
    Bruno Schüller, SJ

35. The Traditional Concept of Natural Law: An Interpretation 413
    Columba Ryan, OP

The Empirical Sciences

36. The Relationship of Empirical Science to Moral Thought 428
    James M. Gustafson

Part 5
THE VOICE OF EXPERIENCE:
THE NATURE, USE AND LIMITS OF MORAL NORMS

The Meaning and Origin of Moral Norms

37. The Meaning of Moral Principle 443
    Denis F. O'Callaghan

Overview of the Debate

38. The Objective Moral Order: Reflections on Recent Research 454
      Philip S. Keane, SS

The Contemporary Debate

39. The Meaning and Limits of Moral Norms 470
      Richard Gula

40. The Absoluteness of Behavioral Moral Norms 48/
      Josef Fuchs, SJ

41. Catholic Ethics: Has the Norm for Rule-Making Changed? 513
      John R. Connery, SJ

Part 6
MAKING MORAL CHOICES:
"WHAT OUGHT I TO DO?"

The Moral Act

42. Ethics: How To Do It 533
      Daniel Maguire

43. Moral Methodology: A Case Study 551
      Lisa Sowle Cahill

Reason and Feeling in Moral Discernment

44. The Reasoning Heart:
      An American Approach to Christian Discernment 563
      William C. Spohn, SJ

45. Moral Discernment in the Christian Life 583
      James M. Gustafson

Acknowledgements

"Does Religious Faith Add to Ethical Perception?" by Richard A. McCormick, reprinted from *Personal Values In Public Policy*, edited by John C. Haughey, © 1979 by The Missionary Society of St. Paul the Apostle in the State of New York. Used by permission of Paulist Press. The Introduction to *What Are They Saying About Scripture And Ethics* by William C. Spohn, S. J. © 1984 by the author. Used by permission of Paulist Press. "The Meaning and Limits of Moral Norms" reprinted from *What Are They Saying About Moral Norms* by Richard M. Gula, S.S. © 1982 by the author. Used by permission of Paulist Press. "Ethics: How To Do It" from *Death By Choice* by Daniel Maguire. Copyright © 1973, 1974, 1984 by Daniel C. Maguire. Reprinted by permission of Doubleday, a division of Bantam, Doubleday, Dell Publishing Group, Inc. "Doctrinal Authority in a Pilgrim Church" from *The Resilient Church* by Avery Dulles. Copyright © 1977 by Avery Dulles. Reprinted by permission of Doubleday, a division of Bantam, Doubleday, Dell Publishing Group Inc. "The Criterion for Deciding What Is Christian" from *On Being Christian* by Hans Küng, translated by Edward Quinn. Copyright © 1976 by Doubleday, a division of Bantam, Doubleday, Dell Publishing Group, Inc. Reprinted by permission of the publisher. Bernard Häring, "Conscience: The Sanctuary of Creative Fidelity and Liberty," in *Free And Faithful In Christ*, vol 1 (New York: Crossroad © 1978). Reprinted by permission of The Crossroad Publishing Company. Bernard Häring, "How Free and Creative Was and Is Moral Theology?" in *Free And Faithful In Christ*, vol. 1 (New York: © 1978). Reprinted by permission of The Crossroad Publishing Company. "In a Different Voice: Visions of Maturity," is reprinted by permission of the publisher from *In A Different Voice: Psychological Theory And Women's Development*, by Carol Gilligan, Cambridge, Mass.: Harvard University Press, copyright © 1982 by Carol Gilligan. "Moral Discernment and the Christian Life," by James Gustafson is reprinted from *Norm And Context In Christian Ethics* edited by Gene Outka and Paul Ramsey with permission of Charles Scribner's Sons, an imprint of Macmillan Publishing Company, Copyright © 1968 Charles Scribner's Sons. "The Use of the Bible in Christian Ethics" is reprinted with permission of the publisher from *The Bible And Ethics In The Christian Life* by Bruce Birch and Larry Rasmussen. Copyright © Augsburg Publishing House. "Basic Freedom and Morality" from *Human Values And Christian Morality* by Josef Fuchs, S. J., is reproduced by permission of the publishers, Gill and Macmillan, Dublin. "The Bible and Christian Morality" by Professor Sean Freyne from *Morals, Law And Authority*, ed. James Mackey is reproduced by permission of the publishers, Gill and Macmillan, Dublin. "The Meaning and the Structure of Moral Experience" from *Gift And Call* by Enda McDonagh is reproduced by permission of the publishers, Gill and MacMillan, Dublin.

Introduction

The Second Vatican Council (1962–1965) was by almost any standard the most important event in the life of the modern church. This historic gathering of Catholic bishops launched changes in theology and practice that were to dramatically affect the lives of Roman Catholics in the decades that have followed.

One of the areas most profoundly affected by this renewal is moral theology. While the revisioning of Catholic moral theology began long before the council, the endeavor received significant impetus from the bishops. In one of their sixteen documents, they pointed to the need for renewal in all areas of theology, but noted particular urgency for a rethinking of moral theology.[1] Efforts in this regard have been proceeding at a rapid pace since the closing of the council in 1965.

What has resulted is not only an abundance of new insights into and reformulations of Christian moral life, but also a change in the audience to whom moral theology is taught. Prior to Vatican II, moral theology was largely the concern of seminaries. This is exemplified by the textbooks of moral theology. They were written by clergy for the training of seminarians especially for their work in the confessional. These textbooks were stylized in format, quite similar in content, and focused on particular moral judgments about this or that act. They were the work of a very few authors and saw numerous editions with slight modifications. The key moral questions seemed to be "Is it a sin?" and, if so, "Is it mortal or venial?"

However, with Vatican II's emphasis on the *universal* call to holiness, moral theology, that is, how one lives the Christian life, became the concern not only of clergy but of all believers. The old textbooks were no longer adequate. They contained an impoverished understanding of the moral life, spoke in a stilted, often legalistic language, and frequently did not address the real life experience of Catholics. Over the past three decades, and especially since the council, numerous efforts have been made to rectify these shortcomings. The efforts have borne fruit. But they have also created new problems, one of which, we believe, is the difficulty of using any single text for an introductory course in Christian ethics.

We are both teachers. One of us teaches at a Catholic liberal arts college and the other is on the faculty of a graduate school of Catholic theology that prepares people for ministry. Together we have nearly twenty years' experience teaching an introductory course in Christian ethics. Virtually every year we have puzzled over which text to use. We know that many of our colleagues have done the same. Over the years there have been a number of very good contributions, ground-breaking publishing efforts, in this area. Yet none has quite accomplished what we had

---

[1] Vatican Council II, "Decree on Priestly Formation," par. 16.

hoped it would. Perhaps it is still too early in this era of moral theology renewal to expect a single synthetic volume. As a result, we have found ourselves directing students to library reserve shelves for journal articles or book chapters that supplemented the texts we were using. This volume is born of our experienced need for developing a set of readings useful in teaching basic Christian ethics.

We have attempted to put under one cover some of the best material available in the revisioning of Catholic moral theology. Our aim has been to provide the advanced undergraduate and beginning graduate student of Christian ethics with a collection of readings that will acquaint him/her with the scope of the discipline, some of the best contemporary scholarship in the field, and a number of the major figures and developments in the renewal of Catholic moral theology.

Several factors have influenced our selection of readings. The volume's contents reflect our commitment to the Roman Catholic theological tradition, and our concern to provide a text for audiences that are primarily Catholic. Hence, by a large majority, the authors included are Roman Catholic. We did not, however, hesitate to include other Christian theologians. It seems clear to us that doing Christian ethics today must be an ecumenical endeavor. While preserving the best of our own tradition, we need to be open to the insights of other faith traditions, particularly those who share our belief in Jesus as Redeemer. Several Protestant scholars, in fact, have made significant contributions to the on-going renewal of moral theology. Some of their works are represented here.

Of the Catholic theologians included, most would reflect what we consider to be a "mainstream" perspective. By that we mean that they share in the theological vision of the majority of moral theologians teaching and writing today. This perspective might be called "revisionist" in that it has taken seriously the mandate of Vatican II to reform the discipline.

We do not wish to suggest that there is a univocal approach to the discipline nor consensus on all issues. On controversial issues, we have included opposing voices. It is important, we believe, that legitimate concerns and objections to revisionist positions be heard and be seriously considered, and that students become acquainted with the arguments and some of the major participants on all sides of debated matters. Two such areas are the exceptionless nature of behavioral moral norms and dissent from official church teaching on moral matters.

The fact that this collection is intended as an introduction to the study of Christian ethics further influenced the selection of articles. A quick glance at the table of contents will indicate that essays dealing with specific moral issues as well as with social ethics have not been included. These are undoubtedly critical areas of Christian moral life and may well be included in an introductory course. Again questions of space prevailed along with our desire to focus on methodology and on the foundational aspects of Christian ethics.

Within these constraints, we have tried to provide a variety of materials. Some selections are the work of established, world-renowned scholars. Others are by second generation revisionist moral theologians and their critics. While a good number of the principal contributors to the renewal of moral theology are represented here, certainly all are not.

Selections were also made with an eye to readability. Many fine essays were not included because of their difficulty and/or technical nature. Of those that have been included, some will be more suitable to the advanced undergraduate student and others to the graduate student. Most, we believe, will be challenging to the good student, but hopefully will not be beyond the capacities of either audience. In places, we have included several articles on a single topic to allow for a professor's discretion as to which reading might be most apt for a given class.

Inevitably, some professors will find that a favorite essay of theirs is not found here. We share in that disappointment. We regret that several authors, whose work we admire and from whom we and our students have learned, are not included in this volume. But at some point practical considerations of size and expense governed our decisions about what to publish in this type of anthology. Still, we believe that what we have included offers a satisfying mix of authors and topics.

The arrangement of the readings reflects the way we teach our own courses—beginning with some historical assessment of where we are in moral theology and what moral theology is, proceeding then to an examination of the nature of the moral agent, and concluding with an investigation of resources and methods for moral decision-making. There is, of course, no implication that this arrangement is the only or the best way to structure a course in introductory moral theology. Professors should feel comfortable assigning readings in any order that fits their own course outline.

There are six major segments to the volume and each of these has subsections. At the beginning of each of the main divisions, there is a brief introduction that provides an orientation to the readings. The introductions are not summaries of the essays, but are rather explanations of what each selection is intended to contribute to the overall aim of the volume.

For many years now, each of us has recognized a void in the area of introductory texts in moral theology for use in colleges and universities as well as in seminaries. We hope this collaborative effort helps to fill that void. For professors, we hope it will provide you with a new resource —primary texts on foundational issues by principal contributors to the revisioning of Catholic moral theology. For students, we hope it will provide you an entry into the discipline of Christian ethics, an opportunity to become acquainted with and dialogue with recent thoughts and thinkers in the field. Above all, we hope it will help to broaden and deepen your commitment to living the moral life in a Christian context. For both students and professors, it is our wish that the pages convey some of the excitement and complexity, the deep faith and intellectual rigor, the joys and the pains of continuously probing the meaning of living morally as a Christian.

Finally, a word of thanks to the scholars whose works are included in this volume. We are grateful not only for their permission to reprint materials, sometimes in an edited version, but also for the contribution these men and women have made to the teaching ministry of the church. We also wish to thank our colleague, Richard Sparks, C.S.P., for his suggestion that we collaborate on this project and for his encouragement, gentle nudgings, advice and editorial assistance throughout. Many other colleagues have made helpful suggestions. To them we are also grateful. And, lastly, we are indebted to Katherine Ruhland, Virginia Lyons, and Jeannine Harff, at the College of St. Thomas, and to William Nolan and John McHugh, theology majors at St. Thomas, for their invaluable technical assistance.

Ronald P. Hamel
College of St. Thomas

Kenneth R. Himes, O.F.M.
Washington Theological Union

Part 1

SITUATING OURSELVES

part 1

Situating Ourselves

Introduction

Without a knowledge of the past it is impossible to understand the present. This is as true for moral theology as it is for any other area of life. Just as a friendship cannot be understood solely by the words and actions of the present moment, so, too, an understanding of moral theology can only be achieved by some awareness of how the present came to be. The difficulty is deciding how far back in history one needs to go in order to have an adequate context for understanding.

In the case of Catholic moral theology, it seemed clear to us that no adequate account could ignore the foundational history of the Christian faith as this is recorded in the Bible. Thus, we have included an essay by Seán Freyne in which he examines how the people of the covenant approached the moral life in the various times and contexts of its history.

The second essay by Bernard Häring is also historical. In it he surveys the history of moral theology in the Catholic tradition, acquainting the reader with many of the important figures and ideas that have shaped the way moral theology has been done within the church.

There is, however, more to situating oneself than knowing how one came to a particular place. Besides knowing something of the shifts that have occurred in moral theology in the past, it is necessary to grasp why developments are continuing to occur today. No one living in our fast-paced world needs to be told of the reality of change in our lives. What may escape notice, however, is that it is not just the things around us that are changing, but we are also subject to change. Perhaps no single factor is more important for understanding moral theology today than an appreciation of how history shapes our self-understanding.

This is precisely the subject of Michael Himes' essay. In it he describes how historical consciousness, an awareness of the time-conditioned nature of human existence, has influenced contemporary theology through a revision of what it means to be human. A particular expression of historical consciousness that has had great impact upon theology, especially moral theology, is the development of feminism. Margaret Farley discusses the particular contribution that feminism can make to a fuller, more complete understanding of the moral life. James Gaffney's brief essay comments upon a number of elements that characterize contemporary moral theology in distinction from its recent past. His reflection on the state of moral theology brings the historical essay of Häring up to the present day.

1

The Bible and Christian Morality

Seán Freyne

In recent times all Catholic theology has had a *crise de conscience* concerning its use of the Bible. Centuries of a tape-and-scissors use in theology manuals has given way to a more accurate determination of the meaning of the Scripture text in the light of historical and literary criticism. But this growing awareness of the need for more refined handling of the Bible by theologians does not always have positive results. Texts no longer say what they appear to say and the overall impression is one of frustration if not futility in this task of relating Scripture to theology. A new approach is called for, one that can do full justice to the exigencies of biblical science and yet has something fruitful to offer theologians as they grapple with contemporary problems. This essay offers the opportunity for such an approach.

One cannot hope to give a detailed treatment of the whole topic of biblical morality. I propose instead to take the Bible as reflecting the beliefs, attitudes and manners of the peo-

ple of the covenant, the people of faith. In it I hope to discover a record of how this people of faith approached the problem of moral living throughout the various circumstances of its history from the Mesopotamia of Abraham to the Rome of Paul. Looking at the Bible in this way one is not so concerned with specific contents of biblical morality, since one can readily recognize the time-conditioned character of much of it. Rather I try to discover what was distinctive about the approach of the people of the Bible to morality. How did faith determine and enlighten its conduct; how much better off is it than its neighbours in discovering how one should lead the good life and in what that good life consists? Such a use of the Bible in theology seems to me best to take account of its historical and time-conditioned nature, on the one hand, and yet accept its normative value as God's word for the Church of every age, on the other.

One could answer the question of what is distinctive about biblical morality briefly by

This article originally appeared in James E. Mackey, ed., Morals, Law and Authority *(Dayton: Pflaum, 1969), pp. 1–88.*

saying that it regards man's behaviour as the direct and immediate response to God's revealed will. On page after page of the Old Testament Yahweh is introduced as the ultimate source of and the sole justification for the conduct that is being demanded from his people. Of course this does not mean that biblical morality is not interested in the dignity of one's fellow humans but such an interest is based on the fact that, as part of God's creation, all enjoy a communal relation of friendship with their creator. In the New Testament God's revealed will has become incarnate in Christ and so the New Testament writers constantly draw attention to the pattern of his earthly life, and his present demands as glorified Lord on those who believe in him, when proposing to them a way of life that is Christian.

Such a general answer opens the way to two further questions which will serve as directions for this essay. Firstly, if biblical morality is concerned with God's revealed will, one immediately asks how is this will revealed to Israel, and how did she discover it? Does Israel consider herself as having an immediate access to this will by contrast with the other nations, and if so, does this dispense her from involving herself in the historical discovery of what that will entails? Secondly and relatedly, how does Yahweh's will impose itself on Israel and how does she consider herself bound by it?

In speaking of Israel here we do not confine ourselves to the people of the Old Testament merely, but include also the people of the new covenant. The name Israel describes the religious reality that is God's people, and can equally well apply to the Christian community, for Christ did not form a new people, but rather he established a new covenant with God's people. In other words there is a basic unity in the people of the Bible, both Old and New Testament, something that is fully recognized by Christ and the New Testament writers after him.

A consideration of the two questions just outlined is of immediate interest to current discussions on morality. If we find that God's people in its formative period has a particular approach to thinking about the good life and the way it proposes this to the man of faith, then clearly the Church of every other age must treat its moral problems in a similar way. Only then is God's will in leaving the Scriptures to the Church as the source of its life and faith, fully respected.

I. The Content of Biblical Morality

A reading of the historical books of the Old Testament gives on the whole a unified picture of Israel's origins, her period of slavery in Egypt and her entry into the promised land. However, historical and literary criticism has shown that this unity is theological rather than historical. Archaeology has shed new light on the varied social conditions of Israel's ancestors of the patriarchal period;[1] the exodus from Egypt may well have involved several separate and unconnected revolts against Egyptian tyranny, the accounts of which were later fused together within the common stream of Israel's faith;[2] the taking possession of Palestine appears to have been the outcome of a long and involved process of settlement rather than the result of a united military onslaught as described in the book of Joshua.[3] Such heterogeneity of origin and social background is clearly reflected in the various laws and customs that we find being presented in one block as God's will for his covenant people in later Israel. This code of behaviour for day to day living has, when examined, all the marks of its origin within the social and cultural milieu of the ancient Near East, and this would seem to indicate that Israel like any other nation discovered it there experientially from the demands of life in that setting. In other words, faith and revelation has not taken early Israel out of its historical setting or rendered the human search for such a code unnecessary or superfluous.

Early Israel

It is well known that there are two different forms of law in the Pentateuch, apodeictic and casuistic. According to the classic study by Albrecht Alt[4] the former is unique in Israel and we shall discuss its significance presently. On the other hand, the casuistic form, i.e. that which proposes a law from the starting point of a particular case, is widespread in the other legal systems of that epoch and region. The Code of Hammurabi (c. 1700 B.C.) from Babylon, for example, is really a collection of such casuistic laws. Thus Israel, for these laws at least, draws on a common tradition, or better is part of a common tradition that determines both the form and the content of her ethical system.

Many of the customs from the pre-Mosaic period, as, for example, a barren wife accepting as heir the child her husband has by a slave girl (Gn 15:1–4), or possession of household gods giving the right of inheritance (Gn 31:19–35), have been paralleled by the discoveries in Mesopotamia dating from the second millennium B.C. The oldest collection of casuistic laws in the Pentateuch is the so-called Book of the Covenant (Ex 21:1–23:19). This collection probably dates from the time when

Israel was already in possession of the land, that is from the early monarchical period, but form critical analysis shows that some at least of its contents date from much earlier. It differs from the two later codes of Deuteronomy and the Holiness code (Lv 16–26), in that it contains very little religious motivation, and is more like a collection of purely secular laws. (See however, Ex 22:21–27; 23:9.) Even a casual glance at these laws, dealing with slavery, property rights, money lending etc. makes it clear that they have to do with everyday occurrences of town (e.g. Ex 22:24) and country (e.g. Ex 21:37) life. The tone throughout is for the most part utilitarian, as is evidenced, for example, in this description of the Sabbath law (Ex 23:12): 'For six days you shall do your work, but stop on the seventh day, so that your ox and your donkey may rest, and the son of your slave girl may have a breathing space'. (Contrast the religious motivation based on the story of creation, Ex 20:8–11.) Clearly therefore, this is popular morality derived from varied circumstances and backgrounds and introduced now into a covenant setting.

The question must now be asked to what extent this popular morality is more refined in Israel than among her neighbours? Clearly, a detailed survey is outside the limits of this study, but some general observations seem pertinent. One notices that the Israelite casuistic law is not as detailed or extensive as the Code of Hammurabi or the Assyrian code. This could mean that many areas were left to the moral sense of individuals or clans with faith in a just and moral God Yahweh as a basis for mutual trust and respect. It would seem also that there was greater respect for human life in Israel: thus property offences do not carry the death penalty; slaves are to be protected from inhuman abuse (Ex 21:20, 26 f.); bodily mutilations as punishment for certain crimes are missing, with the exception of Deuteronomy 25:11 f. There is no class distinction in the administration of Israelite justice and in fact widows and orphans are given express protection by the law (Ex 22:22 f.).

In all these examples it would seem that faith in Yahweh, the God who had liberated Israel from the slavery of Egypt, before whom all are equal, since all are created by him, had the effect of achieving a more refined moral sense. However, this conclusion based on general observations, can yield to contrary proof. The Code of Hammurabi gives to wives many rights which are not mentioned in Israel in regard to divorce, debts incurred by her husband etc. She is therefore given greater protection by the law. Eichrodt sees this merely as a sign of a more highly developed urban life by comparison with the rural and clan civilization in Israel.[5] This may indeed be so, but it still shows that revelation alone did not determine the formal content of Israel's ethical code, or free her from the obligation of purifying her popular morality through the centuries, prompted even by contacts with her pagan neighbours; and that the moral code of the people of faith can in some respects lag behind that of others at least in its explicit formulation.

The Decalogue is the best known group of apodeictic laws (i.e. 'you shall . . .' and 'you shall not . . .') in the Pentateuch (Ex 20:1–17; Dt 5:6–21), but there is evidence of similar lists at Deuteronomy 27:15–26; Leviticus 19:11–18; Exodus 21;12:15–17. To understand the function of such lists it is important to give them their true setting in the cultic life of the people, as can be seen, for example, from Psalm 81. The introduction of this psalm clearly indicates its processional tone on the occasion of the new moon festival; it then goes on to recall Israel's wanderings in the desert, and finally through the psalmist Yahweh proclaims the first commandment to the assembly: there shall be no strange gods among you (verse 9). Probably the whole Decalogue was recited at such gatherings at the central sanctuary when the community rededicated itself to Yahweh.[6] In the book of Joshua, chapter 24 describes one such ceremony in which the Sinai covenant is renewed. Recent analysis of this chapter has discovered beneath the present Deuteronomic reaction an earlier narrative of a gathering, in which the tribes who had not shared in the exodus experience were offered a share in the covenant with Yahweh by Joshua and his house.[7] In all probability tribal law determined conduct at the local level, but it was necessary to have some statement of what belief in the common god, Yahweh, demanded of all Israel, and such lists as the Decalogue indicated the various areas in which Yahweh's will was absolute. Seen in this light one can understand the negative form of most of the commandments, which was probably the form of all originally. They do not attempt to prescribe a total ethical system for Israel, but rather describe what was absolutely displeasing to Yahweh. As von Rad puts it: 'If then these commandments do not subject life to a comprehensive normative law, it is more appropriate for us to say that in certain marginal situations they demand avowal of Yahweh, and this avowal consists precisely in abstaining from doing certain things displeasing to him'.[8]

Once we see the Decalogue in this covenant context as describing the minimum requirements which faith in Yahweh demanded, we shall never be tempted to regard it as a set of immutable principles from which a detailed moral code can be derived. Certainly Israel did not consider it to be such, as can be seen from the existence of several different lists, and the additions and changes which they all underwent in the course of the centuries. Besides, as we have seen, the Book of the Covenant (Ex 21–23), with its detailed prescriptions, was in later times set side by side with the Decalogue (Ex 20). This shows that Israel felt the need to spell out the moral obligations of the covenant people far beyond the situations described by or contained in the Decalogue. By thus introducing popular morality, derived as we have seen from various sources and backgrounds, into the covenant context, Israel was saying that her faith assured her that she was doing Yahweh's will in her moral behaviour. She was also recognizing that the covenant grace did not dispense her from discovering that will historically.

The Prophets

All modern study of the prophets recognizes that they share in the mainstream of Israel's religious tradition, and are concerned with the people's faithlessness to the God who saved them from Egypt. We cannot regard law and prophets as two mutually opposed religious forces in Israel, as some earlier critics have attempted to do.[9] This can be shown, among other ways, from a consideration of the prophets' castigation of Israel's moral failures. They see them as failures to observe the covenant law, and the curses that were the punishment for such failures in the covenant context (e.g. Dt 27), can now be re-interpreted in terms of God's judgements against Israel. Thus the prophet Nathan confronts David with his violation of the commandments on adultery and murder in arranging for the death of Uriah in battle because he desired his wife, Bathsheba (2 Sm 12). The divine judgement

inherent in the law is manifested in this instance by the death of the child who is the offspring of this unlawful union. Elijah likewise confronts the king Ahab and Jezebel, his wife, for taking possession of Nathan's property in direct violation of the Decalogue (1 Kgs 21). The curse is to fall on Ahab's son, Joram, according to the prophet; and when he was actually put to death by Jehu all Israel remembered Elijah's word (2 Kgs 9:26).

The example of these two early prophets is carried on by the later writing prophets. One finds in these a repeated appeal to a collection of apodeictic laws like those of the Decalogue in order to confront Israel with her moral failures: 'Hear the word of the Lord, O people of Israel; for the Lord has a controversy with the inhabitants of the land. There is no faithfulness or kindness, and no knowledge of God in the land; there is swearing, lying, killing, stealing and committing adultery; they break all bounds and murder follows murder' (Hos 4:1 f.; cf. also Jer 7:1–11; Ez 22:6–12).

The striking condemnation of the social ills of his day by the prophet Amos is clearly based on certain prescriptions of the Book of the Covenant relating to unjust treatment of the poor, taking of garments as pledges and taking interest on loans granted to the needy (Ex 22:21 f., 25, 26 f.). These are all specifically mentioned by the prophet as he castigates the rich of the northern kingdom (Am 2:6; 3:10; 5:11; 8:4–8).

In laying so much stress on Israel's failures to observe the law of Yahweh the prophets were making a very important clarification in regard to the nature of her response. Cultic worship meant little to Yahweh as long as his people refused genuine worship of the heart by a life lived in fidelity to the covenant law.[10] The poignant outbursts of Amos, 'I hate, I despise your feasts, and I take no delight in your solemn assemblies' (Am 5:21–24), is re-echoed by all subsequent prophets: Hosea 6:6; Jeremiah 7:21–23; Isaiah 1:11–17; Micah 6:6–8. More than anything else what Yahweh required from his people was the worship of an upright life: 'Wash yourselves; make yourselves clean; remove the evil you are doing from before my eyes; cease to do evil, learn to do good; seek justice, correct oppression; defend the fatherless, plead for the widow' (Is 1:16 f.; cf. Am 5:15).

We must understand this apparent opposition to the cult precisely in the light of its failure to motivate the people to observe the law, which, we have seen, had its original home within the cult at the great yearly gatherings of all the tribes at the central sanctuary. Thus the prophets clearly recognize where Israel's primary responsibility lies, and their major contribution to moral thinking consists in highlighting its absolutely fundamental importance in the covenant relationship between Yahweh and his people.

However, it must be stated that the prophetic movement also contributed greatly to a refinement of Israel's moral sense through the centuries.[11] The more the nation's leaders took a path which led to connivance with foreign powers and ignoring of Yahweh as the director of Israel's destiny, the more the prophets realized that Israel's future as God's people could never lie in great political success. War and the virtues associated with it are no longer a sacred duty as in the earlier period, but are seen to belong to the secular sphere, and even as opposed to God's will. Instead the emphasis is on building up the nation internally through care and concern for the needy and oppressed. These are the special concern of Yahweh, the faithful shepherd of his oppressed flock (Is 7:7 f.; 17:12 f.; Jer 25:15 f.; Ez 25 etc.). Conformity to Yahweh's will demands the same kind of interest in the af-flicted within the community of Israel. Thus an ethic of suffering emerges, and arrogance and power are no longer signs of Yahweh's favour. The ideal he looks for is rather humble submission to life's disappointments, for it is to his *anawîm* that he grants his mercy (Am 2:6–7; Is 3:14–15; Jer 5:28 etc.).[12]

Clearly then, the prophets' contribution to moral teaching in Israel is not based on any special revelation of content from God. Rather, they refined the traditional morality in certain respects, and they stressed the centrality of good moral living, however its details were discovered, in the Israelite's response to the God who had so graciously approached him.

The Wisdom Literature

The Wisdom literature is of special importance for our enquiry since it is largely concerned with the good life. Once again, more important than the actual content is the way in which the Wisdom tradition, with its secular and extra-Israelite origins, came to be accepted as part of all Israel's religious inheritance. This only happened, of course, in the post-exilic community of the law in the wake of the disillusionment of the high hopes at the return from Babylon. The emphasis came to be placed more and more on the problems of everyday living rather than on any immediate hope of a decisive intervention by Yahweh in favour of his people.[13] The older Wisdom material is pressed into service of the law, so that gradually scribe and wisdom teacher come to be identified, as in the writings of Ben Sirach (Ecclesiasticus, c. 190 B.C.), for example. Originally, this tradition had flourished outside Israel, mainly in court circles, so that the recollection that it was Solomon who introduced wisdom to Israel is probably correct, for we know that he organized the court on Egyptian lines.[14] All through the period of the monarchy the relations between the prophets and wisdom teachers are strained, for the latter often advise the reigning king in a way that seems to ignore Israel's firm belief in Yahweh as the only guide for the nation that is his people (Is 10:13; 29:14–16; Jer 8:8 f.).[15]

In the post-exilic period, therefore, many maxims and insights that had been discovered outside Israel were used in the service of her faith. In particular the 'older wisdom', as von Rad calls it, that is found in Proverbs, was fashioned through reflection on the experiences of life and the enigmas which these posed.[16] In Egypt such maxims were often concerned with achieving a successful life at court, but in the religious sphere they have a very different perspective. Avoidance of greed, selfishness or opportunism are important for a young man if he would succeed in life, but motivated by Israel's faith they become expressions of the values of justice, respect for one's neighbour and trust in the God who guides all men's destinies, qualities that are so dear to Yahweh.[17]

The Wisdom tradition is based on experience of life and therefore strives to inculcate respect for the elders in society. Transferred to the religious context this means that the family virtues and esteem for parents are regarded as important, and this makes it a useful commentary on the Decalogue:

> With all your heart honour your father,
> Never forget the birthpangs of your
>   mother.
> Remember that you owe your birth to
>   them;
> How can you repay them for what they
>   have done for you?
>
> *(Sir 7:27–30)*

If a young man wishes to win the confidence of the great ones at court honesty is of paramount importance for him, but this too, is a quality that the Decalogue had demanded from the genuine Israelite:

> Where hatred is, there are dissembling
>   lips,
> but deep within lies treachery;
> The lying tongue hates the truth,
> the fawning mouth brings ruin.
>
> *(Prv 26:24, 28)*

A detailed examination of the whole material is clearly outside the scope of this essay, but these examples may help to show how Israel in the hour of religious need, caused by the apparent failure of her salvation history, could call on such natural insights as those of the Wisdom tradition and use them to deepen the awareness and understanding of Yahweh's will for his community.

Jesus

In discussing the ethical teaching of Jesus, even in outline, it is important to see it against the background of developments in the late Jewish period. It is only thus, by the principle of dissimilarity, as it is called, that we can really determine the originality of Jesus.[18] At the same time we must try to distinguish his own teaching from later adaptation and development by the apostolic community, for form criticism has certainly shown that the words of Jesus were applied to new situations and problems within the life of the post-Easter community.

There are a number of attitudes in late Jewish moral thinking to which Jesus is clearly opposed.[19] In the first place the law had been absolutized to such a degree that each and every part had equal binding authority on the individual, and this was true not just for the written torah, but also for the crop of oral prescriptions that had arisen around it. It would be inaccurate to suggest that the late Jewish ethic was motivated solely by the idea of reward however, as some have suggested. Still, the dominant theme was absolute obedience to the supreme authority of the law, and in this regard in particular Jesus' emphasis lay elsewhere.

In discussing the teaching of Jesus one must begin with his proclamation of the kingdom of God, present in and with his own person. The phrase 'the kingdom of God' refers, not to territory or to overlordship in the secular sense, but to man's acceptance of the God who graciously approached him, and to man's consequent adherence to a certain way of life. It was Jesus who demonstrated what this acceptance meant and what this way of life was. This was the central point of his mission as he understood it, and accordingly his teaching on morality, with regard to both content and motivation, was based on it.[20] We shall return to the question of motivation in the second part of this paper, but it is necessary to refer to it here also since it helps to draw attention to the main concern of Jesus, namely, to live out God's kingdom and its demands to the full in his own life and teaching. He was thereby giving a pattern of behaviour in accord with the nature of the kingdom, on which he could base his authoritative call to men to follow him.

In external form he and his group must have appeared like typical teacher-disciple groups in Palestine and its environs, both Jewish and Hellenistic, but his consciousness of himself and his mission seems to have been that of the longed-for one who finally realized salvation in Israel.[21] Accordingly the ethical teaching of Jesus cannot be regarded as an *Interimsethik*, as has been maintained in the past.[22] It is no irksome burden to be tolerated because the end is near, nor is it merely ascetical preparation for the coming of the kingdom. On the other hand Jesus makes it clear that we can never merit the kingdom: 'When you have done all that is commanded you say: "we are unworthy servants; we have done what is our duty" ' (Lk 17:7–10). Yet once we accept the kingdom as God's gift we must act in accordance with its urgent demands, making full use of all the talents given (Mt 25:14–30). By receiving the kingdom we gain forgiveness of our sins, the cancellation of the great debt (Mt 18:23–34), and yet we are to pray for the growing experience of this forgiveness (Our Father). This in turn increases our sense of forgiveness for our fellow-man. In other words, the grace of the kingdom once received makes demands on us that correspond with its own nature.[23] Little wonder then that we find such expressions as 'receiving the kingdom' or 'entering the kingdom' side by side with others like 'doing the will of my Father' or 'follow me' as general descriptions of the moral behaviour which Jesus expected of all those who listened to his gospel of the kingdom.

Once we make his proclamation of the kingdom our starting point we are in a better position to understand where the emphasis lies in the teaching of Jesus. He was particularly concerned that people should understand the true nature of the kingdom, and it would seem that this was one of the issues on which he was put to death. It is significant that the parables of Jesus, dealing as they do with the true nature of the kingdom, are much more original than his specific moral pronouncements, when both are contrasted with contemporary Jewish sources.[24] We need not expect from Jesus therefore a fully worked out moral system similar to those already existing in Judaism. Indeed his condemnation of the Pharisees seems to centre precisely on this that by their detailed system they made it impossible for 'the people' to enter the kingdom (Mt 23:13). In this connection it is interesting to note that the Qumran covenanters had set themselves an exclusivist ideal of perfection consisting of observance not only of the law but of all the community rules besides. For Jesus on the other hand perfection meant acceptance of the kingdom and its demands, following the pattern of his own life (Mt 5:48; 19:21).[25] And, of course, as Bultmann rightly maintains, we can certainly not expect to find in Jesus's teaching a system of ethics dealing with standards of behaviour or moral values, which would correspond with the Greek idea of a life of virtue, and is quite foreign to the Semitic way of thinking.[26]

At the same time we find that Jesus engaged himself in Jewish discussions about morality, even if these were thrust on him by those who held official positions. His new attitude is not that of an iconoclastic revolutionary with regard to Jewish institutions. Some have gone so far as to suggest that he adopted two different attitudes to the law which can scarcely be made to correspond: sometimes ignoring it, sometimes dealing in almost the same kind of casuistry as Pharisaism. This impression may well be due to the fact that it is to St Matthew's gospel in particular that we must turn for the fullest account of Jesus's teaching on these matters. Matthew paints a conservative picture of Jesus's attitude to Jewish law (Mt 5:17–19), yet it must be recognized that in all probability this gospel was written within a polemical situation in the Jewish Christian wing of the early Church, and may therefore be more conservative than Jesus in regard to the law.[27] At all events we would do well to cross-check our conclusions from the other

sources for the teaching of Jesus, Mark and Q. That Jesus should discuss the ethical implications of his proclamation within the categories of Jewish moral thinking, is only another way of saying that his earthly mission was in the main directed to Israel (Mt 15:24). He saw himself as heir to all that the God of the fathers had done for his people as found in the law and the prophets, and there could be no question of abandoning that inheritance. Yet a new interpretation of the demands that Yahweh's loving kindness made on his people seemed called for in the light of what he was doing in and through Jesus.

In the first place it seems certain that Jesus rejected the formal authority of the Scriptures as absolutely binding. He does not hesitate to interpret the Scriptures for his contemporaries not as a scribe who spells out their every implication, but as one who can oppose one passage to another and show how they correspond with God's kingdom in the present. On the divorce question, for example, Genesis 1:27; 2:24 are set over against Deuteronomy 24:1 (Mk 10:2–9 and par.), thereby explaining what the original will of God was. Scripture is still authoritative, but it must be read in the light of God's final intervention which is to restore things as they were in the beginning, and not be interpreted in any literalistic manner. Even more sweeping is Jesus's condemnation of the Jewish ritual law. It is the heart of man that is important, as the prophets had previously insisted, and ritual prescriptions cannot determine man's total acceptance or rejection of God (Mk 7:14 f.). The precise gospel formulations of this attitude of Jesus are so clear that for some the subsequent struggle in the Church is difficult to explain, if he had pronounced so definitively on the matter. And yet these formulations of his attitude can only be based on Jesus's whole practice and on his associations with Gentiles and sinners during the ministry, something that cannot be denied in view of the amount of evidence in the tradition.[28] Jesus also rejected any legalistic interpretation of the Sabbath command—'The Sabbath was made for man, not man for the Sabbath' (Mk 2:27).

Questions which are sometimes posed to Jesus, such as: 'Which is the greatest commandment?' (Mk 12:28 and par.), or 'What shall I do to obtain eternal life?' (Mk 10:17 and par.) were often discussed in rabbinic circles, and the fact that Jesus is prepared to discuss these shows that he does not reject the idea of the Jewish search for the good life, even if he cannot answer them on conventional lines. The rich young man who had observed the Decalogue from his youth is not far from the kingdom, but he must imitate the total abandonment of Jesus. The greatest commandment is the love commandment, but this is universalized in line with Jesus's own attitude towards all that come to him in his ministry, something that again is in striking contrast to the Qumran community's attitude of love for the brother and hatred for all those who lived outside the community.[29]

Much has sometimes been made of the fact that many of the specific instructions of Jesus, such as those of the Sermon on the Mount, can be paralleled from the rabbinical sources. Bultmann, for example, sees in this a sign that we cannot expect Jesus to formulate concrete requirements or indicate an attitude towards concrete ethical problems.[30] But this is to adopt a much too one-sided approach and to place all the stress on Jesus as the eschatological prophet of the kingdom calling for an immediate decision from men. This aspect is indeed central as we have seen, but Jesus is also a teacher whose words are remembered and regarded as authoritative, precisely be-

cause of his eschatological proclamation. Once we accept that Jesus can combine these two roles, prophet and teacher, in his own person, what is striking is his agreement with and acceptance of the better insights and formulations of the late Jewish moral thinking. Even here at the very climax of God's revelation of his will to man he can and does translate the one fundamental command, acceptance of the kingdom or obedience, into areas of current concern. In doing so Jesus used the insights that he found before him, adding to them now the authority of the one who spoke them. As Davies puts it: 'The acts and words of Jesus compel the same question. They belong together as part of the ethic of Jesus and the mystery of his person: his words themselves confront us with him who utters them.'[31]

Jesus's basic request to men was to 'follow me', to imitate the selfless pattern of his life; this rather than spell out a detailed moral code for them. Hence his definitive contribution belongs more to the second section of this paper, and the Johannine writings, as we shall see in that section, are correct when they put forward Jesus's moral teaching chiefly in terms of the command to love, spelled out mainly in concrete terms of forgiveness, practical caring and unlimited self-sacrifice. As far as codified law is concerned, Jesus inherited and refined rather than innovated.

The Apostolic Church

Our interpretation of the approach of Jesus to morality is borne out by the great variety of moral argumentation to be found in the apostolic communities which are grounded on his life and ministry. Here we can only indicate some examples which show that these communities never considered that they had received a complete code of morality to deal with every situation. The pattern which we discovered earlier in relation to the Old Testament recurs here: the community of faith must discover what its moral response should be in the face of specific moral problems; in doing so it can call on contemporary approaches to such problems, bringing these into line with its understanding of the Lord and the demands he is making on those who have followed him.

Clearly the words of Jesus had an authoritative value, not merely for those who actually heard them but also after his death and resurrection. Occasionally Paul can call explicitly on the 'word of the Lord' to answer a particular problem (1 Thes 4:14 f.; 1 Cor 7:10, 14, 25; 9:14). More often, however, he appeals to the mind of the master by an implicit reference to his words as they are known to us from the gospel tradition.[32] This use of the words of Jesus is not confined to Paul, since it is generally recognized that the epistle of James has also used them quite frequently (e.g. Jas 2:5, 13, 15; 3:12, 18; 5:10, 12). The collection of sayings of Jesus usually designated as Q would also appear to have been compiled for moral instruction in a catechetical milieu.[33] All this is in line with what form criticism has told us about the transmission of the words of Jesus in the oral period.

There is no rigid adherence to the letter of what the master said, for the early Christian teachers, least of all Paul, cannot be regarded as Christian scribes who interpreted the words of Jesus in a casuistic manner. Rather, his sayings could be interpreted, adapted and applied to new situations. Jesus did not discuss every situation or deal with every problem explicitly, but the tradition of his words can be approached in a living and vital way, precisely because Jesus himself is alive and present with

his community (e.g. Mt 28:20). At first sight sayings like Matthew 23:8–10 which declare that there is only one teacher in the community, Christ, appear strange until we remember the extraordinary awareness of the presence of the risen Christ that the primitive community enjoyed. This helps us to understand why discipleship and its co-relative 'following' can be put forward as the ideal for the Christian community even though they can no longer be carried out literally. The longed-for bringer of final salvation had also acted as teacher in line with his gospel of the kingdom, during his earthly life. Now as the risen and glorified Lord he continues the same function confirming in his new status all that he had said to them while he was still with them (Mt 28: 16–20).

Side by side with Paul's use of the words of Jesus, whether implicitly or explicitly, we find that very often he uses the Christian's new life 'in Christ' or their 'life in the Spirit', the idea of a way of life fashioned by the spirit of Christ as a gift received, as the basis for moral argumentation (e.g. 1 Thes 2:10 f.; 5:5 f.; 1 Cor 2:12–16; 6:12–19; Gal 5:1, 16–25; Rom 6; Col 3:1 f.). Indeed some have gone so far as to suggest that this kind of argumentation, imperative based on indicative as it is called, so dominates Paul's ethical thinking that he omits any reference to the earthly life of Jesus.[34] However such a position cannot be maintained. True, it is central to his thought, something that the overall structure of his epistles, exhortation following exposition, makes clear. Such a pattern, moral teaching arising from acceptance of Christ and of his Spirit, corresponds to the preaching of Jesus about the kingdom and his moral teaching arising from this. The fact that Jesus preached the kingdom whereas the Church preached the lordship of Jesus points to a terminological, not, however, a substantial, distinction between the two proclamations.[35]

Within such a Christocentric perspective Paul can use both the words of Jesus and commonplace Jewish or even pagan insights into the moral life and place them side by side as instruction for the new life in Christ. Such a juxtaposition of Christian and pagan insights poses no problem for Paul's theology especially if, as Davies has claimed, he presupposes a set of Noachian commandments[36] binding on Jew and Gentile alike, and this accounts for his castigation of both groups for their moral laxity in Romans 1:18–3:20. God's revealed will is universal and binding on all men, something such prophets as Isaiah (2:2–4) and Zechariah (8:20 f.) had already seen from their reflections on the cosmic lordship of Yahweh.

A good illustration of this combining of the words of Jesus and other moral insights by Paul is to be found in Romans 12–14.[37] 12:1–2 introduces moral instruction which is described as 'the will of God' (the Jewish ideal) and 'what is good and pleasing and perfect' (Stoic overtones; cf. Phil 4:8). Paul goes on to spell out what this ideal implies by means of specific moral directives. We find here clear echoes of words of Jesus: 12:14 (Mt 5:44); 12:17 (Mt 5:39 f.); 12:21 (Mt 5:38); 13:7 (Mt 22:15–22); 13:8–10 (Mt 22:34–40); 14:10 (Mt 7:1); 14:13 (Mt 18:7); 14:14 (Mt 15:11). Fused with this liberal sprinkling of sayings of the master there is other advice which is more in line with the advice of the Stoics and Cynics: 'do not think of yourself more highly than you ought' (12:3); 'live in harmony with one another; do not be haughty, but associate with the lowly' (12:16); 'let us conduct ourselves becomingly as in the day' (13:13) etc. The whole exposition is given a very definite Christological orientation: 'Put on the Lord Jesus Christ, and make no provision for the flesh to gratify its desires' (13:14). We find a similar use of Greek ethical material in a Christian setting in Galatians.[38] Here Paul takes over lists of vices and virtues current in the Greek world and uses them to describe what is opposed to the 'life in the Spirit' and what are the fruits of the Spirit for the one who is in Christ (Gal 5:1, 2, 6, 16–25).

Attention has often been drawn to the lists of household rules to be found not only in the Pauline epistles but in other New Testament writings as well. Colossians 3:18–4:1; Ephesians 5:22–6:9 (assuming both to be Pauline); 1 Peter 2:13 f.; Titus 2:1–10; 1 Timothy 2:8 f.; 6:1 f. are the passages usually mentioned in this connection. These lists concern relations between husbands and wives and those between slaves and their masters. The fact that similar instructions are found in both Pauline and non-Pauline letters may possibly indicate a fixed catechism in the early Church dealing with these matters, though probably it was not as well defined as some scholars maintain.[39] When the New Testament versions of these lists are compared with similar Jewish and Hellenistic ones some case could be made for the claim that the Christian lists have a more developed sense of reciprocal responsibility in relations between husbands and wives. However with the possible exception of the Pastorals, the really distinctive element is that the instructions are introduced with a reminder of the Christian's life in Christ (Col 3:18), or as an invitation to follow his example of self-sacrificing love (Eph 5:25; 1 Pt 2:21).

The possible exception in regard to the Pastorals just mentioned prompts us to look more closely at the moral teaching in these letters. There is a definite shift in emphasis here, for the ideal that is placed before the believer in these letters is couched almost entirely in terms from the Greek ethical teaching.

For those who accept the Pauline authorship of these letters this is an indication of the apostle's final adaptation of his gospel to his audience after he had left Palestine for the last time. Others see it as one of several internal arguments against the Pauline authorship.[40] At all events the Greek colouring in the thought and expression is quite pronounced and it is this that is our chief concern. The Christian is to live 'soberly, piously and justly in this life' (Ti 2:12). These were the virtues by which a Stoic regulated his life with himself, God and his fellow man. All the virtues that were held in high regard by such philosophers as Plato, Epictetus, Plutarch are presented in these epistles as the Christian ideal: truth, goodness, godliness, justice, tranquillity etc. Even more striking, in the opinion of some, is the absence of any motivation from Christ's sufferings and death as in the great epistles. However, we should not overstress this point in regard to the moral teaching of the Pastorals. In the exhortation cited above from Titus there is a reminder that they are awaiting the appearance of our great God and Saviour, Jesus Christ (cf. also 1 Tm 6:14; 2 Tm 4:1, 8). The epistles are addressed to those who are 'called by God' (2 Tm 1:9), who can also be called 'the saints' (1 Tm 5:10). The Christian who is purified and ready for any good work is like a consecrated vessel (2 Tm 2:21), in other words, grace and man's will are both involved in living the Christian life.

We must conclude our survey at this point. In the Christian communities no less than in the Old Testament there is need for the people of faith to formulate their own specific moral directives in the light of the new life in Christ that they considered themselves called on to live. Jesus did not leave a specific code of morality, but rather the example of his own person. His words had a very special authority, but they could scarcely be said to have taken on the character of law, at least not in the way we normally use that term. Other sources of practical moral guidance could also be used to describe a Christian way of behaviour in a world that had been originally created in Christ, and was now redeemed by him as his own possession (Col 1:16–20).

II. Moral Motivation in the Bible

Our rather lengthy examination of the sources of the Bible's moral teaching has already to some degree answered the second question we posed at the outset, namely, how does biblical morality propose itself to the people of faith? We have seen that in both Old and New Testament alike there is a constant search for a deeper understanding of Yahweh's will and its specific content in relation to the varied circumstances of history and environment in which the people of faith finds itself. In this search help can be had from purely human sources, even if sometimes faith will have a purifying influence on the insights of the 'secular' source. Such a process, undefined and subconscious as it often is, means that Israel is always engaged in relating behaviour to faith. Therefore, her moral teaching can never be arbitrary or imposed, without reference to the faith that motivates people to respond to a God, known in faith. This point is well illustrated by the fact that much of the Bible's moral teaching is set in the context of exhortation: Deuteronomy, the prophets, Jesus, Paul. It could never be mistaken as a cold impersonal law alien to the heart. The biblical writers believe that the morality they propose is based on the very nature of the human person 'made in the image of God', and their main preoccupation is to get people, floundering amid all the confusion and obscurity of life, to see where true happiness lies. Repentance, in the sense of returning to one's source, is the very heart of the Bible's moral instruction. People are exhorted to respond from their own hearts rather than imposed upon by legal promulgation.

To this general consideration we may add others in the same line. Firstly, biblical morality is always set in the context of grace. This means that the question of Israel's failure to respond to her God is never seriously considered in the classical periods of her faith. The covenant law comes from the covenant God, as an expression of his love and care for his people. His very name assures Israel of his constant presence with her in each generation (Ex 3:13–15). She is repeatedly reminded that he is the God who brought her out of Egypt, and it is as such that he makes his demands on her. The historical prologue which is part of the classical covenant form serves in the Bible to remind Israel of his gracious acts of kindness in the past (*hesed*), and his loyalty to his pledges in the present (*'emeth*). Thus, e.g. the Decalogue is introduced at Exodus 20:2 with the reminder: 'I am the Lord *your* God, who brought you out of the land of Egypt, out of the house of bondage'. Writing about the Deuteronomic reform, von Rad remarks that there was never any question of Israel not being able to fulfil all the demands; rather, the problem was whether or not Israel was prepared to submit herself to them.[41]

> The law that I enjoin on you today is not beyond your strength or beyond your reach. It is not in heaven, so that you need to wonder, 'Who will go up to heaven for us and bring it down to us so that we may hear it and keep it?' . . . No, the word is very near to you, it is in your mouth and in your heart for your observance.
>
> *(Dt 30:11–14)*

To say that biblical morality is always set in the context of grace means that good moral living is seen as a response that is drawn from humans. What it should consist in is indicated by the generosity of God's action on our behalf. The spirit of legalism, on the contrary, is one which sees the imposed code of precepts as measuring exactly how much is demanded and behaving accordingly.

The legalism of the later Jewish period erred not by asking too much from God's people, but by asking too little. Strangely enough this trend towards legalism was started indirectly by those two great prophets of the new covenant, Jeremiah and Ezekiel. Faced with interpreting Israel's repeated failures and the calamity of the Babylonian captivity (587 B.C.) so soon after the Deuteronomic reform (622 B.C.), they looked forward to a future covenant that would not be like the old one, for it would be written within the hearts of men and not on tables of stone (Jer 31:31 f.; Ez 36:24 f.). This criticism of the old law should not be misinterpreted, however. What was really lacking in Israel was the realization that she was in constant need of her saving God. Thorough though the reform of Josiah set out to be, it never achieved this change of heart. The longing of the prophets for a decisive intervention by Yahweh that would bring about such a conversion was fulfilled with the coming of Jesus for his first Jewish followers. As we have seen, his morality is set in the context of God's kingdom as gift (see e.g. the parables of the wicked husbandmen and the king who made the feast for his son, Mt 21:33–22:10). The New Testament theologians also recognize this intimate link between grace and morality and develop it fully on the personal and community levels. Side by side with the new commandment of love in John we find the admonition to 'abide in my love' and the promises of the indwelling of the Father and Son and the gift of the Spirit (Jn 13:33 f.; 14:15 f.; 15:5–10). Paul combines the images of Jeremiah and Ezekiel to assure the Christian that the *law* (Jer) of the *Spirit* of life (Ez) has set them free, and then develops the idea in terms of the indwelling Spirit and the charity that has been poured forth in their hearts (Rom 8:2–11).[42] This is in line with what we have already seen of imperative based on indicative all through his writings. The Christian has put on Christ in baptism, and yet he must be exhorted to put on Christ by a life modelled on that of Christ (Gal 3:27; Rom 13:14).

This leads on to the idea of morality as imitation of God. 'You shall be holy; for I the Lord your God am holy' (Lv 19:2), 'You therefore must be perfect, as your heavenly Father is perfect' (Mt 5:48) and 'Beloved let us love one another . . . He who does not love does not know God; For God is love' (1 Jn 4:7 f.), are statements which span the whole biblical teaching on morality, and they all insist on the divinizing power found in behaviour that is based on God's own example. The believer is drawn into union with God not through any form of mystical experience or secret knowledge, but by conforming his will to the creator/redeemer God. It was the prophets who first clearly focused attention on morality as central to the God-man relationship in Israel. In doing so they appealed to the human, for they clearly saw that Yahweh was no patronising divinity in showing kindness to Israel. Rather, election meant that Yahweh wanted Israel to make herself into what she really was, a holy people. In the deepest sense possible she could be the maker of her own destiny; he

was helping her and humans as a whole to become their true selves. Motivation was not a matter of imposition, of promulgated precepts, but exhortation to respond to favour and be guided by example.

Old Testament as Tôrāh

From these general considerations we can examine briefly some specific points which illustrate how keenly the Bible is aware of the need to speak to the heart. In the first place it should be noted that the English 'law' corresponds to the Greek idea of *nomos* as 'custom', 'set rule' or 'standard', but it does not do full justice to the Hebrew *tôrāh,* which literally means instruction or guidance.[43] That Israel could call the whole first part of the Bible *tôrāh,* shows how she regarded the details of the law as a gift from Yahweh to help her to fulfil her covenant commitment, and that the divine demands should not be divorced from the narrative of God's saving action. This is further borne out by the fact that the Decalogue is introduced as the 'words' of Yahweh (Ex 20:1), and Israel pledging herself to the covenant *tôrāh* can be described as the listening people or the obeying people since the same Hebrew word *šāma'* covered both ideas (Ex 24:7).

The book of Deuteronomy is perhaps the best example of *tôrāh* in the Old Testament. The actual Deuteronomic code (chs. 12–26) is introduced by two lengthy addresses put on the lips of Moses. These have a very distinctive tone of exhortation and motivation. The detailed prescriptions of the code have to be read in the light of these speeches which give us the author's viewpoint in regard to law and its function within Israel. In the first place it speaks to the heart and it is from the heart that Deuteronomy expects Israel to respond:

6:4–6; 8:2, 5; 11:13, 18; 26:16; 30:11–20. Besides, the setting is clearly cultic, and each generation is confronted anew with Yahweh's command, giving an existential quality to the preaching. 'Today' becomes a key-word, for in and through the cult Israel is confronted with Yahweh's saving action (Dt 5:3; 9:1–3; 29:2–9), and on the basis of this love a decision is called for from each generation (Dt 30:15–20; cf. 7:12; 8:19; 11:13–16).

Secondly, all the commandments are in fact one commandment, in line with the theme of unity that runs through the book at various levels. This can be seen from the way in which singular and plural, commandment-commandments (*entolē-entolai*), can be used interchangeably at various points throughout the work (Dt 6:24, 25, Hebrew text; 30:10, 11).[44] All the various commandments usually described by the triple formula 'laws, statutes and ordinances', can be summed up in the one commandment of love of God, and as such are the expression of the one will of God for his people. They can equally well be described as God's word (30:11–14), thereby emphasizing the revelational character of the commandments in question. The phrase 'walking in the ways of Yahweh' which is found repeatedly (8:6; 10:12; 11:22; 19:9; 26:17; 28:9; 30:16) to describe Israel's observance of the statutes, underlines this same insight into the nature of the laws, as revealing the heart and mind of Yahweh as she has experienced him in her history.[45] Thus, if they are to be gracious and forgiving to slaves, sojourners and orphans, it is because by doing so they are imitating Yahweh who had acted graciously to Israel amid the slavery of Egypt (10:17–19; 15:12–16; 24:17–18). Yahweh commands in accordance with his own nature.

This overall emphasis of Deuteronomy as 'preached law', to use von Rad's phrase, can

be seen in the motivation that within the Deuteronomic code itself is introduced into older statutes previously lacking this.[46] In 14:22, for example, we find an old law about giving a tithe of one's produce to Yahweh, but verses 23–27 is a treatment in homiletic style, explaining now how it may be carried out in the spirit of the present reform. In the later Holiness code of Leviticus 16–26 the same pattern of instruction based on older laws emerges also: at Leviticus 19:17 there is the older negative law: 'You shall not hate your brother in your heart'; to this has now been added a positive instruction: 'But you shall reason with your neighbour lest you bear sin because of him'. Elsewhere in Leviticus we find a similar treatment. Chapter 18 has a structure like that of Deuteronomy. Verses 2–5 give a general instruction to keep the commandments; this is followed by a general commandment (v. 6) which is applied to detailed instances in verses 7–23; the whole is rounded out with a further general exhortation in verses 24–30. It would call for a more detailed study than is possible here to show the changing motivation that was given to various laws throughout the centuries, but for our purposes it is sufficient to show that it was a continual process even within the Decalogue. (Compare Ex 20:8–11 with Dt 5:12–15 on the motivation for the observance of the Sabbath.) In the earliest period it is probable that the mere statement 'I am Yahweh' was sufficient authentication (e.g. the cultic formula in Lv 19). Later a reference to the saving history was a favourite form of such general motivation, as in Exodus 23:15. In the Deuteronomic and Holiness codes we have been examining the fact that individual commands were given separate motivation shows that a growing need was felt to awaken in individual Israelites a sense of obligation to their duties, flowing from their covenant faith. The highest form of motive behind the exhortations is the love of God.

Motivation in the Wisdom Literature

Leaving the Pentateuchal material, then, I should like to turn next to the Wisdom literature once again. The first step in the acceptance of the Wisdom material into Israel's religious tradition was taken with the recognition by Isaiah that Yahweh alone was wise (Is 31:1 f.). The next step is the personification of Wisdom, a feature of almost all the canonical Wisdom books (Prv 8:22–36; Jb 28; Wis 7:22–30; Sir 24; Bar 3:37–4:1). It is important to recognize the function of this personification within the Wisdom writings.[47] It is to present the instructions of wisdom in the most attractive and personal form possible; Wisdom personified is the source of life and nourishment for people; she prepares a banquet for them and invites them to her table.[48] Of particular importance is the fact that she has divine origins, and in Job Yahweh himself is thought of as searching for her, and it was he alone who discovered her.

Wisdom was present with Yahweh at the creation of the world, and consequently she knows the secrets of the world, and the ways of God and men. By accepting her instruction and guidance one can share in these secrets and partake in the divine life that she enjoys with Yahweh. The exact scope of Wisdom's understanding varies from writer to writer. In Proverbs and Job she understands the creation, and so she can share with her followers the mysteries of life and death. In Sirach and Baruch she is identified with the law, and therefore she represents Yahweh's special gift to Israel. This development is in line with the conservative tendencies of late Judaism in Palestine, but such extolling of the law has not degenerated into legalism. The author delights in the law (cf. Ps 119), and there is no question about Israel's inability to fulfil it. Rather, it is her special privilege to possess such a precious gift from Yahweh. By contrast the Hellenistic book of Wisdom sees her as possessing the knowledge of all the sciences, medicine, astrology, zoology etc., so highly cultivated in Alexandria. It is clear then that the personification of Wisdom and the dignity she possesses because of her divine origin are intended by the Wisdom writers to make her and her teaching acceptable to a people who had long been taught to mistrust such maxims as coming from the enemy of Yahweh.

New Testament Morality, a Morality of Love

Finally we turn to the Johannine writings, for in our survey of the New Testament literature in the first part of this essay we did not mention these, precisely because they seem to have little interest in the specific moral teaching of Jesus. The emphasis is centred on the love commandment as the one concrete ethical instruction of Jesus for his disciples. It is called a 'new' command, presumably because it is revealed in and through the ministry of Jesus in a new way. By contrast with the Synoptics it is only love of the brother that is mentioned: John 3:34; 15:12; 1 John 2:8–10; 3:11; 4:7–12. 1 John 4:21 is the one exception, for it also mentions a command to love God, explaining at the same time that this is an empty formula unless one loves the brother whom one sees as a proof of the genuineness of the desire to love.

In discussing this concentration of John on the command to love the brother there are two aspects of his work as a whole that must be kept in mind. In the first place we find a fluctuation between command and commandments, just as in Deuteronomy, and this should put us on our guard against understanding John as having no interest in specific moral directives of Jesus.[49] The disciples are told about a new commandment (*entolē*, sing.) at 13:34 and 15:12, whereas at 14:15, 21 they are told to keep his commandments (*entolai*, plur.). Furthermore, the Spirit is promised explicitly to the disciples to remind them of all that Jesus had said to them (Jn 14:26), and to lead them into all truth (16:12–14). John is far from ignoring the specific words of Jesus but he wants them to be understood in their deepest significance and to integrate them into a higher synthesis.[50]

This gives a clue to the second aspect of John's theology that is of supreme importance for his moral teaching, and again Deuteronomy is a useful background for understanding his thought. We saw how in the Old Testament book the commands given have a revelational aspect, they are the word of God to his community (Dt 30:11–14). The central emphasis of John is, as is well known, the revelation that Jesus, as the Word who was with God, brings into the world (Jn 1:1–4). He has come to bear witness to the truth (Jn 18:37), because he is the truth, in fact the way and the life as well (Jn 14:6). His earthly life has been one of complete obedience to the Father's will (Jn 4:34; 5:30; 6:38), that is a carrying out of the command he received from his Father (10:18 *entolē*, sing.) or a keeping of the Father's commandments, thereby abiding in his love (Jn 15:10 *entolai*, plur.). In other words his life is a model or exemplar of what he is now asking of his disciples. His life of love was a revelation of the God of love (1 Jn 4:7–12), and the new command is to love one another, *as he has loved us* (Jn 15:12 f.). 'By this we

know love that he laid down his life for us; and we ought to lay down our lives for the brethren' (1 Jn 3:16). In other words, Christ's life of love in obedience to the command he received from his Father reveals to us the kind of life we must lead. Our eyes are turned firmly towards the 'life that was made manifest among us' (1 Jn 1:2), that is, towards the Word that became flesh in our midst (Jn 1:14), to discover the pattern our own lives must follow.

In Deuteronomy the Israelites were exhorted to 'walk in the ways of Yahweh', that is to reproduce Yahweh's attitude by imitating him in their dealings with their fellow men. In doing so they became like Yahweh. In John God has come nearer to man in Christ, the Word made flesh, and we are now to imitate him. We must follow him, that is be his disciples, because he has shown us in a unique way 'how to walk in the ways of Yahweh', in selfless giving of himself for others. It is thus that one can attain to the great Other that is God, and this is one's greatest privilege and dignity. It is because John wished to concentrate on this supreme motivation for Christian behaviour that he has focused all the attention on the command to love the brother, to the apparent neglect of the other specific moral directives of Jesus. This one command summarizes perfectly the whole life of him who is the way, the truth and the life.

Conclusion

This enquiry into biblical morality has revealed a number of constants in both Old and New Testament, which answer our questions posed at the beginning. In the first place faith and revelation never dispense God's people from the task of discovering the pattern their behaviour should take in changing historical circumstances. The starting point for this search is always their faith-experience of God, the God of the exodus in the Old Testament, and the God who was in Christ, reconciling the world to himself, in the New. Convinced that their behaviour must always reflect this God who had revealed himself in and through his dealings with them in their history, they may use the contemporary insights into the good life with which they come in contact, refining them where necessary in line with the particular stage of their awareness of God and their current understanding of his nature. The actual content of their morality will thus be often similar to that of their surrounding neighbours, at least in the more lofty formulations of these, but there is now the added assurance that what they are doing is God's will for them, and at the same time the appreciation that by acting in this way, one is attaining to one's true self, which is to be like God.

On the other hand, we must never ignore the fact that this very assurance carried with it real dangers for Israel's moral teaching. The example we cited from early Israel, where her less sophisticated way of life meant that she had not formulated the rights of women as clearly or explicitly as had her urbanized neighbours, points to a danger that the very vividness of the awareness that moral behaviour was the fulfilment of Yahweh's will for his people could cause indifference to exploring all the possible areas of response and failure. It has been suggested by Eichrodt that the relatively few casuistic laws in the Book of the Covenant by comparison with the Code of Hammurabi shows how Israel was prepared to leave many areas to the individual's personal responsibility.[51] This suggestion is, however, open to question. An alternative conclusion would be that early Israel, so deeply conscious of its corporate nature, tended to overlook individual obligations. A case could be made for saying that because she was so keenly aware of her unity before Yahweh as one person, her early laws covered only those areas of moral conduct in which the community harmony and unity was likely to be disrupted. It was only with the breakdown of this corporate moral responsibility in the exilic period (see e.g. Ez 18) that areas of individual rights and duties as such were explored in any depth.

Certainly, the emphasis of the later period with its multiplicity of particular precepts brought with it the danger of blunting the sense of response to a loving God. It was this corrosion of the religiously motivated response from the heart that called forth such vigorous condemnation from Jesus, and other moral reformers such as John the Baptist. Useful though the covenant idea was for expressing the all-embracing character of Israel's relationship with Yahweh, there was always inherent in it certain dangers for a correct understanding of the true nature of that relationship. A covenant of grace and love (Hos 11:1–9) easily became one of contract (Sir 44:20 f.), and once this misplacing of emphasis had taken place, the transition from a response in love to one of formalism and externalism followed inevitably. This danger was not obviated with the advent of the new covenant in Christ, as the bitter judaizing controversy in the early Church shows clearly. Paul's epistle to the Galatians is a vigorous defence of Christian liberty by the apostle, liberty, that is, to serve freely by walking in the Spirit. The law coming much later can never annul the promise made to Abraham, and Christians as children of Abraham, must never allow the personal faith-response to Christ, inaugurated at baptism, to degenerate into a set of practices and observances, however laudable in themselves. Matthew, by building Christ's words into a Messianic torah in the Sermon on the Mount (Mt 5:17–20) may well have obscured somewhat the real originality of Christ as moral teacher. Behind each of the special instructions of the Sermon stands the kingdom as proclaimed by Jesus, that is, God's self-giving gift and his invitation to live out this gift after the model of Jesus's own life. Unless this fact is kept firmly at the centre there is a real danger of reducing the moral teaching of Jesus to a code of morality, a neo-Pharisaism purged of the more extreme elements, but still emphasizing details rather than attitude, the letter rather than the spirit. It would be interesting in the light of this, to trace the extent to which the undoubted popularity of the first gospel in the Church has influenced the subsequent approach to Christian morality.

In the last analysis it is this emphasis on the spirit that is the distinctive and original contribution of the Bible to moral thinking. If members of the people of faith are given the assurance of having the divine goodness as the proper context for moral behaviour, they are also challenged by that goodness to make a free personal choice and a consequent re-orientation of life. The self-disclosure of God, as the people of faith experienced it, was in terms of love, whether covenant love in the Old Testament, or the incarnate love of the historical Jesus in the New. The intensity and the personal quality of the experience is new with the coming of Christ (*kainos*), that is, of a different order, but it still retains the essential quality of love. God's love has been concretized and humanized in Christ, and it is from him that we must learn the demands on self that genuine love makes. His freedom from self that characterized his life unto death, and

his care and concern for human misery in all its forms, even the slavery of the self-opinionated teachers to their own systems, were the features of his life as he was remembered (Jn 2:22; 12:16). It was this that constituted the basis for his radical call to follow him. The Church was keenly aware of the need to retain such a picture of the historical Jesus, with the authority of his truth, wholeness and sincerity, side by side with 'theological' motivation arising from life 'in Christ', as can be seen from the fact that Paul's epistle to the Romans and Mark's gospel were written to the same Roman Church within the space of a few years. This does not mean that Jesus's life and sayings were considered normative in any literalist way, as we have seen. Rather, this gospel record is valid and necessary as showing how within his particular spiritual history God's demand could be lived out to the full, and 'crowned with honour and glory'. It is this that constitutes at once the uniqueness and absoluteness of Christ, and his attractiveness to draw men to imitate his selflessness when faced with the supreme demand of God. The gospel accounts are not merely a record of the past success of Jesus's own historical living out of the demands of the kingdom; they are *anamnēsis,* or representation, witnessing to the possibilities of achieving similar success in their own lives, that Jesus, as glorified Lord, is offering to men in the present.

All this would seem to have very important consequences for the Church as teacher of morals. Her consciousness of herself as bearer of revelation should never cause her to ignore the world and its moral standards or systems of behaviour. Aware of the fact that the people of faith, as reflected in the Bible, discovered much of the content of its moral teaching from 'the world', the Church must never consider herself as a last bulwark against a permissive society, however accurate such generalizations may appear to be at any given time. The exchange with the world in the matter of morality will be much more fruitful for the Church and the world if she realizes that she can on occasion learn from it. Provided she is prepared to observe and listen, she may discover areas, particularly so-called 'human' areas, in which the world has outstripped her in the sharpness of its discovery and formulation of man's dignity and his consequent rights and duties.

Furthermore, the teaching Church must always remember that morality in the Christian context is response from the heart. Accordingly, she must as teacher propose rather than impose. She must never hesitate to present the radical demands of Christ, but this must be done in such a way that the ideal in question is seen as the ideal of Christ, and the radicality of the demand, his radicalness. She will recognize that, like Jesus, her moral teaching must flow from the gospel she preaches, and be based on her own living commitment to that gospel. Here lies her greatest privilege, but also her most urgent challenge as teacher of Christian morals. In particular, she must never succumb to the all too human temptation to become patronising and protective because of human failures and sinfulness, by turning the demand of God into a largely negative and over-elaborate legal system that asks too little of the individual's responsibility. In that event she would be doing less than justice to God's gift. In particular she would be obscuring the fact that Christ's most radical demand was made within the context of repentance and forgiveness, and that the gospel of the kingdom was a message of continuing love and salvation in the present,

without the threat of immediate apocalyptic judgement for failures, something his contemporaries, even John the Baptist, could not fully appreciate or understand (Mt 3:4–12; 11:2–6).

Postscript

It comes as something of a shock to be confronted with one's thoughts of twenty years ago. Nevertheless, I have decided to give permission for republication of my essay because on re-reading it I am even more convinced now of the validity of the position which I proposed then. A thorough revision would have entailed developing or nuancing the argument at several points, so I have contented myself with only minor changes, stylistic for the most part, from the original. I have not attempted to update the references, in the footnotes, but refer the interested student to several recent discussions. Among the many that might be cited I would suggest W. Schrage, *The Ethics of the New Testament*, English translation, T. & T. Clark 1988, and W. Meeks *The Moral World of the First Christians*, Westminster Press 1986, as being the most stimulating. There is something to be learned also for the modern student in recognizing how the emphases in scholarly questions change even from the recent past. On the section on Jesus' approach to morality I refer the reader to my own study *Galilee, Jesus and the Gospels: Literary Approaches and Historical Investigations*, Gill and Macmillan/Fortress 1988, especially the section on "Jesus and the Torah."

I would like to draw the reader's attention to a number of areas in which considerable developments have taken place, pertinent to the matter of this article. Our understanding of the Judaism of the first century has gone through a major paradigm shift, mainly because of the work of Jacob Neusner. The Hellenistic environment of early Christianity has been greatly enriched by the seminal studies of Martin Hengel. Norman Gottwald's and Gerd Theissen's studies on the social world of Israel and the early Christians have underlined that dimension of their ethical experience also, as have the various liberation theologians' reading of the Bible from a very different perspective. Stanley Hauerwas, Dan O. Via and others have pointed to the importance of the narrative dimensions of the Bible for ethical reflection. Finally, the writings of Paul Ricoeur, David Tracy and Werner Jeanrond have underlined the need for an adequate hermeneutical theory in appropriating biblical texts for the construction of a contemporary Christian ethic. In a general way I was aware of all these issues twenty years ago, but they were not then in the forefront of my approach to the Bible to the extent that they would be were I to tackle the question of the Bible and morality afresh today.

Notes

1. The studies of R. de Vaux are fundamental in this area. Originally there were three articles: 'Les Patriarches Hébraux et les découvertes modernes', *Revue Biblique* (43) 1946, 321–47; (45) 1948, 321–47; (46) 1949, 5–36. These have now been summarized and brought up to date in *Theology Digest* (12) 1964, 227–40.

2. This conclusion is based on literary criticism of the Pentateuch and the discovery of various independent traditions concerning the departure from Egypt and entry into Palestine. See e.g. the studies of M. Noth, *Überlieferungsgeschichte des Pentateuchs,* Stuttgart 1948; *The History of Israel,* London 1960, 110–20.

3. See Noth, *The History of Israel,* 53–109.

4. *Die Ürsprunge des israelitischen Rechts,* Leipzig 1934; reprinted in *Essays in Old Testament History and Religion,* Oxford 1966, 81–132.

5. See W. Eichrodt, *Theology of the Old Testament* (E. tr.), I, London 1961, 81.

6. See Alt, *Essays . . . ,* 123 f.

7. See J. L. McKenzie, *The World of the Judges,* London 1967, 68–71.

8. G. von Rad, *Old Testament Theology* (E. tr.), I, London 1962, 195.

9. See W. Zimmerli, *The Law and the Prophets, A Study in the Meaning of the Old Testament,* Oxford 1965.

10. R. E. Clements has shown this in his excellent study of the prophets' contribution to the covenant community, *Prophecy and Covenant,* London 1965.

11. W. Eichrodt, *Theology of the Old Testament* (E. tr.), II, London 1967, 326–37.

12. See A. Gelin, *The Poor of Yahweh* (E. tr.), Collegeville 1963.

13. See J. Bright, *A History of Israel,* London 1960, 413–45.

14. See the articles of M. Noth, N. W. Porteus and R. B. Y. Scott in *Wisdom in Israel and the Ancient Near East,* edited by M. Noth and D. W. Thomas, Leiden 1960 (Essays presented to H. H. Rowley).

15. See J. Lindblom, 'Wisdom in the Old Testament Prophets', in *Wisdom in Israel . . . ,* 192–204.

16. *Old Testament Theology,* I, 418–41.

17. In this regard compare the 'Instruction of Amen-em-Opet' from Egypt (in J. B. Pritchard, *Ancient Near Eastern Texts,* New Jersey 1950, 421–4) with Prv 22:17–24:22.

18. See N. Perrin, *Rediscovering the Teaching of Jesus,* London 1967, especially ch. 1.

19. For a summary account of the position see W. D. Davies, 'Law in first-century Judaism', in *The Interpreter's Dictionary of the Bible,* III, New York 1955, 89–95.

20. The relation between the moral teaching of Jesus and his preaching of the kingdom has been well presented by R. Schnackenburg, in his two studies *Gottes Herrschaft und Reich,* Freiburg 1959, and *Die Sittliche Botschaft des Neuen Testamentes,* Munich 1962.

21. I have discussed this aspect of Jesus's ministry in *The Twelve: Disciples and Apostles,* London 1968, ch. 1.

22. For a discussion of the views of A. Schweitzer and J. Weiss who pioneered the idea see the survey of N. Perrin, *The Kingdom of God in the Teaching of Jesus,* London 1963, 16–28.

23. See J. Jeremias, 'Le Sermon sur la Montagne', in *Paroles de Jésus,* Paris 1963, 16–48.

24. This point has been illustrated by W. R. Farmer, 'An Historical Essay on the Humanity of Jesus Christ', in *Christian History and Interpretation: Studies Presented by John Knox,* edited by W. R. Farmer, C. F. D. Moule, R. R. Niebuhr, Cambridge 1967, 101–26. Farmer gives detailed parallels to the sayings of Jesus, especially those of the Sermon on the Mount, from the rabbinical writings, and also some examples of contemporary parables.

25. See my *The Twelve . . . ,* 160, note 2.

26. See *Jesus and the Word,* Fontana Books, 1958, 66 f. (This is a translation of his famous study *Jesus,* Berlin 1929.)

27. R. Hummel, *Die Auseinandersetzung zwischen Kirche und Judentum im Matthäusevangelium,* Munich 1963, 34–71. Also G. Barth, 'Matthew's Understanding of the Law', in G. Bornkamm, G. Barth and H. J. Held, *Tradition and Interpretation in Matthew* (E. tr.), London 1960, 159–65.

28. C. E. Carlston, 'The Things that Defile (Mk 7:14) and the Law in Matthew and Mark', *New Testament Studies* (15) 1968-9, 75–95.

29. Schnackenburg, *Die Sittliche Botschaft,* 65–71.

30. *Jesus and the Word,* 68.

31. W. D. Davies, *The Setting of the Sermon on the Mount,* Cambridge 1964, 433. See the full discussion, 425–35, for a valid critique of Bultmann's position.

32. Davies, in *Paul and Rabbinic Judaism,* London 1965, 137–45, discusses the better established parallels from the great epistles.

33. This is the general view in regard to Q, e.g. Harnack, Manson, Dibelius, Taylor. Davies, in *The Setting,* 367–85, considers rather that it deals with the crisis nature of Jesus's preaching of the kingdom, and therefore belongs to kerygmatic rather than catechetical circles.

34. See Bultmann, *Theology of the New Testament* (E. tr.), I, London 1955, 188.

35. The object of the 'new quest' for the historical Jesus, is to show the identity between the demands of Jesus's proclamation and those of the early Church. See J. M. Robinson, *A New Quest for the Historical Jesus,* London 1959. In the concluding section (111–25) he describes some positive findings with examples of Pauline passages which were clearly influenced by the tradition of Jesus's words. Compare e.g. Lk 6:20-25 with 1 Cor 4:8-13.

36. See *Paul and Rabbinic Judaism,* 112–19. These were a set of commandments which Jewish tradition believed were given to Noah after the flood, and so passed to all men.

37. See C. H. Dodd's treatment of these chapters in *The Epistle to the Romans,* Fontana Books 1959, 198–217.

38. See L. Cerfaux, *Le Chrétien dans la Théologie Paulienne,* Paris 1962, 424–6.

39. E. G. Selwyn, in *The First Epistle of St Peter,* London 1946, gives a detailed reconstruction of this catechesis.

40. For a detailed discussion of the whole question see C. Spicq, *Les Épitres Pastorales,* Paris 1947, Introduction, especially cxci-cxcix.

41. See *Old Testament Theology,* I, 199 f.

42. See S. Lyonnet, Rom. 8:2-4 à la lumière de Jéremie 31 et d'Ézéchiel 35-39', in *Mélanges Eugène Tisserant,* I, Rome 1964, 311-23.

43. See C. H. Dodd, *The Bible and the Greeks,* London 1935, 25-41.

44. See N. Lohfink, *Höre Ishael, Eine Auslegung von Texten aus dem Buch Deuteronomium,* Die Welt der Bibel 18, Düsseldorf 1965, 61 f.

45. See M. J. O'Connell, 'The Concept of Commandment in the Old Testament', *Theological Studies* (21) 1960, 351-403, especially 379-89.

46. See G. von Rad, *Studies in Deuteronomy,* London 1953, 15-21.

47. See R. N. Whybray, *Wisdom in Proverbs,* London 1965, 90-104.

48. Many exegetes see a similar pattern in Christ's invitation to his disciples to come to him, Mt 11:25-29; Lk 10:21-22; see A. Feuillet, 'Jésus et la Sagesse divine d'après les Évangiles Synoptiques', *Revue Biblique* (52) 1955, 161-96.

49. See R. Brown, *The Gospel according to John, I-XII,* Anchor Bible 29, New York 1966, Appendix 1 (5) *entolē,* 504 f.

50. See N. Lazure, *Les Valeurs Morales de la Théologie Johannique,* Paris 1965 (Études Bibliques), 123-58.

51. *Theology of the Old Testament,* I, 77.

2

How Free and Creative Was and Is Moral Theology?

Bernard Häring, CSsR

I. Creative Fidelity in the Apostolic Church

One of the earliest examples of creative liberty and fidelity in the apostolic Church is seen in the conflict that arose because of the cultural diversities of the believers. The first clash between the Jews born and raised in Judea and those coming from the Diaspora called for a creative solution by giving a greater share in decision-making to representatives of the Hellenistic Jews. The solution, a new ministry of deacon, enriched the early Church through evangelization beyond Judea and Galilee by a pioneering group (cf. Acts 6:1–8). In this paradigm we see a proper, courageous and creative use of authority in resolving the conflict; and it seems not too bold to say that the seven deacons turned out to be the more prophetic group in comparison with the rather static established Church in Jerusalem.

A second important event in apostolic times shows the leader of the apostles, Simon Peter, in a most creative charismatic role. There is spontaneity in his temperament, but it is clear that this is a divine charism that somehow had to be forced upon Peter through a profound God-experience. When, after a vision, Peter was invited to preach the gospel in the house of a gentile Roman officer, Cornelius, he still did not know what the outcome would be. He needed a special intervention of God who bestowed the gifts of the Spirit on the new believers before they were baptized. Under divine inspiration, this motivated Peter not to impose on them the circumcision and all the other Jewish customs that would have ensued. It was not easy for Peter to win the agreement of the Church in Jerusalem. But here, creative freedom goes hand in hand with the patience and gentleness shown by the charismatic leader. This (Acts 10:11–18) is a classical case of genuine salvation knowledge.

The third creative breakthrough shows not Peter but Paul, the prophet among the apos-

This chapter is excerpted from Free and Faithful in Christ, *vol. 1 (New York: Seabury, 1978) 32–58.*

tles, challenging the established Church when Peter had yielded to the pressure of a conservative Jewish group. Thus arose the famous Antioch conflict where Paul publicly withstood Peter (Gal 2:9–21). He did not at all deny the supreme authority of Peter, but he publicly blamed his inconsistency. Peter accepted the challenge humbly, but the conflict continued and nearly fractured the young Church. For Paul, it was a matter of giving the first place to Christ who is our life, our truth and our law. Consciously or unconsciously, others were still giving first place to law in its written form and traditional make-up, while Christ was looked upon more as the law enforcer. Yet the creative liberty of Paul had its bearing on the Church's mission through a common solution reached in the Council of Jerusalem (Acts 15:1–35).

Because of the prophetic word of Paul, the prophetical initiative of Stephen, Philip and the other deacons, and the charismatic leadership in the apostolic Church, Christianity could spread all over the known world of that time. The gospel was not impeded by a canon law like the one which hindered the Church's mission work from the sixteenth to the twentieth century in Asia and Africa.

Whenever theology remains faithful to the biblical approach, there will be no separation between dogma and morality, and no theology severed from evangelization and pastoral ministry. Rather, all theology will affirm and serve the primacy of salvation truth.

II. The Church Fathers

1. The Early Church Fathers

The first who tried a synthesis, a constructive encounter with the prevailing philosophy of Platonism, was Justin (martyred ca. 161).

Being in dialogue with both pagan philosophy and Jewish culture, he presents Christ to Jews and Gentiles as *Logos kay Nomos* (the Word and the Law). The seed of the Word is present in all of creation and in people's hearts. Everywhere there are "the seeds of the Logos". All people have some knowledge of God's love and law. Justin's approach suffered, however, by a certain onesidedness because he ascribes too great a role to Moses whom he considered as the first writer and as influencing all the pagan writers. In his famous *Dialogue with the Jew, Tryphon,* he presents Christ as the *Nómos,* "the Law and the Covenant", in perfect continuity with the central role of the covenant pattern in Old Testament law.[2]

2. Clement of Alexandria

Clement of Alexandria (died ca. 214) is, no doubt, one of the most courageous theologians in creative dialogue with the prevailing thought patterns of his culture. "No one denies his importance for the history of Christian morals".[3] Faithful to the Bible, he develops the main patterns such as discipleship, righteousness, the all-embracing reality of love as gift, goal and commandment, and the relationship between faith and freedom. His chief writings are *Protrepticus* (Exhortation), *Paedagogos* (Instructor) and *Stromateis* (Miscellanies).

The centre and sum of Clement's teaching is the true knowledge of Jesus Christ. Being deeply involved in the fight against Gnosticism, he is creative and constructive in presenting the Christian as the one who lives the true form of Gnosis.[4] He presents a good deal of philosophical speculation (*Seinswissen*) but always integrates it with a salvation perspective and intention. While using Platonic philosophy, he carefully avoids certain pitfalls. He rejects, for instance, the stoic antagonism of body and soul and strongly emphasizes the goodness of the body. However, it is not surprising that he, too, occasionally uses expressions that are characteristic of the patterns of thought in his culture: "The body is only a husk which is wrapped around us for our earthly journey, so that we may be able to enter this common place of correction".[5]

Clement also uses the prevailing ethical idea of the Stoics, *apatheia;* but he gives it a quite new direction. It is no longer the stoic self-sufficiency but the inner freedom and peace that allow creative discipleship. His theology gives place to the primacy of love. "The act of loving the Father with all our strength and power makes us free from decay. For the more a person loves God, the more closely he enters into God".[6]

A main pattern and theme for Clement is that the human person is created in the image and likeness of God. The moral life is seen as responding to this vocation. To him, the perfect "Gnostic" is Jesus Christ, and those who come to know Christ and, through him, the Father, are true "Gnostics". Thus he brings to the foreground the all-embracing goal-commandment, "Let your goodness have no limits, just as the goodness of the heavenly Father knows no bounds" (Mt 5:48).

Clement does not allow Christians to avoid their responsibility to the earthly city: they should, rather, know their vocation to be "salt for the earth". Disciples of Christ can live a truly Christian life in a big city like Alexandria. They are not compelled to renounce wealth, but they will make generous use of it if they really understand the discipleship of Christ. For this purpose Clement wrote his book, *Quis Dives Salvetur?* ("What Rich Man Can Be Saved?"). Faithful to the mystery of the incarnation and redemption, he consistently teaches the mission of Christ's disciples to be light in the world and for the world.[7]

Against Manicheism, Clement purposefully defends the goodness of marriage as well as the vocation of celibacy for the kingdom of God. At times, however, he seems reluctant simply to acknowledge the moral goodness of conjugal intercourse. Some of his restrictions and negative expressions seem to have had more influence on the later tradition than his generally balanced vision. We do not do justice to Clement by quoting only accidental lapses into expressions similar to the Stoics', as, for instance, his description of conjugal intercourse as a "kind of minor epilepsy, an incurable disease. Note the harm it does: the whole person is lost in the unconsciousness of the intercourse".[8] Such expressions as this only prove that even thinkers as creative as Clement do not completely escape the influence of the spirit of their era.

3. Origen

The most creative theologian of the early Greek Church, and surely one of the most influential pioneers in theological synthesis and inquiry, is Origen (born 184 or 185; died ca. 254).[9] He had probably been a student under Clement of Alexandria, and was distinguished by the breadth of his knowledge in profane and sacred literature. True to the rule of faith as it was kept in his time, he looked for a deeper understanding of fundamental questions that still concern us today.

For Origen, Christ is the centre of history. The virtues are mediated by Christ. Against the Valentinians, Origen strongly defends freedom of the will. He teaches the vocation of all Christians to holiness, and can be considered the creator of spiritual theology. All of his theology has a pastoral and spiritual note. He not only taught and preached the gospel of Jesus Christ but also witnessed to Christ under terrible and prolonged tortures. In the search for deeper understanding of faith in the formation of a Christian élite and in the dialogue with unbelievers, Origen proved, again and again, his fidelity and courage. He truly knew what discipleship meant.

The influence of Origen on the early Church was great. During his lifetime he not only suffered from the enemies of the Church but sometimes also from Church authorities. Because in his youth he had castrated himself in a wrong understanding of Matthew's gospel (Mt 19:12), Bishop Demetrius not only refused him ordination to the priesthood but also banned him from Alexandria when a Palestinian bishop had ordained him. However, during most of his life he found a Church and environment favourable to his charism as a zealous and creative explorer of revealed truth.

After Origen's death, and especially after the end of the fourth century, his influence was not always what it might have been. His enemies distorted many of his words, taking them out of context, and his admirers sometimes did no better. By that time, Origenism was feeling the attack of people who had only "knowledge of dominion". The emperor Justinian forced an ecumenical council (ca. 550) to put Origen's name on the list of heretics in Canon 11. That, however, was not approved by Pope Vigilius. The three following councils nevertheless repeated condemnations, always under the influence of knowledge of control and dominion, and not so much on behalf of salvation knowledge.

4. St Basil

St Basil the Great (330–379) was surely one of the most influential Fathers of the Greek Church. He is an eminent example of creative fidelity, concerned about faith and its moral implications. For him, a true believer is seized by an intense desire to follow Christ. At a time when the official Church, and especially the bishops, became too tied up with imperial power—a Church in the service of the emperor—Basil was one of the great leaders of monachism. He is the father of almost all the oriental monasteries throughout the ages.

At its beginning, the monachist movement was a non-violent protest against the worldliness of a Church in service to the empire. St Basil represents the charismatic, the enthusiastic Church. He gives special emphasis to the Holy Spirit and the charisms of the Spirit. He sees clearly that all the charisms, and particularly those of the monks, are for the common good. Since his time, schools, hospitals and other social works have been a part of the religious community.

Basil did not want to set up a sect like that of Qumran, severed from the Church. On the contrary, he wanted the monachism of the religious to become the inspiration of all Christians. He left no doubt that the vocation to holiness is for all; but in view of the concrete situation of his time, marked by a "Church of the empire" and bishops as a superior social class, he insisted that a life in holiness outside the model community was very difficult.

The heart of Basil's spirituality and morality is love in the discipleship under the guidance of the Holy Spirit. His writings are thoroughly nourished by Holy Scripture, and the same is particularly true of his monastic rule. However, where he touches on matters of righteousness, he strongly stresses obedience, although everyone is directed to be obedient to the grace of the Holy Spirit. He greatly influenced the future by his stress on self-denial and a more platonic attitude towards the body as a prison of the soul. His rigorism, however, is tempered by a childlike simplicity and by a healing approach to those who are transgressors of the law. "Basil's faith is more static than Clement's".[10] This applies also to the way he uses moral imperatives of the gospel, although never severed from the gifts of the Holy Spirit.

St Basil was a great admirer of God's creation, even though he does not really include the human body in this admiration. He believed, however, in an inborn law present to all, so he too has influenced positively the tradition of natural law theories.

5. *St John Chrysostom*

In his courage, his vision, his enthusiasm and sanity, and in his charism, John Chrysostom (died 407) embodies the prophetic tradition probably more than most of the great theologians. He truly honours Christ the Prophet. His hero is Paul, the apostle to the Gentiles, and he is Paul's most fervent and faithful interpreter in his emphasis on faith and love in the discipleship of Jesus Christ. Like the prophets, he is clearly on the side of the poor, the oppressed and underprivileged; and, like the prophets of old, he paid in his own body for being a prophet. He was exiled and treated badly. He died when he was led to an even more miserable place of exile on the Black Sea. His guards had been instructed to treat him as harshly as possible and not to let him recover. His last word were "Glory to God for all things".

"As a moralist, he is at the same time creative and profound".[11] All his life and writings manifest the absolute priority of knowledge of salvation. As patriarch of Constantinople he gave striking example of a truly Christian and prophetic exercise of authority, although it cost him enormous suffering and persecution. At the same time, he followed Christ the Prophet, showing great love even to those who persecuted him. He was a prophet also in the way he tried to convert priests who wanted to belong to a superior social class. He praised martyrdom for faith, but gave equal praise to those who offer their lives for any other of God's commandments, especially if commitment to justice and to the rights of the poor and oppressed are involved.[12] It is no wonder that, in the matter of slavery, he was much more clear-sighted than most of his contemporaries. He did not see how slavery could ever be in accordance with God's providence for all humanity or with the dignity of persons created in the image of God. He strongly urged believers either to free the slaves or to treat them as brothers with kindness and reverence.

Chrysostom is also very positive about the importance of work for the Christian's personal development and for service to the brethren. He does not tolerate any gap between faith and daily life. Because of his own prophetic gift and his great veneration for St Paul, he has no tendency towards legalism.

He praises virginity but not in opposition to marriage. "It is wrong to denigrate marriage in order to praise virginity".[13] As a pastor, he greatly values family life: "Make your home a church".[14] He is not anti-feminist. Perhaps only Gregory of Nazianzus among the Church Fathers has a more courageous and positive outlook on marriage. Neither Gregory nor Chrysostom minimize the importance of the body, although they, too, promoted radical self-denial in the discipleship of the Crucified.

Against those who think that monasteries have no meaning, John Chrysostom defends monks. However, he urges monks to be ready for service to others, and especially ready for mission work. "How much better were it for you to become less zealous and to profit others than, remaining on the heights, to look down upon your dying brothers. For how shall we overcome our enemies if one part of us pays no heed to virtue, and those who pay heed to it will stay far from the line of battle?"[15]

Chrysostom's Christian doctrine of natural law is fully developed and in no way severed from the Lordship of Jesus Christ. He insists that all people are endowed with moral knowledge. "When God created man at the beginning he gave to him a natural law. What is natural law? It shapes and corrects the conscience within us when it provides knowledge which is capable, of itself, of distinguishing what is good from what is not good".[16]

External circumstances did not favour Chrysostom's prophetic courage and creativity. He is a sign that God can send prophets under the most unfavourable conditions if those called are truly responsive to the call.

6. *St Ambrose*

St Ambrose (339–397) is one of the great churchmen who combines, in an outstanding way, salvation truth with authentic knowledge of authority. He was so loved as governor of the province Aemilia-Liguria (seated in Milan) that after the death of the Arian bishop the people spontaneously called for him as bishop. He was able to unite the people again in the Catholic faith.

Like Chrysostom, Ambrose was never the "king's priest". His prophetic courage brought him sharp opposition from Empress Justina. He called the mighty ones to penance, to justice and clemency. He was a great teacher of faith. Although not a speculative theologian, he brought the thought of Origen and Basil the Great home to the Latin Church. As a pastor, he addressed many moral problems in a very practical way. He wrote for his priests the book *De Officiis* (on the duties of a good pastor and of all believers), borrowing particularly from Cicero's book of the same

title. He was, however, critical, discerning regarding the use of pagan philosophy. Like others, he adopted the system of the four cardinal virtues from Stoic ethics trying to give them an authentically Christian content. He influenced the Latin Church above all through his disciple, St Augustine, whom he had received into the Catholic Church.

7. *St Augustine*

Augustine of Hippo (354–430) is perhaps the most creative, the most imaginative thinker of Christian antiquity and like Chrysostom is marked by a dedication to Christ and his Church. Augustine, however, had greater influence in the western Church, since he wrote in Latin. Throughout the centuries he has been a fascinating figure, due to his warm humanity, his sincerity, his confidence in God and his capacity to present an attractive synthesis of Christian doctrine and ethics. "He is the crowning end of Christian antiquity, its last and greatest thinker".[17]

St Augustine has treated almost all of the major perspectives of Christian morality, and has done so in great depth and with an unmatched knowledge of the human heart. He has anticipated much of the knowledge uncovered by modern depth psychology. "The genius of Augustine is unique in its versatile mastery of all the literary genres in his ethical writings: vivid description, profound handling of principles, captivating manifestation of emotions, practical moral exhortation, epistolatory admonition, spiritual guidance. Even the diverse methods found within Catholic moral theology, the scholastic and mystic, aesthetic and casuistic, find their models in his work".[18]

Like his personality, Augustine's theology reveals a great complexity. He went a long way from Manicheism to Platonism and finally to

Christ; and only gradually did he free himself from some manichean trends. He always remained a Platonist and so influenced all of western theology until Thomas Aquinas, and even beyond that time.

Always and everywhere, Augustine extols the bounty of God's grace, and faith as an undeserved gift. On the other hand, he has not denied free will, although he realizes that the mystery of predestination on one hand and free will on the other cannot be explained by a human being. Against the Manicheans and Pelagians, Augustine strongly asserts the reality of sin. He calls the Church herself "a mixed body". Sin is a terrifying reality but man cannot excuse himself. God offers his grace to all, and those who pray and put their trust in God will receive freedom in Christ.

Like the Church Fathers of the East of whom we have already written, Augustine teaches a natural law by which God guides the conscience of all people. God never has abandoned humankind. Like Cicero, Augustine defines virtue as "a natural disposition consistent with nature and reason".[19] However, he does not think highly of the virtues of the heathen but thinks that they are, rather, more like splendid vices.

More than many earlier theologians, Augustine succeeds in integrating the four cardinal virtues into the one great vision of redeemed, Christlike love. He sees the divine gift of love, responded to by man, as at the heart of all virtues: "So that temperance is love, keeping the self entire and uncorrupt for the beloved. Courage is love, bearing everything gladly for the sake of the beloved. Righteousness is love, serving the beloved only, and therefore ruling well. And prudence is love, wisely discerning what helps it and what hinders it".[20] Without love, no virtue really counts. Love unites us with God and with fellowman. It makes us truly the Church,

and makes the Church "the one Christ loving himself".[21]

The love of God, always united with the love of neighbour, is for Augustine everywhere visible as the centre of morality. "Virtue is simply nothing but the highest love of God".[22] Probably the most quoted word of St Augustine is "Love and do what you will".[23] However, it must be read in the context and in its original meaning. He does not say "*ama*" but "*dilige*", which means "have a pure and right love". St Augustine's vision of love is not at all that unstructured or agnostic love which Joseph Fletcher and other extreme situation ethicists have in mind. He tells us to be careful about whom we love and how we love, and that we can learn love from Jesus Christ under the guidance of the Holy Spirit.

One of St Augustine's weakest points is his outlook on sexuality and marriage; but there, too, he makes many sensible observations although, especially in his early writings, there is still much of his manichean background. But because he is nevertheless such a creative and faithful theologian, it is not surprising that the Augustinian vision of marriage had a great and often unfortunate impact on the Church in succeeding centuries. In the encyclical *Casti Connubii*, for instance, St Augustine is quoted thirteen times; and it is not uninteresting to read the context of all the quotes made in that encyclical.[24]

III. A Time of Repetition

For theology in general and moral theology in particular, the period from the end of the sixth to the end of the twelfth century was barren. There was little activity beyond the compiling of summaries. Fidelity was not creative; rather, it was frequently misunderstood as never-changing repetition.

To some extent the Iro-Scottish Church was creative in the matter of the sacrament of penance, mitigating and adjusting the rather rigid discipline of the Roman Church. The Irish and Scottish monks did this not without some relation to the oriental monks. However, the penitential books that influenced the whole western Church for almost twelve hundred years were creative in the wrong sense: they added more and more kinds of penance for the various sins. The *Penitential* of Burchard is a pertinent example. It lists not less than twenty varieties of homicide, each with its own appropriate penance determined according to the social rank of the person who was killed![25] In all of this, there was too much knowledge of dominion, of the controller, so that the wisdom of the "knowledge of salvation" was somehow blocked.

IV. A Century of Creative Theology and Renewal

1. *The Blessing of St Francis and St Dominic*

The great religious movements at last brought a new creativity into the theology of morals. Mystical theology was enriched by St Bernard of Clairvaux, Eckart, Tauler, Henry Suso and many others. The greatest contributions were made by members of the two mendicant orders, the Franciscans and Dominicans. Here again, serious learning met with enthusiasm of faith. Alexander Hales (died 1245) and St Bonaventure (1221–1274) and later Duns Scotus (died 1308) enriched the Church by "teaching of wisdom". There was no such thing as a separate moral theology. They studied all of theology as a message of salvation. Union with Christ, the gifts of faith and grace, the sacramental reality: all this was presented in its own richness as bringing fruit in love and justice for the life of the world.

The Dominicans gave to the Church such splendid teachers as Albert the Great (1193–1280) who, in the breadth of his knowledge, is comparable to Clement and Origen, and his disciple, St Thomas Aquinas (died 1274).

2. *A Saint Innovator*

In the recent past centuries, Thomas Aquinas has been presented consistently as the glory and bulwark of the Catholic faith. However, we should remind ourselves of what it meant in those times to be such a creative theologian. Avery Dulles tells of this. To his contemporaries, Thomas Aquinas "was not the 'common doctor' but a controversial innovator, not a canonized saint but the purveyor of a dangerous new brand of secular philosophy, not a strong bulwark but a teacher widely suspected of heresy . . . At Paris, where he did his later studies, the Dominicans were regarded as a strange, unwholesome breed, neither monks nor seculars, defiant of all the traditional categories. Not surprisingly, the Dominican house of studies became a sign of contradiction. The life style of St Thomas and his Dominican brothers might not have excited disapprobation had it not been combined with a second revolutionary stance: the acceptance of Aristotle as the master of theological and scientific method. Thomas had to begin his teaching career in the midst of violent controversy. On many occasions the university students were forbidden to attend his classes. After he died, the bishop of Paris and the archbishop of Canterbury condemned numerous theses which St Thomas had defended".[27]

Thomas Aquinas was truly creative in a

pastoral sense. It was not arbitrariness when he tried to meet Aristotle's thought which was already widespread in Europe and was, for many, a temptation to abandon faith. Instead of presenting sterile apologetics, Thomas entered into a most fruitful dialogue, working out a new synthesis without abandoning what was good in the Augustinian tradition. Aquinas was very well versed in the Bible, and his moral teaching, thoroughly integrated into the whole vision of faith, has at its very heart "the law of the Spirit which gives us life in Christ Jesus".

In a certain sense, Thomas Aquinas was the innovator of a systematic moral theology. However, it is erroneous to present separately the second part of the theological *Summa,* which treats mainly of ethical questions, as a system cut off from the first and third parts. Not only does he treat important moral questions in the third part of the *Summa*—such as "moral life in accordance with the sacraments of faith"—but, above all, the second part was never thought of as an independent moral theology. For St Thomas as for St Bonaventure, there is only one theology and that is the doctrine of salvation that teaches us to know God and to know man, to love God and serve man.

While Thomas Aquinas offers a considerable body of philosophical speculation it is all subordinated to the knowledge of salvation. It is presented with a pastoral mind.

Not unlike Chrysostom, Thomas Aquinas is a model of the creative and faithful theologian in circumstances that did not always favour these qualities. He had much less to suffer than Chrysostom, but it cannot be deplored enough that his beneficial influence was greatly stifled by office holders in the Church at a time when it was most needed. Later, Thomism did not serve its main purpose be-

cause it became too repetitive. The formulations of Aquinas were simply repeated unimaginatively, without his courageous encounter with the spirit of the era and without his sound vision of the signs of the times.

3. *The Impact of Nominalism*

The Nominalism that prevailed after the thirteenth century, largely through the great influence of William of Ockham (1359), can be called creative; yet in many aspects it does not deserve the praise of "faithful in Christ". It emphasized, and sometimes overemphasized, individual freedom and the unique value of the singular and the individual, but it lost sight of the solidarity of salvation.

4. *Thomas Aquinas Vindicated*

In the sixteenth century, the work of Thomas Aquinas was finally no longer suspect and found its great commentators. Some of them, like Thomas De Vio, Cardinal Cajetan (died 1534), and the Dominican Francis of Vitoria (died 1536), are imposing figures of the Thomistic renaissance. Especially Francis Vitoria was most sensitive to the new problems arising in a new era.

V. Origin of the Roman Catholic Moral Theology

1. *A New Purpose and New Environment of Moral Theology*

It is important to remind ourselves that the moral theology that most of us were taught in our seminaries twenty or thirty years ago is a rather recent product. Through fifteen centuries the Catholic Church had nothing like that. It is not "the" tradition but is one late tradition; and as we shall see, it was never unchallenged within the Roman Catholic Church. That there is nothing similar in the Orthodox or Protestant Churches is no wonder, since this type of moral theology came into being only after the great separation.

Although the Thomistic revival of Christian moral theology was concerned with human rights and with international justice—the relations between and among nations—a rather striking privatizing tendency also soon became apparent. And this goes hand in hand with the new purpose of moral teaching: the "administration of the sacrament of penance".

On the one hand, a truly Catholic reform, whose most noble representatives were, among others, St Teresa of Avila and St John of the Cross, was giving the Church profound works on a spirituality that, at least partially, continued the tradition of the great Church Fathers of whom we have spoken. On the other hand there was developing a moral theology just for the solution of cases in the confessional. In this theology, the confessor's role was understood chiefly as a judge. Not only had he to know whether the penitent had sinned but also whether he had committed a grave sin (frequently equated with mortal sin) and to determine accurately the number and species of all these mortal sins. Such a moral theology no longer promotes the patterns of discipleship, of that righteousness that comes from God's justifying action and in loving response to his call to become ever more the image and likeness of his own mercy. All this was left out or at least left to dogmatic or spiritual theology.

The goal of systematic moral theology was now to determine the doctrinal principles underlying the correct solution of cases for the confessional. The result was a gradual development of an independent and self-sufficient moral discipline, although it considered itself self-sufficient only by incorporating all determinations of canon laws and frequently those of civil laws. It became one-sidedly an ethics of obedience while it was also an ethics of control through the confessor.

The new perspective and purpose led to a rapid development of the problematic of "theological opinion"—opinion that could safely be followed by the confessor or/and by the penitent. The source of moral knowledge was no longer Holy Scripture but chiefly law and the declarations of the magisterium which were also conceived in the perspective of abiding laws. The exercise of the magisterium was too much linked with the earthly power of the bishops, especially of the popes.

When the patristic and medieval tradition on natural law was presented in this new framework, it became deeply affected by a legalistic tendency. The emphasis was no longer on the law inborn in man and discovered by conscience in the reciprocity of consciences, but rather on the authoritative decision of what natural law prescribes for all people of all times. There was little consciousness of the interdependence of moral knowledge with the total cultural, social, political structures and environment.

It would be unfair to say that all this endeavour was sterile. There were, throughout all this time, many moralists who tried to integrate the new knowledge of their times about man. But in view of the whole historical context—including the heavy hand of the universal Roman Inquisition and other inquisitions and censorships—a prophetic spirit could not flourish. This moral theology, for instance, presented reasons for the existence of slavery instead of being a prophetic voice for the radical abolishment of such an abominable institution. Most of the manuals showed little interest in matters of social and international justice, for this was not considered a matter for the ordinary penitent. They surely did not foster a consciousness of everyone's responsibility in the cultural, social and political spheres.

The work of theologians has to be seen always within the frame of society and Church and their respective self-understanding. The prevailing concern of one part of this new Roman Catholic moral theology was to enforce the laws of Church and state. The emphasis was on man-made laws. Church law was also understood as being enforced by the political community while, at the same time, the Church enforced the law and order of the political community. And since the self-understanding of the Church was static, as was also the understanding of human nature and natural law, a desire for change was considered one of the greatest sins.

This attitude produced the system of "tutiorism", whereby the literal application of the law was to prevail in all matters of doubt. Close to the same rigid approach came "probabiliorism", which taught that the presumption always favours the literal application of the law unless much stronger reasons can be presented for freedom to seek the good in a different way. Natural law principles were proposed as if they were part of a codified law. Scripture, too, was understood as a static system of laws; hence, any quote from the Bible could enforce a law in a literal, fundamentalist understanding.

On the other side were numerous pastors and theologians—mostly Probabilists—who were much more aware of the dynamic character of history, of human nature and of natural law, and were mainly concerned with respect for the consciences of sincere people.

By no means did they deny the validity of law and order. Under the given circumstances they did not dare to challenge the authoritarian regimes and the staggering number of laws and penal sanctions. Within the given system, however, they gave priority to people's conscience as long as it was sincere. Therefore they taught that in cases where the validity, justice or correct application of a law might be in doubt, creative liberty should prevail.

Frequently these moralists were profoundly compassionate pastors, and their concern in proposing the system of probabilism was to follow the main pattern of the Bible, "Be compassionate as your heavenly Father is compassionate" (Lk 6:36). It cannot be denied that some people would take advantage of their arguments and opinions in order to find the easy way out, but this does not at all diminish the merits of those numerous moralists—especially in the Society of Jesus—who were keenly aware that all too many laws and sanctions stifle the freedom and creativity of the faithful.

They were also concerned not to make it impossible for dedicated Christians to be present in economic and cultural spheres. There was, for instance, the very sharp and clearly defined position of the official Church, prohibiting the taking of any form of interest for loans. In order to avoid guilt complexes or rebellion against the official Church, or withdrawal from the world, many moralists found arguments and reasons for allowing a moderate rate of interest. While their way of arguing, in view of the clearcut teaching of the official Church, was sometimes artificial, their motives, intentions and intrinsic reasons were valid.

Since the rigorists and tutiorists could see no moral value except in the observance of law, they easily labelled these Probabilists as

"laxists", or men aiming to undermine morality. To oppose any part of the codes of law
was, for them, to undermine morality. Even
Blaise Pascal seems to have been not quite free
from this misunderstanding when he under-
took his fight against the moral teaching of the
Jesuits.[28]

The Jansenists, who bitterly fought against
the Probabilists, were perhaps even more entangled in legalistic thinking than those whom
they were blaming. It is true that Probabilists,
even when their concern was clearly for a better understanding of fidelity and in favour of
liberty, did sometimes use arguments that, on
legal grounds, were distorted.

Meanwhile, the Carmelites of Salamanca,
keeping themselves out of the heat of the vigorous theological quarrels, patiently composed their *Cursus Theologiae Moralis*
(1665–1724). This is, without doubt, the most
comprehensive and significant work in moral
theology of that time. However it, too, is affected by the whole situation of a Church in
self-defence, a Church too much linked with a
totalitarian type of political system.

2. St Alphonsus Liguori

St Alphonsus Liguori (1696–1787) is honoured by the Church as patron of moral theologians and confessors.[29] His work and his
contribution to the history of moral theology
can be evaluated only in view of the situation
of Church and society in which he made his
efforts to bring balance into moral theology
and to fight against Jansenism. Alphonsus,
founder of the Redemptorists, was, above all,
a pastor dedicated to the marginal people, the
poor and the oppressed. He and his confreres
bound themselves by an explicit vow to give
preference to these marginal people.

Against Jansenistic pessimism, St Alphonsus' essential message is, "Plentiful is re-

demption with the Lord". When he began to
write, he was not at all intending to propose a
systematic moral theology for all times. On
the contrary, he was simply moved by pastoral
zeal. At that time, the Society of Jesus was
already strongly embattled and the Probabilists were suspect. He himself had been taught
by a Dominican who followed a rather rigid
probabiliorism, but as soon as Alphonsus dedicated himself to the poor and the marginal
people, he saw that this system was not suited
to his purpose. He did embrace probabilism,
but in view of the situation in the Church he
carefully called it "aequiprobabilism", which
means that when an upright conscience has
equally or almost equally good reasons for creative use of freedom in view of present needs,
it is not bound by law which is, in itself or in
its concrete application, doubtful. Law should
have no right to stifle creative freedom unless
it has clearly stronger reasons for doing so.

In spite of warnings on all sides, Alphonsus
also consistently taught that confessors should
not unsettle the good conscience of penitents
by referring to law, whether natural law or
merely Church or state law, when he can
foresee that the penitent cannot truly interior-
ize this law or precept.

The whole theological effort of St Alphonsus against Jansenism is a theology of divine mercy. He therefore strongly opposes the
Thomistic system's teaching about predestination and the distinction between "efficacious"
and merely "sufficient" graces. In that system
it seemed that God would exclude great numbers of people from salvation by his own decrees. While the elect would receive graces
"efficacious" to merit salvation, others would
be given graces called "sufficient", which
would be sufficient for accountability but unproductive of the good works for which they
are given, and therefore would metaphysically
determine unavoidable failure and consequent

condemnation. No wonder that the opponents of this theory responded by the prayer, *A gratia sufficienti libera nos Domine:* "From 'sufficient' grace, deliver us, O Lord!'"

St Alphonsus's theology, like the whole Catholic moral theology of the past centuries, was chiefly concerned with helping confessors to form mature and peaceful consciences. He had given much time to helping scrupulous persons, and therefore instructed confessors not to lead people into unnecessary anxiety. He wrote a number of books specifically destined for confessors, one of which was the *Homo Apostolicus,* "The Apostolic Man". This is probably the most mature of the saint's work in the field of penitential moral theology. It went through one hundred and eighteen editions. Not less helpful is his *Confessor of Country People.* Against the prevailing theological theory that saw the confessor's role above all as a judge, St Alphonsus, in full awareness of the situation, assigned first role to making visible the compassionate love of the heavenly Father, as Christ did.

One can fully appreciate the charism of creative liberty and fidelity in Alphonsus only by giving attention to his more numerous and widespread writings on a truly Christian life. In almost all his books, he repeatedly refers to St Augustine's word, "Have true love and do what love wills". The most beautiful of his works is *The Art of Loving Jesus Christ.* This is a kind of moral theology for lay people as well as for priests. It presents the true countenance of love and applications of love, in the form of a commentary on the thirteenth chapter of the first letter of St Paul to the Corinthians.

This is what St Alphonsus understood as the ideal moral theology. His constant theme is on the vocation of all Christians to holiness; but he was thoroughly against Jansenism which would allow place in the Church only to perfected people. His vision was one of ongoing conversion, and he saw the priest as a patient guide who encourages people to take one step after another.

VI. Renewal of Moral Theology in the Nineteenth Century

1. Reliving the Broader Tradition

As we have shown, the individualistic moral theology was never unchallenged. For instance, Cardinal Berulle, founder of the French school of spirituality which gave the Church great saints, always presented a spirituality and morality based on the sacramental experience of life in Christ, who is the supreme sacrament. Where members of his school preached the gospel, they preserved whole areas from Jansenism and dechristianization.

A scientific and systematic effort to renew moral theology took place in the faculties of German state universities. These efforts were possible because the theological faculties at state universities enjoyed greater academic freedom than teachers in the seminaries. The best known moralists who presented a totally different type of manual from those of the legalistic and casuistic schools are John Michael Sailer (1751-1832), John Baptist Hirscher (1788-1865), and Francis Xavier Linsenmann (1855-1898).

2. John Michael Sailer

Sailer[30] gave to his comprehensive text on moral theology the characteristic subtitle, "Not only for Future Catholic Pastors but also for Every Educated Christian". Like Rosmini in Italy, he was shocked by the gap between the clergy and educated lay people. As the great Church fathers of East and West

have done, so Sailer entered into active dialogue with the thought patterns of his times.
He follows the emphasis on creative fidelity,
righteousness in response to God's own saving
justice, and discipleship and love as the all-
embracing response to God.

Both in the goal he sets for himself and in
the spiritual fervour of his language, he resem-
bles St Francis de Sales whom he greatly admired. But he does not content himself with
imparting practical advice for spiritual progress as did Francis in his masterly treatises.
Sailer's purpose and plan includes the entire
edifice of teaching Christian life, a systematic
presentation of the perfect goal of that life.
But far from Jansenistic harshness, he allows
patient, ongoing progress towards the ideal.
At the heart of his moral theology is the theme
of ongoing conversion.

Sailer must be appreciated in the light of his
times. He belongs to the Romantic period,
and his ideal of personality is influenced by it.
Therefore he insists on the use and development of all of God's individual gifts in all their
diversity, but also in the spirit of solidarity,
since everything is given in view of the up-
building of the mystical body of Christ.

In view of Sailer's creativity as a theologian
and his distinctively Christian fidelity to the
Church, it is almost unbelievable how much
he had to suffer from Church and state estab-
lishments. Even saints were denouncing him as
a controversial and suspect theologian. However, he finally received appreciation from the
official Church and was nominated bishop of
Regensburg.

3. John Baptist Hirscher

Not less creative was John Baptist
Hirscher.[31] He presents the whole Christian
moral teaching in the pattern of the Synoptics:

that is, the realization of the kingdom of God
on earth. In theological depth he yields to
Sailer, whom he greatly admired, but he exceeds him in greater psychological insights.
More realistic and equally aware of the age in
which he lived, he gave a more dynamic and
rigorous presentation of thought, though he
occasionally fell short of Sailer's mystic lofti-
ness.

Sublime in conception and happy in execution, Hirscher's moral theology nevertheless
suffered from the defects which are inevitable
in the enterprise of pioneers. He gratefully accepted critique and improved each of his later
editions. His work found ready acceptance
among Catholics and Protestants; but when
one of his books, in which he blamed the
methods of the Neo-scholastics, was put on
the Index of forbidden books, he was not only
discredited in the eyes of many Catholics but
also suffered a loss of self-confidence. And
this was so because he was not only loyal but
also devout in his fidelity to the official
Church.

4. Francis Xavier Linsenmann

A number of other outstanding and creative
theologians worked in the same direction as
Sailer and Hirscher, and would deserve to be
mentioned. The most important continuer of
this renewal was Francis Xavier Linsenmann
(1855–1898) of the Tübingen school. He dedicated a long series of studies to the fundamental problems of law and liberty.[32] He was
convinced that moral theology should follow
the spirit of St Paul and give primary attention
to the freedom of the sons and daughters of
God. He considered as sterile and futile a
moral theology concerned only with what is
proscribed by law. "Only a tiny portion of the
good expected from us is circumscribed by

law. An immense area of free moral activity lies open before us".[33] Therefore Linsenmann considered it one of the major tasks of moral theology to uncover the deeper meaning of freedom as following of Christ under the grace of the Holy Spirit.

His manual of moral theology (1878) is a happy synthesis of speculative and practical method, with openness to the Spirit and to the opportunities of his age. Always he emphasizes the normative value of growth and ongoing conversion. That his work did not meet with the recognition and success it deserved is most unfortunate. It did not correspond with the static self-understanding of the Church that had prevailed after Vatican I and was, indeed, a strong force since the Congress of Vienna in 1816, and even more since 1848, when many Christians and office holders in the Church decided to withstand all change as if it were sin and danger.

One of the strengths of the German effort to renew Catholic moral theology was its contact with the prevailing spirit of the age, a constructive dialogue with the most influential philosophies, and the fact that the manuals were written in the German language. But in the long run this became also a handicap, since none of the manuals were ever translated into other languages and, therefore, beyond the German-speaking countries, had no major impact on the whole of moral theology in the Catholic Church.[34]

Notes

1. Cf. M. Scheler, *Die Wissensformen und die Gesellschaft,* Leipzig, 1926, reprint Basel-München, 1960.
2. *Dialogus cum Tryphone judaeo,* c. 11, n. 2 PG 6, 497; c. 24, n. 1 PG 6, 528: cf. E. F. Osborn, *Justin Martyr,* Tübingen, 1973.
3. E. F. Osborn, *Ethical Patterns in Early Christian Thought,* Cambridge, New York/Melbourne, 1976, 51.
4. Cf. H. Chadwick, *Early Christian Thought and Classical Tradition. Studies in Justin, Clement and Origen,* New York, 1966; O. Prunet, *La morale de Clement d'Alexandria,* Paris, 1966.
5. Cf. E. F. Osborn, *The Philosophy of Clement of Alexandria,* Cambridge, 1967.
6. *Protrepticus,* 11, 117.
7. E. F. Osborn, *Ethical Patterns of Early Christian Thought,* 52.
8. Clement, *Paidagogos,* II PG 8, 511 A.
9. Cf. H. T. Kerr, *The First Systematic Theologian: Origen of Alexandria,* Princeton, 1958; G. Teichtweier, *Die Sündenlehre des Origines,* Regensburg, 1958; G. Gruber, *Zoë, Wesen, Stufen und Mitteilung des wahren Lebens bei Origines,* München, 1962.
10. E. F. Osborn, l.c., 101.
11. A. Puech, *St-Jean Chrysostome et les moeurs de son temps,* Paris, 1891, 325.
12. Chrysostom, *Against the Jews,* 6, 7, PG 48, 916.
13. On virginity, 9, PG 48, 539–540.
14. In Ps. XLI, 2, PG 55, 158.
15. *Homily on 1 Cor. 6,* PG 61, 53–54.
16. *On Statues,* 12, 3, PG 49, 131.
17. E. Troeltsch, *Augustin, die Christliche Antike und das Mittelalter,* München und Berlin, 1915, 6f; cf. M. T. Clark, *Augustine, Philosopher of Freedom,* New York, 1958.
18. J. Mausbach, *Die Ethik des hl. Augustinus,* Freiburg, 1929, I, 47.
19. *On 63 Diverse Questions,* 31, 1, PL 40, 20.
20. *On the Morals of the Catholic Church,* I, 15, 25, PL 32, 1322.

21. *On the Epistle of John*, 10, 3, PL 35, 2056.
22. *On the Morals of the Catholic Church*, 15, 25, PL 32, 1322.
23. *On the Epistle of John*, 7, 8, PL 35, 2033.
24. See my book *Love is the Answer*, Denville, 1970.
25. Migne, PL 140, 853 DC.
26. E. Gilson, *Saint Thomas d'Aquin*, Paris, 1925; A. Dempf, *Die Ethik des Mittelalters*, München-Berlin, 1927; O. Lottin, *Psychologie et morale aux XIIe et XIIIe siecles*, Louvain, 1942/54.
27. A. Dulles, S. J., "The Revolutionary Spirit of Thomas Aquinas", in *Origins*, Feb. 1975, 543f.
28. Blaise Pascal, *Lettres Provinciales* (1656).
29. Cf. K. Keusch, *Die Aszetik des hl. Alfons Maria von Liguori*, Paderborn, 1926.
30. G. Fischer, *Johann Michael Sailer und Immanuel Kant*, Freiburg, 1953.
31. J. Scharl, *Gesetz und Freiheit. Die theologische Begründung der christlichen Ethik bei J. B. Hirscher*, München, 1941.
32. *Tübinger Theol. Quartalschrift* 53 (1871). 64–114; 221–277; 54 (1972), 3–49; 193–254.
33. I.c., 54 (1872), 45.
34. An abundant bibliography on the history of moral theology and a list of the most used manuals of moral theology is to be found in my earlier work, *The Law of Christ*, I, 53–59. There can be found a more complete sketch of the history. For further bibliography and information, see G. Angelini, A. Valsecchi, *Disegno Storico della teologia morale*, Bologna, 1972; P. Tillich, *A History of Christian Thought from the Judaic and Hellenistic Origins to Existentialism*, edited by C. E. Braaten, New York, 1972; H. R. Niebuhr, *Christian Ethics, Sources of Living Tradition*, edited with introduction by W. Beach and H. R. Niebuhr, 2nd ed., New York, 1973. The most complete and reliable information and bibliography on the history of moral theology can be found in L. Vareecke, *History of Moral Theology*, lectures given at the Academia Alfonsiana, Rome (mimeographed copies are available); Id., *Histoire et morale*, in Studia Moralia, 12 (1974), 81–95; for the latest development of moral theology, esp. in Germany, see the well documented study of J. G. Ziegler, *Die Moraltheologie des 20. Jahrhunderts*, in H. Vorgrimler, *Bilanz der Theologie des 20. Jahrhunderts*, vol. III, Freiburg, 1970, 316–360.

3

The Human Person in Contemporary Theology: From Human Nature to Authentic Subjectivity

Michael J. Himes

The Church must give moral guidance in questions of enormous complexity today. Yet it seems that one of the traditional starting points of moral theological reflection, the notion of a universal human nature, is seriously questioned today even by contemporary theologians. Why is this so? How does contemporary theology understand the human person?

Clearly, one must be very rash to attempt to answer them! And so I begin by carefully indicating what I am about in this paper. If I am to speak of *contemporary* theology, I must indicate what the characteristics are of being contemporary. Therefore, I first intend to examine, however briefly, what I understand to be the hallmark of modernity, namely, his-

torical consciousness, and to note its effects on our (presuming that we are all instances of modernity) idea of humanity. Then recognizing that within this historically-minded and so pluralist context there is no such thing as one theology, but there are rather many theologies, I will attempt to suggest an important concern underlying a great many major streams of contemporary theological thought with regard to the meaning of the human person. I will further suggest a way in which many theologians today, either implicitly or explicitly, have responded to that concern.

At the end of the last century, the great Protestant theologian Ernst Troeltsch wrote of the ever increasing tension between Christianity and modernity. Far too perceptive and

This article is excerpted from A. Moraczewski, ed., Technological Powers and the Person *(St. Louis: Pope John Center, 1983) 270–312.*

honest to trivialize this friction by ascribing it to some one or two causes, Troeltsch concluded:

> This conflict arises not merely from the insubordination of natural reason but clearly and above all from the complete and multifaceted change in modern thought in the last two centuries and its contrast with the thought-forms and perspectives within which Christianity arose in its time and which its ecclesiastical institution has preserved.[1]

Troeltsch's placing of this sweeping change in the ways in which westerners thought about themselves and their universe two centuries before, puts the beginning of this intellectual transformation at the close of the seventeenth century. This corresponds to the period from 1680 to 1715, which Paul Hazard called the age of the crisis of European consciousness.[2] The seventeenth century was an era of scientific and philosophical revolution, a time which saw "the infinitization of the universe," in Alexandre Koyré's words; and the destruction of the cosmos, understood as "a finite, closed, and hierarchically ordered whole."[3]

I wish to suggest a far-reaching aspect of this extraordinary period which too much attention to the giants of the seventeenth century[4]—Bacon, Galileo, Kepler, Harvey, Pascal, Descartes, Locke, Newton, *et al.*, may obscure: the increased speed at which scientific and philosophical ideas become "common sense."

In 1600, the "man in the street" in London or Paris, Frankfurt or Amsterdam, knew that the earth on which he stood was the center of the cosmos and that the sun, moon, planets and stars moved around it. He knew from the Bible that this whole arrangement had come into existence 5604 years before, give or take a year. He knew that his physical well-being depended on the proper balance of four humors within him, each produced by a different organ of his body. "Everyone" knew this. But by 1700, the great-grandson of this "man in the street" knew that the earth was one of the planets revolving about the sun, that the universe containing this solar system was both far larger and far older than had been thought, and that his body was a kind of machine centered about his heart which acted like a pump. And this was what "everyone" then knew. But there was another point which the "man in the street" in 1700 knew: his predecessor in 1600 had not known what he knew now.

It was this last which was truly revolutionary. If the common sense of a generation or two before seemed hopelessly wrong-headed and antiquated, then the intervening years had made a great difference. A new way of understanding oneself and one's world had appeared. But then could not the passage of more time yield more remarkable discoveries which might make our vision of reality seem as quaint as that of our grandparents? The increased rate of scientific and technological change in the seventeenth century made it possible to observe significant differences in common sense from one generation to another or from the beginning of a lifetime to its end: The possibility of the significantly and radically *new* appeared in the western experience. Simultaneously, the past became distant, other, remote from the present and therefore both more interesting and more difficult to fathom; and the future became, in principle, open. For if today is so very different from yesterday, why should tomorrow not be even more different from today? The end of the seventeenth century produced a crisis in consciousness not because it was an age of scientific revolution, but because the people of the time *recognized* that theirs was an age of scientific revolution. They discovered the possibility of revolution, of radical newness.

The discovery of time is the hallmark of modernity. Every aspect of human life and thought, familial and social relations, politics, economics, the human and natural sciences, have been historicized. By this I mean that in all these spheres of activity the principle is now generally accepted that to gain an adequate understanding of any phenomenon or adequately to assess its value, it must be considered in terms of the place which it occupies and the role which it plays within a process of development.[5]

Thus, by the end of the eighteenth century, the historicization of the natural sciences began with geology, a process which became fully accepted in the next century with the work of Sir Charles Lyell. As early as 1778 in *The Epochs of Nature,* a work whose very title would have astonished the generation of Isaac Newton, the Comte de Buffon wrote:

> The surface of the earth has taken different forms in succession. Even the heavens have changed, and all the objects in the physical world are, like those of the moral world, caught up in a continual process of successive variations.[6]

In the nineteenth century, the name of Charles Darwin has come to symbolize the historicization of nature and the natural sciences, and *The Origin of Species* to be the trumpet-call heralding the abandonment of the idea of a static nature. The notion of biological evolution, in the words of R. G. Collingwood,

> is only one expression of a tendency which may work, and has in fact

worked, in a much wider field: the tendency to resolve the very ancient dualism between changing and unchanging elements in a world of nature by maintaining that what had hitherto been regarded as unchanging was itself in reality subject to change.[7]

The extraordinary hold which the idea of evolution took on the imagination of so many in such diverse fields in the nineteenth century was due to its having combined the two most powerful intellectual currents of that century, science and history. By the beginning of this century, it seemed that almost all the sciences had accepted Buffon's dictum that "Nature's great workman is time."[8]

Indeed, our own century has witnessed the extension of the historicization of the sciences to the final bastion of a static mathematicized scientific understanding, physics. From Einstein through Heisenberg to Paul Dirac, the cosmological theories of contemporary physics have moved steadily away from the unchanging and eternal laws of Newtonian physics. So astute and knowledgeable a philosopher of science as Stephen Toulmin can now claim that "at a theoretical level, a Universe whose laws are changing from epoch to epoch is no longer an idle fantasy."[9]

Perhaps as Darwin is the figure who has come to represent the historicization of nature in the nineteenth century, Hegel is the name which represents the historicization of thought. Hegel is so subtle a thinker that any characterization of his work is likely to be a caricature. One might claim that, rather than historicize philosophy, Hegel attempted to philosophize history. "History in general is therefore the development of Spirit in *Time,* as Nature is the development of the Idea in *Space.*"[10] But there is certainly no doubt that, by making philosophy the history of philosophy, Hegel moved from an eternally static to an eternally developing notion of truth.[11]

Thus the claim made by Lord Acton, although it seems almost to make history the queen of the sciences, was, by the time it was written in the 1890's, largely true: history, he wrote,

> is not only a particular branch of knowledge but a particular mode and method of knowledge in other branches. [It] determines their influence on society. It embraces other sciences, records their progress and the tests by which truth has been ascertained. Historic thinking is more than historical knowledge.[12]

And yet, in the latter half of the nineteenth century, even as the historicization of every area of life seemed complete and the emergence of "historic thinking" or historical consciousness an undeniable fact, a concern about the effect of this massive change in western consciousness began to be voiced. Wilhelm Dilthey was one of the most perceptive of those who recognized the ultimate effect of the emergence of historical consciousness.

> The historical thinking of the Greeks and the Romans mainly presupposes a definite human species equipped with definite characteristics. The Christian doctrine of the first and second Adam and of the Son of Man presupposed the same. The natural system of the sixteenth century was still sustained by the same presupposition. In Christianity, it discovered an abstract, permanent paradigm of religion, natural theology; it abstracted the doctrine of

natural law from Roman jurisprudence, and a model of taste from Greek artistic activity. According to this natural system all historical differences contained basic constant and universal forms of social and legal arrangements, of religious faith and of morality. This method of deducing common features from the comparison of historical forms of life by using the idea of supreme types, abstracting natural law, natural theology and rational morality from the varied customs, laws and theologies, still dominated the century of constructive philosophy.[13]

But this world-view had disintegrated by his day, Dilthey believed:

> So the point of view of developmental history could be applied to the study of the whole natural and historical development of man and man as a type dissolved in this process. The evolutionary theory which thus originated is necessarily linked to the knowledge of the relativity of every historical form of life. In the vision which encompasses the earth and its whole past the absolute validity of any individual form of life, constitution, religion or philosophy vanishes. So, more drastically than awareness of conflicting systems, the development of historical consciousness destroys faith in the universal validity of any philosophy which attempts to express world order cogently through a system of concepts.[14]

Or as Dilthey's contemporary, Lord Acton, wrote, "History defeats metaphysics."[15]

This was the alarming result of the shift to historical consciousness in the west, a relativism leading to nihilism. If every world-view, every philosophical system, every moral code, is the product of a particular age with its particular advantages and problems and can make no claim to universal validity, then are we not reduced to organizing our individual lives and our societies, making choices, and evaluating alternatives on the basis of personal preference, advantage, or groundless tradition? What prevents religious indifferentism, philosophical skepticism, moral and political opportunism? Truth, it might well seem, is what the victors decide, and right is what succeeds.

This was the crisis of the intellectual world which began to grip all fields of thought at the end of the last century and the beginning of this. Clearly theology could not refuse to face this challenge without accepting the alternative of irrelevance and incredibility to modernity. Creative and courageous scholars with profound religious concerns dealt forthrightly with the issues raised by historical consciousness. In Protestant circles perhaps the most distinguished such figure is Troeltsch; within Catholicism at that time the names which readily come to mind are Maurice Blondel, Friedrich von Hügel, and Lucien Laberthonnière. Unfortunately their efforts were unable to have their full due effect. On the Protestant side, Barthian Neo-orthodoxy emerged after the First World War with its own agenda and so thorough a rejection of the nineteenth century and all its works that not responding to the exigencies of modern consciousness became virtually the hallmark of truth. On the Catholic side, the Integralist reaction to Modernism led to a doctrinal positivism and theological conformism which relegated the pressing questions of modernity to the status of "contemporary errors" to be refuted, but not taken seriously.

The flowering of Catholic theology in the middle of the century and the passing of the "Barthian interlude" in Protestant theology have brought the questions posed by historical consciousness to the fore once again. Walter Kasper has written that Troeltsch's warning has been proven accurate, that the conflict between theology and science, which seemed so pressing to so many at the turn of the century, would turn out to be merely a symptom of the deeper divorce between theology and history. He cites the judgment of the contemporary philosopher Gerhard Krüger that "history is today our greatest problem. It is so in the threefold sense that it is simultaneously our most pressing, most encompassing, and most serious problem."[16]

Langdon Gilkey has skillfully analyzed the modern context of religious thought in its many aspects. Historicity and relativity are inextricably intertwined, and their combined effect is judged by him to be "central to all we mean by the secular spirit" which is modernity.

> For this modern view, all that is is pinioned within the flux of passage or of history, determined in large part by all that lies behind it, shaped by all that surrounds it, and to be replaced by what follows. Nothing in nature or history, and so by implication nothing at all that is, is thus "*a se*", an unchanging and self-sufficient substance, capable of existing in and by itself and thus exhibiting an essence underived from and so unrelated to the other things that surround it. Nothing anywhere in experience, space, time, or any mode of being is, in that sense, absolute; all is relative to all else and so essentially conditioned by its relevant environment.[17]

The ontological expression of this historical relativity is the philosophical concept of "internal relations", i.e. every existent is formed by its concrete relations to its context. This principle dominates every form of modern philosophy, according to Gilkey, whether idealistic or naturalistic, existentialist or phenomenological. It is presupposed by the natural, social and psychological sciences. Gilkey, like Kasper, proclaims the fulfillment of Troeltsch's and Dilthey's prediction: "The sense of the relativity of all things to one another in the passage of time—of the forms of the cosmos itself, of natural life, of our own species, of political and social structures, of the most significant historical events, the noblest of ideas, the most sacred of scriptures, institutions or creeds—practically defines our era."[18]

This is the context in which all truly contemporary theology must be carried on. The emergence of historical consciousness is the central characteristic of modernity. The meaning of that fact for theology has been very helpfully explored by Bernard Lonergan.[19]

Lonergan has referred to three points which must be recognized if one is to understand contemporary theology. First, whereas theology was at one time understood as a deductive science, it is now largely empirical. In that earlier understanding, conclusions were reached with varying clear degrees of certitude from premises derived from Scripture and tradition. In contemporary theology within the context of historical consciousness, the data of Scripture and tradition are interpreted by the best available hermeneutical procedures and yield results which are, at best, probable.

> An empirical science does not demonstrate. It accumulates information, develops understanding, masters ever more of its materials, but it does not preclude the uncovering of further relevant data, the emergence of new insights, the attainment of a more comprehensive view.[20]

Second, the move from a deductive to an empirical understanding of theology is irreversible because the shift from classical to historical consciousness is irreversible. Although Lonergan does not mention this, I suggest that this irreversibility is seen in the fact that historical consciousness can adequately account for the emergence and dominance of classical consciousness and for its replacement, while classical consciousness has no way to account for the emergence and dominance of historical consciousness, save perhaps in the purely negative category of a mistake. Lonergan notes that one fruit of this irreversible move into a new context is the need for a reorganization of the theological field into specializations, a task which he has attempted in his influential *Method in Theology.*

> Where once the dogmatic theologian was supposed to range over centuries, now Scripture, patristics, medieval and modern studies are divided and subdivided among classes of specialists. Where once the dogmatic theologian could lay down an overall view that echoed the conciliar *tenet atque semper tenuit sancta mater Ecclesia,* now an overall view tends to be either a tentative summary of the present state of research, or a popular simplification of issues that are really not simple at all.[21]

Third, the movement of theology into the context of historical consciousness requires a new conceptual framework and a new vocabulary. The language of Aristotle, so useful for so long within the world of classical consciousness, is inadequate to the new demands. The new framework and language may be derived from a great many possible sources, not least of all, Scripture; personalist, phenomenological, and existential categories are frequent sources.

> Religion is concerned with man's relations to God and to his fellow man, so that any deepening or enriching of our apprehension of man possesses religious significance and relevance. But the new conceptual apparatus does make available such a deepening and enriching. Without denying human nature, it adds the quite distinctive categories of man as an historical being. Without repudiating the analysis of man into body and soul, it adds the richer and more concrete apprehension of man as incarnate subject.[22]

It is noteworthy that understanding man as an historical being does not deny the category of nature. This is because, within the context of history, one recognizes the usefulness of that category at certain times for certain purposes. Lonergan has described the shift from a classical to an historically conscious worldview, happily for our purposes, employing the understanding of man as an example.

The classicist begins by abstracting from all the differences distinguishing one man from another and so is left with a residue called human nature. Obviously, on the basis of this procedure this human nature will be always and everywhere the same.

> One may fit out the identity, human nature, with a natural law. One may

complete it with the principles for the erection of positive law. One may hearken to divine revelation to acknowledge a supernatural order, a divine law, and a positive ecclesiastical law. So one may work methodically from the abstract and universal towards the more concrete and particular, and the more one does so, the more one is involved in the casuistry of applying a variety of universals to concrete singularity.[23]

In such a procedure one will never arrive at a demand for a change of law or form or method because abstract universals do not change. Like mathematical principles, they are what they are defined to be and so cannot alter.

The starting point for a consideration of the human person in the context of historical consciousness is quite different.

> One can begin from people as they are. One can note that, apart from times of dreamless sleep, they are performing intentional acts. They are experiencing, imagining, desiring, fearing; they wonder, come to understand, conceive; they reflect, weigh the evidence, judge; they deliberate, decide, act. If dreamless sleep may be compared to death, human living is being awake; it is a matter of performing intentional acts; in short, such acts informed by meaning are precisely what gives significance to human living and, conversely, to deny all meaning to human life is nihilism.[24]

A similar approach can be applied to human communities. Within a common field of experience, shared ways of understanding complement one another and create a community of mind. The common judgments arrived at within such a community create a consensus to which common commitments are given which enables the community to affirm its destiny and its faith in providence.

But, as Lonergan notes, these individual intentional acts and communal meetings are not timeless abstractions.

> They are the hard-won fruit of man's advancing knowledge of nature, of the gradual evolution of his social forms and of his cultural achievements. There is such a thing as historical process, but it is to be known only by the difficult art of acquiring historical perspective, of coming to understand how the patterns of living, the institutions, the common meaning of one place and time differ from those of another.[25]

The difficult art of acquiring historical perspective has been the work of every generation since the seventeenth century discovery of the remoteness of the past, the openness of the future, and the possibility of newness. Historical consciousness has become the common sense of modernity which has altered the procedures, standards, and goals of all the sciences. Modernity is conscious of being modernity, of being different from the past. "So to modern man it seems self-evident that he has made his own modern world and, no less, that other peoples at other times either have done the same or else have made do with a world fashioned by bolder ancestors and inertly handed on."[26]

The contrast then is between two ways of trying to understand the human being, one "abstractly through a definition that applies *omni et soli* and through properties verifiable

in every man", the other "as a concrete aggregate developing over time, where the locus of development and, so to speak, the synthetic bond is the emergence, expansion, differentiation, dialectic of meaning and of meaningful performance."[27] Since abstractions do not change, the first view will never find within itself either a demand or even a possibility for change. Intentionality and meaning are, by contrast, never static, always dynamic, always developing, sometimes declining, constantly capable of reformation. Thus not merely the possibility of change but the insistence upon it is built into the second method of apprehending human being. And not only is this second approach in harmony with contemporary consciousness, as the first is not, but it is also in far greater consonance with the normative foundational witness of the Christian tradition. In Lonergan's judgment, the abstractness which is at the heart of the understanding of human nature within a classicist world-view

> is not theological; it is grounded simply upon a certain conception of scientific or philosophic method; that conception is no longer the only conception or the commonly received conception; and I think our Scripture scholars would agree that its abstractness, and the omissions due to abstraction, have no foundation in the revealed world of God.[28]

Clearly one of the salient features of the historically-minded approach to the study of the human being is its insistence that such study be multi-dimensional and inter-disciplinary. Thus, while theology can and must add a necessary element to our understanding of the human being, it cannot pretend to speak the full or only word on the human person. Nor can it, on the basis of its own resources, respond to every question which may be raised about the human person. Thus the theologian cannot respond to the question of the precise beginning or end of human life purely and simply as a theologian. He *can* and *must* participate in the response to such a question by reflecting theologically on the data supplied by other sciences. This is, I believe, a major implication of theologizing in an historically-minded context. David Tracy has noted that while a major strength of a theologian operating in an essentially classicist world-view is the ability "to develop sophisticated models for providing systematic understanding of the basic beliefs of his church community", the principal weakness of such a theologian is "his inability to make intrinsic (i.e., inner-theological) use of the other scholarly disciplines."[29] Questions regarding genetic manipulation consequently impel the theologian into conversation with the fields of medicine, sociology, and public policy, a conversation in which the theologian does not "lay down the law" in advance, but makes the contributions of these other disciplines an "inner-theological" element in his own reflection.

The theological task is to bring the interpretive power and insight of the symbols of the Christian tradition to the inter-disciplinary dialogue, thus giving form and meaning to the data supplied by other disciplines and simultaneously allowing that data to expand our understanding of the meaning of those symbols. This is the perennial work of theology: the mutual interpretation of the symbols drawn from tradition (with Scripture as the normative record of the originating stages of the tradition) and contemporary experience. These symbols are the powerful persons, events, objects, ceremonies, images and stories in which the Christian community, and Israel before it,

has understood its mission and the divine self-gift which it has received. Among the most important of these symbols are God, Christ, Spirit, Trinity, incarnation, redemption, resurrection, Church, eucharist, grace, Mary, baptism, sacrifice, atonement, etc. The Church has to protect these meaning-giving symbols, and thus has translated many of the most important ones into credal statements, normative doctrines, and laws. But certainly no one—under pain of idolatry—can claim that such translations are exhaustive. The symbols always remain richer than their doctrinal formulations, which is why they have traditionally been referred to as "mysteries."[30]

But there is a great problem here. If the theological contribution to the discussion of the ethical problems confronting us as we move into the last years of the twentieth century is the interpretation of the experience, formulated by the natural and social sciences, in light of the symbols of the Christian tradition, and those symbols are the expressions of the Christian experience of revelation, the God-man relationship, is not this entire project undercut by the radical historicization of all thought and experience which we have described as the chief characteristic of modernity? The responses to the pressing ethical issues of our time must affirm and protect the value of the human person. Moral theology operating in the classicist world-view described by Lonergan rooted its answer to moral dilemmas in a universal human nature. But the existence of such a nature, or at very least its knowability, is precisely what is denied by the scientific and philosophical understanding of historically conscious modernity. Does this not reduce the possible responses to ethical questions to prudential judgments as to what may work for the moment? Indeed, does not the entire theological enterprise come into question? For, if the symbols of the Christian tradition are expressions of the God-man relation, the thorough historicization of the understanding of human being must make that relation so fluid that no total or unsurpassable symbol of that relation can exist. What does this do to the incarnation, the atonement, or the resurrection?

Edward Schillebeeckx has raised this question of the status of Christian theology in historically conscious modernity with great sharpness and clarity. He notes that theologians' attempts to enter creatively into the context of historical-mindedness have introduced the term "salvation history" which was virtually unknown prior to the Second World War. This has radically altered the plan of content in every theological treatise.

> God accomplishes in history his intentions with regard to man. God's activity is history in that it reveals itself, and it reveals itself by becoming history. Revelation is a growing historical process set in motion anonymously in the concrete life of every human being in the world. It acquired a more concrete form in Israel and finally reached the constitutive phase of its maturity in Christ and in the early apostolic Church. Whenever a present-day theologian wishes to enquire about the content of divine revelation in connection, for example, with faith in creation, he turns first of all to Israel, to see how this people—and they precisely as the people of God—experienced the reality of creation and interpreted it in the religious sense. Then he considers Christ and how he, conscious of his Sonship, actively experienced this reality. Finally, he investigates the way in which the

earliest Christians, as the people of God redeemed in Christ, concretely experienced and interpreted this same reality of creation.[31]

Furthermore, theology, which once had philosophy as its primary dialogue partner, now has entered into a conversation with history which has opened new insights into the implications of Christian faith. "Not only is eschatology, for example, actively forming the basis for a *theology* of Church history—a similar development is also taking place in the creation of a theology of earthly values, of history, of work, of the physical cosmos as the environment of man, and so on."[32]

But, Schillebeeckx observes, there is a danger in this new theological orientation. Whereas the theological manuals of an earlier day presented theology apart from the economy of salvation, there can be today too often the presentation of the economy without any properly speculative theology.

> Phenomenology, which correctly stresses the historical character of all human life, has not always appreciated the fact that this historical character in man is accompanied by a *consciousness* of time in the strict sense of the word. And a consciousness of time implies a rising above time. This does not mean that we somehow come to stand outside time and the world, but that there is a *transhistorical orientation* in the historical character of our human life.[33]

Here Schillebeeckx raises a point of enormous significance: historical consciousness is *consciousness* not only within but *of* history. Any analysis of historical process which reduces human agency to the product of historical forces, whether social or economic, psychological or physical, fails as historical explanation because it cannot account for the historian. For the historian maintains that he *knows* the truth, in however limited a degree, about the events which he studies. What he thinks about the past he seeks to justify by historical data; the judgments which he makes he supports by properly historical warrants. He does not accept that his reconstruction of the past is the product of external forces determining this judgment so that his historical conclusions are those which he must draw given his own historical circumstances. To some extent, however limited, he maintains that he transcends his present so that he may, in some measure however small, know the past. He cannot be merely the product of history, for he knows history.

Thus the historical consciousness of modernity with its sweeping claims of universal relativization still rests, often tacitly as Schillebeeckx observed, on a claim to transcendence. This permits me to suggest an understanding of the human person which must emerge from any self-reflective and consistent historical consciousness: the human being is, first and foremost, a creative participant in history. Humanity, understood within modern historical consciousness which does not lapse into the outmoded historicism of the turn of the century, is the ability to respond to one's circumstances by grasping one's past, determining one's present, and shaping one's future. The distinctively human mode of existence is an interplay of given factors—biological, psychological, social, economic, political, linguistic, geographical, etc.—and intentions, goals, purposes, understanding, misunderstanding, determination and courage, weakness and cowardice, altruism and selfishness.

The human being is both product and producer, creature and creator. Obviously there is a given into which we come or, better, out of which we come, but there is also our response which has some greater or less degree of spontaneity. We are both in history and transcendent to it.

This fundamental characteristic of being human, namely, the ability creatively to participate in historical process, shifts the category for understanding what is permanent in the human person from human nature to subjectivity. Human nature is a static, because abstract, concept; subjectivity is a center of intelligence, decision, and action, and so presupposes change, growth, and development. The turn to the subject is a study of the human being in so far as he is conscious.

Such study cannot proceed by abstraction, because abstraction prescinds from the concrete, and it is only in the concrete that the operations of the subject, i.e. inquiry, reflection, deliberation, action, occur. It is precisely by setting such concrete operations aside that classical consciousness arrived at the abstraction "human nature." In order to turn to the concrete subject, one must employ a transcendental reflection.

The use of the term "transcendental" in this context began with Kant, who thus designated "all knowledge which is occupied not so much with objects as with the mode of our knowledge of objects in so far as this mode of knowledge is to be possible *a priori*."[34] The transcendental method is closely identified in philosophy and Catholic theology today with the school of thought which traces its origin to Joseph Maréchal and has included Joseph de Finance, André Hayen, André Marc, Emerich Coreth, Bernard Lonergan, and Karl Rahner.[35] In fact, however, while these scholars do represent a quite consistent and recognizable intellectual tradition, transcendental reflection in a broader sense has been employed by a vast array of quite diverse philosophers and theologians from Maurice Blondel to David Tracy, from John Henry Newman to Johannes Baptist Metz. This broader sense is, in Rahner's description, the examination of an issue "according to the necessary conditions given by the possibility of knowledge and action on the part of the subject himself."[36] For example, when I speak of this sheet of paper before me, I am speaking of this paper *as I perceive it*. To speak of anything outside of me is also implicitly to speak of me. Transcendental reflection turns our attention to what must be true of me if I can perceive and speak of this sheet of paper at all. It asks what the conditions of my being must be if I can perform these operations.

Thus, if the context of modern historical consciousness presupposes tacitly or explicitly the human person's transcendence to history and so necessarily understands man as capable of creative participation in history, transcendental reflection on man must inquire what conditions hold within human being which allow such creative participation. What must be true of the human subject if he is able to grasp the past and shape his future and, to do so, is able to enter into political, social, and economic co-operation with other subjects?

It is by such a transcendental reflection as this on the concrete historical subject that we arrive at the concrete operations which we call, when taken together, authentic human existence. Our capacity for these operations makes us human. Our fulfillment of these capacities is an obligation which calls us to be moral beings. Lonergan has formulated this obligation to be human by performing these operations in imperatives which he names "the transcendental precepts": Be attentive, Be in-

telligent, Be reasonable, Be responsible, Evaluate and, if necessary, change.[37] Thus the human being is no longer understood by reference to faculties, qualities, or obligations, but rather by the operations of intentionality which render him a subject capable of performing those operations and so entering into the specifically human world of shared meaning. It is here that we discover the permanent dimension of human being.

The response of moral theology to this fact cannot be based on a timeless human nature if it is to be intelligible and therefore applicable to modernity radically and irreversibly marked by historical consciousness. I cannot say concretely what the moral theological response may or should be to the many questions which now confront us, or the many more which soon will. But I do suggest what the basis of any response must be in the context of modernity. That which is in accord with and furthers authentic subjectivity, i.e. which makes us more attentive, intelligent, reasonable, and responsible, is morally acceptable. That which violates such authentic subjectivity, i.e. which inhibits attentiveness, intelligence, reason, and responsibility, is immoral. This is, in the context of contemporary theology, the principle which holds universally and grounds all our moral theological judgments.

Notes

1. Ernst Troeltsch, "Die christliche Weltanschauung und ihre Gegenströmungen," *Gesammelte Schriften,* 4 vols. (1922; reprint ed., Aalen: Scientia Verlag, 1962), 2:325.
2. Paul Hazard, *La Crise de la Conscience Européenne* (Paris: Boivin, 1935); Eng. trans., *The European Mind, 1680–1715*

(New York: New American Library, 1963).

3. Alexandre Koyré, *From the Closed World to the Infinite Universe* (Baltimore: Johns Hopkins University Press, 1957), p. 2.

4. Bernard Lonergan mentions Hazard's judgment and Herbert Butterfield's placement of the birth of modern science in this period, as well as Yves Congar's opinion that dogmatic theology finds its beginning at this same time; see Bernard Lonergan, "Theology in Its New Context," *A Second Collection*, ed. William F. J. Ryan and Bernard J. Tyrrell (Philadelphia: Westminster Press, 1974), p. 55.

5. This meaning of historicization of thought and evaluation is derived from Maurice Mandelbaum's definition of historicism, although I am obviously applying it more widely than he does; see Maurice Mandelbaum, *History, Man, and Reason: A Study in Nineteenth-Century Thought* (Baltimore: Johns Hopkins University Press, 1971), p. 42.

6. Georges Louis Leclerc Comte de Buffon, quoted in Stephen Toulmin and June Goodfield, *The Discovery of Time* (Chicago: University of Chicago Press, Phoenix Books, 1982), p. 145.

7. R. G. Collingwood, *The Idea of Nature* (Oxford: Oxford University Press, 1960), p. 10.

8. Buffon, quoted in Loren Eiseley, *Darwin's Century: Evolution and the Men Who Discovered It* (Garden City, New York: Doubleday and Co., Anchor Books, 1961), p. 41.

9. Toulmin and Goodfield, p. 265; see also Ginestra Amaldi, *The Nature of Matter: Physical Theory from Thales to Fermi* (Chicago: University of Chicago Press, Phoenix Books, 1982); Werner Heisenberg, *Physics and Philosophy: The Revo-lution in Modern Science* (New York: Harper and Row, Harper Torchbooks, 1962); and Jagjit Singh, *Great Ideas and Theories of Modern Cosmology* (London: Constable, 1961).

10. G. W. F. Hegel, *The Philosophy of History,* trans. J. Sibree (New York: Dover Publications, 1956), p. 72.

11. See G. W. F. Hegel, *Lectures on the History of Philosophy,* 3 vols., trans. E. S. Haldane and Frances H. Simson (London: Routledge and Kegan Paul, 1955), 1:27: "It is only the living and spiritual which internally bestirs and develops itself. Thus the Idea as concrete in itself, and self-developing, is an organic system and a totality which contains a multitude of stages and of moments in development. Philosophy has now become for itself the apprehension of this development, and as conceiving Thought, is itself this development in Thought. The more progress made in this development, the more perfect is the Philosophy."

12. Lord Acton, Cambridge University Library, Add. 5011, 340, quoted in Herbert Butterfield, *Man on His Past: The Study of the History of Historical Scholarship* (Cambridge: Cambridge University Press, 1969), p. 97.

13. Wilhelm Dilthey, *W. Dilthey: Selected Writings,* ed. and trans. H. P. Rickman (Cambridge: Cambridge University Press, 1976), p. 134.

14. Ibid., p. 135.

15. Lord Acton, Cambridge University Library, Add. 5011, quoted in Butterfield, p. 97.

16. Walter Kasper, "Kirche und Theologie unter dem Gesetz der Geschichte?" in *Glaube und Geschichte* (Mainz: Matthias-Grünewald-Verlag, 1970), p. 49.

17. Langdon Gilkey, *Naming the Whirlwind: The Renewal of God-Language*

(Indianapolis: Bobbs-Merrill Co., 1969), p. 48. See also the same author's discussion of the contemporary context for theology in his *Religion and the Scientific Future* (New York: Harper and Row, 1970); *Catholicism Confronts Modernity: A Protestant View* (New York: Seabury Press, 1975); *Reaping the Whirlwind: A Christian Interpretation of History* (New York: Seabury Press, 1976), esp. pp. 188–208; and *Society and the Sacred: Toward A Theology of Culture in Decline* (New York: Crossroad Publishing Co., 1981).

18. Gilkey, *Naming the Whirlwind*, p. 48.
19. The references in Lonergan's work are numerous. Especially pertinent are: "The Transition from a Classicist World-View to Historical-Mindedness," "The Future of Thomism," "Theology in Its New Context," and "Revolution in Catholic Theology," in *A Second Collection;* "Time and Meaning," and "Healing and Creating in History," in *Bernard Lonergan: 3 Lectures,* ed. R. Eric O'Connor, Thomas More Institute Papers/75 (Montreal: Thomas More Institute for Adult Education, 1975); and *Method in Theology* (New York: Herder and Herder, 1972), esp. pp. 175–234.
20. Lonergan, "Theology in Its New Context," in *A Second Collection,* p. 59.
21. Ibid., p. 60.
22. Ibid., p. 60f.
23. Lonergan, "The Transition from a Classicist World-View to Historical-Mindedness," in *A Second Collection,* p. 3.
24. Ibid., p. 3f.
25. Ibid., p. 4.
26. Ibid., p. 5.
27. Ibid., p. 5f.
28. Ibid., p. 5.
29. David Tracy, *Blessed Rage for Order: The New Pluralism in Theology* (New York: Seabury Press, 1975), p. 25.
30. See the important article by Karl Rahner, "The Concept of Mystery in Catholic Theology," *Theological Investigations* IV (Baltimore: Helicon Press, 1966), pp. 36–73. For a brief but useful statement of the major points of this article, see Rahner's entry, "Mystery" in *Encyclopedia of Theology: The Concise Sacramentum Mundi* (New York: Seabury Press, 1975), pp. 1000–1004.
31. E. Schillebeeckx, *Revelation and Theology,* 2 vols. (New York: Sheed and Ward, 1967–68), 2:141.
32. Ibid., 2:143.
33. Ibid., 2:144.
34. Immanuel Kant, *Critique of Pure Reason,* trans. Norman Kemp Smith (New York: St. Martin's Press, 1965), p. 59.
35. A general study of this "transcendental school" in Catholic thought is Otto Muck, *The Transcendental Method,* trans. William D. Seidensticker (New York: Herder and Herder, 1968). A brief but good presentation of the school is given by Helen James John, *The Thomist Spectrum* (New York: Fordham University Press, 1966), pp. 139–192.
36. Karl Rahner, "Theology and Anthropology," in *Theological Investigations* IX (New York: Herder and Herder, 1972), p. 29.
37. The references to the transcendental precepts are frequent in Lonergan's work. For their introduction in the context of method, see *Method in Theology,* p. 20.

4

New Patterns of Relationship: Beginnings of a Moral Revolution

Margaret A. Farley, R.S.M.

Patterns of relationship between women and men are changing. Why they are changing, and how rapidly, are matters of debate. It may be that the chief forces for change are, e.g., economic.[1] Industrialization and the accompanying trend toward smaller, independent families accounts in part for husbands having to share in domestic tasks which stand-in female members of larger, extended families would have assumed. Technological development, which eliminates the requirement of physical strength for many occupations, accounts for the decrease in sex differentiation in portions of the work force. Mass media make feminist ideas accessible to otherwise isolated women, facilitating an unprecedented broadening of the base of challenge from women no longer willing to live within past role definitions. Rising affluence eliminates the need for parents to choose to educate sons in preference to daughters.

It may also be, however, that much of the change in patterns of relationship between men and women is more apparent than real. Some researchers claim, e.g., that despite the seeming loss of authority on the part of fathers, husbands still retain the preponderance of power in the family.[2] Feminist interpreters of life in society and the churches call attention to the fact that since the 1920's women have lost more ground than they have gained in their struggle to share in the public world.[3] Statistics show that in the United States women's growth numerically in the work force has not significantly changed their economic status vis-à-vis men.[4]

Whatever the actual changes already realized in women's and men's social roles, there can be no doubt that there is an important change in persons' assessment of those roles. Sex roles have ceased to be unproblematic, accepted as a given. They are everywhere subject to critical appraisal—whether there is consensus on the critique or not. They have thus at least changed in so far as they have been raised to a level of reflective awareness.

This article originally appeared in Theological Studies 36 (December 1975): 627–646.

Often they have been changed in terms of legal rules, even if they have not yet really altered because of custom or attitude. In any case, for many persons profound conceptual and symbolic shifts have occurred in relation to gender differentiation and sex roles. Indeed, so profound are these changes and so far-reaching their consequences that one is tempted to say that they are to the moral life of persons what the Copernican revolution was to science or what the shift to the subject was to philosophy.

My concern in this essay, however, is less with what has already happened in interpersonal relationships than with what ought to happen. Patterns of relationship, self-understanding, sex roles, and gender differentiations ought to change. They ought to change because over-all they have been inadequate, based on inaccurate understandings of human persons, preventive of individual growth, inhibitive of the common good, conducive to social injustices, and in the Christian community not sufficiently informed by or faithful to the teachings of Christ.

The reasons for past inadequacies and inaccuracies of understanding regarding the relations between men and women are many. It is important to try to understand those reasons, for they help to disclose the need for present and future changes. We may, however, never be able finally to settle questions of, e.g., whether the Judeo-Christian tradition in the past was ultimately responsible for sexism in religion and culture, or whether it only suffered along with other components of human history under limitations imposed by economic, cultural, or psychological factors.[5] What is more important now, given a kind of fulness of time in human history (however prepared for by economic exigencies, technological supports, or whatever else), is to understand the reasons why patterns of relation ought to change.

Role for Theology and Ethics: Filling the Hiatus

Christian theology and ethics have an important role to play in articulating reasons for changes in patterns of relationship and in clarifying what the changes should be. They also have an important role in translating reasons into motives, in providing a climate within which conceptualization and symbolization can facilitate experiences of moral obligation. It is, after all, incumbent upon the Christian community no less than any other group in society (given its fundamental premises, perhaps more so) to consider what is right and just, loving and wise, called for by the gospel regarding human interpersonal relationships. Christian theology is the effort of the Christian community to articulate its faith, and Christian ethics is the effort of the Christian community to understand and articulate how its faith should be lived. But Christian faith does have something to do with relationships between persons, and Christian theological and ethical traditions have offered insights and guidelines, even principles and rules, regarding these relationships. They have done so, in fact, with some degree of specificity regarding sex roles.

Hiatus in the Revolution

We are not now in a situation where Christian theology and ethics must simply provide a Christian commentary on general societal patterns which are questioned and/or in fact changing. We are rather in a situation where, precisely within the Christian community, for whatever reasons, many persons' ideas about sexual identity and gender roles have already changed. To understand the present task of theology, we need to look at the hiatus between past assumptions regarding fundamentally hierarchical patterns for relationship between men and women and today's growing acceptance of egalitarian patterns of relationship.

The "old order" was clearly one in which women were considered inferior to men and in which women's roles were subordinate, carefully circumscribed, and supplementary. Numerous studies have already documented the tendency of Christian theology to undergird this old order by identifying women with evil, by refusing to ascribe to women the fulness of the *imago dei,* and by defining women as derivative from and wholly complementary to men.[6] Beyond this, Christian theological ethics offered theories of justice which systematically excluded the possibility of criticizing sexism. Given the interpretations of women's "nature" as inferior, there was no question of violating the principle of giving "to each her due" when women were placed in subordinate positions or denied rights which were accorded to men. And given a concept of "order" in which one person should hold authority over others, justice was served precisely by the maintenance of a hierarchy—in family, church, or society—in which a male person stood at the head.[7]

The "new order," however, is based upon a view of women as autonomous human persons, as claimants of the rights which belong to all persons, as capable of filling roles of leadership in both the public and private spheres, as called to equality and full mutuality in relation to both men and women. It is difficult to exaggerate the radical nature of the shift in the perception of the reality of women and the consequent potential changes in relationships between persons (between men and women, but also between women and women and between men and men). Rilke spoke of a time when woman "will have stripped off the conventions of mere femininity in the mutations of her outward status," when "there will be girls and women whose name will no longer signify merely an opposite of the masculine, but something in itself, something that makes one think, not of any complement and limit, but only of life and existence: the feminine human being."[8] The "new order" is characterized by the belief that such a time has at least begun to be.

Now the hiatus between the old and the new orders is first of all one of understanding. For some Christians the process has been one of awakening, of unfolding, of conversion of thought if not of heart. For others, there has been no process at all. The new order of understanding is tacitly accepted, or at least not actively denied; but its implications are not at all seen. The new order cannot, however, either in logic or in persons' lives, simply be spliced to the old order as if it were another frame in an unwinding film. If there is to be growing clarity regarding social roles and individual identity, Bergson's "between" of process is as important as the beginning and the end. What is at stake is not only a Copernican revolution, where insight may be achieved in the flash of an eye, but a moral revolution wherein the Christian community's first obligation is to try to discern the claims of persons qua persons and the true common good of all persons.

The hiatus is also, of course, a hiatus between thought and reality and a hiatus between persons who behold a new order and those who do not. The gap in these senses is characterized differently in the different

Christian traditions, so I shall limit my generalizations to the Roman Catholic tradition.[9] Here new understandings of the nature and role of women have not yet penetrated the pastoral teachings of the Church.[10] Unlike most other Christian traditions, even formal legal barriers to women's fuller participation in the life of the Church still remain. And obviously not all persons in the Church share the new understandings of social roles and interpersonal relationships or the new experiences of moral ought which are grounded in these understandings. Even those who do, readily admit that new patterns of relationship are not fully clear and that achievement of new self-understandings has not finally been realized.

Filling the Hiatus

The task of theology has obviously something to do with bridging the gap. Nowhere is the hiatus more visible, in fact, than in theology itself. The work of transition from old to new understandings has hardly begun, and the revolution in thought which it entails cannot come full circle until the meaning and consequences of the new order are more adequately probed. What is needed, therefore, is not simply a further promulgation of new understandings, or a move by the theological community from tacit to spoken acceptance of new models of interpersonal and social relationships, or even exhortations of the community by theologians and ethicists. The task of theology is to engage precisely as theology and as theological ethics in the process whereby new understandings are born and develop.

The most obvious beginning work for theology in this regard is the self-critical work of disclosing past inaccuracies and distortions in theological interpretations of, e.g., the nature of woman and the role of sexuality in human life (a work well begun primarily by some few feminist theologians).[11] But theology has also a reconstructive task (if part of the movement in a revolution can be reconstructive as well as constructive) which will entail, e.g., efforts at a resymbolization of evil and a further probing of the doctrine of the *imago dei.* The reconstructive task of Christian ethics is derivative from and dependent upon the fruits of theological reflection, but it will inevitably involve new efforts to discern the moral imperatives rising from new understandings of the indicative regarding relations between persons. It is still the principles of Christian love and justice which must illuminate and regulate these relationships. There are, however, crucial considerations to be taken into account in the elaboration of these principles if they are to be faithful to Christian revelation as it is received in the concrete experience of the contemporary Christian community. What I should like to do in the remainder of this essay is to suggest key ways in which further considerations precisely of Christian love and justice can aid the process from old to new understandings of patterns of relationship between women and men and can thereby inform and give impetus to the moral revolution which now promises to touch and reshape these relationships from the ground up.

Ethical Reconstruction

New Patterns of Relationship: Relevance of Christian Love

At first glance it seems a simple matter to apply the norms of Christian agape to patterns of relationship between persons. If agape means equal regard for all persons, then it requires that women be affirmed no less than men. If agape means a love that is self-sacrificing, then men as well as women are to yield one to the other, to know the meaning of sacrifice and surrender at the heart of their love for God and for human persons. If agape includes mutuality—as the gift it receives, if not the reward it seeks—then some form of equality is assumed in every Christian love.

Yet in the context of male-female relations, there have appeared throughout the centuries countless ambiguities regarding the form of agape when it is for a person precisely as man-person or as woman-person. Among other things, the very notions of equal regard, self-sacrifice, and mutuality become problematic. When agape has been understood as a graced love called forth and measured by the reality of the one loved (as it has been largely in the Roman Catholic tradition), then affirmation of a lesser share in life and in being for women than for men has been justified on the grounds that women are simply inferior to men.[12] When agape has been understood as indifferent to the reality of the one loved, coming forth "unmotivated" from the graced power of the one loving (as it has been in many of the Protestant traditions), then inequality in what is affirmed for women in relation to men has been justified by making love for women as women a "preferential" love, not under the norm of agape.[13] And while Christian love in all persons has indeed always included the notion of self-sacrifice, there have been ways of attributing that element of love especially to women—reinforcing, on the one hand, a sense of subservience in women, and leading, on the other hand, to such strange conclusions as that the woman is the "heart" of the family and the man is the "mind."[14] Finally, the mutuality of love envisioned between men and

women has seldom in theory included the full mutuality which is possible only in a relation marked by equality. It has, more often than not, found its analogues in the mutuality of relationships between parent and child, ruler and subject, master and servant.[15]

Many aspects of Christian love could be examined in an effort to reconstruct a Christian ethic which would aid the process to new patterns of relationship between women and men. The notions of equal regard, self-sacrifice, and mutuality offer particularly relevant areas for consideration, however, and it is in these areas that I would like to raise and to consider representative issues.

Equal Regard and Equality of Opportunity

The notion of equal regard as a component of Christian agape has generally meant that all persons are to be loved with Christian love, regardless of their individual differences or their individual merit. They are to be loved, so the Roman Catholic tradition generally holds, because they are lovable precisely as persons (all beloved by God, all objects of the command to love them as we love ourselves).[16] Equal regard has not had sufficient content in the past, however, to save agapeic ethics from sexism; for, as we have seen, it is possible to affirm all persons as persons in a way that maintains a gradation among persons. All are loved as equal before God but not necessarily as equal before one another. When the norm of the objective reality of the person loved is added to the notion of equal regard, then the affirmation of persons as equals depends on the perception of their reality. Now it is just here that Christian ethics has suffered from an inadequate theology of the human person; for as long as the reality of woman is considered to be essentially lesser in being than the reality of man, she can be affirmed as personal but as essentially subordinate to men (in much the same way as children can be loved as persons without love demanding that they be affirmed in all the ways that adults are affirmed).

No one would argue that there are no differences between individual persons or that there are no differences between men and women. The question, of course, for a right love of women as human persons, is whether or not the differences between men and women are relevant in a way that justifies differentiating gender roles and consequent inequality of opportunity for women to participate in the public sphere or to determine the mode of their participation in the private sphere.

The primary method that theology used in the past to come to conclusions regarding the differences between women and men was a method of extrapolation from biological and sociopsychological data.[17] If theology is today consistent in its method in this regard, it has no choice but to reject its earlier position regarding the nature of woman. Evidence from the biological and behavioral sciences, from history and current practice, is overwhelmingly in contradiction to old claims regarding the intellectual superiority of men, the innate suitableness of women and men for gender-specific social roles, the physiologically determined psychological patterns of women and men, etc.[18] What differences there are between women and men are not differences which justify gender-specific variations in a right to education, to work, to access to occupational spheres, to participation in political life, to just wages, to share in the burdens and responsibilities of family, society, and church. History clearly shows that efforts to restrict social roles on the basis of sex inevitably lead to inequities, to circumscription of persons in a way that limits the possibilities of growth in human and Christian life. A love which abstracts from the fundamental potentialities and needs of persons qua persons (in the name of attending to specific differences among persons) cannot finally be a Christian love which is a love of equal regard.

Self-Sacrifice and Active Receptivity

Self-sacrifice and servanthood go together as important concepts in Christians' understanding of a life of Christian love. In general, there is no difficulty in seeing them as part of the call of every Christian to a love which is like the love of Christ. Yet women have become conscious of the potential falsification of these concepts when they are tied to a pattern of submissiveness to men. As members of the contemporary Christian community, they have thus experienced grave difficulty in sharing the new enthusiasm of men for an understanding of Christian life and ministry in terms of servanthood and surrender. Women have long known their ministry (in home, society, or church) as a ministry of service, but they are painfully aware that for too long they have been primarily the servants of men, subject to the regulations of men, surrendered to the limitations imposed upon them by men. Thus it is that for women theological reflection on servanthood has come to focus importantly on the revelation of service as a form of divine help, a role of privilege and responsibility, never "an indication of inferiority or subordination."[19]

Such clarifications would seem sufficient to restore a needed balance in patterns of relationship and ministry, preserving the fundamental elements of a surrendered and effective, free and whole love. But the ambiguities of sexual identity and culturally conditioned sexual roles are not so easily removed from actual efforts to live lives of Christian love. The process toward a "new order" calls for more careful analysis of the problems and opportunities in integrating sexual identity with agapeic love.

At the root of the difficulty in correcting false emphases in both women's and men's understandings of self-sacrifice, surrender, servanthood, etc., in Christian love, are false notions of receptivity. There is, I suggest, an implicit but direct connection between historical theological interpretations of woman as passive and historical difficulties in interpreting agape as active. In both cases receptivity constitutes a stumbling block.

It is, of course, a favorite theme in traditional interpretations of male-female relations to consider the feminine as passive and the masculine as active, the woman as receptacle and the man as fulfiller, the woman as ground and the man as seed. No other interpretation of the polarity between the sexes has had so long and deep-seated an influence on both men's and women's self-understanding. The source of this interpretation was primarily reflection on the reproductive structures of men and women. These structures served not only as symbols of male and female nature and roles, but they determined the meaning of the reality they symbolized. A perception of the function of bodily organs molded the consciousness of men and women for centuries. And there was no question that he who was an active principle was somehow greater in being

than she who could be only a principle of passivity.[20]

Now in the history of Christian conceptualizations of agape, two trends are apparent. On the one hand, there has been a tendency to describe agape as wholly passively received in the human person from God and wholly actively given by the human person to his or her neighbor.[21] The primacy of the active principle is maintained in such a way that in the relation between God and the human person, only God can be active, and in the relation between the Christian and his or her neighbor, Christian agape must be wholly active.[22]

On the other hand, where there has been a theology of grace which allows for secondary causality and freedom, both activity and receptivity are allowed in the response of Christian agape to God and to neighbor. That is to say, love of God is receptive not only in the sense that the power and the act of love are received from God as grace, but in the sense that love for God is awakened by the received revelation of God's lovableness and responds in active affirmation; and love of neighbor is likewise awakened by the lovableness of the neighbor, and only when it is so awakened (when it has so received the beauty of the neighbor) is it an actively affirming response.[23] It is an important irony, however, that those theological traditions which have tended to allow both receptivity and activity in the integral reality of Christian love have also tended to identify woman with love and man with active mind.[24]

Now the fact that receptivity has been a stumbling block both in the self-understanding of women and some theologies of Christian love is readily apparent. We can see it first in the effort of women to transcend "old order" understandings of themselves. A major part of this effort has been the struggle of women to reject identification in terms of bodily structures. Voices raised in the women's movement five or six years ago were more often than not stressing the unacceptability of the "anatomy is destiny" dictum. They had come to see the inadequacies of traditional interpretations of the structure of the human self which tied sexual identity and social roles too closely to biological givens. A certain kind of identification with the body had to be transcended if women were to achieve the personal identity which had so long eluded them. A body objectified by the other had become objectified for the self; and too simple interpretations of bodily structures led to conclusions about women's identity which were in contradiction to women's own experience. The old understandings of body and woman and receptivity had to be left behind.

Similarly, flight from receptivity in modern theologies of Christian love parallels a general fear of receptivity in a modern age when for Sartrean man "to receive is incompatible with being free,"[25] and for "protean man" everywhere there is a "suspicion of counterfeit nurturance."[26] But such fears are the result of an experience and an interpretation of receptivity which is oppressive, deceiving in its illusory offer of meaning and happiness, destructive in its enforced passivity. It is not only women but all persons who can sense that certain forms of receptivity, of passivity and submission, are not appropriate for the human person and never truly constitutive of Christian love.

New light can be shed, however, on the meaning of receptivity for all persons. Women have found important access to that light, paradoxically, by returning to considerations of bodily structures. Their move to transcend

reference to bodily structures and processes was never complete; for at the same time that women were rejecting anatomical determinism, they were also taking more seriously their relation to their own bodies, seeking a way to integrate embodiment with personal selfhood and womanhood. The very forcefulness of the negation of the body as sole determinant of identity and social function allowed an undercurrent of interest in a feminist rediscovery of the body to emerge dialectically as a major theme for today's voices in the women's movement.

In their efforts to reclaim their bodies, women finally took seriously the scientific discoveries of the nineteenth and twentieth centuries which showed, e.g., that even at the physiological level the female body is never only a receptacle for male sperm. Knowledge about the ovum, and the necessity of two entities (sperm and ovum) meeting in order to form a new reality, forever ruled out the analogy of the earth receiving a seed which was whole in itself and only in need of nourishment to grow.[27] Suddenly enwombing took on a different meaning, and inseeding had to be conceptualized in a different way. Even the passivity of the waiting womb had to be reinterpreted in the face of discoveries of its active role in aiding the passage of the sperm. Receptivity and activity began to coincide.

There are dangers, of course, in women's new efforts to understand and to live their embodiment. First, if it is only women who take seriously human existence as embodied, they may simply reinforce past stereotypes which identify woman with body and man with mind. Secondly, if women fall into the trap which Freud did—i.e., by taking account of the body in only some of its manifestations and not the body as a whole—distortions will once again be introduced into the self-understanding of both men and women. Thus, e.g., to fail to see all the ways in which, even at a physical level, men's bodies receive, encircle, embrace, and all the ways women's bodies are active, giving, penetrating, is to undermine from the start any possibility of growing insight into patterns of mutuality in relationships between persons.[28] Finally, there is the danger of forgetting that bodily structures and processes, whether in themselves or as symbolic of something beyond themselves, cannot provide the key to the whole of personal identity. They do, after all, demand to be transcended, so that we come to recognize all the possibilities of activity and receptivity which belong to both men and women, not as masculine and feminine poles of their beings, but as full possibilities precisely as feminine or precisely as masculine.

But if insight can be gained into active receptivity and receptive activity at the level of human embodiment, there is also a way to further insight in the experience of Christian agape. Receptivity is indeed at the heart of Christian love, and it does indeed lead finally to receptive surrender and to a life of active and receptive self-sacrifice. But it may be that we can grasp the meaning of receptivity in Christian agape only by seeing it in the broader context of Christian faith. Theological interpretations of Christian beliefs have pointed to a mystery of receptivity in the life of God Himself, in the incarnation of the Son, his life, death, resurrection, and return to the Father, in the dwelling of the Spirit in the Church, in the life of grace which is the sharing of human persons in the life of the triune God. "The Father, who is the source of life, has made the Son the source of life" (Jn 5:26). "I can do nothing by myself . . . my aim is to do not my own will but the will of Him who sent me" (Jn 5:30). "God gives the Spirit

without reserve. The Father loves the Son and has entrusted everything to him" (Jn 3:34–35). The Son's incarnate existence as God-man is an existence of receiving, of utter openness to the Father, of finally receptive surrendering unto death, and in death beyond death into life, and into new assumption into the life of the Father.[29] The Church is alive with that same life only because and in so far as it receives the Spirit of Christ, the Spirit of the Father (Jn 4:14, 6:37, 14:15–19, 15:5–15). Human persons, subsistent receptors of their very being, awaken into life and consciousness, into love and communion, even into the love of God and communion with Him and all persons in Him, only through the mystery of their capacity to receive, their possibility of utter openness to the creative and created word of God.

Christian love, no less and indeed radically more so than any other form of human love,[30] is essentially receptive in relation to both God and neighbor. It is God's self-communication which enables Christian love, and that self-communication includes the manifestation of His lovableness for the conscious reception in and response of Christian love. And Christian love of neighbor is radical love not in that it involves no reception of the one loved, but because the one loved is received according to his or her deepest reality (her existence in God in Christ Jesus) and responded to with an active affirmation that reaches to that reality.

But all this receptivity at the heart of Christian existence is not in any way only passivity. "To receive," as Marcel has noted, can mean anything from passive undergoing to a receiving which is an active giving, as when a host "receives" a guest.[31] The receiving which is the Son's in relation to the Father is an infinitely active receiving. The receiving which is each human person's from God, and from one another within a life shared in God, is an active participation in the active receptivity of Christ, awakening, growing, reaching to the coincidence of peak receptivity with peak activity. Theologians who worry that if agape is active in relation to God, God's power will not be preserved, or theologians who worry that if agape is receptive of neighbor it will inevitably be a self-centered love, fail to understand that receiving can be self-emptying, and giving can be self-fulfilling. They fail to see the meeting between lover and beloved (whether God or a human person) which is utterly receptive but utterly active, a communion in which the beloved is received and affirmed, in which receiving and giving are but two sides of one reality which is other-centered love. Theologians or any persons who persist in identifying woman with love and man with knowledge, or who neglect to find in self-sacrificial love the coincidence of opposites (giving and receiving), fail to understand the reality of either man or woman and fail to see the absurdity of withholding the possibilities of great Christian love from the heart of all persons.

Mutuality on a Trinitarian Model

There is a further step that we can take in trying to understand the reality of women and men, the nature of the love which can be between them, and the model of interpersonal relationship which is offered to them in Christian revelation. That step is to the doctrine of God. It is suggested by the fact that Christian theology has failed to grant equality to women precisely in so far as it has failed to attribute to women the fulness of the image of God. All persons are created in the image and likeness of God, but men participate in the

imago dei primarily and fully, while women have long been thought to participate in it secondarily and partially. It is not surprising, then, that the only way to move beyond a long-standing inability to conceptualize and actualize patterns of relationship which do not depend upon a hierarchical model is to see whether sexual identity does indeed give graded shares in the *imago dei*. At the same time we may see whether God's own self-revelation includes a revelation of a model of interpersonal love which is based upon equality and infinite mutuality.

If we are to pursue the question of whether women as women can be understood to be in the image of God, we must ask whether God can be imaged in feminine as well as masculine terms.[32] The Christian community has traditionally tried to articulate its understanding of the inner life of God in the doctrine of the Trinity, and it is here that we might expect to find also the fullest meaning for the *imago dei*. Certain cautions, however, are in order. First, the Christian doctrine of God has never ceased to affirm that God is a transcendent God whose reality is beyond all of our images and who cannot be understood to be either masculine or feminine. Nonetheless, we do use images to help our understanding of God; and since God holds all the fulness of being, it is as legitimate to say that the perfections of masculinity and femininity are in God as to say that they are not in God. There will, of course, be radical limitations to any use of masculine or feminine images of God; but there are radical limitations to the use of any images-including those of fatherhood and sonship, or those of word and wisdom, or those of memory, understanding, and will.

It is important for us to bear in mind, however, two special limitations of masculine and feminine imagery. (1) Given no history of careful delimitation of the imagery (such as we do have for the images of fatherhood and sonship), constant care must be taken to place it within a clear affirmation of the unity of God.[33] (2) Any use of masculine or feminine imagery, whether in relation to God or not, runs the risk of being caught once again in reifying notions of the masculine and the feminine. I shall say more about this second concern later.

There are, I suggest, in traditional Roman Catholic Trinitarian theology,[34] grounds for naming each of the persons in the Trinity feminine as well as masculine. "Fatherhood" is the image traditionally used for the First Person of the Trinity. In the first two centuries of Christian thought it connoted primarily the Godhead as the creator and author of all things,[35] but it soon began to signify the unoriginated "begetting" by the First Person of the Second Person. The exclusive appropriateness of the image of fatherhood is beyond question in an age when the sole active principle in human generativity was thought to be male. No absolute necessity remains for limiting the image to that of masculine generativity, however, when it becomes clear (as it has in our own day) that the feminine principle of generativity is also active and self-contributing. There is, in other words, no reason why the First Person of the Trinity cannot be named "Mother" as well as "Father," no reason why creation cannot be imaged as coming forth from the ultimate womb, from the ultimate maternal principle. Neither image is sufficient (since in the human analogue neither male nor female principle can be the whole source of life), but either is appropriate; and perhaps only with both do we begin to return the power to images which they had in a simpler day.

"Sonship" is the image traditionally used for the Second Person of the Trinity. Once again, the appropriateness of this image is unquestionable in an age when human sons were the always desired human offspring, and when relationships between fathers and sons could often be marked with greater equality and mutuality than could those between husband and wife.[36] But there is, again, no absolute reason why the Second Person cannot be named "Daughter" as well as "Son." There is, on the contrary, good reason to suggest that the Second Person is better imaged when both the images of sonship and daughterhood are used.[37]

There is, however, another way in which feminine imagery may be ascribed to the Second Person of the Trinity. A large part of the history of the doctrine of the Trinity is a history of attempts to express the relationship between the First and Second Persons in a way that avoids subordinationism. From the Apologists to the Council of Nicaea the attempts were unsuccessful. Nicaea affirmed the equality and the unity of the two Persons, but the images still faltered.[38] "Fatherhood" and "sonship" (even when elaborated upon in terms of Father and Logos or light, etc.) were simply not capable of bearing the whole burden of the reality to be imaged.

With Augustine new images were introduced (being, knowing, willing; mind, self-knowledge, self-love; memory, understanding, will) which described a triune life in which all that the Father is is communicated to the Son, and all that the Son receives is returned to the Father, and the life of utter mutuality, communion, which they share, is the Spirit.[39] This life—imaged by analogues from the human mind—is still attributed, however, to Persons whose primary names are "Father" and "Son" (and "Spirit"). It is the further elaboration of this same basic description which is to be found in the rest of the history of the theology of the Trinity in the Western Church and in the official teachings of the Church.[40]

Given this articulation of the life of the Trinity, however, is it not possible to introduce images of masculinity and femininity which are no longer those of parent and child? Does not a feminine principle of creative union, a spousal principle, express as well as sonship the relation of the Second Person to the First? Is not the Second Person revealed as infinite receptor, in whom peak receptivity is identical with peak activity? Is it not possible on this account to describe the First Person as masculine and the Second Person as feminine and the bond which is the infinite communion between them (the Spirit of both) as necessarily both masculine and feminine? Do we not have here revealed a relationship in which both the First Person and the Second Person are infinitely active and infinitely receptive, infinitely giving and infinitely receiving, holding in infinite mutuality and reciprocity a totally shared life? Do we not have here, in any case, a model of relationship which is not hierarchical, which is marked by total equality, and which is offered to us in Christian revelation as the model for relationship with Christ and for our relationships in the Church with one another?

But let me return here to the caution I noted earlier, namely, that to use the images of masculinity and femininity to represent the Godhead runs the risk of sealing yet more irrevocably the archetypes of the eternal masculine and the eternal feminine. The God of Christianity is a transcendent God, one who breaks all archetypes and who can continually call us beyond their limitations in our own lives. It is surely the case that we do not want to find yet one more way to imprison women or men in what are finally falsifying notions of gender identity. We began these consider-

ations, however, as part of a process—a process which may in fact lead necessarily beyond all sexual imagery to notions only of transcendence. What is important is that there be room in the process for women to know themselves as images of God, as able to be representatives of God as well as lovers of God. In addition, we cannot dismiss out of hand the possibility of finding in God's self-relevation grounds for understanding femininity in a way that begins to shatter its previous conceptual limitations, and that begins even to revolutionize archetypes. Finally, both the struggle of Trinitarian theology through the centuries to deny any subordination of the Second Person to the First, and the struggle of women and men to achieve equality and mutuality in more and more patterns of relationship, may well be served by adding the image of masculine-feminine polarity to past images of fatherhood and sonship.

New Patterns of Relationship: Relevance of Christian Justice

The Good of the Individual

There is a sense in which, once we have considered the norms of Christian love vis-à-vis patterns of relationship between women and men, we have already also considered the norms of Christian justice. At least in the theory of Christian justice to which I would subscribe, justice is itself the norm of love. What is required of Christians is a just love, a love which does indeed correspond to the reality of those loved. Thus, in a strict sense, justice requires that we affirm for persons, both women and men, what they reasonably need in order to live out their lives as full human persons and, within the Christian community, what they need in order to grow in their life of faith. It is therefore clear that to refuse to persons, on the basis of their sex, their rightful claim to life, bodily security, health, freedom of self-determination, religious worship, education, etc., is to violate the norms of a just love. Any pattern of relationship, in home, church, or civil society, which does not respect persons in these needs and claims is thereby an unjust pattern of relationship.

We have already seen the demand which a just love then makes for rejecting institutionalized gender differentiations and for affirming equality of opportunity for all persons regardless of their sex. Feminists have sometimes gone beyond an egalitarian ethic, however, to a "liberation" ethic in their delineation of the norms of justice for society and the churches.[41] The liberation ethic, in this sense, asserts that equal access to institutional roles is not sufficient to secure justice, since institutions and roles are themselves at present oppressive to persons. The reality of both men and women is such that "the social institutions which oppress women as women also oppress people as people"[42] and must be altered to make a more humane existence for all. While the goal of a liberation ethic is ultimately the common good, it nonetheless asserts important claims for a just love in terms of the reality of individuals who are loved.

The Common Good

If traditional principles of justice are to be brought to bear in forming new patterns of relationship, then it is not only the good of individuals which must be taken into account but the common good of all. It is just here that moral discourse often breaks down when arguments are advanced for basic egalitarian patterns of relationship between men and women. At least three important areas of consideration suggest themselves if we are to discern seriously the moral imperatives in this regard.

1) From the standpoint of the Roman Catholic ethical tradition, it is a mistake to pit individual good against the good of the community, or the social good, when what is at stake is the fundamental dignity of the individual. If it is the case, then, that the reality of woman is such that a just love of her demands that she be accorded fundamental personal rights, including equality of opportunity in the public world, then to deny her those rights is inevitably to harm the common good. "The origin and primary scope of social life is the conservation, development and perfection of the human person. A social teaching or reconstruction program . . . when it disregards the respect due the human person and to the life which is proper to that person, and gives no thought to it in its organization, in legislation and executive activity, then instead of serving society, it harms it. . . ."[43] On the basis of such a view of the common good, all arguments for refusing women equality of opportunity for the sake of safeguarding the "order" of society, church, or family must fall.

2) In the "old order," as we have seen, it was argued that the common good (which consisted primarily in some form of unity) could best be achieved by placing one person at the head of any community. Strong utilitarian rebuttals can now be offered against this view of the nature of authority.[44] The tradition from which it comes has itself shifted, through the adoption of the principle of subsidiarity, from a hierarchical to an egalitarian model of social organization in contexts of

civil society.[45] To extend the shift to include relationships between men and women, it is necessary to argue that in fact the good of the family, church, etc, is better served by a model of leadership which includes collaboration between equals.

Thus, e.g., it can be argued that present familial structures which give major responsibility for the rearing of children to the mother do not, after all, provide the greatest good for children.[46] Or familial structures which entail a sharp split between the public and private worlds entail also strains on marital commitment[47] and a dichotomy between public and private morality.[48] Similarly, ecclesiastical structures which reserve leadership roles to men do not provide the needed context for all persons to grow in the life of faith. Within the confines of such structures God is not represented in the fulness of triune life, and the vacuum which ensues is filled by false forms of chauvinism in the clergy and religiosity in the congregations. On the basis of this form of argument, hierarchical patterns of relationship are judged unjust not only because they violate the reality of individual persons but because they inhibit or undermine the common good.

3) If the ultimate normative model for relationships between persons is the very life of the Trinitarian God, then a strong eschatological ethic suggests itself as a context for Christian justice. That is to say, interpersonal communion characterized by equality, mutuality, and reciprocity may serve not only as a norm against which every pattern of relationship may be measured but as a goal to which every pattern of relationship is ordered. Minimal justice, then, may have equality as its norm and full mutuality as its goal. Justice will be maximal as it approaches the ultimate goal of communion of each person with all persons and with God. Such a goal does not merely beckon from the future; it continually impinges upon the present, demanding and promising that every relationship between women and men, and between women and women and men and men, be at least turned in the direction of equality and opened to the possibility of communion.

The kinds of changes that are needed in the patterns of relationship between women and men are changes which are finally constituted in and by a moral revolution. It is difficult to imagine how such changes can be effected without a continuing process of conversion of thought and of love in the individual and in the community. I began this essay by suggesting that theology and ethics have an important role to play in such a process. Theological and moral insight do not come easily, however, in areas where centuries of thought and behavior have skilled us in selective vision. Surely some structures will have to change before minds and hearts can change. Surely laws and structures can begin to change without filling the hiatus between old and new understandings. We are talking, however, about a revolution that must occur in the most intimate relations as well as the most public. Without continuing changes in understanding and love, I doubt that we shall be able to effect sufficiently radical structural changes in the public sphere or structural changes at all in the world of our private lives. "We may sometimes decide to act abstractly by rule . . . and we may find that as a result both energy and vision are unexpectedly given . . . but if we do leap ahead of what we know we still have to try to catch up. Will cannot run very far ahead of knowledge, and attention is our daily bread."[49]

Notes

1. See studies such as Harriet Holter, "Sex Roles and Social Change," in Hans Peter Dreitzel, ed., *Family, Marriage, and the Struggle of the Sexes* (New York, 1972) pp. 153–72. It must also be noted that there are economic causes which reinforce old patterns of relationship. See, e.g., the analysis of the effect of the Industrial Revolution on familial structures in Viola Klein, *The Feminine Character: History of An Ideology* (London, 1971) p. 10.

2. See D. L. Gillespie, "Who Has the Power? The Marital Struggle," in Dreitzel, pp. 121–50.

3. See, e.g., Beverly Wildung Harrison, "Sexism and the Contemporary Church: When Evasion Becomes Complicity," in Alice L. Hageman, ed., *Sexist Religion and Women in the Church: No More Silence!* (New York, 1974) pp. 195–216.

4. Figures in U.S. Bureau of Census Report 1970 show that median income of full-time employed women is half that of men.

5. See Elizabeth Gould Davis, *The First Sex* (Penguin, 1973).

6. See, e.g., such studies as Mary Daly, *The Church and the Second Sex* (New York, 1975); George Tavard, *Woman and the Christian Tradition* (Notre Dame, 1973); Rosemary Radford Ruether, ed., *Religion and Sexism* (New York, 1974).

7. For Aquinas' position in this regard, see, e.g., *Sum. theol.* 1, q. 92, a. 1; q. 93, a. 4; q. 96, a. 3; *On Kingship* 2, 17–20. It is almost superfluous to note here that so-called "pedestalism," whereby women were in some sense exalted as paragons of virtue, etc., served only to finally reinforce their subordination to a woman's "place."

8. Rainer Maria Rilke, *Letters to a Young Poet,* tr. M. D. H. Norton (New York, 1962) p. 59.

9. Thus far, more efforts have been made to analyze such situations in the Protestant churches than in the Roman Catholic; see Harrison, *art. cit.*

10. This is eminently visible in even the 1975 statements of Paul VI regarding the International Women's Year.

11. See references in n. 6 above.

12. *Sum. theol.* 1, q. 92, a. 1, ad 1 and 2.

13. Such is the conclusion which can be drawn from, e.g., the theories of Kierkegaard or Nygren.

14. "As he occupies the chief place in ruling, so she may and ought to claim for herself the chief place in love" (*Casti connubii,* no. 27).

15. These analogous polarities must not be thought to appear only in the Roman Catholic tradition. Reformation views of relationships between men and women did not revolutionize the pattern of hierarchy and subordination. See, e.g., Martin Luther, *Commentary on Galatians 1535* (WA 40, 543); *Commentary on Genesis 1535–45* (WA 44, 704).

16. For a general analysis of the meaning of "equal regard" see Gene Outka, *Agape: An Ethical Analysis* (New Haven, 1972) chap. 1.

17. This is not to deny that scriptural exegesis of, e.g., the story of creation has played an important part in theological reflection on the nature of woman. I would argue, however, that such exegesis served until recently proof-text conclusions drawn largely from other sources.

18. It is, I hope, superfluous to document such an assertion, but it may be helpful to point to such studies as Margaret Mead, *Male and Female* (New York, 1949) and Jean Strouse, ed., *Women and Analysis* (New York, 1974).

19. Letty M. Russell, "Women and Ministry," in Hageman, pp. 54–55.

20. Were there space here, it would be interesting to speculate on the reasons for some variations on this theme. Thus, why did the seventeenth century sustain the myth of female passivity, yet give rise to a belief that women's sexuality was insatiable?

21. See, e.g., Anders Nygren, *Agape and Eros,* tr. P. Watson (New York, 1969) pp. 75–80, 92–95, 127; Outka, pp. 49–52; Norman Snaith, *The Distinctive Ideas of the Old Testament* (New York, 1969) pp. 174–75.

22. The major difficulties which this position sees with allowing agape to be active vis-à-vis God and receptive vis-à-vis one's neighbor are the difficulties of preserving total divine causality in grace and the difficulties of the emergence of egocentricity in "preferential" love.

23. This view of agape is found most representatively in the Roman Catholic tradition of a theology of Christian love.

24. See n. 14 above.

25. Marcel puts these words in the mouth of the early Sartre; see Gabriel Marcel, *The Philosophy of Existentialism,* tr. M. Harari (New York, 1964) p. 82.

26. Robert Jay Lifton, "Protean Man," in *The Religious Situation: 1969,* ed. D. Cutler (Boston, 1969) p. 824.

27. While the ovum was discovered only in the nineteenth century, Hippocrates had taught that woman's participation in reproduction includes a positive contribution. This was taken up into philosophy and theology by the Franciscan school in the Middle Ages, but there was as yet no acknowledgment of equal contributions from male and female principles. The male contribution was considered "efficient cause," and the female contribution still "material cause." See Bonaventure, *In Sent.* 2, d. 20, q. 2.

28. This, I take it, constitutes a morally significant factor in understanding homosexuality as well as heterosexual relations. There is not the opportunity here to pursue this topic, but it is of utmost importance to juxtapose these insights with the testimony of the contemporary gay community that the "new generation" of homosexuals does not reject their given sexual identity even though their sexual preference is for persons of the same sex.

29. For a brief but excellent summary of the element of receptivity in the life of Jesus, see Hans Urs von Balthasar, *A Theology of History* (New York, 1963) pp. 25–30.

30. See Jules J. Toner, *The Experience of Love* (Washington, D.C., 1968) p. 95.

31. See Marcel, *Creative Fidelity,* tr. R. Rosenthal (New York, 1964) pp. 89–91.

32. This does not eliminate the need to consider woman as person participating in the *imago dei.* To go to this without considering also woman as woman participating in the *imago dei* does not, however, meet the historical problem of identifying man as the primary sharer in the image of God.

33. In other words, not only must modalism be eschewed but "social" theories of the godhead as well; see Claude Welch, *In This Name: The Doctrine of the Trinity in Contemporary Theology* (New York, 1952) pp. 29–34, 133–51, 252–72.

34. These same reflections could be applied to the Trinitarian theology of, e.g., Karl Barth.

35. See J. N. D. Kelly, *Early Christian Doctrines* (New York, 1958) pp. 83–95.

36. I am passing over here the question of the influence of reflection on the Incarnation on these views; see Kelly, chaps. 4–5.

37. Tavard suggests the view that the Holy Spirit be considered as imaging daughterhood in the Trinity. This does not, it

seems to me, adequately account for the theology of spiration. See Tavard, p. 198.

38. Athanasius, e.g., still needed to draw upon such images as "stream" and "source" to try to express the relation of Father and Son. The Cappadocians still referred to the Father as cause and the Son as caused.

39. *De trin.* 5, 12; 5, 15–17; 8, 1; 15, 5 and 10; *In Ioan tract.* 99, 6.

40. For a concise summary of the official doctrine of the Church regarding the Trinity, see Karl Rahner, *The Trinity,* tr. J. Donceel (New York, 1970) pp. 58–79.

41. See analysis in Jo Freeman, "The Women's Liberation Movement: Its Origins, Structures, and Ideas," in Dreitzel, pp. 213–16.

42. *Ibid.,* p. 214. This is the argument given by some women against ordination of women in the Roman Catholic Church.

43. Pius XII, Christmas Address, 1942, in Vincent A. Yzermans, ed., *The Major Addresses of Pope Pius XII* 2 (St. Paul, 1969) 54.

44. Other forms of rebuttal, on deontological grounds, can be offered as well. These may be inferred, however, from our discussion thus far.

45. See the historical analysis of this shift in David Hollenbach, *The Right to Procreate and its Social Limitations: A Systematic Study of Value Conflict in Roman Catholic Ethics* (unpubl. diss., Yale University, 1975) chap. 3.

46. See Alice S. Rossi, "Equality between the Sexes: An Immodest Proposal," in Robert J. Lifton, ed., *The Woman in America* (Boston, 1964) pp. 105–15.

47. See Martha Baum, "Love, Marriage, and the Division of Labor," in Dreitzel, pp. 83–106.

48. See Beverly Wildung Harrison, "Ethical Issues in the Women's Movement," address given to the American Society of Christian Ethics, 1974.

49. Iris Murdoch, *The Sovereignty of Good* (New York, 1971) p. 44.

5

Values, Victims and Visions

James Gaffney

A little more than a century ago, as a tribute to his recently deceased wife, a great English poet wrote an extraordinary poem. It is admirable in a number of respects, not least its telling of a truly fascinating story. But what continues to interest me is that, from start to finish, it is a poem about moral thinking.

The masterpiece called *The Ring and the Book,* which Robert dedicated to Elizabeth Barrett Browning, is about the once very famous murder of an adolescent Italian girl and her elderly parents by her middle-aged husband, allegedly to avenge the girl's infidelity with a young local priest. Because the defendant himself had received minor orders, he succeeded in having the case transferred from civil to ecclesiastical jurisdiction. The case was eventually decided in a criminal tribunal of the Vatican.

The connection of all this with moral thinking is the remarkable way Browning constructed his dramatic monologue. He causes the entire story to be re-told, time after time, by very different people, each with contrasting social positions, backgrounds, interests, assumptions, ambitions, and degrees of personal involvement. We are compelled to view the same crude facts from a variety of personal and social moral viewpoints. We discover that what one account presents as momentous appears trivial in another. We find motives not even suspected in one taken for granted in another. We see heroes transform into villains and villains into non-entities. Virtues turn into vices, bystanders into participants, and neutral circumstances into compelling influences. Each account is a peculiar mosaic of lights and shadows, and the pattern of vividness and obscurity constantly changes. Hence, for the reader, even though a definite fabric of facts remains substantially unaltered, the moral picture is repeatedly transformed. What causes the transformations are the different human viewpoints from which it is perceived. G. K. Chesterton characterized *The Ring and the Book* as a "spiritual detective story." When the mystery is concluded in the final scene what assures us of the verdict is neither knowledge of facts nor knowledge of law, but the spiritual discernment of an aged saint, ded-

This article originally appeared in Commonweal 113 (August 15, 1986): 426–429.

icated to justice, trustful of God, close to death, and unconcerned about anything this world could bestow or withhold.

To me, it has come to seem fairly clear that changes in the way modern Catholics think about morality are explicable, to a considerable extent, in much the same way as those transformations of moral perception that are the most original feature of Browning's poem. Moral cases, including typical ones look different, and therefore are analyzed and judged differently, depending on the perspective in which they are viewed. And that perspective depends on who the viewers are, and how they are enabled and accustomed to do their seeing. In this respect, moral judgment is similar to legal judgment, and the practical significance of differing perspectives for legal judgment is something of which we all become acutely aware whenever we watch trial lawyers in a selection of jurors.

For a very long time, nearly since the Protestant Reformation, and until quite recently, Catholic moral judgments exhibited a remarkable degree of uniformity. A major reason for that was the control exerted on such judgments by a body of doctrine called moral theology, censored and authorized by the church, and developed for the most part to assist priests in administering the sacrament of Penance. The main assistance it offered was twofold: first, to identify the kinds of sins being confessed; and second, to ascertain the guilt of the person who confessed them.

Many things, both favorable and unfavorable, can be said about that confessional system and the moral theology that derived its character from it. But it also had a confining effect on moral perspective, and therefore on moral thinking.

That confinement depended on both the setting and the characters. Because the setting was juridical, it had to rely on a definite set of statutes, in effect criminal and penal laws official specifications of punishable offenses. Penitents had the task of translating their recent moral histories into terms of infractions of these laws. The confessor was there to help them do so, and moral theology was his equipment for that function. From the nature of the case, the laws had to be stable and uniform, and so did the procedures for interpreting them. Under such circumstances, moral theology had every reason to be conservative and dogmatic. It had no reason to be original or philosophical.

The confessional orientation confined moral thinking for other reasons as well. Among them must be included the fact that the whole procedure was directed not only by a quite rigid set of norms, but also by a highly specialized set of persons. All of them were men; none women. All of them were celibate; none spouses, and none parents. Nearly all had received a very similar, and quite peculiar, education. All were full-time functionaries of a vast, hierarchical institution. None of these characteristics is objectionable in itself. But even with maximum allowance for individuality, and maximum resistance to clerical stereotyping, it remains obvious that no random assortment of Roman Catholic priests could be seriously regarded as a cross-section of humanity at large. Yet no one else was ever allowed to have much to do with formulating or administering moral theology, until very recently.

In still other ways, the penitent's role contributed to a confinement of moral thought. Penitents, of course, included all sorts of people. Yet each penitent appeared alone, as the doer of certain morally objectionable deeds. Hence, the only moral picture readily obtainable in the confessional was a picture taken of—or from the viewpoint of—an individual moral agent. Most of the sins confessed were, of course, actions that offended and injured other people, sometimes great numbers of other people and in extremely complicated ways. Yet, because none of those people was heard from, their moral perspectives could scarcely be introduced. Not surprisingly, then, Catholic moral thinking habitually understood sin in relation to sinners more than in relation to the victims of sinners. There were no plaintiffs and, apart from the defendant, who confessed and pleaded guilty, there were no witnesses. Even with maximum sincerity, such an arrangement is hardly calculated to generate a comprehensive picture of moral realities.

Penitents, it should also be recalled, came always, until very recently, as isolated individuals, to confess the particular individual deeds for which they sought forgiveness. Under such circumstances moral vision is seriously incapacitated for perceiving either morality or immorality as socially organized, institutionally entailed, ideologically sustained, or culturally perpetuated. To adopt familiar jargon, moral theology, as shaped by the exigencies of the confessional system, tended greatly to emphasize what may be called micro-morality, and to overlook macro-morality. Social sin, as it has come to be called, tended to slip through the meshes of the confessional system, and consequently to slip the minds of moral theologians and of Catholics who took their moral cues from them.

One last consideration along the same lines: what penitents were expected to report, and what confessors were expected to interpret, were not traits or tendencies of moral character, but particular misdeeds. One confessed what one was doing, not what one was becoming. Moral theology focused on rules

rather than on virtues, and on the intermittent breaking of rules rather than on the progressive deterioration of character. By the same token, moral theology typically gave far more attention to doing things one should not do, than to not doing the things one should. The only sins of omission commonly attended to were those involving very precise, usually ritual, obligations.

The functional relationship between moral theology and the confessional system had far-reaching effects, both in assuring the relative invariance of Catholic moral thinking, and in skewing that thinking in a number of important ways. To recapitulate, among the changes in moral thinking that have recently been most conspicuous among Catholics, we can plainly see a number of reversals of, or compensations for the following five broadly-stated tendencies, separately or in combination:

- First, moral norms were regarded as a definite and permanent set of fixed statutes.
- Second, moral issues were interpreted with both insights and oversights typical of celibate, male clergy.
- Third, moral perspective was dominated by the viewpoint of agents of wrongdoing rather than that of sufferers from it.
- Fourth, sins were identified with individual misdeeds, with little attention to their involvement in social practices, policies, and structures.
- And fifth, immorality was thought of rather as a quality of actions than as a disposition of character.

It should be noted that the recent wave of change and diversification in Catholic moral thinking has been simultaneous with a rapid decline of moral theology, at least as traditionally understood, and with widespread neglect of sacramental confession, despite some interesting experiments in changing its procedures.

1. For quite some time now, there has been a widespread reluctance to attribute absolute validity to any but the most comprehensive moral norms. The most extreme reaction has been to discredit moral generalizations altogether, and then replace them all by a sweeping injunction to love. Very often, the obvious practical inadequacy of such an approach leads to interpreting love as that which contributes to happiness, thereby turning Christian morality into a pure consequentialism indistinguishable from secular utilitarianism. In more moderate circles, the tendency is to pay much more attention than formerly to proportional consequences, while honoring certain other norms as well.

2. For a somewhat shorter time, doubt has been cast on a number of familiar moral assumptions by a growing suspicion that they embody prejudices rooted in ignorance of typical female and conjugal experience, intensified by institutionally encouraged attitudes of authoritarian paternalism. Here the most extreme reactions have taken the form of ideological feminism and anti-clericalism. More balanced reactions have explored the effects of sexism on distributive justice, and cultivated a sexual and conjugal morality more sensitive to the realities of family life.

3. A subtler, more profound reassessment of moral priorities has been broached by deliberately adopting the outlooks and evaluations proper to those who may be described as morally victimized, those, that is, whose sufferings are intensified and whose decent aspirations are frustrated by the moral indifference and social irresponsibility of others, more fortunately situated.

4. Catholics are steadily becoming aware of the extent to which moral wrongdoing is rooted in corporate action or inaction, facilitated by social systems, and supported by underlying ideologies, mainly political and economic. Indeed, such wrongdoing may even be so effectively disguised by these same factors as to be commonly overlooked by the moral criticism of conscientious people. Altering those factors has come to be seen as a primary demand of social justice.

5. Several lines of thought, psychological and theological as well as ethical, have conspired in recent years to recommend the centering of moral assessment not on rules but on virtue. The basic idea is that moral goodness is primarily a quality of human lives, constituted not by a record of unbroken regulations, but by the cultivation and integration of certain basic habits, attitudes, and outlooks, of which conformity to rules is only one indication. Such goodness is adequately demonstrated only by the story of a life, in which not only overt action, but vision and expectation shape the evolution of a character within the unfolding of a plot.

What answer can be given to the very basic, practical question of whether Catholic moral thinking in recent years has been getting better or worse? I can only answer: both. All five of the trends I have described are, in my opinion, progressive. But at the same time, because they are a response to a given historical moment, they can be too readily exaggerated, and allowed to supersede rather than supplement elements of moral wisdom from the past.

In my own view, the most celebrated of modern trends in Catholic moral thinking, often called situation ethics, is the most superficial and least innovative. After all, throughout the entire history of Christianity, circumstantial limits to most moral rules have been readily admitted. Even the most venerable Christian moralists, for example, made lots of exceptions to "Thou shalt not kill," and at least a few to "Thou shalt not steal." The same cannot be said of "Thou shalt not commit adultery," and it is notorious that when situation ethicists get down to cases, it is very largely in the realm of sexual morality that they draw controversy and condemnation. We are thus reminded of that peculiar inflexibility which overtakes the traditional Roman Catholic moral theological mind whenever moral rules are rules affecting sexual behavior. Here, I suppose, is the most deplorable effect of a centuries-old hegemony of male celibates in moral theology.

Looking again at the kinds of exceptions to moral norms that have long been taken for granted, one notices that most of them have obviously been based on some kind of consequentialism and proportionalism, that is, on comparing, in particular circumstances, the values of what would happen if the norm were conformed with. That, for example, is clearly the basis on which moral approval has been given to thefts by the very poor from the very rich, and to lethal violence by defenders against aggressors. There is nothing new in principle about consequentialism and proportionalism, but only about certain of their applications. And it cannot be overlooked that here too, at least in official Catholic circles, it is about sex that nearly all the fuss is made.

Up to a point, consequentialism and proportionalism express sound common-sense morality. Obviously the foreseeable results of our actions should be major factors in judging their moral rightness or wrongness. It is elementary morality to try to do more good than harm. But it is not the whole of even elementary morality. The serious problems about consequentialism are not in the realm of sex,

but in the realm of justice. For no one can realistically doubt that occasions can arise when doing something plainly unjust really is likely to accomplish more good than any alternative just behavior. That is not only how tyrants defend their disregard of human rights, but how terrorists opposing those tyrants defend their massacres of the innocent. It is also how governments defend mining foreign harbors, how tax-evaders defend cheating the public, how disciplinarians defend indiscriminate punishment, and how ideologues defend suppressing the truth. Within limits, consequentialism is indispensable to reasonable morality. Beyond those limits, it annihilates the sense of justice.

Subtler and more innovative than these trends is the tendency in modern Catholic moral thinking to adopt the perspective not only of those who perform moral or immoral actions, but also of those who are chiefly affected by them. Phrases like "option for the poor" and "solidarity with victims" are significant expressions of this perspective in recent Catholic social ethics. There is a growing awareness that, from the receiving end of morality and immorality, one gets a different view, and in some respects a clearer and truer one. Demands on our generosity or responsibility take on a completely different moral quality as we shift our focus from concentrating on our own limited resources to entering into the predicaments of those who ask us to share them. The closer one gets to the sufferer, the harder it becomes to refuse help. And the farther one stays from the sufferer, the farther one remains from the central moral reality of the situation. Thus we chase the beggars off our streets, keep the slums off our itineraries, and usher the helpless off our premises because their near presence mocks the complacency of our consciences.

Yet, even this wholesome trend of thought has, perhaps, a dark side in moral thinking. For, given our congenital egocentrism, it is an easy step from paying moral attention to the victimization of others, to thinking about our own moral situations more in passive than in active terms, that is, thinking of ourselves as the objects of other people's moral or immoral behavior.

I think there is reason to fear something of this kind of recurring. The main indication I would point to is a change in the prevailing language of ordinary moral discourse. I have in mind the rapidly increasing frequency of references to rights, and a corresponding diminution of references to duties and obligations. This is a transferral of properly legal language to the realm of ethics. One thing to be said for the confessional system was that it required Catholics regularly to interrupt preoccupation with their rights and pay serious attention to their obligations. We may need to recall that. In a world where all moral thoughts were concerned with rights, and none with obligations, moral life would inevitably cease. The converse is not true.

Perhaps no recent trend has had greater impact on Catholic moral thinking than that which emphasizes the collective and socially structured nature of so much ethical behavior. The practical corollary is that our own responsibility concerning such actions depends on what we can do about the collectivities and social structures involved, and about our personal relations with them. Social justice, as a moral virtue, has come to be understood as a disposition, on the one hand, to try to make societies more just and, on the other, to detach oneself from societies bent on injustice. The velocity of progress in this regard is well demonstrated by attitudes towards conscientious objection, such a short time ago reprobated by the entire fraternity of Catholic moral theologians, and now enjoying praises and blessings from bishops, popes, and an ecumenical council. At the present time, the moral reinterpretation of political, economic, and professional life seems to be well under way.

The least developed, and in some ways the most interesting of the trends I have listed is the last one, with its reinterpretation of moral goodness as the development—over a course of time, experience, and choice—of a certain kind of human being. The interesting thing is that this point of view is not in the least *new* to Catholic thought, even though it is rather new to Catholic theorizing about morality and ethics. The fact is, if one wants to find Catholic thought of the kind here recommended, one can easily find it in any well-stocked Catholic library. To get to it, though, you must make a wide berth of the sections labeled "moral theology" and settle down among the volumes marked spirituality and hagiography. A long, long time ago, spirituality and moral theology went separate ways, eventually separating even more widely. Bringing them together again would be a natural result of addressing questions about what we ought to do with questions about what we are supposed to become. That, it seems to me, is the only possible way a distinctively Christian morality might come into being.

Part 2

MORAL THEOLOGY: THE NATURE OF THE DISCIPLINE

part 2

Moral Theology:
The Nature of the Discipline

Introduction

What is moral theology? What are its major concerns? What is the source of moral obligation? How does one's faith commitment affect one's perception of morality and one's living of the moral life? These are some of the questions that the essays in this part of the text address.

Too often, Christian ethics is understood as almost exclusively concerned with behavior, with the evaluation of a person's acts. In the first essay, Charles Curran, a prominent though controversial Catholic moral theologian, suggests a much broader approach to the discipline. He identifies four areas that he believes must be considered in any systematic reflection on Christian moral life. This wider perspective makes it clear that living morally is both more complex and richer than simply deciding what actions are right or wrong. It also helps make clear how a person's beliefs about God, salvation, human nature and other fundamental realities have a bearing on one's moral life.

While Curran paints the broad picture, McDonagh focuses in on one foundational aspect of ethics—the experience of being confronted with moral claims that are independent of our own wishes and preferences.

The next three essays discuss the relationship of revelation to moral theology. This broad category encompasses more specific issues. Some are epistemological. For example, do Christians know something about the moral life that non-Christians do not know? Or is moral truth knowable only by faith? Others are theological. One major concern here would be precisely what it is that revelation brings to ethics. Still others are political. Here the question is whether and how Christians can participate in public discourse in a pluralistic society if their moral positions are theologically informed.

The Swiss Catholic theologian, Hans Küng, discusses what is distinctive about Christian morality in contrast to non-Christian or non-religious perceptions of moral life. James Gustafson, one of the most respected American Protestant ethicists today, offers his reflections on the same issue. We conclude this section with suggestions by Jesuit moral theologian, Richard McCormick, who explains the dynamic of how faith complements yet informs moral reasoning.

6

Method in Moral Theology: An Overview From an American Perspective

Charles E. Curran

Moral theology, like all theology, bases its reflections on the Word of God in the scriptures, on the tradition, on the teaching of the Church, on the signs of the times and on the eschatological pull of the future. In the last few years great attention has been paid to the signs of the times. The signs of the times, which are important for moral theology in the United States, include both the cultural milieu with its understanding of moral problems and the thematic and systematic reflection, which is the discipline of ethics, both in its religious and philosophical contexts.

To read the signs of the times always involves a prudential discernment and the risk of being wrong. Traditionally American life and ethos have given great importance to freedom in all aspects of life, but there has also been a recognition of the limits of freedom which has especially come to the fore in recent years.

The contemporary American scene has witnessed the end of an era in which easy optimism and even naïveté characterized much of the country's self-understanding. Self-criticism and doubt have been more apparent ever since the Vietnam War, Watergate, continuing world crises and the energy shortage. At times there is a feeling of pessimism and even helplessness, but this self-critical attitude has raised in the public consciousness a greater interest in ethics and the morality of the decisions that must be made to guide our future life. No one is unaware of the multitude of problems calling out for a solution—nuclear energy and weapons, poverty throughout the world and at home, hunger in the world, human rights and wars of liberation, the contemporary trouble spots in the globe—the Near East, Indochina, Africa, Central and South America, world trade and economic

This article originally appeared in Studia Moralia 18 (1980): 107–128.

policies, multinational corporations, technology, energy, the environment. There appears to be a widespread feeling that America must be willing to face these problems and also to change their own life styles away from the consumerism and materialism which have so often characterized our society. At the same time there exists a great interest in contemplation, in the personal struggle for growth and in the meaning of life and death.

The influence of specifically Catholic thought and theology on the American cultural and intellectual life has not been great. Over twenty years ago, JOHN TRACY ELLIS criticized American Catholicism for its failures in making any noticeable contribution to the wider scene of American intellectual and cultural life.[1] Since that time, individual Catholics and groups have made some contributions, but generally speaking there has been little that is specifically theological in these individual contributions.

On the reflective level of ethics as such, Catholic moral theology in the United States is related to and influenced by religious ethics, especially Protestant Christian ethics, and philosophical ethics. Protestant ethics has had a significant influence in the United States. Perhaps there is no intellectual figure who had a greater impact on American foreign policy in the middle years of the twentieth century than REINHOLD NIEBUHR.[2] Before the Second Vatican Council there was little or no dialogue between Protestant and Catholic ethicists, but that situation has changed dramatically since the 1960s. Not only dialogue but also rapprochement characterizes the relationship between moral theology and Protestant ethics. As one very knowledgeable and competent Protestant scholar has pointed out, Catholic moral theology now gives more stress to

aspects of ethics that were previously identified as typically Protestant emphases—becoming, process, dynamism, change, freedom, history, grace and gospel. On the other hand, Protestants have striven to give more importance to Catholic concerns such as being, structure, order, continuity, nature and law.[3] Close contact and dialogue with Protestant Christian ethics characterizes moral theology in the United States, but moral theology still attempts to remain firmly rooted in its own tradition. At the same time there is increasing communication with philosophical ethics both on methodological and on substantive questions. Philosophical ethics is no longer dominated by an analytic approach which shuns substantive and content questions. Now there is a growing interest of philosophers in the ethical questions facing society and in theoretical issues such as justice and the justification of moral norms.[4] Catholic moral theology exists in an intellectural milieu in the United States in which it is in contact and dialogue with Protestant and philosophical ethics.

I approach the question of method in moral theology with the presupposition that errors and mistakes in method generally arise not so much from positive error as from the failure to consider all the aspects which deserve discussion. In moral theology itself in the last few years, there has been an unfortunate tendency, readily understandable in the light of the contemporary controversies, to reduce moral theology merely to the question of norms and the morality of specific actions. The questions of specific actions and of norms are significant questions in moral theology, but there are other questions which are of greater or equal importance. In my judgment the following areas must be investigated in any systematic reflection on Christian moral life: the perspective or stance; the ethical model; Christian anthropology; concrete Christian decision making and norms. These different aspects will now be discussed in greater detail.

I. Stance

The question of stance, perspective or horizon is the most fundamental and logically first consideration in moral theology. Catholic moral theology has not explicitly posed the question of stance, but in the American Protestant tradition JAMES SELLERS has insisted on stance as the first consideration in moral theology, logically prior to any other consideration and the sources of other criteria.[5] JAMES GUSTAFSON employs a similar concept of perspective or posture to indicate the fundamental angle of vision which directs the entire enterprise of Christian ethics.[6] Some contemporary Catholic theologians speak of horizon, which for our purposes can be understood as the way in which moral theology looks at the reality of the Christian moral life and structures its own understanding of moral reality.

Two cautions should be kept in mind in any discussion of stance. First, it is impossible to say that one stance is right and another wrong. The adequacy of the stance depends on how well it accomplishes its purpose as being the logically prior step, which structures our understanding of moral reality, serves as a critique of other approaches and is a source of other ethical criteria. Second, although stance as a logically prior step seems to have something of the a priori about it, in reality my own stance developed in an a posteriori way based on a critique of other positions. To properly fulfill its critical function and be proved adequate, the stance cannot rest merely on an a priori deduction or assumption.

My stance consists of a perspective based on the fivefold Christian mysteries of creation, sin, incarnation, redemption and resurrection destiny. The reason for accepting these as aspects of the stance are obvious for the Christian, but the adequacy of this fivefold stance must be shown. The stance functions both methodologically and substantively. From a methodological viewpoint the stance both serves as a negative critique of other methodologies and provides a positive approach of its own.

Roman Catholic natural law theory rightly recognized that the Christian finds ethical wisdom and knowledge not only in the Scriptures and in Jesus Christ but also in human nature and human reason. On the basis of creation by a good and gracious God, human reason reflecting on human nature can arrive at ethical wisdom and knowledge. Insistence on the goodness of the natural and the human, with its corollary that grace builds on nature and is not opposed to nature, stands as a hallmark of the Catholic theological tradition. Some Protestant theologians deny the goodness of creation and the possibility of ethical wisdom and knowledge based on human nature and human reason for a number of different reasons—Scripture alone is the source of ethical wisdom for the Christian; a narrow Christomonism sees Christ as the only way into the ethical problem; sin so affects human nature and human reason that they cannot serve as the basis of true knowledge; an unwillingness to accept an analogy between creation and the creator.

However, from the viewpoint of the proposed stance, the natural law approach is deficient because it does not integrate the natural or creation into the total Christian perspective. The natural law theory rightly recognizes creation and incarnation; but sin, redemption and resurrection destiny do not receive their due. Catholic moral theology may have overstressed sin in terms of particular actions; but it never paid sufficient attention to the reality of sin as present in the world and affecting, without however destroying, human nature and human reason. Likewise, natural law theory gives no place to grace, or redemption and resurrection destiny as the stance describes this reality, so that often Catholic moral theology became based exclusively on the natural to the neglect of what was then called the supernatural.

On the contrary, a Lutheran two realm theory recognized the reality of sin but overemphasizes sin and fails to give enough importance to the reality of creation and to moral wisdom based on it, to the integrating effect of the incarnation, to the recognition that redemption also affects the world in which we live and to a more positive appreciation of the relationship between resurrection destiny and the present world.

Protestant liberalism arose in the nineteenth century and its most significant ethical manifestation in the United States was the Social Gospel school.[7] This approach, especially in its more extreme forms, stressed the goodness of creation, the integrating effect of the incarnation on all reality, and the presence of redemption in the world, but sin and resurrection destiny as a future gift at the end of time were neglected.

Liberalism was succeeded in Protestant theology by Neo-Orthodoxy with its Barthian and Niebuhrian approaches. Barthian ethics flourished in Europe, but its most significant American exponent is PAUL LEHMANN.[8]

Barthian ethics emphasized the centrality of redemption and of Christ and made Christ the sole way into the ethical problem. There was no place for philosophical ethics or natural law for the Christian. Within such a perspective, sin, incarnation, redemption and resurrection destiny could all be given due importance, but creation and its ethical ramifications in terms of human reason were denied. Niebuhrian Neo-Orthodoxy, which ultimately exerted such a great influence on American thought and foreign policy, recognized the ethical import of creation even though it was infected by sin, but in the final analysis gave too much to the presence of sin and failed to appreciate the effects of incarnation, redemption and a more positive relationship between the world of the present and the fullness of resurrection destiny in the eschaton. However, in many ways NIEBUHR tried to account for all the elements in the stance but overemphasized the role of sin and downplayed the others.

In the 1960s in Protestant theology, some approaches similar to the older liberalism came to the fore in the form of the theologies of the death of God and of secularization. Once again there was a tendency to overstress creation, incarnation and redemption and to neglect the reality of sin and the fact that resurrection destiny is future and its fullness comes only as God's gracious gift at the end of time. In the light of the proposed stance subsequent developments were healthy. A theology of secularization gave way to a theology of hope with the primacy on resurrection destiny as future. However, at times there was still not enough emphasis on sin and on some discontinuity between this world and the next. MOLTMANN as a Protestant and METZ as a Catholic both went through a development similar to that outlined above and then put greater emphasis on discontinuity by highlighting the role of suffering as MOLTMANN wrote about *The Crucified God* and METZ talked about the future «*ex memoria passionis eius*».[9]

In the 1960s in conjunction with the Second Vatican Council, Roman Catholic theology rightly attempted to overcome the dichotomy between nature and grace, between gospel and daily life, between Church and world. But in overcoming the dichotomy there emerged the danger of making everything grace and the supernatural. In other words there was a tendency to forget sin and the fact that resurrection destiny is future and exists always in discontinuity, as well as in continuity, with present reality. Catholic thinking in this period often suffered from a collapsed eschaton because of which people thought that the fullness of the kingdom would come quickly, readily and without a struggle or suffering.

In contemporary Catholic theology, liberation theology, with its attempt to integrate redemption and the gospel into our understanding of political and economic life in society, marks an improvement over the exclusive natural law approach that formerly characterized Catholic social ethics as exemplified in the papal social encyclicals. However, in liberation theology there exist among some a tendency to forget the reality of sin as affecting to some extent all reality (too often the impression is given that sin is all on one side) and a tendency to think that the fullness of the eschaton will come too readily and quickly. On the contrary, liberation will involve a long, hard, difficult struggle and will never be fully present in this world. At times liberation theology fails to reorganize complexity in this world, for among some there is a great confidence in being able to know quite easily what

God is doing in this world. The opposite danger maintains that reality is complex and sin so affects all reality that one cannot know what God is doing in the world. I want to avoid both these extremes.

The stance embracing the fivefold mysteries of creation, sin, incarnation, redemption and resurrection destiny not only serves as a critique of many other theories in moral theology as pointed out above, but at the same time it provides a positive methodology and perspective for approaching moral theology. Creation indicates the goodness of the human and human reason; but sin touches all reality, without however, destroying the basic goodness of creation. Incarnation integrates all reality into the plan of God's kingdom. Redemption as already present affects all reality, but resurrection destiny as future exists in continuity with the redeemed present but also in discontinuity because the fullness of the kingdom remains God's gracious gift at the end of time.

The stance also addresses some substantive issues; but, since the stance is the logically prior step in moral theology and by definition remains somewhat general, one cannot expect the stance to provide specific and detailed substantive content. A primary contribution of the stance is in giving a direction and general perspective to our understanding of some of the most basic issues in Christian ethics. The first question refers to the meaning of human existence in this world and to the relationship between this world and the kingdom. In the past, Protestant theology often addressed the same basic question in terms of the relationship between Christ and culture as illustrated in the book by H. RICHARD NIEBUHR, who points out five different typologies for understanding this relationship.[10] The position derived from the stance corresponds to

NIEBUHR'S type of Christ transforming culture. The fullness of the kingdom will only come at the end, but in this world the kingdom strives to make itself more present. The individual Christian and the community of believers must recognize that the mission of the Church and of the gospel calls for them to struggle for peace and justice in the world.

The stance also sheds light on the meaning of death for the Christian. Death seems to point to total discontinuity between this world and the next for the individual person, but in the light of the stance death can be seen in a transformationist perspective. All created reality will die, but sin has added an important negative dimension to the Christian understanding of death. Even more importantly, death is understood in the light of the mystery of the incarnation, death and resurrection of Jesus so that death is neither the end nor the beginning of something totally discontinuous but rather the transformation of earthly life and reality into the fullness of life and love.

The stance serves as an interpretative tool in understanding the basic mysteries of the Christian life. Especially in a sacramental and mystical perspective the Christian life is often described in terms of living out the paschal mystery of Jesus into which we are baptized. The paschal mystery can be interpreted in different ways depending on the stance. Some have interpreted it in paradoxical terms to show that life is present in the midst of death, joy in the midst of sorrow and light in darkness. A transformationist understanding recognizes that there are some paradoxical aspects to the Christian life, but also at times God's life is known in human life, God's love in human love, God's light in human light and God's joy in human joy. The paschal mystery understood in this perspective gives us a better understanding of Christian life and death and the relationship between the two. Life involves a constant dying to selfishness and sin to enter more fully into the resurrection, and so death itself can be seen as the moment of growth par excellence—dying to the present to enter most fully into life itself.

Perhaps this is the best place to briefly mention the debate about a distinctively Christian ethic. I deny that on the level of material content (actions, virtues, attitudes and dispositions) there is anything distinctively Christian because non-Christians can and do share the same material content of morality even to the point of such attitudes as self-sacrificing love. Unlike some others, I do not base this on a common human nature abstractly considered, but rather on the fact that in the present existential order all are called to share in the fullness of God's love. However, Christians thematize their understanding in a specifically Christian way. Since ethics, as distinguished from morality, is a thematic and systematic reflection, moral theology and Christian ethics must be based on Christian realities even though some of these (e.g. creation) are not distinctively Christian.

II. Ethical Model

The second logical step in the systematic reflection, which is moral theology, concerns the model in view of which one understands the Christian life. Three different models have been proposed in both philosophical and theological literature. The teleological model views the ethical life in terms of the goal or end to be achieved, but in the complexity of existence one distinguishes ultimate goals from intermediate and subordinate goals. Something is morally good if it is conducive to achieving the goal and is evil if it prevents the attainment of the goal. It should be pointed out that these models are very broad umbrellas. THOMAS AQUINAS, who begins his ethical consideration with a discussion of the last end, serves as a good example of the teleological model; but utilitarians also fit under the same model. A deontological model views the moral life primarily in terms of duty, law or obligation. The categorical imperative of IMMANUEL KANT well illustrates a deontological approach to ethics. Popular Christian piety frequently adopts such an approach by making the ten commandments the basis of the moral life. The manuals of moral theology, although thinking they were in the tradition of THOMAS AQUINAS, by their heavy emphasis on law as the objective norm of morality and conscience as the subjective norm, belong to the deontological model. A relationality-responsibility model views the moral life primarily in terms of the person's multiple relationships with God, neighbor, world and self and the subject's actions in this context.

I opt for a relationality-responsibility model as the primary ethical model. Such an option does not exclude some place for teleological and deontological concerns, but the relationality-responsibility model is primary and constitutes the basis upon which the ethical life is discussed. There are a number of significant reasons supporting the primacy of such a model. Contemporary Scriptural studies indicate that the primary ethical concept in the Old Testament is not law but covenant. The New Testament emphasis on love as, at least, an important ethical concern, despite its different understanding by different authors, argues for a relationality-responsibility approach. The Scriptures often describe the moral life as our response to the gracious gift of God. Contemporary hermeneutics reminds us of the difficulty of finding universal moral norms in the Scriptures.[11] Among Protestants, a Barthian approach argued against a fundamentalistic reading of the Scriptures often associated with legalism and replaced it with an understanding of the Scriptures as the description of the mighty acts of God to which the believer responds. The stance reminds us of the call for the Christian to respond creatively to the contemporary situation and to make the kingdom more present. Philosophical emphases on historical consciousness, the importance of the subject and personalism argue against the more static notion of morality as the plan of God worked out for all eternity which so often characterized Catholic understandings in the past. Although the teleological model might be more open to historicity, personalism and the importance of the subject, still one does not have as much control over one's life as this model often supposes.

Within a relationality-responsibility model one must avoid the danger of a narrow personalism which views the moral life only in terms of the perspective of an «I-thou» relationship. The Christian is related to God, neighbor, the world and self. The failure to give due weight to all these relationships will distort the meaning of the Christian life. The basic reality of the Christian life has been described in different ways—love, conversion, life in Christ, the law of the Spirit. All of these descriptions can be used, but they must be understood in terms of a relationality model which includes all the aspects mentioned above.

Just as the fundamental, positive understanding of the Christian life is viewed in relational terms, so too the negative aspect of sin should be seen in the same perspective. A deontological model defines sin as an act against the law of God. A teleological model views sin as going against God, the ultimate end. But, from the earliest pages of Genesis, sin is described in terms of our relationship with God, neighbor, the world and self. A contemporary theology of sin in terms of the fundamental option should also be interpreted in relational terms. Mortal sin is not primarily an act against the law of God or going against the ultimate end but rather the breaking of our relationship of love with God, neighbor, world and self. Venial sin is the diminishing of these fundamental relationships. In this perspective all the aspects of sin become apparent especially social sin and its influence on our political, social and economic structures.

Changes in the understanding of the sacrament of penance will illustrate the shift to a more relational model of the Christian life. In the context of a deontological ethical model, the sacrament of penance was called confession from the name of the primary act—the confession of sins according to number and species. Today the sacrament is called reconciliation—a relational term which includes our multiple relationships with God, neighbor, world and self.

The general notion of relationality-responsibility needs to be developed and spelled out as accurately as possible. On the American scene, H. RICHARD NIEBUHR has attempted a further elucidation of this basic concept. NIEBUHR understands responsibility as involving four elements—response, interpretation, accountability and social solidarity.[12] My own development of relationality-responsibility, especially in comparison with NIEBUHR, gives more significance to the ontological grounding of relationality and to the creative role of the subject. Without using the term relationality-responsibility, DANIEL C. MAGUIRE has recently proposed a method which fits under such a model. According to MAGUIRE one

seeks to discover the moral reality on the basis of four sets of questions—What?; Why? How? Who? When? Where?; Forseeable effects?; Viable alternatives? The evaluation of this moral reality involves a number of factors including creative imagination, reason and analysis, principles, affectivity, individual experience, group experience, authority, comedy and tragedy.[13]

A relationality-responsibility model also influences our approach to particular questions. Take the example of lying. An older approach, based on the teleology inscribed by nature in the faculty of speech, defined the malice of lying as frustrating the God-given purpose of the faculty of speech, which according to God's plan is to express on one's lips what is in one's mind. Within such a context, it was necessary to resort to a casuistry of mental reservations to deal with some of the problems that arise. Lately, a different approach employing a relationality model has seen the malice of lying in the violation of my neighbor's right to truth. There are cases in which the neighbor does not have the right to truth, and my false speech does not involve the moral malice of lying. Similarly, sexual morality is no longer based on the innate teleology inscribed in the sexual faculty. A more relational approach sees the sexual faculty related to the human person and the person related to others, especially to the marriage partner. A relationality-responsibility model not only determines our understanding of basic moral considerations but also results in different solutions to concrete ethical questions.

III. Christian Anthropology

A third step in the development of a method for moral theology concerns Christian anthropology or the subject existing in the midst of these multiple relationships. In ethics the basic importance of the person as subject is twofold. First, individual actions come from the person and are expressive of the person. Actions are ethically grounded in the person placing the actions. As the Scriptures remind us, the good tree brings forth good fruit or those who live in the Spirit should produce the fruits of the Spirit. Second, the person, through one's actions, develops and constitutes oneself as a moral subject. In the transcendental terms to be developed later, through one's actions, one fulfills the drive to authentic self-transcendence. Individual acts are not the most fundamental ethical category because they are both expressive of the moral subject and constitutive of the moral being of the subject.

The importance of the moral subject underscores the place of growth and development in the Christian life. The Christian is called to be perfect even as the heavenly Father is perfect. Although the fullness of response to God's gracious gift will never be achieved, the Christian strives to grow in wisdom, age and grace before God and human beings. The call to continual conversion also highlights the importance of growth in the Christian life. Philosophically, this growth is grounded in the drive of the subject toward authentic self-transcendence. Through actions the subject continually transcends self and thereby contributes to true growth. Psychologists, too, have been paying much attention to the importance of moral growth in human life. In the United States, LAWRENCE KOHLBERG has proposed his theory of moral development involving six stages with the last stage exemplifying post-conventional morality and described as the full development of an interior, self-directed moral sense with an orientation of conscience toward ethical principles

which appeal to logical comprehensiveness, universality and consistency.[14] Catholic thinkers are appreciative of KOHLBERG'S work but are beginning to deal with KOHLBERG in a critical way.[15] In my judgment, KOHLBERG'S basic limits come from the formal aspects of his approach which is conditioned both by his Kantian philosophy and by his attempt to come up with a model of moral development acceptable and usable in a pluralistic context. As a result, his approach is based on the formalities of justice but does not give enough importance to content, to questions of dispositions and virtues, and to aspects other than a rationalistic understanding of justice.

Intimately connected with the subject are the attitudes, virtues and dispositions, which are expressed in action and which also constitute the subject as morally good and form an essential part of the growth and development of the moral subject.[16] These dispositions or virtues affect the various relationships within which the subject finds oneself. It is impossible to describe in detail all the dispositions which should characterize the different relationships within which the Christian person exists as subject, but some of the more significant ones can be mentioned.

Traditionally the relationship of the individual to God is characterized by the three theological virtues of faith, hope and charity. In the light of a better integrated view of the moral life of the Christian based on the stance, some other important dispositions and attitudes should be developed. The attitude of worship and thanksgiving must characterize the Christian, who recognizes God as the author of love, life and all good gifts. The Christian is primarily a worshipper. Here one can see the intimate connection between liturgy and the moral life of the Christian. The liturgy with its celebration of the encounter of God's giving and of human response mirrors the basic structure of life. A second very fundamental attitude for the Christian is openness and receptivity to the word and work of God. The Scriptures frequently allude to the importance of this basic virtue—be it done unto me according to your will. This disposition is the true humility of spirit which the Scriptures portray as the great characteristic of the poor of Yahweh. The privileged people in the kingdom—the poor, children and sinners—underscore the importance of this disposition of openness to God's saving gift. A self-sufficiency, which so often characterizes the rich, the proud and the important, is the antithesis of the disposition of openness or true humility of spirit.

Within the traditional triad of faith, hope and charity more importance must be given to hope than was true in the manuals of moral theology. This emphasis comes from the contemporary theological highlighting of eschatology and of the pilgrim nature of our existence. Struggle and suffering are an integral part of our existence.

Relationships to neighbor are characterized by the generic dispositions of love and justice. These general attitudes are then specified by the different relationships one has to specific neighbors—parent, friend, teacher, coworker, client, boss, employer, person in authority. In this context one cannot underscore enough the Christian insistence on love for the poor, the needy and the outcast. This habitual attitude constantly calls one out of one's own narrowness and selfishness and strives to make ever broader and more universal the horizons of our love.

The relationship to the world and to earthly realities involves a number of specific relationships. The basic Christian attitude is that the goods of creation exist to serve the needs of all. The purpose of the goods of creation is to serve all God's people, and no one has a right to arrogate superfluous goods to oneself at the expense of the neighbor in need. Unfortunately an overemphasis on private property has too often blinded us to the basic attitude toward the goods of creation.[17] Selfishness and sinfulness have too often turned the goods of creation into the means of personal gratification and aggrandizement at the expense of others. The question of the best economic system is complex, but the guiding principle must be how well the system fulfills the basic principle that the goods of creation exist to serve the needs of all. An attitude of respectful gratitude for the gifts of creation serves as the basis for an environmental ethics. Our relationships with the different types of material goods will make more specific and spell out this general understanding of their universal destiny.

Our relationship to self is governed by the basic attitude of stewardship, using our gifts, talents and selves in the living out of the Christian life. Here, too, the individual must always struggle against the opposite attitude of selfishness. As in our other relationships there is place for a proper Christian asceticism, which uses our lives, our gifts and our bodies for the service of the kingdom and our own development.

IV. Decision Making and Norms

The fourth and final level of ethical reflection in describing a method for moral theology concerns concrete decision making and the morality of particular actions. In the contemporary context the two most important questions are the grounding of moral norms and the role and function of conscience.

There has been much discussion in Catholic moral theology, in Protestant Christian ethics and in contemporary philosophical ethics about norms and the grounding of moral norms. Among a good number of Roman Catholic theologians throughout the world there has been a dissatisfaction with the existence of certain negative moral absolutes and the grounding of these norms in a particular understanding of natural law. In my judgment the problem arises from a concept of natural law as coinciding with the physical structure of the act so that the physical structure of the act becomes morally normative—an act described in physical terms is said to be always and everywhere wrong. I am not saying that the physical structure of the act and the moral reality of the act cannot coincide, but the moral must include much more than just the physical structure of the act and the grounding of the moral meaning involves more than just a consideration of the physical structure of the act.

Many revisionist Catholic moral theologians at the present time solve the problem distinguishing between moral evil and premoral, physical or ontic evil, which, in the understanding of the manuals on questions such as double effect or sterilization, was called moral evil. Physical, ontic or premoral evil can be justified if there is a commensurate or proportionate reason.[18]

In my view such an approach is on the right track but does not go far enough. The physical is but one aspect of the moral, which is the ultimate human judgment and includes all the other aspects—the psychological, the sociological, the pedagogical, the hygenic, etc. It is necessary to unpack what is meant by premoral or ontic evil and commensurate reason. This raises the question of the different values involved. In general, norms exists to protect and promote values. But the question arises of how norms are arrived at and grounded?

Before discussing the precise way in which norms as the safeguard of values are to be grounded, a word should be said about the source of conflict situations, which bring about the tensions existing between and among different values. Again, in keeping with a general presumption in favor of complexity, there appears to be a number of sources for the conflict situations that arise and might call for modifications or exceptions in moral norms. From a strictly ethical perspective, Catholic moral theology has recognized one source of conflict in its distinction between the objective moral order and the subjective. Objectively a particular act is morally wrong (e.g., drunkenness), but for this individual subject in these particular circumstances (e.g., an alcoholic) there is no subjective guilt or the guilt is greatly diminished. Philosophical ethics recognizes the same reality in its distinction between circumstances which justify an act (make it right) and circumstances which excuse an act (take away guilt without making it right).

There exist other sources of conflict situations in moral theology which can be reduced to three—eschatological tension, the presence of sin and human finitude. Eschatological tension results from the fact that the fullness of the eschaton is not here, and in this pilgrim existence the eschatological exigencies cannot always be fully met. In this light I have argued against an absolute prohibition of divorce and remarriage.

The presence of sin in the world also causes some conflict situations. There can be no doubt that the presence of sin in the world has justified certain moral actions which would not be acceptable if there were no sin. Think of the justifications given for war, capital punishment, revolution, occult compensation. An older Catholic theology explicitly recognized that the justification of private property was grounded in the fact of original sin and not in human nature as such. In the light of my stance and contention that at times Catholic moral theology has not explicitly given enough importance to the reality of sin, it seems there might be other cases in which the presence of sin might justify an action which could not be justified if sin and its effects were not present. In the past I have referred to this as the theory of compromise. Such a theory is more a theological explanation of the source of the conflict and tension rather than a tightly reasoned ethical analysis of how it is to be applied in practice. Compromise was chosen to describe this reality in order to recognize the tension between justifying such actions because of the presence of sin and the Christian obligation to try to overcome sin and its effects. However, at times in this world sin and its presence cannot be overcome—a fact which the Catholic tradition has recognized in its discussion of war and private property; but perhaps a greater emphasis on the compromise aspect of these two ethical realities might have made us more cautious in dealing with them.

A third source of tension and conflict in establishing moral norms as preservers of values stems from human finitude. Values will at times conflict and clash because it is impossible to obtain or safeguard one value without losing or diminishing another value. At the very least, moral theology should recognize the sources of the conflict situations which often arise in questions involving norms. However, the recognition of the different sources of conflict does not help to resolve the question of how norms are grounded and the question of modifications or exceptions in some norms that have been accepted as absolute in the manuals of moral theology.

In approaching the question of grounding norms, much can be learned from a dialogue with contemporary philosophical ethics. The question is often phrased in terms of a deontological or teleological grounding of norms. According to the deontological grounding of norms, certain actions are right or wrong no matter what the consequences. No matter how much good might result, suicide, for example, is always morally wrong. Such an approach has been called a Catholic position and certainly coincides with what has often been presented in Catholic philosophy and theology. However, some revisionist Catholic moralists maintain that norms are derived teleologically and this was true even for the Catholic understanding in the past. Norms were based on whether or not the particular action was judged good or evil for the human person and for society.

Many of the revisionist Catholic theologians, who have proposed a teleological grounding for norms, have employed an approach according to which commensurate reason can justify premoral or ontic evil and, thereby, have challenged some of the absolute norms defended in the manuals of moral theology. As a result some other Catholic theoreticians claim that such approaches are consequentialist, basing morality solely on the consequences of the action.[19]

An overview of the contemporary philosophical discussion about the grounding of norms indicates there are three different positions and not just two, but the terminology is confusing and not uniform. The one position is clearly deontological—some actions are always wrong no matter what the consequences. A second position is truly consequentialist, utilitarian or strictly teleological and derives norms and the morality of actions solely on the basis of consequences. In this context there has been much debate about the difference between act and rule utilitarianism.

However, it is evident that there also exists a third position mediating between the two and called by different names including teleology and *prima facie* obligationalism.[20] This position rejects deontology but also disagrees with a strict teleology or consequentialism. In disagreement with strict consequentialists or utilitarians this middle position maintains the following three points: (1) Moral obligations arise from elements other than consequences, e.g., promises, previous acts of gratitude or evil; (2) The good is not separate from the right; (3) The way in which the good or the evil is obtained by the agent and not just the end result is a moral consideration.

The existence of three different positions on the grounding of the moral norm indicates there are more than just two different approaches to this question. In my judgment the middle position is best described as a distinct approach based on a relationality-responsibility grounding of norms. Such a position grounds the norm on the basis of what is experienced as good for the person and for the total human society but understood according to a relational criterion which gives importance to consequences but also gives moral value to aspects other than consequences.

In general, a relational grounding of the norm sees the norm as protecting and promoting values. Such an approach avoids the absolutism of a deontological approach and also the oversimplistic approach of a consequentialism which gives moral significance only to consequences. By highlighting the continued importance of the social dimension of human existence, such an approach recognizes that often norms are required for the good of all living together in human society.

The difference between my approach and that of GERMAIN GRISEZ, a contemporary Catholic deontologist, helps to give a clear understanding of how my approach works. According to GRISEZ, there are eight basic human goods which the individual person can never directly go against.[21] My relational approach does not see the individual face to face with eight separate, basic goods but rather views the individual in multiple relationships with others and sees these goods as also related among themselves. At times there might be a conflict among these eight basic goods, and one might have to be sacrificed for other important values. In my methodology, a relationality-responsibility model not only serves as the basic model of the Christian moral life but also grounds and establishes moral norms.

Conscience is the guide and director of the moral life of the individual. The understanding of conscience found in the manuals of moral theology can be criticized for being legalistic, minimalistic, overly rational and too deductive. A better notion of conscience must be integrated within the understanding of the stance, model and anthropology described above. For example, a relational model will not accept as primary the deontological understanding of conscience as the subjective norm of morality trying to conform to the objective norm of morality, which is law in all its different aspects—divine, natural and positive. Conscience is grounded in the subject, who is called to respond to the gospel message in the midst of the multiple relationships of human existence and thereby live out the trust for authentic self-transcendence. Conscience thus partakes of the dynamism of the self-transcending subject.[22] The authentic life of the person as subject calls for self-transcendence which on the moral level reaches its fulfillment when the subject exists in a loving relationship with God, neighbor, the world and self. An older faculty metaphysics situated conscience in the practical intellect. In my perspective conscience should be seen as an operation of the subject. In this way one can better integrate the creative and affective aspects of conscience and avoid a one-sided rationalism.

Conscience is the operation of the subject guiding and directing the moral life. Conscience is stimulated in many different ways —through parables, stories,[23] symbols, the liturgy, through the example of others as models and through a myriad of life experiences. In its pursuit of values and self-transcendence the subject in many different ways comes to know, appreciate, love and create the attitudes which should mark the life of the Christian. Conscience is seriously impoverished when it is reduced merely to a knowledge of the law for it should be seen as an operation of the self-transcending subject trying to live out the fullness of the relationship with God, neighbor, the world and self.

What about the decision of conscience about a particular action to be done here and now? In accord with a transcendental approach in the context of a relational model of ethics, the judgment of conscience is grounded ultimately in the self-transcending subject. The ultimate criterion of the truth of conscience is not conformity to the truth existing out there but is the self-transcendence of the human subject striving for authentic development.

The judgment of conscience is virtually unconditioned. The self-transcending subject with its thrust towards the true and the good

constantly asks questions. The criterion of a true judgment exists when the subject rests at peace because there are no more pertinent questions to ask. The subject is always dealing with the data and reality before it and asking questions precisely to comprehend the moral meaning. Of course, there are dangers that the drive for authentic self-transcendence and the questioning based on it will be blunted and short-circuited, but the mature moral subject will be aware of these possible pitfalls and struggle against them.

The Christian tradition has talked about the peace and joy of conscience as being the sign of a good conscience. A transcendental theory grounds this peace and joy in the judgment of conscience as a virtually unconditioned in which the subject, constituted by its dynamic thrust toward self-transcendence, arrives at the true and the good and is at peace. The subject rests in the achievement of the true and the good. In this whole process the self is constantly asking questions about the entire moral act, end and circumstances and takes all the steps which are appropriate in a discerning process including prayer, reflection, and counsel.

The dilemma of conscience has always arisen from the recognition that the individual must act in accord with personal conscience, but conscience might be wrong. The generic limitations of conscience, especially in the light of the stance, are finitude and sinfulness. The person striving for true self-transcendence must be aware of these limitations and strive to overcome them. In this context, from a purely ethical viewpoint, which is obviously strengthened in the light of Catholic ecclesiology, one can see the importance of the Church as a moral teacher because by definition the community of believers guided by the Spirit through various offices and charisms exists in diverse times and places and is aided in the struggle against sin. The Church helps to overcome the twofold generic limitation of human conscience.

This study has attempted to sketch the method which should be employed in moral theology especially in the light of the cultural and academic situation in the United States. On the basis of a presupposition recognizing great complexity in the moral life in general and in the systematic reflection on that experience, four general areas of reflection have been considered—the stance, the ethical model, anthropology and norms and concrete decision making.

Notes

1. John Tracy Ellis, *American Catholics and the Intellectual Life*, Thought 30 (1955), p. 351–388.
2. See Ronald Stone, *Reinhold Niebuhr: Prophet to Politicians*, Nashville, 1971; also *Reinhold Niebuhr: His Religious, Social and Political Thought* (ed. Charles W. Kegley and Robert W. Bretall), New York, 1956.
3. James M. Gustafson, *Protestant and Roman Catholic Ethics: Prospects for Rapprochement*, Chicago, 1978.
4. See, for example, *Ethics and Problems of the 21st Century* (ed. K. E. Goodpaster and K. M. Sayre), Notre Dame, Indiana, 1979. On questions of justice much discussion has been sparked by John Rawls, *A Theory of Justice*, Cambridge, Mass., 1971.
5. James Sellers, *Theological Ethics*, New York, 1966, p. 29–68.
6. James M. Gustafson, *Christ and the Moral Life*, New York, 1968, p. 240–248.
7. The standard account of this movement

remains, Charles Howard Hopkins, *The Rise of the Social Gospel in American Protestantism, 1865-1915*, New Haven, Conn., 1940.
8. Paul Lehmann, *Ethics in a Christian Context*, New York, 1963; *The Transfiguration of Politics*, New York, 1975.
9. Jürgen Moltmann, *The Theology of Hope*, New York, 1967; *The Crucified God*, New York, 1974; Johannes B. Metz, *Theology of the World*, New York, 1969; *The Future in the Memory of Suffering*, New Concilium 76 (1972), p. 9-25.
10. H. Richard Niebuhr, *Christ and Culture*, New York, 1956.
11. (The way in which moral theology employs the Scriptures in moral theology constitutes another very significant methodological question. I distinguish different ways in which the Scriptures have an impact on the four levels discussed here—stance, ethical model, anthropology and concrete actions and norms. For a recent discussion of this question in American Christian ethics, see Bruce C. Birch and Larry L. Rasmussen, *Bible and Ethics in the Christian Life*, Minneapolis, Minn., 1976. These authors do not consider any Catholic literature coming from outside the United States.
12. H. Richard Niebuhr, *The Responsible Self: An Essay in Christian Moral Philosophy*, New York, 1963.
13. Daniel C. Maguire, *The Moral Choice*, Garden City, New York, 1978.
14. Kohlberg has published his stage of moral development in many different places. For a recent elucidation, see Lawrence Kohlberg, *The Implications of Moral Stages for Adult Education*, Religious Education 72, 2 (March–April 1977), p. 183–201.
15. Illustrative of this critical approach are

the following: Paul J. Philibert, *Conscience: Developmental Perspectives from Rogers and Kohlberg, Horizons* 6 (1979), 1–25; Walter E. Conn, *Post-conventional Morality: An Exposition and Critique of Lawrence Kohlberg's Analysis of Moral Development in the Adolescent and Adult, Lumen Vitae* 30 (1975), p. 213–230.

16. A significant factor on the American scene is the interest by Protestant ethicians in the subject and in character. See James M. Gustafson, *Christian Ethics and the Community*, Philadelphia, 1971, pp. 151–216; also in his *Christ and the Moral Life*; Stanley Hauerwas, *Character and the Christian Life: A Study in Theological Ethics*, San Antonio, Texas, 1975.

17. The universal destiny of the goods of creation to serve the needs of all has been highlighted in more recent statements of the hierarchical magisterium; but John A. Ryan, the leading figure in American Catholic social ethics in the first half of the twentieth century, insisted on such a first principle in his discussions of the goods of creation and the system of private property. See John A. Ryan, *Distributive Justice*, New York, 1916, p. 56–60. See also Reginald G. Bender, *The Doctrine of Private Property in the Writings of Monsignor John A. Ryan*, (S.T.D. dissertation, The Catholic University of America, 1973).

18. For a book of readings in English of significant articles originally written on this topic in various languages, see *Readings in Moral Theology, No. 1: Moral Norms and the Catholic Tradition* (ed. Charles E. Curran and Richard A. McCormick), New York, 1979. On the American scene Richard A. McCormick has done the most to carry on a dialogue on this question of norms both with Catholic moral theologians throughout the world and with Protestant and philosophical ethicians in the United States. See especially his *Notes on Moral Theology* which appear regularly in *Theological Studies* and also *Doing Evil to Achieve Good: Moral Choice in Conflict Situations* (ed. Richard A. McCormick and Paul Ramsey), Chicago, 1978.

19. John R. Connery, *Morality of Consequences: A Theological Appraisal, Theological Studies* 34 (1973), p. 336–414; reprinted in *Readings in Moral Theology, No. 1*, p. 244–266.

20. This third or mediating position is held by a large number of philosophers. See, for example, Rawls, *A Theory of Justice*, p. 25ff; William K. Frankena, *Ethics*, Englewood Cliffs, New Jersey, 1973, p. 13ff.

21. Germain Grisez, *Abortion: The Myths, The Realites and The Arguments*, New York, 1970, p. 311–321; Germain Grisez and Russell Shaw, *Beyond the New Morality: The Responsibilities of Freedom*, Notre Dame, Indiana, 1974. For his critique of what he calls consequentialism, see Germain Grisez, *Against Consequentialism, The American Journal of Jurisprudence* 23 (1978), p. 21–72.

22. For a detailed development of this notion of conscience, see Walter E. Conn, *Conscience and Self-Transcendence* (Ph. D. dissertation, Columbia University [Ann Arbor, Mich.: University Microfilms, 1973, no. 72 — 20554]). A revised version of this dissertation will be published by Trinity University Press.

23. For a strong insistence on the importance of story, see Stanley Hauerwas, with Richard Bondi and David B. Burrell, *Truthfulness and Tragedy: Further Investigations into Christian Ethics*, Notre Dame, Indiana, 1977, especially p. 15–98.

7

The Structure and Basis of the Moral Experience

Enda McDonagh

I. The Starting Point: Experience of Moral Call

Values or systems of moral criteria do not appear to me as primary in the experience I wish to explore here. They emerge at a level of analysis and reflection which is subsequent to the experience of moral call or obligation with its consequent acceptance or refusal, a call which occurs for all of us in actual situations. The moral dimension in one's experience of the actual situation which impinges on one first of all as challenge, obligation or call, duty or command provides one useful starting point, as one can check on it in the actual situation in which one finds oneself. The different words obligation, call, duty, command plus others can express different nuances of meaning or appear more apt to different persons or in different situations. The basic experience is, I believe, the same. For reasons that will appear later I prefer the word call but will use obligation interchangeably with it at this stage as it is more commonly accepted.

II. The Situation

The obligation or call is experienced in a particular situation. It is not always easy to define the exact limits of the situation, although some 'situationists' seem to assume that it is. In the sense that one experiences morality in its basic form as obligation or call in situations, one can fairly describe morality as situational and use the situation as the starting point for further reflection on the experience. The 'moral situation' is not a peculiar type of human situation any more than the 'moral experience' is a peculiar type of human experience. There is a moral dimension, more or less important, more or less evident, in all human situations and one's experience of them. In the situation of writing this article

This article is excerpted from the Irish Theological Quarterly 38 (1971): 3–20.

one may not attend consciously to this moral dimension but various aspects of it may be quickly invoked. My undertaking to write a series of articles on this topic; my promise to the editor to have this one ready at a particular time (the failure to do that qualifies my further obligation but does not remove it); my obligation to the reader to present my understanding of the structure and basis of morality as honestly, as carefully and as intelligibly as I can; my professional obligation as a moral theologian to make some contribution to a Christian understanding of morality; my general obligation as a human being and Christian to pursue and communicate the truth in the life-situation in which I find myself. Some of these are derivative obligations from a personal undertaking or professional commitment. They specify the more general commitment for me. The relation between these different aspects will require further study but here I am concerned with calling attention to them as forming the moral dimension of the immediate situation at my desk in which I find myself. And some such implicit moral dimension occurs in every human situation; in every situation in which the human being finds himself. It may be more or less important. The clarity for instance with which I am called to express myself evidently applies more rigorously to the working out and ordering of my thoughts and to my use of words than to my use of the typewriter or pen: a totally illegible typescript or manuscript would of course frustrate the whole attempt to respond to my obligation and so legibility does form a subordinate part of that obligation.

(a) The Interpersonal Character of the Situation

This situation as experienced by the human being is particular and concrete, but it is not, unlike my obligations to editor, readers or the Church, always immediately and directly concerned with other human beings. The contemporary preoccupation with conservation reflects a moral dimension in our relation with the cosmos and its resources. The moral obligations which one experiences in relation to property is a more familiar example of an impersonal immediate term of moral obligation. In this latter example the mediate personal term is very influential. Because this property belongs to somebody, is of service to somebody, one must respect it. A somewhat similar case could be advanced for the respect for the cosmos and its forces of which we are now becoming conscious. The appeal is being made in the name of the people, present or future. If one were alone in the universe it would be difficult to make sense of the call to conservation. There are some further problems here about how one treats one's own property, about respect for animals and about a call to respect for the cosmos which seem to go beyond the immediate aims of the conservationists and which require further and fuller elucidation. Yet I believe that not only is the moral experience human and personal in the sense that it is experienced by human persons but also in the sense that its ultimate source as it impinges on one is also personal. The situation itself is interpersonal, although the medium through which the obligation is experienced may be impersonal such as somebody else's property or other cosmic entities and forces as they are related to and available to humans.

In describing the moral situation as interpersonal, as existing between people, whether directly or indirectly, one has to recognize some very important characteristics of the situation, which might easily be overlooked with harmful consequences to its overall moral understanding.

(b) Interpersonal and Intergroup: The Social Character

The personal centre which experiences the obligation or is the source of it may be too easily confined to the individual person. In many situations today where one experiences moral obligation the source is not an individual but a group or society. One has only to think of the feeling of moral obligation towards the victims of natural disaster such as the people subjected to cyclones in Pakistan or earthquakes in Peru; or of the people suffering from injustice, violence, war, for racial, class or ideological reasons in South Africa or South America, the U.S.S.R. or the U.S.A., Great Britain or Ireland; or of the personally handicapped such as the ill or blind or slow learners; or of all those everywhere who are short of food, clothing, housing, educational opportunity, employment opportunity, development opportunity, freedom. In so many places the people involved constitute massive groups from which the moral call to the more prosperous or educated or healthier comes and to which the moral response must be made. Indeed these situations and obligations may be said to be the most important and most urgent facing people in the more affluent countries as well as many privileged people in other countries.

And the situations confront them not just as individuals but as groups. This becomes more evident when one observes that very little response can be made to the situations by single individuals. It is only in organized groups, voluntary such as Gorta or Oxfam, or statutory and governmental that any effective response can be made. If such obligations exist and if they can be met only by group activity, then the interpersonal character of the moral situation clearly means intergroup in some instances. And the *subject* as well as the *source*

of the moral call is not only the individual but the group.

A sharp criticism of the manual tradition of moral theology maintained that it was very individualistic as exemplified by its concentration on commutative justice at the expense of social justice. This was, in recent decades at least, compensated for to some extent by the development of papal social teaching from Leo XIII to Paul VI. However, the wider and deeper issues of the social dimension of morality as a whole have not yet been sufficiently developed in a systematic way. And one of the great deficiencies here is the deficient understanding of the group as subject of moral obligation and moral response.

The passing attention given to this after World War II in discussing the collective guilt of the Germans under Hitler for example did not contribute very much. Its idea of collectivity was undeveloped and guilt is not a happy starting point for fruitful discussion of the moral subject. A somewhat similar critical and negative reaction has appeared in Europe and the U.S. in criticism of particular activities such as the Vietnam War. The War Trials of the Americans in Stockholm provide one example of a growing awareness of collective responsibility and collective failure. Yet very little awareness of the need for a further analysis of the group-subject of morality has appeared in moral writing. Social responsibility tends to be discussed in terms of the individual's obligation to society or to the group, which is indisputable and more easily handled. The group itself as moral subject has received little attention. In what I have to say about the interpersonal character of the moral situation I will have in mind the group to group situation and the individual to group (including group to individual) as well as the individual to individual situation. Not all of what I say will be applicable in exactly the same way to each of these situations but it will be applicable. There can be no reduction of all interpersonal moral situations to the face-to-face, I-thou (or you) situation of two individuals.

Of course the interpersonal situation of two individuals has its own social aspect which will be ignored only at the risk of misunderstanding the situation and its obligation. Each of the personal poles belongs to a social setting which enters into his being and into the call and response which define the moral situation. At the various levels the individual belongs to a family, local community, linguistic group, racial group, professional or working group, age-group, national group, state, etc., etc. All these overlapping patterns of relationships help to make him what he is and at least some will be relevant in the particular situation. If he is confronted with somebody dying after an accident for example, his call or obligation will vary with his professional group. If he is a doctor he will quite clearly have a different obligation from the obligation he has as a bus-conductor. In a quite different situation say of a sexual kind, the fact that the parties are married to each other or that one is the wife or husband of somebody else is clearly relevant.

Even in a person to person situation the social dimension of each person enters in but its precise relevance depends on the particular situation. Some situational discussion of morality unfortunately ignores this. To define the situation correctly (never an easy task) the relevant social setting or relationship of each person must be taken into account.

(c) The Historical Character

So far the picture presented of the moral situation has been a static one: group or individual facing group or individual captured in a still photograph rather than a moving film. Of course the situation and the people in it are not static but moving or changing. One cannot stop the world even to focus on one's moral obligations. With his social relationships, both personal and structural, each person is in historical movement. Because this movement is part of his being just as his social relationships are, it is better to speak of his movement or development as historical than to speak of him moving through history. He is a history. And this applies to group as to individual. So in any given moral situation the historical movement of the two poles, personal source and personal subject, has to be taken into account if the situation is to be properly understood. This again is no easy task.

Source and subject emerge from the past and through the present move into the future. The moral situation which arises and the obligation of the one to the other cannot be defined in terms of a momentary or more extended present. To understand the needs of the one some awareness of how he arrived at this particular stage of development will, sometimes at least, be necessary. So a patient's previous history may be important to understanding and treating his illness. In group terms some understanding of the historical background to the divisions in Northern Ireland, for instance, is demanded of anyone who seeks to heal them. Some urgent needs have to be met without time for consideration of previous history. And the appeal to history could be used as an excuse for inactivity. Yet at the individual and group level some grasp of how the present need developed is necessary, if the hungry or the homeless, the victims of religious, racial or class discrimination, the lonely or the sick are to be effectively helped and not just have their symptoms alleviated for the moment.

Here the further stage in the historical movement obtrudes itself. The need which is to be served may have developed out of the past but it is anchored in an individual or group moving into the future. The service called for then must be directed towards future development or growth. In lecturing or writing about the meaning of morality one must be aware of the historical tradition from which the present understanding of audience or reader has developed but one is seeking to promote a better understanding for the future. The obligation in this situation as in others is directed towards the future.

The past-present-future elements apply to the subject of the obligation as well as the source and so enter into defining the situation and obligation. His previous professional training and experience influence how far a doctor or a moral theologian has the resources to respond to a particular call of himself and how far he should invoke the help of another professional. In any moral situation the resources of the subject which have developed in the past are clearly important in defining a situation in which he will be called on to serve another for some short time at least in the future. As will be pointed out later these resources are to some extent always potential but one has to consider how far that potential can be realized to meet the needs facing one. So while anybody might in the very broad sense be a potential medical doctor some already acquired medical expertise is demanded in face of serious illness.

The historical aspects of the situation and its personal poles make it difficult to define it exactly. It cannot, as I said, be captured precisely in a photographic still. It is necessary to consider the relevant elements of the past as well as the relevant possible consequences in the future in relation to source and subject, although as in the social context relevance is not always easy to decide. This is so partly because so much must remain unknown about the past if any response is ever to be made and inevitably about the future. Even the doctor with the most detailed case-history realizes that he may not have all the relevant data and subsequent developments may clearly show this. In a less controllable and less professional situation the risks of ignorance are much higher. However, in the human condition these risks must frequently be accepted and the situation defined and understood as fully as possible in the circumstances, yet in that openended way that permits one to take account of new data from the past, should it appear and of unforeseen consequences in the future, should they occur.

(d) The Situation as Medium

In seeking to describe and define the moral situation one must take into account the relevant cosmic (e.g., biological in sex or chemical in conservation), social and relational, and historical elements of both personal centres, whether individuals or groups. The situation occurs between the personal centres and the call or obligation and the response relate centre to centre at the core of their being. Otherwise it would be my mind recognizing the obligation and not me. It would be my hand or tongue making the response not me and so on. Similarly I would be feeding stomachs but not people. In the professional surgical situation for example the concentration may be on a stomach but only in the context of response to a person. Stomachs in themselves would not merit such attention. Any decline in attention to the personal context in medicine as in other fields must negatively affect the human value of an elaborate technical service.

For all its basic importance the personal centre does not confront one in any pure form. Constituted as it is cosmically, relationally and historically with a complex series of capacities and needs, which are in turn cosmic, relational and historical, one person centre confronts another, under some particular aspect defined by the particular situation.

In the situation of writing and reading this article the aspect of verbal communication emerges and is made concrete in this article, which in this sense acts as a medium and gives rise to mutual obligations. (In the earlier part of this essay I used a simpler model derived from one's awareness of moral obligation arising from relationship with another in a situation. But the relationship and obligation are always in some sense reciprocal. This reciprocity will receive fuller treatment later. I mention it here as necessary to understanding how the two poles of the moral interchange meet in the situation.) In the moral situation created by writing and reading this article the medium is defined by the article itself and my obligations to the reader, referred to earlier, include careful preparation and intelligible expression with a view to enabling the reader to understand what I am saying, relate it to his own life-experience of morality and his understanding of it in the hope that it may enlarge that understanding. The cosmic elements of the medium of which physical signs or words are the most important, must combine with the social and historical to make sense to the reader of the *Irish Theological Quarterly* in so far as he can be defined or described. The reader in turn owes it to me once he enters into relationship by reading the article, to read it carefully and intelligently with a view to understanding exactly what I am saying and so to assessing its value in the context of analysis of morality at this level. I have to reach him; he has to reach me; both through the medium of the article.

In different type situations the situational medium will be entirely different. In another type of situation it may be not communication at the conceptual and verbal level but at the sexual level for example. Where the medium is sexual as defined by the situation clearly the sex of the parties is relevant as well as their historical sexual relationships. To be somebody's wife or husband or fiancée or merely casual acquaintance will be relevant to understanding the moral situation characterized by sexual need or call.

The moral situation arises between people but it focuses their conjunction in a particular way, provides, to use a different optical metaphor, a filter for the cosmic, socio-relational and historical aspects of their existence which are relevant. It is important to define situation as carefully as possible because it specifies the content of the particular moral call as obligation.

III. The Moral Call as Unconditional

The specific character of the call as distinct from its content is a certain unconditionality or absoluteness. Again the exact word to be used is hard to find. What I am trying to express is the way in which the moral call impinges on one as a call to which one ought to respond. There is nothing inevitable or unavoidable about the response. One is conscious of one's freedom when confronted by the call. Yet there is an unavoidable character about the call if not the response, and one is no less conscious of this in exercising one's freedom by responding or refusing. The sense of obligation or oughtness does not take away one's freedom. It presupposes it. But neither can one's freedom dissolve the sense of obligation. For different people and in different situations the sense of obligation, of the unconditional character of the call will vary. It may be increased or diminished. Some types of call will be regarded as unconditional in this sense by some people and as merely conditional, dependent on what one wants, by others. In some situations, the driver of a car confronted by somebody lying on the road and feeling obliged not to run over him, the unconditional call seems to arise directly. In other situations, by contract or promise or marriage for example, the call is dependent on some relationship undertaken freely and to which at some stage one had no obligation. John might not have married Mary or I might not have undertaken to write this article for the *Irish Theological Quarterly*. Once one has undertaken however, certain unconditional calls will arise.

I think it is important to insist on this aspect of the moral call in face of a certain relativisation of morality. This is more commonly understood in terms of a relativity of content but there is a deeper relativity which influences the relativity of content. We are all aware of the differences even in our own culture about practical and important issues like war, poverty, revolution, political dishonesty, tax evasion, advertising, pornography, euthanasia, etc., etc. What is not always realized is that part of the difficulty arises from relativising the moral obligation itself by insisting too much on a teleological model, whether that is salvation of one's soul, the greatest happiness of the greatest number or some other individual or social goal. To somebody not interested in particular goals, the linking of particular or all moral obligations with them may easily lead to an 'if' or 'conditional' approach to morality. If I wish to attain this goal, I should do this, but only 'if'.

In my view the moral obligation is an aspect of experience which in some situations occurs as something which one may not evade or refuse. Evading or refusing it does not abolish it. It remains with one at least in the sense of judgement on failure. Of course, it is possible to dull the sense of obligation and of failure in some or all areas in which one encounters it. But the moral analyst is primarily interested in the moral reality itself in a clearly recognisable form and in this form it emerges as independent of one's own desires or projections. It constitutes a primary experience which may not be reduced to or produced by some other experience. This is not the place for an extended discussion of the is-ought question or the naturalistic fallacy. My own experience suggests that the route to be taken is from 'ought' to 'is' and not the other way round. One can and should investigate one's experience of ought or obligation or moral call in order to define more precisely its content, to understand the medium and to understand the base on which it rests, that which the medium mediates. The second of these tasks will occupy the rest of this essay.

In insisting on the unconditionality of the actual and proper moral experience of the situation, in appealing to its primacy as a datum of experience I am not suggesting that it is some kind of mystical or mysterious experience available only to the few or closed to further investigation. It is a common experience, I believe, and demands further investigation. I do not believe that it is best described as intuition when it is simply an awareness of a certain dimension of one's experience which develops in the course of one's life. It may have, as is sometimes suggested nowadays, certain affinities with literary or artistic discernment. This has much more to do with refinement in deciphering the contents of the obligation than with the experience of the obligation itself and such a model may be very misleading.

IV. Human Otherness as Source

Further reflection on the unconditional call in the situation anchors it very firmly in the personal poles, individual or group, which may be described as subject and source. The subject is aware of this call through the medium defined by the particular situation but he is aware of it as coming from the personal source. Through the situation and the call it articulates subject encounters source and encounters source as source of the unconditional call. Whether it is a situation calling for respect for life or property, for verbal or sexual communication, the personal source of the call is at the same time source of its unconditionality.

The moral interchange through the medium of the situation between personal subject and personal source (individual or group in either case) has a number of important characteristics. One obvious one, that of reciprocity, may be left aside for the moment while I concentrate on the subject's experience of the personal source in the call or obligation. I stressed earlier that the encounter was between two personal centres and not between a need and a service. In many situations the experience itself sufficiently indicates this: one's obligation and response to hunger or illness is experienced as personal obligation and response to the hungry and the ill, to the persons. In other situations the encounter may be mediated through property or social structures (e.g. voting, taxation) or through some aspects of the cosmos itself but the ultimate term is another personal centre, individual or group.

(a) Human Otherness and Unconditionality

The personal term of the encounter throws light on the unconditionality of the moral call described above. Irrespective of or rather prior to any particular need the person calls for a recognition and respect that may not be directly explicit but implicit in the particular call and built into the particular situation. Very little reflection will make explicit the peculiar call to recognition and respect which each personal centre embodies. As compared with a non-human, cosmic entity the human person (as individual or group) calls for a recognition and a respect which will not permit one to use (or abuse) this person as simply an instrument and so an extension of oneself. One may not manipulate him as subordinate to oneself, one's possession. One may not indeed possess or strive to possess him or simply eliminate him. He confronts one calling for recognition and respect with an independence which one may not ignore. Positively this independence makes him a different source of knowledge and understanding, freedom and initiative, activity and love. He is another world. Negatively one may not (and indeed on further reflection cannot) use or possess or eliminate. He remains *finally other* than oneself. The primary generic call in any situation is to recognize and respect this otherness. It manifests itself through some specific call in the situation and is the source of unconditionality in the specific call.

(b) Human Otherness and Uniqueness

In any situation the subject of the moral experience is personal and so is the source, to be recognized, respected and responded to in the particular demand mediated by the situation. The human otherness of the source, its quality as this different, insubordinable, unpossessable centre of life and knowledge and love, as this particular human world makes it finally and irreducibly different from the human subject (in its otherness) and all other human centres in the wider community. It makes it in that sense a unique world of its own. So moral exchanges occur between unique personal centres which not only may not, but ultimately cannot, be reduced the one to the other. This final difference or otherness emerges in the actual moral situation as the unconditional or unavoidable quality of the particular moral call itself.

The otherness and uniqueness are of course two-way. They apply to the subject as well as the source. The call emanating from the source is to an irreducibly different and unique subject. The uniqueness of the personal centres or poles in any moral situation gives the situation itself a uniqueness that cannot be denied but which does not exclude it entirely from continuity with similar situations involving other people or the same people at different times. It is the denial of this continuity which makes the otherwise valuable insistence of certain situationists on the uniqueness of the situation ultimately indefensible because it is unintelligible. If there is no continuity between human situations, if they share no common elements at all, then there are no words to describe, indeed no way of recognizing them. If the words used have a totally different meaning in each situation one has no way of telling what this meaning is, of recognizing what they describe. The love of every husband and wife is different, unique because of the unique personal poles involved. Yet how can one describe John's attitude to Mary as love and Michael's attitude to Jane also as love, if one maintains there are no features common to both? And how can one describe John's action in a particular situation as loving or unloving if one denies any continuity between this situation and another situation in which one would want to describe his action also as loving or unloving. Continuity between situations and sharing of common elements

are implied by the intelligibility of the situations themselves. To deny this intelligibility is to deny one's right to discuss the situations at all and to opt out of all that is called human discourse about morality.

It is not to my purpose here to launch into a full-scale discussion of all contemporary versions of 'Situation Ethics'. I felt it necessary however to call attention to the uniqueness which undoubtedly exists in the moral situation but in the context of its relation to other situations. The features of continuity with historical overtones, and of shared elements (perhaps commonality) with social overtones, apply not to just the situation but the personal poles meeting in it. Indeed the meeting in the situation, for all the emphasis that has been placed on their otherness, is possible at all because they have something in common; they are in communion or community and so can communicate with or encounter each other. The otherness exists and emerges within a common bond in some community however elementary. It is the extension of the community, at a very elementary level admittedly, through the communications media, that brings Irish people into contact with Biafrans or Pakistanis and so creates a moral situation in which they experience a call to help these people.

Human otherness within community, within some actual and possible communication, provides the basis of the moral situation. Although it has been treated here from the point of view of subject and source as corresponding to the conscious experience of moral call in one of the poles, there is at this basic level a clear reciprocity. Each is called to recognize and respect the other as other within the community, whatever might be the particular concrete response in which recognition and respect are expressed. One will have to return to this reciprocity between human others in communion again and again in the further analysis of the moral experience. The concept of otherness for all its importance must not obscure community as the context in which it exists; communication as the method of recognizing, respecting and responding to it; communion or deeper community as the crowning achievement of response. Without the 'commun'—dimension, human otherness could provide no insight into the experience of morality. And the 'commun'—dimension seems necessarily reciprocal. To be in community, to communicate, to achieve communion —all involve mutual recognition, respect and response.

V. Othercentredness as Criterion of Moral Response

If one may concentrate for the sake of simplicity on one of the personal poles in the moral situation, his experience of the moral call to response as emanating from the other through the medium of property or bodily need or whatever, with its implicit call for recognition and respect, reveals the direction of the moral response. It must follow the call in the direction of the other. It must be other-directed or other-centred, if it is to be faithful to the call. To turn back on the self by refusing the call or to respond to the other as a means of promoting the self and so fail to recognize and respect the other as other is what I should call moral failure. The inherent dynamism of responding to the call is to break out of the self to reach the other by recognizing, respecting and responding to him through the medium in which one encounters him in the particular situation. In brief then, one behaves morally when one responds in an other-centred way; one behaves immorally when one behaves in a self-centred way.

There are very many problems about this which I prefer to discuss later. I may mention that the response in its totality requires time. It has a history. It moves from understanding of the past through the present to serve the development of the other in the future. The historical dimension of the whole situation has to be taken into account and a refusal to give something to the other in the present may be other-centred if referred to the future as so frequently happens with children, for example; just as to give in the present may be self-centred, to rid ourselves of some irritation or nuisance. The social dimensions of the two poles, their various relationships at the personal and structural level, are no less important. And they may lead to even more acute difficulties as one recognizes the other in his social setting and the self in his and tries to decide whether the limited resources of the self may be directed to this other for the present in view of one's many different commitments. The family man has to think of his commitments to wife and children when he encounters another in need. Of course his concern for them may not necessarily be decisive in the actual situation as for example when he is faced with somebody drowning or barely relevant if it is some small or short-term demand for money or care. The social dimension of the other as source of the call applies in innumerable ways also. Recognition of his world in a way relevant to the situation will frequently call for some recognition of his other relationships—that he is somebody's husband, for example, in a sexual situation.

The call one experiences in the moral situation is first of all a call to understand the situation correctly, to understand the other as he encounters one through the particular moral situation in order to respond to it as effectively as possible. Anything less than that kind of recognition is a failure to respect the other as other and ensures failure to make the further appropriate response.

VI. Gift-Call Character of Moral Situation

In all this the subject's moral experience of the other in the situation may very easily have given an impression of the other as burden, simply source of moral demand or call. On reflection I think this impression should be corrected to seeing the other primarily as gift but gift embodying call. The world of the other with which one is confronted comes to one as gift in both senses of that expression. He is given: he is not in any sense one's own achievement but freely presented to one. He is present as *present* and in the second sense associated with gift he is present as *enriching* or at least potentially enriching one's own world. Any encounter with the world of another has this potential. Every other man or group comes to one first of all as gift.

The gift aspect has its root in the otherness-in-community already discussed. Human otherness has its biological, psychological and sociological dimensions. The individual genetic code with its physiological consequences in height, weight, colouring and even psychological as in temperament, the familial and wider social environment (including climate), the historical interaction of all these contribute to the gift-otherness of the individual human as he confronts his fellow-humans. They contribute to the different individual world which he constitutes within the wider

human world in which he exists, is present to and communicates with his fellow men. But the difference and the irreducible otherness are not explicable simply in these terms. His ability to recognize and organize these elements in the face of all other worlds, personal, social or environmental; his ability in other words to determine his own life and relationships by his powers of personal knowledge and freedom, decision, and self-giving, reveal more exactly how his otherness is at once gift, offering entry to a new world and call, asking for recognition and respect.

Yet the other is primarily gift, a free and enriching offer. Of course the gift of the other implies offer by him, invitation to enter his world. It is possible only in community and communication. One may not force an entry into the world of the other. However his very presence always involves some sharing however minimal in his world. It changes one's own world in however limited a way. It enriches one in very varying degrees admittedly. It is not however by seeking such enrichment in itself by a passive reception of the other, or by exploitation or using of him but as indicated already, in discussing the moral direction of our activity, by active attempts to recognize, respect and respond to him. This is how one enters his world and is enriched by it. The gift embodies call. It is as gift that it involves a call to move out of the world of the self in recognition and exploration of new worlds. The basic biological, psychological and sociological differences with their personal realization and transformation in the individual, social and cultural developments clearly enrich all of us but their supreme and unique manifestation as *gift* in the people one meets, might well be overlooked.

The primacy of the other as gift in the moral

situation precludes the understanding of morality or of the other as burden. The first reaction called for is one of thanksgiving for the gift, of celebrating its presence. Indeed the richest human exchanges are of this kind. And the call which the gift undoubtedly involves, includes, apart from any further specifications, a call to recognize the other as gift and rejoice in his presence. In some situations this may be very evident although the common celebration may not be seen as answer to a moral call, with consequent impoverishment of the meaning of morality. If this gift element is not recognized as always present and is not sometimes explicitly attended to, moral call and the existence of others as source of moral call become increasingly and exclusively burden. How morality can degenerate in this way may be traced perhaps in one's own history, in the story of a breaking marriage or in the story of Covenant and Law in Israel.

VII. Threat-Fear Character

It is the other as gift who embodies the call and summons one out of self to recognition, respect and particular response. Yet it would be very unrealistic to describe the other and one's awareness of the other exclusively in terms of gift embodying call. The presence of the other precisely as this different and irreducible world of its own may also constitute a *threat provoking fear*. There is ample evidence of this from every kind of human interchange between groups, states or races or classes or religions and between individuals, even individuals in such ostensibly favourable situations as the family or the religious community or the Church.

The existence of the other as threat may be due to his seeking to eliminate his opposite number by murder for example or at least to refusing to accept his independent existence, seeking to absorb him (even temporarily) into his own world. Conversely the other may emerge as threat because the self refuses to recognize his existence or sees his independent existence as upsetting his own controlled and controllable world. This is not due then to any moral fault on the part of the other but on the part of the self who cannot tolerate the existence of this separate and independent world. Because he is self-centred and will not recognize or tolerate other worlds except in so far as they are subordinate to his own, their existence becomes threat.

One seldom finds such a pure situation where the other or the self are simply threat. More usually there will be elements of threat mixed with elements of gift on both sides. In daily living the relationship between husband and wife, parents and children, professional colleagues, neighbours, even fellow-religious or fellow-Christians is a mixture of gift and threat. How often has one seen the threat element gradually predominate in a situation which started as gift on both sides whether in marriage or in the church. The relationship between different groups in the church today is too often predominantly one of threat-fear instead of gift-call. Theologians constitute a threat to and feel threatened by the hierarchy in a situation where the gift-call dimension should predominate if anywhere. In the teaching situation between teacher and student the same element exists and sometimes predominates. In the business organization of our world for all the sophistication of modern managerial methods or Madison Avenue advertising, the underlying element of threat can too easily predominate. It is scarcely necessary to draw attention to this danger at the political level, national and international.

VIII. Ambiguous Character

In the actual moral situation, whether of group to group, of group to individual and of individual to individual, the gift-embodying-call is always combined with threat-provoking-fear. Given the reciprocity of the relationship and the moral direction of the relationship on both sides as recognition of, respect for and response to the other as other, then it would appear that the moral direction of the call is also towards enabling the gift to triumph over the threat and so towards enabling the genuine communion and mutual enrichment of the two worlds and not towards the elimination or subordination of one or both.

This will not be easily or always achieved as far as one can judge from human experience of morality. And it will take time and patience and effort. Total surrender to threat is no more moral than total imposition of it. It is the transformation of threat into gift and so of the hostile confrontation of different worlds into their developing communion which is the moral task of all men in their different situations.

Conclusion

In seeking to outline the structure and basis of morality, I have taken as my point of departure the situation in which the moral dimension emerges in one person's (the subject's) experience of moral obligation which I prefer to describe by the wider term 'call'. The other pole (the source) of the situation and the call is also personal, although the relationship may be more or less direct or immediate. And both poles may be personal as groups or individuals.

The situation while interpersonal has cosmic, historical and social dimensions arising from the conjunction of the personal poles which exist in the cosmos, in history and in a network of relationships. Which of these elements are relevant to defining the moral call in the situation will vary with the particular need of the source as expressed in the call and the resources which the subject has to meet it. And while the two personal poles do make contact with each other at their personal centres, it must be through some of the many facets of their personal existence which act as medium and define the situation in some general way, such as verbal communication or sexual endowment or physical health.

The call as properly moral has a certain unconditional element about it. One ought to respond; one is free not to. But as the 'ought' or call does not take away one's freedom, one's freedom and one's use of it responding or refusing to respond does not abolish the 'ought'.

At this level also the moral call seems to me a primary datum of experience. It may be misinterpreted or weakened or scarcely developed. (As with all our capacities to discern some aspect of reality it develops in some social context.)

The experience of moral call in a concrete situation under a particular form, as unconditional or unavoidable, as interpersonal and as a primary mode of experiencing yields on further investigation the concept of the personal source as finally other. This quality of irreducible otherness is of course reciprocal but in the subject-source model underlies the unconditional call of the source and reveals that whatever the particular situation and particular call, there is always a call to recognition of and respect for the other as other which then seeks fulfilment in the further response to the particular call. This recognition, respect and response are only possible in the context of community, where in other words communication is possible and they are directed towards fuller communion of the different worlds. The moral direction of one's response then is towards the other. If it is a proper moral response it is, according to this analysis, other-centred.

The other does not on deeper reflection confront one first of all as call but as gift. The gift of this freely bestowed and potentially enriching different world of the other embodies the call to recognition, respect and response which leads to the enrichment of the subject (as a consequence). The gift-embodying-call view of the other and its recognition as structuring the moral situation could have an important liberating effect on one's approach to morality.

However gift embodying call is not the only way in which the other reveals himself in the moral situation. He can also appear as threat provoking fear, either because he wants to take over one's self and one's world or because oneself will not tolerate the existence of such another independent world. In most moral situations the gift embodying call and enrichment aspect is mixed with threat provoking fear. And the correct moral direction in this ambiguous situation is towards the predominance of gift-call over the threat-fear.

8

The Criterion for Deciding
What Is Christian

Hans Küng

Only relatively few people—of this we can be quite certain—are capable of using the many modern opportunities of information and communication in such a way as to be able to adopt a completely independent, critical attitude in society. And even the most critical and independent person is not guided simply by the norms which he has himself discovered and substantiated by reason. For no one begins at zero. Nor is this only because he is determined by his environment, pre-programmed and driven by instinct. He belongs to a community, to a tradition. Even before him, people in very diverse conditions tried to live in a manner befitting human dignity. Normative human conduct is essentially made known by human beings, in a genuinely human way by words, deeds, achievements and attitudes, which cannot be deduced from general truths but emerge in a very concrete way out of a complex tension between intellectual reflection and immediate involvement. A risk is always taken with an ethos which can

be proved by its results to be sustainable, which can be measured by its "fruits." We might have gone into a lengthy and complex analysis at this point, but we must be content to say briefly that *knowledge of the good, its norms, models, signs, is conveyed to the individual by society.*

Hence neither philosophical nor theological ethics can simply create an ethos and impose it as binding on a large group of people. As a science, theological ethics—like theological science as a whole—can define scope and limits, remove impediments, utilize experiences, clarify prejudices, bring out the true or false, genuine or hypocritical ethos. It can help to give rational guidance to the reception of new ethical norms. By integrating the multifarious conclusions of the human sciences it can offer new impulses, questions and opportunities, as a result of which a human ethos acquires new dimensions, becomes better and more quickly adapted to the present and the imminent future. But, through all this, free-

This article is extracted from On Being a Christian *(Garden City: Doubleday and Co., 1976) 540–553.*

dom of consent, strength of experience and particularly the power of convincing speech should not and cannot be replaced, but in fact stimulated.

Would it not therefore be a good thing for someone to make use of the experiences and maxims of a community, of the great human and religious traditions, of the wealth of experience of his own ancestors, in order to illuminate his own problems, the questions raised by the organization of his own life, his own norms and motivations? It is true that he can never get out of his personal responsibility for his actions and the maxims which govern his life. But for that very reason it is extraordinarily important for him to decide *who* is to tell him anything, to whom he will listen on *decisive issues*. From all the foregoing it is completely clear that the Christian lets *Christ* tell him what is essential even for practical action. But does this solve all problems in practice?

Specifically Christian Norms?

As with the ambiguous understanding of God, it might also be said of the ambiguous ethical norms that they cease to be ambiguous in the light of the biblical proclamation. We may recall the Old Testament, especially the Ten Commandments (Decalogue), which are important also for the Christian tradition: "You shall honor your father and mother. You shall not kill, not commit adultery, not steal, not bear false witness . . ." But precisely at this point it becomes obvious that at least a brief elucidation is necessary. Even the biblical precepts and prohibitions are norms conveyed by human means. What was said about norms in general still holds.

a. The *distinguishing feature* even *of the Old Testament ethos* did not consist in the individual precepts or prohibitions, but in the *Yahweh faith* which meant that all the individual precepts and prohibitions were subordinated to the will of the God of the Covenant.

The ethical requirements of the Old Testament—here we may rely on the results of Old Testament studies[1]—did not fall from heaven either in content or in form. What can be proved for the ethos of the prophets and correspondingly for that of the wisdom literature holds most of all for the earlier ethos of the law. The whole, lengthy Sinai story[2] contains some very complex material in the form of divine ordinances which reflect the different phases of time. Yet even the Ten Commandments—the "Ten Words,"[3] which are extant in two versions[4]—passed through a long history. The directives of the "second tablet" for interpersonal relationships go back to the moral and legal traditions of the pre-Israelite semi-nomadic tribes and have numerous analogies in the Near East. There was a long period during which they were put into practice, shaped and tested until the Decalogue had become so general and concise in content and form that it could be regarded as an adequate expression of the will of Yahweh.

These fundamental minimal requirements then are not specifically Israelite and they originated before faith in Yahweh. All that is specifically Israelite is the fact that these requirements are subordinated to the authority of Yahweh, the God of the Covenant, who is the "object" of the "first tablet" (duties to God). The new faith in Yahweh had its effect on the former ethos: like other sets of precepts incidentally, these requirements insofar as they are compatible with faith in Yahweh outline as succinctly as possible Yahweh's will in regard to men. Now it is Yahweh himself who makes provision in the Ten Commandments for the rudiments of authentic human existence, as in the "second tablet" with reference to honoring parents, protecting life, to marriage, ownership and one's neighbor's honor. The peculiarity of Old Testament morality therefore consists not in finding out new ethical norms, but in placing traditional directives under the authority and protection of Yahweh and his covenant: in the assumption of the existing ethos into the new association with God. This theonomy presupposes the autonomous development of ethical norms and at the same time starts them on a new course: the existing norms undergo a further development and correction—admittedly, not consistently in all fields (marriage and the position of woman, for example)—in the light precisely of this God and his covenant.

The *consequences* of giving the Decalogue a religious setting within the covenant scheme are plain to see.[5]

Moral behavior acquires a new motivation: gratitude, love, the prospect of long life, the gift of freedom become decisive motives.

At the same time *moral life gains a new dynamism:* ancient pre-Israelite and recent extra-Israelite norms are increasingly if not completely adapted to the new relationship with God; new moral and legal norms are developed and there is a significant concentration and unification insofar as the "Ten Words" cease to be merely minimal ethical requirements and become pithy statements of God's will possessed of absolute validity and applying in principle to wider areas.

Finally, *moral obligation becomes more clearly defined*. It is true that the precepts and prohibitions retain their social meaning and remain indispensable postulates of a genuinely human existence. But at the same time they acquire a new religious character: Yahweh himself appears as advocate of humanity. Thus

the fulfillment of the law becomes an expression of a union in faith and love with the divine Partner to the Covenant. And, although the norms have arisen autonomously out of the evaluation of human experiences, Israel has not now an impersonal law, but simply requirements of the God of the Covenant speaking and acting in history. Just like the ethos of the law, the existing (now Israelite) ethos of the prophets awaiting the eschatological reign of God and of the wisdom literature is taken up into the individualistic theological idea of wisdom.

b. The *distinguishing feature* in particular *of the Christian ethos* does not consist in the individual precepts or prohibitions, but in *faith in Christ* for which all the individual precepts or prohibitions are subordinated to Jesus Christ and his rule.

The ethical requirements of the New Testament—here we may rely on the results of New Testament studies[6]—did not fall from heaven either in content or in form. What holds for the ethos of the New Testament as a whole can be made clear particularly from the ethical requirements of the Apostle Paul. Not that we can really speak of a Pauline "ethic," since Paul did not develop either a system or a casuistry of morality. What he did was to draw his admonitions (paraenesis)—and this is important here—largely from Hellenistic and especially Jewish tradition.

Of course we cannot ascribe to him the "house tablets" with exhortations to the different classes, current in contemporary popular Graeco-Roman ethics (Epictetus, Seneca), as they are found first in the epistle to the Colossians[7] and in the epistle to the Ephesians dependent on it, as also in the pastoral epistles and the works of the Apostolic Fathers. But Paul certainly makes use of concepts and ideas from the Hellenistic popular philosophy of the time. And, although he uses only once the term "virtue" which is central to that ethic, he places it in this one text of Philippians in the midst of so many Greek—especially Stoic—ethical terms that the whole thing reads almost like a summary of current Greek ethics: "Whatever is true, whatever is noble, whatever is just, whatever is pure, whatever is lovable, whatever is reputable, if there is any virtue, anything worthy of praise—think over these things."[8] In the other lists of virtues and vices[9] Paul keeps to the Jewish more than to the Hellenistic tradition.

The consideration in the New Testament of some particular ethical requirement does not mean that this is specifically Christian[10] and as such without parallel. The ethical requirements taken over by Paul from Jewish or Hellenistic tradition can be justified for other reasons. Paul has no special principle of synthesis or selection, but justifies his ethical demands with a variety of motives: kingdom of God, imitation of Christ, eschatological kerygma, body of Christ, Holy Spirit, love, freedom, being in Christ. Although he uses catchwords like obedience or freedom, these are not meant to be systematic main themes but simply express the wholeness and indivisibility of the obligation on the part of the believer and the believing community to its Lord.

What is specifically Christian therefore is the fact that all ethical requirements are understood in the light of the rule of the crucified Jesus Christ. It is then not a question merely of what is moral. The gift and the task coincide under the rule of Jesus Christ; the indicative already contains the imperative. Jesus, to whom we *are* subordinated once and for all in baptism by faith, *must* remain Lord over us. "In following the Crucified it is a question of manifesting the rule of the risen

Christ. Justification and sanctification go together in the sense that both mean assimilation to Christ. They are distinguished, since this does not happen once and for all, but must constantly be freshly experienced and endured in varying situations from the time when it all began with baptism."[11] Thus Pauline ethics is nothing but "the anthropological reverse side of his Christology."[12]

In these basic questions of ethical action, therefore, we are brought back to the central issue: the proclamation and conduct, the suffering, death and new life of this Christ Jesus. And it is now confirmed retrospectively in the light of ethics how right it was, in determining what is Christian, to start out from this concrete Jesus Christ.

Concrete Person Instead of Abstract Principle

Christian proclamation and Christian action remain tied to his person, not merely historically but also essentially. Platonism as a doctrine can be separated from Plato and his life, Marxism as a system from Marx and his death. With Jesus of Nazareth, however, as we saw from beginning to end, his teaching forms such a unity with his life and death, with his fate, that an abstract system of universal ideas does not reproduce what was really involved. Even for the earthly Jesus and most of all for the Jesus who has entered into God's life and been confirmed by God, person and cause completely coincide. If the end of his proclamation, his action, his person, had been simply a fiasco, nothingness and not God, his death would have been the disavowal of his cause: nothing then would have been left of that cause which, it is claimed, is God's cause (and only as such man's cause). But if his end is eternal life with God, then he himself is and remains in person the living sign of the fact that his cause has a future, demands effort, deserves to be followed. No one then can claim to believe in the living Jesus without expressing in deeds his allegiance to that cause. Nor, on the other hand, can anyone support his cause without in practice entering into a bond of discipleship and fellowship with him.

The *following* of Christ is what distinguishes Christians from other disciples and supporters of great men, in the sense that Christians are ultimately dependent on this person, not only on his teaching, but also on his life, death and new life. No Marxist or Freudian would want to claim this for his teacher. Although Marx and Freud personally composed their works, these can be studied and followed even without a special commitment to their authors. Their works, their doctrines, are separable in principle from their persons. But we understand the real meaning of the Gospels, the "teaching" (message) of Jesus only in the light of his life, death and new life: in the New Testament as a whole his "teaching" cannot be separated from his person. For Christians then Jesus is certainly a teacher, but at the same time also essentially more than a teacher: he is *in person the living, archetypal embodiment of his cause.*

As long as Jesus remains in person the living embodiment of his cause, he can never become—like Marx and Engels, for instance, in totalitarian systems—a vacant, impassive portrait, a lifeless mask, the tamed object of a personal cult. This living Christ is and remains Jesus of Nazareth as he lived and preached, acted and suffered. This living Christ does not call merely for inconsequential adoration or even to mystical union. Nor of course does he call for literal imitation. But he does call for practical, personal discipleship.

For this it is notable that only the verb is used in the New Testament: "following" means "walking behind him."[13] It is a question of being active, no longer visibly accompanying him around the countryside as in Jesus' lifetime, but of binding oneself to him in the same spirit of allegiance and discipleship, of joining him permanently and making him the measure of one's own life. This is what following means: *getting involved with him and his way and going one's own way*—each of us has his own way—*in the light of his directions.* This possibility was seen from the beginning as the great opportunity: not a "must," but a "may." It is therefore a genuine vocation to such a way of life, a true grace, which requires us only to grasp it confidently and *adapt our lives* according to it.

The important thing is one's *attitude to life.* People so often have difficulty in finding convincing reasons for a particular decision. Why? Because no decision is ever explained merely in the light of immediate dispositions and motivations, but is rooted in a certain basic attitude, a basic approach, a basic orientation. In order to give a completely rational justification of a decision we would have to set out, not merely all the principles on which it was based, but also all the consequences which might result from it. This would mean giving a detailed description of our attitude to life (life-style, way of life), of which this one decision is part. But how can this be done in practice? "This complete specification is impossible in practice to give. The nearest attempts are those given by the great religions, especially those which can point to historical persons who have carried out the way of life in practice."[14]

The Christian faith is one of those great religions the strength of which lies in being able to justify and substantiate in detail an attitude to life, a way of life and a life-style, by pointing to a quite definite, authoritative, historical figure. In the light of Jesus Christ—with complete justification, as we saw—the basic attitude and basic orientation of a person, his form of life, life-style and way of life, can be described both comprehensively and concretely. In fact there is no doubt that the whole Christian message aims not merely at certain decisions, enterprises, motivations or dispositions, but at a wholly new approach to life: at an awareness transformed from the roots upward, a new basic attitude, a different scale of values, a radical rethinking and re-turning (*metanoia*) of the whole man. And in this respect a historical figure is undoubtedly convincing in a way that is impossible to an impersonal idea, an abstract principle, a universal norm, a purely ideal system. Jesus of Nazareth is himself the *personification* of this new way of life.

a. As a concrete, historical person, Jesus possesses an *impressiveness* which is missing in an eternal idea, an abstract principle, a universal norm, a conceptual system.

Ideas, principles, norms, systems lack the turbulence of life, the vivid perceptibility and the inexhaustible, inconceivable richness of empirical-concrete existence. However clearly defined, simple and stable, however easy to conceive and express, ideas, principles, norms, systems appear to be detached, abstracted from the concrete and individual, and therefore colorless and remote from reality. Abstraction results in uniformity, rigidity, relative insubstantiality: all "sicklied o'er with the pale cast of thought."

A concrete person however does not merely stimulate thinking, critical-rational conversation, but also continually rouses fantasy, imagination and emotion, spontaneity, creativity and innovation: in a word, appeals to the whole man, of flesh and blood. We can depict a person, but not a principle. We can enter into an immediate existential relationship with him. We can talk about a person and not only reason, argue, discuss, theologize. And just as a story cannot be replaced by abstract ideas, neither can narrating be replaced by proclaiming and appealing, images replaced by concepts, the experience of being stirred replaced by intellectual apprehension. A person cannot be reduced to a formula.

Only a living figure and not a principle can *draw* people, can be "attractive" in the most profound and comprehensive sense of the term: *verba docent, exempla trahunt,* words teach, examples carry us with them. It is not for nothing that people speak of a "shining" example. The person makes an idea, a principle, visible: he gives it flesh and blood, "embodies" this idea, this principle, this ideal. Man then not only knows about it, he sees it in a living shape before him. No abstract norm is imposed on him, but a concrete standard is set up for him. He is not only given a few guidelines, but is enabled to take a concrete, comprehensive view of his life as a whole. He is not therefore expected merely to undertake a general "Christian" program or merely to realize a general "Christian" form of life, but he can be confident in this Jesus Christ himself and attempt to order his life according to his standard. Then Jesus, with all that he authoritatively is and means, proves to be far more than simply a "shining example,"[15] proves in fact to be the true "light of the world."[16]

b. As a concrete, historical person, Jesus possesses an *audibility* which makes ideas, principles, norms and systems appear to be mute.

Ideas, principles, norms and systems have neither words nor voice. They cannot call, cannot appeal. They can neither address us nor make demands on us. In themselves they have no authority. They are dependent on someone to give them their authority. Otherwise they remain unnoticed and ineffective.

A concrete, historical person has his unmistakable proper name. And the name Jesus— often uttered only with an effort and hesitatingly—can signify a power, a protection, a refuge, a claim. For this name is opposed to inhumanity, oppression, untruthfulness and injustice, and stands for humanity, freedom, justice, truth and love. A concrete, historical person has words and a voice. He can call and appeal. And the following of Christ is based essentially on being summoned by his person and way, that is, on a vocation —today conveyed by human words. A concrete, historical person can address us and make demands on us. And the following of Christ means being required by his person and his fate to commit ourselves to a specific way. Through the transmitted word a historical person can make himself heard even over the span of the centuries. And man with his perceptive reason is called, led by the words of Jesus in understanding faith, to attempt an interpretation of human life and to develop this human life.

Only a living figure and not a principle can make sweeping *demands*. Only such a figure can invite, summon, challenge. The person of Jesus Christ is characterized, not only by impressiveness and luminosity, but also by practical direction. He can reach a man's personal center and stir him to enter on a free, existential encounter; he can activate that basic trust,

that trust in God, in virtue of which man is capable of giving his heart to this person with his invitation and demands. He rouses the desire to act according to his will and shows the way in which this desire can be realized in ordinary life. And he provides that authority and assurance which enable us to act in accordance with his will even if it cannot always be proved completely rationally that such behavior is meaningful and worthwhile. So Jesus, with all that he is and means, then proves to be not only "the light," but the "Word" of God dwelling with men.[17]

c. As a concrete, historical person, Jesus displays a *realizability* which makes ideas often appear to be unattainable ideals, norms unrealizable laws, principles and systems unrealistic Utopias.

Ideas, principles, norms and systems are not themselves the reality which they exist to regulate and set in order. They do not offer realization, they demand it. Of themselves they have no reality in the world, they are dependent on someone to realize them.

A historical person however is indisputably real, even though this personality is open to different interpretations. There is no doubt that Jesus Christ existed, that he proclaimed a very definite message, displayed a particular attitude, realized certain ideals, suffered and survived a very specific fate. With his person and his way we are dealing, not with a vague possibility, but with a historical reality. And, unlike an idea or a norm, one historical person cannot simply be rendered obsolete by another: he is irreplaceably, once and for all, himself. In the light of the historical person of Jesus man can know that he *must* go on his way and keep to it. There is no question therefore of an imperative being simply imposed on us: you shall go on this way and be justified, liberated. An indicative is presupposed: he went by this way and—in view of this—you *are* justified, liberated.

Only a living figure and not a principle can be *encouraging* in this comprehensive fashion. Only such a figure can attest in this way the possibility of realization. Only he can stimulate people to follow him: inspiring and strengthening their confidence that they too can go his way, dispelling doubts about their ability to do good. All this means of course that a new standard is set: not only an external goal, a timeless ideal, a universal norm of conduct, but a reality, a promise fulfilled, which only has to be trustfully accepted. Norms tend to require a minimum, Jesus a maximum—but the way remains always within man's power and in accordance with his nature. So Jesus himself, with all that he is and means, then proves to be not only "light" and "word" for man, but quite plainly "the way, the truth and the life."[18]

Jesus therefore acts as the authoritative concrete person: in his impressiveness, audibility and realizability, attracting, demanding, encouraging. And do not these very words— "light," "word," "way," "truth," "life"— themselves clearly state what is essential for Christian action, for Christian ethics: the criterion of what is Christian, the distinctively Christian reality, the much discussed "Proprium Christianum"?[19]

The Distinctive Christian Element in Ethics

In ethics too we shall not find the distinctive Christian feature in any abstract idea or in a principle, not simply in a special mentality, a background of meaning, a new disposition or

motivation. And others too—Jews, Muslims, humanists of all types—can act out of "love" or in "freedom," in the light of a "creation" or "consummation." The criterion of what is Christian, the distinctive Christian feature— this holds both for dogmatics and consequently also for ethics—is not an abstract something nor a Christ idea, not a Christology nor a Christocentric system of ideas: it is *this concrete Jesus as the Christ, as the standard.*

It is quite legitimate, as we saw, to track down the autonomous discovery or even acceptance of ethical norms and establish the different connections with other systems of norms. It is also legitimate therefore to follow up different traditions within the ethos of Jesus and to note what they have in common with the ideas of other Jewish or Greek teachers. Jesus was not by any means the first to put forward simple ethical instructions (for example, rules of prudence) or even certain higher ethical requirements (for example, the golden rule): all these are found elsewhere. But, in examining all this, it is easy to overlook the unique context of Jesus' ethical requirements, which are not to be regarded as isolated peaks and lofty statements in a wilderness of ethically worthless propositions, allegorical and mystical speculations and trivialities, sophisticated casuistry and ossified ritualism. And it is particularly easy to overlook the radicality and totality of Jesus' requirements: the reduction and concentration of the commandments to a simple and final statement (Decalogue, basic formula of love of God and neighbor); the universal and radical significance of love of neighbor shown in service regardless of precedence; endless forgiving; renunciation without a quid pro quo; love of enemies. The important thing however is that we shall never see the full meaning of all this if we do not see it in the *totality of Jesus' person and fate*. What does this mean?

In the music of Wolfgang Amadeus Mozart we can observe the roots of his style and all the points at which he is dependent on Leopold Mozart, on Schobert, Johann Christian Bach, Sammartini, Piccinni, Paisiello, Haydn and so many others; but we have not thereby explained the phenomenon of Mozart. Although he was intensely occupied with the whole musical environment and the whole available musical tradition, we find in amazing universality and differentiated balance all styles and genres of music of his time; we can analyze "German" and "Italian" elements, homophony and polyphony, the erudite and the courtly, continuity and contrast of themes, and nevertheless lose sight of the new, unique, specific Mozartean feature: this is the *whole* in its higher unity rooted in the freedom of the spirit, it is *Mozart himself* in his music.

So too in Jesus' ethos all possible traditions and parallels can be detected and again brought together in unity, but this does not explain the phenomenon of Jesus. And we can emphasize the pre-eminence and universality of love in Jesus' message and bring out the radicality of the theocentrism, of the concentration, intensity, spiritualizing of the ethos of Jesus by comparison—for instance—with Jewish ethics; we can distinguish also the new background of meaning and the new motivations: but we are still far from grasping clearly what is new, unique, about Jesus. What is new and unique about Jesus is the *whole* in its unity; it is this *Jesus himself* in his work.

Yet even then we have only begun to define what is distinctive about Jesus and have not even begun—and here the analogy with Mozart ends—to define what is the distinctively Christian feature, although this is based of course on what is different about Jesus. Nor

do we catch sight of this *distinctive Christian element,* particularly with reference to Christian ethics, if we look merely at Jesus' proclamation, the Sermon on the Mount (ethos), and then transfer this directly to the present day —as if nothing had happened in the meantime. Between the historical Jesus of the Sermon on the Mount and the Christ of Christendom however there are death and resurrection, which come within the dimension of God's action and without which the Jesus proclaiming would never have become the Jesus Christ proclaimed. Just what is distinctively Christian therefore is the *whole* in its unity, it is this *Christ* Jesus himself as proclaiming and proclaimed, as crucified and living.

Any attempt to reduce the cause of Jesus Christ to a cause understood exclusively as that of Jesus, assuming that God's dimension in this event can be disregarded, must lack any final binding force. Christian ethics too is then exposed to arbitrary ethical pluralism. And even an "Ethics of the New Testament" acquires a unity only with difficulty[20] if it treats successively Jesus, primitive community, Paul, the rest of the New Testament, as if there were—so to speak—four new Gospels, as if there could ever be any talk in this respect of a juxtaposition—theological or historical. And Christian ethics too must be worked out in the light of the fact that its foundation *is* laid and that this foundation is not simply the commandment of love or the critical relationship to the world, or the community, or eschatology, but solely Jesus the Christ.[21]

The reference to this name is anything but an empty formula even and indeed particularly for the working out of human action. We may be permitted therefore to dispense with concrete details and be content to refer back in general and in principle to all that has been said. It is all summed up in the words of Dietrich Bonhoeffer, who not only taught discipleship but practiced it to the very end. On the meaning of the following of Christ he says: "It is nothing else than bondage to Jesus Christ alone, completely breaking through every program, every set of laws. No other significance is possible, since Jesus is the only significance. Beside Jesus nothing has any significance. He alone matters."[22]

The Basic Model

At this point, however, we must preclude two possible misunderstandings.

First: We have depicted Jesus Christ as a historical figure in his impressiveness, audibility and realizability. But, however impressive, audible and realizable, Jesus' person and cause are not from the outset so unmistakably discernible and so conclusively evident to anyone that it is simply impossible to reject them. On the contrary. This very impressiveness is so attractive, this audibility so demanding, this realizability so encouraging, that man finds himself faced with a clear and inescapable decision which in fact can only be a *decision of faith:* a decision to trust this message, to commit himself to Jesus' cause, to follow Jesus' way.

Second: Even for someone who has decided in the light of faith for him, for his cause and his way, Jesus does not become an easy, universal answer to all the ethical questions of ordinary life: methods of birth control, education of children, control of power, organizing co-determination and assembly-line production, environment pollution. He is not an optional model simply to be copied in every detail, but a *basic model* to be realized in an infinite variety of ways according to time,

place and person. Nowhere in the Gospels is he described in terms of his virtues, but always in his actions and in his relations with others. What he is, is shown in what he does. This Jesus Christ permits discipleship in response and in relation to himself, but no imitation, no copies of himself.

If someone commits himself to Jesus as the standard, if he lets himself be determined by the person of Jesus Christ as the *basic model for a view of life and a practice of life,* this means in fact the transformation of the whole man. For Jesus Christ is not only an external goal, a vague dimension, a universal rule of conduct, a timeless ideal. He determines and influences man's life and conduct, not only externally, but from within. Following Christ means not only information, but formation: not merely a superficial change, but a change of heart and therefore the change of the whole man. It amounts to the fashioning of a *new man:* a new creation within the always diverse, individually and socially conditioned context of each one's own life in its particularity and singularity, without any attempt to impose uniformity.

We might then summarily define Jesus' unique significance for human action in this way: with his word, his actions and his fate, in his impressiveness, audibility and realizability, he is himself *in person* the *invitation,* the *appeal,* the *challenge,* for the individual and society. As the standard basic model of a view of life and practice of life, without a hint of legalism or casuistry, he provides inviting, obligatory and challenging *examples, significant deeds, orientation standards, exemplary values, model cases.* And by this very fact he impresses and influences, changes and transforms human beings who believe and thus human society. What Jesus quite concretely conveys and makes possible both to the individual and to the community who commit themselves to him may be described as follows:[23]

A new basic orientation and basic attitude, a new approach to life, to which Jesus summoned men and whose consequences he indicated. If a man or a human community has in mind this Jesus Christ as concrete guiding principle and living model for their relations with man, world and God, they may and can live differently, more genuinely, more humanly. He makes possible an identity and inner coherence in life.

New motivations, new motives of action, which can be discovered from Jesus' "theory" and "practice." In his light it is possible to answer the question why man should act just in one way and not in another: why he should love and not hate; why—and even Freud had no answer to this[24]—he should be honest, forbearing and kind wherever possible, even when he loses by it and is made to suffer as a result of the unreliability and brutality of other people.

New dispositions, new consistent insights, tendencies, intentions, formed and maintained in the spirit of Jesus Christ. Here readiness to oblige is engendered, attitudes created, qualifications conveyed, which can guide conduct, not only for isolated and passing moments, but permanently. Here we find dispositions of unpretentious commitment for one's fellow men, of identification with the handicapped, with the fight against unjust structures; dispositions of gratitude, freedom, magnanimity, unselfishness, joy, and also of forbearance, pardon and service;

dispositions which are tested in borderline situations, in readiness for complete self-sacrifice, in renunciation even when it is not necessary, in a readiness to work for the greater cause.

New projects, new actions on a great or small scale, which in imitation of Jesus Christ begin at the very point where no one wants to help: not only universal programs to transform society, but concrete signs, testimonies, evidence of humanity and of humanizing both the individual and human society.

A new background of meaning and a new definition of the goal in the ultimate reality, in the consummation of man and mankind in God's kingdom, which can sustain not only what is positive in human life, but also what is negative. In the light and power of Jesus Christ the believer is offered an ultimate meaning, not only for man's life and action, but also for his suffering and death; not only for the story of man's success, but also for the story of his suffering.

In a word: for both the individual human being and the community Jesus Christ in person, with word, deed and fate, is
invitation ("you may"),
appeal ("you should"),
challenge ("you can"),
basic model therefore of a *new way of life, a new life-style, a new meaning to life.*

Notes

1. For the Old Testament theologies cf. especially W. Eichrodt, *Theology of the Old Testament,* Vol. II, London, 1967,

§22; G. von Rad, *Theology of the Old Testament,* Edinburgh/London, Vol. I, 1962, pp. 190–202; W. Zimmerli, *Gundriss der alttestamentlichen Theologie,* Stuttgart, 1972, p. 11. In addition H. van Oyen, *Ethik des Alten Testaments,* Gütersloh, 1967. On the Decalogue A. Alt, *Die Ursprünge des israelischen Rechts,* Leipzig, 1934, is still basic reading; then, in addition to the lexicon articles, H. Haag, "Der Dekalog" in J. Stelzenberger (ed.), *Moraltheologie und Bibel,* Paderborn, 1964, pp. 9–38; G. O. Botterweck, "The Form and Growth of the Decalogue," in *Concilium,* May 1965, pp. 33–44; N. Lohfink, "Die zehn Gebote ohne den Berg Sinai" in his miscellany, *Bibelauslegung im Wandel,* Frankfurt, 1967, pp. 129–57.

2. Ex 19–Nb. 10.
3. Ex 34:28; Dt 4:13; 10:4.
4. Ex 20:2–17; Dt 5:6–21.
5. A. Auer, *Autonome Moral,* pp. 63–68, deduces these consequences clearly from the Old Testament material.
6. On the problems discussed here see L. Nieder, *Die Motive der religiös-sittlichen Paränese in den paulinischen Gemeindebriefen. Ein Beitrag zur paulinischen Ethik,* Munich, 1956; W. Schrage, *Die konkreten Einzelgebote in der paulinischen Paränese. Ein Beitrag zur neutestamentlichen Ethik,* Gütersloh, 1961; A. Grabner-Haider, *Paraklese und Eschatologie bei Paulus. Mensch und Welt im Anspruch der Zukunft Gottes,* Münster, 1968. On New Testament ethics as a whole, among the New Testament theologies, see especially K. H. Schelkle's systematic treatment in Vol. III, "Ethos." As typical historical-systematic presentations may be cited on the Catholic side R. Schnackenburg, *The Moral Teaching of the New Testament,* London/New York, 1964, and on the Protestant side H.-D. Wendland, *Ethik des Neuen Testaments. Eine Einführung,* Göttingen, 1970.
7. Col 3:18–4:1.
8. Ph 4:8.
9. Lists of virtues in Ga 5:22–23 and Ph 4:8. Lists of vices in Rm 1:29–31; 1 Co 6:9–10; 2 Co 12:20–21; Ga 5:19–21.
10. On what follows see E. Käsemann, *An die Römer,* Tübingen, 1973.
11. Ibid., p. 166.
12. Ibid.
13. In addition to the exegetical literature mentioned in C IV, 1, see D. Bonhoeffer, *The Cost of Discipleship,* London/New York, 1959; K. Barth, *Church Dogmatics,* IV, 2 §66, 3; A. Schulz, *Nachfolgen und Nachahmen,* Munich, 1962; E. Larsson, *Christus als Vorbild,* Uppsala, 1962; G. Bouwmann, *Folgen und Nachfolgen im Zeugnis der Bibel,* Salzburg, 1965; H. D. Betz, *Nachfolge und Nachahmung Jesu Christi im Neuen Testament,* Tübingen, 1967; M. Hengel, *Nachfolge und Charisma,* Berlin, 1968.
14. R. M. Hare, *The Language of Morals,* Oxford, 1952, p. 69; also P. W. Taylor, *Normative Discourse,* Englewood Cliffs, N.J., 1961, pp. 151–58.
15. Even the English expression, "The Paradigmatic Individuals," is not an adequate translation of Karl Jaspers' term, *die massgebenden Menschen.* Cf. the otherwise very sound article by A. S. Cua, "Morality and the Paradigmatic Individuals" in *American Philosophical Quarterly,* 6 (1969), pp. 324–29.
16. Jn 8:12.
17. Jn 1:14.
18. Jn 14:6.
19. On this whole chapter see the important works: by A. Auer, *Autonome Moral und christlicher Glaube,* Düsseldorf, 1971; the same author, "Die Aktualität der sittlichen Botschaft Jesu" in A. Paus (ed.), *Die Frage nach Jesus,* Graz, 1973,

pp. 271–363; F. Böckle, "Was ist das Proprium einer christlichen Ethik?" in *Zeitschrift für Evangelische Ethik* 11 (1967), pp. 148–57; the same author, "Theonomie und Autonomie der Vernunft" in W. Oelmüller (ed.), *Fortschritt wohin? Zum Problem der Normenfindung in der pluralen Gesellschaft*, Düsseldorf, 1972, pp. 63–86; the same author, "Unfehlbare Normen?" in H. Küng (ed.), *Fehlbar? Eine Bilanz*, Zürich/Einsiedeln/Cologne, 1973, pp. 280–304; J. Fuchs, "Gibt es eine spezifisch christliche Moral?" in *Stimmen der Zeit* 185 (1970), pp. 99–112; J. Gründel/H. van Oyen, *Ethik ohne Normen? Zu den Weisungen des Evangeliums*, Freiburg/Basle/Vienna, 1970; W. Korff, *Norm und Sittlichkeit. Untersuchungen zur Logik der normativen Vernunft*, Mainz.

20.　This holds with some reserve even for H. D. Wendland's very thorough "introduction" to the "Ethics of the New Testament."

21.　1 Co 3:11.

22.　D. Bonhoeffer, *The Cost of Discipleship*, p. 49.

23.　For a number of the following points I gained some valuable ideas from a conversation with J. M. Gustafson on the occasion of his lecture in Pittsburgh, "The Relation of the Gospels to the Moral Life," published in D. G. Miller/ D. Y. Hadidan (eds.), *Jesus and Man's Hope*, Pittsburgh, 1971, Vol. II, pp. 103–17. Cf. the same author, *Christ and the Moral Life*, New York/London, 1968.

24.　"When I ask myself why I have always aspired to behave honourably, to spare others and to be kind wherever possible, and why I didn't cease doing so when I realized that in this way one comes to harm and becomes an anvil because other people are brutal and unreliable, then indeed I have no answer." Sigmund Freud, Letter to J. J. Putnam, 8.7.1915, in *Letters of Sigmund Freud 1873–1939*, edited by Ernst L. Freud, London, 1961, p. 315.

9

Can Ethics Be Christian?
Some Conclusions

James M. Gustafson

Can ethics be Christian? The answer is negative if certain restrictive concepts of "ethics" are used. If the concept stipulates that any reflection on morality that finds justification or warrants for moral values and principles which are themselves grounded in "private," "historically particularistic," or "nonrational" assumptions is not ethical reflection, then in principle ethics cannot be Christian. If a pattern of thought, in order to be ethics, must in each order of moral discourse be exclusively rational, and if Christianity (or any other religion) is classed as irrational or nonrational, and if particular religious warrants are appealed to in any order of moral discourse, Christian moral thought is not ethics. For example, if the principle "you shall love your neighbor as yourself" is justified on the basis that it is in the Torah and in the Christian scriptures, or that it is a revelation from God, or that it is an action-guiding principle that is inferred from the theological assertion that God is love, then on the basis of the restrictive

concept the process is not in the domain of ethics. If, however, that principle were justified on the grounds that it is a universalizable principle, and therefore one on which presumably all rational persons can agree, the process would be in the realm of ethics. Indeed, the biblical language might be interpreted to mean that one ought to respect each person as an end in himself, or in some similar way, in order to cleanse it of its particular historical religious overtones.

Can ethics be Christian? The answer is affirmative on the basis of two different points of view. They are, first, that ethics must be Christian and *is* Christian in a universally applicable sense because it is in Christ that all things are created, and he is the Lord of all things. The second is that the ethics *of Christians* is and must be exclusively Christian because the community is called to absolute obedience to Jesus as Lord; all of the moral actions of the community must be determined by his lordship.

This article is extracted from Can Ethics Be Christian? *(Chicago: University of Chicago Press, 1975), pp. 169–179.*

From the first point of view, Christian ethics and universal human ethics are convertible terms. What is ethically justifiable to do (in a purely rational sense) is the Christian thing to do, and vice versa. This is given theological legitimacy by the doctrine of the Trinity in which Christ, the second person, is the one in and through whom all things are created. From this point of view, in principle there is no distinctive Christian morality, but all morality that is rationally justifiable is Christian. The historical particularity of the source of the life of the church has no particular ethical significance, though its theological significance is tremendous, for Jesus is the revelation of God. Christians have special obligations perhaps, for example, to follow Jesus in lives of self-sacrificial service, but these are not ethical obligations. They are particular religious obligations. Christians have distinctive ideals, but these cannot be called, in a strict sense, moral ideas, for they are not rationally justifiable. If one chooses to call these obligations and ideals "moral," necessarily one has a double ethics, a minimalistic one that is Christian in a grand theological sense, and a more demanding one that is Christian in a special historical sense. With modifications, this point of view can be found in St. Thomas, Luther, and Calvin.[1]

From the second point of view that comes to a strong affirmative answer, not only can ethics be Christian, but the ethics of Christians *must be* Christian. The pattern for this has two distinctive points of orientation. One is that the Christian community has a particular vocation to follow Jesus and the way of life that he exemplified and taught; it is obligated to be fully obedient to his lordship, to be a distinctive people with a distinctive way of life. The second is that while Christ is confessed to be the savior of the world, the sorts of philosophical speculations that give grounds for the convertibility of the Christian and the rational are eschewed. The Christian community has its significant grounding in a historical event, and its history and conduct are to be determined by that historical revelation. This point of view does not imply that every moral act of Christians is distinctively different from the acts of other persons. The honesty of Christians, for example, in their personal or business relations has no visible difference from the honesty of other persons. Indeed, the immediate moral intention of their actions (the intention to be honest) is not distinctive; they would also justify honesty on rational ethical grounds. What is characteristic, however, is that the final justification for honesty would be its consistency with a Christian way of life; a people could not be obedient to the lordship of Jesus and be dishonest. Very important for understanding this point of view is this: Jesus, who is Lord, is known through the gospel accounts of his life and teachings; on the basis of these accounts there are distinctive obligations for his followers and these are of equal authority to the more ordinary moral obligations that also follow from his lordship. "Christian" ethics then is highly distinctive, though not unique in all respects, and to be Christian is to be obliged to follow the distinctive as well as the ordinary morality that is part of a Christian way of life. The ethics of Christians is and must be Christian ethics; all of their moral actions are under Jesus' lordship; since he is Lord, the distinctive aspects of his way of life and teaching are as morally obligatory on those who confess him as Lord as are the ordinary aspects. With some modifications this point of view is present in the early stages of monastic movements (Franciscan morality is one example), in various Anabaptist movements of the sixteenth century, and in "radical" religious movements of the Puritan period (the Quaker movement is one example).

On the basis of a highly restrictive concept of ethics, the latter point of view is not ethics at all; it offers a religious way of life with religious obligations some of which are ethically defensible. The first point of view would, on the basis of a restrictive concept, be ethical throughout until the final justification, the gracious gift of God's creation, is invoked. (Whether "decision is king" only for religious persons at the point of an affirmation or choice either of the "ultimate grounds" of morality or of a definable "way of life" even the philosophers dispute. Certainly it is clear that all moral philosophers, not to mention all rational persons, do not agree on these matters.)

A more proper conclusion, stated in most general terms, is that religion *qualifies* morality, and that ethics can be Christian in the senses (*a*) that the morphology of religious morality can be explicated, and (*b*) that certain action-guiding values and principles can be inferred from religious beliefs as normative for those who share some common Christian experience of the reality of God. The religious qualification of morality can be rather thorough in its consequences, but it does not create an exclusive Christian morality or ethics. This general statement will be developed subsequently; it is important to note that the bases for drawing distinctions used in the answers above are not totally applicable to how my conclusions are drawn. Indeed, the basic question of the title must be refined to, "In what senses is it intelligible to speak of ethics as Christian?"

For the sake of organization and economy of words, attention is given here to three crucial aspects of morality that are qualified by Christian experience and belief, and thus three aspects of ethics. They are (1) the reasons for being moral, (2) the character of the moral agent, and (3) the points of reference used to determine conduct.

It is intelligible to speak of morality, and by derivation of ethics, as Christian in the sense that Christianity offers reasons for morality itself, and reasons for persons to be moral. That morality can be interpreted to have other ultimate grounds than Christian theological ones cannot be gainsaid; social conventions, biological necessity, systems of nontheistic metaphysics, and others have been developed. That persons and communities can have reasons for being moral other than those of the Christian faith and tradition is equally uncontradictable; to be happy, to have peace in society, and other reasons have been given. In Christian experience, however, the religious dimensions have priority over the moral. The existence of God is not posited in order to have an ultimate ground for morality; rather the reality of God is experienced, and this experience requires morality; or, by inference from this experience, the reality of God requires morality. One is not a religious person in order to have reasons of mind and heart to be moral; rather, one is religious as a consequence of experience of the reality of God, and this experience requires that one be moral.

In the religious consciousness of the serious Christian (and I believe also of the devout Jew and Moslem), every moral act is a religiously significant act. To act for the sake of justice for the oppressed is not only a moral act; it is a moral act done for religious as well as moral, indeed for religious-moral reasons, and thus is an act both of fidelity to God and of honor to God. Some Protestant theologians have equivocated on the word "good" to make this point; Luther, for example, believed that an act was truly good only if it was done "in faith." The morally good and the theologically good were collapsed into each other. Such an extreme position does not follow from my analysis. The moral act is qualified by the religious significance it has for the agent in the light of his or her reasons for being moral without collapsing the two references of "good." It is a good act for two distinctive but "overlapping" reasons; it is a morally right or good act because of its consequences or because of the immediate moral principles that governed it. It is also a "good" act for the more ultimate "theological" and "religious" reasons it was done; it was done in fidelity to God, or done to honor God. Since moral intention (for the well-being of creation) is one aspect of the reality of God as experienced, the two distinctive reasons overlap.

If morality is qualified by religion in this sense, then Christian ethics is possible in two aspects. One is making clear the morphology of Christian experience of being moral for "religious" reasons (as I have tried to do). The second is to develop action-guiding principles and values that can be inferred from these reasons; the ethical task is to answer the question, "If one is moral for these reasons, what sorts of moral action ought one to do?" "What values and principles guide the discernment of what God is enabling and requiring me (us) to do?" Theology does not only provide "ultimate grounds" for morality; the morality that it grounds is qualified by the theological beliefs. Christian religious beliefs do not only ground morality; since the reality of God has compelling clarity through Jesus, the morality that it grounds is qualified by that medium. Thus inferences of principles and values, and the ordering of priority of them, are qualified by him.

It is intelligible to speak of morality and ethics as Christian in a second sense, namely, that the experience of God's reality through the Christian "story" qualifies the characteristics or the "characters" of moral agents. That others than Christians have morally commendable characters cannot be contradicted; they emerge from their life experiences and from their commitment to worthy moral values and principles. In Christian experience, however, the religious dimensions have priority over the moral. An experience of God's reality is not sought to prop up moral character; rather, the reality of God is experienced, and with compelling clarity through Jesus; this experience both engenders and requires characteristics of moral agents that are morally commendable. Persons do not worship God, for example, to shore up weaknesses of moral character; rather, to participate in worship is to express and to evoke an experience of the presence of the ultimate power. This experience has consequences for the moral "sort of person" one is becoming.

In Christian experience of God and its persisting consequences for persons, it is not possible to separate the "religious" characteristics from the "moral" characteristics of persons. Consciousness cannot be *separated* along a line that distinguishes the moral from the religious. That persons who do not share Christian experience can be loving, hopeful, and faithful cannot be gainsaid; to experience the reality of God with special clarity through the Christian story, however, has, and ought to have, the consequences of nourishing (if not creating) loving, hopeful, and faithful dispositions in Christians. There are "readinesses" to act in certain ways, to seek the interests of others rather than one's own for example, that are nourished and sustained not only by actions in accordance with principles that would direct such action but also by participation in the Christian community with its common memories and its central person. To affirm that dispositions, affections, and intentions of a marked Christian sort are the fruits of Christian experience is not to affirm that other "virtues" like courage and justice are not also nourished by it. Indeed they are, for the ultimate power whose reality is experienced wills them as well.

If moral agents are qualified by the religious dimensions of experience in this way, then Christian ethics is possible in its two aspects. First, an intelligible account of these qualifications can be rendered, as I have attempted to do. Second, there are imperatives directed toward the sort of persons Christians ought to become that can be inferred from such an account. The normative, like the analytical, task of ethics includes attention to agents as well as acts. This second aspect of the ethical task is to answer the questions, "If one experiences God's reality, particularly informed by the Christian story, what sort of moral person ought one to become?" "What intentions and dispositions ought to be characteristic of Christians?" Quite reasonably, the answer to these questions is likely to resort to illustrations, by pointing to persons whose own life stories seem to embody those characteristics; this is one basis for the imitation of Christ theme in the history of Christian ethics, and for hagiographies both ancient and modern. The sort of person Christians ought to become is informed and influenced (that is, qualified) by the Christian story.[2]

It is intelligible to speak of morality and ethics as Christian in a third sense, namely, that distinctive points of reference are used to give guidance to moral action. These distinctive points of reference function in two ways in Christian moral reflection. First, religious symbols and theological concepts are used to interpret the moral and religious significance of events and circumstances; they are used in the process of forming a descriptive evaluation, or evaluative description, of the occasions for action. That other symbols and concepts can be used no one can dispute, and that the interpretations forthcoming can be accurate is disclosing the crucial moral issues in political, social, or interpersonal circumstances is equally clear. In the Christian community, however, the authorization for the selection of symbols and concepts is not only their potency in disclosing the moral issues; it is also that the confirmation in experience of the power of these symbols and concepts to articulate the experience of God's reality and of man's life in relation to God authorizes their use. These symbols might be highly specific in a historical sense; the use of the cross is one example. What the cross elucidates can be elucidated by other symbols; again, the use of the symbol of the crucifixion is authorized primarily by the compelling clarity it evokes in Christian experience of God as self-giving and self-sacrificing love.

The second function of distinctive points of reference is to infer and to state action-guiding principles and values that aid the Christian community and its members in discerning what God is enabling and requiring them to be and to do. To find such principles and values is not to guarantee that the actions of Christians are "morally better" than the actions of others whose principles and values are derived from "purely rational" bases. To claim, as the churches seem often to do, that the reason for using Jesus' teachings, or for inferring principles to govern action from theological beliefs, is to develop a "higher" or better morality is a mistake. The prime significance of the Christian experience is its apprehension of God's reality through the Christian story with compelling clarity. A fidelity to God follows which gives distinctive though not exclusive authority to the media through which that experience occurs. Thus there is confidence, though not blind trust, that these historically particular media are a trustworthy basis for finding moral values and principles that are in accord with God's will and reality.

That these values and principles might be distinctive, in the sense that there are claims on the Christian community that appear to be "irrational" and certainly "imprudent" is part of my argument. From a highly restrictive philosophical concept of ethics such claims as that the Christian community ought to be willing to give up its own immediate interests for the sake of others are not moral but religious claims. On the basis of the assumption that certain values and principles have an obligatory character within a "way of life" and that the Christian history and community call for a way of life grounded in the Christian story, it is fitting to call these Christian ethical principles and values. This is clearly not to insist that persons who do not share in that religious way of life must follow those principles or honor those values. While theologically an argument might be made for their universality, the confirmation of their authority is in the history of the Christian community and in personal experience. It is unreasonable to assume that those who do not share the "believing" should be obligated to follow the principles and honor the values that are distinctive to that community. Others may be quite prepared to adhere to these more rigorous demands for other reasons, such as personal ideals or the sustaining ethos of another religious community.[3] But the strength of the claim to engage in such action is qualified by the Christian experience and ethos.

Thus, it is intelligible, and I hope plausible and persuasive, to argue that ethics can be Christian in the senses that have been developed.[4] If the argument is not persuasive, at least it might locate where the crucial issues are. Its import I believe, is not only for ethical theory but also for the Christian communities and churches. They are deeply concerned about human well-being, prone to make moral judgments on all sorts of events, developing rules of behavior and recommendations for policy, and stimulating moral action among their members. All too frequently, however, they are not very clear and precise about the grounds or reasons for their authorizing all this activity.

If one is Christian or religious in order to be moral, just as if one is Christian in order to be happy, the heart of religion is not yet grasped. The heart of religion is the experience of the reality of God, mediated through all sorts of other experiences. The distinctiveness of the Christian experience of the reality of God is that he is experienced with compelling clarity in Jesus and in the Christian story. The confirmation of this (not an uncritical one) in experience grounds Christian morality. Christian ethics is the intellectual discipline that renders an account of this experience and that draws the normative inferences from it for the conduct of the Christian community and its members. The practical import is to aid the community and its members in discerning what God is enabling and requiring them to be and to do.

Notes

1. The Christology, the ethics, and the relations of the church to the world involved in this point of view are those of

Ernst Troeltshch's "Church-type"; those involved in the second are his "sect-type." See Ernst Troeltsch, *The Social Teaching of the Christian Churches* (Glencoe, Ill.: Free Press, 1949), I, pp. 331–43.

2. See James M. Gustafson, "The Relation of the Gospels to Moral Life," in Donald G. Miller and D. Y. Hadidian, eds., *Jesus and Man's Hope* (Pittsburgh: Pittsburgh Theological Seminary, 1971), 2:103–17.

3. See, for example, L. Jacobs, "Greater Love Hath No Man . . . The Jewish Point of View on Self-Sacrifice," *Judaism* 6 (1957): 41–47.

4. I believe the formal pattern of my analysis will bear the weight of a more inclusive range of materials. Thus, ethics can be "religious" in this way, when religion refers to generalizations based either on the characteristics of various historical religions or on some "generic" or functional concept of religion. Further, the formal pattern might function as a basis for "comparative" religious ethics. My own research has concentrated on Catholic and Protestant ethics, with Jewish ethics and law increasingly in view; I am not competent to make a range beyond these. Other scholars, happily among them are former students and colleagues of mine, are gaining the competence to do such work. See, for example, David Little, "Comparative Religious Ethics," in Paul Ramsey and John F. Wilson, eds., *The Study of Religion in Colleges and Universities* (Princeton: Princeton University Press, 1970), pp. 216–45.

10

Does Religious Faith Add to Ethical Perception?

Richard A. McCormick

The particular question I want to raise can be posed in any number of ways. Does one's faith add to one's ethical perceptions, and if it does, what does it add? Is not a morally wrong judgment morally wrong independent of religious belief? Is not a right decision right whether one is a believer or not?

Theologians have been deeply concerned with this question in recent years. They formulate the question variously. For example is there a specifically Christian ethics? Does Christian faith add material content to what is in principle knowable by reason? Is Christian morality autonomous? Is Christ the norm for the morally good and right, and in what sense? These questions may appear academic, at the margin of real life. Actually, the proper answer to them is of great importance.

For instance, if Christian faith, rooted in God's revelation, tells us things about right and wrong in human affairs that we would not otherwise know, then it is clear that decision-making risks integrity unless it is Christianly informed and inspired. Furthermore, the answer to the question raised affects public policy. For example, if Christians precisely as Christians know something about abortion that others cannot know unless they believe it as Christians, then in a pluralistic society there will be problems with discussion and decision in the public forum.

Moreover, the answer to these questions affects the churches' competence to teach morality authoritatively, and how this is to be conceived and implemented. Thus, if Christian faith and revelation add material content to what is knowable in principle by reason, then the churches conceivably could teach moral positions and conclusions independently of the reasons and analyses that recommend these conclusions. This could lend great support to a highly juridical and obediential notion of Christian morality. The very processes we use, or do not use, to judge the moral rightness or wrongness of many concrete projects (e.g., donor insemination, in

This article is excerpted from John Haughey, ed., Personal Values and Public Policy *(New York: Paulist Press, 1979), 155–173.*

vitro fertilization, warfare, poverty programs, apartheid) would be profoundly affected. The question, then, is of enormous importance.

Origins of Moral Judgments

The first thing to be said is that moral convictions do not originate from rational analyses and arguments. Let me take slavery as an example. We do not hold that slavery is humanly demeaning and immoral chiefly because we have argued to this rationally. Rather, first our sensitivities are sharpened to the meaning and value of human persons and certainly religious faith can play an important part in the sharpening. We then *experience* the out-of-jointness, inequality and injustice of slavery. We then *judge* it to be wrong. At this point we develop "arguments" to criticize, modify, and above all communicate this judgment. Reflective analysis is an attempt to reinforce rationally, communicably, and from other sources what we grasp at a different level. Discursive reflection does not *discover* the right and good, but only *analyzes* it. The good that reason seems to discover is the good that was already hidden in the original intuition.

This needs more explanation. How do we arrive at definite moral obligations, prescriptions, and proscriptions? How does the general thrust of our persons toward good and away from evil become concrete, even as concrete as a code of do's and don't's, and caveats? It happens somewhat as follows—and in this I am following closely the school of J. de Finance, G. de Broglie, G. Grisez, John Finnis, and others who are heavily reliant on the Thomistic notion of "natural inclinations" in explaining the origin of basic moral obligation. We proceed by asking what are the goods or values man can seek, the values that

define his human opportunity, his flourishing? We can answer this by examining man's basic tendencies. For it is impossible to act without having an interest in the object, and it is impossible to be attracted by, to have interest in something without some inclination already present. What then are the basic inclinations?

With no pretense at being exhaustive, we could list some of the following as basic inclinations present prior to acculturation: the tendency to preserve life; the tendency to mate and raise children; the tendency to explore and question; the tendency to seek out other men and obtain their approval—friendship; the tendency to establish good relations with unknown higher powers; the tendency to use intelligence in guiding action; the tendency to develop skills and exercise them in play and the fine arts. In these inclinations our intelligence spontaneously and without reflection grasps the possibilities to which they point, and prescribes them. Thus we form naturally and without reflection the basic principles of practical or moral reasoning. Or as philosopher John Finnis renders it:

> What is spontaneously understood when one turns from contemplation to action is not a set of Kantian or neoscholastic "moral principles" identifying this as right and that as wrong, but a set of values which can be expressed in the form of principles as "life is a good-to-be-pursued and realized and what threatens it is to be avoided."[1]

We have not yet arrived at a determination of what concrete actions are morally right or wrong; but we have laid the basis. Since these basic values are equally basic and irreducibly attractive, the morality of our conduct is determined by the adequacy of our openness to these values. For each of these values has its self-evident appeal as a participation in the unconditioned Good we call God. The realization of these values in intersubjective life is the only adequate way to love and attain God.

Further reflection by practical reason tells us what it means to remain open and to pursue these basic human values. First we must take them into account in our conduct. Simple disregard of one or other shows we have set our mind against this good. Second, when we can do so as easily as not, we should avoid acting in ways that inhibit these values, and prefer ways that realize them. Third, we must make an effort on their behalf when their realization in another is in extreme peril. If we fail to do so, we show that the value in question is not the object of our efficacious love and concern. Finally, we must never choose against a basic good in the sense of spurning it. What is to count as "turning against a basic good" is, of course, the crucial moral question. Certainly it does not mean that there are never situations of conflicted values where it is necessary to cause harm as we go about doing good. Thus there are times when it is necessary to take life in the very defense of life, in our very adhering to this basic value. That means that taking life need not always involve one in "turning against a basic good." Somewhat similarly, one does not necessarily turn against the basic good of procreation (what Pius XII called a "sin against the very meaning of conjugal life") by avoiding child-bearing. Such avoidance is only reproachable when *unjustified*. And the many conflicts (medical, economic, social, eugenic) that justify such avoidance were acknowledged by Pius XII. Suppressing a value, or preferring one to another in one's choice cannot be simply identified with turning against a basic good. My only point here is

that particular moral judgments are incarnations of these more basic normative positions, which have their roots in spontaneous, prereflective inclinations.

Even though these inclinations can be identified as prior to acculturation, still they exist as culturally conditioned. We tend toward values as perceived. And the culture in which we live shades our perception of values. Philip Rieff in *The Triumph of the Therapeutic* notes that a culture survives by the power of institutions to influence conduct with "reasons" that have sunk so deeply into the self that they are implicitly understood.[2] In other words, decisions are made, policies set not chiefly by articulated norms, codes, regulations, and philosophies, but by "reasons" that lie below the surface. This is the dynamic aspect of a culture, and in this sense many of our major moral problems are cultural. Our way of perceiving the basic human values and relating to them is shaped by our whole way of looking at the world. (Cf. Clarke.)

Let me take an example from another area of concern, that of bioethics. In relating to the basic human values several images of man are possible, as Callahan has observed.[3] First there is a power-plasticity model. In this model, nature is alien, independent of man, possessing no inherent value. It is capable of being used, dominated, and shaped by man. Man sees himself as possessing an unrestricted right to manipulate in the service of his goals. Death is something to be overcome, outwitted. Second, there is the sacral-symbiotic model. In its religious forms, nature is seen as God's creation, to be respected and heeded. Man is not the master; he is the steward and nature is a trust. In secular forms, man is seen as a part of nature. If man is to be respected, so is nature. We should live in harmony and balance with nature. Nature is a teacher, showing us how to live with it. Death is one of the rhythms of nature, to be gracefully accepted.

The model which seems to have "sunk deep" and shaped our moral imagination and feelings—shaped our perception of basic values—is the power-plasticity model. We are, corporately, *homo technologicus*. The best solution to the dilemmas created by technology is more technology. We tend to eliminate the maladapted condition (defectives, retardates, and so on) rather than adjust the environment to it. Even our language is sanitized and shades from view our relationship to basic human values. We speak of "surgical air strikes" and "terminating a pregnancy", ways of blunting the moral imagination from the shape of our conduct. My only point here is that certain cultural "reasons" qualify or shape our perception of and our grasp on the basic human values. Thus these reasons are the cultural soil of our moral convictions and have a good deal to say about where we come out on particular moral judgments.

Once the basic values are identified along with their cultural tints and trappings, theologians and philosophers attempt to develop "middle axioms" or mediating principles. These relate the basic values to concrete choice. The major problem any professional ethic faces is to reinterpret the concrete demands of the basic values in new circumstances without forfeiting its grasp on these values.

The Christian Perspective and Moral Judgments

There may be many ways to explain the influences of Christian faith on the moral norms that guide decision-making. For in-stance, the very notion one entertains of the Supreme Being can influence normative statements. If one thinks of God above all as the creator and conserver of order, then this yields a certain attitude toward human interventions into the givenness of the world. If, however, one also believes God is the enabler of our potentialities, then a quite different normative stance becomes feasible, as James Gustafson has pointed out.[4]

My own view on the relation of Christian belief to *essential* ethics would be developed as follows. Since there is only one destiny possible to all men, there is existentially only one *essential* morality common to all men, Christians and non-Christians alike. Whatever is distinctive about Christian morality is found essentially in the style of life, the manner of accomplishing the moral tasks common to all persons, not in the tasks themselves. Christian morality is, in its concreteness and materiality, *human* morality. The theological study of morality accepts the human in all its fullness as its starting point. It is the *human* which is then illumined by the person, teaching and achievement of Jesus Christ. The experience of Jesus is regarded as normative because he is believed to have experienced what is to be human in the fullest way and at the deepest level.

The Second Vatican Council stated something similar to this when it asserted that "faith throws a new light on everything, manifests God's design for man's total vocation, and thus directs the mind to solutions which are *fully human*."[5] It further stated: "But only God, who created man to His own image and ransomed him from sin, provides a fully adequate answer to these questions. This he does through what he has revealed in Christ His Son, who became man. Whoever follows after Christ, the perfect man, *becomes himself more of a man*."[6]

Traditionally, theologians referred to moral knowledge as originating in "reason *informed* by faith." The word "inform" is important. It does not mean *replaced* by faith. It is in explaining the term "inform" that we may hope to see more precisely how faith influences moral judgments at the *essential* level.

I have noted that our concrete moral judgments are applications originating in insights into our inclinations toward basic human values or goods. I have also suggested that our reasoning processes about these basic values can be distorted by cultural biases.

Let us take an example. It can be persuasively argued that the peculiar temptation of a technologically advanced culture such as ours is to view and treat persons functionally. Our treatment of the aged is perhaps the sorriest symptom of this. The elderly are probably the most alienated members of our society. More and more of them spend their declining years in homes for senior citizens, in chronic hospitals, in nursing homes. We have shunted them aside. Their protest is eloquent because it is helplessly muted and silent. But it is a protest against a basically functional assessment of their persons. "Maladaptation" is the term used to describe *them* rather than the environment. This represents a terribly distorted judgment of the human person.

Love of and loyalty to Jesus Christ, the perfect man, sensitizes us to the meaning of persons. The Christian tradition is anchored in faith in the meaning and decisive significance of God's covenant with men, especially as manifested in the saving incarnation of Jesus Christ, his eschatological kingdom which is here aborning but will finally only be given. Faith in these events, love of and loyalty to this central figure, yields a decisive way of viewing and intending the world, of interpreting its meaning, of hierarchizing its values. In this sense the Christian tradition only illumines human values, supports them, provides a context for their reading at given points in history. It aids us in staying human by underlining the truly human against all cultural attempts to distort the human. It is by steadying our gaze on the basic human values that are the parents of more concrete norms and rules that faith influences moral judgment and decision-making. That is how I understand "reason informed by faith."

In summary, then, Christian emphases do not immediately yield moral norms and rules for decision-making. But they affect them. The stories and symbols that relate the origin of Christianity and nourish the faith of the individual, affect one's perspectives. They sharpen and intensify our focus on the human goods definitive of our flourishing. It is persons so informed, persons with such "reasons" sunk deep in their being, who face new situations, new dilemmas, and reason together as to what is the best policy, the best protocol for the service of all the values. They do not find concrete answers in their tradition, but they bring a world-view that informs their reasoning—especially by allowing the basic human goods to retain their attractiveness and not be tainted by cultural distortions. This world-view is a continuing check on and challenge to our tendency to make choices in light of cultural enthusiasms which sink into and take possession of our unwitting, preethical selves. Such enthusiasms can reduce the good life to mere adjustment in a triumph of the therapeutic; collapse an individual into his functionability; exalt his uniqueness into a lonely individualism or crush it into a suffocating collectivism. In this sense I believe it is true to say that the Christian tradition is much more a value-raiser than an answer-giver. And it affects our values at the spontaneous, prethematic level. One of the values inherent in its incarnational ethos is an affirmation of the goodness of man and all about him—including his reasoning and thought processes. The Christian tradition refuses to bypass or supplant human deliberation and hard work. For that would be blasphemous of the Word of God become human. On the contrary, it asserts their need, but constantly reminds men that what God did and intends for man is an affirmation of the humans and therefore must remain the measure of what man may reasonably decide to do to and for himself.

The Influence of Faith

If this is a satisfactory account of the relation of Christian faith to decision-making (at the *essential* level), it means that faith informs reason because the reasoner has been transformed. This transformation means practically: (1) a *view* of persons and their meaning; (2) a *motivation* in the following of Christ; (3) a *style* of performing the moral tasks common to persons (communitarian, sacramental, cross of Christ, Holy Spirit). I think it quite possible that persons with such a view, motivation, style, might come to some different practical conclusions on moral matters, as indeed the historical Christian churches have. But these conclusions will not be in principle unavail-

able to human insight and reasoning in the broadest sense. That is what is meant, I believe, by the two assertions we find in Catholic Christian tradition. The first admits that our reasoning processes are "obscured by the sin of our first parent" and that revelation is necessary so we can know "expeditiously, with firm security and without error those things that are not in principle impervious to human reason." (DB 1286) Second, notwithstanding this realism about our sinful (even if redeemed) condition, this tradition refuses to bypass or supplant human deliberation and hard work in normative ethics.

Notes

1. John M. Finnis "Natural Law and Unnatural Acts" *Heythrop Journal* 11 (1970) 365–387.
2. Philip Rieff, *The Triumph of the Therapeutic* (New York: Harper & Row, 1966).
3. Daniel Callahan "Living with the New Biology" *Center Magazine,* 5 (July-Aug. 1972) 4–12.
4. James Gustafson, *The Contributions of Theology to Medical Ethics,* (Milwaukee: Marquette University, 1975).
5. *The Documents of Vatican II* (New York: America Press, 1966) p. 209.
6. *Ibid.,* p. 240.

Part 3

The Moral Self
and the Sort of Person
One Is and Becomes

part 3

The Moral Self
and the Sort of Person
One Is and Becomes

Introduction

Upon hearing the terms "ethics" or "morality," most people think of judgments about the rightness or wrongness of actions and/or the moral codes that communicate these judgments. While these are undoubtedly essential elements of what ethics is about, they are not the only nor perhaps even the most important. Focusing on behavior first is in many ways putting the cart before the horse. According to many Christian ethicists today, what is primary is the moral agent, the person who engages in moral choices and moral action. For example, early on in his three volume work, *Free and Faithful in Christ,* the ground-breaking German moral theologian, Bernard Häring, writes: "Moral theology is interested not only in decisions and actions. It raises the question, 'What ought I to do?' but asks, first of all, 'What ought I to be: What kind of person does the Lord want me to be?' "[1]

This concern with the quality of being of the moral agent is not new to moral theology. It is very much present in the Christian tradition's emphasis on virtue. But over the past few centuries, it has suffered some neglect because of the major new emphases in contemporary Christian ethics. Much of the impetus for retrieving and further developing this pivotal dimension of moral life comes from Protestant ethicists James Gustafson and Stanley Hauerwas, as well as Roman Catholic moral theologian, Bernard Häring.

Under the umbrella of the "moral self," we have included selections having to do with a variety of aspects of moral agency. The first three have to do with moral character. In his essay, Stanley Hauerwas articulates what is meant by "character" in the moral context, how it comes to be, and its relationship to what we choose and how we act. The Gustafson and Saliers articles both deal in one way or another with the formation of character. Gustafson explores the significance of one's spiritual life (i.e. one's experience of and orientation toward God) for one's moral life. It is his belief that the experience of the Holy engenders and nourishes certain qualities of spirit or character, and that the sense of the Holy is kept alive through worship and prayer. Saliers' concern

---

[1] Bernard Häring, *Free and Faithful in Christ,* 3 vols. (New York: Seabury Press, 1978), p. 85.

is similar. He wishes to examine the relations between liturgy (including prayer) and ethics. He maintains that liturgy allows individuals and communities to rehearse and re-enter the narratives that define them. This should result in a new way of understanding oneself and the world. Furthermore, it should help the individual to incorporate distinctively Christian affections and virtues into his/her character and way of life.

In a tightly written essay, Josef Fuchs focuses on an extremely important concept in contemporary Roman Catholic moral theology—fundamental option. The term refers to a moral agent's use of his or her most basic freedom to choose how he or she will stand before God. Fundamental option consists essentially in the giving or the refusal of the self in love before God. Upon it rests one's self-determination as good or evil.

Many moral theologians today regard a negative fundamental option as the true meaning of sin. The next grouping of articles deals with various aspects of this reality. Bruce Vawter discusses sin from a biblical perspective, while Josef Fuchs explains both sin and conversion in more theological terms as choices of one's basic freedom. As we are becoming increasingly aware, sin is not merely an individual reality. It has a social dimension particularly in its embodiment in social structures and institutions. Peter Henriot delineates the meaning of social sin and what the church's response to it should be.

The existence of sin in the individual and society calls for transformation or conversion. This is a foundational experience of Christian life and so of Christian ethics. Using the work of a number of developmental psychologists and of the theologian Bernard Lonergan, Walter Conn reflects on several dimensions of the conversion experience in the life of the Trappist monk, Thomas Merton. He then ties this psychological analysis to biblical understandings of conversion and to the theological notion of fundamental option. James Hanigan offers yet another perspective on this core Christian experience. He examines what conversion entails concretely for the Christian and argues that it should result in the converted Christian's seeing morality differently.

Two final aspects of the moral self dealt with in this section are conscience and moral development. Bernard Häring provides a biblical, theological, and psychological overview of conscience and its development. The last two selections focus on growth toward moral maturity. Carol Gilligan offers a feminist perspective on moral development. Taking issue with Lawrence Kohlberg's stage theory, which she finds to be too male-oriented, Gilligan argues that a woman's journey toward moral maturity has more to do with responsibility and care in her relationships than with rights, equality and fairness. Craig Dykstra approaches moral growth more theologically, seeing it primarily as a formation in discipleship. This formation requires training in three disciplines of the Christian life—repentance, prayer, and service. His discussion actually brings us back to where we began this section—the moral self and its formation in a Christian context.

11

Toward an Ethics of Character

Stanley Hauerwas

No ethic is formulated in isolation from the social conditions of its time. The contemporary emphasis in Christian ethics on the dynamic and self-creating nature of man is a reflection of the kind of society in which we live. Perhaps our ancestors were born to pre-established roles in a world where faithfulness to those roles guaranteed the fulfilment of moral duty. But we are born into a social world that forces us to be free, to be autonomous; for now the moral imperative is to actually fashion our lives by choosing among the numerous alternatives our social world presents to us.

In such a world it is not surprising that current moral discourse employs the language of freedom and responsibility to focus on man as self-creator.[1] The moral life is not constituted by correspondence to an objective moral order; rather it is to be constantly readjusted to the nuances and ambiguities of our ethical choices and experiences. Modern ethicists recognize that there is often more to our moral situation than our principles and rules contain; so much of our significant moral experience and life simply does not fall within the areas marked off by clearly defined roles or principles. "Responsibility" names the fact that often we are simply forced to fall back on ourselves in order to make decisions that have no relationship to objective standards of right and wrong.

In a social situation that seems to force the individual to be on his own, it is no surprise that the subject matter of ethics is centered around "problems," i.e., situations in which it is difficult to know what one should do.[2] Ethical discussion then focuses on the best way to respond to such "problems": Should an ethical decision be determined primarily in relation to principles and rules, or by a loving response to the peculiarities of the immediate situation? Those who argue for "principles" suggest that only their approach assures objectivity in morals, or that love is sentimentalized if it is not "imprincipled." Contextualists maintain that adherence to principles results in a false security that makes one insensitive to the complexity of modern moral issues.

Ethicists on both sides of the "context versus principle" debate have made the same error: in focusing on "the problem," both

---

This article is excerpted from Theological Studies *33 (December 1972): 698–715.*

have tended to ignore the ethics of character. "Problems" or "situations" are not abstract entities that exist apart from our character; they become such abstractions to the extent that we refuse to be other than we are. Perhaps the ethics of character has won a distasteful reputation because "having character" is associated with being set in one's ways, inflexible, or unbending.[3] But unless the positive significance of character is appreciated, freedom and responsibility cannot be understood in their proper moral context; for we are more than just the sum total of our responses to particular situations, whether the moral significance of such responses is determined by the situation itself or by its lawfulness.

To emphasize the idea of character is to recognize that our actions are also acts of self-determination; in them we not only reaffirm what we have been but also determine what we will be in the future. By our actions we not only shape a particular situation, we also form ourselves to meet future situations in a particular way. Thus the concept of character implies that moral goodness is primarily a prediction of persons and not acts, and that this goodness of persons is not automatic but must be acquired and cultivated.[4]

Exactly how is the relationship between a person and his acts to be understood? Is there a difference between what the person is and what he does? Do a person's actions follow from the kind of person he is, or does his character depend on the kind of action he engages in? Beyond even these questions is the problem of what it means to act at all.

These are extremely hard questions, but their difficulty does not excuse the failure of contemporary moralists to consider them. In the Protestant context, this failure may reflect the traditional concern to deny that the actual shape of a man's life has any efficacy in the attainment of his righteousness. Protestant ethics has taken seriously its mission to guard against "the temptation to confuse the shaping of life in accord with one's belief with the attainment of grace and God's righteousness."[5] In order to do this, Protestants have tended to emphasize the dual nature of the self: the "internal" justified self is divorced from the "external" sinful self, the passive self from the active. This has been more than just a theological description; there are enormous practical consequences if what a man does and how he acts have relatively little to do with his real "internal" justified self,[6] if man's "external" acts are only the ambiguous manifestations of his "true internal" self. Because of this emphasis, Protestant ethics has paid relatively little attention to how men's disposition, intentions, and actions actually embody whatever is considered to be the normative "style" of the Christian life.

Roman Catholic moral theology has continued to be more open to the language of character and virtue, as these concerns have played so important a role in the Catholic tradition as it has been shaped by Aristotle and Thomas. Moreover, recent Catholic moralists have emphasized the "whole person" rather than judgments of particular acts divorced from the total development of the moral agent.[7] Yet even in the Catholic context it is hard to find sustained analysis of the nature of the idea of character that its ethical significance would seem to demand. I am sure any explanation for this would be extremely complex, since it would have to combine sociological insight with a history of moral theology. Even if I were competent to supply such an account, it would direct me too far away from the main purpose of this essay. Rather I want to try to begin the kind of analysis of the nature of the idea of character and its moral significance that is required if we are to adequately account for this aspect of the Christian moral life. I do not pretend to say anything that Aristotle and Thomas did not say as well or better.[8] But perhaps this essay will at least provide the impetus to read their work with fresh eyes.

Meaning of Character

It is no accident that the concept of character is most appropriately used in contexts suggesting individuality; for, etymologically, the word "trait," which is often closely associated with it, is connected with making a distinguishing mark.[9] In this sense a character may be a distinctive figure in arithmetic or it may be used to point out a particular feature of an inanimate object. Therefore it is not surprising that character is also used to mark off the distinctive in a human being.

However, character takes on an added meaning when it is applied to persons. It denotes not only what is distinctive but what is in some measure deliberate, what a man can decide to be as opposed to what he is naturally. Because a man chooses to have a kind of character, we can assume that by knowing his character we have some indication about what he is likely to do. For example, we think of a man as naturally and incurably slow, but we feel that one can choose to be more or less honest or selfish. A man's

> inclinations and desires, which are part of his "nature," may suggest goals but such inclinations and desires only enter into them in a certain manner, in accordance with the rules of efficiency like persistently, carefully, doggedly, painstakingly or in accordance with rules of social ap-

propriateness like honestly, fairly, considerately, and ruthlessly.[10]

Probably because the notion of character seems to have this fundamental connection with personal effort, it is often thought of an implying effort done for moral praise or blame. Nowell-Smith expresses this by saying: "Pleasure and pain, reward and punishment, are the rudders by which moral character is moulded; and 'moral character' is just that set of dispositions that can be moulded by these means."[11] Supporting this argument is the fact that so many individual character words imply a moral judgment. Yet, as R. S. Peters points out, the relationship between the descriptive and evaluative aspects of character language is actually much more complex than this. An indication of this is the fact that we may be quite hazy about the spheres in which praise and blame apply and yet talk with some assurance about a person's character.[12]

This kind of ambiguity is clarified if we distinguish between "character traits" and "having character." A "character trait" usually refers to a distinctive manner of carrying out certain activities. Thus we can describe a person as being a perfectionist in his work without implying that he exhibits this trait in all his activity. Sometimes we use certain trait words to characterize the way a person carries out all the various activities of his life. We sometimes use such trait words to imply a negative evaluation of a person whose adherence to one particular style of behavior causes him to act inappropriately in certain situations.

The notion of "having character" is clearly set apart from the idea of a "character trait." To speak of a man "having character" is not to attribute to him any specific traits; rather the point is that, whatever activity he takes part in or trait he exhibits, there "will be some sort of control and consistency in the manner in which he exhibits them."[13] We often speak of integrity of character, thereby closely identifying integrity and consistency with the meaning of having character. We talk of strength or weakness of character as a way of indicating whether a man may be relied upon and trusted even under duress. Character in this sense is what Hartmann calls moral strength, which is the capacity of "the person to speak for himself, to determine beforehand his future conduct not yet under his control, therefore to guarantee for himself beyond the present moment."[14]

Character understood in this way implies that man is more than that which simply happens to him; for he has the capacity to determine himself beyond momentary excitations in the acts.[15] This is not just a matter of being able to will one's present decision as determinative in and for the future; as Hartmann argues, this volitional possibility ultimately depends on the identity of the person himself.

> One who promises identifies himself as he now is with what he will be later. . . . The breaking of a promise would be a renunciation of himself, its fulfillment a holding fast to himself. On this personal identity depends a man's moral continuity in contrast to all natural and empirical instability; on it, therefore, depends at the same time the ethical substance of the person.[16]

Thus it is character that gives a warrant for our expectation of a link between what the individual is and the sequence of his actions and attitudes.[17]

Once the distinction between "character traits" and "having character" has been made clear, we can better appreciate the complexity of the evaluative and descriptive aspects of character language. When we think of a person's character, a distinguishing trait such as honesty or kindness is usually what we have in mind; but when we speak of a man as "having character," we are more apt to be thinking of something like integrity, incorruptibility, or consistency. The former denotes more the common meaning of "virtues," while the latter indicates a more inclusive and unitary concept. Both usages denote the distinctive and both require effort on the part of the agent. They not only differ in level of generality, but having character also denotes a more basic moral determination of the self.

The use of "character" (mainly implied in specific character words such as "honesty") in the sense of denoting specifiable traits usually suggests an immediate moral evaluation, whereas to say a man "has character" is much more ambiguous; for even though normally to say that a man has character is to praise him, we do not think it odd to say that a man has character and yet deplore a large part of his conduct. For example, we might well say that a thief has character (he can be trusted to be a thief, and perhaps one who is clever or courteous), but we would not wish to imply by this that he is thereby a good man. This simply makes the point that, though most of us would give positive valuation to the consistency, integrity, and reliability that "having character" implies, yet these alone do not completely specify either the nature or the moral value of the traits which are part of such character.

Character as Qualification of Our Self-Agency

We have already indicated in several different contexts that man's capacity for self-determination is crucial if he is to "have character."

At the very least, this capacity implies that a man is more than that which happens to him. Though the importance of physiological and environmental factors is not to be underestimated, a man is not simply formed by the interaction of these forces. Rather man is in his essence self-determining; through his heredity and environment he acts to give his life its particular form. A man's present choices and actions control his own future by shaping the kind of man he is. Man is at the mercy of external forces only if he allows himself to be, for man is not just acted upon but agent. To be a man is to be an autonomous center of activity and the source of one's own determinations; all he knows, all he wills, all he does issues from that very act by which he is what he is.

This strong sense of agency, however, does not deny the aspects of man's life that can be thought of as his destiny. We do not have unlimited possibilities, we are "destined" to a certain range of choices by our culture, society, and our particular biographical and psychological situation. It is our destiny to be born at a particular time in a certain society rather than another. In this sense we do undergo much, and much happens to us in our lives. However, we recognize that a man can gain character by responding in significant ways to events beyond his control. In so responding, he is not just being a passive agent, but he is actively forming himself to endure what he is undergoing in a particular way. Though it is undeniably true that we are destined men, we are also agents who have the capacity to give that destiny a form appropriate to our character. Though character may grow out of what we suffer, its main presupposition and condition must remain the agency of man.

Man's capacity for self-determination is dependent on his ability to envision and fix his attention on certain descriptions and to form his actions (and thus his self) in accordance with them. A man's character is largely the result of such sustained attention. His reasons for his action, his motives and intentions are really explanatory because they are the essential aspect in the formation of the act and consequently in his own formation. His reasons do not "cause" him to act, but by embodying them he as the agent effects the corresponding action.[18] Man's agency may not be determined by any external cause, but it is only effective when it is determined in one direction rather than another, i.e., when a man chooses to live his life by certain beliefs and intentions rather than others, and embodies this fundamental choice in his concrete choices. Man chooses within an indeterminate range of possibilities by ordering them in accordance with his intentions. To be free is to set a course through the multitude of possibilities that confront us and so to impose order on the world and one's self.

Character is thus the qualification of our self-agency, formed by our having certain intentions (and beliefs) rather than others. Character is not a mere public appearance that leaves a more fundamental self hidden; it is the very reality of who we are as self-determining agents. Our character is not determined by our particular society, environment, or psychological traits; these become part of our character, to be sure, but only as they are received and interpreted in the descriptions which we embody in our intentional action. Our character is our deliberate disposition to use a certain range of reasons for our actions rather than others (such a range is usually what is meant by moral vision), for it is by having reasons and forming our actions accordingly that our character is at once revealed and moulded.

In emphasizing the agent's perspective, I am not recommending ethical solipsism. Thinking something right or wrong does not make it so. Kurt Baier has rightly suggested that the minimal condition for being a morally serious person is willingness to judge our action from the point of view of anyone—i.e., we are willing to defend our action on grounds that are open to public debate.[19] Only as we are willing to subject our reasons (descriptions) for our actions to something like the universalizability principle is ethical judgment and argument possible at all.[20] This emphasis on the agent's point of view, then, does not undercut the importance of moral argument, judgment, and practical reasoning; it does indicate that the moral life involves more than these issues. Willingness to examine our actions from a moral point of view is certainly a condition of morality; but such investigation makes no sense unless we are willing to first engage in certain actions or ways of life. A man is good not only because his acts are justifiable, but because he is willing to face hard decisions entailed by his embodiment of commitments that go beyond the minimal conditions for moral argument.[21]

To understand character as the qualification of our agency is not to affirm that we can and should become whatever we wish. To strongly emphasize our agency is not to deny the significance of the passive aspects of our existence. Much that we are is that which "happens to us." Our intentions embody the "given" aspects of our existence as elements in the envisaged project. Through such an embodiment we conform our lives to what we think to be "reality," in its descriptive as well as its normative mode. The point I have tried to make, however, is that part of what constitutes "reality" for men is what we are able to contribute through the active ordering of reality by our intentional action.

These last two points can be brought together, since our society and its stock of public descriptions form large parts of the passive aspects of our existence. Yet no man can simply be passively formed by his society. He may find it easier to simply acquiesce in the expectations and demands of his society. But such a conformity is not completely passive, for it must still become a qualification of his agency. His resulting character is still uniquely his, as much as the character of other members of the society who have interacted more creatively with that society and are more visibly different from the society's normal expectations. It is certainly true that much of our life consists in assuming societal roles or patterns of behavior, which may be good or bad. Yet it must still be our agency that embodies and enacts these roles.

It is not possible to establish abstract criteria that can accurately indicate how much our character is determined and how much we determine ourselves. These obviously vary from society to society, from one position in society to another, from individual to individual. Our original genetic temperament and social position largely determine the range of descriptions which will be possible for us. My point is the more general one that, regardless of the way our character is actually formed in its concrete specification, it must be nonetheless our character if, as I have argued, men are fundamentally self-agents.

Character as Moral Orientation of the Self

Character is tremendously important for our moral behavior; for what we do morally is not in itself determined by the rules we adhere to or how we respond to one particular situation, but by what we have become through our past history, by our character. Experiences like facing death and falling in love are very important for what we are and do; yet they are often ignored in the analysis of moral experience simply because they are not in propositional form. It is our character that gives orientation and direction to life. The clarity and singleness of men's characters vary greatly in their concrete manifestations. Perhaps the clearest example of character is one in which a life is dominated by one all-consuming purpose or direction. The moral value of such a character depends on the substance of the purpose to which it is dedicated. Most of our characters do not exemplify such an all-consuming aim; rather each of us has a set of intentions and descriptions integrated in some hierarchy of priority which provides a general orientation.

If character is understood as the orientation of our self-agency, it cannot be finished once and for all; it is impossible to perceive beforehand all that is implied in the descriptions which we have made our own. We often find that the patterns we use to form our actions have more to them than we originally suspected. To have character is necessarily to engage in discovery: by our continuing action we discover unanticipated new aspects and implications of our descriptions. For example, we may find that we have embodied two different descriptions which we originally felt to be in harmony, but which prove to be contradictory as they are further specified in concrete actions. We discover the conditions for the success of the other. Thus we may find that we cannot wish to gain as much money as we can and at the same time treat all men fairly. At some point, in relation to a particular situation, we discover that though our agency can be determined by either one of these descriptions, they cannot both be harmonized in the same act. We must choose one or the other, and thereby become as we have chosen.

It is possible, of course, that we shall simply be inconsistent, one time acting to gain money and the other time to be fair. Such inconsistency does not mean that we do not have character, it only means that there are inconsistent elements in the character we do have, or that our character is determined primarily in view of expediency, accommodation, etc. We may think that this does not provide a very successful or particularly attractive way to be, but nonetheless it is the way we are. Of course, it is possible that both these ways of being, gaining money and acting fairly, may be harmonized in terms of a further goal, such as ambition. Thus one may find that he can further his ambition by acting in one situation to gain money, in another to leave the impression that he is a fair person. But his criterion for being one or the other is determined by his ambition.

I have thus tried to clarify the idea of orientation that I am associating with character. Character may be a general direction without necessarily being conceived in a highly specific manner or in terms of a definite goal. We may consider such definite formation morally important, but this is not a conceptual necessity. Our character may consist of simply meeting each situation as it comes, not trying to determine the direction of our lives but letting the direction vary from one decision to another. Or we might even approve of the man who at times acts inconsistently with his character.

Such inconsistency may be important in providing a transition from our past to our future, especially when our character is so formed that we are closed to the future and fail to acknowledge the significance of new elements that confront us and challenge our past determinations. We may expressly try to protect ourselves in some narrow way from the vicissitudes of living life in a creative manner. This can be done by simply limiting our actions to a well-laid-out routine which allows a safe boredom and protects us from the ravages of the unknown. But it is equally true that our character can be formed in such a way that it provides the means by which we reach new appreciation of the possibilities of our future. Indeed, if we are to determine our own future, it is precisely upon our character that such an openness depends.

Character is morally significant because, if rightly formed, it provides a proper transition from our past to our future; for the task of this transition is not to accept the future unconditionally, but to respond and remake the future in the right kind of way. Our future is what we determine it to be from the depths of who we are; it can be as rich or as narrow as we make it. It is not enough that we as moral agents take into account all that is in the situation objectively understood, for what is also "in" the situation is the possible change we can make by the fact that we are certain kinds of persons. Our moral life is not limited to passive accommodation to the good; it includes changing the world through intentional activity rooted in our character. Moreover, the kind of person we are, our character, determines to a large extent the kind of future we will face. Only if we have a morally significant character can we be relied upon to face morally serious questions rather than simply trying to avoid them.

Especially since character is formed in freedom, no one type of character is normative for all men. The actual character of a man is too much the product of the contingencies of his life for such a concrete recommendation to be viable. Men are simply different, and the difference does not necessarily denote degrees of goodness or badness. Individuals have formed themselves differently in relation to their individual circumstances. Such variety of goodness frustrates the philosopher's desire for a simple description of the moral life, but the reality is undeniable.

To accept the variety of the good embodied in our actual lives, however, is not to refuse all recommendations about the kinds of character a man should have. It is simply to recognize that such recommendations do not necessarily determine their concrete specifications. In this essay I have attempted to describe the significance of the idea of character for the moral life, but a descriptive argument is not enough. The question of the kind of character one *ought* to embody cannot be avoided. This normative question involves such complex issues that it is best discussed in another context. However, I would like to make two brief normative suggestions, one moral and one theological.

The question of how our character is acquired and developed is a morally significant question. The most general statement about the character of morally serious people is that it has not been left to chance. One of the constant themes running through moral philosophy has been that the unexamined life is not worth living. This theme is very much at the heart of the moral significance of character, for it is through consciousness (intentionality) that we shape ourselves and our actions. And what else does consciousness mean but the effort to see and understand our actions in terms of their most significant moral descriptions? For the idea that the moral life is the examined life is but a way of saying that we can choose to determine ourselves in terms of certain kinds of descriptions rather than others. Thus, to live morally we must not only adhere to public and generalizable rules but also see and interpret the nature of the world in a moral way. The moral life is thus as much a matter of vision as it is a matter of doing.[22]

This recommendation that we consciously strive to develop our character does not imply an unwarranted concern for the moral man with his own perfection or righteousness. I wish to give no comfort to the prig or prude. Character as I have analyzed it is not an end in itself but that which gives our lives moral orientation by directing us to certain kinds of activities. The possible moralizing misuses of character in no way detract from the moral value of character properly formed. It is not finally a question of whether we have or do not have character, but rather the kind of character that results from our way of seeing the world. The moral importance of the idea of character is not that good men think a great deal about acquiring and having character; rather it is that the concerns represented by the idea of character play an essential part in their being good men.

On a theological level, the idea of character provides a way of explicating the normative nature of the Christian life. The Christian life is not simply a matter of assuming a vague loving attitude, but rather it is a concrete determination of our being developed through our history. The Christian is one so formed as he assumes the particular description offered him through the Church. This formation is the determination of our character through God's sanctifying work. Sanctification is thus the formation of the Christian's character that is the result of his intention to see the world as redeemed in Jesus Christ.[23]

The Christian life so understood is not made up of one isolated "loving" act added to another. Rather it ought to be the progressive growth of the self into the fuller reality of God's action in Christ. Such growth in the Christian life is necessitated not only by the new contingencies we face as individuals; it is called forth by the object of the Christian's loyalty. The Christian tradition possesses rich images to characterize such a life. The primacy of one image or set of images is a theological question I cannot settle here. Rather I have developed a position from which such an argument can be meaningfully carried on.

Notes

1. For a much fuller account of the idea of responsibility and its use in contemporary theological ethics, see Albert Jonsen, *Responsibility in Modern Religious Ethics* (Washington: Corpus, 1968).
2. For an extraordinarily perceptive article that makes this point in a philosophical context, see E. Pincoffs, "Quandary Ethics," *Mind* 80 (1971) 552–71.
3. For an extended discussion of character viewed primarily as an "armour" or limiting aspect of our human freedom, see Wilhelm Reich, *Character Analysis* (New York: Noonday, 1949).
4. Robert Johann, "A Matter of Character," *America* 116 (Jan. 21, 1967) 95.
5. Gustafson, p. 14.
6. This kind of problem can already be found in Luther, especially in *The Freedom of the Christian.* See *Three Treatises,* tr. W. A. Lambert (Philadelphia: Muhlenberg, 1957) p. 297.
7. See, e.g., Charles Curran, *A New Look at Christian Morality* (Notre Dame: Fides, 1968) pp. 204–7; and John Milhaven, *Toward a New Catholic Morality* (New York: Doubleday, 1970) pp. 22, 87, 107. Milhaven, in a recent article "Objective Moral Evaluation of Consequences," THEOLOGICAL STUDIES 32 (1971) 407–30, emphasizes Thomas' under-

standing of the relation between virtue and moral knowledge, but he thinks psychological analysis is now more appropriate for such issues. While this may be the case, it certainly is a matter that must be demonstrated rather than assumed. It is not clear how completely Milhaven integrates the emphasis on the significance of the agent into his general position; he continues to defend a form of consequentialism in which the impersonal moral judgment of the spectator makes irrelevant the agent's own understanding of what he was doing. One cannot help but get the feeling that many of the so-called "new-liberal Catholic moralists" still continue to accept the "old morality" presupposition that ethics is primarily concerned with judgments about particular problems. If this is the case, the difference between the new and old moral theology is not primarily in method but in style and specific conclusion. Put in historical terms, this means that the new Catholic ethics, like the old, has not provided an adequate account of the relation between the virtues and the more "objective" and problem-oriented ethics traditionally associated with the confessional.

8. For an analysis of Aristotle and Thomas on virtue and character, see my *Moral Character as a Problem for Theological Ethics* (New Haven: Yale Ph.D. dissertation, 1968).

9. R. S. Peters, "Moral Education and the Psychology of Character," *Philosophy* 37 (1962) 38.

10. *Ibid.,* p. 38.

11. P. H. Nowell-Smith, *Ethics* (Harmondsworth: Penguin, 1961) p. 304.

12. Peters, p. 39.

13. *Ibid.,* p. 43.

14. Nicolai Hartmann, *Ethics* 2 (tr. Stanton Coit; London: Allen and Unwin, 1963) 287.

15. In the light of this understanding of the idea of character the problem with situation ethics is that, in spite of its claim to provide men with autonomy, it is working with a very passive model of the self. The self is always lost amid the contingencies of the particular situation. For men to have autonomy in any meaningful sense, they must be able to meet "the situation" on grounds other than those which the situation itself provides. Such grounds must be based on their character. Situation ethics seem but a secular restatement of the passive view of man associated with the traditional Protestant insistence on the centrality of justification by faith.

16. Hartmann, p. 288.

17. Martin Buber, *Between Man and Man* (Boston: Beacon, 1955) pp. 104–17.

18. "Cause" here appears in inverted commas to indicate an issue of controversy. Philosophers such as Melden, Anscombe, and Richard Taylor argue that since actions are only intelligible in terms of reasons or motives, they are not open to an account in terms of Humean causality (Melden, p. 53; Taylor, pp. 9–98). They argue that since Humean causality presupposes a contingent relation between cause and effect, the relation of logical necessity between the agent and his act precludes causal explanation; for the intention of the agent is necessarily connected with the external act simply because the intention to do a certain thing cannot be described without making reference to its object. But even if this argument is sound, it need not preclude that "reasons"—insofar as they are wants and desires—are still properly thought of as the "cause" of our action. For two excellent discussions that argue this way, see Alvin Goldman, *A Theory*

of Human Action (Englewood Cliffs: Prentice-Hall, 1970) pp. 76–85, and Georg Henrik von Wright, *Explanation and Understanding* (Ithaca: Cornell Univ., 1971) pp. 95–131. For the purpose of this essay it is not necessary to make a decision about this issue; however, it is obviously of great significance for any full theory of agency and especially for basic methodological questions concerning the nature of the social and behavioral sciences and their relation to ethics; for at the least the agency theory of human behavior makes clear that the social sciences cannot model their explanatory patterns after the natural sciences. See, e.g., Charles Taylor, *The Explanation of Behavior;* Peter Winch, *The Idea of a Social Science* (New York: Humanities Press, 1958); *Readings in the Philosophy of Social Science,* ed. May Brodbeck (New York: Macmillan, 1968); and Alasdair MacIntyre, *Against the Self-Images of the Age* (New York: Schocken, 1971) pp. 211–279. In the context of these methodological questions the kindest thing that can be said of Milhaven's statement that "the use of the behavioral sciences *is* morality" is that it displays a rather shocking naïveté and innocence (*Toward a New Catholic Morality,* p. 125). The important relation between ethics and the social sciences is not well served by the ethicist's accepting at face value the procedure and conclusion of the social scientist on the grounds they are "empirical."

19. Kurt Baier, *The Moral Point of View* (New York: Random House, 1966) pp. 100–109.

20. My affinities with the Kantian tradition are obvious. However, for the exposition of the generalization principle closest to my own, see Marcus Singer, *Generalization in Ethics* (New York: Knopf, 1961).

21. As Richard Price observed, most men whose behavior is in the main decent and regular "are perhaps what they appear to be, more on account of the peculiar favorableness of their natural temper and circumstances; or, because they have never happened to be much in the way of being otherwise; than from any genuine and sound principles of virtue established within them and governing their hearts. The bulk of mankind is not composed of the grossly wicked, or of the eminently good; for, perhaps, both these are almost equally scarce; but of those who are as far from being truly good, as they are from being very bad; of the indolent and unthinking; . . . the wearers of the form without the reality of piety; of those, in short, who may be blameworthy and guilty, not so much on account of what they do, as what they do not do" (*A Review of the Principle Questions In Morals,* ed. D. Daiches Raphael [Oxford: Clarendon, 1948] pp. 230–31). The ethics of character is an attempt to indicate that "what men do not do" is important for the kind of men they are; and "what men do not do" is not just their failure to judge their own individual actions from a "moral point of view," but their failure to take a stance out of which all their action develops.

22. Iris Murdoch has written persuasively on the importance of "vision" for the moral life; see her "Vision and Choice in Morality," in *Christian Ethics and Contemporary Philosophy,* ed. Ian Ramsey (New York: Macmillan, 1966); and "The Idea of Perfection," *Yale Review* 53 (1964) 343–80. For a full exposition of Miss Murdoch's thought, see my "The Significance of Vision: Toward an Esthetic Ethic." *Studies in Religion,* June 1972. Also see my suggestion about the relat-

ing of language and ethics, "Situation Ethics, Moral Notions, and Theological Ethics," *Irish Theological Quarterly,* July 1971, pp. 242–57. For an extremely suggestive article that indicates how some of the implications of this article might be developed, see James McClendon, "Biography As Theology," *Cross Currents* 21 (1971) 415–31.

23. For a fuller exposition of the relationship between character and the doctrine of sanctification as it appears in Calvin and Wesley, see my *Moral Character as a Problem for Theological Ethics.* Also see the last chapter of James Gustafson's *Christ and the Moral Life* (New York: Harper & Row, 1969) for some similar suggestions.

12

Spiritual Life and Moral Life

James M. Gustafson

Moral theologians have often been too busy attending to the demands for rigorous thinking about practical problems to reflect much upon the well-springs of disposition and action in the Christian community and its members. Ascetic theologians have often been so occupied with the opening of man's vision of God that they have not said much about the relation of the mystical to the moral, of the practice of corporate and private spiritual discipline to the practice of the moral life. It is, however, the "interface" between ascetical and moral theology that I wish to examine; or perhaps more accurately, it is the relationship of man's orientation to God and his moral orientation to the neighbor that I want to explore.

I wish to look at something that Catholicism and Protestantism, and Judaism as well, have assumed all through their histories, namely that there is an intrinsic and significant relation between piety and morality, between the spiritual life and the moral life, between the practice of one's devotion to God and his service to his neighbor. It is interesting to note that the book whose title comes closest to

what I wish to examine, *Worship and Ethics,* is Max Kadushin's account of their relationship in rabbinic Judaism.[1] The apparent reason for writing this book, which is important for our understanding of Jewish ethics, is that, left to philosophical and legal minds, the *halakah* loses its vitality and communal significance as engendering the worship of God as well as right behavior to others.

Worship and Morality

Scripture provides ample evidence that the people of God could never separate what philosophers sometimes wish to distinguish as "religious acts" and "moral acts." That the community and its members were doing something different at the altar than they were when they justly paid the hireling his wages at the end of the day is clear, but it is also clear that they assumed a significant connection between the two. (I have, in a paper as yet unpublished, "Religion and Morality from the Perspective of Theology," sought to indicate that the facile distinction between the two

This article is excerpted from Theology Digest 17 (Winter 1971): 296–307.

made by contemporary philosophers simply founders on the texts of the great Western religions.) Both the most sophisticated theologians of the Christian tradition and the writers of the manuals of piety and devotion, though not all in the same way, assumed that there are reciprocal relations between the spiritual life and the moral life. We might find the claim of Bishop K. E. Kirk to be too sweeping, but his great book *The Vision of God* is a major source in non-Roman Catholic theology for grasping what these relations are. Kirk wrote:

> The doctrine "the end of life is the vision of God" has throughout been interpreted by Christian thought at its best as implying in practice that the highest prerogative of the Christian, in this life as well as hereafter, is the activity of *worship;* and that nowhere except in this activity will he find the key to his ethical problems. As a practical corollary it follows that the principal duty of the Christian moralist is to stimulate the spirit of worship in those to whom he addresses himself, rather than to set before them codes of behavior.[2]

Too sweeping indeed. But if the *principal* duty of the Christian moralist is not to stimulate the spirit of worship, perhaps in fact it is the *most neglected* among his duties.

Experience of and Orientation Toward God

The more problematic that God as an object of belief and experience for man becomes, the more meaningless that worship becomes. The more problematic that experience and belief in God become, the more fragile the tone and quality of the moral life of the Christian community become. Indeed, the moral arguments and actions of the community and its members take place in a different context when awareness of the transcendent is lost: persons become means rather than ends, sin becomes infraction of moral rules rather than a denial of God; the end of action becomes an increased quantity of moral goodness rather than the glorification of the goodness of God; casuistry becomes computer-like, problem solving rather than man's earnest search for God's will and purposes; the spirit of technical logic and technical manipulation evaporates the spirit of awe, of wonder, and of mystery. Man loses his sense of finiteness, not to mention sin, and displaces God, the Absolute. Without the experience of the Holy, Christian moral life withers.

The principal point of distinctiveness for the moral life of religious communities is precisely their openness to and awareness of God. It is the recognition that man's dependence is not merely on other persons, on the world of nature of which he is a part, on legal and social institutions, but also in and through these on the power and goodness from which all things flow, in which all things are grounded. Man's gratitude is given not only to those whose love and care bring him into being and sustain his life, but to God who brings all life into being and is its ultimate sustainer. Man's guilt is caused not only by the suffering he causes others through his misdeeds, but by his failure to relate himself conscientiously in trust and in faithfulness to God's purposes for him and for all of creation. Man's repentance is not only before those who are the victims of his heedlessness, his insensitivity, and his overt and selfish wrath and destructiveness; his repentance is before God who wills and enables that he be other than as he is. Man's obligation is not only to those who have some social authority over him, or those whose very being in dependence upon him makes a moral claim; his obligation is to God as God's deputy in the care and nurture of life. Man's orientation is not only toward what will restrain evil in the world, or what will bring moral well-being to his fellows; his orientation is toward God that his goodness might be glorified in the order of life in the world and in the deeds of individual men. Man's love is not only for his wife, his family, his friends, his country, his church, the beauty of nature and of humanly created things around him, or even for humanity itself; God whose love makes possible all other objects of human life is the ultimate object of man's loves. Man's respect for the rights of others, his concerns to overcome injustices in the world, are grounded not merely in his perceptions that human well-being will come from adhering to these, but also from the conviction that others have rights because they are creatures of God's goodness, and that justice is a fundamental requisite for human peace because it is in accord with God's purposes for man.

Thesis

It is the single and simple thesis of this lecture that, apart from the individual and corporate disciplines of the spiritual life of the Christian community, its sense of the Holy, of the transcendent, withers; when its sense of the transcendent withers, the distinctive tone and quality of its moral activity is lost. Indeed, not only *how* it decides and acts is altered; the ends that it seeks to achieve and the limits on means that it imposes on itself might also be altered. *What* it does might also be altered. I

am not prepared to assert and argue that a "spiritual" community is necessarily a better moral community, or that the "spirit of worship" (to use Bishop Kirk's terms) is in itself the sufficient condition for a morally praiseworthy Christian community. The history of piety and morality in the Christian community is replete with evidences that would counter such assertions. Too often a consciousness of orientation toward God has led to insensitivity to the needs of men; too often men who have claimed a special and privileged access to God have claimed also a moral certitude which has often been distorted and even perverse. Nor am I prepared to assert and argue that the moral conditions of the world—the injustices in social structures, for example— would be rectified if only the spiritual life of the Christian community were vivified. That would make the worship of God a technique for moral improvement, which is clearly a distortion of the reasons for worship, and would also be a mistaken prediction.

Basic Assumption

It is clear that the resolution of the problematic of "God-talk" (the term is itself a trivialization of the seriousness and passion that I would assume it would have for anyone for whom much is at stake) is crucial for the thesis of this paper. Minds of far greater power and learning than mine have addressed and continue to address that issue. If unbelief turns out to be truer than belief, if atheism turns out to be more honest than trust in God, all I will have said in this lecture could be subsumed under "the consequences of a useful fiction for the moral life." Similarly it is clear that if persons who have an awareness and experience of the transcendent are merely the victims of their individual or collective unconscious, and that the spiritual life is "caused" by culturally available symbols for controlling and directing psychic drives, all I will have said could be subsumed under "the consequences of a relatively harmless neurosis for the moral life." We shall beg these prior and important questions. We work from the platform assumption that experience and awareness of the transcendent is a real relationship between human subjects and the reality of God, a "power bearing down" on them.[3]

The focus of our attention, in any case, is primarily upon the human subjects, that is, on the significance of their spiritual lives in their awareness of an orientation toward God for their moral lives. That the meaning of God is given in Christian and Jewish terms is, of course, crucial. To be aware of and oriented toward God as known in Hindu tradition leads to different sorts of both spiritual and moral life. But that is not our primary concern.

A Correlative Enterprise

In developing the theme more specifically, I wish to correlate three points of reference in the Christian life. The central point is certain senses, sorts of awareness, or qualities of spirit, which the spiritual life engenders, sustains, and renews. The terms that I use here are not exhaustive: they are neither precisely fixed on the theological virtues nor on the gifts of the Spirit as these have been developed in Catholic theology. Nor is there time to develop all the ramifications even of the terms I choose, and their relations to each other. But central in our correlative enterprise are the following sorts of awareness and/or qualities of spirit: a sense of radical dependence, a sense

of gratitude, a sense of repentance, a sense of obligation, and a sense of direction. It is my primary assertion that the life of worship and devotion to God as he is known in the Jewish and Christian tradition, that the Christian experience of the Holy, engenders and nourishes these senses, or qualities of the human spirit.

While I desire not to be mechanically schematic about things which are organic in their relationships, for purposes of clarity I shall correlate each of these senses with the second point of reference, namely certain experiences of God and beliefs about God. Thus, to provide outline: the sense of radical dependence is correlated with our experience of and belief in God as Creator; the sense of gratitude is correlated with the experience of God as beneficent, as good, in his creation, sustenance, and redemption of the world; the sense of repentance is correlated with the experience of God as judge; the sense of obligation with the experience of God as orderer and sustainer of life; the sense of direction with the experience of God as the end, the *telos,* of all creation.

The excessive schematization of this, it must be forewarned, is humanly and theologically dangerous, for on the theological side it is *one* God whom we experience, whose being, presence, activity, and relatedness to man cannot be separated into discrete aspects of creator, judge, end, and so forth, and into distinctive moments of being creator at one time and end at another. Theology, and even morality, often get into trouble when useful distinctions become separate aspects or moments, such as those that are made between God as Creator and God as Redeemer, between moments of his activity as being creative at one time and being redemptive at another. The schematization is humanly dangerous as well, and in principle for the same reason, namely that, while there are moments when the sense of gratitude is more overwhelming than the sense of repentance, the two are intrinsically related to each other in the experience of God.

The third point of reference in our three-way correlation is the predispositions to view life and to act in certain ways morally. Precision and clarity of terminology is extraordinarily difficult at this juncture. There are certain dispositions or tendencies which have significant consequences for how one lives morally that are correlated with these senses of dependence, gratitude, and so forth; "how one lives morally" not only in terms of what one does, but in one's perspective, outlook, deliberation, and motivation. Again, schematization is dangerous, but it provides an outline for further development. The sense of dependence is correlated with awareness of both finiteness and trust. Finiteness engenders self-criticism, knowledge of limitations, recognition of relativity, reins on claims to moral certitude. Trust engenders confidence even within finiteness; it engenders responsibility as deputies of the creator. The sense of gratitude engenders both a reason to be moral and a movement of the will to do: it provides a reason and an empowering of the will to be imitators of God, to be doing with and for others deeds in accordance with what God has done for man. The sense of repentance engenders again self-criticism, but also a returning toward the moral purposes that are in accord with God's will. The sense of obligation engenders awareness of both duties and opportunities in the moral sphere, and an awareness of the accountability of the community before God. The sense of direction opens the path through the thickets of human moral experience toward an end which is both spiritual and moral at once.

Our task now is to develop briefly, but hopefully in a suggestive way, each of these correlations, and finally to indicate that the disciplines of the spiritual life, individual and collective, are a necessary condition for them all, and thus for the Christian moral life.[4]

A Sense of Dependence

Man's situation is experienced as one of being dependent upon the author, power, and purpose of life, that is, on God. We have not chosen to be; we have come into being. To be sure, there are increasingly precise explanations of how not only we as individuals, but also of how the world itself came into being. The significance of our sense of dependence is not that of a causal explanation of how we and the world have come into being. Rather, it is in the experience of necessarily being reliant upon others than ourselves. We live in reliance upon our parents, upon our families and friends, upon the order of nature, and upon the cultural order that men have developed. In the Christian experience of life, these are experiences which open our awareness of the Holy, of our reliance upon a power and purpose on whom all things depend.

The sense of dependence, it must be admitted, is a morally ambiguous one. It can become oppressive if it entails a coercive domination of the dependent creature by the one on whom he relies. It can stifle initiative and freedom of action by providing subtle life-destroying forms of paternalism. It can foster immaturity. It can paralyze a needed sense of self-confidence, for with it comes awareness of human limitations.

The experience of God in Jewish and Christian traditions is construed, however, in ways which can engender a morally worthy sense of dependence. The creator who brings into being and sustains the world is one whose creation is fundamentally good, whose purposes are the well-being of the world and of persons. Our experience of God creates and preserves a double response: first, that God is God and man is man, that his ways are not our ways, and his thoughts our thoughts; but also that God is worthy of our trust, our confidence, for his power and purpose ultimately favor the fulfillment of creation. Thus our moral lives are lived in awareness of our finiteness, but also in a sense of trust and confidence.

A Sense of Limit

Our awareness of finiteness keeps us from falsely absolutizing any of our moral values and principles, from claiming for ourselves as individuals or for our communities and institutions a dogmatic moral certitude that cannot err, and to which all men are obligated to pay homage. Our finiteness forces upon the community constant critical self-evaluation, constant need for the use of the subjunctive mode, constant willingness to admit moral mistakes. But it also creates the resources of openness to change, the readiness to learn what are the moral requirements under new and changing conditions in our lives and in the circumstances in which we are called to act. In short, it restrains our tendency to impose uncritically upon tomorrow the moral certitudes that fill another time, another cultural place, another historical condition; yet at the same time it evokes the disposition to search for the moral requirements that are concretely related to our conditions, the developments in our society and culture, the path through the entangled moral forest in which we live.

But dependence also evokes trust, or confidence. The biblical pastoral imagery may still resonate the point better than more abstract terms. To be dependent upon God is to be like the sheep who can rely upon the sheep-herder; it is to live in a confidence that there is one who accepts accountability for their conditions, who wills to provide their care, who seeks their well-being. Indeed, as the Christian community is reliant upon God, so are others reliant upon its members, that is, not only is there a ground for confidence, but (to indicate the interrelation of things) obligations to others come into being as we are obligated to God in whom we have confidence. Confidence in God provides a ground for living morally, even in finiteness, with courage, with willingness to risk, with a sense of inner freedom to seek the good and the right even under the conditions of finiteness.

A Sense of Gratitude

It is difficult in our experience of God to speak of dependence without at the same time speaking of gratitude, for the reality on whom we ultimately rely is one whose purposes for his creation are good, who wills the fulfillment of that which has been brought into being. If the experience of an ultimate power were not the experience of a beneficent power, there would be no occasion for gratitude.

There is in this particular aspect of believing and experiencing, as in others, a matter of trust and of hope which is only in part confirmed in human experience, both individually and collectively. Honesty requires the admission that it is difficult to be grateful to God for life when it gives no concrete opportunities for human fulfillment, when those who have been sustaining and meaningful to us are brutally taken away, and when whole communities are suppressed and destroyed by the demonic and destructive activities of men, and indeed, of nature. Conscientious religious men have a quarrel with God, not only after Auschwitz, but after earthquakes, not only in the midst of an unjust war, but after assassinations of leaders who have symbolized hope and justice and peace. Like Job and Jeremiah, we too have occasion to curse God for the day that we were born. To gloss over such human experiences would be to engage in cheap religious rhetoric.

Nonetheless the occasions for gratitude, though they come in small sizes and with less frequency than we might desire, remain as some testimony to the goodness of life and even evoke our celebration. For all our anxieties and struggles, we are grateful to be, to exist. Most of us have been loved beyond our deserving, forgiven when we dared not believe it possible, sustained by the patience of others when they have had grounds to reject us. We have received from the sustaining powers of the sun and the earth, the social order and the culture, more than we could ever claim to deserve. These experiences point to the goodness of God, and they confirm the goodness which we dimly apprehend. And we are grateful.

Gratitude, like dependence, can be oppressive and destructive if it carries also an obligation to cower before those who have given life to us. But it can be liberating if the gifts we receive are given freely, graciously, and in love, rather than as bribes or for the self-glorification of the giver. This is the importance of the experience of God as beneficent and gracious: what is given is freely given in love. It is not merely what we earn by our accomplishments, but it is already there for us to respond to, to appropriate, to participate in.

The experience of gratitude is a pivot on which our awareness of God's goodness turns toward our life as moral men and communities. What is given is not ours to dispose of as if we created it, nor ours to use to serve only our own interests, to mutilate, wantonly destroy, and to deprive others of. Rather, if life is given in grace and freedom and love, we are to care for it and share it graciously, freely, and in love. I believe this is at the heart of religious morality in the Western world; God has been good to us, and in gratitude to him we have reason enough to seek the good of others, and are moved to do so. This is a central theme in the ethics of both Judaism and Christianity: the imitation of God, "Go and do likewise."

A Sense of Repentance

Throughout the recorded history of man's experience of God there are indications of man's need for, and experience of, repentance. We have denied our dependence on God and his goodness, and have used his gifts not only for our own interests, but to destroy and cripple the lives of others. We have assumed dominion over the earth, as we are called to do, but have ignored the dependence that is involved in this vocation: we have been the spoilers rather than the tenders of nature, we have been dictators rather than deputies in our relations to others, we have acted as masters rather than as servants, we have put other gods before the beneficent Creator. In this God is experienced as the Judge. Life is wantonly taken that God wills be treated honestly, the teaching which shows a way of life has been violated, injustice in both the patterns of life and in individual deeds is dissonant with the justice of God. The call of the prophets, of Jesus, of the Jewish and Christian communities is a call to repentance. It strikes a responsive note, for there is already there in man an awareness of the abrasiveness between what he has done and the goodness of God. We experience God as Judge.

The sense of repentance is not only a sense of guilt; it is a call to return to the Lord, to the purposes of personal and common life that are consonant with God's goodness. It is a turning to those ways which sustain and enhance the moral well-being of the human community. Like the sense of gratitude, it grounds not only a reason for moral concern and action (I ought to be reoriented toward those ends which are in accord with God's goodness because God wills and enables not only my forgiveness but my renewal) but it also grounds the will to act. Like the sense of gratitude, it has an existential or sense aspect that has moving power.

A Sense of Obligation

The experience of the reality of God engenders a sense of obligation in persons and in the religious community. In part this arises out of the sense of dependence. To be reliant on God whose goodness is experienced is not only to be grateful to him, but to recognize that one has obligations to him for sustaining and caring for life. But the particular aspect of the experience of God that evokes a sense of obligation is that of an ordering and sustaining power reflected in the ordering and sustaining requirements of creation both in nature and in human societies. In more specifically profane experience we gain the recognition that there are obligations and duties that we must fulfill in order for personal and communal well-being to exist. We know, for example, that if

we do not order the common life in such a way that justice prevails more than injustice, persons and whole communities are deprived of the opportunities to share in the benefits of creation, and in their frustration are rightfully moved to unpeaceful activities for the sake of their common good. We know that the presence of others in our relationships in family, or in academic communities, or anywhere, whose well-being depends upon us is itself a claim of obligation upon us. We recognize that we must conform our actions to that ordering of life that is required if we are not to destroy the natural world upon which our lives and those of future generations depend. While we cannot say that evidence of the need for sustaining and ordering activities and structures is evidence for God's reality, we can say that in our experience of God, we recognize that he is present in such ordering, and that we are obligated to him to attend to the proper ordering of life about us.[5]

We must acknowledge that the language of duties and obligations is often resisted in our current culture. There are ample evidences that many persons believe they ought to do only what they immediately desire to do. And there are good as well as bad reasons to support such an outlook; for the moral life has too frequently been taught to be one of bending one's desires and wills to the extrinsic authority of others, who by reason of their social position or claims to absolute moral truth have dictated what ought to be done and have demanded obedience only by threat of punishment. Consciences have been deformed, spontaneity has been repressed, and morality has been seen to be negative rather than positive in its ultimate aims. The Eichmanns of this world have claimed moral rectitude because they obeyed orders.

A Sense of Just Ordering

In the face of this, a claim is made in the religious moral life that the ordering and sustaining forces to which man is called to conform seek the well-being of persons, human communities, and the whole of creation. We are obligated and accountable to God, the power and purpose who grounds life, as he is experienced and known through the developments in understanding that come through historical experience. Thus order*ing*, rather than order. His purposes do not come with full clarity in a single moment of history but through our participation in life together with our conscientious wrestling with the moral purposes of God. We are obligated to seek to discern God's ordering and sustaining purposes and to shape our moral intentions in their light. We are obligated to seek just orders because God's purposes are just, and justice is a requirement of the fulfillment he wills for man. We are *obligated* to seek justice, even when it obstructs our own immediate interests, or those of our people, or even our generation. To experience God as Orderer and Sustainer is to have a sense of obligation, not only to him, but to the creation he orders and sustains. It is to be morally conscientious in developing and preserving those human orderings which sustain the good of man. It is to be obligated to the one to whom we are grateful, of whose love we are the beneficiaries; it is obligation within the context of grace and love.

A Sense of Direction

If a gross distinction is at all warranted between the Catholic understanding of the moral life and that which came from Luther (Calvin is more complex), it is that for the Lutheran tradition the moral life of the man of faith was an expression of his trust in the graciousness of God and took the form of an inwardly motivated love of the neighbor, whereas in the Catholic tradition man's natural orientation toward his end and his graced orientation toward the vision of God both motivated and directed the moral life of the community. Put even more crudely, one can conceive of moral life in Lutheran terms as being moved from within to do expressive acts of love with little attention given to the object of the act; one can conceive of moral life in Catholic terms as being drawn by the object toward those acts which are appropriate to it, the ultimate object being God.

The experience of God as the end and as the object toward which life is oriented provides a sense of direction. Insofar as each of us has coherence and integrity in our lives, it is in part dependent upon a consistency in his intentions, an orientation of his will toward certain ends. We look forward toward an end, as well as backward toward the antecedents of our actions. We are creators of vision, drawn by aspirations for the future of man; we are creatures of love drawn toward the objects of our deepest desires. In our behavior over a period of time we express to others what our visions and aspirations are, what the objects of our most profound loves are. In the experience of religious men there is an awareness of aspiration to fulfill the vocation of humanity in accord with the purposes of God; there is a love of beings which opens to a love of Being itself, to allude to the vision of Jonathan Edwards. Indeed, we can sing with Charles Wesley of a "Love divine, all loves excelling," which we have received and which evokes in turn our love of God, our orientation toward him. God, as the ultimate object of our love and loves, is the end toward which our lives are oriented, our intention turned, our desires directed. And not only individual loves and desires—since we are members of a community, he is the object of our social actions as well.

Catholic theology has long understood that the wrong object of our intentions and our loves leads to wrong actions in the moral life. If the fundamental purpose of life is to fulfill maximally the desire for sensual pleasure, and persons are means to that fulfillment, life may have a consistency, a sense of direction, but it does not redound to the benefit of the human community, but only to that of the individual. If one is driven by the aspiration to tyrannize over others, to dominate as much of the world as one can, there might well be a consistency, but its end does not lead to the fruits of justice and peace and love. If the ultimate objective of our scientific enterprises is to bring all things under our control, to be God, then our actions are likely to be destructive. We can then learn from the aphorism of Paul Ramsey, "Men ought not to play God until they have learned to become men, and when they have learned to become men they will not play God." The object of our deepest longing, the object of our most pervasive desire, our ultimate end, is to a great degree determinative of the moral worthiness of our acts. It is not that man is a creature oriented toward an end that is important to consider, but that the end toward which he is oriented be the proper one for him and his community.

The experience of the Holy, of the presence of God, in and through others whom we more immediately know and respond to, is central to the religious life. Beyond the good of the human community which we seek is the goodness of God to which we respond in love for him. Beyond our orientation toward the needs of the neighbor is the presence and power of God which is glorified in meeting those needs. The experience of God as the end of all our actions, as the object toward which life is oriented, provides a sense of direction.

If nothing could be affirmed about his reality and characteristics from the religious life of the ages, there would be little we could infer for our moral direction. But in the history of our community's life with him, in the moments in which there is an acute disclosure of him, there is insight into what is ultimately a mystery. To be oriented toward God is to seek those moral ends which are consistent with his reality, with our knowledge of his purposes for creation. As the Johannine epistles make so clear, to love God who loves us, and yet to be creatures whose acts are those of hatred is a lie. Put positively, to be oriented toward God who is loving, who is just, who wills the fulfillment of his creation, is to be oriented in our moral lives toward the needs of near and distant neighbors, to seek justice for all men, to be aimed in our actions toward what benefits the well-being of the human community in its interdependence with nature.

Worship, Meditative Prayer, and Moral Life

I think it is abundantly clear how these explorations will be completed in this lecture. The existential question is how to keep the experience of the Holy alive and vital in our preoccupations with all the specific activities that conscientiousness requires from day to day. It is how to keep that sense of reverence and respect for other persons and for nature alive when most of our relationships are those of use. It is how to maintain a sense of awe in the midst of cultural successes in which we manage and manipulate everything from human genes to arriving on the moon. I hope I have established that the awareness and experience of God is important as a ground for these "senses" of which I have spoken, and that these "senses" are significant for our moral lives. I am not prepared to say with Bishop Kirk that "the *principal* duty of the Christian moralist is to stimulate the spirit of worship in those to whom he addresses himself," but I am prepared to say that worship and meditative prayer are fundamental requisites of the Christian moral life.

It is in worship and meditative prayer (or prayerful meditation, if you will) that the presence of the Holy, the sense of the sacred, the awareness of the transcendent, can be evoked and renewed in individuals and in the community. It is in the freedom from immediate demands that one is open to the reality of God in a compelling and moving way. It is in the focus of attention upon the Reality in whom all realities exist, upon the Power on whom all powers depend, on the events in which God's love has been peculiarly disclosed to men, that the community is renewed and nourished in its spiritual life, and thus in its moral life as well. The senses of dependence, gratitude, repentance, obligation, and direction become atrophied, warped, undernourished, apart from their evocation and refreshment in attentive meditation, and worship of God. This is not to make worship and prayer means to a better moral life. But it is to affirm that apart from worship the spiritual roots of the moral life of the Christian community, the spirit out of which and in which its members act, loses its distinctive character.

Notes

1. Max Kadushin, *Worship and Ethics: A Study in Rabbinic Judaism* (Evanston: Northwestern Univ. Press, 1964).

2. Kenneth E. Kirk, *The Vision of God: The Christian Doctrine of the* Summum Bonum (London: Longmans, Green, 1931) pp. ix–x.

3. In a critique of "ultimate concern" and comparable theories of religion, Julian N. Hartt has written that "We ought to say that [man] is not really religious unless he feels that some power is bearing down on him, unless, that is, he believes that he must do something about divine powers who have done something to him."—Julian N. Hartt, *A Christian Critique of American Culture* (New York: Harper and Row, 1967) p. 52.

4. Given an opportunity for further development, I would extend the discussion to further refinements of the affective, volitional, and intellective consequences. Indeed, the relation of believing in and experiencing God to human actions is central to the enterprise, and requires sophisticated analysis. Julian N. Hartt's Cardinal Bea Lecture provides a suggestive way of proceeding by arguing that belief in God is a "construing belief": "A construing belief is rather more a *believing* than it is a finished product commonly suggested by *belief.* Thus a construing belief is an interpretation of some aspect of experience. But may also be a program, a mandate, as it were, for interpreting all of experience and the world. Such I take *believing in God* to be." "*It means an intention to relate to all things in ways appropriate to their belonging to God.*"—Julian N. Hartt, "Encounter and Inference in our Awareness of God," in Joseph P. Whelan, S.J. (ed.),

The God Experience (New York: Paulist/Newman Press, 1971), pp. 30–59 (quotations from p. 49 and p. 52).

5. This sentence compacts a whole argument similar to that made by John E. Smith, in *Experience and God* (New York: Oxford Univ. Press, 1968), in his discussion of the functions of the traditional proofs for the existence of God, pp. 121–157. "The Absolutely Exalted is grasped by the reflecting self able to understand its own experience; only through understanding and interpreting can the self discover in these signs [awareness of the contingent, awareness of death, awareness of freedom and responsibility] the presence of a reality whose nature it is to be present and directly experienced, but not immediately known" (p. 157).

13

Liturgy and Ethics: Some New Beginnings

Donald E. Saliers

Questions concerning Christian ethics and the shape of the moral life cannot be adequately understood apart from thinking about how Christians worship. Communal praise, thanksgiving, remembrance, confession and intercession are part of the matrix which forms intention and action. This matrix of personal agency constitutes a focal point in any investigation of the liturgical life of a religious community. Concepts such as remembering, praising and giving thanks to God rightly belong to the study of liturgy, and have come increasingly to occupy the forefront of research and constructive work in liturgical theology. But there has to date been a paucity of dialogue between liturgical studies and ethics, even though it seems obvious that there are significant links between liturgical life, the confession of faith, and the concrete works which flow from these.

How we pray and worship is linked to *how* we live—to our desires, emotions, attitudes, beliefs and actions. This is the normative claim of all communities intending to be faithful to

Scripture and to the inner norms of the Church's declaration of faith. Yet how we pray and worship is, empirically considered, often radically in conflict with how we live. Such is the description of what is the case sociologically. Upon this gap between the "rhetoric" and the "reality" of liturgical worship we have recently had no end of commentary. In fact, most views of the connection between liturgy and ethics picture the relation as external or causal. This approach is reinforced by the easy assumptions of sociology and psychology of religion in our time.

Our question is, therefore, how to effect the dialogue between liturgical studies and ethics. This essay is one attempt to open the conversations at a level beyond the recital of the slogan: *lex orandi, lex est credendi.* The fundamental conviction undergirding these pages is that, properly considered, there is an internal, *conceptual* link between liturgy and ethics. At the foundations of Christian faith and throughout Jewish teachings, liturgy and ethics are bound together internally. That is,

---

This article is excerpted from Journal of Religious Ethics 7 *(Fall 1979): 173–189.*

the link is not causal and extrinsic, but conceptual and intrinsic. Our problem is how to articulate this without doing injustice to the complexity of other relationships between liturgy and ethics which can be described.

A second assumption undergirding these pages is that norms and practices in ethics are never *simply* ethical. The concretization of the moral life requires a vision of a world, and the continuing exercise of recalling, sustaining and reentering that picture of the cosmos in which norms and practices have meaning and point. In short, the possibility of religious ethics (or, for that matter, of any significant societal understanding and practice of the good) rests upon available *mythoi*—stories and narratives of human existence in which a picture of the moral good and associated ideas are expressed. In particular, Christian moral intention and action is embedded in a form of life which is portrayed and shaped by the whole biblical story. Such a narrative understanding of the world found in Hebrew and Christian Scripture provides a way of placing human life *in conspectu dei,* before the face of God. Such narratives are not ethical systems or lists of rules and principles as such; rather they portray qualities of being-before-God which are focused upon features of God such as holiness, righteousness, and lovingkindness.

It may be objected that a description of the moral life can indeed be given in complete independence from liturgical considerations. This may be empirically possible. But if this is done, certain essentials fall away; indeed, certain conceptual confusions concerning religious ethics result. Thus my central thesis is: *the relations between liturgy and ethics are most adequately formulated by specifying how certain affections and virtues are formed and expressed in the modalities of communal prayer and ritual action. These modalities of prayer enter into the formation of the self in community.* Beliefs about God and world and self which characterize a religious life are dramatized and appropriated in the mode of the affections and dispositions focused in liturgical occasions.

I

Worship is something Christians do together, not just because of religious duty, but because it is *their way* of remembering and expressing their life unto God. But it is also a characterizing activity. It takes time and place and people. When worship occurs, people are characterized, given their life and their fundamental location and orientation in the world. Worship characterizes human beings who recall and give expression to a story about the world. The language of this story teaches us to describe all creatures in the world as God's. Worship forms and conveys the awareness of God and the orders of creation and history.

To put the point in a slightly different way, worship both forms and expresses persons in the beliefs, the emotions and the attitudes appropriate to the religious life. It shapes the Christian affections, and provides a way of expressing the perceived realities of existence as received by those who are at the disposal of such beliefs, emotions and attitudes. In any adequate explication of the meaning and point of Christian worship, both the forming and expressing side must be made clear.

Worship, then, is something Christians do together, not just from religious duty (though this may be a sociological fact), but because it is the primary communal mode of remembering and expressing the Christian faith and the Christian story. In the very activity of re-presenting and rehearsing features of existence described in the Scriptures, worshippers articulate their fundamental relations to one another and to the world. Worship is thus necessarily normative. At the same time, not all who participate in its language and action are shaped by it. This is a remark about the concept of "understanding" the world in and through the Christian story. Not all who say the words and participate in the stylized activities fully understand what it is to say and do these things and to *mean* them. Faith is related to "understanding," but in complex ways.

In corporate worship, Christians engage in activities which articulate and shape how they are to be disposed toward the world. Those who say they love God but who are *not* disposed to love and serve the neighbor are misunderstanding the words and actions of worship. In *I John* we read that anyone who claims to love God and hates the neighbor is a liar. That is a conceptual remark and not an empirical observation about what Christians may or may not do most of the time. It links saying, doing and understanding in worship with a way of life. "Not everyone who says to me, Lord, Lord, will enter the kingdom." To speak of and to address God in the vocative of prayer means to undertake a certain way of existing, and to be a certain way towards other persons. This linkage between learning to address God in worship and learning to be disposed toward the world and other human beings "in his name" is easily neglected.

To this point, we have spoken of prayer and worship interchangeably. Obviously, not everything in worship is, strictly speaking, a prayer. There are lessons, hymns, sermons, gestures of giving and receiving, acts of reconciliation and exhortations. But surely the heart of corporate worship is prayer. We can learn what to say about the nature of Christian worship by thinking about the range and scope of what it means to pray. Prayer covers the entire range of human experience, from extremity to extremity, and much everydayness between. The Lord who teaches the church to pray himself ranged from "hallowed be thy name" to "My God, why?" The psalms provide the great common hymnal and prayerbook for the praise of God, as well as describe experience of those struggling to live with God in faith.

Regarded from a human point of view, prayer is the activity in which human beings explore their life "unto God." It is much more than words. In uttering the words of prayer, we are doing something, performing an act. To thank God, to praise God, to confess, to intercede—all these are ways of gesturing the self in and through words. What is done with the words is part of the meaning of what is said. Unless we grasp the point of saying such things to God and about God, we will not have fully understood the language of Scripture and theology, or at least its fundamental *telos*. Let us recall briefly, then, something of the primary range of prayer so that we may better describe the meaning and point of worship.

The primary mode of prayer in all Jewish and Christian liturgy begins in praise and thanksgiving. The formulary of the Jewish *berakah* underlies the gesture of common prayer: "Blessed art Thou, O Lord our God. . . ." This form of words speaks God's name in gratitude and praise for who God is, and for the specific occasions in the world given to us. Inherent in this mode of praying is a fundamental receptivity to the world as God's domain—a world bestowed. Liturgically we may wish to distinguish the logic of praising from the logic of giving thanks; but for our purposes they can be assimilated under the more generic *berakah,* or blessing prayer.

Christian eucharistic prayers display their origin and shape in this primordial acknowledgement of God.

The prayer of praise and thanksgiving is intrinsic to understanding the nature of God within the religious life; it is essential to human self-understanding as well. In learning to pray this way, human beings are disposed in gratitude toward the world and their place in the orders of existence. Such praying mitigates against the natural fear of regarding everything as having strings attached. So far as prayer is first and last speaking God's name in thanks and praise, it is required for truthfulness in Christian life and theology. Worship is, in this sense, a continual practice in naming God, thereby keeping an essential aspect of the concept of deity in both thought and affection: God is the giver of life, the source of good.

But prayer is also recalling and retelling. Prayer in corporate worship recalls who God is and what God has done. It is grounded in the corporate memories of the religious community. Huub Oosterhuis (1968:8) has put this point well.

> When the bible prays, the whole of creation is listed and the whole of God's history with man is brought up again. When we pray, with the bible, we appeal to creation and to the covenant. We call God to mind and remind him who he is and what he has done. What God used to mean . . . in the past includes a promise for the future, the promise that he will mean something for us as well, that he will be someone for us.

So prayer is praise and thanksgiving: the acknowledgement of God for who God is. But secondly, prayer recalls and re-presents the story of God's mighty deeds in relationship to the world and to humanity.

In the classical eucharistic prayers of the first six centuries, both East and West, the shape and substance of prayer is *anamnetic*. That is, Christians give thanks to God in the action of the eucharist or Lord's Supper precisely by reciting the story of creation and redemption in the vocative of addressing God.[1] Such prayers of great thanksgiving are recitals of the *mirabilia dei,* rendering the past as present: "Do this, for my *anamnesis.*"

Thirdly, prayer is acknowledgement and confession of who we are in God's sight. For to address God and *mean* what we say is to recognize our status. Praying thus explores and continually reveals the infinite qualitative difference between God and human beings. A central paradigm for this feature of communal worship is found in the language of Isaiah in the temple. In response to the vision of God's transcendent holiness he exclaims, "Woe is me, for I am a man of unclean lips, and I dwell in the midst of a people of unclean lips. . . ." This same modality of prayer is found in various confessional sequences and is reflected in the Collect for Purity, "cleanse the thoughts of our hearts by the inspiration of thy Holy Spirit, that we may perfectly love Thee. . . ."

Confessing sin and untruth to God occasions insight into the indelibly human features of the moral life. If praising and thanking are essential to our humanity, so is confession. The language of confessing unto God gives shape to our own self-description: "We have followed too much the devices and desires of our own hearts, we have offended against thy holy laws. . . ." "Lord, have mercy upon us." What interests us here is the manner in which descriptions and ascriptions of God are intrinsic features of the language of repentance, desire, praise and longing. The emotions of the believer—sorrow over sin, gratitude, joy in the forgiveness of God—are made clear in and through language which attributes holiness and mercy to God. Praying brings an entry into the language such that dispositions to feel, intend and to act are formed.

Finally, though not exhaustively, liturgical prayer is found in the mode of intercession. Praying for others requires looking clearly and honestly at the world as it is, and entails awareness of the suffering of others. In interceding for the world, the liturgical community identifies with others and, at the very least, is formed toward pity and compassion. In this sense, communal prayer, rightly exercised, covers the entire range of circumstances and events, good and evil. As a corporate act of intercession, praying holds the world in its actuality, before God. It is a worldly activity. The strenuousness of true intercessory prayer results in a truthful perception of the world's moral ambiguity. We will return in more detail to the relationship of intercessions and the moral imagination in section III.

Christian worship, through a complex symbolic pattern of words and gestures in its ritual actions, both forms and expresses dispositions belonging to the life of faith in God. These dispositions show a double aspect discerned in the four modes of prayer just observed. The affections take God as their ground and object, and they are ingredient in the moral regard toward the neighbor and toward the world as the arena of God's activity. Thus, love of God and neighbor are correlate in the very forms of language and action addressed to God—especially so in the eucharistic context. Such dispositions are requisite features of understanding who God is and what God commands from those who worship him. In tracing out the grammar of the language and action of specific liturgies—*e.g.,* rites of

initiation, daily offices, rites for marriage and burial, the eucharist, *et al.*—we begin to encompass the inner logic of the Christian life.

Specific rites also express the community's life before God and thus bring to consciousness a wide range of life experience in the world of lived moral conflict. There are tensions between the meanings articulated in such rites and the life-meanings which persons bring to worship. On the one hand, there are normative patterns of affection and virtue commended and formed in the liturgical prayer of the community. As God is holy, so the worshippers are called to be holy. On the other hand, the worshippers' intentions and actions fall short, and their affections never become pure motives for well-doing in everyday life. There is always a gap between the ideal values inherent in the prayers and rites and their existential realization. But just at this crucial point, a dialectic is built into adequate forms of communal prayer. Recognition of the gap is itself part of what is formed and expressed in the affections belonging to repentance.[2]

II

The Christian life can be characterized as a set of affections and virtues. There are limits and possible misunderstandings in such a characterization, but for purposes of drawing attention to the internal relations between liturgy and ethics, it is essential. From the outset we must conceive virtues and affections in their specific determination in response to the person and work of Jesus Christ. The Christian moral life is the embodiment of those affections and virtues which are intentional orientation of existence in Jesus Christ.

We cannot understand the moral life here

simply as conformity to a set of rules, even though teachings and rules for appropriate attitudes and actions are involved. Nor is it sufficient to speak of the imitation of the pattern of behavior given in the gospel portraits of Jesus. Neither the achievement of moral ideals *per se* nor the adoption of a view of life adequately accounts for the shape of the Christian moral life. An actual reorientation of sensibility and intentional acts is involved, as well as a new self-understanding and a "world-picture." How we understand ourselves in the world and how we ought to live in relation to society, the neighbor and the self—all these are ingredient in our conception of the Christian moral life.

Affections and virtues grounded in the saving mystery of Christ constitute a way of being moral. Thus gratitude to God, joy in the saving works of Christ, hope, penitence and love of God and neighbor are all grounded in the narrative of who Jesus was and is. The exercise of such affections requires a continual re-entry of the person into the narrative and the teachings which depict the identity of Jesus Christ. As I have proposed, the modalities of prayer and liturgical action are the rule-keeping activities of the affections. Liturgy provides both a rehearsal of the narratives and a continual re-embedding of persons in the language of faith.

In a recent study, Stanley Hauerwas (1975) has argued persuasively that the continuity and identity of self embodied in our character has profound moral significance. The individual Christian character, he contends (Hauerwas, 1975:210), "is formed by his association with the community that embodies the language, rituals, and moral practices from which this particular form of life grows." The heart of the matter in the form of the Christian life is coming to understand who God is and what his intentions for human beings are

as revealed in Jesus Christ. This coming to understand is precisely what good liturgy and faithful communal prayer provide. Hauerwas (1975:213–214) borrows a phrase from John Dewey—"deliberate rehearsal"—to express the necessary process of bringing every aspect of character into harmony with God's intention for us in Christ. This phrase, I contend, is an apt description of the imaginative power of good liturgy for the formation of character. The various modalities of prayer discussed above are linked with the deliberate rehearsal of the great narratives of creation and redemption in Christian liturgy. Patterns of prayer, reading, proclamation and sacramental action are precisely such occasions of communal rehearsal of the affections and virtues befitting "life in Christ." This is no mere *mimesis;* no simple "imitation of Christ." Rather such worship is best understood as a participation in the symbols of faith which is effected and signified by the words and actions of Christ.

Responding to some remarks on the fundamental symbols of faith made by H. Richard Niebuhr, Hauerwas (1975:233) speaks of the "enlivening of the imagination by images that do justice to the central symbol of our faith." The primary formation and expression of the enlivened Christian imagination is worship. Normatively considered, good liturgy is the fundamental imaginal framework of encounter with God in Christ which forms intentions in and through the affections which take God in Christ as their goal and ground.

Yet it is also true that Christian liturgical prayer must respond to a world in which moral ambiguity abounds. Archbishop Anthony Bloom (1966:123) has reminded us that "Prayer is not simply an effort which we can make the moment we intend to pray; prayer must be rooted in our life and if our life contradicts our prayers, or if our prayers have nothing to do with our life, they will never be alive nor real." Not only does prayer shape intentions in accordance with the central symbols of faith, it must be accountable to the way we make actual decisions.

The connection between liturgy and the ethics of character we have been sketching leads to the inner connection between praying and being. How honestly such a form of life confronts the suffering and gladness of the world is something which liturgy itself cannot guarantee. Spiritual self-deception is always possible because praying is always done in the human sphere of forces. Prayer and praise in heaven, we may assume, no longer fall prey to deceit. In hell, self-deception has become a way of life. Prayer that seeks withdrawal from the realm of human forces—social, economic and otherwise—and seeks only to enjoy the symbols of faith, fails to exercise fully the religious affections as motives in well-doing. To be moved by the love of God in Christ requires engagement with the principalities and powers of the world.

A powerful expression of this point is given in the high priestly prayer of Jesus which appears in John's gospel. In addressing the Father Jesus says, "I do not pray that thou shouldst take them out of the world, but that thou shouldst keep them from the evil one" (Jn 17:15). The prayer of Christian liturgy faces the world's ambiguity and evil. But it is precisely in the world that God is to be glorified by doing the works of Christ. Worship ascribes glory to God alone; but unless the glorification is shown in works of justice, mercy and love faithful to God's commands, Christ's liturgy is not fully enacted. At times the tension between cultic and ethical activity must be rediscovered. At other times, their coinherence and mutual reciprocity must be

shown forth. The glory and holiness of God is shown *both* in the otherness of God as the object of prayer and worship, *and* in the servanthood of those who are formed in the central symbol of the faith.

In our time, there is a tendency to define prayer primarily by its effects and by our own consequent actions in the world. The prayerful life is shown by its fruits, though it can never be reduced to its results. When praying becomes a special instrument for getting things done, such a conception is not far from magic. A one-sided concern for the effectiveness of prayer leads, in Urban Holmes' (1977) phrase, to a spirituality of "prayer as production."

Despite such misunderstandings, prayer and worship do respond to a broken and often inexplicable world. Christian prayer is beholding the world in light of the narrative, told, enacted and pondered in Scripture, proclamation and liturgical rites. It is linked both to the raw needs of conflict and to the world beheld as the arena of God's activity. The question may not be "to what?" does prayer respond but, "to whom?"

The issue is whether we pray what we mean and mean what we pray without being drawn into the way in which God views the world. The meaning of praying is not a simple matter of saying the words. To pray is to become a living text before God. In this sense, meaning what we pray requires more than the onset of lively emotions. Meaning what we pray involves sharing a form of life in which the affections and dispositions are oriented toward God. Discovering the meaning of what we pray in communal worship includes the discovery of our loves, fears, hopes, and the situations over which we will weep and rejoice together.

Prayer begins in gratitude, and its constancy

in season and out of season is linked to the constancy of its object—God's love in Christ. As the Psalmist sings, "For his love endureth forever." This holds, I think, for all Christian prayer. To pray is to give oneself to the Christian story in such a way that there is an internal link between the emotions and virtues exercised in that life and the meaning of the texts, prayer and symbols enacted in the rites. Prayer will be on occasion, and perhaps for long periods of time, dry and "meaningless" in the popular sense of that term. Where affectivity is lacking, we may lose sight of the story, and its power and reach may be in eclipse for such periods in one's life. Such a lack of meaning cannot itself be overcome by cultivating "feelings" apart from recovering the depth of the story in allowing our moral lives to be qualified and shaped by it. The "meaninglessness" here must always be met with a waiting, an attending to the Word of God.

To pray to God in the various modalities entailed in communal worship requires living in light of the Christian Gospel such that we may rejoice whatever the circumstances and persist in hope. To pray constantly is to be disposed in this world before the face of God. Prayer is thus not an *aid,* psychological or otherwise, to the living of a spiritually healthy or ethically sensitive life. It is not a motivating set of techniques. Rather, prayer is part of having a life formed in joy, gratitude, awe and compassion. These capacities, which one learns to call "gifts" when they are rightly understood, are directed toward God and all God's creation. We respond to the world and to others because we behold them before the face of God. Yet God is never "contained" in prayer. After all this has been said, the connection between liturgy and ethics is qualified by the fact that liturgy is an eschatological gesture and utterance—it is proleptic and does not presume to "possess" or to "dispense" God.

III

We have explored how the prayer of Christian liturgy is formative and expressive of the ethics of Christian character. Liturgy as cultus must bear within itself a prophetic self-awareness because *how* and *what* we pray is also a response to the world as the arena of moral ambiguity and agency. It is time to render an implicit question explicitly: to what extent ought the church as liturgical community make moral and ethical transformation of persons and society the purpose of worship? Is the ultimate thing to be said about the liturgy of Jesus Christ that it is service and love toward mankind? The answer, of course, can only be framed in terms of the double focus of liturgy—the glorification of God and the sanctification of man. The glory of God is shown both in right praise and in the servanthood of those who worship in the name of Jesus Christ.

Let us consider a specific mode of prayer-action which raises these questions most clearly, namely, the intercessions or "prayers of the faithful."

The restoration and renewal of the prayers of the people in recent liturgical reforms helps focus a central reality: Christ is in the midst of his people praying with and for them. Here is an explicit mode of prayer in which the attention is upon the needs of the world. This mode of prayer, as we established in the previous section of the essay, comes in response to the divine identification with the lowly, the suffering and the forsaken. The prayers of intercession are themselves a declaration that God in Christ identifies with the suffering needs of a fallen humanity. Here is a specific place of formation of identity as those who pray with Christ the intercessor.

Without prayers for others, our worship cannot discern the fullness of how God is to be glorified by doing his works in the world. The presence and self-giving of God in the liturgy of Word and sacraments cannot be disassociated from the neighbor in need. St. Paul makes this clear, for example, in his criticism of the church at Corinth whose eucharists were a profanization of the body and blood precisely because they did not attend to another. To forget the others in the presence of Christ's self-giving is to participate unworthily. To recognize Christ's power and presence in Word and eucharist is to confess his presence in the hurt and suffering of the neighbor as well. The former, rightly acknowledged and praised, discloses the latter. In this sense, intercessory prayer is linked to the continuing action of Christ both in liturgy and in the world. This link gives us an insight into the relation between true liturgical spirituality and Christian moral vision.

Prayers for others in the context of Christian worship show forth a fundamental Christological orientation: As Christ had compassion, so must we; as he encountered the brokenness of others, so must we; as he loved even in the face of death, so must we. In these specific ways we are being formed, not simply in the rhetoric of the prayer texts (whether liturgical or "free"), but in a way of regarding the world. The meaning and direction of our affections is always two-fold, toward those in need whom God in Christ loves; and with Jesus who prays in our midst—the mediator and high priest. Intercessions are the practice and exercise of being turned to discern and act in the direction in which God's love looks and moves.

Four aspects of intercessory prayer constitute its "grammar" and require rediscovery in every age. First, we encounter dimensions of ourselves as praying with and for others. Prayer, for the early church, was never an isolated action. The notion of "closet" prayer—the interior prayer of the purified heart—focuses upon the integrity of praying not its personal privacy. Praying was always in community, even when it was prayer alone. The distinction between individualistic devotional prayer and the church's common prayer is foreign to the early church.

Prayer for others requires a truthfulness about who we are in relation to others as well as a vulnerability born of empathy. There are religious communities of prayer where counterfeit vulnerability of self-indulgence abounds. Spiritual pulse-taking can and should never substitute for being disposed in love toward others. Thus, encounter with these dimensions of the self are part of understanding and praying.

Secondly, only in and through solidarity with those in need can we mean what we pray in intercession. In exercising the human capacity for identification with others, this mode of praying can grow in maturity and insight into God's grace. The meaning of prayers for others, therefore, is not so much the style of praying as it is the manner of being disposed in compassion.

Thirdly, we gain a moral intentionality in addressing the world to God. We ask God to remember those for whom we pray. We cannot simply "enjoy" the forms of prayer and the affections of empathy. Those who pray must learn, outside the rooms of prayer, the reality of commending others to the grace and mercy of God. The development of this capacity can only be learned over time and circumstances as we engage the needs of others. The most difficult thing is that those who pray are called to trust God beyond their own highest capacity for pity and compassionate service. To intercede is to be attentive to God's hidden ways with the world.

Finally, to intercede without allowing the ministries of the community to be visibly represented in the body renders prayers inadequate to their intent and object. "The community of the people of God," Karl Barth (1963:38) reminds us, "speaks to the world by the fact of its very existence as a community of prayer." It serves the world and speaks "by the simple fact that it prays for the world." Thus is manifest the *reason* for praying—Christ goes before us and promises to be encountered in the hurt and the needy. Where encountering the reality of human need is *not* part of the experiential background in intercessory prayer, no amount of lovely text—said or sung—will suffice.

Intercessory forms of prayer force us to recognize that religious faith must be lived in the world of power, conflicting passions and moral ambiguity. In our age and cultural circumstances prayer as praise must be connected with prayer as love of neighbor. This, we may observe, is the perennial tension between prayer and action in the Christian life. But our argument implies two further points relevant to this tension. First, the stress on love of neighbor does not entail the diminishment of love and adoration of God. Love of God and love of neighbor are not two sides of a balancing scale of affections. The commandment cannot be taken this way. The summation of law and prophets does not put love of God and neighbor in inverse ratio one to the other.

Secondly, we should not assume that the tension between prayer and action is the same as the contrast between contemplation and action. This identifies prayer completely with "contemplative prayer." It is far more illuminating to speak of the contemplative and envisioning dimensions of all genuine Christian prayer in the liturgy.

Here we see that tensions are built into the Christian moral life shaped by common prayer. This is because the concept of praying is internally connected with the call to holiness at the heart of the Christian gospel. This constitutes the focal point of Christian existence: Christ's own life is one of active prayer and prayerful action. It is thus fitting to speak of his whole life as a prayer—a continual self-offering in love and obedience to the Father. In exploring what Christ's life (liturgy) signifies, we ponder anew the necessity of understanding prayer and action not in opposition, but in tension required by living particular moments in the stream of life which is oriented toward the full stature of God in Christ.

Prayer is itself one activity among others within the Christian life. So there is a temporal contrast: now the community prays and worships, now it engages in works of love and mercy. But this assumes a connection between faith and works which is conceptual and not merely causal or consequential. In light of our thesis concerning liturgy and the formation of Christian affections, faith without works is not so much "dead" as it is self-preoccupied and self-stultifying. Holy affections which do not become the well-spring and motive for action turn in upon themselves; in short, they are not holy affections.

It is crucial to mark a contrast between being and doing within the Christian life. But we also need a contrast between the prayerful life and a life without prayer. These are not conflicting but complementary contrasts. The pervasiveness of prayer can be construed as a mark of Christian moral maturity only insofar as it expresses a whole-hearted orientation of life in the person and work of Christ. We are led therefore to extend the concept of prayer (and worship) from its application as specific acts of piety to its application over the whole of one's life. As the early patristical theologians are fond of saying, the whole of the life of a saint is one continuous prayer. We began with praying in the ordinary sense of specific acts of worship and find ourselves necessarily drawn to a sense of prayer which encompasses all of one's feeling, knowing and doing. "The glory of God is the living man." Thus Irenaeus of Lyons asserted once for all against future heresies the fundamental truth we have been exploring in our reflections on the intercessory modes of prayer.

Christian prayer in each of its modes— praise, thanksgiving, confession, intercession, and others—manifests the double focus of glorification and sanctification. Thus we cannot oppose the joy of contemplating heavenly things (the enjoyment of the divine moral excellency of God) and the grim courage of active mission in the world. Both contain a joy which flows forth from having one's affections fixed upon the creating and redeeming self-giving of God.

Human persons are formed in myriad ways. But in the Christian life, the mystery of redemption in the death and resurrection of Christ is the basis and source of the formation of the person. The orientation and process of maturation is therefore never a matter of adopting right behavior or conforming to *a priori* systems of ruled actions. The qualities of formed character and the exercise of the virtues require the on-going deliberate rehearsal of the identifying stories and actions of God. What remains to be done is the detailed analysis and specification of how the context of liturgy—rightly prayed and celebrated—is the school of the affections; and, more particularly, what constitutes faithful and unfaithful liturgy in the formation of the Christian life.

When liturgy is regarded primarily as a means to moral exhortation or ethical motivation, it loses its essential character as praise, thanksgiving and anamnetic enactment of the mystery of faith. Instrumentalist definitions of worship, whether Protestant or Roman Catholic, founder upon this rock. As it has been observed, when the Church marries the spirit of the age, she will be left a widow in the next generation.

Surely the worship of God in forms which call forth obedience to the Gospel and open ears and hearts to the prophetic Word of God forces the issue upon us. Worship is not merely *cultus*—it cannot be and remain faithful to its ground and goal. In the New Testament it is clear that all of Christian existence is a rendering of service unto God. The sacrifice of praise and thanksgiving is already ingredient in the formation of moral dispositions. In fact, the biblical concept of sacrifice is more than a merely cultic concept—it has immense ethical ramifications. There is a unity of *leitourgia* and *diakonia*—of worship and the doing of good works—implied by the narrative recital of God's covenant and history with the world. The focal point remains God's gracious turning toward humankind. The human response of worship articulates a glorification of God in and through all that is human.

All this being said, it is stubbornly the case that the liturgical life of the Christian community cannot be reduced to ethical implications of the cultus, either. Liturgy is the non-utilitarian enactment of the drama of the divine-human encounter. At the heart of this is our response to the divine initiative and to the divine goodness into which the prayerful life is drawn. As James Gustafson has remarked

(1975:75), ". . . when one's being is rightly tending toward or intending God, when one's love is rightly directed, there will also be a right intention and direction of specific projects. Thus, what one is by virtue of God's creation, . . . can become realized to some extent in the moral life as one has the right objects of love." How the life of worship and prayer helps to give direction toward the good and toward those right ends has been, in part, the burden of these remarks.

Notes

1. A detailed study of these eucharistic prayers yields a rich set of data for our inquiry. The recital of creation and redemption serves to portray the world in which human response to God has point and meaning. Different liturgical traditions or families of eucharistic prayers show differing relations between praise of God for creation and specific thanksgiving for the works of redemption. The West, generally speaking, concentrates upon the redemptive work of Christ, while the Eastern liturgies accent the glory of God and the extent of God's power and splendor in the created order.

2. This is why reformed rites in our time must continue to struggle with penance and confession of sins, even though we have rightly restored in several traditions (Roman Catholic, Episcopalian, Methodist and Lutheran), the non-penitential and joyous sense of thanksgiving in the texts and actions of the eucharistic rites.

14

Basic Freedom and Morality[1]

Josef Fuchs, SJ

The freedom we have in mind here is not the psychological freedom of choice nor moral freedom nor Christian freedom, but that contemporary concept called *basic freedom (liberté fondamentale*[2]) or *transcendental freedom* (K. Rahner[3]).

As regards *freedom of choice,* modern psychology attempts to sound the depths of the human ego in order to discover the ultimate principle that governs man's actions and the aims he pursues, and the extent to which these aims and actions are freely chosen. Basic freedom, on the other hand, denotes a still more fundamental, deeper-rooted freedom, not immediately accessible to psychological investigation. This is the freedom that enables us not only to decide freely on particular acts and aims but also, by means of these, to determine ourselves totally as persons and not merely in any particular area of behaviour. It is clear that man's freedom of choice and his basic freedom are not simply two different psychological freedoms. As a person, man is free. But this freedom can, of course, be considered under different aspects. A man can, in one and the same act, choose the object of his choice (freedom of choice) and by so doing determine himself as a person (basic freedom).

Our inquiry into basic freedom obviously presupposes the conviction that it is not the good and the evil aims and actions in themselves or the measure of good in man's exercise of his freedom of choice that determine his goodness or wickedness. Here the decisive factor is rather the extent to which an individual as a person, in his freely chosen good or evil aims and actions, determines himself as a whole, i.e., in basic freedom, thus determining himself as good or evil, and ordering his aims and acts in accordance with that determination. The question of basic freedom, therefore, ultimately becomes the question of the moral goodness and wickedness of man.[4] It will be dealt with here under four heads:

I. Basic freedom and man as person.
II. Basic freedom and freedom of choice.
III. Basic freedom and self-awareness.
IV. Basic freedom and grace.

This article is excerpted from Human Values and Christian Morality *(Dublin: Gill and Macmillan Ltd., 1970) 92–111.*

I. Basic Freedom and Man as Person

Basic freedom stands for our freedom in so far as it enables us to ascertain not only the morality of particular aims and actions but also the morality of the person who pursues or performs them. It brings home to us, accordingly, the full meaning of morality. Our first task, then, will be to inquire into the relation between basic freedom and man as person.

The ultimate objective of our inquiry will be to obtain an answer to the question: what does the freedom of myself as a *person* amount to, over and above my actions and my aims? Granted that my ego, that dynamic unity which is myself, is more than the sum of my acts and aims and that the latter are but the fitful expression and manifestation of the ego and not the personal ego itself, what is the morality of my personal ego, over and above the morality of my various actions?

Individual moral acts and aims are the object of moral knowledge and volition on the part of the person who performs or pursues them; they proceed from the person's objective, categorical knowledge and volition. But the personal ego can function not only in objective, categorical knowledge and volition but is itself—as subject—knowledge and freedom. For knowledge and freedom, so far as I myself as a person am concerned, are inextricable parts of that integrated, dynamic organism. A person is conscious of himself as a subject without reflecting on himself as an object. As a subject a person is committed in freedom without realizing himself in action as an object. This self-consciousness—consciousness of himself—and freedom, of the person as a subject, evidently lie much deeper than the subconscious or the unconscious as understood by psychologists, because the sub-

conscious and the unconscious are categorically and objectively defined.

What then do we mean by self-consciousness and self-determination of the person as a subject? Now this person with which we are dealing is the human person and the human person is not a monad turned in upon, and locked up in, itself. On the contrary the human person is by its very nature oriented towards other human persons, obviously not to ward them off but to enter into relations with them. (We can be sure that no man is an island!) Self-realization in openness towards others—love—is the true moral commitment of the basic freedom of the person; withdrawal into oneself is negative self-commitment. Finally, basic freedom enables us, indeed presses us, to place ourselves as persons unreservedly at the disposal of him who has the greatest claim on us, because he—who is God—created us as persons.

The reason why *basic* freedom or *transcendental* freedom is so called will now be clear. The free self-commitment of ourselves as persons is more than any particular action or actions and more than the sum of them; it underlies them, permeates them, and goes beyond them, without ever being actually one of them.

A man's free and basic self-commitment, consisting ultimately of the gift or refusal of the self in love to God, should not be equated with any particular moral act. The act of basic freedom is the realization of the person as a whole. He means to follow out his intention to its ultimate depth and intensity, and to build into it every particular personal development in time and space, past and future. Love of God—the positive act of basic freedom—would not amount to this effort to commit the entire person if the person were content with a minimum of self-giving, or were indifferent to past moral failure or to conversion to concrete good behaviour in the future, or took no trouble to integrate the resistant forces of human concupiscence. Self-realization in basic freedom is thus a total act, in so far as it means the self-determination of the person as a whole in face of God's total demand upon him. On the other hand this self-commitment of the person as a whole in basic freedom is always immature and imperfect, not a complete self-commitment of the whole person, since it can become deeper and more intensive, has to be maintained and made manifest in countless different situations, and has to prevail against the still continuing hostile tendencies of the concupiscent ego. Similarly the negative use of basic freedom, the closing of the self against God, is still not a total disposal of the entire person. Here too not every possibility of self-determination is realized, not all of the past is worked through and absorbed, not all the tendencies towards good that remain are integrated. And when will the realization of the person as a whole, for good or ill, finally be total, complete, and thus definitive?

One should not think of the person in his basic freedom as pure possibility, as if one day he discovered his basic freedom and with it the possibility of self-determination and then was able to consider, while in possession of himself simply as a free person, how he should commit himself. No one exists simply in the *possibility* of basic free decision, since an adult has already come to freedom, a freedom that is already in action, has become a self already freely engaged.[5] Basic freedom exists only in the concrete act. The mature adult who has grown into created freedom, has already decided upon the meaning of what life

requires of him, whether to be open or closed to the absolute demand God makes of him. This basic freedom of a person as a whole in face of the Absolute should not be confused with freedom of choice in particular moral acts. It must be understood that we are basically free always and only as loving or sinning —but loving or sinning freely.

Accordingly we are never undecided about the ultimate meaning of our existence, which is either a total surrender of the self to the Absolute, or a refusal of such surrender. Moreover this does not mean an act of surrender in the past, but a continuing activation of our basic freedom. It is clear that this continuing free activation in a particular moral direction is a fundamental force in the moral formation of our life, as it takes shape in successive acts (H. Reiners, *Grundintention*[6]). If moral life follows the line of the basic free option, this is further developed and strengthened. If it takes the opposite direction, either as a superficial inconsistency or as a fundamental free choice, then this means not simply the self-commitment of a hitherto neutral person, but a contradiction of the self already freely activated.

II. Basic Freedom and Freedom of Choice

Obviously there exists a significant interaction between the basic free option of the person as a whole and the particular moral acts and efforts that to a greater or lesser extent derive from freedom of choice.

We speak of freedom of choice in so far as we are able, in particular acts, to apply ourselves freely to the many possibilities and requirements of life as it unfolds before us in space and time. We must choose freely to be just, loyal, merciful, and so on. The moral act of free choice can be expressed in an external act, or in an inner act of free will. But when we bring to realization, in our free choices, the values of justice, loyalty, mercy, and so on, at the same time we engage ourselves as persons. The personal realization of justice, loyalty and mercy through free choice always means an effort to engage the person as a whole in basic freedom. Only to the extent that justice and loyalty and mercy constitute a striving for the self-realization of the person are they in fact moral at all. And only where justice and loyalty and mercy express and signify the person who is truly acting in basic freedom, only there are they moral in the full and real sense. So long as they are 'merely' personal, but do not spring from a true commitment of the person, they are indeed moral acts, but only by analogy and not in the full sense.[7]

Conversely there can be no particular, categorical act of basic freedom—for a person can never grasp and engage the totality of himself categorically, as an object. As soon as the self, as subject, grasps at the self as object, the subjective self that acts is no longer to be found within the self confronting it as object. Therefore the basic, free self-realization of the subject always takes place in particular acts related to an object distinct from the person as a whole. The spiritual person can only attain basic, free self-realization when he emerges from his spiritual unity into the physically conditioned diversity of his development in space and time, to which his personal freedom of choice is directed.

The various free moral acts are accordingly a constitutive element of self-realization in basic freedom, but at the same time they are also—at least in themselves—a sign of this self-realization. They are particular acts of free choice—justice or loyalty or mercy—which

express and derive from the total act of basic freedom, the radical opening out of the self to the Absolute. Only, of course, 'in themselves'. For particular acts of free choice can also spring from a more superficial level of the personality and not express its basic, freely chosen attitude. A trivial lie, for example, does not derive from the fundamental decision of the man who loves God.

If we are right to consider and assess separately the two aspects of our freedom—basic freedom and freedom of choice—then it follows that the actual value of a moral act depends more on the basic free self-commitment of the person than on the various virtues arising out of free choice. The real value of morality lies in a person's self-commitment in relation to the Absolute. Of course this is realized and demonstrated in freely chosen virtuous acts which specify categorically the transcendental self-commitment of the person. Conversely the proper use of basic freedom can only occur and be made plain in an act which is specified as morally good.

It is accordingly love that lends merit to the particular moral act of justice, loyalty or mercy which it fills and penetrates. It is not justice and loyalty and mercy as such that are meritorious, but only justice, loyalty and mercy as expressing the gift of self to the Absolute. The specific act of free choice—justice, loyalty, mercy—may be carried out as a *preliminary* movement towards God without true self-commitment (love) for him. But the particular act of free choice is only meritorious if it expresses the real commitment of the self in an act of basic freedom, that is love. When the Church's teaching authority lays down that not only love, but also justice and other moral acts earn merit (DS 2455 f.), what is meant is this: not only a specific act of love of God freely chosen is meritorious, but also a specific act of other virtues, pre-supposing that it is permeated with the transcendental exercise of the love of God in basic freedom.

Here we can see again that the relationship of the various moral virtues to the virtue of love corresponds to the relationship of specific free choice to basic freedom. The love that commits a person as a whole is not a specific act of love distinct from other specific moral acts, but a transcendental self-commitment in basic freedom that is realized and demonstrated in particular specific acts of free choice. When Christ both distinguishes between his disciples' love for him and their keeping of his word and also sees the two as one, so that love indeed includes the keeping of his word and the observance of his commands (Jn 14:15, 21, 23), this really means the same thing. It is not a specific act of love but the transcendental love acting out of basic freedom that necessarily lives and expresses itself in the keeping of his word through the various acts of free choice. This difference between the person as a whole, whom we have at our disposal in basic freedom, and the person's acts, which we determine by free choice, is also meant when Scripture says that God looks not only at a man's deeds but also at his heart, that the holy Spirit by grace gives us a new heart; and this is the sense wherever the biblical speech of the Old and New Testaments uses the concept of the heart to signify the depths of the human person. It is, however, also a matter of the relation between basic freedom and freedom of choice when Paul speaks of sin in the singular and of sinful acts in the plural (Rom 5–7), or when he interprets the many and various vices of the heathen as the expression of the single sin of culpable godlessness (Rom 1:18–31). In the same way, according to John, every sin—all sins—are fundamentally this single sin: malice,

that is, the self-sufficient rejection of God as the source of our salvation (1 Jn 3:4). For in all these texts the same theme seems to be dealt with, that is that the many sins of all kinds are really and ultimately more than they indicate in their specific classification: they express a man's fundamental free disposition of himself as a whole in face of the God of salvation, a total disposition therefore, that is present at the deepest level of the many individual sins.

A short reference should be made to a further phenomenon of freedom in the moral life, that concerns the relation between basic freedom and freedom of choice. The man who is realizing himself in basic freedom and in freedom of choice builds up for himself in the many specific fields of morality certain fundamental tendencies—virtues and vices. That means immediately and above all that the will to follow a particular good or bad course of conduct, freely chosen, is and continues to be activated in such a way that good and bad acts will follow as a result of the freedom thus activated, and continuing to be activated. Secondly, it means that practice increasingly integrates the various layers of a man's being with his freely-chosen basic tendency of conduct (virtue or vice), so that the performance of individual acts meets with less resistance. Freedom activated in virtue or vice, that is moral freedom, does not give rise to particular acts in such a way, it seems to us, that they are only free because of the freedom (moral freedom) that has already been set in motion. For so long as man is a pilgrim (viator) and his freedom has not yet been definitively committed, freedom of choice is always required for individual free acts. Only in this way can it be understood how there is the possibility of intensifying or moderating basic tendencies, and even the possibility of choosing freely in contradiction to a free basic tendency. (Thus indeed the basic freedom that has been activated can also be re-activated and reaffirmed, or can even be turned around in an opposite direction.)

A short reference should be made to a further meaning of the relationship between basic freedom and freedom of choice. Every world view, so long as it is fully human, has its origin in those depths of the person in which knowledge and freedom are indivisible, in man's commitment of himself as a person. The formation of a world view takes place basically in responsibility and therefore in moral acts—these, however, are grounded, as acts of free choice, fundamentally in the person as such, acting in basic freedom. Basic freedom expresses itself in the world through freedom of choice, but in a world that shows itself to be a world of human persons.

Obviously there exists in moral life an interdependence between basic freedom and freedom of choice. Above all, morality in the true and full sense only exists, as we have said, where our freedom, as basic freedom and freedom of choice, simultaneously determines our action. The basic freedom of personal self-commitment can be activated only in acts of free choice. Such acts, however, when they do not correspond to the depths of self-commitment in basic freedom, are not moral in the real and full sense, but only by analogy. For not every act of free choice necessarily corresponds to that self-commitment of the person —even when the moral quality of the act is recognized and its commission freely willed. A lie, recognized in its sinfulness, considered and freely willed, does not usually determine a self-commitment of opposition to God in basic freedom; for the intrinsic opposition to God of the lie, the No before God, which is always grave in itself, is in practice usually not

sufficiently evaluated and is therefore not personally realized as such. An exceedingly large gift of alms by a sinner, made in full knowledge and freedom, will very often express the beginning of change in him, often too, but by no means necessarily and always, true conversion in basic freedom from sinner to lover. Thus both the materially costly act of almsgiving and the materially light act of lying remain, seen in personal terms, 'light', 'superficial' acts, moral acts only by analogy, because the self-commitment of the person in basic freedom does not enter into them. Many of our daily good or bad deeds do not involve the self-commitment of the person as a whole in basic freedom and are therefore—as acts only of free choice—merely 'light' moral acts, acts performed at the surface level of the person, moral acts by analogy.

We are accustomed to dividing moral acts into those that are fully human (*actus perfecte humani*) and those that are not (*actus imperfecte humani*). Is it in fact sufficient to let fully human acts be defined solely by clear knowledge concerning their morality and their performance in free choice? In that sense the lie, and also the costly alms of the sinner who has not yet been converted, are fully human actions. But is this not to understand the *actus perfecte humanus* in an altogether too formal way? Must we not, in order to speak in real rather than formal terms, regard as the essential condition of a fully human act that it be the expression of the person's self-activation, in basic freedom, before the Absolute? But if we understand the *actus perfecte humanus* in this way, then it is always—whether good or bad—an *actus gravis,* a moral act in the true sense and not merely by analogy. Both the *materia levis* of the lie and the *materia gravis* of an exceedingly costly alms-gift can be realized without the activation of basic freedom. Is not occasionally a *materia levis* ('good' or 'bad'), perhaps some lack of love or small proof of love, realized in the simultaneous activation of basic freedom, that is, as a 'gravely' good or bad deed? Thomas took this to be the case when man made his first moral choice.[8] Others hold this to be possible for the mystics,[9] or at some point in the course of a long series of such actions:[10] when, that is, there comes about at the centre of the person full existential understanding and evaluation of the relationship of the person to the Absolute that is involved.

Let us make yet another, and final, remark concerning the mutal influence upon each other of basic freedom and freedom of choice, which indeed has already been briefly touched upon. The free choice and realization of good or bad acts and the creation by free choice of good or bad tendencies may decide or occasion the intensification or diminution of the basic intention arising out of basic freedom, and even indeed the reversal into its opposite —always according to whether they correspond to or contradict the basic intention. Total lack of concern in the sphere of venial sins will diminish love of God (the basic intention) or could even endanger it. The sinner's renewed attention to the fulfilment of good will lessen his abandonment to evil and clear a way for his conversion in basic freedom. Conversely basic freedom will have its influence upon the performance of free choice. The man who, because of his self-commitment in basic freedom, lives in grace and love will not come so easily to serious sin as another who has not made the basic decision of surrender to God. For he does not only have to carry out the evil deed in free choice, but he has also to reverse, in basic freedom, his

basic free attitude to God. Therefore it cannot be assumed that someone continually—'seven times a day'—changes from mortal sin to the love of God and *vice versa*, not only because of the bias of grace,[11] but also because of the effective power of love. Where the specific acts—grave sins or acts of sorrow—seem to indicate the contrary, one has to deal with more or less free acts of choice without the involvement of self-commitment in basic freedom. That is to say, the person is presumably in a continuous state either of sin or of justification.

III. Basic Freedom and Self-Awareness

Obviously we are conscious in different ways of the activation of basic freedom and the realization of freedom of choice, although the activation of basic freedom is performed not as a distinct act in itself but in and through an act of free choice. The problem to which we must now turn is that of awareness of the activation of the person as a whole in basic freedom.

That there is an awareness of basic, free self-commitment can hardly be questioned, since a free process can only be a conscious one. While, however, the performance by free choice of a particular moral action makes possible an objective knowledge of this—whether it be more in a conceptual and reflexive or more in an intuitive manner—this is not possible in relation to the person's basic and free activation to love or to sin. We have already noted that objective reflection on the self can never take in the whole self as subject; the subjective 'I' which reflects and acts in this reflection remains, precisely as such, outside the 'I' that is the object of reflection. It cannot be fully established by my objective reflection whether I am lover or sinner in fulfilment of basic freedom. There can be no adequate objective knowledge of this matter. This corresponds to the declaration of the Council of Trent (DS 1534 f.), that no one has a certain knowledge of the state of grace—and that indeed means also of his basic free love of God. And yet basic free self-commitment—love and sin—cannot be other than conscious—precisely because it is an act of freedom. This consciousness is not objective, or even reflexive, but transcendental and unreflexive. The person acting in basic freedom is totally present to himself,[12] not as object but as subject, not perceived but self-aware, not seen from outside but experienced in himself.

The same consideration applies when Scripture, as well as our own reflection, leads us to distinguish between love as total surrender and good works, as also between sin (in the singular) as refusal of surrender to the God of salvation, and sins (in the plural) as evil works. In the objective and reflexive consciousness of the man who carries out good works in grace and love, these good works—perhaps some service of love to his neighbour—are related to an act of free choice. If it were otherwise, if in his objective consciousness he referred to his self-commitment in loving God, then the good work for his neighbour would perhaps not be achieved, or would be experienced as less than true love of neighbour as such. Self-commitment in love is not specifically 'known', but transcendentally 'conscious'. This manner of perception is not less than the other but more deeply-rooted and richer. That too is why the man who, in his good works, reflects on his own act of love of God does not really see it in its fullness—as a transcendental process—but only a specific and inade-

quate expression of it. In the same way the sinner does not refer, objectively and reflexively, to his basic free self-commitment as he shuts himself off from God, but to the specific, freely chosen act of sin. Yet he is conscious of his refusal of love in basic freedom. The assertion often heard that sinners only want the sinful act but are not aware of any refusal of love of God and moreover, do not want this, overlooks the fact that the real and fundamental withholding of the self, because it is a commitment of basic freedom, takes place in the realm not of objective knowledge but of transcendental self-awareness.

What is said here also answers, basically, the question of how a person can really take a stand in relation to God in love or in sin as commitment of himself as a whole. In intensive good work, or in abandonment to sin, specific thinking about God tends more or less to disappear, though it somehow remains present as unreflecting awareness. But the decisive factor is something else: specific knowledge about God and the taking up of a specific attitude towards God by free choice do not constitute the really fundamental relationship to him. Deeper, more fundamental, is the transcendental—and therefore not objective —awareness of God as the absolute horizon of human reality. So also the surrender or the withholding of the self as a basic free act is not a specific but a transcendental process. And as we are inclined to assume that the atheist who, whether in good faith or in culpable suppression of the truth (Rom 1:18), declares that he does not have to take a God into account, also has a transcendental awareness of God, we should equally be justified in thinking that his good works and evil deeds, too, if performed not only by specific free choice but also in transcendental basic freedom, represent a certain self-surrender, or its refusal, to the God of whom he is transcendentally aware.

The answer that the basic free activation of the person—love or sin—is known in a transcendental and unreflexive manner but is not adequately carried over into specific, reflexive knowledge, does not satisfy us. How and to what degree can basic free self-commitment be translated into our specific consciousness? What knowledge of this kind do we have of our sinfulness or of our life in grace? What do we mean by our explicit opinion or statement that we are 'in a state of grace and love' or 'not in a state of grace but of (mortal) sin'?

Thomas Aquinas[13] puts it that we come, in our specific consciousness, to a knowledge of the state of our soul—that is, of the basic free position of the person as a whole before the Absolute—by means of a 'conjecture'. He gives criteria for such a conjecture: the consciousness of joy in God or of contempt for the world, the experience of divine consolation, the certainty that one can remember no mortal sin. We should like to put it in another way: we can conclude from various signs in the realm of free choice what is the manner of our basic free commitment. The material gravity of a sin, for example, is a sign, and leads us to suppose that in the committing of this sin the activation of the person in basic freedom has also taken place. But the gravity of the matter is only a *sign,* and only *one* sign. Perhaps we can establish at the same time a lack of sufficient moral and existential perception, or a lack of consent. This lack of freedom of choice in carrying out the deed would be another sign. For without the activation of free choice there is no activation of basic freedom and thus no realization of one's own self. 'Conjecture', therefore, based on 'signs', gives us that moral certainty with which we judge

reflexively ourselves and others, the moral certainty which is characteristic of and adequate for our actions and conduct in the sphere of the specific acts of daily life.

IV. Basic Freedom and Grace

If the activation of the person's basic freedom is love or sin, total self-giving or self-refusal in face of the Absolute, we should not definitively abstract from this the fact that the required self-surrender exists only in overcoming the egoism of human concupiscence and in abandonment to God as Father, after the example of his Son-become-man, that is, that it is possible only in grace. Were it to be otherwise, salvation would lie within a man's own power. Accordingly the relationship between basic freedom and grace should be briefly dealt with.[14]

Here we understand grace as that which justifies a man and re-forms him in the pattern of the God-man. It is—in the mature man—not a 'something' to be received passively, but a gratuitous transformation of the person. It is the working of grace which commits the person in his totality, tears him free of the egoistic course of human concupiscence and makes him respond in loving self-surrender to the love of God—after the manner of the incarnate Son of the Father. The grace that achieves this is obviously not only offered but also freely accepted grace. As, however, the loving self-disposal of the person as a whole is the activation of basic freedom, it comes about that the offer of grace occurs in that centre of the person in which he is totally present to himself, in undivided self-awareness and freedom. Precisely in this centre there takes place the acceptance or rejection of grace as the activation of basic freedom. Acceptance or rejection of grace are more than simple acts of free choice, a simple Yes or No. They are a self-commitment of the person as a whole. And the transforming grace of Christ is offered only in acts in which the person at the same time acts in basic freedom.

Accordingly specific, individual moral acts as such are not the acceptance or rejection of grace. Acceptance and rejection, as self-activation in basic freedom, occur much more *through* specific acts of free choice. And individual acts that are moral in the full sense, in which a man disposes of himself as a whole, are, rather, as specific and individual acts (justice, loyalty, mercy), the expression and outcome of the free acceptance or refusal (in basic freedom) of grace, and with it the effect of grace or the consequence of lack of grace.

If we are inclined to assume, following a well-founded theory, that the grace of Christ is offered also to the man, as an individual, who does not (specifically) know or recognize Christ[15]—otherwise how could he attain salvation?—then it follows for the non-Christian also that the call of grace is offered to him too in that centre of the 'I' in which the person is present to himself in a transcendental, unreflexive awareness, and disposes of himself. As he experiences it in non-specific consciousness, so he will accept or reject it in the same consciousness and in basic freedom, that is, in non-specific self-disposition. Thus his self-realization in basic freedom in making himself open to the Absolute is also acceptance of the grace of Christ and therefore in some sense Christian love of God—and his sinful closing up of himself within himself is a sin against the grace of Christ. The love that according to the saying of Christ enables us to keep his word, is the grace offered and accepted in basic freedom or else its effect. Sin (in the singular)

which is present in all sins (in the plural) as their fundamental reality is the self-sufficient refusal to accept the love of the God of our salvation that is offered us.

A further consequence follows from the fact that acceptance or refusal of grace comes about through activation of basic freedom. We are thinking of those people whose way of life does not conform at all to the moral standard. This can be the outcome of a basic negative decision, that is, of rejection of grace. But what if the far-reaching lack of psychological and social formation—one thinks of 'a-social' people—leads one rather to think that such conduct is far from corresponding to true freedom of choice? Then it is indeed not impossible that such people, despite their outwardly immoral and a-social way of life, have not refused the grace of Christ in basic free self-activation, but have accepted it—or, after willed failures, have accepted it anew.[16]

But with reference also to those unambiguously good and outstanding Christians who without doubt accept God's grace in basic freedom and strive to correspond to it in daily life, visibly and in all seriousness, some raise this question, and not without reason: if at some weak point in their life there are repeated failures, cannot sometimes the manner of their life as a whole become a sign that the individual failures do not always correspond to a rejection of grace in the depths of basic freedom—that such acts, perhaps, do not arise from sufficient freedom of choice?

Finally let us refer to the many daily sins and good works which remain only on the edge of personal commitment (venial sins and minor good works). Since they are 'superficial' and therefore moral only in an analogous sense, that is, causing no activation of basic freedom, such acts do not mean a simultaneous acceptance or refusal of grace. They may well be linked to the acceptance or refusal of grace in earlier acts. It is above all, when they lie along the line of the basic direction—as its 'superficial' expression—that they are 'superficial' signs and effects of grace freely accepted or refused.

Grace, therefore, calls, and is accepted or refused, in the centre of the person. For this very reason the grace that transforms a man can influence him in every sphere. For the man activated in basic freedom seeks to integrate with his basic intention every part of his being and life. Thus grace makes its way from the centre of a man and his basic freedom into all areas of life, into the many acts of free choice and beyond these into the formation of the world.

*   *   *

It seemed to us important that in the discussions of moral theologians about man's freedom this central area of freedom which we term basic freedom should come to be more regarded. The concept of basic freedom must necessarily have arisen, in recent times, in connection with such other concepts as basic decision, basic intention, self-disposition, total decision, transcendental awareness, etc. Obviously all these classifications point in the same direction: what is visible in individual free acts and efforts is not the whole, not the essence, of morality. If modern psychology gives us information about freedom and lack of freedom in human behaviour, it is doing an inestimable service to the better judgement of man's morality. But beyond this help from psychology we need the insights of philosophical and theological anthropology—and the classification of 'basic freedom' belongs here —in order better to understand the phenom-

ena respectively of morality and of Christian morality. Our brief exposition should have shown that such anthropological reflections have not only theoretical but also practical value.

Notes

1. Lecture at the Second National Congress of the Association of Italian Moral Theologians, Assisi, Italy. 16–19 April 1968.
2. See P. Fransen, 'Pour une psychologie de la grâce divine', *Lumen Vitae* (12) 1957, 209–40.
3. *Passim;* e.g. in 'Theology of Freedom', *Theological Investigations* VI (tr. K. H. Krüger), 179–96. Cf. also J. B. Metz, 'Freiheit', in *Handw. theolog. Grundbegriffe* (H. Fries), I, 403–14.
4. The activation of basic freedom takes place as a basic decision (*option fondamentale*). There is an extensive bibliography on this in H. Reiners, *Grundintention und sittliches Tun*, Freiburg/Br. 1966; J. Maritain, *Neuf leçons sur les notions premières de la philosophie morale*, Paris 1949, 119–28; Z. Alszeghy and M. Flick, 'L'opzione fondamentale della vita morale e la grazia', *Gregorianum* (41) 1960, 593–619; P. Fransen, *art. cit.* (note 2 above); J. B. Metz, 'Befindlichkeit', in *Lex. f. Theol. u. Kirche*, 2 111, 102–4. While we regard the basic decision as a mature act of self-determination, others (e.g. Fransen) understand it more as a preliminary, as yet immature, groundwork. On the other hand, we do not understand by it an almost definitive decision (Maritain's formulations are too one-sided for us), but an act that grows and deepens, that can, however, also become blunted and can even be turned into its opposite.

5. Cf. the work already cited, J. B. Metz, 'Befindlichkeit' (note 4 above).

6. See note 4.

7. Cf. B. Schüller, 'Zur Analogie sittlicher Grundbegriffe', *Theologie und Philosophie* (41) 1966, 3–19.

8. *S. theol.* 1–11, q. 89, a. 3; and *passim*. Cf. Maritain, *op. cit.* (note 4).

9. Thus e.g. B. Häring, *The Law of Christ*, 1, Cork 1967, 362.

1C. Thus K. Rahner, 'Gerecht und Sünder zugleich', *Geist und Leben* (36) 1963, 434–45; H. Rondet, *Notes sur la théologie du péché*, Paris 1957, III f.

11. *De verit.* q. 27, art. I ad 9: 'quanvis per unum actum peccati mortalis gratia amittatur, non tamen facile gratia amittitur; quia habenti gratiam non est facile illum actum exercere, propter inclinationem in contrarium.'

12. Certainly the being present to himself of the person as a whole is not a consciousness in unbounded fullness, for the human spirit is a finite spirit.

13. See *S. theol.* 1–11, q. 112, a. 5c.

14. Cf. the works already cited of Alszeghy-Flick, Dianich and Reiners (note 4 above), also Fransen (note 2 above).

15. On this question cf. e.g. Karl Rahner's essay on the teaching of the Second Vatican Council on Atheism in *Concilium* (3), March 1967, 5–13.

16. Cf. Karl Rahner, 'Der Christ und seine ungläubigen Verwandten', *Geis und Leben* (27) 1954, 171–84.

15

Missing the Mark

Bruce Vawter

Etymologies are handy things. They frequently tell us what our fathers, who first coined the words that we nowadays use so casually, really meant by what they said, which is sometimes a little different from what we mean. On the other hand, etymologies can just as often be misleading, since it is use that really determines a word's meaning for those who use it, and use may have parted company with etymology even from the very beginning. Ordinarily we will find that it is at least instructive to examine etymologies, even though in the end we may not have to treat them too seriously. The classic Scholastic approach to a new term has always been through *quoad nomen* and *quoad rem,* the etymological definition first, then the real meaning.

At the outset, then, it is interesting to observe that none of the words used in the Bible for 'sin' has of itself that exclusively moral association to which hundreds of years of Christian use have accustomed us. It is interesting, because this fact throws some light on certain aspects of the biblical idea of sin and especially on some attitudes adopted by later

Judaism. It cannot, however, give us any adequate appreciation of the biblical theology of sin.

In the Hebrew Old Testament the word most commonly used for sin, the word that we customarily translate 'sin' in our Bibles, is *hattah,* which literally means 'to miss the mark'. The mark that is missed need not be a moral mark, nor need it be missed immorally. The author of Prv 19:2 uses 'missing the mark' of the hasty traveller who loses his way through inadvertence to road signs.

The Hebrew word used most commonly after *hattah* in the biblical vocabulary of sin, *pesha,* is entirely of the same order. It means 'overstep' or 'rebel'. In 2 Kgs 8:20, when the author states that Edom successfully rebelled against the rule of Judah, he is passing no moral judgement on the revolt but simply recording a political fact. Other Hebrew words that are used on occasion to signify a moral lapse—such as 'err', 'wander', and the like—also have of themselves no necessary moral application.

The same must be said of the Greek word

This article originally appeared in The Way 2 *(January 1962): 19–27.*

hamartano, used in the Greek Old Testament to translate *hattah,* and in the New Testament in its own right as the word for 'sin'.

Hamartano is the exact equivalent of *hattah.* It, too, means 'miss the mark', and in profane Greek it often refers to a man's losing his way on the road. For that matter, the Latin *peccare, peccatum,* with which our own liturgy has made us so familiar and which have as their root meaning 'stumble', originally did not necessarily connote anything moral. When the Italian says *che peccato!,* he is not saying 'what a great sin!' but rather, 'what a pity!' Thus it is that terminology alone cannot tell us a great deal about the biblical theology of sin. We must see, rather, how the terminology is used. The terminology doubtless assisted what was a tendency of the later Judaism, to make of the notion of sin something purely formal and legalistic. Wellhausen was able to assert that what the Law of Moses demanded was not rightdoing, but rather the avoidance of wrongdoing. With respect to the later legalism, Wellhausen's charge was well founded. He was certainly wrong, however, in extending this indictment to the Law itself and to the way it was understood in the biblical period. This much we can easily see, I believe, by examining a few of the passages that go to make up the biblical theology of sin.

See, for example, how the word *pesha* is used by the prophet Amos, one of the earliest of our biblical authors. If we read his first oracles we find that the 'transgressions' of which he repeatedly speaks embrace inhumanity, cruelty, social injustice, violation of contract, acceptance of bribes, violation of the public trust, greed, lust, and hypocrisy, on the part of Gentiles as well as of Israelites.[1] There is obviously no question here of sin as the merely formal, mechanically computed, violation of a law. Rather, it is clear that for Amos *pesha* is a transgression of the moral law, a rebellion against God's moral will, a will that had been made known to the Gentiles as the norm of rightdoing. Amos does not, it is true, elaborate any doctrine of natural law, to explain how Israelite and Gentile alike were under the same moral obligations; no such doctrine is anywhere elaborated in the Hebrew Old Testament, which addressed itself always and exclusively to the people of God who were recipients of his revelation. Yet in 6:12 Amos does state that the rejection of the justice and rightdoing which God required of Israel—here in specific reference to the corruption that had taken place in Israelite courts of law—was as absurd and unnatural as tracking horses over rocks and ploughing the sea with oxen. Sin for the Israelite, certainly, was the violated will and law of the Lord. But it was will and law that found a response in man's mind and heart; it was never arbitrary whim or caprice.

This conception of *pesha* that we first encounter in Amos is common to the rest of the prophets. It is not incorrect to do as we are doing, to find the spirit of the Law expressed in the prophets. The criticism of the past century tried to oppose the two, as though the spiritual, prophetic religion and the priestly religion of the Law had been separate, mutually antagonistic developments in Israelite history and tradition. Criticism now recognizes that in this attempt it, too, had taken the wrong track and missed the mark. Prophecy and Law were, of course, two different emphases of Israelitic religion, which correspondingly spoke two different languages. But they were emphases of the same religion and were directed towards broadly the same ends. If we do not expect to find the moral and devotional teaching of Catholicism in the Code of Canon Law or the Roman Ritual, neither do we oppose what we do find there to the *Summa* of St. Thomas or the *Introduction to the Devout Life*. In much the same fashion, it is now agreed that we rightly interpret prophetic teaching as supporting in its way a doctrine that the Law upheld in its own.

In the Law the favoured word for sin is *hattah*. The 'mark' or norm that was 'missed', in the mind of the Israelite authors, was that of the Covenant of Sinai, of which Israel's Law was the spelling out of the people's obligations with respect to its covenant God.

Here, too, if we would understand rightly in what this covenant duty consisted, we must have a clear idea of what covenant meant, first and foremost, in the ancient Near East. The closest analogy to covenant in our own society is the bilateral contract; but while the analogy is valid as far as it goes, we have sometimes tended to overlook the fact that analogy is not identity. In other words, covenant was *like* a contract in some ways, but covenant was not precisely a contract. Specifically, whereas the binding force of a contract consists in legal justice, the covenant obligation was not conceived primarily as one of justice but as one of love.

The word customarily used in the Old Testament to convey the notion of the covenant bond is *hesed,* translated variously as 'mercy', 'loyalty', 'devotion', 'lovingkindness', or simply 'love'. It was in *hesed* that God had chosen Israel and bound it to himself; *hesed,* correspondingly, was the duty of every Israelite in return, towards God and towards the other members of the covenant community. The covenant idea, therefore, was modelled after a family rather than a legal relationship. When an Israelite committed *hattah*, sinned, his offence was not terminated by the letter of the law which he had violated, but by the familial piety which he had ruptured, the *hesed* of

which the Law was a formulated norm and expression.

Sin and evil to the Semite were not the negation, the 'deprivation of good' that they have achieved in our thinking under the influence of other thought-forms. Sin was a positive thing that had been done, that therefore continued to exist until done away with. What we think of as 'guilt', the condition of the sinner as the result of sin, and the punishment that we conceive of as a kind of act of reciprocity on the part of God or offended authority taking vengeance on the sin, were to the biblical authors hardly distinguishable from the sin itself. In Nm 32:23 'sin' and 'the consequences of sin', as we would have to render the thought in English, translate the same Hebrew word, and this is typical of the biblical viewpoint. It is from this viewpoint that we must understand the Old Testament conception of sins committed in ignorance, for which expiatory rites and sacrifice were provided by the Law. From this viewpoint, too, we can see how a whole community could share in the guilt of one of its members, or generations yet unborn in the guilt of their progenitor. It was not that they were being 'held' guilty of another's wrongdoing, but that they were caught up in the consequences of an act that were actually the continued existence of the act itself. The Deuteronomic law of personal responsibility[2] that was laid down as a necessary rule in the human administration of justice, and its application by Jeremiah[3] and Ezekiel[4] to the divine dispensation under the new covenant, were restrictions placed by God on the 'natural' extension of guilt.

Similarly, punishment was not so much a retribution 'visited' upon the sin (though this idea of retribution is also, at times, the biblical conception) as it was the inexorable running of sin's course. God, it is true, could forestall this consequence—there is nothing in the Bible akin to the fatalism of Greek tragedy. For sins of ignorance he did so by accepting the expiatory sacrifices of the Law. For other sins there was the recourse of prayer, coupled with the contrition and the confession of the sinner, of which we have so many examples in the Psalms. But God's forgiveness of sin did not automatically entail his remission of punishment, as can be seen from the famous judgement passed on David's sin with Bathsheba.[5] The Catholic teaching on the temporal punishment of sin is a true echo of this biblical doctrine.

Finally, we can see from this 'objective' nature of sin as it was understood by the Old Testament why that which is sinful was broader in its extent than that which is immoral. Legal purity, by which was meant the external holiness of a people consecrated to God, a reminder, in turn, of the need of interior holiness,[6] could obviously be violated without the performance of any immoral act. A woman had to make a 'guilt offering' after the 'uncleanness' of childbirth because legal purity had been offended; but no question whatever of morality was involved in the matter.

Here we may pause to note the difference between the world of the Old Testament and that of the New. While most of what has been said above applies equally well to the thinking of the Old and the New Testaments, there is in the New Testament, for reasons that we shall explain more fully later on, no trace of the conception of purely legal holiness. The old formulas are used, but they are used within the new dimension of a salvation and a regeneration of which the former figures were but a type and a foreshadowing. The 'holy ones' to whom St. Paul writes are not those merely consecrated to God, but those of

whom personal holiness is expected as a consequence of the indwelling Spirit. With the entire apparatus of formal sanctity superseded in a new and spiritual covenant, sin and immorality are fully identified. The law of Christians is the code of conduct that befits those removed in principle from this world and joined to the Source of all that is holy and to Holiness itself. Charity is the *hesed* of the new covenant.

The nature of sin in the Bible can aptly be perceived in the effects that are attributed to it. These are described in various ways and under various figures, but the idea that emerges is much the same. In the Law, sin is represented as an *obex,* an obstacle that stands between God and people—once again we see the relevance of the 'objective' conception of sin. The rites of expiation are not directed to God in the thought that he is to be placated or changed from an unfavourable to a favourable disposition; God is never the object of the verb that we translate 'expiate'. Expiation, rather, has sin for its object. Sin must be removed, this obstacle in the path of man's approach to the Holy. Man, not God, must change. When sin has been wilful, committed 'with a high hand', a sin of mind and heart, then the mind and heart of man must be changed. This is contrition or repentance.

In the famous sixth chapter of Isaias we find this same notion of sin as it was experienced by the prophet at the time of his call to prophesy. If this chapter is read attentively, it is apparent that, despite the awesome and grandiose terms in which God is described in theophany, it is in the moral order rather than in the order of being that man is seen to be most separated from God. Sin, in other words, the sin that Isaias confesses of himself and of his people, is what lies behind his recognition that he is 'lost' in the presence of the Holy.

Much the same idea must be in the background of the English word 'sin' (cf. the German, *Sünde*) that has been formed by Christian thinking, namely that it *sunders* one from the other.

One of the most fruitful sources of the biblical theology of sin are the penitential psalms of the Old Testament. The New Testament would certainly open up a wider vision of the riches of God's salvation and his grace, but not even the New Testament can tell us more about the sense of sin and of the lostness and meaninglessness which are its inevitable concomitant. Among the penitential psalms none is richer in its content than Psalm 50(51), the well-known *Miserere*.

This psalm begins with a plea to God, the covenant Father, to honour his *hesed* in responding to the sinner's appeal. Three words are used for sin throughout the psalm: the two of which we have already spoken above, together with *awon*, 'guilt', the state of a sinner who has transgressed the will of God and who now stands in a condition of disharmony with that will. Sin, in other words, appears as a rebellion, an offence against the covenant bond, and therefore a state of aversion from the God of the covenant. Correspondingly, three different words are used to express the sinner's conviction of what God alone can and must do with regard to his sinful state.

It is important to see precisely what these words mean, since all of them involve vaguely the same figure, and it would be easy to conclude mistakenly that they are more or less arbitrary synonyms. 'Blot out', 'wash', and 'cleanse' are their usual English equivalents. The 'blotting out' in question is a ritual obliteration or washing away: in this sense the same verb appears in Nm 5:23. The 'washing' that the psalmist has in mind does mean this, certainly, but we need to recall the type of washing with which he was familiar. The washing of clothes,[7] not of the hands or feet, is what the verb denotes. More literally still, it could be rendered 'tread out'—the Oriental flung his soiled clothing in a stream and stamped on it enthusiastically. The 'cleansing', finally, to which the psalmist refers is a ritual or declaratory cleansing of the kind provided for in Lv 13:6.

The psalmist petitions of God, therefore, what a later theology would distinguish into a forensic and a real justification. Justification is forensic: God must simply forgive, declare the sinner to be a sinner no more. There is a simple truth preserved in this conception, for the committed sin, of course, is a reality that is never annulled or annihilated. The historical fact that is a past human act cannot be done away with as though it had never occurred. But justification is also real: the guilt that has remained in the sinner and that prevents his access to the God of holiness must be stamped out and obliterated.

The nature of this real justification is brought out beautifully and profoundly towards the middle of the psalm. The psalmist calls upon the Lord to *create* in him a clean heart, and to *renew* within him an upright spirit. The same word (*bara*) is used that we translate 'create' in the creation narrative of Gn 1:1. It is a word reserved in the Old Testament exclusively for the wonderful, unique action of God alone. For the Israelite, 'heart' was much more than a metaphor for the emotions or, as we sometimes use it, for a kind of better self or good will. The heart was conceived as the seat of *all* emotion, will, and thought; for the Semite, we must always remember, thought or 'said' things in his heart, not in his head. The heart was the Self. The 'spirit', or breath, was the power residing within man, a power that could come from

God only, by which he was able to think and will in his heart. It, too, therefore, might be called the Self. The psalmist clearly knew, as a consequence, that the justification of the sinner entailed a divine work of re-creation, the renewal of a personality that had been distorted and turned aside from its true purposes by the act of sin. Create, he says, a new *me*. Such an idea is boundless in its commentary on what he believed the effect of sin to be in the sinner, an effect which obviously far transcends any notion of purely formal or legal rectitude. Sin was, in his eyes, an involvement from which man could not emerge without an alteration in his inmost being.

Because of the similarity of this passage to the language of Jeremiah[8] and Ezekiel,[9] some authors have concluded that the psalmist must have been dependent on the teaching of these great prophets. In their preaching about the new covenant, however, Jeremiah and Ezekiel seem merely to have articulated an ancient Hebrew conception. Similarly, the psalmist's conviction (expressed in v. 6) that every sin is a sin against God, contains nothing that was new in Israel, as can be seen from the ancient Joseph story[10] and David's confession at the finding out of his sin with Bathsheba.[11]

One other value Psalm 50 has in setting forth for us the biblical theology of sin. In v. 7 the psalmist declares, 'Behold, I was brought forth in guilt, and in sin did my mother conceive me'. He makes this utterance as a motivation to God to be merciful, as a reminder that man's proclivities are sinful—Gn 8:21 has God himself acknowledge this and accept it in his announced plan or his economy of dealing with man. The biblical authors were well aware that the introduction of sin into the world and its continuation were the achievement of human malice against the will of God. They testified that man's disposition to sin

was not of God's designing, but was part of a consistent history in which the will of a saving God had from the first been resisted and thwarted.[12] It was this belief that St. Paul would further develop[13] and which we understand more comprehensively as the doctrine of original sin. The Bible does not profess this belief, of course, to excuse man's continued sinfulness; it merely seeks to explain it.

As we have mentioned above, most of the Old Testament theology of sin is discernible in the thinking of the New Testament authors, who had been formed completely in the tradition of their biblical fathers. There is, however, a decisive difference that results from the new and definitive revelation of Christianity. For while sin was taken for granted and elaborately provided for in the life of the old covenant, the New Testament Church saw in itself the fulfilment of the prophets' prediction of a new covenant,[14] which was to be an everlasting covenant in which sin should have no part.

The New Testament writers were well aware, of course, that Christians could and did commit sin—the apostolic epistles and the letters to the churches in the first chapters of the Apocalypse testify to a refreshing and total lack of naïveté in this respect. Sin, however, together with the Law, and the 'flesh', and death, and everything imperfect, belonged to this sinful world in which the Christian by rights no longer had any share. It was only by returning to this sinful world or to any of its works—and hence St. Paul's polemic against the attempt of the 'Judaizers' to impose the Mosaic Law on Christians—that the Christian could become guilty of sin. Sin was, therefore, always a kind of apostasy. The salvation achieved by Christ, the new covenant ratified in his blood, had freed mankind in principle, through grace, from the reign of sin and this world. Because what was done now in principle would be accomplished definitively only at the end of all, in the final fulfilment of the divine economy;[15] because, therefore, the Christian though freed of this world continued to live in it and could always relapse into its ways, sin was an ever present possibility. Yet he could sin only by abandoning the total commitment involved in Christian faith, which he could regain only through the new heart and spirit that must once more be bestowed on him by divine grace.

The sense of horror and of enormity in the presence of sin[16] never deserts the New Testament, even though it is under no illusion as to the weakness of Christians and to their consequent recurring need of the forgiveness of Christ and the ministration of his Church. If we today can summon a somewhat more casual attitude to the function of the confessional in the sacramental life of the Church, undoubtedly this is partly due to the fact that modern man, even Christian man, has to a greater or less extent forgotten what sin really is.

Probably man can never really lose his sense of sin, though today he seems to have great difficulty in defining for himself what he means by it. When we look about us at a world in which men give witness, by action far more eloquently than by word, to a feeling of rootlessness and purposeless existence, to a life bereft of meaningful experience in which event follows event in witless sequence and where men can achieve no community together, we perceive, in a groping sort of way, what biblical man understood as sin.

Notes

1. Amos 1:3–2:8.
2. Deut 24:16.
3. Jer 31:29f.
4. Ezek ch. 18.
5. 2 Sam 12:10–14.
6. Cf. Lev 11:44 ff.
7. Cf. Exod 19:10.
8. Jer 24:7; 31:33; 32:39.
9. Ezek 36:25 ff.
10. Gen 39:9.
11. 2 Sam 12:13.
12. Cf. Gen 3 ff. and similar passages.
13. Rom 5:12 ff.
14. Cf. Jer 31:31–34; 32:37–41.
15. 1 Cor 15:53–56.
16. Cf. 1 Cor 6:13–20.

16

Sin and Conversion

Josef Fuchs, SJ

The topic to which I address myself is a consideration of sin and conversion. In dealing with these issues I propose to discuss the more fundamental, existential and personal dimensions of the moral Christian life. Sin and conversion are only two examples; namely, what is going on in the human person as sinner and in the human person as convert? In this consideration we shall delineate four points: First, the moral and the theological relevancy of sin; secondly, the theological aspect of sin; thirdly, the existential aspect of sin; and fourthly, conversion itself in its moral, theological, existential aspects.

Now to the first point: the moral and theological relevancy of sin. We know what the nature of sin is. Sin, morally considered, is a violation of a supposed material moral order. Violation of this order has as one of its constituents parts a certain "matter"; and this matter can be more or less important. As human beings we are obliged to bring order into our own lives, and through such activity to bring order into human society and the

entire world. In a very real sense the entire world belongs to us; it is an extension of what we are as human beings.

A sin is precisely a defect; by sin we refuse to put order into this world. Therefore a sin, objectively considered, is against the Creator of this world and the order of this world, against the Creator of the human person and the order of the human person. Sin is a violation and this violation is brought about by a free choice, a psychologically free act. In this psychologically free act we make a choice of this or that reality out of all the realities of the world (*Liberum arbitrium*). Here we find the *moral* relevancy of sin.

The *theological* relevance of sin affects the personal relation of a human person to God; so we speak of theological relevancy. A sin is not so much an individual act about a particular object. It is much more a disposition of myself as a person, not merely one single act. True, sin involves an individual act about a particular object, but far more important is the realization that in sin I bring about a cer-

---

This article is excerpted from Theology Digest *14 (Winter 1966): 292–301.*

tain self-realization. Here we find the central reality in sin; it is much deeper than simply introducing moral disorder into this world.

In every moral act a person tries much more to realize himself as a whole, as a person, than to realize a particular act. Even if he is thinking explicitly only about this particular act with its supposed good for him, still through the particular act he is much more engaged in realizing *himself* as a person. A person, however, is not without his own purpose, his own ultimate end, as we say in scholastic terminology. He is not without a relationship to his God, for without that he does not exist. Therefore, if in a sinful moral act a person is realizing not only one particular act but himself as a person, then in this moral-act this person is realizing his personal relationship to his ultimate end, and therefore to God. Here we find the theological relevancy of sin.

We must note that this realization of myself in personal relationship to God will not be achieved by the same psychological liberty as the realization of the particular act itself. To dispose of myself *as a whole* I need another liberty; today we call it fundamental liberty. It is a liberty that makes it possible for me precisely to *actualize myself*, not merely an *act* of mine. There is a major distinction between these two liberties: the particular liberty to make a choice between one good or another and the fundamental liberty that makes it possible for me to dispose of myself as a whole, as a person. With this fundamental liberty I am not only committing a sin, an act, but I am also making *myself a sinner*. By this act, by this liberty of the sinful act, I am actualizing my own person with my own will. In this act my will is actualized as the will of a sinner, permanently refusing to God my own self-donation, denying to God my love. For love is not only

giving something, not only giving this or that particular good. Love is giving oneself as a whole with a whole future insofar as this is possible. The sinner by one act refuses this self-giving love to God. From this moment a sinner is really a sinner: *a person* refusing himself to God. Surely there is much more here than a simple act of moral disorder.

Autonomy Is Withdrawal

For what I say now, perhaps we may turn for some help to the NT. For instance, let us take Luke's narrative of the prodigal son (5:11–32). The prodigal son withdraws himself as a whole from the charity and the love of his father. Why? He wishes to be perfectly autonomous before his father and to be independent of his charity. Likewise sin is not only an act refusing *something* to my Father; rather it is the basic withdrawing of *myself* from my Father, God, and from his charity. I do not want to depend on his charity. I desire to be *autonomous*. Here we have the true character of sin.

St. John in his first letter (3:4), according to the recent interpretation of biblical scholars, points to the essential nature of sin: iniquity. In John iniquity means the autonomy, the hostility of a man against God, and precisely against God as the Saviour from whom we could have salvation. Every sin is that. All the variations of particular sin culminate in as well as originate from precisely this hostility. The only distinction between different sins consists in the fact that they are different expressions of what sin is—an autonomy, an hostility, against God our Saviour.

St. Paul in his letter to the Romans (for instance, in chapter 1) speaks about the fact that all men are sinners. This is true of the Christian, the non-Christian, the atheist. Why does St. Paul consider atheists as sinners? Atheists are aware of God, according to Paul, but they are suppressing their deeper knowledge of him. By suppressing within themselves the explicit knowledge of God, they are in fact refusing to acknowledge him. This is their sin: They do not acknowledge God. From this fact, according to Paul, from this inner core of sin, there follow all the different sins we know. The first example in St. Paul is homosexuality and thereafter in the same chapter we find many other sins as well. All these different sins issue from what is at the very heart of sin: the refusal to acknowledge God.

Later on in his letter to the Romans Paul considers sin in the singular. Thus sin is, for Paul, the free acceptance of what we are, our tendencies, our egoisms, all rooted in original sin. That is sin, in the singular. But in the very same letter Paul also speaks of sin in the plural. These sins are transgressions of the moral order and so the expressions of sin in the singular. The true nature of sin is its theological character: refusing God my personal love. And this root character of sin has manifestly different expressions in the world.

I now turn to my second point, the theological aspect of sin. First of all, sin is a personal self-realization apart from and against God. Objectively, I think there is no difficulty in understanding this point. Sin is against the order created and established by God our Creator and Saviour. Sin is against the natural as well as the Christian order. This is to consider sin objectively, but our precise problem is not located in the objective order at all. The problem is that sin is always a *personal* matter, a subjective reality, a sin against God. Or is it? That is the question. Is a sinner always aware of the theological aspect of what he is doing?

Is he always aware that he is acting against his God and Saviour? Sometimes a sinner is aware of his sin as sin. Often he knows it explicitly; he knows what he is doing and he does it. Much more commonly, however, a sinner in doing what in some sense appears good to him does not think of God—at least not explicitly. Conceptually he does not think of the personal God; he thinks of other things. Therefore the question arises: when man sins, is he really unaware of God?

Levels Are Distinct

We have to distinguish levels of consciousness. I can be conscious of myself and what I am doing in a conceptual way, of sinning against my God. But I can also be conscious of myself and what I am doing in a non-conceptual way. Thus in sinning I would not be aware of God in the order of conceptualization, but I would be conscious of God as the background of my whole life. In *this* way, I think, the inner person, Christian or non-Christian, can be aware of his God. I also believe that without being explicitly and conceptually conscious of God, he could act consciously against his God. The real disposition of myself in relation to God is not on the conceptual level of my consciousness. I can posit my whole personality only if, as St. Thomas says, I am present to myself as a whole, as a person. Only thus can I posit my personality as a whole. Hence the full disposition of my self is on a deeper level where I am present as a whole to myself.

But on this level complete conceptual reflection is impossible. I can be aware of what I am doing: I am actualizing myself as a person and in this person my own relationship to God. But I am also aware of much that escapes conceptual reflection. If I could exploit in conceptual reflection what I am doing about myself as a whole, as a person, whether I am refusing or accepting God's love, then I would know with conceptual clarity and certitude whether I am in the state of grace or not. Or, on the other hand, if I am a sinner, I would know with conceptual clarity and certitude that I am not in the grace of Christ. To claim such certitude, I believe, is against the teaching of the Council of Trent.

So it follows, on the one hand, that I cannot dispose of myself as a whole without being aware of what I am freely doing. On the other hand, I cannot know myself and my actions exhaustively in conceptual reflection. Therefore, I am aware of what I am doing before God, but not with complete conceptual reflection. Also from a philosophical and anthropological point of view, in any moral act made with conceptual reflection, in order to dispose of myself as a whole, I should be present to myself as a whole. But in conceptual reflection there is a distinction between the *self reflecting* and the *self as reflected;* therefore, I never possess myself in the totality of my personality in conceptual reflection. On the other hand, if I am expressing my whole person, realizing myself, for instance, by a sin, I have to know what I am doing; otherwise I am not sinning. Hence, I am aware, I am conscious of myself sinning. I am freely disposing of myself as a person but not with exhaustive conceptual reflection. Moreover, it is not possible for me to grasp fully what is going on inside of me in sinning because of my pride and the disorientation of my free will.

This thought leads us to a special question. There is much concern in the world today about atheism. St. Paul, as we know, was speaking about atheists in the first chapter of his letter to the Romans. The real question here is: Is an atheist able to sin in the theolog-

ical sense against God? If not, it is not a true sin. I think atheists are able to sin against God. I think that if they are living on a moral level, if they have the knowledge of an absolute, they also have an understanding of what an absolute is, though perhaps not on the conceptual level. On the conceptual level such a person will say: "I am an atheist." But on a deeper level he is not capable of making an analysis; he is not able to reflect on this level. However, he is aware of what he is doing, realizing himself in relation to what is an absolute; otherwise he would not be performing a moral act. He does not acknowledge an absolute, but he is aware of it. Precisely in regard to sin, we find that its fundamental dynamism is not on the level of conceptual reflection. But on the same level where sin is found, there also is an awareness of God—not of God as a person categorically known, perceived through a concept, but a general awareness. On the same level that the atheist is aware of God, on that same level is the fundamental possibility of sin. Is the atheist guilty or not guilty? According to St. Paul, the atheist is guilty, because he has suppressed his awareness of God. Because of this suppression he does not acknowledge his God. The atheist is aware of God, but he refuses to give himself to him. That is precisely his sin in the theological sense.

Secondly, sin is a personal self-realization against Christ the Redeemer. Again, the objective aspect presents no difficulty. It is clear that in a world created in Christ and redeemed by the God-man every sin in this world is objectively a sin against his world, against his order, and therefore against him.

But here again the problem manifests itself on the subjective level. Is every sin subjectively a sin against Christ? The answer is yes. But how? We have today a very sound theological principle that is accepted by all Catholic theologians. Each and every man is called by Christ. He has his vocation not only in the sense that Christ is calling the entire world, but in another sense, indicated by the Second Vatican Council. Christ is calling every man *personally*. Therefore every man, it seems to me, is aware somehow of this vocation and this call of Christ. Otherwise, how is it possible for him to be called personally by Christ? Hence, each man must have an experiential awareness, a consciousness of the call of Christ; this "I am called" belongs to me. It affects me as a person. Therefore if I am realizing myself as a person, I am not realizing myself in an abstract way. Rather I am realizing my personality as it is existentially affected by this call of Christ my Saviour. Perhaps I do not have any explicit reflex knowledge of this call. It may well be true that the Christian sinner does not very often think explicitly that he is sinning against Christ. But he is always aware that in his moral actions he is realizing himself as a person called by Christ and therefore his sin is consciously, if not with conceptual reflection, a sin against Christ.

Christ Calls Atheists

We come now to the same problem we encountered before about the atheist. The atheist does not know Christ in explicit conceptual knowledge, but Vatican II indicates that he is called personally by Christ. All men, atheists included, are affected by grace —the call of Christ is a grace—the grace of Christ. If they are affected by this grace, they have an awareness of that grace. Thus the non-Christian also is aware that he is sinning against Christ: not on the conceptual level but on a deeper, more personal level where the fundamental possibility of sin exists. There he is aware of himself refusing to answer his call by Christ. So for the non-Christian also sin is subjectively sin against Christ.

Thirdly, sin is a self-oriented declaration of autonomy. On the conceptual level of consciousness a sinner indicates through his freedom of choice what has appeared to him as a good. Perhaps he knows, even explicitly, perhaps reflectively, that his action is really a sin. On this conceptual level of consciousness the sinner does not accept his salvation from God and from Christ. He knows very well that what he is doing is against his own nature and that as a human being he has his salvation only from God in Christ. What happens then on the deeper level of consciousness? On this level, he is destroying himself, emasculating his own nature, because he can be saved only by God in Christ but he refuses this salvation.

Sin, therefore, is the utterly destructive affirmation of self. By so acting the sinner loses his Christian liberty, the freedom by which Christ and his Spirit enable us to love the Father, and to give ourselves totally as persons to him. By his sin the sinner has forfeited his Christian liberty, and this from the very moment that his will is actualized in sin. It is not only in the actual moment of sin, but from this initial moment on, his will is actualized in opposition to God, against Christ, and against the acceptance of his salvation in Christ. He is a sinner. He cannot go back by himself. He cannot become alive again all by himself; that would be self-redemption, which we know from revelation is not possible. Hence from the moment of a true sin the sinner has lost his Christian liberty. He is and will remain with his will set against his God. He cannot change unless Christ by his grace restores to him his freedom to come back, to make a new choice for God, and on this deeper level to love God once more.

Thirdly, let us consider the existential aspect of sin. Any voluntary moral disorder is in itself objectively a *no* to God and to Christ. My question now is this: Is it possible that a human *no* to one's Creator and Redeemer would not be a mortal sin? My answer: I cannot think so.

A fully human *no* to God or to Christ is a mortal sin. The important matter in a sin is not ten cents or a million dollars; the main element in any sin is a *no* to God; if you really say *no* to God, that is mortal sin. This is true whether such a denial deals with a light matter or a million dollars. If this *no* really is a personal *no,* if this *no* is clearly self-realization, if this *no* is really a total disposition of myself in relation to God, then this *no* is always a mortal sin. Therefore whether a sin is a mortal sin or not depends on the answer to this question: In this sin am I fully engaged and really involved as a person? If my person as a whole (*tota persona*) is involved in this act, I am finished. That is mortal sin. What I am doing is refusing my personal self-donation to God and insofar as I am refusing to love God, I am in mortal sin. I not only refuse *some thing*—ten cents or a million dollars or whatever I might give to someone else. But in such an act where I am fully engaged as a person, I am refusing myself, closing off my whole being to God.

Venial Sin Differs

But what about venial sin? Why is venial sin only venial? Why is it not a mortal sin? A venial sin seems also to be a *no* to God. We argue by analogy. In venial sin, a person is not engaging himself as a whole. There are so many superficial acts in which the center of personality where the whole person is present to himself is not engaged. In these acts the center of the person, as a matter of fact, is not involved; they cannot in any true sense be called fully personal. The full engagement of personality is on another level. In venial sin a "just" man does not really dispose of himself in relation to God. He remains a person who loves God, whose fundamental liberty is still intact, but on a more superficial level, he is going in the opposite direction. However on this level, since his person as a whole is not engaged, the *no* of venial sin must be understood in some other sense than as a fully personal *no*. In such a situation I am not refusing my love or closing up my personality to God, and it is only because this objective *no* of venial sin is not realized in the center of my person that it is not a mortal sin.

Let us take an example: for instance, lying. What is the material character, the "matter" in lying? Why is the matter in a lie light matter? Is lying a sin involving freedom and liberty? Yes, it is. But we must examine which liberty is involved here—the liberty to make a choice of this or that good, or the liberty to dispose of myself as a whole? Perhaps a person is clearly free here and now to make the choice between telling a lie and doing some other act. Even if he tells the lie, I do not think his *fundamental* liberty is involved, that liberty by which he is able to dispose, not merely of his acts, but of himself.

A second question arises: What about the matter in the sin? It is easy to distinguish light matter, grave matter, etc., and this distinction is not without importance. But much more important is the existential engagement of the person in saying *no* to God. I think that in regard to what is called light matter, such as a lie, a person normally at least will not be able to engage existentially the center of his personality. In this act, then, he will not be able to dispose of himself. This is so because a small disorder in this world is usually not so important that a person will be aware that his whole person and therefore his whole life is engaged in such an act. On the other hand, if a person is faced with a choice in some matter of importance, he will normally realize that his person as a whole is involved. Since his whole person and his whole life is engaged, he will understand without reflection that in what he is doing he is disposing of himself. Therefore, usually but not always, in any free choice involving grave matter, the action itself will most probably be a mortal sin.

Can we then say that telling a lie is a perfect human act with full freedom? We must distinguish. There is the full freedom to choose between one or another road; but this is *not* the freedom, the liberty, to dispose of oneself. Is a venial sin then a perfect human act? Yes or no? It is not a perfect act such as would be the case in mortal sin, because a mortal sin is precisely an engagement of the whole person in this action; a venial sin is not. However, in venial sin insofar as it is the choice between this or another act, there can be full conceptual freedom, and *only* in this sense is it a human act.

Thirdly, by a full disposition of self, a person takes a stance in relation to God. His will is and will remain committed to loving or refusing to love him. So sin, as a grave act (or as theologians say today, a fundamental option), becomes a permanent orientation of the will. This fundamental option brings about an abiding fundamental intention. The whole person is committed in this direction. Consequently, I believe it is not so easy—not as easy as our moral textbooks seem to indicate—to change ourselves, to change what we are. It is easy to change an act; but it is not easy to change ourselves, a sinner or a man who at the center of his being loves God.

Therefore, when we are considering venial sin, whether it be venial sin in a just man or in a sinner, we may say in both cases that it is an act that does not engage the entire person. In the just man his already actualized good will is not engaged; in the sinner his actualized hostility toward God is not fully reasserted. That is precisely what makes a venial sin venial.

What Is Conversion?

Let us now consider our fourth point: the nature of conversion. It is a more interesting subject, easier to speak about after having spoken about sin. First then, what is conversion? Conversion is not any good act, such as "O my God, I am sorry," not just some other act which follows upon an act of sin. No, conversion is a change in the whole person, for the whole person is a sinner, enduringly committed to be a sinner. Conversion means to change the whole thrust of one's life. In other words, conversion means recapitulating and transforming the basic orientation of a person who has been so against God that he cannot come back to God by himself. Conversion is the total person changing himself. Once a sinner, he is now committing himself totally to the love of God, giving himself as a person to the Father. So conversion is not the sum or substance of many good acts—not, for example, the gift or gifts of a millionaire to the church. Perhaps by such acts a sinner gives something; yes, but he is not giving himself. He is taking some necessary steps with God's help to pass out of his situation as sinner, but he remains in his person as a whole against God.

Therefore conversion is not achieved by just *any single good act*. Conversion takes place on the deep personal level where a man is able to dispose of himself as a whole; this disposition of self is not possible through a superficial act. In principle, we may say that conversion is possible only on the same level where the fundamental possibility of sin is found. Just as a person becomes a sinner only on the deep personal level, so it is also only there that a sinner can experience conversion. Conversion therefore contains contrition for all sins committed, precisely because it is a turning away from the fundamental orientation to sin. Thus contrition for some sins and not for all mortal sins is impossible. For if the sinner would exclude one sin from his contrition, he would not be converted; he would not be changing himself on the deep personal level where he is a sinner. He would still retain in his will his fundamental option against God. He would not be giving himself as a whole to God.

Somewhat in the same way conversion also contains a promise, at least implicitly, or virtually as we say in theology; likewise a true promise involves true contrition. We might say that very often this is not the case. For instance, suppose that a sinner who is getting married tomorrow is as a matter of fact getting out of the occasion of sin; he will not be committing the sins that he has been committing. Obviously for such a man this change is very easy because he no longer will be in an occasion of sin. Is this change a conversion? Is this a true promise? He says he will not sin again. But is this promise a true promise not to sin; that is, not to do anything against the will of God? If he rejects in the depth of his person his sinful orientation, we have a promise in the true sense. In this promise we have conversion, since his promise contains contrition, at least virtually.

Self-Realization

Conversion evidently is the disposition of the whole person—a self realization. This self realization is to be achieved through an explicitly conceptualized act realizing some particular good action. Through this act on its deeper level, i.e., at the center of the person, conversion is achieved. Hence, once again, conversion is always on the level where a person is present to himself, where you *cannot* fully reflect on it. Consequently, in conversion we are conscious that we are converting, that we are now moving from sin to a love of God above all else. I cannot love God without knowing it; as subject I am aware and conscious of it but this love of God is not as an object of reflection. For full reflection is impossible. It would mean that I would have to go out of myself; when that occurs I as a whole am not present to myself. I cannot go out of myself and with conceptual clarity and certainty know that I am living in grace. True conversion occurs in the subject as subject, not as object of reflection. Suppose a sinner says; "Oh my God I regret my sins." Is he really regretting his sins and his being a sinner? On the conceptual, reflex level, I cannot tell you with certainty. The sinner cannot do this himself. But in the center of his person, he is aware of whether he is really loving God or not.

But even though full reflection on this conversion is not possible, we do have signs of it just as we have signs for a mortal sin. Normally if we know we are doing wrong in a matter of importance and if we are psychologically free in making the choice, most probably we are committing a mortal sin. But most likely in such an act grave matter is only *one* sign. There are also other signs of what I am in the very inmost being of my soul. For instance, during such acts I am aware of the degree of my psychological freedom to make a true choice of this or another act. So also in conversion, I have signs whether I am really converted or not: e.g., I am sincere with myself; I recognize the fruits of my conversion; or as St. Ignatius says, I look for signs of true consolation, etc. We do have signs. However, it still remains true that we cannot fully grasp in conceptual reflection whether we are converted or not. Christian life does not have this certainty whether I am in grace and love my God or whether I am a sinner and am refusing myself to God. We know this only "by conjecture," as St. Thomas says. Christian joy is not the joy of a possessor but of a man who has hope in Christ. This state is typical for the Christian.

Secondly, how is conversion possible? This is a crucial question! If a person is a sinner with his whole person committed to hostility against his God, how can he come back? Is it possible? You may say, "Yes, by grace." But this working of grace also poses the same question. How can this person who in the self realization of his person stands against God be changed and become a different person? Here we must observe that although this person did dispose of himself as a whole, he did not and could not do so *totally*. Why? A human person lives his life successively by moments and days, by months and years. He cannot realize himself totally in any single moment. Hence, if a sinner disposes of himself as a whole but not totally, and does so continuously during his entire life, much of his total reality still remains to be integrated in him as a sinner, and in this life he will never accomplish it totally. In him other tendencies always remain—e.g. not to be a sinner. It is at this point that the grace of Christ can help him.

The good man is in a similar situation. He too has disposed of himself as a whole, but not totally; hence he can become a sinner. You are familiar with St. John's phrase, *justus non peccat*. But still it is true that the Christian does sin sometimes? How is this possible? It is possible precisely because the justified man, while loving God with his whole person, has not as yet integrated into this love the whole reality of his long life. As a fallen man he has many tendencies against God, and throughout his whole life he is called upon to integrate all that his life means and is into his love of God. But as long as he lives in this world, there is always the possibility that his contrary tendencies may lead him back to a life of sin. Therefore, sin is possible in the just man just as conversion is possible for the sinner. Conversion, however, requires the grace of Christ; otherwise there would be the possibility of self redemption, which is excluded.

Examples

How should we describe this always-given grace of Christ? Can it be that Christ is *in every moment* offering the grace of conversion? I do not think that this is possible. Why not? Conversion is not possible in or through a superficial act. Conversion is possible only in an act which engages the entire person. It is in such an act that the grace of conversion is offered by Christ. In this way Christ helps the person to become free once more and to accept his grace as a son of God.

Thirdly, I wish to offer a few thoughts by way of analogy on "conversions," as we commonly use the term. A first type of conversion *per analogiam* can take place in the first perfect human act of a person, whether he be baptized or not. In this first perfect human act a person becomes involved in the entire disposition of himself. Before this moment such a person is not as yet a sinner in a personal way. But neither at this moment is he totally indifferent; he is not a zero. He is a human person, tainted by the sin of Adam and possessing all the egoistic tendencies of fallen man. Now at a single moment of time he has to dispose of himself as a person, to set the direction of his life. Will he accept the inclinations of his fallen nature? Or will he resist and in this sense convert to the other side, giving himself as a whole to his God and to Christ who is calling him by his vocation, by grace? If he resists and decides to give himself to God, then this first act is in a true sense an act of conversion by analogy. In such an act of conversion a person is involved as a whole in a fundamental option (*optio fundamentalis*). This is a free act, realized perhaps by choosing one or another good, but more deeply a giving of oneself to God within the center where the whole person is present to himself. Such a person could thus actualize his whole being in the direction of God, and although he would be aware of what he is doing, he could not capture it in full conceptual reflection.

There is another analogous type of conversion, the so-called continual conversion which occurs in three different forms: 1) the radical neo-conversion, 2) continuous verification of one's self-gift to God, and 3) conversion from venial sin.

Conversion Can Grow

What is radical neo-conversion? A man has committed himself to love God. That is his will, enduringly. But in a certain moment, for instance in a retreat, he substantially deepens the intensity of his own option for Christ and God. His subsequent life would then be an expression of this deeper self realization in relation to God. This would be a new conversion. This person really would be a new man thereafter.

The second form of *conversio continua* is the continuous verification of what we are, of our self-giving to Christ and to God. It is continuous verification because we have to verify successively throughout our lives what we are in our relationship to God. We have given ourselves to God. Depending on different situations there is a successive growth that must be realized. Some of these acts of verification will perhaps be deep enough to justify the use of the term, fundamental act; other acts will be superficial expressions of what we are. In all these acts we are integrating the whole reality of our lives into the personal disposition of ourselves. It seems to me that by this continuous verification of what we are as converted men, we will also grow in what we are and not remain merely what we were. We shall grow, develop, and mature in love.

Finally, the third form of this *conversio continua* is conversion from venial sin. This much is clear: Insofar as venial sin is not a fundamental act engaging the entire person, conversion from venial sin need not be on the level of the disposition of myself as a person, as a whole.

Let me now conclude this consideration of sin and conversion. Sin is a fundamental reality of the Christian life. It is a powerful reality, a reality full of consequence. A true sin—not venial sin which is sin only by analogy—involves the whole person. In this sin a person is constituting himself through his will in an actualized, permanent resistance against God and the grace of Christ.

Conversion is not possible without the help of the grace of Jesus Christ. Christ's grace makes the sinner once more able and free to change himself, to overcome his resistance against the Father. In converting the sinner, Christ enables him to change the orientation of his whole person and his whole will in relation to God and to Christ. Not every sinful act nor every good act is in the full sense of the word either sin or conversion, but only those acts which engage the person precisely as person, as a whole. From the moment of his first perfect human act, an adult person is always, continuously, freely, and as a whole engaged, either giving himself as a whole to God, or refusing himself as a whole to God. A morally adult man is never indifferent; he is always committed as a total person. This is true whether he has been converted from a true sin or has just made his first perfect human act in coming from his situation as fallen man. By his conversion he becomes a "spiritual man" (*homo spiritualis*); the sinner is a "carnal man" (*homo carnalis*); the fallen man is *inclined* to be a sinful man (*homo carnalis*). A convert is, by the grace of Christ, a spiritual man. Every man is either a spiritual man, in St. Paul's sense, or a carnal man. It is in the human act in which our person as a whole is engaged that we actualize ourselves fully as spiritual men or as sinful men. It is a case of either/or; there is no middle ground. In other acts, superficial acts, we do not engage our personalities fully. Indeed, so many of our human acts are, as a matter of fact, not acts in this full personal sense at all. They are neither sin (in the full sense) nor conversion.

17

Social Sin and Conversion:
A Theology of the Church's
Social Involvement

Peter Henriot, SJ

Certainly there are few topics as exhaustively worked over as the topic of Christian social involvement. Pontifical pronouncements and theological treatises, sociological surveys and political polemics: all seem to have said already whatever could—or should—possibly be said on the topic. Why do I so boldly dare to take up this topic anew?

My daring comes in response to an emphasis found in the work of the 1971 Synod of Bishops. The Synod produced the document, "Justice in the World," a stirring call for the Church's active social involvement. What makes the Synod document uniquely important, and worth more than the usual passing notice, is its emphasis upon the theme of *social sin*. That emphasis is the key to what I argue can be considered a "new" theology of the Church's social involvement—"new" at least in the sense that it has never before been so clearly explicated in an authoritative Roman document. Theologically, it helps us

to understand more completely and adequately both (1) *why* the Church is socially involved, and (2) *how* the Church is socially involved. We will consider these two questions in detail here.

I. Why Is the Church Socially Involved?

"Gathered from the whole world, in communion with all who believe in Christ and with the entire human family, and opening our hearts to the Spirit who is making the whole of creation new, we have questioned ourselves about the mission of the People of God to further justice in the world." In these introductory words, the Bishops of the Synod expressed their effort to discern anew the social implications of the Gospel which the Church is mandated to preach to all nations. Since the days of Leo XIII, the Church's social doctrine has developed along fairly consistent lines.

This article originally appeared in Chicago Studies 11 *(Summer 1972): 115–130.*

Basic human rights have been emphasized, traditional scholastic teachings on social justice explained, and—more recently—biblical theology brought to bear on Church ministry.

It is the element of biblical theology which has made significant impact in recent development of the social doctrine of the Church. This is particularly evident in *Gaudium et Spes*, Vatican II's Constitution on the Church in the Modern World, and in Paul VI's *Populorum Progressio*. The first part of the Vatican II document (#'s 11–45) spells out the social implications of the biblical themes of the dignity of the human person, the community of mankind, the value of human activity in the world, and the role of the Church in the world. The encyclical of Pope Paul—rejected by the *Wall Street Journal* as "warmed-over Marxism"—treated the topic of worldwide development and its demands on the rich nations within a framework of explicit biblical lessons.

Key to this new biblical emphasis has been a healthy stress upon the importance of serious engagement with the things of this world. I say "healthy" because all too often there has been a stated or unstated presumption that the really deeply spiritual person, the truly religious individual, did not become mixed up with social issues. Somehow it came to be accepted by many Christians that it was possible to respond to the Gospel and yet be unconcerned with social responsibilities. Although love of neighbor was always seen as basic to Christian life, effective social action and involvement to implement that love through the works of justice was not considered a necessary requisite. *Gaudium et Spes* rejected this view out of hand: "They are mistaken who, knowing that we have here no abiding city but seek one which is to come (Heb 13:14), think that they may therefore shirk their earthly responsibilities. For they are forgetting that by the faith

itself they are more than ever obliged to measure up to these duties, each according to his proper vocation (2 Thes 3:6–13; Eph 4:28)."

But as strong as was this teaching by Vatican II for social involvement, it needs to be moved still further. The theological topic which provides impetus for this further movement is the topic of *social sin*. This became an explicit topic of the Second Roman Synod, mentioned again and again in the debates, and referred to three times by the Bishops in the final document: 1) After reviewing the serious gap between the rich and the poor of the world and the consequent injustices which are structured into global society: "In the face of the present-day situation of the world, marked as it is by *the grave sin of injustice,* we recognize both our responsibility and our inability to overcome it by our own strength." (Part II) (emphasis added). 2) In urging a genuine reform of educational approach in order to promote a vital education to justice: "But education demands a renewal of heart, a renewal based on the recognition of *sin in its individual and social manifestations.*" (Part III) (emphasis added). 3) In emphasizing the role of the liturgy in educating Christian people to the demands of justice: "The practice of penance should emphasize *the social dimension of sin* and of the sacrament." (Part III) (emphasis added).

Sin and redemption are, of course, major biblical themes. The Old and New Testaments are filled with accounts of man's infidelities and God's mercies. For the Christian community the sin-redemption theme is central. Gathered in the Eucharist, we proclaim a redemptive mystery of faith which has particular meaning because we "all have sinned, and have need of the glory of God" (Rom 3:23). The Gospel which the Church joyfully proclaims is a "Gospel for the remission of sins."

If we are honest with ourselves, however,

we must admit that by and large we have tended to restrict the category of sin to a very narrow *personal* sense. Evidence of this can be easily obtained from a quick glance at the standard forms for the examination of conscience available in catechisms and prayer books: "Have I missed my morning and night prayers? . . . Have I failed in my Sunday obligation? . . . Did I lie? . . . Did I steal? . . . Did I entertain impure thoughts? . . . Did I swear?" We might object that such forms of examination are very passé in the Post-Vatican II Church of the 1970's. Yet for the overwhelming majority of adult Roman Catholics, these truly did serve as "forms"—profoundly formative of moral sensitivities.

The Bishops of the Synod appeared keenly aware of this fact and voiced their concern that such a narrow focus on sin in a personal sense was the major reason for the failure of Catholics to see the situation of the modern world as truly a "sinful situation." The official synthesis of the Synod debates noted: "Here, indeed, there emerged a major preoccupation of the Synod. How is it, after eighty years of modern social teaching and two thousand years of the Gospel of love, that the Church has to admit Her inability to make more impact upon the conscience of Her people? But it was stressed again and again that the faithful, particularly the more wealthy and comfortable among them, simply do not see *structural social injustice as a sin,* simply feel no personal responsibility for it and simply feel no obligation to do anything about it. Sunday observance, the Church's rules on sex and marriage tend to enter the Catholic conscience profoundly as *sin.* To live like Dives with Lazarus at the gate is not even perceived as *sinful.* It was this very strong reaction of the Synod that the whole social teaching of the Church has to be removed from the high level of doctrinal pronouncements and forced into

the consciences of the People of God." (#7) (emphasis added)

The theme of social sin was well focused for emphasis at the Synod by the opening section of the pre-synodal working paper. Men of our times, the paper states, "demand profound changes in the very structures of society, structures which often constitute in themselves an embodiment of the sin of injustice." (#2) That sin is somehow related to social structures is the very essence of "social sin," and to understand this we need to look at some recent developments both in theology and in sociology.

In recent theological development, sin has more and more been viewed as a state rather than an act, as stance, orientation, direction, attitude rather than deed, incident, transgression. (See Piet Schoonenberg, S.J., *Man and Sin: A Theological View,* Notre Dame, Indiana: University of Notre Dame Press, 1965; and Louis Monden, S.J., *Sin, Liberty and Law,* New York: Sheed and Ward, 1965.) Biblical scholarship has shown that in its more refined treatment in John and in Paul, "sin" is used in the singular to imply state or condition. Such a biblical interpretation of sin challenges moral theology to be more *actor-oriented* than *act-oriented* in its discussion of sin. The social implication—indeed, the social incarnations —of sin are more readily put in perspective by this understanding.

Concomitant with this theological development has been a heightened sociological appreciation of the reality of social structures. In modern society these structures—systems and institutions, socio-economic-political arrangements—are very real entities with a life of their own, embody highly influential norms and sets of values, and have immense potential for an impact that can be either good or bad. Sociologist Peter Berger, for example, has emphasized that an understanding of the dialectic between man and society, a dialectic made explicit in the constitution and operation of social structures, is critical to a realistic understanding of man today. Hence it is critical to any viable theological understanding. Berger sums up this dialectic: "Society is a human product. Society is an objective reality. Man is a social product." (Peter L. Berger and Thomas Luckmann, *The Social Construction of Reality: A Treatise in the Sociology of Knowledge,* New York: Doubleday Anchor Books, 1967, p. 61.)

One of the problems which arises when the reality of social structures is insufficiently recognized is that social ethics tends to be very underdeveloped. Bryan Hehir has noted this fact as a consequence of an over-focus by Catholic moralists upon the birth-control question. The high visibility of the question in Catholic circles in the past decade tended to constrict natural law thinking as an institutional ethic apt to deal with the moral issues which arise in the structural problems of our society at the national and international level.

Examples of Social Sin

Given this theological understanding of sin and this sociological emphasis upon structures, we can now begin to appreciate why certain situations and structures can be referred to as instances of social sin. It will be helpful to look at three examples of social sin.

1. A social structure which oppresses human dignity and stifles freedom is a sinful structure. For example, a welfare system based on the premise that the poor are somehow bad and therefore not to be trusted or given a say in what happens to them is a structure which oppresses the dignity of the poor. It is a structure which victimizes those obliged to follow its patterns and customs: minimal payments, excessive surveillance, demeaning interviews, the ever-present fear of a cut-off of necessary funds. As we would refer to personal action of such an oppressive nature as sinful, so we must refer to action of this structure as sinful.

2. A social situation which promotes and facilitates individual acts of selfishness is a sinful situation. For example, zoning and tax systems which allow individual citizens to preserve their privileges at the expense of the poor and powerless provide situations wherein the selfishness of these individuals is made easy. Zoning legislation which makes it impossible for the less economically advantaged to seek more habitable surroundings outside of the central city facilitates the selfishness of the more privileged. A tax system which places a disproportionate burden of paying for public goods upon lower- and middle-income people (through numerous loopholes for higher-income brackets) is clearly a system which promotes the individual selfishness of some citizens in our society.

3. A social structure or situation which is unjust also becomes sinful when one is aware of the injustice but refuses to exert efforts to change it. This is the social sin of complicity. For example, the silent acceptance of an international monetary and trade system which severely injures the legitimate interest and aspirations of the developing countries in the 1970's is certainly an instance of social sin. With 20% of the world's population controlling 80% of the world's wealth, major decisions are made every day which affect the quality of life of the inhabitants of the Third World without their having the least say in the character of these decisions. A startling instance of this was the decision in the fall of 1971 to devalue the American dollar, a decision costing the voiceless poor nations some

$500 million in precious international reserves. Silent complicity as we enjoy the benefits of such a decision constitutes an instance of social sin.

If it is true that it is possible for some of the very structures of our society to constitute in themselves an embodiment of the sin of injustice, then we have the key to discerning a deeply theological reason for the Church's involvement in social action. In the *Constitution on the Church in the Modern World*, Vatican II had clearly stated the single intention of the Church's mission: "that God's kingdom may come, and that the salvation of the whole human race may come to pass." (#45) This mission is accomplished in the preaching of the Gospel of Jesus Christ, in fulfillment of the mandate, "Go into the whole world, preach the Gospel to every creature" (Mk 16:15). The Kingdom is established and salvation comes only in the face of a struggle against sin—personal and social.

The theological foundation for *why* the Church is socially involved—not only has the *right* but the *obligation* to be so involved—can be summed up in two propositions: (1) the Gospel that the Church preaches is a Word that frees from sin, and (2) the world is marked by the evil of situations and structures of social sin. This foundation was clearly expressed by the Synod: "Action on behalf of justice and participation in the transformation of the world fully appear to us as a constitutive dimension of the preaching of the Gospel, or, in other words, of the Church's mission for the redemption of the human race and its liberation from every oppressive situation" (Introduction).

It is helpful to note that this explicit linking of social involvement with the preaching of the Gospel is made in at least three other places in the Synod document. The citations are worth quoting in full. "The mission of preaching the Gospel dictates at the present time that we should dedicate ourselves to the liberation of man even in his present existence in this world." (Part II) "The Church, indeed, is not alone responsible for justice in the world; however, she has a proper and specific responsibility which is identified with her mission of giving witness before the world of the need for love and justice contained in the Gospel message, a witness to be carried out in Church institutions themselves and in the lives of Christians." (Part II) "At the same time as it proclaims the Gospel of the Lord, its Redeemer and Savior, the Church calls on all, especially the poor, the oppressed and the afflicted, to cooperate with God to bring about liberation from every sin and to build a world which will reach the fullness of creation only when it becomes the work of man for man." (Part IV)

We can answer the first question, *why* is the Church socially involved, by offering a theological explanation which is rooted in a new emphasis on social sin. This emphasis ties the Church's social involvement directly and essentially to its mission of preaching liberation from sin.

II. How Is the Church Socially Involved?

Sinners are called to *conversion*. Liberation from sin comes in the process of "metanoia." Conversion is the call of the prophets to Israel to return as a people to the worship of the one God, Yahweh; it is the message of John the Baptist, the opening expression of the Good News proclaimed by Jesus ("Repent and believe, the Kingdom of God is at hand," Mk 1:15), the repeated exhortation of the kerygmatic sermons in *Acts*. A central religious experience, the process of conversion implies a change of heart, a reorientation of life's direction, the acceptance of a new set of values.

I believe it is possible to discuss a theology of *how* the Church is socially involved in terms of conversion, in terms of the actions the Church—as individuals and as community—takes to bring about conversion from social sin. For our purposes here, I suggest three approaches to conversion: prophetic word, symbolic witness, and political action.

A. *Prophetic word.* The Church's primary tool in social involvement is the Word of God. A "two-edged sword," this Word must be spoken fearlessly in situations of social sin and against sinful structures wherever found. According to the Synod document, "Like the Apostle Paul, we insist, welcome or unwelcome, that the Word of God should be present in the center of human situations. . . . Our mission demands that we should courageously denounce injustice, with charity, prudence and firmness, in sincere dialogue with all parties concerned." (Part III) Thus is the Christian community called to speak the "two-edged sword" of denouncing and encouraging, the prophetic word.

A concrete prophetic word helps to bring about conversion primarily because it challenges our view of "the way things are" and "the way things are done." Certainly the chief obstacle to social change, the main hindrance to remedying conditions of injustice, is our failure to perceive the sinfulness of a situation. Our perceptions are very contingent upon the prevailing set of images and patterns of perception, the values and behavioral standards, which are inherent in our culture. What the prophetic word does is shatter the images or mindsets by which we are accustomed to perceive reality, especially social reality. As the

synthesis of the Synod debates suggests, "We are all to some degree prisoners of the perceptions and visions to which we are educated— by formal schooling, by the pressures of the media, by special propaganda." (#19) The Gospel message of liberation frees us from this prison by offering alternate perceptions and visions.

For example, American society places great stress on the ethic of *competitiveness* and exalts being "number one," whether in business, sports, or foreign policy. By and large, this is an accepted value in our society, with children being socialized to it and adults judging events by it. But the Gospel ethic of *sharing*—with consequent emphasis upon moderation, concern for the other, etc.—is in sharp conflict with the ambition of being "number one." Where a prophetic word for sharing is spoken, then, conversion from sinful structures—unjust economic systems, for instance, or unjust foreign policies—based on competitiveness is made both a challenge and possibility for Christians.

Social involvement of the Church by way of speaking a prophetic word seems to be what Johannes Metz refers to as the "critical liberating function" of the Church (*Theology of the World,* New York: Herder and Herder, 1971, p. 117). Precisely because the Church's message is eschatological, it points to the future and judges all institutions, ideas, and images as *provisional*—that is, as subject to radical change. Metz's emphasis upon the institutional role of criticism is echoed by Eduard Schillebeeckx, who adds the specification that the Church's prophetic word about social change must arise from concrete situations. Ethical imperatives thus emerge "from a concrete experience of life and impose themselves with the clear evidence of experience" (*God the Future of Man,* New York: Sheed and Ward, 1968, p. 153.)

Something which Schillebeeckx says about the character of this concrete prophetic word is important for us to recall at this point. At times we in the Church are prevented from speaking out—or at least we plead that we are so prevented—by our "lack of knowledge of all the facts." But Schillebeeckx has noted that the ethical content of the stands that we might take even on complex political issues can and frequently do arise from what he has called a "contrast-experience." A "contrast-experience" is the experience of a very concrete social evil—such as war, racism, torture, exploitation, world hunger—to which the Christian can only respond: "This should not be so, this must not go on!" I may not have all of the facts to know what the alternatives should be, but I can know—from the values which the Gospel expects to be integral to the life of a follower of Jesus—that this particular evil must simply not be allowed to continue. And thus the prophetic word is spoken.

Granting what I have just said in the preceding paragraph, there is still need—if conversion is to be promoted and exercised through an effective prophetic word—for serious research into critical social questions. If Church leadership, for example, is to expect a hearing, then it must show the authenticity of its commitment by the seriousness of its effort. A specific instance comes to my mind. Again and again in the 1960's, groups of American Catholics petitioned individual bishops and the National Conference of Catholic Bishops to speak out in moral condemnation of the Vietnam War. Repeatedly the Bishops refused to say anything specific, on the grounds that they lacked sufficient information to make a concrete judgment. As legitimate as this excuse

might have been the first time it was uttered, its legitimacy faded with constant repetition. The Bishops failed the test of authenticity by making no effort whatsoever to gain sufficient information to make a moral judgment. No study group was set up, no experts were consulted. What we in the American Church did not hear from our Bishops was the response of a group clearly committed to value leadership in our country at a critical time: "We do not have sufficient information to make a proper moral judgment about the Vietnam War at this time and *therefore* we appoint a special commission of political scientists, moral theologians, ordinary citizens, etc., to assist us in making that judgment as soon as possible." We can hope that the experience of the 1960's will have taught the Bishops—and indeed all of us—of the need to take seriously the call to speak prophetic words.

B. *Symbolic witness.* Immediately after urging the Church's social involvement by way of prophetic words, the Synod document notes, "We know that our denunciations of injustice can secure assent to the extent that they are an expression of our lives and are manifested in continuous action" (Part III). This call to witness symbolically—that is, to act out concretely—the values of which the Church speaks is evident in other places in the Synod document and is essentially related to the task of conversion from social sin. The symbolic deed not only manifests our conversion but also in turn deepens our conviction.

The integral link between the prophetic word and the symbolic deed has been cogently explained by Paulo Freire. Designing a "pedagogy of the oppressed," a method of education for liberation, Freire stresses that a word not only conveys information but also effects change. "Within the word we find two dimensions, reflection and action, in such radical interaction that if one is sacrificed—even in part—the other immediately suffers. . . . An unauthentic word, one which is unable to transform reality, results from the dichotomy imposed upon its constitutive elements. When a word is deprived of its dimension of action, reflection automatically suffers as well; and the word is charged into idle chatter, into *verbalism,* into an alienated and alienating 'blah.' It becomes an empty word, one which cannot denounce the world, for denunciation is impossible without a commitment to transform, and there is no transformation without action." (*Pedagogy of the Oppressed,* New York: Herder and Herder, 1970, pp. 74–75.)

Lest Church pronouncements on social matters become an "alienated and alienating 'blah,' " it is crucial that the Christian community witness through symbolic deeds its commitment to transformation through action for justice. Thus the Synod document states: "While the Church is bound to give witness to justice, she recognizes that anyone who ventures to speak to people about justice must first be just in their eyes." (Part III) To achieve a semblance of justice in the eyes of others, the Church is urged by the Synod to an examination of its modes of actions, its possessions, and the life style of all: bishops, priests, religious, and lay people.

Especially noteworthy in this call to symbolic witness is the challenge for a "sparing and sharing" life style (See William R. Callahan, S.J., "The Quest for Justice: Guidelines to a Creative Response by American Catholics to the 1971 Synod Statement, 'Justice in the World,' " Washington, D.C.: Center of Concern, 1972). The Bishops at the Synod stressed that the possessions of the Church must never compromise the preaching of the Gospel to the poor, and that "our faith demands of us a certain sparingness in the use" of goods. The theme is taken up with particular relevance to the Catholic Church in the United States— since we Americans are six percent of the world's population but consume forty percent of the world's resources—"Those who are already rich are bound to accept a less material way of life, with less waste, in order to avoid the destruction of the heritage which they are obliged by absolute justice to share with all other members of the human race." (Part III) Studies such as that of the Club of Rome (Dennis Meadows *et al., The Limits of Growth,* New York: Universe Books, 1972) have recently pointed out the *finite* character of our globe and emphasized the limited natural resources and interrelated ecology of our planet. This makes the Synod's call for sparingness all the more urgent and the practice of an austerity of life style all the more dramatic a manifestation of conversion from social sin.

The challenge is particularly relevant for priests. The life style of the priest is of critical importance in this country both in its symbolic value and in its ability to sensitize the priest himself and his community to the needs of others. I am not speaking here of an "ascetical ideal" but of a social necessity. The synod document is very explicit: "If . . . the Church appears to be among the rich and the powerful of this world its credibility is lost." (Part III) Hence it is essential that the priest as a public person of the Church makes a serious effort to practice the "sparingness of use" urged by the Synod. Simplicity of life style is surely called for today in the priest's residence, food and drink, car, recreation, vacations, protocol and privilege, etc. We priests need to be very honest with ourselves, and in very practical ways test the authenticity of our commitment to social justice, our conversion from the social sin of a wasteful consumer society.

C. *Political action.* Sooner or later in a discussion of *how* the Church is to be socially involved, the issue of the Church and politics must be squarely faced. In the United States this is an especially sticky issue, one which has been clouded emotionally by disputes inside the Church and between the Church and society at large. The reason why political action must be considered in these theological reflections, however, is precisely because social sin is a structural phenomenon. Conversion from social sin is possible only if efforts are made to see that structures are changed—and in the United States, major social structures are changed through the political process. According to the Synod document "This desire [for justice] however will not satisfy the expectations of our time if it ignores the objective obstacles which social structures place in the way of conversion of hearts." (Part I) Social involvement taken seriously, then, of necessity means that political action is taken seriously.

It is at this point that the true meaning of conversion takes on a special significance. The Christian who pursues just social change through political action must do so because of his or her own justice. The 1968 Medellin documents, statements of renewal by the Second General Conference of Latin American Bishops, make this point lucidly: "The originality of the Christian message does not consist directly in the assertion that it is necessary to change structures, but in the insistence on the conversion of man which in turn calls for this change." (Conclusions, Justice, #3) First personal conversion, then conversion of structures; but no authentic personal conver-

sion without genuine commitment to change structures.

That the Church in the United States is socially involved through political action is a fact which can hardly be denied. Individual Catholic citizens acting on their own do, in the words of the Synod, "involve the responsibility of the Church whose members they are" when they act in the political area "under the influence of the Gospel and the teaching of the Church." (Part II) And certainly the U.S. Catholic hierarchy has been deeply involved in politics in such issues as aid to education and abortion legislation. What is being called for by the Synod, and appears to be supported by our theological discussion of social sin and conversion, is the acceptance of political action as a *religious imperative,* a Christian responsibility. If some social structures in the United States are instances of social sin and are to be remedied, then political action to change them becomes the concrete implementation of that "constitutive dimension of the preaching of the Gospel" identified by the Synod as "action for justice and participation in the transformation of the world." (Introduction)

Conclusion

John Gardner, one of those unique figures who is a public philosopher engaged in practical political action, has noted somewhere that our society continues to be preoccupied with specific evils to be corrected, rather than the development of a society responsive to the need for continuous change. It has been my contention here that for the Church to be socially involved is for it to be concerned about the structures of society—and whether or not those structures are in need of and open to that continuous change which is movement from social sin to conversion to justice. The theological foundation for the Church's social involvement and the theological explanation of its manner of involvement can be found in the 1971 Synod's emphasis on social sin. It should be clear from my discussion that I have been using "Church" in a variety of senses, sometimes referring to the Church as an institutional force, but most of the time meaning simply all the People of God. All of us have the common task of getting the Church socially involved in response to the call to preach the Gospel through "action on behalf of justice and participation in the transformation of the world."

18

Christian Conversion:
Developmental and
Theological Reflections
on Young Thomas Merton

Walter E. Conn

While the history of Christianity is filled with accounts of remarkable conversions, perhaps the best documented conversion we have is the contemporary story of Thomas Merton's personal journey of transformation—a strikingly vivid and sharply focused example of the complex dimensions of Christian conversion. Though Merton's life story is the narrative of a conversion process extending over some thirty years, this essay will focus on the early period recounted in *The Seven Storey Mountain,* the young Merton's conversion to Catholicism and decision for the monastic priesthood.[1] This is not the place to retell the story of Merton's life, something the autobiographical and biographical writings have done with some thoroughness. Rather, presuming familiarity with his conversion experience, the emphasis here—from the perspectives of developmental psychology and foundational theology—will be on an analysis of that experience as reflective of the fundamentally moral dimension of Christian conversion.

Employing the insights on personal transformation of Erik Erikson, Jean Piaget, Lawrence Kohlberg, and James Fowler, as well as of Bernard Lonergan, Part I will reflect on the cognitive, affective, moral, and faith dimensions of Merton's conversion experience.[2] Part II will then consider how Merton's experience is reflected in several foundational themes of contemporary theologians.

I. Developmental Perspective

Merton's spiritual journey to Gethsemani offers us several opportunities to reflect on significant cognitive, affective, moral, and faith dimensions of development and conversion.

This article originally appeared in The Perkins School Journal of Theology *(Fall 1983): 11–23.*

Cognitive Transformation

Clearly, Merton's Christian conversion had a strong cognitive dimension—so powerful, in fact, that Merton was for a time deceived into overestimating its efficacy. From his adolescent atheism Merton traces his journey of cognitive conversion while a student at Columbia through encounters with Etienne Gilson and Aldous Huxley, William Blake and Jacques Maritain, first to an intellectual appreciation of the Christian God and then finally to personal belief in this God.[3] The explicitly intellectual component of this belief, and of Catholic Neo-Scholastic theology generally, provided the cognitive foundation for conversion which Merton had previously lacked, and had failed to find, for example, in his brief flirtation with communism.

From a developmental perspective, there seems to be no question about Merton's advanced cognitive status. The power of abstract, hypothetico-deductive reasoning—the normal operations in which cognitive development culminates, according to Jean Piaget—clearly marked his cognitive orientation. Exceptionally perceptive, even his reflective power of self-criticism was extraordinary for a young man. What Merton required for Christian conversion, then, was not greater or more sophisticated cognitive abilities, but a liberation of his intelligence for a more authentic grasp of reality. If Gilson provided him with his first intelligible, coherent concept of God, Huxley, Blake, and Maritain together brought Merton to the personal insight that allowed him to break out of his closed, naturalistic realism in order, finally, to be able to embrace that God. Whatever the ultimate philosophical merit of these perspectives, they did open Merton's horizons to the supernatural, and by thus exploding the former limits of his world,

revolutionized his thinking and eventually his life. By the end of the summer, 1938, after Blake had during the course of many months worked himself into Merton's system through the medium of a master's thesis, Merton was convinced at least intellectually of the necessity of living in a world "charged with the presence and reality of God."[4] By Merton's own calendar, then, it had taken about a year and a half, beginning with his reading of Gilson's *Spirit of Medieval Philosophy* early in 1937, for the transformation of the self-described atheist into "one who accepted all the full range of possibilities of religious experience right up to the highest degree of glory."[5]

Affective Transformation

But this embrace of God is never a purely intellectual affair. It is, rather, a fully personal reality, at once thoroughly affective and thoroughly cognitive. The author of *The Seven Storey Mountain* was as acutely aware of this as anyone could be, and he rightly stressed, along with his intellectual journey, the long and difficult course of development in his affective life that led him to ever greater transcendence of himself, and finally to conversion.

Bernard Lonergan has suggested that a person is affectively self-transcendent when the isolation of the individual is broken and he or she spontaneously acts not just for self but for others as well. Further, when a person falls-in-love, his or her love is embodied not just in this or that act or even in any series of acts, but in a dynamic state of being-in-love. Such being-in-love is the concrete first principle from which a person's affective life flows: "one's desires and fears, one's joys and sorrows, one's discernment of values, one's decisions and deeds."[6] Falling-in-love, in other words, is a more or less radical transformation of a person's life: affective conversion. Such conversion turns one's self, shifts one's orientation, from an absorption in one's own interests to concern for the good of others. If moral conversion is the recognition of the possibility, and thus the felt challenge, to become a living principle of benevolence and beneficence, affective conversion is the transformation of personal being which actualizes that possibility, which makes effective response to that challenge a reality. Affective conversion, therefore, is the concrete possibility of overcoming moral impotence, of not only being able to make a decision to commit oneself to a course of action or direction of life judged worthwhile and personally appropriate, but of being able to execute that decision over the long haul against serious obstacles.

The reality of falling-in-love, of course, has as many versions as there are love stories. There is the beaming love of young parents for their newborn child; there is the love of sons and daughters for mothers and fathers which grows through years of responding to the wonders of parental self-transcendence. Such familial self-transcendence grounds the possibility, too, of the intimate love between a woman and a man—from the boundless dreams and reckless self-giving of young lovers to the gentle touch and knowing smiles of a peaceful couple looking back over a half-century through which they have grown together in each other's love.

Life, of course, is made of more than love stories. Right alongside are ugly tales of hatred and brutality, misunderstanding and resentment, indifference and bitter disappointment —tales which too often end without a hint of forgiveness, reconciliation, hope. At the end of a century that has witnessed human atroci-

ties of the most staggering proportions, a story that ignores the full potential of the human heart for evil is less credible than a fairy tale. Still, if life is not an innocent story in which prince charmings and fairy godmothers always emerge triumphant, there *are* instances of self-transcending love. As the lives of individuals as different as St. Thérèse of Lisieux and Mother Teresa of Calcutta remind us, when the mutual love of families and friends is authentic it does not remain absorbed in an *égoisme à deux* or three or more, but reaches out beyond itself to the neighbor, not to "humanity," but to the concrete person in need, whoever or wherever that person is.

Two examples from Merton's early life are to the point: his involvement in Communism and his attraction to Friendship House. While the author of *The Seven Storey Mountain* described the young Merton's participation in Communism as a moral conversion, his own final estimate of the episode was that his "inspiration to do something for the good of mankind had been pretty feeble and abstract from the start."[7] Pretty much an isolated individualist in 1935 as he entered Columbia after some difficult, lonely school years in England, he was really interested only in doing good for himself, despite his weak attempt at something more. In contrast, the affectively converted person is not primarily interested in the abstract "good of mankind," but in responding to the specific needs of concrete persons.

When we turn our consideration to Merton's attraction to Baroness de Hueck's Friendship House in Harlem six years later, just before his decision to go to Gethsemani, we get a quite different picture. Here we see Merton dealing with the injustice of society by responding to the real needs of suffering people he had worked with and knew as individuals. Events quickly conspired to lead Merton along a different path, toward an end which he perceived as greater, so there is no story of "Merton at Friendship House." How such a story might have turned out is not the point here, however, for there is no reason to doubt that his commitment to Friendship House was much more like his decision for Gethsemani than it was like his earlier decision for the Young Communist League.

Without intending a pun, the difference is best understood, I think, in terms of six years of *friendship*. Despite all the difficulties and uncertainties of his years of confusion in New York, one constant that stands out clearly is the importance in Merton's life of his friends. Merton the autobiographer saw the hand of God very clearly at work in the small group of friends that formed during those student days at Columbia. Together these truly good friends provided the support each needed to realize themselves in moving beyond the boundaries of their narrow, private worlds. All the prods to sanctity were not as explicit as Bob Lax's suggestion that Merton should desire to be a saint, but even the most common doings of friends were important: a recommendation of Huxley's book at one right moment, an introduction to Bramachari, the contagiously spiritual Hindu monk, at another. And it does not seem accidental that this group of friends had a special relationship to Mark Van Doren, Merton's favorite professor. A life of self-transcendence does not grow and flourish without the nourishment of a strong model, and, perhaps more than anyone else, Van Doren was this for the young Merton. Bramachari and Dan Walsh, another professor, and certainly the Baroness were important. But the quiet influence of Van Doren on Merton's intellectual, moral, and affective life appears to have been singular in the depth of its effect. It does not seem inap-

propriate that in the end it was Van Doren's question to him about the priesthood that finally brought Merton to his decision.

"Falling-in-love," it must be stressed, refers not to an easy soap-opera sentimentalism, but to a radical personal capacity for self-transcendence, for reaching out beyond oneself to the good of others. While the personal dynamic state of "being-in-love" is normative for authentic human living, the affective dimension of the personal subject is clearly developmental. No one familiar with Erik Erikson's pattern of psychosocial development, therefore, will expect normative affective development, and thus the possibility of effective, sustained self-transcendence, in an adolescent, for example. If ethical capacity, in Erikson's view, is the criterion of identity, it is the criterion of identity not as an adolescent crisis but as an adult consolidation. Reversing the lens, we can see that a successful resolution of the identity crisis is a condition for mature ethical capacity, which is to say, for the intimate love of the young adult and the responsible caring of the generative adult. For only a person confident in his or her identity can risk losing that identity in going out to others. While one can fall-in-love with everything from puppy dogs to God, the meaning here is the normative one of an adult love that is caring and responsible.

In Merton's spiritual journey from Cambridge through the period in New York and finally to Gethsemani, we see the sharply etched lines of an identity crisis that required several years of difficult negotiation for Merton to bring to a basically successful if not perfect resolution in his conversion and decision for the priesthood. If the end of one's twenty-seventh year seems a bit late to be finally getting a real purchase on one's identity, we must remember that Merton had bitten off a very large piece to resolve. He would be satisfied with nothing less than the full commitment of himself in fidelity to the Truth he finally discovered to be God. A modest crisis with an easy resolution was not for Merton; after all, his was an identity reaching out for the Ultimate.

A central factor in Merton's identity resolution, of course, was his very discovery of God —the discovery of a living God to whom Merton reached out in an affective self-transcendence which for the rest of his life would continue to deepen through even the most difficult days and darkest nights. Such a loving relationship would go a long way toward resolving the critical issue of intimacy in Merton's life. In all, Merton's experience manifests most lucidly the structure of affective conversion as a shift from the instinctive, spontaneous egocentrism of self-abortion to the personal, reflective caring for others of self-giving love.

Moral Transformation

Having considered the cognitive and affective dimensions of Merton's conversion, we must turn now to see how they came together to effect transformation in his moral life. For, clearly, Merton's years in New York constituted a period of sustained development in his moral judgment and decision-making powers. He was, after all, engaged for much of that time in an almost single-minded effort to reach a decision—not just an important decision in his life, or even about his life, but a decision constitutive of his very life, of the kind of person he would be.

Earlier we considered points of contrast between Merton's conversion to Communism and his Christian conversion. In focusing now on Merton's moral development, it may be helpful to examine the two specific moral

judgments he made about war in those different version contexts.

In 1935 Merton, along with several hundred others participating in a Peace Strike meeting in the Columbia gymnasium, solemnly took the Oxford Pledge against fighting in any war. The basic attitude of the meeting's speeches, as Merton later reported, was that there was no justification for any kind of war by anybody, and if a war did break out, it would be the result of a capitalist plot and should be resisted. This was exactly the kind of position that appealed to his mind at that time. "It seemed to cut across all complexities by its sweeping and uncompromising simplicity. All war was simply unjust, and that was that. The thing to do was to fold your arms and refuse to fight. If everybody did that, there would be no more wars."[8] The Pledge was strongly supported by the Communists, of course. The next year, when the Spanish Civil War broke out, Merton was no longer actively involved in Communism, but Communists who had taken the Pledge were now either fighting against Franco or picketing anybody who did not see that the war in Spain was a holy crusade for the workers against Fascism. Reflecting on all this, the author of *The Seven Storey Mountain* admitted that the Pledge would not have been intended by him (or probably the others) as anything more than a public statement, as in his (and their) mind there was no real basis of moral obligation or principle of justice. In fact, Merton saw his younger self and Communist associates as unprincipled opportunists who recognized no law but their own wills.[9] This stinging judgment from the monastery, in terms of Lawrence Kohlberg's Stage of instrumental-relativism may not be fully justified, but the simplistic, ideological character of Merton's 1935 judgment on war seems evident enough.

In contrast, six years later, as Merton was moving towards his decision for Gethsemane in 1941, the character of his judgment on war is significantly more nuanced. If Merton's earlier, unconditional objection to war had been based mostly on emotion, his response to the draft in 1941 was the product of a conscience carefully formed in just war theory and rooted in a sense of moral duty.[10] Assessing America's anticipated participation in the war as both defensive and necessary, Merton judged that he could not absolutely refuse to go if drafted. But though the intent of the war would be necessary self-defense, and thus morally legitimate in purpose, there still remained the crucial question of means. Though Merton had little doubt that the indiscriminate slaughter of noncombatants in modern war was immoral, the morality of the means was the most difficult for him to decide. In fact, he did not have to decide it. For, fortunately, as a monastic autobiographer still interpreted several years later, the draft law left him a loophole: he could apply as a noncombatant objector. In this way he would be able to "avoid the whole question" and follow what seemed the much better course. Putting aside the "practically insolvable question of cooperation," Merton saw service in something like the medical corps as an opportunity to perform works of mercy, to overcome evil with good.[11]

Placed next to his participation in the Oxford Pledge, the reasoning leading to Merton's moral judgment here is clearly superior. In the Oxford Pledge we saw Merton taking a simplistic, absolute stand based more on the abstract, totalitarian logic of ideology than on a perceptive understanding of the concrete realities of the situation. And while his enthusiasm for Communist ideology represented a desire to move beyond egocentric interests to a concern for value, we also noted how, according to the autobiographical interpretation, this short-lived enthusiasm conveniently masked a continuing fundamental self-interest.

By 1941, however, Merton had, as he put it, developed a conscience. Now it was his genuine, tested commitment to value, wedded to intelligence that demanded careful, realistic analysis of the concrete situation, that motivated and guided his decision, not an emotionally charged will whose final form was self-interest.

If the significant development in Merton's moral reasoning and decision-making powers between 1935 and 1941 is apparent, however, the limitations of his moral development as manifested in his 1941 decision on the draft should also be clear. In 1935 he had "borrowed," for his own purposes, the communist ideology on peace. In 1941 his morality is still "borrowed," but now from standard Catholic moral theology: the just war theory. Merton's application of this theory to his situation was fairly sophisticated, to be sure, but the theory's warrant for Merton lay finally in the Church's authority. Evidence of this is found, for example, in Merton's failure to pursue and resolve what seemed to be something of a discrepancy between his interpretation and "the mind of the Church" on the meaning of the gospel teaching, "Whatsoever you have done to the least of these my brethren, you did it to me." In Merton's understanding, at least, it was "not the mind of the Church that this be applied literally to war—or rather, that war is looked upon as a painful but necessary social surgical operation in which you kill your enemy not out of hatred but for the common good." For Merton, this was "all very fine in theory." Whatever difficulties it involved in practice he was willing to avoid by using the legitimate option of the non-combatant objector. This also avoided a personal confrontation with traditional Catholic moral theology. The mind of the Church and civil law combined nicely for Merton into a satisfying conventional solution, which gave him "an ineffable sense of peace."[12]

The fact, of course, which even Merton the autobiographer did not fully realize several years later, is that under the surface of this conventional solution a radical challenge to the traditional just war theory was beginning to take shape. Its development into an autonomous principled morality would require many years, but the seed was growing and already beginning to make its subterranean presence felt in 1941. For, while Merton's stated objection to the war, and thus his explicit reason for application as a non-combatant objector, was the indiscriminate slaughter of civilians through the ruthless bombing of open cities, his own words show that he was really concerned not just about that modern barbarism, but about being involved in any killing: he would willingly enter the army" so long as he "did not have to drop bombs on open cities, or shoot at other men."[13] Clearly, Merton only *thought* he agreed with the just war theory. The truth is that he had only borrowed it; he would never really own it. Whatever the real limitations of Merton's moral development at this point in his life, though, what seemed indisputable are the real gains he had made. By 1941 Merton had not only "developed a conscience," as he put it, he had also committed himself to Christian values in a solidly conventional way through a fundamental moral conversion.

Faith Transformation

We have considered significant cognitive and affective developments in Merton during the crucial years of young adulthood, and how they combined to effect a profound transformation in the moral dimension of his life. But while Christian conversion touches the moral dimension deeply, as a full personal reality it clearly involves even more than the moral dimension. In order to do at least some justice to this "more than," we must now turn to the personal reality which James Fowler calls "faithing," the constructing of and relating to an ultimate environment of meaning.[14]

For anyone attempting an interpretation, a conversion to Catholicism such as Merton's is a complex, ambigious reality, despite the fact that faithing in such an instance is explicitly religious. On the one hand, such a Christian conversion is clearly a deliberate, personal choice of value, a decision, indeed, constitutive of one's character, definitive of one's very being. On the other hand, conversions to the Catholic Christian faith are often characterized by a marked dependence on the authority of the Church. Merton, clearly, is no exception here. We have just seen, for example, how Merton's acceptance of the official Catholic teaching on the just war overshadowed his own incipient pacifist intuitions.

Through the lens of a cognitive-developmental stage theory of faithing, however, Merton's conversion is brought into sharper focus by Fowler's descriptions of Stage 3 Synthetic-Conventional Faith and Stage 4 Individual-Reflective Faith. Several defining elements of both stages of faithing aptly characterize Merton during the conversion period inasmuch as he is in a transitional phase, beginning to move out of the third stage but not yet fully into the fourth. Clearly, Merton takes seriously the burden of responsibility for his own commitments, life-style, beliefs, and attitudes. His identity is taking on a clearer measure of self-definition. And he expresses his intuitions of ultimate coherence in explicit, conceptual systems of meanings. While these factors point toward movement to a Stage 4 Faith perspective, the defining element Fowler names "Locus of Authority" sharply indicates the limits of this transition. In Stage 4 Faith authority is located critically in one's own judgment. Despite his clear gains in explicit definition of self and world view, there is no evidence to suggest that his faith orientation at this time is truly critical. On the contrary, evidence such as his decision about participation in the war clearly indicates the precritical orientation of faith Stage 3.

Merton's conversion faith is clearly personally chosen. But just as clearly, his choice is of an "ideologically established perspective," that of the Catholic Faith. His appropriation is not the critically self-chosen faith of a postconventional orientation. Like moral conversion at moral Stage 4, Christian conversion at faith Stage 3 is an uncritical conversion. A person at faith Stage 3 may or may not experience conversion, but if he or she does, the experienced conversion is uncritical, occurring within and depending upon an unquestioned, given world of values and beliefs. Such a conversion may be conceptually sophisticated, affectively rich, and personally profound, yet uncritical because of its inability to question its fundamental values and beliefs. And as personally authentic and life transforming as Merton's 1939–41 Christian conversion was, then suggesting that it was essentially a conventional, uncritical conversion to the then, unquestioned values and beliefs of the Catholic Church.

Preceding pages have discussed, in order, Merton's cognitive, affective, and moral conversions. The fact, of course, is that during the 1939–41 period Merton experienced one conversion—extended in its realization to be sure—but still one conversion: a single Christian conversion with cognitive, affective, moral, and faith dimensions.

II. Theological Interpretations

Conversion as Fundamental Option

The understanding of Christian conversion we have constructed from Merton's experience corresponds in many ways to what contemporary theologians have called fundamental option or decision. In fact, some theologians have considered conversion precisely as fundamental decision. Karl Rahner, for example, interprets conversion as, "the religiously and morally good fundamental decision in regard to God, a basic choice intended to commit the whole of life to God. . . ." This fundamental turning to God, is seen, of course, "as a response, made possible by God's grace, to a call from God."[15]

Josef Fuchs places this fundamental option of conversion in the explicit context of sin. For him, "conversion is a change in the whole person, for the whole person is a sinner. . . . Conversion means to change the whole thrust of one's life." Because conversion is the deposition of the whole person, it occurs on the deep personal level where one is able to dispose of oneself as a whole. "Just as a person becomes a sinner only on the deep personal level, so it is only there that a sinner can experience conversion." Thus conversion is much more a "turning away from the fundamental orientation to sin" than from any particular definite sin of the past. Still, if conversion is achieved on the deepest level at the center of a person, it is always realized in and through a particular concrete good act.[16]

From this point of view, Rahner insists that conversion is primarily unselfish love of the neighbor, "because only in conjunction with this can God really be loved, and without that love no one really knows with genuine personal knowledge who God is." Most simply, then, conversion is "a resolute, radical and radically conscious, personal and in each instance unique adoption of Christian life."[17]

Jesus' Call to Conversion

Turning from sin to love of neighbor points to the central moral dimension of Christian conversion. Jesus' preaching clearly called for moral conversion: "Repent and believe in the Gospel!" (Mk 1:15). But just as Christian conversion is more than moral conversion, so Jesus' call to conversion is more than a call to moral obligation. Jesus' call to repentance is a call to Christian conversion only in the context of the immediately preceding proclamation: "The time is fulfilled and the reign of God is at hand!" As Franz Böckle explains, the order of presentation here is important, since, for Jesus, the demand for conversion followed upon God's anticipatory salvific move.[18] As Charles E. Curran points out, the "motive for conversion is the presence of the reign of God in Christ."[19] Christian conversion is the joyous and grateful change of heart that results from hearing the good news of salvation: God's offer of love. This good news of God's salvific love both requires—and makes possible—the joyful change of heart, the grateful acceptance of God's reign of love. The misery of the sinner, God's offer of love, and the appropriate response of conversion is poignantly depicted in the parable of the prodigal son. Bernard Häring helps us to understand the meaning of conversion here by noting that the Hebrew word for conversion, *schub,* means returning home. The good news is the possibility of returning home to God's unconditional love. To

accept this good news, of course, one requires a vivid sense of the wretchedness of sin and the need of redemption. Homecoming is for the homesick. One reaches conversion not through increasing evil, says Häring, but through growing insight into one's sin and into the misery of being cut off from God.[20]

Theological Interpretations and Merton

Häring and the other theologians we have been considering were not writing with Merton in mind. But they might have been. For Merton's experience of conversion concretely exemplifies their theological interpretation of Christian conversion just as vividly as it illustrates the psychological analyses of conversion. Indeed, the intrinsic religious dimension of Merton's experience demonstrates the necessity of a specifically theological interpretation to complement the psychological analysis of genuine Christian conversion. Clearly, Merton's conversion cannot be understood without reference to the complex dimension of personal identity. Just as clearly, it cannot be adequately understood *only* in relation to personal identity. More precisely, Merton's identity cannot be understood properly except in religious terms. For him the conflict of the divided self was an ultimate conflict. Merton understood that his decision was a radical decision for the fundamental orientation of his life—a turning from sin to God.

In fact, while Merton's experience supports the view that Christian conversion should be understood as a fundamental option, it also suggests that the reality of fundamental option should be understood much more explicitly as an *experience.* Contemporary theologians commonly assert that an adult has a fundamental orientation or stance either for or against God. From this premise it is argued that this fundamental stance could only have been established through a fundamental option. Therefore every adult has made a fundamental option of one kind or another, whether he or she knows it or not. This view was developed in order to shift the focus of modern moral theology away from a preoccupation with individual acts to a more biblically oriented concern with the pattern and direction of a person's whole moral life.

Basic developmental insights, however, require that we specify the meaning of "adult" in a critical way. All chronological adults are not moral adults. By definition, moral adults have made a fundamental option. Many chronological adults of long standing, however, have never come into their moral adulthood. They have never confronted themselves and taken possession of their lives at a deep enough level to make any kind of fundamental decision. These persons merely drift. They are often good people, doing many good things. But to claim for them a fundamental decision about their lives is to deny psychological reality for the metaphysical fantasy of ideology. Rahner is correct in emphasizing the radically conscious character of fundamental Christian decision as a personal experience. There may be good doctrinal reasons for positing the existence of a pre-conscious determination of a person's life, but such an alleged reality should not be confused with the conscious, experiential reality of personal conversion. People do not stumble into a conversion. Personal conversion involves a conscious, deliberate decision. Many important changes may be occurring in a person's moral and religious life of which he or she is unaware. But, if conversion is to mean anything as an empirical concept, it must be distinguished from such changes, however profound they may be. Biblical witness as well as modern psychological analyses support the view that only persons who have experienced transformation have been converted. It need not be a sudden, dramatic experience of conversion, but for characterizing someone who cannot identify such transformation in his or her experience, conversion is an inappropriate category. No one has to be told that he or she has been converted!

The contemporary theological interpretation of Christian conversion is also corroborated by Merton's experience in its emphasis on the biblical data. More than anything else, Merton experienced his conversion as a response to God's call: "And He called out to me from His own immense depths." How beautiful and how terrible are the words with which God speaks to the soul of those He has called to Himself, and to the Promised Land which is participation in His own life. . . ." "This was the call that came to me with my Baptism, bringing with it a most appalling responsibility if I failed to answer it."[21]

The very structure of Merton's autobiography highlights the fact that he heard God's call at a time of utter wretchedness. The final paragraph in Part One of *The Seven Storey Mountain* sums up the first phase of the conversion process, and anticipates the second: "I had come very far, to find myself in this blind-alley: but the very anguish and helplessness of my position was something to which I rapidly succumbed. And it was my defeat that was to be the occasion of my rescue."[22]

Merton prefers the imagery of the Jews being called out of Egypt into the Promised Land, but he is obviously, too, the Prodigal Son. And it was in this condition of anguished helplessness, when, as he would reflect, he "had been beaten into the semblance of some kind of humility by misery and confusion and secret, interior fear," that he was able to recognize the gracious offer of God's own life, which is Love. As he began to accept that offer, he "walked in anew world."[23]

Christian Conversion as Love of Neighbor

As we have seen, this gift of God's love was extended first of all through Merton's friends. In the same way, with the help of the Baroness, one of Merton's first responses to God's call was concern for the poor of Harlem—for his neighbor. Like Rahner, Dom Marc-François Lacan emphasizes that the faith of Christian conversion must be realized in love of the neighbor. Because Jesus, in Matthew's version of the Last Judgment, invites us to see him in the least of the little ones who are his brothers, the Christian is not to ask "Who is my neighbor?" as if some people could be excluded from our love. Christian conversion implies a conversion in the way one sees.[24] So, in the parable of the Good Samaritan, Jesus turns the question around: "How will I show that I am a person's neighbor, whoever that person may be?" "By being merciful" (Lk 10:29, 36, 37). To be merciful is to be perfect like the Father. Lacan points out how in Matthew's version of the Beatitudes the merciful are connected with those who search for justice. But this justice is not simply the human justice of loving those who love us; it is the transformed justice of universal love and forgiveness without limit. The root of this transformed justice is the humility which Jesus, the model of true justice, calls his disciples to: "Shoulder my yoke and learn from me, for I am gentle and humble in heart" (Mt 11:29). Humility, indeed, is at the heart of the new law: "If anyone wants to be first, he must make himself last of all and servant of all" (Mk 9:35). In so doing, the disciple will be imitating the Son of Man, who "did not come to be

served but to serve . . ." (Mk 10:45). It is this loving service of the neighbor in the daily lives of his disciples that Jesus points to in the image of the cross: "If anyone wants to be a follower of mine, let him renounce himself and take up his cross and follow me" (Mk 8:34).

Christian Conversion and the Transformation of Social Structures

Loving service of the neighbor, then, is the concrete form taken by the moral dimension of authentic Christian conversion. In order to specify this moral dimension for the contemporary world more sharply, Gustavo Gutierrez has insisted on the need for a spirituality of liberation which focuses conversion to the neighbor on "the oppressed person, the exploited social class, the despised race, the dominated country." For Gutierrez, Christian conversion means committing oneself to the liberation of the poor and oppressed. It means not only committing oneself generously, but lucidly, realistically, concretely, "with an analysis of the situation and a strategy of action."[25]

Taking his lead from social analysts such as Paulo Freire, Gutierrez emphasizes that the "conversion process is affected by the socioeconomic, political, cultural, and human environment in which it occurs. Without a change in these structures, there is no authentic conversion." All conversion requires a break. And not just in the private sphere of personal piety. "We have to break with our mental categories, with the way we relate to others, with our way of identifying with the Lord, with our cultural milieu, with our social class, in other words, with all that can stand in the way of a real, profound solidarity with those who suffer, in the first place, from misery and injustice."[26]

This view was strongly endorsed by the document of the 1971 Synod of Bishops, "Justice in the World." Because sin exists not only in personal consciousness, but just as powerfully in unjust social structures, the Bishops declared that "Action on behalf of justice and participation in the transformation of the world fully appear to us as a constitutive dimension of the preaching of the Gospel, or, in other words, of the Church's mission for the redemption of the human race and its liberation from every oppressive situation."[27]

What, then, is the relationship between the radical personal reorientation I have called Christian conversion, and the transformation of unjust social structures? In 1968 the Latin American Bishops addressed a key aspect of this question at their Medellin Conference: "The originality of the Christian message does not consist directly in the assertion that it is necessary to change structures, but in the insistence on the conversion of man which in turn calls for this change." On this basis, Peter Henriot answers our question this way: "First personal conversion, then conversion of structures; but no authentic personal conversion without genuine commitment to change structures."[28] Though certainly correct in affirming a connection which insists on genuine social commitment, this view's incompleteness oversimplifies the issue.

Coming at the question from the opposite direction, the Bishops of the 1971 Synod stressed that the desire for justice "will not satisfy the expectations of our time if it ignores the objective obstacles which social structures place in the way of conversion of hearts. . . ."[29] This point makes clear the inadequacy of any "first, then" sequential connection. Personal conversion does demand the transformation of social structures. But the transformation of social structures is also required for personal conversion. The Gospel calls us to work for both simultaneously. Ultimately, of course, this private/public dichotomy is untenable; society is not a collection of discrete individuals. Persons are social, through and through; and society is personal. Private conversion is really no conversion. Authentic Christian conversion is fully personal; it is thus shaped by, and shapes, the structures of its social context. This is not meant to discredit partial conversions; persons are not transformed totally in even the most intense moment. The point, rather, is to recognize the limits of any conversion, and to press for its expansion into the fullness of one's life.

Indeed, recognition of the limits of a conversion experience, and the necessity of expanding it, is one way of stating the fundamental Christian insight that conversion is not just a momentary, once-and-for-all experience; that authentic Christian life requires continuing conversion. As Curran points out, the vitality and dynamism of the Christian life demands continual openness to the call of God and neighbor. Even while the Christian shares in the work of bringing God's reign to final perfection, he or she remains a "spiritual schizophrenic," at once just and sinful. Thus the Christian's need for continual growth, through the redeeming work of overcoming sin by love, toward complete union with God and neighbor.[30]

Empirical Criterion of Conversion: Doing God's Loving Will

Our brief consideration of the theological perspective on Christian conversion recalls William James' psychological approach to conversion in his classic *Varieties of Religious Experience*.[31] For despite the significant differences between them, both views agree that the ultimate test of a conversion is in its living. James was interested in judging a conversion not in terms of its origin, but empirically, by its fruits for life. And this, finally, is the Biblical criterion, too. The mark of Christian authenticity is not saying "Lord, Lord," but doing God's will. And for Jesus, as Hans Küng rightly emphasizes, "God wills nothing but man's advantage, man's true greatness and his ultimate dignity." God's will, then, is nothing for himself; it is simply "man's well-being." Jesus' radical identification of God's will and human well-being means that God cannot be seen apart from men and women. To be for God is to be for one's neighbor. If the "universal and final criterion," as Küng says, is "man's well-being," then the test of Christian conversion can be nothing else than the empirical one of love for one's neighbor.[32]

For Jesus, of course, the call to love one's neighbor has no limits, as we have noted. To follow Jesus means to be the servant of all. Indeed, a radical transformation is necessary in one's understanding to have any sense at all of what God's will requires of us in our loving commitment to the neighbor's good. Human thoughts are not God's thoughts. It is not an easy saying, therefore, that follows Jesus' rebuke of Peter in Mark's Gospel. To follow Jesus in loving service is to lose one's life. But only the person who loses his or her life in loving service will save it. Therefore, as Lacan points out, to follow Jesus is "to walk in a direction diametrically opposed to that which men spontaneously follow."[33]

Such a radical turn from the spontaneously chosen path to follow God's will in Jesus clearly heads one beyond a moral conversion. The genuine Christian conversion involved in such a following of Jesus quite definitely starts one along the path to the profound reorientation of a life centered in God's love that is truly called religious conversion. As Rudolf Schnackenburg put it, the greater justice demanded by Jesus was a "religious demand, calling on man to hand himself over to the God who was greater than him and to be subject to him in obedience to his call and in readiness to become pure in heart and radical in action, but also in trust, that he will help and save him."[34] In one's response to Jesus' demand for unconditional service, the reign of God that is still to come becomes a present reality. As Böckle strongly emphasizes, the fundamental decision to respond to Jesus is in the final analysis, of course, a matter of faith, and therefore is a response to a call which is not "simply a demand, but primarily a gift."[35]

When Rahner, discussing this religious dimension of Christian conversion, speaks about trustingly accepting one's "existence in its incomprehensibility and ultimate unmanageableness as incomprehensibly meaningful, without claiming to determine this ultimate meaning" or to have it under control, and of successfully "renouncing the idols of . . . mortal fear and hunger for life,"[36] he is pointing to the possibilities in the power of God's gift for the lives of those who risk the first step of response in leaving all behind and following Jesus.

III. Conclusion: Following Jesus Towards Religious Conversion

This essay has focused on Merton's youthful conversion to Christianity in order to concretize through a specific example the moral dimension of Christian conversion. We have seen how the affective, cognitive, moral, and faith dimensions of Merton's life were transformed through his discovery of God and his response to God's love. Psychological and theological interpretations allowed us to appreciate Merton's conversion as a fundamental decision, a radical reorientation of life in terms of the values concretely embodied in the person of Jesus. Truly Christian conversion, we noted, is never merely moral, but through its response to God's love in Jesus always includes a religious dimension. Love of God through love of the neighbor perceived as Jesus is the Christian version of an affective conversion which wrenches a person out of self-absorption and throws him or her into a caring love of the least of the brethren. Such a conversion of life, of course, is never finished. So to suggest that Merton's youthful Christian conversion of 1939–41 is only the beginning of a life-long journey is not to diminish its reality and significance. It is, rather, to recognize the necessity of following the continuing journey which will bring Merton to the possibility of full religious conversion: absolute surrender in a total, unqualified love of God. For Christian conversion is not just another step along one's pre-set path. It is an about-face which sets one on a new, previously unknown path, following the footsteps of Jesus. To follow Jesus along that difficult path in constant fidelity is not just to learn more about God's love, but to discover the loving God in the depths of one's own being, as Jesus did. Merton, the autobiographer, realized that with his youthful commitment he "had entered into the everlasting movement of that gravitation which is the very life and spirit of God: God's own gravitation towards the depths of His own infinite nature, His goodness without end."[37]

Notes

1. Thomas Merton, *The Seven Storey Mountain* (Garden City, NY: Doubleday Image; first published 1948).

2. For convenient statements of these approaches to personal transformation, see Erik H. Erikson, *Childhood and Society* (2nd ed.; New York: Norton, 1963); Jean Piaget, *Six Psychological Studies* (New York: Random House Vintage, 1968); Lawrence Kohlberg, *The Philosophy of Moral Development* (San Francisco: Harper & Row, 1981); James Fowler, *Stages of Faith* (San Francisco: Harper & Row, 1981); and Bernard Lonergan, *Method in Theology* (New York: Herder and Herder, 1972), esp. pp. 104–05, 237–43. For an integration of Erikson, Piaget, Kohlberg, and Lonergan on cognitive, affective, moral, and religious development and conversions, see Walter E. Conn, *Conscience: Development and Self-Transcendence* (Birmingham, AL: Religious Education Press, 1981).

3. In addition to Blake's works, on which Merton wrote his master's thesis, the key books are Gilson's *The Spirit of Medieval Philosophy,* Huxley's *Ends and Means,* and Maritain's *Art and Scholasticism.*

4. Merton, p. 233.

5. *Ibid.,* p. 249.

6. Lonergan, *Method in Theology,* p. 105.

7. Merton, p. 184.

8. *Ibid.,* p. 180.

9. *Ibid.,* p. 181.

10. *Ibid.,* p. 376.

11. *Ibid.,* pp. 378–79.

12. *Ibid.*

13. *Ibid.,* p. 378.

14. See Fowler, *Stages of Faith,* pp. 151–83.

15. Karl Rahner, "Conversion," *Encyclopedia of Theology: The Concise Sacramentum Mundi,* ed. K. Rahner (New York: Seabury, 1975), pp. 291–95, at 291–92.

16. Josef Fuchs, "Sin and Conversion," *Theology Digest* 14 (Winter 1966): 292–301, at 297–98.

17. Rahner, pp. 292–93.

18. Franz Böckle, *Fundamental Moral Theology* (New York: Pueblo, 1980), pp. 152–53.

19. Charles E. Curran, "Conversion: The Central Moral Message of Jesus" in his *A New Look at Christian Morality* (Notre Dame, IN: Fides, 1968), pp. 24–71, at 27.

20. Bernard Häring, "The Characteristics of Conversion" in his *This Time of Salvation* (New York: Herder and Herder, 1966), pp. 217–28.

21. Merton, pp. 274, 275, 276.

22. *Ibid.*, p. 204.

23. *Ibid.*, pp. 256, 207, 257.

24. Dom Marc-François Lacan, "Conversion and Kingdom in the Synoptic Gospels" in *Conversion: Perspectives on Personal and Social Transformation*, ed. Walter E. Conn (New York: Alba House, 1978), pp. 97–118, at 117. Edited versions of cited essays by Rahner, Fuchs, Curran, Häring, Gutierrez, Henriot, and Küng are also included in this *Conversion* collection.

25. Gustavo Gutierrez, *A Theology of Liberation* (Maryknoll, NY: Orbis, 1973), pp. 204–05.

26. *Ibid.*, p. 205.

27. 1971 Synod of Bishops, "Justice in the World" in *Renewing the Earth: Catholic Documents on Peace, Justice and Liberation*, ed. David J. O'Brien and Thomas A. Shannon (Garden City, NY: Doubleday Image, 1977), pp. 390–408, at 391.

28. Peter J. Henriot, "Social Sin and Conversion: A Theology of the Church's Social Involvement," *Chicago Studies* 11 (Summer 1972): 115–30, at 128 (the Medellin Conference, Conclusions, Justice, No. 3, is quoted here).

29. "Justice in the World" in *Renewing the Earth*, p. 393.

30. Curran, pp. 49–50.

31. William James, *The Varieties of Religious Experience* (New York: Random House Modern Library, 1929; first published 1902), esp. chs. 8–10 on "Divided Self" and "Conversion."

32. Hans Küng, *On Being a Christian* (Garden City, NY: Doubleday, 1976), pp. 251–52.

33. Lacan, p. 106.

34. Quoted in Böckle, p. 166 from R. Schnackenburg, "Die Vollkommenheit des Christen nach Matthäus" in *Christliche Existenz nach dem Neuen Testament*, I, 146.

35. Böckle, p. 166.

36. Rahner, p. 292.

37. Merton, p. 274.

19

Conversion and Christian Ethics

James P. Hanigan

Conversion is the foundational experience of Christian life and so of Christian ethics. What follows in this article attempts to explore this claim. The intent is to investigate what conversion entails rather than the processes or dynamics through which it may be elicited or invited. To express the matter somewhat differently, we will not be dealing here with how people are or may be converted, but with what it means to be converted in the Christian sense.

I

Conversion is, in the language of Charles Curran, "the central moral message of Jesus,"[1] and, consequently, the foundational experience of the Christian way of life.[2] All the biblical symbols that point to the basic structure of the divine-human relationship or which suggest how one enters upon the Christian way of life make this clear.[3] What is called for is a death and a rebirth, a turning away from the darkness to walk in the light, a putting off of the old self to put on the new, a change of mind and heart so as to put on the mind of Christ, and so on. Conversion is a principle, then, in the literal sense of *principium;* it is a beginning on which all that follows is based. It is not, of course, an intellectual principle but an experimental one, which is why we can refer to it as the foundational experience of Christian ethics. The biblical symbolism can surely be multiplied at great length to confirm this initial point, but we can also explore this foundational experience in a more substantive way by using biblical examples of individuals who encounter the living God, or who are awakened to a consciousness of the presence of transcendent reality in their lives. I restrict myself here to three such examples, but there are certainly many others, an analysis of which would provide similar results.

(1) The prophet Isaiah gives us a dramatic account of his prophetic calling (Is 6:1–13).[4] The initial vision or experience of the prophet is one of the holiness and glory of Yahweh whose glory fills all the earth. This experience

This article originally appeared in Theology Today 40 (April 1983): 25–35.

evokes the profound feelings of awe, reverence, and holy fear and immediately elicits from him the response of his own and his community's wretched and sinful state. "What a wretched state I am in! I am lost, for I am a man of unclean lips and I live among a people of unclean lips, and my eyes have looked at the King, Yahweh Sabaoth" (6:5b).

This insight, this awakening to a consciousness of his wretched condition is incomplete, however, for immediately a seraph flies to the prophet with a live coal taken from the altar of Yahweh. With it he touches the prophet's lips and says, "See now, this has touched your lips, your sin is taken away, your iniquity is purged" (7b), and with this purging comes Yahweh's question: "Whom shall I send? Who will be our messenger?" (8b). The prophet is emboldened to volunteer—dare he not?—"Here I am, send me" (9a). He is promptly sent; "Go and say to this people. . . ." (9b).

There is noticeable in this story a basic structure of an experience of the living God which, I suggest, begins to point us toward the normative meaning of conversion. There is first the unlooked for awakening to the presence of transcendent reality in the prophet's own life—not just an awareness of God, but God for him. This awakening provokes a new consciousness of both the divine and the human and their relationship. As an immediate consequence there is a reorientation of the self, a reorientation which is initially painful and unwelcome—it is not pleasant to recognize that one is lost, wretched and unclean—but which ends up in comfort and hope.

Both moments or sides of the experience, the death and rebirth are provoked not by any insight into or awareness of the self and its shortcomings and possibilities, nor by a re-

flection on the world and its problems. The experience follows upon Isaiah's awareness of the holiness of Yahweh. We might, by way of illustration, contrast the prophet's experience to the human experience of awakening to one's own limits, failures, and inadequacies or those of one's society in the light of either one's own ideals and values or the abilities, achievements, and social standing of others. For this latter experience the best answers our modern culture seem able to generate are either cries for revolution or some version of the therapeutic principle, "I'm okay, you're okay," whereas it was abundantly clear to Isaiah that none of us is okay at all.

(2) We find the same basic structure of experience in *Peter's* awakening to a consciousness of the presence of divine reality in his life as he encountered that presence in the person of Jesus. The experience is recounted for us in an especially clear way in Lk 5:1–11 and in less explicit fashion in Mt 4:18–22. As Luke tells the story, it was the miraculous catch of fish that awakened Peter's consciousness to an awareness that there was more to Jesus than meets the eye. Peter found himself in the presence of someone or something which elicited from him that most natural of all gestures of awe, reverence, and holy fear—he fell on his knees. This gesture was accompanied by a confession of his own wretched condition: "Leave me, Lord; I am a sinful man" (5:9). Once again, however, this insight is incomplete. Immediately a new life, a new direction is held out to Peter. "Do not be afraid; from now on it is men you will catch" (11a). And Peter followed Jesus, leaving everything behind.

In this example of Peter, despite a rather different social setting and a different content of experience, we find a basic structure of experience that is readily recognizable as similar in meaning to Isaiah's experience. There is the unlooked for awakening to the presence of transcendent reality in his life, which provokes in him a new awareness of both the divine and the human and their relationship. There is the reorientation of the self which involves the initially painful acknowledgment of his own sinful condition but which terminates in comfort and hope. Neither moment of the experience is self-provided or self-initiated, but elicited by the encounter with the divine presence. There is, once again, considerably more involved here than taking stock of one's self and one's failures and possibilities, or of comparisons of the self with the abilities and achievements of others, or of honesty about one's deepest fears and aspirations. Despite the confession about himself, Peter, like Isaiah, is not self-focused but other-focused.

(3) As a third and final example we can detect the same basic structure of experience in Paul's conversion experience which is similar on the surface to Isaiah's in that it takes the form of a private vision. The account of Paul's experience can be found in Acts (9:1–19, 22:1–16, 26:12–23), and in a shortened form in Gal 1:11–24. For no particular reason, I follow here the account in Acts 9.[5] While on his mission of zeal to preserve the integrity of Judaism, Paul is surrounded by a light from heaven and falls to the ground. This time a voice other than his own makes not a confession but an accusation, "Saul, Saul, why are you persecuting me?" (9:4). The voice then orders Paul to proceed to Damascus where he will be given further instructions. In Paul's case the experience initially leaves him blind and there is a three day wait before Ananias appears with the good news that he is to see

again and be filled with the Holy Spirit. He eats, drinks, regains his strength, and after a few days begins to proclaim the Gospel.

Again there is the same structure of experience; the unlooked for awakening to the presence in his life of transcendent reality, a new awareness of the divine and the human and their relationship, a new orientation of the self that is initially painful but which terminates in comfort and hope.

I have elaborated these examples in some detail because I am concerned to illuminate as clearly as possible what I have repeatedly called a basic structure of experience. And it is that basic structure of experience that I wish to propose as *normative* for the meaning of Christian conversion. Obviously the three examples are portrayed biblically in a somewhat dramatic fashion and so suggest that the awakening of consciousness to the presence of transcendent reality in one's life is something abrupt, unlooked for, and well-marked. But that does not mean that there was no previous psychological and spiritual preparation for such experience nor that, if we had the biographies of our three exemplars, we would be unable to fit these experiences coherently into their lives. It does mean, however, that the awakening is experienced with a degree of serious intensity and sufficient newness that warrant calling it a conversion experience or describing it as a decisive event.[6]

We can understand events such as we have described as events of cognitive and psychological disequilibrium.[7] They involve a process of being thrown off balance—it is noteworthy, that both Peter and Paul fell down—and then restored to equilibrium on an entirely new basis, which requires considerable getting used to. One way, then, of describing the Christian way of life is as a gradual and complete change in the equilibrium of the self.[8] The attempt of Peter to walk upon the water (Mt 14:22–33) serves as a useful biblical illustration of how difficult it is to establish this new equilibrium. Such an understanding also suggests why conversion is only a beginning of the Christian life, or if one prefers, why conversion might also be understood as a continuous process in which we are likely to be thrown off balance more than once.

Understanding conversion as a process of disequilibrium and restoration to balance on a new basis is similar to the theoretical understanding of cognitive and moral development of psychologists like Jean Piaget and Lawrence Kohlberg. Both men see such development taking place as a result of a series of cognitive disequilibrium events and the persistent tendency of the human organism to seek equilibrium.[9] This way of looking at the matter helps us to understand why the simple experience of being knocked off balance is sufficient neither for conversion nor moral growth. For a person might well seek to restore equilibrium on the same old basis. It also makes clear why not just any change or new basis is sufficient for Christian conversion, since only faith in Christ can serve as the foundation for the Christian way of life, a fact which supports the claim for a normative conception of conversion.

But it is important to stress that the awakening of the consciousness of the human person to the presence of the God revealed in Christ results in a disturbance of the present equilibrium of the self. It disturbs the at-home-ness in my world which I have so carefully established for myself on my own terms. It reveals to me not only that I am lost or mistaken, but that I have no excuse to offer, no defense to make for being lost. If this painful condition is faced and acknowledged,

it leads to the confession of one's wretched state or sinfulness. This confession, then, is the first normative element in the meaning of Christian conversion to explore for its ethical implications.

II

The popularity of Kohlberg's theory of moral development with its strongly Kantian understanding of morality,[10] and which, incidentally is coming under increasing criticism from theologians, has familiarized most educators with stages of moral growth that lead the individual away from heteronomy toward autonomy.[11] Such stage theory holds out as the goal of moral development the Enlightenment moral ideal of the fully autonomous human agent. My teaching experience with students is that they readily accept such an ideal, harbor a varying degree of self-doubt, guilt, and resentment toward authority figures —including God—because they have not yet realized the ideal, and generally interpret the ideal to mean that they are or should be accountable to no one but themselves for their moral decisions. But if my depiction of conversion is at all accurate, such students have badly missed the mark. Autonomy in Kohlberg's sense is not a Christian ideal but an illusion and a rather subtle form of idolatry. What the awakening of consciousness to the presence of the God revealed in Christ makes explicitly clear, ethically, is that we are accountable to someone beyond our own consciences. We are called, and rightly called, to respond to a truth, a beauty, a goodness beyond our own making or imagining, and woe is me if I do not respond.[12]

While it is, then, properly speaking, a religious conversion which stands at the foundation of the Christian way of life, such a conversion has also an inescapable ethical dimension. The religious conversion can be described accurately in the language of a Paul Tillich as being grasped by ultimate concern or with Bernard Lonergan as an other-worldly falling in love,[13] or in sundry other ways, but in any case Christian conversion involves also a demand for total, permanent self-surrender, without conditions, qualifications, or reservations. God is not some sentimental blob who does not care what we do, but rather the One who cares passionately and demands an accounting. The call to such surrender is not for an action but for a new dynamic orientation of the self that is logically prior to and the principle of all subsequent understandings and actions. While this new orientation can be explicated philosophically, as Lonergan does, as the undertow of existential consciousness,[14] or in terms of a fundamental option,[15] it can also be expressed in the language of Vatican II as the vocation to holiness[16] or in simple biblical terms as the call to discipleship. But it is precisely only over-against this call, this demand for response, that our confession and need for continual conversion find their meaning and possibility.

This experience—or better, this aspect of the experience I am describing as conversion —does not seem to be what is generally understood as being born again, and it is certainly not the experience which answers Luther's question of where one will find a gracious God.[17] For while it includes the joyful acceptance of God's healing grace, it also involves facing up to and acknowledging both my own sinfulness and the demand of God that I be responsible.

Nevertheless, it is both beside the point and possibly dangerous to try to proclaim the central moral message of Jesus by pointing out to individuals or groups how sinful or wretched or wicked they are, or how far short they fall from Gospel ideals or commands, or by urging them to cultivate an excessively introspective conscience.[18] For the sinfulness—and the sins —for which we are asked to repent are not primarily illuminated by comparisons with other people, past or present, who seem more generous than ourselves, or by examining how short we fall from our own rules or ideals. Our lostness is made manifest in the face of the awesome holiness of God and "the harsh and dreadful love"[19] revealed in Christ.

III

The other normative aspect of the conversion experience, beyond the confession of our sinful condition, is the call to holiness, the discipleship to which we are summoned which encompasses the more particular but inescapable ethical demands of Christian existence. There is something God wants us to be, calls us to be, and repentance and faith are both meaningless and impossible without the call to discipleship and holiness of life. Yet this call, while expressed here in general, abstract terms, is not itself abstract, but always concrete, rooted in a specific history and society with quite specific referents. Christian conversion always implies a community referent, a narrative referent, a rational referent, and a personal referent.

The *community* referent reminds us that Christian conversion entails church membership, that is, association with a normative community, not merely in a voluntary group that constructs its own norms and purposes, or in one that happens to be personally agreeable. God's call in Christ means that one is called to join the Church. Church membership, then is a moral duty, not an optional element or a utilitarian need. And the church, while sociologically understood as a voluntary association, is theologically a moral community to which one is called to belong and serve. To express the same notion differently, Christian conversion recognizes that we become God's children, members of his family, by grace and adoption, not by nature. Those who are converted, therefore, find that they must answer not only to God, but also to and for the community of the faithful.

This community referent is vividly clear in the examples of Isaiah, Peter, and Paul. It is also clear that the nature and the extent of the responsibility to and for the community is a function of the unique call with the different gifts individuals have received. For many people this responsibility will be exercised first and most immediately in the family, the *ecclesiola in ecclesia*.

Secondly, there is the *narrative* referent. I borrow the term narrative from Stanley Hauerwas and I used it to mean what I understand him to mean by it, that Christians have a normative story in accord with which they are called to form their character and their common life.[20] A willingness to submit to the story, to allow one's purposes and intentions, one's character and relationships to be shaped by the story is a normative aspect of Christian conversion. And, of course, since the normative story is not my story and not under my control (I am called to enter into the story and make it my own), to insist that I am the sole authentic interpreter of the story is, in effect, to refuse submission to the story. The Christian story is the story of Jesus and the story of his people. Consequently the community referent and the narrative referent go hand in hand, which is why, in more formal theologi-

cal terms, one must acknowledge and wrestle with the authority of Scripture, tradition, and the church.[21]

The rational referent to Christian conversion suggests the authority embedded in the natural, created, and developed resources of human persons. In saying this I no doubt reveal my penchant for some version of natural law morality, but I am not concerned at the moment to defend such an extensive claim. I only wish to suggest that a normative aspect of Christian conversion is the acceptance and embracing of God's creation and so of God the Creator. What that means can be made more specific by pointing to an acceptance of what one is in terms of the givens of one's life, one's race, ethnic heritage, color, sex, size, human talents, limitations, and so on. It would include an acceptance of human finitude, sociality, historicity, and physicality. It would accept and value the human capacity for intellectual, aesthetic, emotional, and spiritual growth. It would mean the acceptance of the world as world with all its diversity, challenge, and unfinished nature. I am suggesting that a conversion that is not in principle open to the future and the need for human growth in all dimensions is as little a Christian conversion as one that is in principle not open to the Cross or to membership in the community of the faithful.

Finally, a fourth referent of the call to holiness is what I would call the *personal* referent. By this I mean the acceptance of the responsibility for one's own judgments of conscience or, in more religious terms, for one's personal response to God. There are numerous biblical texts and examples that convey the meaning intended here, but the story of the rich young man (Mk 10:17–22) will serve as well as any to illustrate the need for a personal response to the call of God, even though others may not be asked to sacrifice as much or respond in a similar way. The example of Peter in John 21, where he is told to follow Jesus and not worry about God's plan for John, also illustrates the point. The three examples with which I began make the same point. Isaiah, Peter, Paul were called to carry out individual tasks unique to themselves. They did not ignore the other three referents I have mentioned—that way lies madness and fanaticism—but neither did they use them to protect themselves from the radically personal call of God.

IV

We have argued that the normative meaning of Christian conversion is to be found in a basic structure of human experience, involving the initiative of God's action and provoking a two-sided, inseparable response. This response involves the acknowledgment and confession of one's lostness and sinfulness as well as the acceptance of a call to holiness. This call in turn has four clear concrete referents or ethical aspects, involving the authority of: the Christian community, the Christian story, reason, and personal conscience. These submissions are, of course, in principle only, since every individual has to work out in life the conflicts and tensions that arise in daily living among these authorities. But to refuse one or more of these authorities in principle is to refuse to respond to the central moral message of Jesus.

What this foundational conversion experience means for Christian ethics, I believe, is that the converted inevitably will understand morality differently from the non-converted. In practice, what will appear to some as only a psychological or social problem will for the Christian have a primary moral significance,

and it will make sense to say about some issues that Christians don't behave that way.[22] To that extent I am in full agreement with Stanley Hauerwas' claim for a distinctively Christian social ethic and that what can only be seen as one choice among many by the non-Christian will be perceived by Christians as a duty.[23] Accordingly, it should be possible to show how Christian conversion casts moral problems in a different light.[24] Let me conclude, then, by trying this on one area of social justice, the question of unequal wealth.

It has become a truism to say that the American consumer ethos conflicts with the Gospel warning that one cannot serve both God and mammon (Lk 16:13), that materialism stands in sharp contradiction to the Gospel ideals of stewardship and preferential concern for the poor and disadvantaged. At the same time, the practical implication of the Gospel ideal remains elusive for the average middle-class American Christian. Short of the total renunciation of all possessions, we seem able to recommend little more than spiritual detachment from one's material possessions and generous personal giving to worthy causes. In some cases, tithing has again become fashionable as a useful practical guide for what is generous, or as the only biblical guideline available. The normative experience of conversion which I have tried to describe would want to say at least five things about this problem.

First, the accumulation and use of material possessions is not a matter of moral indifference in the Christian way of life. We are not the owners but the stewards of our possessions and so we need to recognize that we can, do, and have sinned in this regard. An essential correlative to this acknowledgment, moreover, is the demand to listen meaningfully to the cries of the poor, the hungry, the naked who are the mediators of God's presence among us (Mt 25:31–46). While I think such meaningful listening is the intelligible intent of contemporary liberation theologians in demanding solidarity with the oppressed, I find this way of putting the matter both less ideological and also more realistic.

Second, the spiritual detachment from material possessions counselled in the Christian tradition must have as part of its external embodiment a responsible support of the Christian community's concrete mission in the world. What constitutes responsible support is having shared reasons for giving and using one's wealth, in company with the Christian story, so that almsgiving or charity or giving from one's surplus to the needy is not a work of supererogation but a Christian duty.[25]

This leads to the third thing to be said, namely, that spiritual detachment from material possessions also needs to be fostered in repeated confrontation with the Christian story and the biblical texts that challenge our greed and our supposed right to a given standard of living.

These three points largely shape an attitude toward material possessions and wealth, but they are not without practical import. At least one student of mine was profoundly shocked to discover that the Christian Gospel challenged his desire and ambition to make as much money as he could and so undermined his fundamental reason for being in school at all. Other students have been equally shocked to learn that material aid to the poor and disadvantaged is biblically not a matter of sentimental and paternalistic good will but of strict duty and justice. Doubtless many other examples will come readily to mind.

The last two things to be said about the issue of wealth also ask for recognition rather than providing answers. In submitting to the authority of personal conscience, we open ourselves to the real possibility that God may well be calling us—or even our families—to live and work in ways that will demand sacrifices and afford a standard of living considerably different and lower than what is considered to be average or normal. This is a situation many of us who teach or work in church-related institutions already experience, though not always with the sense of mission and the absence of resentment and complaint faith would seem to call for. Before the call of God, there is no such thing as a right to a certain standard of living.[26]

Submission to the authority of reason, which conversion entails, warns us against either sentimental or ideological responses to the problem of material inequality. It is the tradition of reason in Christian faith which argues for the relative importance of human activity in the world and which makes it clear that people are not fed, homes are not built, clothes are not produced and distributed by sentimental good will and pure hearts, but by intelligence and hard work. It is also the tradition of reason which argues that while Christians may find capitalism or socialism or some other economic system here and now a more just and equitable system, they may not embrace such a system on the grounds of faith and give it the absolute loyalty which only the Kingdom of God may claim.

It is the tradition of reason that refuses to identify the Christian way of life with the American way of life, or the socialist way, or any other political option.[27] It is, to conclude, the tradition of reason that insists human beings take responsibility for their political and economic choices and not see in their affluence or poverty either the cruel hand of fate or the benign finger of God. The normative conception of conversion which we have proposed cannot tell any of us what use to make of our material goods, but it does provide the foundation on which such decisions can be made in a way that has some claim to be called the Christian way.

Notes

1. Charles E. Curran, "Conversion: The Central Moral Message of Jesus," *A New Look at Christian Morality* (Notre Dame: Fides, 1970), pp. 25–71.
2. Rudolf Schnackenburg, *The Moral Teaching of the New Testament* (New York: Herder and Herder, 1965), pp. 15–53.
3. Jim Wallis, *The Call to Conversion* (San Francisco: Harper & Row, 1981), pp. 1–17; see especially the notes to chapter 1, pp. 170–174; and A. Hulsbosch, *The Bible on Conversion* (De Pere, Wisc: St. Norbert Abbey Press, 1966).
4. All biblical citations are from *The Jerusalem Bible.*
5. David Stanley, "Paul's Conversion in Acts: Why the Three Accounts?" *Catholic Biblical Quarterly* 15 (July 1953), pp. 315–338.
6. Krister Stendahl, *Paul Among Jews and Gentiles* (Philadelphia: Fortress Press, 1976), pp. 7–23, is more impressed with the continuity of the before and after of Paul's experience than the difference and so prefers to describe the experience as a call rather than a conversion. I am in full agreement with his discussion, but will argue that call is an indispensable aspect of authentic conversion.
7. Walter E. Conn (ed.), *Conversion: Perspectives on Personal and Social Transformation* (New York: Alba House, 1978) is indispensable for exploring various dimensions of conversion that are outside the immediate interests of this essay.
8. Evelyn Underhill, *Mysticism* (New York: E. P. Dutton, 1961 ed.), pp. 176–177.
9. For a popular treatment of Piaget and Kohlberg see Ronald Duska and Mariellen Whelan, *Moral Development: A Guide to Piaget and Kohlberg* (New York: Paulist Press, 1975), esp. p. 49. See also Craig R. Dykstra, "Transformation in Faith and Morals," THEOLOGY TODAY, XXXIX, 1 (April 1982), pp. 56–64.
10. Lawrence Kohlberg, *Essays on Moral Development: Volume 1, The Philosophy of Moral Development* (San Francisco: Harper & Row, Publishers, 1981).
11. See, e.g. Craig Dykstra, *Vision and Character: A Christian Educator's Alternative to Kohlberg* (New York: Paulist Press, 1981); Stanley Hauerwas, *A Community of Character* (Notre Dame, London: University of Notre Dame Press, 1981), pp. 129–152; Paul J. Philibert, O.P., "Conscience: Developmental Perspectives from Rogers and Kohlberg," *Horizons* 6 (Spring 1979), pp. 1–25.
12. The Catholic way of expressing that, in the words of Vatican Council II, is "within his conscience man discovers a law which he has not laid upon himself . . ." Austin Flannery, O.P. (ed.), "The Church in the Modern World," *Vatican Council II: The Conciliar and Post Conciliar Documents* (Collegeville, Minn: The Liturgical Press, 1975), 16, p. 916.
13. Bernard Lonergan, *Method in Theology* (New York: Seabury Press, 1979), pp. 104–107.
14. *Ibid.,* p. 240.
15. Franz Böckle, *Fundamental Moral Theology* (New York: Pueblo Publishing Company, 1980), pp. 105–112.
16. Flannery, *"Lumen Gentium,"* 9–17, pp. 359–369.
17. Stendahl, pp. 12–13.
18. Both Stendahl, pp. 23–40 and Gerard S. Sloyan, *Is Christ the End of the Law?*

(Philadelphia: The Westminster Press, 1978), pp. 74–104, make it a point that Paul himself was in no way obsessed with his own sins nor did he find keeping the law particularly difficult. For Paul that was not the human predicament.

19. The phrase is borrowed from Dorothy Day. See her biography, William Robert Miller, *A Harsh and Dreadful Love: Dorothy Day and the Catholic Worker Movement* (New York: Liveright, 1973).

20. Hauerwas, pp. 36–71, 89–152.

21. The relationship of the authority of the Scriptures, tradition, and the present church community is not simply a Catholic problem. See, e.g., Bruce C. Birch and Larry L. Rasmussen, *Bible and Ethics in Christian Life* (Minneapolis, Minn: Augsburg Publishing House, 1976), pp. 125–159.

22. *Ibid.*, p. 220. For the sense it does make, see Richard A. McCormick, "Notes on Moral Theology: 1981," *Theological Studies* 43, 1 (March 1982), p. 90.

23. Hauerwas, pp. 1–5.

24. *Ibid.*, pp. 135–229 tries to do this in regard to having children and abortion. Andrew M. Greeley, *The New Agenda* (Garden City, NY: Doubleday 1973), pp. 159–160, does something similar in regard to the issue of pre-marital sex.

25. Jacob Viner, *Religious Thought and Economic Society* (Durham, N.C.: Duke University Press, 1978).

26. There is, of course, such a right before our fellow human beings.

27. This is the important point made repeatedly in an otherwise disappointing book, James V. Schall, S. J., *Christian and Politics* (Boston: St. Paul Editions, 1981).

20

Conscience: The Sanctuary of Creative Fidelity and Liberty

Bernard Häring, CSsR

The Second Vatican Council makes a pro-
grammatic and profound statement on our
understanding of conscience. "In the depths
of his conscience, the human person detects a
law which he does not impose on himself but
which holds him to obedience. Always sum-
moning him to love good and avoid evil, the
voice of conscience can, when necessary,
speak to his heart more specifically: do this,
shun that. For man has in his heart a law written by God. To obey it is the very dignity of
the person; according to it he will be judged
(cf. Rom 2:15–16). Conscience is the most secret core and sanctuary of a person. There he
is alone with God whose voice re-echoes in his
depths. In a wonderful manner conscience reveals that law which is fulfilled by love of God
and neighbour (cf. Mt 22:37–40; Gal 5:14). In
fidelity to conscience, Christians are joined
with the rest of men in search for truth and for
the genuine solution to the numerous problems which arise in the life of individuals and
from social relationships. Hence, the more a
correct conscience holds sway, the more persons and groups turn aside from blind choice
and strive to be guided by objective norms of
morality"[1].

Conscience and Discipleship

1. To Know Together and Be Free for Each Other

The word "conscience" derives from the
Latin *cum* (together) and *scientia, scire* (to
know). Conscience is the person's moral faculty, the inner core and sanctuary where one
knows oneself in confrontation with God and
with fellowmen. We can confront ourselves
reflexively only to the extent that we genuinely encounter the Other and the others.

Within us re-echoes the call of the Word in
whom we are created, the call of the Master

This article originally appeared in Free and Faithful in Christ, *vol. I (New York: Seabury Press,
1978) 223–284.*

who invites us to be with him. Our conscience comes to life through this Word that has called us into being and now calls us to be with him as his disciples, through the power of the Holy Spirit, the giver of life.

In the depth of our being, conscience makes us aware that our true self is linked with Christ, and that we can find our unique name only by listening and responding to the One who calls us by this name. The sensitivity and truthfulness of our conscience grow in the light of the divine Master who teaches us not only from without but also from within by sending us the Spirit of truth.

Although conscience has a voice of its own, the word is not its own. It comes through the Word in whom all things are made, the Word who became flesh to be with us. And this Word speaks through the inner voice which presupposes our capacity to listen with all our being. Of itself, conscience is a candle without a flame. It receives its truth from Christ who is Truth and Light; and through him it shines forth with his brightness and warmth.

In the search for truth, man's conscience is the focal point for sharing experience and reflection in a reciprocity of consciences. There is a truthful encounter of consciences to the extent that we are free for each other, free to receive and to give not only some knowledge but to give, along with the knowledge and experience, ourselves. When we know each other in the sight of God, and accept each other as belonging to one another in the divine Word, then our consciences are fully alive and creative.

2. The Biblical Vision of Conscience

a) Conscience in the Old Testament

If we were to study the problem of conscience in the Old Testament, relying only on the vocabulary and seeking Hebrew or Greek concepts for our word "conscience", we would be greatly disappointed. Only in the late Book of Wisdom (17:10f) do we find the Greek word *syneidesis,* which indicates the unquiet or bad conscience. But the Old Testament knows the reality to which we refer when we speak of conscience in a profound way.

As in other cultures, so in Hebrew thought, there is a development. We can see from the older parts of the Bible that the Israelites looked upon the experience of good and evil in an extrinsic, objective and sometimes collective perspective. God's will is mediated by traditions and religious leaders. However, they experience God's voice also as calling them from within. This understanding of conscience as internalized was one of the great contributions of Israel's prophets. It is a person's innermost being, called to fidelity to God and to the people of the covenant. It is the spirit within the person who guides him if he is willing to open himself to it.

So we turn our attention, above all, to the great biblical vision of "the heart" of man. We have spoken of it in relation to the fundamental option. Through the Spirit of God, man receives, in his whole being, an inner disposition and call to do good, to search honestly for God's will, in readiness to do it. His "heart", his innermost being, is shaken if he has disobeyed that inner voice of his best self. "For the Semites, the heart was the seat of thoughts, desires and emotions, and also of moral judgment[2]".

The believer in Israel knows that God "searches the heart and reins". He believes that there the Spirit of God can touch him and call him. Therefore, the heart praises or blames one's deeds. "My heart does not reprehend me in all my life" (Job 27:6). When

King David begins to show his own and Israel's power by a census, his "heart struck him after the people were numbered" (2 Sam 24:10). The evildoer knows in his heart that he has done wrong against God and his fellowmen. It is not just an intellectual knowing; it is a deep pain of heart. And in this pain the person still stands before God although he has turned his face away from him as Cain did. "Cain said to the Lord, 'My punishment is too great to bear . . . From your face I shall be hidden. And I shall be a fugitive and a wanderer on the earth' " (Gen 4:13f).

We do not find in the Old Testament any reflection like that of modern theologians and psychologists on "antecedent" and "following" conscience; but the reality is most evident in the inspired writers. The heart can do more than accuse the person after he has done the evil. It can also listen to the prompting of the Spirit that illumines him, guides him to righteousness and, if he has done wrong, calls him to meet God again. "You with sad hearts, cry aloud, groan in the heaviness of your spirits" (Is 65:14). From his inmost being, shaken by the spirit, the Psalmist prays, "Create in me a clean heart, O God, and put a new and right spirit within me. Cast me not away from your presence, and take not your holy Spirit from me" (Ps 51:12–13). Conversion begins with the affliction of one's heart (cf. 1 Kgs 8:38).

The profound vision of man's heart, where he is touched and moved by the Spirit, overcomes all merely extrinsic morality. It is the great message of the prophets that God will write his law into the person's heart, in his innermost being (cf. Jer 31:29–34; Ez 14:1–3 and 36:26). "The sin is engraved in the tablet of their hearts" (Jer 17:1). Man's heart can be hardened; but the message of the prophets is that God can renew even the hardened hearts and give them a new sensitivity and openness to God's loving will and to their fellowmen's burdens.

b) Conscience in the New Testament

The reality of experience of conscience in the New Testament should be seen in the light of the Old Testament which is brought to completion. The Gospel message is that now the time has come when God takes away the hardened heart and gives sinners a new heart so that they can live a life renewed in heart and spirit: the time when God gives them not only a new spirit but his own Spirit. If they do not respond with a renewed heart, it is their own fault. The light shines with new brilliance on them and they can be light in the Lord. But they can, instead, be lacking in docility and can become stubborn. "If the light that is in you becomes darkness, how great will the darkness itself be?" (Mt 6:23; Lk 11:33f).

What we have said earlier about liberation from falsehood and for the truth in Christ infers that inner renewal, the experience of a new heart and a new spirit. God's calling that resounds in our heart is at the same time a religious experience and an experience of conscience. It is always marked with wholeness. The whole person is called by God, for God and for the good.[3] We can be at peace only if we respond with our whole heart to this call. This is the law of love of God and of neighbour that is written into the human heart.

As apostle, Paul brought to his ministry the vision of the Old Testament and the experience of the Lord calling him and renewing his heart. "His sensitivity in dealing with the consciences of others springs from the delicacy of his own conscience (2 Cor 1:12), from his constant awareness of divine mercy for himself and God's presence (2 Cor 4:1–2), and from the fear of the Lord (2 Cor 5:11)".[4] Paul conveys this message to the Gentiles in their own language, building upon their own experience of conscience and religiousness, while trying at the same time to bring them into the full light of Christ. He not only accepts and approves "all that is lovable and gracious, whatever is excellent and admirable" (Phil 4:8; cf. 1 Thes 5:21), he also takes up a key concept of the Stoic ethics, *syneidesis*.

Biblical scholars and historians discuss how much Paul actually took over from the Stoic tradition. Surely, he was not ignorant about what this concept meant to his audience.[5] And, surely, he did focus on what he found acceptable and positive in the Greek concept of *syneidesis*.[6] "Even if Paul actually did borrow the term from the philosophical language of his time, he fortified it with the whole biblical tradition on the role of the 'heart' and further enriched it with the dynamic presence of the divine Pneuma".[7] What he thinks, preaches and writes is deeply rooted in the biblical tradition of Israel, yet he is able to bring the message home in the language of his listeners.

It is highly probable that, until the time of Paul, the Stoic ethics used the concept *syneidesis* exclusively for the consciousness of the evil that followed the decision; but even so, it is understood as a cry of the innermost being for wholeness and for existential knowledge of oneself confronted with good and evil. Several times Paul uses *syneidesis* for the conscience that accuses the sinner, which fits into both the biblical and the Greek traditions. However, even in direct dialogue with the Gentiles, he explicitly broadens the understanding of conscience in the light of the prophetic tradition. Perhaps no other text shows better than Romans 2:14–15 how Paul can blend together the old and the new: "When Gentiles, who do not possess the written law, carry out its precepts by the light of nature,

then, although they have no law, they are their own law, for they display the effects of the law inscribed in their hearts. Their conscience is called as witness, and their own thoughts argue the case on either side against them or even for them".

While using the concept *syneidesis,* Paul intends to convey the message of the prophets about the heart of man wherein God makes known his law of love. *Syneidesis* is brought explicitly into the context of the essential message that God writes his law into man's heart. It is not only a question of remorse or of an accusing conscience; the heart or *syneidesis* argues the case "on either side". Today it is more and more agreed among biblical theologians that Paul uses the word *syneidesis* also to point out the constructive, creative quality of the human heart to grasp what is good and right. "He also uses it to cover decisions in advance of what should be done".[8]

For Paul, the question is not only whether the heart speaks out only as a wounded conscience after sin or speaks also while the decision is being worked out; his special concern is about the integrity of conscience. He notes that the good conscience is expressive of one's wholeness; and his core message is always that the Spirit renews the heart of man, that there is repentance and conversion which includes a rebirth of the "heart". Clearly, he means what we mean when we speak of "conscience".

Paul describes the split in one's innermost self if one professes to acknowledge God but withstands the grace and calling of faith. "Nothing is pure to the tainted minds of disbelievers, tainted alike in reason and conscience. They profess to acknowledge God but deny him by their actions. Their detestable obstinacy disqualifies them for any good work" (Ti 1:15–16).

Redemption includes not only liberation

from falsehood in the mind and reasoning but reaches deeper, even into the person's conscience. If we believe in Christ and trust in him, then "his blood will cleanse our conscience from the deadness of our former ways and fit us for the service of the living God" (Heb 9:14). The conscience also gives witness to the believer about the sincerity of faith and life. "We are convinced that our conscience is clear; our one desire is always to do what is right" (Heb 13:18; cf. 2 Tim 1:3). A good conscience, however, is not self-assurance or self-affirmation. The apostle stands before God, his divine Saviour and Judge (cf. 1 Cor 4:4). And a person who truly lives before the Lord never judges his conscience individualistically. Rather, he lives the reciprocity of consciences in constant concern for the integrity of the other (cf. 1 Cor 10:25-29). All this accords with Paul's insistence that the law of mutual love is inscribed in our "hearts" (consciences).

Anthropological and Theological Reflexion

1. The Act of Conscience and the Abiding Endowment of Conscience

The Apostle of the Gentiles could fulfil his role as messenger of the Good News and of the moral message only by entering into dialogue with the respective cultures. The basis of our understanding of conscience is always Holy Scripture, read, understood and reflected on, however, in the community of believers. This makes the dialogue with each culture and each era imperative.

A history of moral theology could well be written in the main perspective of how conscience was understood, presented, and how the whole life manifested a concrete under-

standing of conscience. Helmut Thielicke is right when he asserts that the understanding of conscience mirrors always a concrete anthropology.[9] Therefore, we can never simply repeat the formulations of previous theologians, and cannot even understand their purpose without being aware of their different context.

The theological reflections of Scholastic theology and later moral theology are greatly influenced by a sharp distinction between *conscientia* (corresponding etymologically to our "conscience") and *synteresis* or *synderesis*. Conscience was treated only as the judgment or the act by which man reaches the conclusion that this or that is good or evil. *Synteresis,* however, meant the abiding endowment that urges man to seek truth and to put it into practice, to do the good and avoid evil. This word came into theological reflection probably through the commentary of St. Jerome to Ezekiel, by a corruption of *syneidesis*.[10]

The Scholastic tradition took from Jerome *synteresis* as that profound quality which makes man have conscience and qualifies him to perceive the moral order and moral values as his obligation. Thomas Aquinas sees it as the most profound inborn disposition (*primus habitus*) of the practical intelligence.[11] All Scholastics agreed that it is that unique and most relevant endowment or inborn disposition that makes man a moral being.

2. Incomplete Theories Regarding Conscience

a) Emphasis on the Practical Intellect
For Albert the Great and Thomas Aquinas, the *synteresis* is the practical intellect's inborn endowment with the highest moral principles,

insofar as they are immediately perceived as binding one's self and every human being. The moral principles are not abstractions, good only for drawing conclusions, although they enter as the main subjects into all moral reflection. *Synteresis* tells the person that "the good is to be done", or "love your neighbour as yourself".

The judgment of conscience is an actual conclusion from the *synderesis* and from a concrete moral judgment about what is actually the good or right expression of love of neighbour, justice and so on. Later, Thomists and moralists, who did not know Thomas Aquinas, conceived this theory in a merely intellectual way and, in practice, frequently combined it with "knowledge of dominion". Thus, the uniqueness of the person and the depth of the person's heart were no longer seen.

However, this was not Thomas Aquinas' doctrine. His vision put great emphasis on knowledge of the good, but in the sense of the biblical understanding of "knowing". It is a knowledge that comes from the depth of the heart, a knowledge of salvation, of wholeness. "We must bear in mind that, according to Thomas, the natural inclination of the will is always bound up with the knowledge of the practical reason. Thus, by the very nature with which it is created, there is in the will a profound disposition that urges it, of itself, to strive for the good conceived by reason . . . It presses towards the good as known by reason (*bonum rationis*)".[12]

Moreover, it should not be forgotten that, for St. Thomas, a right moral reasoning and weighing of the values requests the virtue of prudence. So the outcome of a sincere judgment of conscience is the harvest of the inborn disposition called "synderesis", and the virtue of prudence which, for its very being

and functioning, presupposes the fundamental option for the good. As theologian, Thomas Aquinas does not forget that the gifts of the Holy Spirit can give a kind of connaturality to the loving will of God and permit an intuitive grasp of the good.

b) Emphasis on the Inborn Disposition of the Will

Alexander of Hales, St. Bonaventure, Henry of Ghent, and many others, see in the *synderesis* the inborn disposition of the will, to love and to desire what is known as the good. The mystics understood it as the *scintilla animae,* the spark of the soul, the passionate love that sets man's innermost being on fire for the good. Thus, what is recognized as corresponding to right reason receives its dynamic force in each particular instance from the profound and inborn tendency of the will to love and to do what is understood, here and now, as the good. Through the *synderesis,* the human will is a little spark of love kindled by the divine love. The will, in its innermost disposition, is touched by God, the source of all love. Here, the religious depth of this theory of conscience becomes manifest.

St. Bonaventure has no intention of devaluating the intellectual aspect so strongly emphasized by St. Thomas Aquinas, for the will is never conceived as a blind force but as a power drawn to the known good. It seems to me that the two theories, when proposed by the great teachers Thomas and Bonaventure, are not opposed but complete each other. Or, let us say that they manifest the same vision but from different angles. However, as soon as the two schools became antagonistic, there was a militant emphasis on one aspect as against the other, and thus the wholeness was shattered.

3. *The Holistic Understanding of Conscience*

a) The Innermost Yearning for Wholeness and Integrity

Most moral theologians today agree with outstanding psychologists and therapists who insist that conscience is not just one faculty. It is not more in the will than in the intellect, and it is a dynamic force in both because of their belonging together in the deepest reaches of our psychic and spiritual life.

The dynamic of our conscience is "the reaction of our total personality to its proper functioning and disfunctioning, not to the functioning of this or that capacity but to the capacities which constitute our human and individual existence".[13] We are created for wholeness biologically, psychologically and spiritually. The deepest part of our being is keenly sensitive to what can promote and what can threaten our wholeness and integrity.

The concrete judgment of prudence, accepted as judgment of the conscience, depends on many conditions. But what gives urgency and attractive appeal to the judgment of prudence is conscience's own longing for wholeness. Being created for wholeness, we can dynamically decipher and experience the good to which God calls us in the particular situation. One's conscience is healthy only when the whole person—the emotional as well as the intellectual elements and the energies of the will—is functioning in a profound harmony in the depth of one's being. This innermost depth is the locus where we are touched by the creative Spirit and brought to ever greater wholeness. It is "the pivotal personal centre of man's total response to the dynamics, direction and personal thrust of the divine claim on him".[14] Conscience has to do with man's total selfhood as a moral agent.[15]

The intellectual, volitional and emotional dynamics are not separated; they mutually compenetrate in the very depth where the person is person to himself.

In the wholeness and openness of our conscience we are a real sign of the promptings of the Spirit who renews our heart and, through us, the earth. Even though in the depths of the human spirit, intellect and will are somehow distinct, they cannot really thrive without each other. It is, however, the mark of their finite nature that intellect and will can oppose each other, although not without unleashing profound grief in the innermost depths in which they are united. The rift that is created is painfully perceived. It is in this wound that the soul cries out for healing; and this cry is itself a sign of the presence of the Spirit who summons the person to close the dreadful gap of dissension through restoration of that unity and harmony which makes him or her a true image and likeness of God.

Because of the profound integration of intellect, will and affectivity in our very nature, the intellect's longing for truth and goodness is shaken when, out of sinister motives, the will struggles against it. And the will, in its turn, must agonize when it tries to withstand the intellect's yearning for better knowledge and realization of the good. The person suffers in his whole being if there arises a kind of split into different selves, the true self that longs for wholeness and truth and the selfish self that seeks a mere image of the good. As root and source of unity of all one's powers, the depth of the soul is tortured, torn by the dissension.

Here is the profound reason for the first elemental agony of conscience, a spontaneous unreflected pain. Theologically, we might dare to say that the image of the Trinity within us recoils in horror at the distortion of the divine likeness in us.

b) Wholeness and Openness for Truth and Solidarity

The call to unity and wholeness pervades our conscience. It is a longing for integration of all the powers of our being that, at the same time, guides us towards the Other and the others. The covenant reality is inscribed in our heart.[16]

There cannot be peace in our heart (or conscience) unless our whole being accepts the longing of the intellect and reason to be one with the truth. Since our very substance unites these powers with the will and with all our being, there can be genuine inner wholeness only in that openness to the light that is in the world from the beginning. This includes openness also to our fellowmen, since our self-understanding and growth in the knowledge of the good depend greatly on the symbols created by the interaction of many minds in mutual human relationships. We come to know ourselves in our depths and wholeness in that interaction which responds to the same longing for dignity and wholeness in everyone else. We need, from those around us, love and respect as persons with consciences, and we can explore the depth and dynamics of our conscience only if we respond to that love in a creative way.

The law that re-echoes in our being is the golden rule that simply deserves the name "law". "Love your neighbour as yourself": this is the sum of the law. "Treat others as you would like them to treat you: that is the law and the prophets" (Mt 7:12; Lk 6:31). It is the distinctive quality of the mature Christian that he understands the inner law in the light of Christ who manifested for us the all-embracing law of the covenant, "Love one another as I have loved you" (Jn 15:12). We are sealed with this understanding of the law, written in our hearts, when we receive the Spirit and are open to him. We celebrate it each time we take the cup of salvation. What Jesus proclaims re-echoes in our hearts, "This is the blood of the New Covenant" (Lk 22:20). If the Eucharist, which is at the centre of our faith, becomes also the rule of our life, then we will reach wholeness in our conscience and unity with our fellowmen.

Our conscience has only two basic choices, either for solidarity of salvation in authentic covenant morality or for solidarity in collective sinfulness. At this point, we can relate the theological insight on solidarity to the findings of psychology about the functioning of the superego.

In childhood and early adolescence, the temporary strength of the superego is a normal phase of transition. It can play an important role in the process of socialization. And if, at the proper time, the person works out a deeply rooted fundamental option for solidarity in the good, the energies of the superego are directed into the same course. The result is a mature, peaceful conscience, the integration of the person in his inner core and integrity in covenant morality.

However, if the education tactics are wrong, if they distort the dynamics of the superego for the mere enforcement of obedience, it can become a prepotent agent of all the dark powers that draw persons eventually into collective sinfulness, hypocrisy, belligerent group egotism and the slavery of falsehood. Even at best, superego morality tends to be sterile, repetitive, degrading, whereas covenant morality opens one to ever new and creative responses to God and neighbour.

c) Conscience in its Creative Fidelity and Liberty

The way we have approached the problems of conscience shows that our main concern is to make the tree good so that the fruits may be good. We are, indeed, interested in the mature and right judgement of conscience but then we have to give our attention to its conditions.

The creative judgment of conscience, with its strong tendency towards living in the truth and acting on it, depends on several conditions: first, on the God-given dynamics of the conscience, the inborn yearning for wholeness and openness; second, on the firmness and clarity of the fundamental option which confirms the natural yearning for those qualities but which should be honoured as the harvest of the Spirit; third, on the strength of the dispositions towards vigilance and prudence and all the other dispositions that embody a deep and good fundamental option; fourth, on the mutuality of consciences in a milieu where creative freedom and fidelity are embodied and there is active and grateful dedication to them; fifth, on the actual fidelity, creativity and generosity in the search for truth in readiness to "act on the word".

Many theologians who have reflected on the creative quality of the conscience have especially noted Thomas Aquinas' teaching on intuitive knowledge of the good, made possible by connaturality with the good. This is always the work of the Holy Spirit, who enables us to bear fruit in abundance according to our openness (1 Cor 2:14–15, 1 Jn 2:20 and 2:27).

Reflecting on the dynamic element in the Church, Karl Rahner gives particular attention to intuitive knowledge.[19] His description of it reminds us of Abraham Maslow's theme of "peak experience"[20] Bernard Lonergan also speaks of this dimension: "Faith is the knowledge form of religious love. First, then, there is a knowledge born of love. Of it Pascal spoke when he remarked that 'the heart has reasons which reason does not know'. The meaning of Pascal's remark would be that, besides the factual knowledge reached by experiencing, understanding and verifying, there is another kind of knowledge reached in love".[21]

An aspect of the creativity of conscience becomes evident in the growth of one's conscience into new dimensions. It is conscience itself that teaches the person to overcome the present stage of development and to integrate it into a higher one. In other words, the openness manifested in intuitive knowledge is also the process of the person's self-realization in his or her conscience.

4. Wholeness and the Erring Conscience

Vatican II has reaffirmed a classical Catholic tradition regarding an erring judgment of conscience. "Conscience frequently errs from invincible ignorance without losing its dignity. The same cannot be said of a person who cares but little for truth and goodness, or of a conscience which by degrees grows practically sightless as a result of habitual sin".[22]

As far as objective truth and values are concerned, the human conscience is surely not infallible. The Council acknowledges that error in evaluation happens rather frequently. But more important is the acknowledgement that it happens frequently without personal guilt, without conscience losing its dignity. This is so whenever the intentions are right and the conscience is sincerely seeking the best solution. By "best solution", I do not mean the abstract best, but what is for the person here and now, in this particular situation, the most fitting step in the right direction.

There is something unique—one might even say "untouchable"—about the conscience, because it is the judgment of a person on his or her journey towards ever fuller light. To err in one's judgment of conscience in an important matter can be a great misfortune;

but it is much worse, a moral evil, if the conscience errs because of lack of sincerity. The greatest evil is when the conscience becomes dull and sightless. The Council speaks sharply of this happening when a person "cares but little for truth and goodness", is careless in the very search for moral knowledge, careless especially in situations that are morally relevant, and finally becomes practically blind as a result of habitual, unrepented sins.

When a person is truly looking for what is good and right, there is a kind of indefectibility in the conscience. With unwavering certainty, it orders the will to conform with the intellect, following its light, as the two are rooted together at the core of one's being. This imperative, written in the heart, has moral majesty even though it may have a background of defective moral knowledge, indeed even if it makes a fully erroneous judgment. If the error in evaluation is in no way due to negligence or ill will, there is nothing in the faculty of conscience itself which would murmur against acting on the ground of that erroneous judgment. Rather, it is sustained by the whole sound dynamic of conscience.

An inculpably erroneous dictate of conscience obliges in the same way as a correct conscience, just as a servant feels obliged to carry out the order of his master as he has understood it after listening attentively, even though the order was actually different. If we really seek to discover the Lord's will in a sincere search for truth and with the intention to act on the truth, then the Lord sees into our heart. Hence, Cardinal Newman is correct in his famous statement, "I have always contended that obedience even to an erring conscience was the way to gain light".[23]

On this point, we find the same emphasis in the moral and pastoral theology of St. Alphonsus de Liguori.[24] He speaks of the invincibly erring conscience, where a sincere conscience cannot internalize a positive law of the Church or of the secular authorities, or even a valid aspect of natural law teaching. From an existential point of view, it might not be so much an erroneous assessment as an impossibility to take the third step before the second in one's progress towards a more profound knowledge of the good. From an objective, abstract point of view, we might, as outsiders, say that the person's conscience is erring, but existentially it might indicate the best possible step in the direction towards more light. It would be a most serious fault against the dignity of the conscience if a pastor, a confessor, or anyone else were to press the person to act against his sincere conscience, or indiscreetly try to inculcate the objective norm if this would disturb the person who simply cannot accept a particular precept or norm.

An erroneous judgment of conscience can be culpable in varying degrees and for various reasons. There can be a lesser or greater negligence in searching for what is truth and goodness, or there can be the blinding influence of past sins insufficiently repented, or the misguided power of passions not sufficiently controlled.

St. Thomas Aquinas held that, in the case of a culpably erroneous dictate of conscience, the person sins whether he follows its dictate, or acts contrary to it; but the sin is more immediate and evident if he acts contrary to his erroneous conscience, even if, in so doing, he does what is objectively right. By acting against the dictate of conscience he wounds and jeopardizes even more his inner wholeness and his union with what he sees as the objective good and truth.

Although an erroneous verdict of conscience can be rectified, still, as long as it persists, it is actually binding.[25] And yet, according to Thomas Aquinas, it would not be correct to say that the person with a culpably erroneous conscience has only two choices and, therefore, unavoidably commits sin. There exists a third choice, which is to correct the verdict of conscience by purging the sources of error in their very depth,[26] by a deeper conversion. And if one delays conversion or refuses to be converted at all, this attitude contaminates all one's decisions of conscience.

St. Thomas teaches also that if anyone professes faith in Christ and/or the Church, although he is firmly convinced that it is wrong to do so, he is sinning against his conscience.[27] However, St. Thomas could not conceive that a Catholic who had once come to faith would ever, without personal guilt, reach the conviction of conscience that he has to leave the Church.[28] Today we have to consider many more psychological and sociological influences in approaching this and other complex problems of the erroneous conscience.[29]

To any such difficult problems we can apply the general criterion that a particular decision has the unconditioned dignity of a judgment of conscience if the person is sincerely seeking the truth and is ready to revise the decision as soon as he realizes that new pertinent questions call for his consideration. The sign of a truly conscientious decision is the inner peace and a growing sensitivity to all the new opportunities to do what love and justice demand.

5. *The Perplexed Conscience*

The disturbed or perplexed conscience is a particular type of erroneous conscience arising from a transitory but violent disturbance of the person's capacity to form a serene judgment. Faced with the necessity of having to make a decision, the person can see no apparent choice free from sin. If the decision can be delayed, then one must postpone the solution in order to deliberate on it more quietly. But if it cannot be delayed, the conscientious person will choose what he thinks is "the lesser sin" and thus manifest his correct attitude. In fact, there is no question of sin in this matter, for sin is not merely a matter of intellectual judgment but is also an evil act of free will, which is evidently lacking here.

A moral theology that has multiplied the absolutes that can conflict with each other in concrete situations has produced many cases of "perplexed conscience". A moral education that helps to discern both the urgency and the priority of values will greatly alleviate such pain for conscientious people. It is not enough to tell people that, on the subjective level, they will not be guilty if they make certain choices; we must also insist that there is always an objectively right way to resolve these cases.

Developmental Psychology and the Stages of Conscience

Developmental psychology's great contribution towards a better understanding of conscience and of moral education is welcomed by a moral thology concerned with creative freedom and fidelity and a dynamic understanding of the person. Especially helpful are the studies of Erik Erikson, Erich Fromm and Lawrence Kohlberg.

Erikson distinguishes three phases in the development of moral awareness and conscience. "I will speak of moral learning as an aspect of childhood, of ideological experimentation as a part of adolescence, and of ethical consolidation as an adult task".[30] He describes the dangers and chances of each stage. In the first stage, the danger is that education lords over the child by prohibitions reinforced by frowning faces and moral threats—if, indeed, moral learning is not actually beaten into the child by physical punishment before the child can possibly understand the meaning of it all. But where guidance is given with love and respect, the child can already learn to internalize moral prohibitions.[31]

Adolescence is a time when the critical mind awakens. "The adolescent learns to perceive ideas and to assent to ideals, to take, in short, an ideological position for which the younger child is cognitively not prepared".[32] The adolescent and the young adult are seeking for a worldview coherent enough to attract a total commitment.

In all stages, Erikson sees an affirmative chance for the superego: it can and must be integrated into higher levels of moral awareness if it is to foster genuine socialization through discerning self-commitment. However, both he and Erich Fromm warn also about the negative possibility, a wrong direction taken during the first stages, if the superego serves mainly the goals of the caretaker. In these cases the prescriptions of authoritarian conscience—their commands and taboos—are not determined by experience of values; they simply echo the pronouncements of external authority.[33]

The child needs more guidance than the adolescent. However, guidance can be given in such a way that the first stage anticipates the second. External sanctions give way to internal perception; prohibition and fear give way to joy and preferences in self-respect; habits of obedience give way to genuine self-guidance and creative responses.[34]

If we understand the contribution made by Erikson for a better understanding of the fundamental option, then we are helped to appreciate also Lawrence Kohlberg's contribution towards a deeper understanding of the moral development of conscience.[35] It seems to me most fortunate that Kohlberg has found such a ready audience among ethicians and educators.

He distinguishes six stages at three levels of development:

I.   The pre-conventional level
     Stage 1: Obedience and punishment orientation
     Stage 2: Instrumental relativistic orientation
II. The conventional level
     Stage 3: Interpersonal concordance of "good boy/ nice girl" orientation
     Stage 4: "Law and order" orientation
III. Post-conventional, autonomous or principled level
     Stage 5:
              Social contract orientation (with utilitarian overtones)
     Stage 6: Universal-principle orientation.[36]

Kohlberg repeatedly insists on the dynamic aspect indicated by the fact that each stage contains some horizon and some tendency towards the next stage. During the first stage, children experience the good chiefly by the physical consequences which they perceive as reaction. During the second stage there arises a clearer perception of values like fairness and reciprocity, but perception is still on a rather pragmatic level. During the third stage, "good behaviour is that which pleases or helps others and is approved by them. There is much conformity to stereotyped images of what is majority or 'natural' behaviour. One earns approval by being 'nice' ".[37]

During stage four, the growing person especially perceives the values of authority, maintenance of order and reliability. There is already a beginning discernment between good and poor exercise of authority. On this level, danger arises if those in authority are not able to share the knowledge of salvation and prefer to operate on the level of knowledge of control-dominion. Thus, they oppose the inner dynamic of this stage towards the next.

Kohlberg assesses stage five as more or less that of the official morality of the United States' government and constitution. "There is a clear awareness of the relativism of personal values and opinions and a corresponding emphasis on procedural rules for reaching consensus . . . an emphasis on the legal point of view but also with an emphasis upon the possibility of changing law in terms of rational considerations".[38] However, there is gradually developing a sense of the moral good beyond law. In stage six, the universal ethical vision takes over. Right is defined by the decision of conscience in accordance with self-chosen ethical principles.

While all education, if conceived as truly moral education, tends clearly to the sixth stage, the dynamic is best utilized if special attention is given to the gradual transition to the next possible stage. With Dewey and Piaget, Kohlberg is convinced that children can learn early to accept authority when they are helped to understand its goodness and to see the reasons behind the rules. On this point he firmly dissociates himself from Emile Durkheim and his followers who, in their understanding of common life, remain substantially on the level of mere order and discipline.

The growing person is able, and therefore has a right, to be helped to understand ever better that there are ethical principles clearly distinguishable from arbitrary conventional rules and beliefs. It is important to listen to children and their way of arguing. "We all, even and especially children, are moral philosophers. By this I mean the child has a morality of his own".[39] If we respectfully listen to and talk to children, we can discover "that they have lots of standards which do not come in any obvious way from parents, peers or teachers".[40]

From this cross-cultural research, Kohlberg has found that the stages of moral development are common to all cultures. Each child goes, step by step, through the various stages but with varying speed according to the help or hindrance he finds in the world around him. Kohlberg and Piaget emphasize the cognitive development but also affectivity. "All mental events have both cognitive and affective aspects. It is also evident that the presence of strong emotion in no way reduces the cognitive component of moral judgment".[41]

The development of moral thought moves forward in one direction, but it can be blocked at an earlier stage so that it never reaches the fifth or sixth stage. The person who reaches moral maturity recognizes universal values. This does not mean that all values are universal; but the basic one of justice, common to all people, should be expressed towards all. The golden rule is basic and common: "Do unto others as we would have them do to us. Love your fellowmen as you want them to love you". For Kohlberg, this is the most universal principle.[42]

In stimulating moral development through stages five and six, the aim of moral education is to give the individual the capacity to engage in moral judgment and discourse rather than to impose on him a specific morality.[43] The heart of the matter is discernment, based on the knowledge of man and on a recognized hierarchy of values. The great psychologists have abundantly proven how dangerous it is to consider moral life as static. An education based upon such a static concept leads to lack of integration and presents the danger of regression.

A Distinctively Christian Conscience

The recent discussions on a distinctively Christian ethics were frequently sterile and frustrating because they centred all around the concept of normative ethics, and in a rather narrow and all too static vision. The following pages suggest a shift of focus.

Christians should be distinguished by their true humanity and co-humanity, for at the centre of faith is the dogma of the incarnation of the Word of God. God reveals himself in full humanity and co-humanity in Jesus Christ, true God and true man. Therefore, if we take seriously our identity as Christians, we develop a distinctively Christian conscience whereby we think, above all, of our solidarity with all of humankind. We believe that Christ is the Redeemer and Lord of all, and that his Spirit works in all, through all and for all.

The great privilege that, through faith, we know Christ and have our life in him does not allow us any superiority complex or exclusiveness. Rather, it gives us a mission to be and to become ever more light to the world and servants to the world. We cannot help others to reach out for the fullness of explicit faith unless we know our own name and live according to the One who calls us by that name.

1. In Christ—Under the Law of Faith

The conscience and conscientiousness of a Christian are marked by his encounter with Christ, by his joy at being a new creation in Christ, and by his knowledge, through Christ, of the Father and of his fellowmen. "This is the eternal life, to know you who alone are truly God, and whom you have sent, Jesus Christ"(Jn 17:3).

It is important to understand what the word "know" means. It is a gift of the Holy Spirit who reaches into the innermost depths of our soul. A salvific knowledge of Christ includes confirmation of our fundamental option that gives us wholeness of conscience and a knowledge by connaturality.

A truly Christian conscience is marked by that creative liberty and fidelity that arises from faith in Christ. Faith is the joyous, grateful and humble reception of him whom the Father has sent, and who is our Life, our Way, our Truth. It is total surrender to him who draws us to the Father, a new, liberating experience of friendship with Christ that gives us also a new and intimate relationship with God the Father, in the Holy Spirit, and with our fellowmen, as well as a new self-understanding.

The foundation and the firmness of this Christian conscience lie in faith. The Apostle of the Gentiles contradicts emphatically those who feel that his preaching about the "law of faith" undermines the law or morality. "Does this mean that we are using faith to undermine morality? By no means! We are placing morality itself on a firmer footing" (Rom 3:31). It seems to me that we can replace Paul's word "law" or "morality" by "conscience" without changing his meaning. "To St. Paul, faith is the whole attitude of the Christian, assimilating his judgments of moral worth too. The Christian is not divided within himself between a natural economy and a supernatural one; there is only one judgment of conscience and it is determined by his faith".[44]

The Revised Standard Version translates

Romans 14:23 as, "Whatever does not proceed from faith is sin". The New English Bible translates it simply, "What does not arise from conscience is sin". Both these translations are right, for St. Paul sees the human conscience and the conviction of conscience illumined and confirmed by faith. Especially in his Pastoral Epistles, "faith" and "conscience" have almost the same meaning. "The aim and object of this command is the love which springs from a clean heart, from a good conscience, and from faith that is genuine" (1 Tim 1:5). For Paul, faith and good conscience are inseparable. "So fight gallantly, armed with faith and a good conscience" (1 Tim 1:19). Christian leadership can be exercised only by persons "who combine a clear conscience with a firm hold on the deep truths of our faith" (1 Tim 3:9). Those who desert faith and spread falsehood are men "whose own conscience is branded with the devil's sign" (1 Rom 4:2; cf. Ti 1:15–16).

A mature Christian conscience will not think of faith as a catalogue of things and formulations. What shapes all the moral dispositions, gives wholeness to the conscience and firmness to the Christian's fundamental option is the profound *attitude* of faith and its responsiveness. Faith, as a profound relationship with Christ, awakens in us a deep longing to know Christ and all that he has taught us and expects from us. This faith is marked by gratitude and joy that give direction and strength to all our life (cf. Neh 8:10). Faith can be defined as an all-embracing Christ-consciousness.[45]

A mere inculcation of various doctrines, without a synthesis in Christ and without a sharing of the joy of faith, does nothing to help the formation of a distinctively Christian conscience. Indeed, an over-emphasis on control of doctrines and a militant theology about doctrines can become an obstacle to an integrated faith. Only a joyous sharing of faith and a building up of a profound disposition of faith can guarantee the synthesis between orthodoxy and orthopraxis that unites all believers in Christ.

2. "No Longer Under the Law But Under Grace" (Rom 6:14)

Whoever gives first place to law and moral obligation while assigning only a second place to the grace of Christ perverts the right order and undermines the authenticity of a Christian conscience. Life in Christ means to be drawn to him and to the Father by his Spirit, and into a life that is praise and thanksgiving. Grace and faith take the first place.

Faith itself is a gratuitous gift that can only be received and welcomed in gratitude. It gives us a vista that makes us see everything in the light of the love of God and his graciousness. Grace (*charis*) means, above all, the attractive love of God the Father. He who has given us his life-giving Word and bestows on us the life-giving Spirit turns his face to us, blesses us. It is in this way that he makes us sharers of the covenant and engraves his law—his loving will—in our hearts.

Moral teaching becomes Good News if it is presented as an integrated part of faith-experience (of course, without making everything an unchangeable "dogma") and received in gratitude for God's infinite self-giving love. This is the central message of St. Paul's moral teaching. In view of our sharing in Christ's death and resurrection, we understand that "we are no longer under a regime of law but under grace" (Rom 6:14). "The law of the Spirit who gives us life in Christ Jesus has set me free from the law of sin-solidarity and from death" (Rom 8:2). The Christian conscience is marked by faith in the Holy Spirit and by an all-pervading gratitude that keeps us on the level of the Spirit and frees us from the web of incarnate selfishness.

We repeat the same truth when we insist that a Christian's profound dispositions and outlook are thoroughly formed by the celebration of the Eucharist, which evokes thanksgiving in view of all that God has done for us and promises us. One cannot live under grace without a grateful memory. Openness to the Spirit guides the Christian conscience in the evaluation of every situation. We see at the same time all the gifts God has bestowed on us and the needs of our fellowmen to which we can respond by using rightly all that we have received from God. Only in this readiness to meet the responsibilities of our co-humanity can we praise God and pray, "What can I render to the Lord for whatever he has given me?"

The legalist stands before an abstract law and will ever be tempted to get around it without a full commitment to the Lord, or else to impose it ruthlessly on others, with no knowledge of salvation. He fixes his attention on the minimal requirements of the universal laws. But, whether he becomes more a laxist or a rigorist, he will always be a captive of legalistic thinking. Only if the believer turns his attention to the love of God and to all the many signs and gifts of God's love, can he be set free for his neighbour and become faithful in Christ. When this boundless love of God becomes his main orientation, he no longer looks for the minimum response but aspires, rather, to "let your goodness have no limits, just as the goodness of the heavenly Father knows no bounds (Mt 5:48).

To live under grace means a shift from the prohibitive laws to the orientations of the goal-commandments, the affirmatives pre-sented in the whole gospel, in the words of Christ and the Letters of St. Paul. It is a dynamic morality that never allows the Christian to settle down, content with himself. His gratitude becomes the new noödynamics that gives clear directions to his psychodynamics.

The Lord has expressed this morality of gratitude in his parables about the talents and in practically all the parables about the kingdom of God. A conscience formed by faith and grace knows that all the gifts come from the one God and Father, and that not to use them responsibly and to the full is to show ingratitude to God and injustice to the human community, for every gift is given for building up the kingdom of God. The person who has received two talents and uses them well receives the same praise as the one who has received five and used them profitably. And if the person who has received one talent would have used it, he, too, would have matched the fidelity of the others.

We discover then that all that we are and all that we have are signs of God's love. All our life is then taken up by the dynamics of the goal-commandments: "Love each other as I have loved you" (Jn 15:12) or, as expressed in the beatitudes and in the solemn words that follow the beatitudes, the repeated, ". . . but I tell you . . ." (Mt 5:17–48). If we live according to a kind of normative ethics that is mainly limitative, prohibitive or static, we have not yet truly entered into the new covenant.

We have not yet fully overcome the split between a static moral theology and a lofty ascetical and mystical theology. Moral theology for the use of confessors and penitents was almost unavoidably guided by the knowledge of dominion and control. Since such a theology, written mostly for controllers, could threaten the freedom of believers in the realm of things solicited by grace, it seemed best to leave out or bypass spirituality or ascetical mystical theology.

The dichotomy between moral theology as static normative ethics and a totally different spiritual theology led frequently also to an ethics for two classes: one for those who wanted to become "perfect" (the religious) and the other for those who only lived under the commandments, understood as static norms. Thus, not only the unity of the people of God could fall apart, but there was danger that consciences, too, could separate into two different departments, one for moral norms and the other for "superfluous works".

The beatitudes, all the goal-commandments and the "harvest of the Spirit" were considered as a mere ideal or as *parenesis* and, therefore, not as a part of normative Christian ethics. Surely, we must carefully distinguish what is an abiding orientation and normative ideal from what is time-bound moral or religious exhortation in a particular situation. But it would be most harmful for the specifically Christian self-understanding if all the goal-commandments of the Bible were reduced to mere ideals or even only to *parenesis*.[46]

To love God with all our hearts and to love each other as Christ loved us is not just an ideal but a *normative* ideal that requests that all our desires, deeds and endeavours be energized in this direction. Christ has revealed the true countenance of love to us, and there can be no rest or self-satisfaction for the Christian, since this lofty ideal draws us constantly closer to Christ and reveals itself as both ever more demanding and ever more rewarding.

It is detrimental to the very fundamental norms of Christian ethics, but especially to the formation of a distinctively Christian consciousness, if the law of growth and the criteria for a deeper understanding of Christian

love are relegated to another discipline or, in moral theology, only considered as *parenesis*. But it should be equally clear that a distinctively Christian formation of conscience does not belong to those who specialize in "knowledge of control". For it is at the very heart of knowledge of salvation.

3. *Filled with Hope*

Not only the development and rootedness of a genuinely Christian fundamental option but also each act of conscience and the whole formation of conscience should be seen in that same light of the eschatological virtues that allows and calls for creative fidelity and liberty. Ours is a pilgrim ethics. Hope brings this home to our consciousness and inscribes it in our conscience.

In view of false forms of secularization we give special attention to a distinctively Christian hope. It arises from faith in the resurrection from the dead and God's promise to grant us a new heaven and a new earth, if we faithfully work to incarnate love, justice and peace in all of life. The sharp conscience of Christians for social justice, their non-violent and most active involvement, and a Church that is watchful for the "signs of the time" should be a real symbol of our hope of the world to come.

A distinctively Christian hope that gives a new and unifying noödynamic to the psychodynamics of our conscience will never ignore the cross of our Lord Jesus Christ and his calling us to follow him on the way of the cross. As the strength of our fundamental option grows, we accept in the depths of our conscience the still remaining need to put to death our selfish self and to take up every day our burden and a part of the burden of our fellowmen. The Eucharist that nourishes the expectation of the coming of our Lord will give us joy, strength and orientation for our mission in this time on this earth.[47]

4. *Vigilance and Prudence*

Vigilance results from the creative tension between the "already" and the "not yet", perceived and responded to in thanksgiving and hope. The vigilant conscience is symbolized by the virgins who are always ready for the coming of the Lord; for his call reaches us in the here and now, in the *kairos*. Each Christian and the whole Christian community are meant to share in the charism of John, "the man waiting for the coming of the Lord" (Jn 21:22-23), recognizing him under whatever disguise he is coming. Through vigilance a distinctively Christian conscience is seized by the wealth and the tensions of the history of salvation.

The formation of conscience depends a good deal on how the virtue of prudence is understood. It should be seen thoroughly in the light of the eschatological virtues, especially of vigilance. Vigilant prudence gives the conscience the delicate tact for the situation and deciphers even in the most confused and confusing events the present opportunities and needs despite all the darkness that arises from past sins and from the allurements of a sinful world. Thus, the conscience is sensitive for the Lord's calling and trustful of his grace. That gives true creativity and fidelity. The task of vigilant prudence is twofold: to appraise correctly the objective realities, and to discern and command the actions which are appropriate as a response to God's gifts and human needs. Joseph Pieper says that prudence has "two faces, one turned to the objectively real, the other to the good to be made real".[48]

To the degree that a decision of conscience is the certain voice of a sincere conscience, it is neither more nor less than the verdict of prudence. As to the content, the dictates of conscience correspond exactly to the prudential judgment. However, the existential inner awareness of the calling, and the urgency to do the good, come from the whole moral condition and wholeness of conscience.

In St. Thomas Aquinas' teaching, we note the strong insistence on vigilance for the moment of grace. He holds that this is a distinctive function of prudence or, more specifically, a distinctive virtue which is assigned to the virtue of prudence. He calls it *"gnome"*, which is a sensitivity to the wealth of the present situation, which always offers something more than the ordinary.[49]

Thomas Aquinas relates the distinctively Christian character of prudence to the gifts of the Holy Spirit. It is at least partially understood as a fruit of wisdom that gives the person a taste for heavenly things and joy in the service of the Spirit. The special gift of the Holy Spirit which brings prudence to perfection is counsel. Through this gift the Holy Spirit directs deliberation—the first act of prudence—with such perfection that subsequent acts are assured of a solid basis.[50]

Under the inspiration of the gift of counsel, the conscience rejoices in the divine dispositions and directives and thus becomes more sensitive to all the possibilities of the here and now.[51] If the conscience is solidly guided by the Spirit and trusting in the Lord, serenity and courage will guarantee the spiritual atmosphere that provides the proper judgment and joyous fulfilment.

5. *Discernment: The Virtue of Critique*

More than ever, we have to ask the question, "Whom shall we follow?" The emphasis on reciprocity of consciences makes discernment regarding ourselves and our partners an important aspect of a mature conscience. Besieged by so many ideologies, we have to heed Jesus' warning, "Beware of false prophets . . . you will recognize them by the fruits they bear. Can grapes be picked from briars or figs from thistles? In the same way, a good tree always yields good fruit and a poor tree bad fruit" (Mt 7:15–17).

Paul mentions a special charism in the Church, "the ability to distinguish true spirits from false" (1 Cor 12:13). But all Christians are admonished to exercise discernment. "But do not trust any and every spirit, my friends; test the spirits, whether they are from God" (1 Jn 4:1). The criterion, "every spirit which acknowledges that Jesus Christ has come in the flesh is from God" (1 Jn 4:2), is pronounced by John against the Gnostics. They denied the incarnation in true humanity and, therefore, they also disregarded commitment to the bodily world. We might draw the conclusion that all who are not willing to cooperate for the embodiment of freedom, fidelity, goodness and non-violence in the world around them are not true prophets.

Whoever is inspired by the Holy Spirit does not contradict the doctrine of Christ transmitted by the apostles (1 Jn 2:24; 4:6). For Paul, the condition of discernment is conversion of heart and mind, which is the work of the Holy Spirit. "Adapt yourselves no longer to the pattern of this present world but let your minds be remade and your whole nature thus transformed. Then you will be able to discern the will of God and to know what is good, acceptable and perfect" (Rom 12:2).

These words of Paul can easily be related to what we have said about fundamental option and the transforming power of fundamental dispositions. We can easily be deceived by the falsehood in the world unless we live fully in the light of Christ. "Let no one deceive you

with shallow arguments . . . Live like people who are at home in daylight, for where the light is, there all goodness springs up, all justice and truth. Try to find out what would please the Lord" (Eph 5:6–10).

Discernment depends upon one's wholeness and the openness of one's conscience to the Spirit. "This is my prayer, that your love may grow ever richer and richer in knowledge and insight of every kind and may thus bring you the gift of true discernment" (Phil 1:9–10). Profound faith experience and the fulfilment of Christ's law of love are the conditions for recognizing what things are most worthwhile.

The uniqueness and creativity of conscience is not just for one's own sake; it is for co-humanity in and for the reciprocity of consciences. Hence, discernment concerns the common good in Church and society, and the good of each of our fellowmen. Church and world need a critical conscience. (The word "critique" comes from the Greek *krinein*, which approximates our "discernment".) In a pluralistic society and world, Christians should be an active leaven of the virtue of critique. There are three options. Either we choose critique in the sight of God or we fall into one of the two extreme deviations of idle conformism or vicious critique. We must also be ready to accept criticism from others and to acknowledge our own shortcomings and faults. We have to listen to the prophets even if they shake us and unmask our errors. Towards community and society, critique must be exercised as a ministry in continuing service for the common good. However, one should have given a hundred signs of solidarity and cooperation before proffering one effective and credible protest.

The virtue of critique presupposes gentle persuasion, self-control and commitment to non-violent speech and action. Generalizing accusations and lamentations do more harm than good; they become part of the confusion. Our critique must be detailed, clear, and always against a background of appreciation expressed for all the good. It becomes virtue only if we believe in the inner core, the divine spark, and the resources of those whom we criticize. As expression of enmity, it is vicious. The virtue of critique is a part of the ongoing dialogue and reconciliation in the world. On this road we must be ready to accept an open-ended compromise, but with the understanding that we continue our shared ministry of discernment and peaceful striving for a healthier community and society.[52]

Summing up, we can say that we have a distinctively Christian conscience if we are deeply rooted in Christ, aware of his presence and his gifts, ready to join him in his love for all his people. Everything will be tested as to whether it can be offered to Christ as fitting response to his love, his gifts, and to the needs of our fellowmen.

Sin and Sanity

Once we have realized that conscience is the inner core, the deepest wellspring of integration and wholeness, it becomes evident that many forms of mental and physical unhealthiness are caused by a corrupted conscience. Whoever has quenched the light that comes from within, and has allowed his will and intelligence to disintegrate through indulgence of the selfish self, has a corrupted conscience. Gradually he has lost freedom for truth and goodness. "To the pure all things are pure, but nothing is pure to the tainted minds of disbelievers, corrupted alike in reason and conscience. They profess to acknowledge God but deny him by their actions. Their detest-

able obstinacy disqualifies them for any good work" (Ti 1:15–16).

I do not intend now to cover all the dimensions of the interrelation of sin, health and sanity, but it is important to see how health and sanity are related to the healthy or unhealthy conscience.

Since the longing for inner wholeness and the yearning for truth and goodness are the most important dimensions of our human existence, there cannot be full human health and wholeness if conscience is corrupted. As we saw earlier, it is an evil if we make an erroneous assessment about an important decision. But it is a much greater evil for us and for the world around us if our inner integrity is destroyed or handicapped.

Not each ailment or psychic defect has to do with sin. There can be suffering as a truly human condition and a way to greater maturity. We should never judge suffering people in a moralistic way. But by its very nature each sin is an enemy of sanity. It would be a grave error and, for Christians, a sin to consider health and sanity only in a perspective of the functioning of our various organs. A biochemical understanding of health, therapy and sickness is not only simplistic but is dangerous reductionism. The wellspring of human health rises from an inner wholeness and openness; and sin contradicts and diminishes the yearning for these qualities.

I am not speaking here, of course, of the hundreds of "mortal sins" invented by legalists and ritualists, but of sin as acting against one's conscience, and especially the gradual destruction of the integrity of conscience itself. Sin is alienation from one's better self, loss of knowledge of the unique name by which we are called, a plunging into darkness, and a split in the depth of our existence. If our conscience is tainted, we cannot build up healthy relationships with others but, rather, will contaminate the world around us with all the symptoms of alienation, falsehood and abuse.

The relatedness of sin with unhealthiness has been noted down through the ages. And today, what the Bible says about the inner and outer destruction caused by sin is confirmed, illustrated and presented in scientific terms by great psychologists and therapists like Erikson, Fromm, Frankl and many others.[53] Only gradually do we understand scientifically how grave is the noögenic neurosis caused by a negative response to the inner longing of the conscience for wholeness and openness. And how can a person consider himself healthy on a human level, if he has missed finding his true identity and integrity?

Each sin negatively affects man's wholeness and creative liberty. It contradicts the very meaning and purpose of our conscience and our freedom. By losing our own inner freedom and integrity, we are doomed to become slaves of the powers from which Christ has freed us if we believe in him. Sin contradicts our faith and, therefore, our liberation in Christ. Especially habitual sin and lack of repentance deepen the wound in our inmost self, while conscience still cries out for wholeness and health. "The experience of a so-called 'bad conscience' may be viewed as a profound rift in the depth of man's being, leading to a sense of disunity in oneself".[54]

Different types of corruption of conscience have different consequences regarding wholeness, integration and integrity.

Repentance and Rebirth of the Integrity of Conscience

Our discourse on conversion and reconciliation would be somewhat abstract if it did not relate to the rebirth of consciousness, wholeness and integrity.

Max Scheler's treatise on repentance is presented in the great perspective of rebirth.[55] Conscience that is tainted and corrupted by sin can be restored because it is never totally destroyed except in the case of "sin against the Holy Spirit", where all wholeness and integrity are thoroughly destroyed. God calls to repentance and thus to a new life by touching, through his grace, the depth of our conscience where the wound still cries for healing. And if the sinner turns to God with all his heart, God's powerful action grants him wholeness and integrity again. If the sinner repents, the blood of the covenant "will cleanse his conscience from the deadness of his former ways and fit him for the service of the living God" (Heb 9:14).

This promise of God, offered by his grace, should be the most urgent calling to the sinner to desire his own inner wholeness, integrity and openness. Even if we have not definitely turned away from God but realize that our conscience has been obscured and weakened, we hear the insistent call of grace: "So let us make our approach in sincerity of heart and full assurance of faith, our guilty hearts sprinkled clean, our bodies washed with pure water"(Heb 10:22).

If the sins, although grave, were "only" venial, there remains still a precious alliance between one's inborn desire for wholeness and one's fundamental commitment, freely affirmed, towards the good. Our remorse of conscience can then much more easily become a salvific contrition, though always only through God's healing forgiveness and purifying grace.

But if it is a case of mortal sin, then the fundamental option was made for evil and the chaos is so great that repentance is indeed a great miracle of God's grace, a rebirth in the full sense. Yet, man is so much God's good creation that even after a mortal sin there is still in him a remnant of God's image and likeness, a natural longing for wholeness on which grace can build. Rebirth, however, is not possible without profound sorrow, without a contrition in which the whole soul is shaken by the acknowledged insight about the terrible injustice committed against God and good. All good resolutions are weak and inefficient if they are not born of a profound contrition.

"Contrition is the most revolutionary force in the moral world".[56] It is a new encounter with God and good, and a new espousal between the will, longing for true love, and the intellect searching for truth and goodness. But this is not possible without the pangs of a new birth. "The Christian knows that every resolution which is not born in the pain of sorrow for sins remains stale and sterile, because it did not arise from the ultimate depth and, above all, did not come from God, was not conceived in God. Only sorrow softens the hardness of our nature so that a permanent 'new orientation of will' towards God, founded on that which is ultimate, can be impressed on us".[57]

The honour of God requests that each time we have sinned even venially we repent and ask forgiveness and healing as soon as possible.

There is no greater danger for our wholeness than to postpone repentance and conversion. Unrepented venial sins prepare the downfall of the good fundamental option. And we should realize how difficult it is to return to God and find inner wholeness and integrity again after a fundamental option against God.

Reciprocity of Consciences

1. *The Meaning of Reciprocity of Consciences*

The root words, *con* and *scientia* (to know together) already indicate a mutuality of con-

sciences. We have to see the reciprocal action. The healthy conscience allows wholesome relationships with neighbour and the community. Equally and perhaps more fundamentally, wholesome relationships in mutual love and respect, and a healthy community and society, greatly promote the development and health of the individual conscience.

Surely, conscience also means self-reflection, self-awareness, to be at peace with oneself, to experience one's growing wholeness or the threat against it. But genuine self-awareness and self-reflection are existentially not possible without the experience of encounter with the other.

This is the theme of a profound book by Maurice Nédoncelle on the reciprocity of awareness, consciousness and conscience.[58] The person comes to his or her identity and integrity only in the reciprocity of awareness and conscience. One knows about one's own unique self only through the experience of relationship between Thou and I, which leads to the experience of the We. It is a matter of genuine love and respect when the other is accepted in his selfhood, his uniqueness. "Any kind of love that has another purpose or reason than the openness of I and Thou for a reciprocal communion is an illusion about love".[59]

Genuine reciprocity of knowledge, awareness and conscience enters into the other's perspectives or, better said, two distinct perspectives enter into a collegial conscientiousness.[60] This meeting of people in each one's singularity and identity, in mutual respect for each other's conscience, is a process of reciprocal liberation.[61] Where this bond of fidelity to the other's true self is established, each person can be freed from his mask.[62]

The two who have mutually accepted their diversity and their equal dignity in the profound sharing of conscientiousness, and with radical respect for their conscience, are no longer slaves of the superego; they are no longer just playing roles to please each other. They have come to genuine creative liberty and fidelity, free from that boring repetition which characterizes the mask of the superego.[63] When persons can enter into that ultimate solidarity without giving up their own identity, but rather in profound reverence and cooperation in the Spirit, then they are best prepared to discover the horizon of the divine.[64]

Through mutuality of consciences, a true ego-strength and self-respect arises that allows an ever greater respect and freedom for one another's conscience. Without this synthesis between the reverence that allows the other to be who he is and the solidarity by which the persons are a source of identity, integrity and authenticity for each other, there can be neither true freedom nor creative fidelity. The reciprocity of consciences is disturbed not only by lack of love and respect for others; it is a most painful experience for our own conscience to realize that we are, ourselves, unable to love. Thus bridges that sustain our own worth are destroyed.[65]

2. *Reciprocity of Consciences in Paul's Letters*

An individualistic concept of conscience it totally alien to Holy Scripture. Paul shows us how sensitive is the conscience of those who are freed by the law of the Spirit. They understand the deep desire of all people and even of all creation to have a share in the liberty of the sons and daughters of God. Those who live on the level of the Spirit are no longer under the power of the superego; they are not looking just for approval by others but are responding to their deepest desire to come to fullness of life and a full experience of saving solidarity. This is particularly a theme of the Epistle to the Romans, chapter 8.

Paul's call to be renewed in heart and mind in order to "be able to discern the will of God and to know what is good, acceptable and perfect" (Rom 12:2) is followed by a vision of building up the Body of Christ through all the gifts that God has bestowed on people. "Care as much about each other as about yourselves" (Rom 12:16). This concern extends equally, and even particularly, to those who are hostile to us. "If your enemy is hungry, feed him; if he is thirsty, give him a drink; by doing this you will heap live coals on his head. Do not let evil conquer you, but use good to defeat evil" (Rom 12:20). The Church becomes a visible sign of Christ's presence on earth—as it were, the Body of Christ—insofar as the disciples use all their talents and charisms in complementarity (Rom 12; 1 Cor 12:14; Eph 4).

In Romans 14 and 1 Corinthians 10, Paul discusses a very specific example of reciprocity of consciences: the loving attention which those who have progressed in faith give to the weaker consciences of their fellow Christians. Paul himself is convinced that there is no distinction between ritually clean and unclean food, yet he reminds the Christians to respect the conscientiousness of others. "For instance, one person will have faith enough to eat all kind of food, while a weaker one eats only vegetables. The person who eats must not hold in contempt the other who does not, and he who does not eat must not pass judgment on the one who does; for God has accepted him" (Rom 14:2–3).

This mutuality of conscience is rooted in our faith relationships with Christ. If we live for the Lord, we also live for each other in concern and respect for one another's conscience. "For no one of us lives and no one dies for himself alone. If we live, we live for the Lord; and if we die, we die for the Lord" (Rom 14:7–8). "Let no obstacle or stumbling block be placed in a brother's way. I am absolutely convinced, as a Christian, that nothing is impure in itself; only if a man considers a particular thing impure, then to him it is impure. If your brother is outraged by what you eat, then your conduct is no longer guided by love. Do not, by your eating, bring disaster to a person for whom Christ died" (Rom 14:13–15).

While Paul appreciates his own freedom from taboos and traditions that are no longer meaningful, he warns that it is something quite different to have contempt for fellow Christians who are still wavering or still have strong convictions about laws and traditions that, by one's own values, would no longer be binding. "Happy is the man who can make his decision with a clear conscience! But a man who has doubts is guilty if he eats, because his action does not arise from his conviction, and anything that does not arise from conviction (conscience) is sin. Those of us who have a robust conscience must accept as our own burden the tender scruples of weaker men, and not consider ourselves. Each of us must consider his neighbour and think what is for his good and will build up the common life" (Rom 14:22–15:2).

Again, in the First Letter to the Corinthians, chapter 10, Paul shows how he understands the reciprocity of consciences. The Council of the Apostles in Jerusalem had decided that Christians should "abstain from things polluted by contact with idols" (Acts 15:20). Paul does not conclude that it is intrinsically and absolutely evil to eat meat that was sacrificed to the idols and then sold on the market. He approaches the problem in a perspective of the reciprocity of consciences. The liberals, who were insisting on their own insight that the food is always the gift of the good God, ignored the injunction of the Council of the Apostles. They bragged of the freedom of their consciences, saying, "We are free to do anything". But Paul asks them, "But does everything help the building of the community? Each of you must regard not his own interests but the other person's" (1 Cor 10:23–24).

If nobody's conscience is hurt, he agrees that they can eat the meat with thanksgiving to God. "You may eat anything sold in the market without raising questions of conscience; for the earth is the Lord's and everything in it. If an unbeliever invites you to a meal and you care to go, eat whatever is put before you, without raising questions of conscience" (1 Cor 10:25–27). But the situation is quite different if the fact that the meat is sacrificed becomes a part of the context of eating. Even if an illumined conscience sees it only as a gift of the one God, the person must consider the conscience of the other. "But if somebody says to you, 'This food has been offered in sacrifice', then, out of consideration for him, and for conscience's sake, do not eat it: not your conscience, I mean, but the other person's. 'What?' you say, 'Is my freedom to be called into question by another man's conscience? If I partake with thankfulness, why am I blamed for eating food over which I have said grace?' Well, whether you eat or drink, or whatever you are doing, do all for the honour of God: give no offence to Jews or Greeks or to the church of God" (1 Cor 10:28–32).

According to Paul, it is evident that we cannot honour God from the depth of our conscience unless we are thankful but also respectful about the impact of our action on the wavering conscience of our fellowmen. Those who were not yet completely freed emotionally from their ancient cult might well have thought that those stronger characters took a double insurance, one with Christ and one with the pagan gods. For Paul, it is the conduct, and not the material thing itself, that is always to be judged in the reciprocity of conscience, in the collegial solidarity for wholeness and salvation.

Church Authority and the Reciprocity of Consciences

A sincere conscience is, for everyone, the supreme authority under God. It is by respecting this authority that we can adore God in spirit and truth. However, we have seen that our conscience comes to its fullness only in reciprocity with other consciences. We receive light and strength through the authority of conscientious persons, the saints, the prophets, who are at the same time competent in important areas of life.

Our conscience does not receive so much light and impulse from abstract laws as from the exemplary person who lives truthfully under the authority of his conscience and respects wholly the conscience of others. We live the communion of saints by sharing our reflections and our moral and religious experiences, by encouraging each other to ever greater depth of conscience. The greatest gifts to the Church and to each of us are the saints who have brought themselves totally under the authority of the loving God through a pure heart, a sincere conscience.

The creativity of God's people depends on the prophetic people who are always vigilant for the coming of the Lord and can communicate to our conscience their experience: "It is the Lord who calls you". The office-holders will enjoy greater authority in the Church if they are grateful for the "authority" of the prophets and the many humble saints who live fully the reciprocity of consciences under God and in full co-responsibility with and for all of God's people.

Christ has sent apostles as witnesses, people who have lived with him, have come to know him and have allowed themselves to be guided by the Holy Spirit. The Church flourishes when popes and bishops are truly charismatic, zealous shepherds and proclaimers of the Good News. Their authority for the conscience of all open-minded people grows if they are outstanding observers and listeners, able to learn from the example of the saints and from the voices of the prophets and of men and women competent to speak by their learning and by their spirit of prayer.

In our difficult times of transitions and worldwide meetings of various cultures, the cooperation of the papal and episcopal magisterium with theologians is of paramount importance for a better understanding of the signs of the times. Headed by the pope, bishops and theologians stand together in the service of the Word of God. All are guardians and promoters of the faith in mutual complementarity. They can be leaders of the people only if they are the most outstanding listeners, listening to the word of God, listening to each other, listening to the faithful, especially to those who embody the moral and religious authority of life, competence and experience, while listening always to the Spirit who prompts their hearts to search, in absolute sincerity, for truth.[66]

Only where and when this reciprocity of consciences comes to its full bearing will magisterial interventions and the ongoing research of theologians strengthen the teaching authority of the Church.[67] The hierarchical authority and the theologians are, together, leaders and learners in a pilgrim Church. Nobody possesses a monopoly of truth, and nobody can hope to be inspired by the Spirit unless he honours the Holy Spirit who works in all and for all.

Nobody should be distressed or surprised when neither the pope nor the theologians have always ready responses to all new problems, but have to go through painstaking effort to discern the abiding truth, to decipher the signs of the times, and to free themselves and their fellow Christians from ossified formulations and partial ideologies.[68]

There must be the authority of those who teach and make decisions, and there must be a spirit of loyalty and obedience towards them. But in order to understand the specific quality of authority and obedience in the Church we must think, above all, of the truth embodied in Jesus Christ and in his communion of saints, the apostolic faith passed on, confessed, celebrated and preached. It is the common faith of all Christians, that can be shared and better understood in the reciprocity of consciences. The more consciences express purity of heart, and the more authority of the upright conscience is recognized, the more all will come to a deeper understanding and a greater moral authority.[69]

The magisterium of the Church, in all its forms and on all levels, is authentic and faithful to Christ when the overriding concern is not for submission but for honesty, sincerity and responsibility. The Church is present where the superego morality is unmasked and where mere acceptability yields to co-responsibility in reciprocity of consciences. All the saints, the prophets, those who enjoy particular competence, and the hierarchical authorities have to join energies to withstand all kind of manipulation of consciences, and to educate persons who are open to the Spirit and have the courage to shoulder together their responsibilities. Thus the earth will be filled with the knowledge of the Lord.

Notes

1. *Gaudium et spes,* 16.
2. R. Schnackenburg, *Moral Teaching of the New Testament,* New York, 1965, 69f.
3. Cf. C. A. Pierce, *Conscience in the New Testament,* London, 1955, 113.
4. D. Stanley S. J., *Boasting in the Lord,* New York, 1973, 131.
5. Cf. J. Stelzenberger, *Syneides im Neuen Testament,* Paderborn, 1961; Id., *Die Beziehungen der früchristlichen Sittenlehre zur Ethik der Stoa,* München, 1973.
6. Cf. J. L. McKenzie, "Conscience in the New Testament", in his *Dictionary of the Bible,* Milwaukee, 1965, 147; C. H. Dodd, *The Epistle of Paul to the Romans,* London, 1959, 61f.
7. Ph. Delhaye, *Christian Conscience,* New York, 1968, 36.
8. R. H. Preston, "Conscience", in J. Macquarrie, *Dictionary of Christian Ethics,* Philadelphia, 1967, 67; cf. Ph. Delhaye, l.c., 42; P. Spicq, "La conscience dans le Nouveau Testament", in *Revue Biblique* 47 (1938), 63–67; E. D. D'Arcy, *Conscience and the Right to Freedom,* New York, 1961, 4–12.
9. H. Thielicke, *Theological Ethics,* vol. I, Philadelphia, 1966, 298; cf. D. Capone C.Ss.R., "Antropologia, coscienza e personalità", in *Studia Moralia* IV (1966), 73–113.
10. Cf. H. Schär, "Protestant Problem with Conscience", in E. Nelson (ed.), *Conscience: Theological Perspectives,* New York, 1973, 86;M. B. Crowe, "The Term Synderesis and the Scholastics", in *Irish Th. Q.* 23 (1956), 151–164; 228–245; see Jerome, *Commentarium in Ezechielem,* lib. I c. 1 PL 25, 22.
11. S.Th., I II, q 79, a 13.
12. R. Hofmann, *Die Gewissenslehre des Walter von Bruegge und die Gewissens-*

lehre in der Hochscholastik, Münster, 1941, 107–108.

13. E. Fromm, l.c., 162.

14. P. Lehmann, *Ethics in a Christian Context,* New York, 1963, 253f. We find the same emphasis on a holistic vision in C. J. Van Der Poel, *The Search for Human Values,* New York, 1971, 106ff; J. Fuchs, *Theologia moralis generalis,* Rome, 1971, 154ff; Ph. Delhaye, l.c., 51–58.

15. E. Mount, *Conscience and Responsibility,* Richmond, Va., 1969, 33.

16. J. Mullrooney, "Covenant and Conscience", *The Way* 2 (1971), 283–290.

17. Cf. S. Breton, *Conscience et intentionalité,* Paris, 1956; D. Capone, La verità nella coscienza morale, *Studia Moralia* VIII (1970), 7–36; R. May, *Man's Quest for Himself,* 174–222: "The Creative Conscience".

18. S.Th., I II, q 45, a 2.

19. K. Rahner, *The Dynamic Element in the Church,* New York, 1964, 13–41.

20. See especially A. Maslow, *The Farther Reaches of the Human Nature,* New York, 1973, 299–340.

21. B. J. Lonergan S. J., *Method in Theology,* New York, 1977, 115.

22. *Gaudium et spes,* 16.

23. J. H. Newman, *Apologia Pro Vita Sua,* New York, 1950, Part VI, 212.

24. St. Alphonsus de Liguori on "invincible ignorance", *Theologia moralis,* lib. I, tr. 2, ch. IV, dubium 1; pastoral conclusions, see *Praxis confessarii,* n. 8. It is for St. Alphonsus not so easy to accuse another of error of conscience, since not only man-made laws but even formulations of natural law allow *epikeia;* that means that a concrete judgment not conforming with a natural law formulation in conflict situation might well be a truthful judgment; see *Theologia moralis* I, 4, n. 170.

25. *De Veritate,* q 17 a 4; cf. a 5.

26. S.Th., I II, q 19, a 6 ad 3.

27. S.Th., I II, q 19, a 5; cf. *De Veritate,* q 17, a 4, and Th. Deman OP, "The Dignity of Conscience", in *Blackfriars* 34 (1953), 115–119.

28. This opinion is clearly proposed by K. Adam, *One and Holy,* New York, 1951, and by M. Laros, "Autorität und Gewissen", *Hochland* 36 (1938/39), 265–280; however, the argumentations based on Thomas Aquinas, *De Veritate* q 17, are not conclusive.

29. Cf. X. G. Colavecchio, *Erroneous Conscience and Obligations: a study of the Teaching from the Summa Halesiana, Saint Bonaventure, Saint Albert the Great, and Saint Thomas Aquinas,* Washington, 1961; F. Kaiser, *The Concept of Conscience According to John Henry Newman,* Washington, 1958.

30. E. Erikson, *Life History,* 206.

31. l.c., 261.

32. *Insight and Responsibility,* 225.

33. E. Fromm, *Man for Himself,* Greenwich, 1969, 149. Cf. R. May, l.c., 187ff.

34. Cf. G. Allport, *Becoming,* New Haven, 1955, 71–72.

35. Cf. L. Kohlberg, *Collected Papers on Moral Development and Moral Education,* Cambridge/Mass., 1973; L. Kohlberg and E. Turiel (eds.), *Moralization Research; the Cognitive Developmental Approach,* New York, 1971; L. Kohlberg, "Stages of Moral Development: a Basis for Moral Education", in *Moral Education: Interdisciplinary Approaches,* edited by C. M. Beck and others, New York, 1971; Id., "Education for Justice: a Modern Statement of the Platonic View", in *Moral Education,* Five Lectures (J. Gustafson, R. S. Peters, L. Kohlberg, B. Bettelheim, K. Kenston), Cambridge/Mass., 1970, 56–83; R. Duska and M. Whelan, *Moral Develop-*

ment: A Guide to Piaget and Kohlberg, New York, 1975; J. Piaget, *The Moral Judgement of the Child*, New York, 1962 (first published 1932); C. E. Nelson (ed.), *Conscience: Theological and Psychological Perspectives*, New York, 1973.

36. L. Kohlberg, "Stages of Moral Development", 86f.
37. l.c., 87.
38. l.c., 88.
39. l.c., 34.
40. l.c., 35.
41. l.c., 44.
42. l.c., 65.
43. l.c., 54. The religious educator should be aware of the limited scope of L. Kohlberg's theories. He does not refer to a distinctively Christian formation of conscience (cf. the following section of this chapter). We should also take a critical look at his Kantian philosophical approach and the one-sided emphasis on the cognitive dimension of the conscience. Cf. W. E. Conn, "Postconventional Morality: An Exposition and Critique of Lawrence Kohlberg's Analysis of Moral Development in the Adolescent and Adult", in *Lumen Vitae* 30 (1975), 213–230; P. Philibert, "Lawrence Kohlberg's Use of Virtue in His Theory of Moral Development", in *International Philosophical Quarterly* 15 (1975), 455–479; P. Philibert, "Some Cautions on Kohlberg", in *The Living Light* 12 (1975), 527–534.
44. R. Schnackenburg, *Moral Teaching of the New Testament*, 294.
45. Cf. J. Leclercq, *Christ and the Modern Conscience*, New York, 1962; J. Coventry S. J., "Christian Conscience", in *Heythrop Journal* 7 (1966), 145–160; X. G. Colavecchio, "Conscience: A Personalist Perspective", in *Continuum 5* (1967), 203–210; T. E. O'Connell, "A

Theology of Conscience", in *Chicago Studies* 15 (1976), 149–166.
46. This is to a great extent the thought pattern of B. Schüller; see his article "Zur Diskussion über das Proprium der Christlichen Ethik", in *Theologie und Philosophie* 51 (1976), 321–343. In his overview of the latest discussion on this subject R. McCormick synthesizes this tendency—seemingly approving it—in the following way: "Where morality is concerned, Schüller argues, Scripture is largely parenesis. That is why so many rich and excellent studies in biblical ethics never come to grips with the problem of normative ethics", "Notes on moral theology" (regarding the specificity of Christian Ethics), in *Theological Studies* 38, (1976), 64–71, quote from p. 67.
47. Cf. my book *Hope is the Remedy,* New York and Slough, 1972.
48. J. Pieper, *Prudence,* New York, 1969, 27.
49. S.Th., II II, q 51, a 4; q 57, a 6 ad 3; cf. R. Doherty, *The Judgement of Conscience and Prudence,* River Forest/Ill., 1961.
50. II II, q 52.
51. I II, q 68, a 1.
52. Cf. P. Freire, *Education for Critical Consciousness,* New York, 1973; G. Goulet, *La Conscience critique,* Paris, 1971.
53. Cf. E. Fromm, *Anatomy of Human Destructiveness,* New York, 1973; Id., *Esscape from Freedom,* New York, 1941.
54. G. M. Regan, *New Trends in Moral Theology,* New York, 1971, 167.
55. Cf. Max Scheler, "Reue und Wiedergeburt", *Vom Ewigen im Menschen,* Berlin, 1933 (3rd ed.), 5–58.
56. l.c., 41.
57. D.v. Hildebrand, *Transformation in Christ,* New York, 1948, 31.
58. M. Nédoncelle, *La réciprocité des consciences; essai sur la nature de la per-*

sonne, Paris, 1942. Id., *De la fidelité,* Paris, 1953; *Love and the Person,* New York, 1966. The French word "conscience" has a much broader meaning than the English "conscience"; it is awareness, self-awareness, consciousness but not without relationship to the moral conscience and consciousness.

59. *Réciprocité des consciences,* 11f.
60. l.c., 18.
61. l.c., 23ff.
62. l.c., 51. The French word "masque" and the English "mask" remind of the Greek word "persona" which meant the mask one used in the play. The word "mask" in Nédoncelle's writing comes close to the meaning of the superego, that drives people to play the social game without attention to their authenticity and conscience.
63. l.c., 64ff.
64. l.c., 86–90.
65. K. B. Clark, *Pathos and Power,* New York, 1974, XIV.
66. Archbishop Robert Coffi, "Lehramt und Theologie—Die Situation heute", in *Orientierung* 40 (1976), 63–66.
67. Cf. R. McCormick, "Notes on Moral Theology", in *Theol. Studies* 38 (1977),

84–114, esp. p. 90; cf. also International Theol. Commission, "Theses de magisterii ecclesiastici et theologiae relationibus ad invicem", in *Documentation cath.* 73 (1976), 658–665; M. Flick S. J., "Due funzioni della teologia secondo il recente documento della commissione teologica internazionale", in *Civiltà Cattolica* 127 (1976), 472–483; Bishop A. L. Descamps, "Théologie et Magistère", in *Ephem. Theol. Lov.* 52 (1976), 82–133; A Dulles S. J., "What is Magisterium?", in *Origins* 6 (1976), 81–87.
68. Cf. B. C. Butler, "Letter to a Distressed Catholic", in *Tablet* 230 (1976), 735f and 757f.
69. Cf. Y. Congar O. P., "Pour une histoire sémantique du terme 'magisterium' ", in *Revue des sciences Phil. et Theol.* 60 (1976), 85–98; Id., "Bref historique des formes du 'magistère' et de ses relations aec les docteurs", *ibid.,* 99–112; A. B. Calkins, "John Henry Newman on Conscience and the Magisterium", in *The Downside Review* 87 (1969), 358–369; Associazione dei moralisti italiani, *Magistero e coscienza,* Bologna, 1971, with an article of mine under the same heading, 319–345.

21

Visions of Maturity

Carol Gilligan

Attachment and separation anchor the cycle of human life, describing the biology of human reproduction and the psychology of human development. The concepts of attachment and separation that depict the nature and sequence of infant development appear in adolescence as identity and intimacy and then in adulthood as love and work. This reiterative counterpoint in human experience, however, when molded into a developmental ordering, tends to disappear in the course of its linear reduction into the equation of development with separation. This disappearance can be traced in part to the focus on child and adolescent development, where progress can readily be charted by measuring the distance between mother and child. The limitation of this rendition is most apparent in the absence of women from accounts of adult development.

There seems to be a line of development missing from current depictions of adult development, a failure to describe the progression of relationships toward a maturity of interdependence. Though the truth of separation is recognized in most developmental

texts, the reality of continuing connection is lost or relegated to the background where the figures of women appear. In this way, the emerging conception of adult development casts a familiar shadow on women's lives, pointing again toward the incompleteness of their separation, depicting them as mired in relationships. For women, the developmental markers of separation and attachment, allocated sequentially to adolescence and adulthood, seem in some sense to be fused. However, while this fusion leaves women at risk in a society that rewards separation, it also points to a more general truth currently obscured in psychological texts.

In young adulthood, when identity and intimacy converge in dilemmas of conflicting commitment, the relationship between self and other is exposed. That this relationship differs in the experience of men and women is a steady theme in the literature on human development and a finding of my research. From the different dynamics of separation and attachment in their gender identity formation through the divergence of identity and inti-

This article is excerpted from In a Different Voice, *(Cambridge, Harvard University Press, 1982) 151–174.*

281

macy that marks their experience in the adolescent years, male and female voices typically speak of the importance of different truths, the former of the role of separation as it defines and empowers the self, the latter of the ongoing process of attachment that creates and sustains the human community.

Since this dialogue contains the dialectic that creates the tension of human development, the silence of women in the narrative of adult development distorts the conception of its stages and sequence. Thus, I want to restore in part the missing text of women's development, as they describe their conceptions of self and morality in the early adult years. In focusing primarily on the differences between the accounts of women and men, my aim is to enlarge developmental understanding by including the perspectives of both of the sexes. While the judgments considered come from a small and highly educated sample, they elucidate a contrast and make it possible to recognize not only what is missing in women's development but also what is there.

This problem of recognition was illustrated in a literature class at a women's college where the students were discussing the moral dilemma described in the novels of Mary McCarthy and James Joyce:

> I felt caught in a dilemma that was new to me then but which since has become horribly familiar: the trap of adult life, in which you are held, wriggling, powerless to act because you can see both sides. On that occasion, as generally in the future, I compromised.
>
> (*Memories of a Catholic Girlhood*)

I will not serve that in which I no longer believe, whether it calls itself my home, my fatherland or my church: and I will try to express myself in some mode of life or art as freely as I can and as wholly as I can, using for my defense the only arms I allow myself to use—silence, exile and cunning.

(*A Portrait of the Artist as a Young Man*)

Comparing the clarity of Stephen's *non serviam* with Mary McCarthy's "zigzag course," the women were unanimous in their decision that Stephen's was the better choice. Stephen was powerful in his certainty of belief and armed with strategies to avoid confrontation; the shape of his identity was clear and tied to a compelling justification. He had, in any case, taken a stand.

Wishing that they could be more like Stephen, in his clarity of decision and certainty of desire, the women saw themselves instead like Mary McCarthy, helpless, powerless, and constantly compromised. The contrasting images of helplessness and power in their explicit tie to attachment and separation caught the dilemma of the women's development, the conflict between integrity and care. In Stephen's simpler construction, separation seemed the empowering condition of free and full self-expression, while attachment appeared a paralyzing entrapment and caring an inevitable prelude to compromise. To the students, Mary McCarthy's portrayal confirmed their own endorsement of this account.

In the novels, however, contrasting descriptions of the road to adult life appear. For Stephen, leaving childhood means renouncing relationships in order to protect his freedom of self-expression. For Mary, "farewell to childhood" means relinquishing the freedom of self-expression in order to protect others and preserve relationships: "A sense of power and Caesarlike magnanimity filled me. I was going to equivocate, not for selfish reasons but in the interests of the community, like a grown-up responsible person" (p. 162). These divergent constructions of identity, in self-expression or in self-sacrifice, create different problems for further development—the former a problem of human connection, and the latter a problem of truth. These seemingly disparate problems, however, are intimately related, since the shrinking from truth creates distance in relationship, and separation removes part of the truth. In the college student study which spanned the years of early adulthood, the men's return from exile and silence parallels the women's return from equivocation, until intimacy and truth converge in the discovery of the connection between integrity and care. Then only a difference in tone reveals what men and women know from the beginning and what they only later discover through experience.

The instant choice of self-deprecation in the preference for Stephen by the women in the English class is matched by a child-like readiness for apology in the women in the college student study. The participants in this study were an unequal number of men and women, representing the distribution of males and females in the class on moral and political choice. At age twenty-seven, the five women in the study all were actively pursuing careers —two in medicine, one in law, one in graduate study, and one as an organizer of labor unions. In the five years following their graduation from college, three had married and one had a child.

When they were asked at age twenty-seven, "How would you describe yourself to yourself?" one of the women refused to reply, but the other four gave as their responses to the interviewer's question:

This sounds sort of strange, but I think maternal, with all its connotations. I see myself in a nurturing role, maybe not right now, but whenever that might be, as a physician, as a mother . . . It's hard for me to think of myself without thinking about other people around me that I'm giving to.

(Claire)

I am fairly hard-working and fairly thorough and fairly responsible, and in terms of weaknesses, I am sometimes hesitant about making decisions and unsure of myself and afraid of doing things and taking responsibility, and I think maybe that is one of the biggest conflicts I have had . . . The other very important aspect of my life is my husband and trying to make his life easier and trying to help him out.

(Leslie)

I am a hysteric. I am intense. I am warm. I am very smart about people . . . I have a lot more soft feelings than hard feelings. I am a lot easier to get to be kind than to get mad. If I had to say one word, and to me it incorporates a lot, *adopted*.

(Erica)

I have sort of changed a lot. At the point of the last interview [age twenty-two] I felt like I was the kind of person who was interested in growth and trying hard, and it seems to me that the last couple of years, the not trying is someone who is not growing, and I think that is the thing that bothers me the most, the thing that I keep thinking about, that I am not growing. It's not true, I am, but what seems to be a failure partially is the way that Tom and I broke up. The thing with Tom feels to me like I am not growing . . . The thing I am running into lately is that the way I describe myself, my behavior doesn't sometimes come out that way. Like I hurt Tom a lot, and that bothers me. So I am thinking of myself as somebody who tried not to hurt people, but I ended up hurting him a lot, and so that is something that weighs on me, that I am somebody who unintentionally hurts people. Or a feeling, lately, that it is simple to sit down and say what your principles are, what your values are, and what I think about myself, but the way it sort of works out in actuality is sometimes very different. You can say you try not to hurt people, but you might because of things about yourself, or you can say this is my principle, but when the situation comes up, you don't really behave the way you would like . . . So I consider myself contradictory and confused.

(Nan)

The fusion of identity and intimacy, noted repeatedly in women's development, is perhaps nowhere more clearly articulated than in these self-descriptions. In response to the request to describe themselves, all of the women describe a relationship, depicting their identity *in* the connection of future mother, present wife, adopted child, or past lover. Similarly, the standard of moral judgment that informs their assessment of self is a standard of relationship, an ethic of nurturance, responsibility, and care. Measuring their strength in the activity of attachment ("giving to," "helping out," "being kind," "not hurting"), these

highly successful and achieving women do not mention their academic and professional distinction in the context of describing themselves. If anything, they regard their professional activities as jeopardizing their own sense of themselves, and the conflict they encounter between achievement and care leaves them either divided in judgment or feeling betrayed. Nan explains:

> When I first applied to medical school, my feeling was that I was a person who was concerned with other people and being able to care for them in some way or another, and I was running into problems the last few years as far as my being able to give of myself, my time, and what I am doing to other people. And medicine, even though it seems that profession is set up to do exactly that, seems to more or less interfere with your doing it. To me it felt like I wasn't really growing, that I was just treading water, trying to cope with what I was doing that made me very angry in some ways because it wasn't the way that I wanted things to go.

Thus in all of the women's descriptions, identity is defined in a context of relationship and judged by a standard of responsibility and care. Similarly, morality is seen by these women as arising from the experience of connection and conceived as a problem of inclusion rather than one of balancing claims. The underlying assumption that morality stems from attachment is explicitly stated by Claire in her response to Heinz's dilemma of whether or not to steal an overpriced drug in order to save his wife. Explaining why Heinz should steal, she elaborates the view of social reality on which her judgment is based:

By yourself, there is little sense to things. It is like the sound of one hand clapping, the sound of one man or one woman, there is something lacking. It is the collective that is important to me, and that collective is based on certain guiding principles, one of which is that everybody belongs to it and that you all come from it. You have to love someone else, because while you may not like them, you are inseparable from them. In a way, it is like loving your right hand. *They are part of you;* that other person is part of that giant collection of people that you are connected to.

To this aspiring maternal physician, the sound of one hand clapping does not seem a miraculous transcendence but rather a human absurdity, the illusion of a person standing alone in a reality of interconnection.

For the men, the tone of identity is different, clearer, more direct, more distinct and sharp-edged. Even when disparaging the concept itself, they radiate the confidence of certain truth. Although the world of the self that men describe at times includes "people" and "deep attachments," no particular person or relationship is mentioned, nor is the activity of relationship portrayed in the context of self-description. Replacing the women's verbs of attachment are adjectives of separation—"intelligent," "logical," "imaginative," "honest," sometimes even "arrogant" and "cocky." Thus the male "I" is defined in separation, although the men speak of having "real contacts" and "deep emotions" or otherwise wishing for them.

In a randomly selected half of the sample, men who were situated similarly to the women in occupational and marital position give as their initial responses to the request for self-description:

Logical, compromising, outwardly calm. If it seems like my statements are short and abrupt, it is because of my background and training. Architectural statements have to be very concise and short. Accepting. Those are all on an emotional level. I consider myself educated, reasonably intelligent.

I would describe myself as an enthusiastic, passionate person who is slightly arrogant. Concerned, committed, very tired right now because I didn't get much sleep last night.

I would describe myself as a person who is well developed intellectually and emotionally. Relatively narrow circle of friends, acquaintances, persons with whom I have real contacts as opposed to professional contacts or community contacts. And relatively proud of the intellectual skills and development, content with the emotional development as such, as a not very actively pursued goal. Desiring to broaden that one, the emotional aspect.

Intelligent, perceptive—I am being brutally honest now—still somewhat reserved, unrealistic about a number of social situations which involve other people, particularly authorities. Improving, looser, less tense and hung up than I used to be. Somewhat lazy, although it is hard to say how much of that is tied up with other conflicts. Imaginative, sometimes too much so. A little dilettantish, interested in a lot of things without necessarily going into them in depth, although I am moving toward correcting that.

I would tend to describe myself first by recounting a personal history, where I was born, grew up, and that kind of thing, but I am dissatisfied with that, having done it thousands of times. It doesn't seem to capture the essence of what I am, I would probably decide after another futile attempt, because there is no such thing as the essence of what I am, and be very bored by the whole thing . . . I don't think that there is any such thing as myself. There is myself sitting here, there is myself tomorrow, and so on.

Evolving and honest.

I guess on the surface I seem a little easy-going and laid back, but I think I am probably a bit more wound up than that. I tend to get wound up very easily. Kind of smart aleck, a little bit, or cocky maybe. Not as thorough as I should be. A little bit hardass, I guess, and a guy that is not swayed by emotions and feelings. I have deep emotions, but I am not a person who has a lot of different people. I have attachments to a few people, very deep attachments. Or attachments to a lot of things, at least in the demonstrable sense.

I guess I think I am kind of creative and also a little bit schizophrenic . . . A lot of it is a result of how I grew up. There is a kind of longing for the pastoral life and, at the same time, a desire for the flash, prestige, and recognition that you get by going out and hustling.

Two of the men begin more tentatively by talking about people in general, but they return in the end to great ideas or a need for distinctive achievement:

I think I am basically a decent person. I think I like people a lot and I like liking people. I like doing things with pleasure from just people, from their existence, almost. Even people I don't know well. When I said I was a decent person, I think that is almost the thing that makes me a decent person, that is a decent quality, a good quality. I think I am very bright. I think I am a little lost, not acting quite like I am inspired—whether it is just a question of lack of inspiration, I don't know—but not accomplishing things, not achieving things, and not knowing where I want to go or what I'm doing. I think most people especially doctors, have some idea of what they are going to be doing in four years. I [an intern] really have a blank . . . I have great ideas . . . but I can't imagine me in them.

I guess the things that I like to think are important to me are I am aware of what is going on around me, other people's needs around me, and the fact that I enjoy doing things for other people and I feel good about it. I suppose it's nice in my situation, but I am not sure that is true for everybody. I think some people do things for other people and it doesn't make them feel good. Once in awhile that is true of me too, for instance working around the house, and I am always doing the same old things that everyone else is doing and eventually I build up some resentment toward that.

In these men's descriptions of self, involvement with others is tied to a qualification of identity rather than to its realization. Instead of attachment, individual achievement rivets the male imagination, and great ideas or distinctive activity defines the standard of self-assessment and success.

Thus the sequential ordering of identity and intimacy in the transition from adolescence to adulthood better fits the development of men than it does the development of women. Power and separation secure the man in an identity achieved through work, but they leave him at a distance from others, who seem in some sense out of his sight. Cranly, urging Stephen Daedalus to perform his Easter duty for his mother's sake, reminds him:

> Your mother must have gone through a good deal of suffering . . . Would you not try to save her from suffering more even if—or would you?
> If I could, Stephen said, that would cost me very little.

Given this distance, intimacy becomes the critical experience that brings the self back into connection with others, making it possible to see both sides—to discover the effects of actions on others as well as their cost to the self. The experience of relationship brings an end to isolation, which otherwise hardens into indifference, an absence of active concern for others, though perhaps a willingness to respect their rights. For this reason, intimacy is the transformative experience for men through which adolescent identity turns into the generativity of adult love and work. In the process, as Erikson (1964) observes, the knowledge gained through intimacy changes the ideological morality of adolescence into the adult ethic of taking care.

Since women, however, define their identity through relationships of intimacy and care, the moral problems that they encounter pertain to issues of a different sort. When relationships are secured by masking desire and conflict is avoided by equivocation, then confusion arises about the locus of responsibility and truth. McCarthy, describing her "representations" to her grandparents, explains:

> Whatever I told them was usually so blurred and glossed, in the effort to meet their approval (for, aside from anything else, I was fond of them and tried to accommodate myself to their perspective), that except when answering a direct question, I hardly knew whether what I was saying was true or false. I really tried, or so I thought, to avoid lying, but it seemed to me that they forced it on me by the difference in their vision of things, so that I was always transposing reality for them into terms they could understand. To keep matters straight with my conscience, I shrank, whenever possible, from the lie absolute, just as, from a sense of precaution, I shrank from the plain truth.

The critical experience then becomes not intimacy but choice, creating an encounter with self that clarifies the understanding of responsibility and truth.

Thus in the transition from adolescence to adulthood, the dilemma itself is the same for both sexes, a conflict between integrity and care. But approached from different perspectives, this dilemma generates the recognition of opposite truths. These different perspectives are reflected in two different moral ideologies, since separation is justified by an ethic of rights while attachment is supported by an ethic of care.

The morality of rights is predicated on equality and centered on the understanding of fairness, while the ethic of responsibility relies on the concept of equity, the recognition of differences in need. While the ethic of rights is a manifestation of equal respect, balancing the claims of other and self, the ethic of responsibility rests on an understanding that gives rise to compassion and care. Thus the counterpoint of identity and intimacy that marks the time between childhood and adulthood is articulated through two different moralities whose complementarity is the discovery of maturity.

The discovery of this complementarity is traced in the study by questions about personal experiences of moral conflict and choice. Two lawyers chosen from the sample illustrate how the divergence in judgment between the sexes is resolved through the discovery by each of the other's perspective and of the relationship between integrity and care.

The dilemma of responsibility and truth that McCarthy describes is reiterated by Hilary, a lawyer and the woman who said she found it too hard to describe herself at the end of what "really has been a rough week." She too, like McCarthy, considers self-sacrificing acts "courageous" and "praiseworthy," explaining that "if everyone on earth behaved in a way that showed care for others and courage, the world would be a much better place, you wouldn't have crime and you might not have poverty." However, this moral ideal of self-sacrifice and care ran into trouble not only in a relationship where the conflicting truths of each person's feelings made it impossible to avoid hurt, but also in court where, despite her concern for the client on the other side, she decided not to help her opponent win his case.

In both instances, she found the absolute injunction against hurting others to be an inadequate guide to resolving the actual dilemmas she faced. Her discovery of the disparity between intention and consequence and of the actual constraints of choice led her to realize that there is, in some situations, no way not to hurt. In confronting such dilemmas in both her personal and professional life, she does not abdicate responsibility for choice but rather claims the right to include herself among the people for whom she considers it moral not to hurt. Her more inclusive morality now contains the injunction to be true to herself, leaving her with two principles of judgment whose integration she cannot yet clearly envision. What she does recognize is that both integrity and care must be included in a morality that can encompass the dilemmas of love and work that arise in adult life.

The move toward tolerance that accompanies the abandonment of absolutes is considered by William Perry (1968) to chart the course of intellectual and ethical development during the early adult years. Perry describes the changes in thinking that mark the transition from a belief that knowledge is absolute and answers clearly right or wrong to an understanding of the contextual relativity of both truth and choice. This transition and its impact on moral judgment can be discerned in the changes in moral understanding that occur in both men and women during the five years following college (Gilligan and Murphy, 1979; Murphy and Gilligan, 1980). Though both sexes move away from absolutes in this time, the absolutes themselves differ for each. In women's development, the absolute of care, defined initially as not hurting others, becomes complicated through a recognition of the need for personal integrity. This recognition gives rise to the claim for equality embodied in the concept of rights, which changes the understanding of relationships and transforms the definition of care. For men, the absolutes of truth and fairness, defined by the concepts of equality and reciprocity, are called into question by experiences that demonstrate the existence of differences between other and self. Then the awareness of multiple truths leads to a relativizing of equality in the direction of equity and gives rise to an ethic of generosity and care. For both sexes the existence of two contexts for moral decision makes judgment by definition contextually relative and leads to a new understanding of responsibility and choice.

The discovery of the reality of differences and thus of the contextual nature of morality and truth is described by Alex, a lawyer in the college student study, who began in law school "to realize that you really don't know everything" and "you don't ever know that there is any absolute. I don't think that you ever know that there is an absolute right. What you do know is you have to come down one way or the other. You have got to make a decision."

The awareness that he did not know everything arose more painfully in a relationship whose ending took him completely by surprise. In his belated discovery that the woman's experience had differed from his own, he realized how distant he had been in a relationship he considered close. Then the logical hierarchy of moral values, whose absolute truth he formerly proclaimed, came to seem a barrier to intimacy rather than a fortress of personal integrity. As his conception of morality began to change, his thinking focused on issues of relationship, and his concern with injustice was complicated by a new understanding of human attachment. Describing "the principle of attachment" that began to inform his way of looking at moral problems, Alex sees the need for morality to extend beyond considerations of fairness to concern with relationships:

> People have real emotional needs to be attached to something, and equality doesn't give you attachment. Equality fractures society and places on every person the burden of standing on his own two feet.

Although "equality is a crisp thing that you could hang onto," it alone cannot adequately resolve the dilemmas of choice that arise in life. Given his new awareness of responsibility and of the actual consequences of choice, Alex says: "You don't want to look at just equality. You want to look at how people are going to be able to handle their lives." Recognizing the need for two contexts for judgment, he nevertheless finds that their integration "is hard to work through," since sometimes "no matter which way you go, somebody is going to be hurt and somebody is going to be hurt forever." Then, he says, "you have reached the point where there is an irresolvable conflict," and choice becomes a matter of "choosing the victim" rather than enacting the good. With the recognition of the responsibility that such choices entail, his judgment becomes more attuned to the psychological and social consequences of action, to the reality of people's lives in an historical world.

Thus, starting from very different points, from the different ideologies of justice and care, the men and women in the study come, in the course of becoming adult, to a greater understanding of both points of view and thus to a greater convergence in judgment. Recognizing the dual contexts of justice and care, they realize that judgment depends on the way in which the problem is framed.

But in this light, the conception of development itself also depends on the context in which it is framed, and the vision of maturity can be seen to shift when adulthood is portrayed by women rather than men. When women construct the adult domain, the world of relationships emerges and becomes the focus of attention and concern. McClelland (1975), noting this shift in women's fantasies of power, observes that "women are more concerned than men with both sides of an interdependent relationship" and are "quicker to recognize their own interdependence" (pp. 85–86). This focus on interdependence is manifest in fantasies that equate power with giving and care. McClelland reports that while men represent powerful activity as assertion and aggression, women in contrast portray acts of nurturance as acts of strength. Considering his research on power to deal "in particular with the characteristics of maturity," he suggests that mature women and men may relate to the world in a different style.

Like the stories that delineate women's fantasies of power, women's descriptions of adulthood convey a different sense of its social reality. In their portrayal of relationships, women replace the bias of men toward separation with a representation of the interdependence of self and other, both in love and in work. By changing the lens of developmental observation from individual achievement to relationships of care, women depict ongoing attachment as the path that leads to maturity. Thus the parameters of development shift toward marking the progress of affiliative relationship.

The implications of this shift are evident in considering the situation of women at mid-life. Given the tendency to chart the unfamiliar waters of adult development with the familiar markers of adolescent separation and growth, the middle years of women's lives readily appear as a time of return to the unfinished business of adolescence. This interpretation has been particularly compelling since

life-cycle descriptions, derived primarily from studies of men, have generated a perspective from which women, insofar as they differ, appear deficient in their development. The deviance of female development has been especially marked in the adolescent years when girls appear to confuse identity with intimacy by defining themselves through relationships with others. The legacy left from this mode of identity definition is considered to be a self that is vulnerable to the issues of separation that arise at mid-life.

But this construction reveals the limitation in an account which measures women's development against a male standard and ignores the possibility of a different truth. In this light, the observation that women's embeddedness in lives of relationship, their orientation to interdependence, their subordination of achievement to care, and their conflicts over competitive success leave them personally at risk in mid-life seems more a commentary on the society than a problem in women's development.

The construction of mid-life in adolescent terms, as a similar crisis of identity and separation, ignores the reality of what has happened in the years between and tears up the history of love and of work. For generativity to begin at mid-life, as Vaillant's data on men suggest, seems from a woman's perspective too late for both sexes, given that the bearing and raising of children take place primarily in the preceding years. Similarly, the image of women arriving at mid-life childlike and dependent on others is belied by the activity of their care in nurturing and sustaining family relationships. Thus the problem appears to be one of construction, an issue of judgment rather than truth.

In view of the evidence that women perceive and construe social reality differently from men and that these differences center around experiences of attachment and separation, life transitions that invariably engage these experiences can be expected to involve women in a distinctive way. And because women's sense of integrity appears to be entwined with an ethic of care, so that to see themselves as women is to see themselves in a relationship of connection, the major transitions in women's lives would seem to involve changes in the understanding and activities of care. Certainly the shift from childhood to adulthood witnesses a major redefinition of care. When the distinction between helping and pleasing frees the activity of taking care from the wish for approval by others, the ethic of responsibility can become a self-chosen anchor of personal integrity and strength.

In the same vein, however, the events of mid-life—the menopause and changes in family and work—can alter a woman's activities of care in ways that affect her sense of herself. If mid-life brings an end to relationships, to the sense of connection on which she relies, as well as to the activities of care through which she judges her worth, then the mourning that accompanies all life transitions can give way to the melancholia of self-deprecation and despair. The meaning of mid-life events for a woman thus reflects the interaction between the structures of her thought and the realities of her life.

When a distinction between neurotic and real conflict is made and the reluctance to choose is differentiated from the reality of having no choice, then it becomes possible to see more clearly how women's experience provides a key to understanding central truths of adult life. Rather than viewing her anatomy as destined to leave her with a scar of inferiority (Freud, 1931), one can see instead how it gives rise to experiences which illuminate a reality common to both of the sexes: the fact that in life you never see it all, that things unseen undergo change through time, that there is more than one path to gratification,

and that the boundaries between self and other are less clear than they sometimes seem.

Thus women not only reach mid-life with a psychological history different from men's and face at that time a different social reality having different possibilities for love and for work, but they also make a different sense of experience, based on their knowledge of human relationships. Since the reality of connection is experienced by women as given rather than as freely contracted, they arrive at an understanding of life that reflects the limits of autonomy and control. As a result, women's development delineates the path not only to a less violent life but also to a maturity realized through interdependence and taking care.

As we have listened for centuries to the voices of men and the theories of development that their experience informs, so we have come more recently to notice not only the silence of women but the difficulty in hearing what they say when they speak. Yet in the different voice of women lies the truth of an ethic of care, the tie between relationship and responsibility, and the origins of aggression in the failure of connection. The failure to see the different reality of women's lives and to hear the differences in their voices stems in part from the assumption that there is a single mode of social experience and interpretation. By positing instead two different modes, we arrive at a more complex rendition of human experience which sees the truth of separation and attachment in the lives of women and men and recognizes how these truths are carried by different modes of language and thought.

To understand how the tension between responsibilities and rights sustains the dialectic of human development is to see the integrity of two disparate modes of experience that are in the end connected. While an ethic of justice proceeds from the premise of equality—that everyone should be treated the same—an ethic of care rests on the premise of nonviolence—that no one should be hurt. In the representation of maturity, both perspectives converge in the realization that just as inequality adversely affects both parties in an unequal relationship, so too violence is destructive for everyone involved. This dialogue between fairness and care not only provides a better understanding of relations between the sexes but also gives rise to a more comprehensive portrayal of adult work and family relationships.

As Freud and Piaget call our attention to the differences in children's feelings and thought, enabling us to respond to children with greater care and respect, so a recognition of the differences in women's experience and understanding expands our vision of maturity and points to the contextual nature of developmental truths. Through this expansion in perspective, we can begin to envision how a marriage between adult development as it is currently portrayed and women's development as it begins to be seen could lead to a changed understanding of human development and a more generative view of human life.

References

Erikson, Erik H. *Childhood and Society*. New York: W.W. Norton, 1950.

Gilligan, Carol, and Murphy, John Michael. "Development from Adolescence to Adulthood: The Philosopher and the 'Dilemma of the Fact.'" In D. Kuhn, ed. *Intellectual Development Beyond Childhood*. New Directions for Child Development, no. 5. San Francisco: Jossey-Bass, 1979.

Joyce, James. *A Portrait of the Artist as a Young Man* (1916). New York: The Viking Press, 1956.

Levinson, Daniel J. *The Seasons of a Man's Life*. New York: Alfred A. Knopf, 1978.

McCarthy, Mary. *Memories of a Catholic Girlhood*. New York: Harcourt Brace Jovanovich, 1946.

McClelland, David C. *Power: The Inner Experience*. New York: Irvington, 1975.

Miller, Jean Baker. *Toward a New Psychology of Women*. Boston: Beacon Press, 1976.

Murphy, J. M., and Gilligan, C. "Moral Development in Late Adolescence and Adulthood: A Critique and Reconstruction of Kohlberg's Theory." *Human Development* 23 (1980): 77–104.

Perry, William. *Forms of Intellectual and Ethical Development in the College Years*. New York: Holt, Rinehart and Winston, 1968.

Piaget, Jean. *The Moral Judgment of the Child* (1932). New York: The Free Press, 1965.

Rubin, Lillian. *Worlds of Pain*. New York: Basic Books, 1976.

Stack, Carol B. *All Our Kin*. New York: Harper and Row, 1974.

Vaillant, George E. *Adaptation to Life*. Boston: Little, Brown, 1977.

22

Disciplines: Repentance, Prayer and Service

Craig Dykstra

Moral growth involves the increasing apprehension of mystery. This takes place when we no longer put ourselves at the center of the universe, succumbing to the illusion of moral egocentrism. To move out of the center requires a transformation of our imaginations. The evil imaginations of our hearts must be purified and reformed. This is accomplished, sometimes in sudden and striking ways and more often in prolonged and more subtle ways, through revelation.

The transformation of our imaginations through revelation is not something we can accomplish by our own powers alone or achieve by force of will. It is a gift that is given to us. It is an effect of grace. But this does not mean we have no responsibility for our own moral growth. Only if we are willing to receive can we do so. And, as Diogenes Allen points out, "we have to change in quite specific ways to get into the condition which allows us to perceive mysteries."[1] Getting into that condition requires that we undertake certain disciplines.

The importance of discipline in the moral life has become obscured in our culture and in the church as well. The stress on autonomy in the moral life has led to an emphasis on the independent powers of the individual, which we are afraid might be stifled or restricted by too much training or dependence on the guidance of others. Creativity in morals and almost everything else results, we think, from allowing what is inside a person to be freely expressed. And true expression depends more on leaving people alone than on helping them to be molded through the disciplines of the "school figures."

But Christians have historically understood the formation of the moral life as formation in discipleship. To be a disciple is to be an adherent of the way of Christ. It is to be a follower of his, and to have one's life formed through the strenuous discipline of going where he went, looking at things the way he did, trusting as he trusted, making ourselves vulnerable as he was vulnerable. If we believe that reality is revealed to us through the eyes

---

This article is excerpted from Vision and Character *(New York: Paulist Press, 1981) 89–114.*

of Christ and that our lives are transformed by being with him, then the way to grow morally is to undertake the discipline of becoming disciples.

There are, I am sure, many ways to describe the disciplines of the Christian life. Each different way will highlight some aspects and ignore others. But there are three disciplines that seem to me to be fundamental and generic. They are the disciplines of repentance, prayer, and service.[2] Through these disciplines, the church has trained its people for discipleship—for active engagement in the world as persons formed by Christian faith. I believe these disciplines merit our renewed attention if we are to be effective Christian educators for the moral life.

Repentance

One of the differences between juridical ethics and visional ethics is that the former does not take sinfulness very seriously while the latter does. There is a corollary to this. Juridical ethics finds no place for the discipline of repentance. For visional ethics repentance is utterly essential.

If our problem is really sin—a fundamental breach in human existence—then repentance, not self-improvement, is the first requirement. This is the biblical view of the foundations of morality. The prophets, John the Baptist, Jesus, and Paul all beckoned their hearers to a new life by calling them first to give up the old in repentance (Mk 1:15; Lk 13:3, 5; Acts 26:20; Rom 2:4; II Cor 7:9–10). Repentance is the absolutely inescapable first step of the Christian moral life. Without repentance, the Christian moral life is impossible.

Repentance is often thought of in terms of being sorry for, and asking forgiveness for, particular transgressions. This, admittedly, is

often the biblical context for the mention of the idea. But, if this were all there is to it, repentance would be perfectly compatible with the concept of the self-sufficiency of the independent reasonable person. After all, even reasonable people make mistakes, and it is appropriate for them to admit them. But Jesus and Paul regarded sinfulness and the need for repentance as something much deeper. For them, sinfulness was a profound alienation from God, and, therefore, from reality. In our sinfulness, we do not know reality as mystery. It is reduced to a mere object and distorted in fantasy. So we cannot be related to the world as it is.

Repentance, in the New Testament, refers to a reorientation of the whole self. We have talked of sin as our striving to establish and sustain ourselves by our own power against the threats to our existence and security. Repentance is a *metanoia,* a turning from the self to God as the source of our establishment and sustenance. As such, it is a recognition of one's sinfulness, of one's utter incapacity to make oneself good and whole by one's own powers, and of one's utter dependency on God and constant need for grace. The reorientation is thus a displacement of our own self-establishment and self-sustenance from the focal point of our psychic and physical energy. It is a "letting go" of all that, leaving it in the hands of Another.

But repentance is not only a reorientation. It is also a transformation of the self. As Jean Calvin puts it, "Departing from ourselves, we turn to God, and having taken off our former mind, we put on a new."[3] This transformation involves a sacrifice, a kind of death:

> Therefore, my brothers, I implore you by God's mercy to offer your very selves to him: a living sacrifice, dedicated and fit for his acceptance,

the worship offered by mind and heart. Adapt yourselves no longer to the pattern of this present world, but let your minds be remade and your whole nature thus transformed. Then you will be able to discern the will of God, and to know what is good, acceptable, and perfect.
(Rom 12:1–2; NEB)

We are called, in repentance, not only to turn in a new direction, but to allow a great change to take place in ourselves. This is perhaps the most frightening and difficult thing about repentance. We are not being called to *make* a great change in ourselves; that would be hard, but at least we could maintain control over it. We are to give up control and allow something to happen within ourselves that we cannot foresee. We are to give up "the pattern of this present world," which tells us who we are, what is expected of us, what the rewards and punishments will be of acting and thinking in certain ways, and let ourselves be remade from top to bottom. The great fear in all of this, of course, is that we will lose ourselves—that we will disappear.

Repentance, if it is this kind of turning and openness to transformation, requires two things: humility and trust. Repentance requires the humility involved in the confession that I am a sinner, one whose life is not whole and who lacks the power both to find either the direction to wholeness or the resources for wholeness on my own. Repentance requires trust in a power that can and will ultimately sustain and establish me if I let go of myself into that power's hands. Without both trust and humility, repentance is impossible.

But, as Donald Evans makes clear in considerable detail in his book *Struggle and Fulfillment,* trust and humility come only as the fruit of struggle. Trust is a struggle against anxiety, wariness, idolatry, despair, and apathy, which

"is personally experienced as a disorderly daily scrimmage between forces which usually do not identify themselves until there is a temporary truce and the dust of battle has settled for a while."[4] Humility is a realistic acceptance of both my actual powers and my actual limitations. It is a struggle against both pride ("a self-deceptive attempt to act out my infantile fantasies of infinitude, of unlimited strength and status"[5]) and self-humiliation ("a self-deceptive attempt to ignore my real though modest powers and achievements, preferring instead to wallow helplessly in shame"[6]).

These struggles, as Evans and, before him, Erik Erikson show, are struggles that begin in our earliest years and continue in different ways throughout our lives. Repentance is something we are not capable of until trust and humility have to some degree become characteristic of our lives. We must be able to bring ourselves to repentance in humility and trust. But in repentance, our trust and humility are tested, refined, and deepened. The trust and humility that I have make it possible for me to offer myself to God—trust and mistrust, humility, pride, self-humiliation, and all. And what I find then, according to the promise of the Gospel and the witness of the church, is that my trust is grounded in the trustworthiness of God and that my humility has its basis in God's acceptance of me. I offer myself, risking the possibility that my trust will be shattered and my self-acceptance found unacceptable. I find instead that I am given myself back again as a gift. I find myself established and sustained by One who has established and sustained me before and through my struggles, and who can be depended on to establish and sustain me for all time.

The fruit of repentance is the availability to me of the mystery of myself, the world, and God. The availability to me of the mystery of myself allows me to be free with respect to myself and to tap depths within myself that are beyond my direct control. In the freedom to be myself that repentance brings, I can let go of willful control of myself and be receptive to what lies deep within me. Evans puts it this way:

> A man allows himself to be changed by an upsurge of vital energies which impel him in unforeseen directions. When a man is open to the inner dynamism of the psyche he loses the security of the order which he has already imposed on his life. If he empties his mind of the orderly structures which he has concocted as his defense against inner chaos, and waits expectantly for something to happen, he somehow overcomes his anxiety, somehow trusts the forces within him in spite of the risk. The new freedom which then may come is a spontaneous, creative freedom.[7]

If, in repentance, I give up self-establishment and self-sustenance, I also become more free to see others as they are because I am less captive to the need to distort them for my own purposes. I am free to perceive and accept the world as it is and to give myself to it without fearing that I will lose myself in doing so. Here we see most clearly the vital connection between repentance and morality. Repentance is becoming unself-conscious in a way that allows me to become receptive to the world. The persistent need of the unrepentant ego to establish and sustain itself builds up indestructible walls between ourselves and the world, making it impossible to relate in appropriate and responsible ways without selfish distortion. But when the diabolical process of

fattening the ego is given up in repentance, we are able to accept and respect the inexhaustible particularity of others and to shape our attitudes and actions to their fundamental needs.

Finally, repentance makes the activity of God available to me. Repentance is not making; it is allowing. Repentance allows me to be receptive to myself. It allows me to be met and shaped by others as they really are. It also allows God to work God's transforming craft in me. To quote Evans again:

> God cannot act in a man unless the man permits it. Instead of being receptive to divine activity a man can block, impede, and resist it. Instead of allowing God to liberate him, a man can reinforce his own self-imprisoning defenses. God does not help those who help themselves; he helps those who realize their own need of help. God creates new life in those who acknowledge the destructive elements in their lives and let go of them. God speaks to those who are willing to listen to him. God is present to those who are open to receive him.[8]

So repentance is a "letting go," in trust and humility, of our striving to control everything in order to establish and sustain ourselves. It is a turning to God to allow God to meet our needs in a way that makes possible a transformation of ourselves.

Repentance is a crucial movement in the Christian moral life and one that is never completed. It is a continuing discipline that we undertake at increasingly deeper levels, bringing more and more of ourselves to God in humility and trust. We repent by bringing our ideas, our desires, our offenses and offended-ness, our plans and goals, our values and convictions as living sacrifices to be taken from us and returned to us, transformed and made new. Saints never cease repenting, but repent more and more deeply as they increasingly recognize the depth and breadth of their dependence on God and of the mystery of the world.

Prayer

Repentance and prayer are deeply related. We need to pray for our repentance, and repentance makes possible better prayer. The two build on and nourish each other. But there is a sense in which prayer follows on repentance. We must see this in order to understand what prayer is and how it shapes us morally. In repentance, we let go of ourselves in order that we may be receptive to God and to the mysteries of reality. Through repentance God's power becomes available to work in us. Prayer moves us further. More than receptivity to God, it is attention to God. Repentance is the discipline of opening ourselves. Prayer is the discipline of paying attention to what, by our repentance, God gives to us.

If this idea that prayer consists of attention to God seems strange to us, perhaps it is because we have given up the discipline and no longer really know how to pray. In most of our praying, our attention is neither focused nor on God. What we attend to is largely our own selves, and this in a rather generalized and ambiguous way. Prayer, both public and private, and particularly among Protestants, tends to be almost totally prayer of petition. We have some need, and we pray that it will be met. We are in some trouble, and we pray that God will take it away. Even when we do pray prayers of praise, thanksgiving, and confession, we do so with our attention turned to what we are pleased with, thankful for, and guilty of. We find it extremely difficult to allow our praise, thanks, confession, petition, and intercession to be formed by attention to God, and awfully easy to allow the God to whom we pray to become a mere reflection of our own concerns. At least this is what I experience myself as a prayer and what I perceive in most public worship. "Simple attentiveness" is most difficult. It is also very important.

Prayer shapes us morally. Murdoch tells us, "The religious believer, especially if his God is conceived of as a person, is in the fortunate position of being able to focus his thought upon something which is a source of energy."[9] The reason religious believers are fortunate is that attention to sources of energy that are good provides the power and direction to move away from evil. If we are involved in a destructive relationship with someone, if we are addicted to a way of living that is making it impossible to live fully, if we are at war with ourselves and with others, it does little good to tell ourselves to stop. "What is needed," says Murdoch, "is a reorientation which will provide an energy of a different kind, from a different source."[10] What we require "is the acquiring of new objects of attention and thus of new energies as a result of refocusing."[11] When we become absorbed in something else, the original object of our attention no longer has its pull on us. We are almost automatically obedient to what absorbs our attention.[12] This is why prayer is the necessary discipline for obedience to God.

Prayer, or attention to God, is the most difficult form of attention. We have not seen God, and it is very hard to pay attention to what we have not seen. Furthermore, we are compulsive idolators, and our attention to

God is easily diverted to attention to idols. We do not start, then, in the discipline of prayer, with attention to God. That is our goal. We start by learning to pay attention to what God has given us, the reality before us. Such attention is practice in prayer. It is also an implicit form of prayer. To really attend to and love the natural world, art, ideas, and other people is indirectly to attend to and love God.

Jesus shows how this is so by telling the parable of the sheep and the goats (Mt 25:31–46). Those who receive the Lord's blessing are those who, in the course of their lives, are able to pay attention to the hungry, the thirsty, the stranger, the ill, and the imprisoned. It turns out that, unwittingly, they had all along been attending to God in Christ. Prayer, in its implicit form, is the act of attention to realities that are before us. By such acts, we attend, indirectly, to God. Through such acts, God's very self is made known to us, and we are thus more able to pray explicitly.

"Attention," according to Simone Weil, "consists of suspending our thought, leaving it detached, empty, and ready to be penetrated by the object; it means holding in our minds, within reach of this thought, but on a lower level and not in contact with it, the diverse knowledge we have acquired which we are forced to make use of."[13] Paying attention means holding back our preconceptions and our desires for how things should be until the object of our attention has had a chance to make an impact on us. It allows the reality before us to move us and change us. Once the object of our attention is seen, we allow it to change our preconceptions if necessary and to reaffirm what truth we previously knew. Attention takes us out of ourselves, and then changes us to bring us more in accord with reality. When this happens we are thankful and joyous—both for the reality we have come to know and for our relationship to it.

Attention to human beings is more difficult. To love persons is to attend to them just as they are. In attention to persons, "the soul empties itself of all its own contents in order to receive into itself the being it is looking at, just as he is, in all his truth."[14] This means withholding conventional labels, refusing to compare the other's status or prestige with my own, allowing the other to accept or reject what I have to give, refraining from manipulating the other into meeting my needs, granting the other his or her separateness and independence from me. All of this is very hard to do, and is possible only if we are free to do it because our own needs are met by God. But doing it is something we can learn by discipline.

As we practice these disciplines, we come closer to prayer itself. But prayer as attention to God is not the occasion for the disappearance of attention to the world. Attention to God purifies our attention to the world and provides the energy and light we need in order to do it. Murdoch says that there is a place for "an attention which is not just the planning of particular good actions but an attempt to look right away from the self towards a distant transcendent perfection, a source of uncontaminated energy, a source of new and quite undreamt virtue."[15] Attention to God in prayer requires that we turn our attention from the world for a time. But this, as Murdoch goes on to say, "may be the thing that helps most when difficulties seem insoluble, and especially when feelings of guilt keep attracting the gaze back towards the self."[16]

Service

The theme of service is a prominent one in the Bible, and particularly in the Gospels. Several times the Gospels report that the disciples argued about who would be nearest to Jesus in the coming Kingdom. In response to these arguments, and in other situations, Jesus always made it perfectly clear that those who would be near him, those who would follow him and be his disciples, would be servants.[17] Likewise, we who would undertake the disciplines of discipleship must undertake the discipline of service.

One of the most powerful images of service in the Bible is Jesus washing the feet of his disciples (Jn 13:1–17). At our seminary, we have chapel services every Tuesday and Thursday morning. The text for one of these days happened to be John 13, and the worship leader planned not only to preach on that text but also to have us celebrate the "sacrament" of foot-washing. But through a typographical error, perhaps inspired, the announcement went out that we were to have a "fool-washing." The slip seemed right. The brightest and the best, the powerful and authoritative in our world, do not wash people's feet; only fools do. To become a servant is to undertake a foolish discipline.

The Christian idea of service is distinctive in that it buys nothing. It is a "good for nothing" kind of service. It is service that is obedient simply to the fact of a person in need who requires our attention whether what we have to give will ameliorate that person's need or not.

In our culture, service is tied intimately to effectiveness.[18] That is, we do not consider a service to have been rendered to someone unless that service changes that person's condition in a material way. We have not served the ill unless we cure their illness. We have not served the weak unless we make them strong. We have not served the lonely unless they are no longer lonely. We have not served social outcasts unless we make them socially acceptable. Now I am not suggesting here that it is

necessarily better to remain ill, weak, lonely, or socially outcast. Nor am I suggesting that we should not help people toward health, strength, and fellowship with others. But I do want to point out that, where our sole aim is effectiveness, certain diabolical dynamics are set in motion.

Effectiveness requires power and the use of power. And if we are to be effective, the power must be in our hands. Power and the use of power are not in themselves evil. But the gathering of power into our own hands in order to be effective regularly turns into the gathering of power in order that we may be and remain powerful. When this takes place, we are no longer servants; we are masters. We find ourselves no longer obedient to the needs of others; we are obedient instead to the demand of maintaining and exercising power.

This has an undercutting effect on the ones whom we initially wish to serve. For, if service is linked too closely with effectiveness, we become the ones who must decide what effectiveness means. In taking power into our own hands in order to be effective, we must determine what the one in need will become when our service is accomplished. We become the definers of health and strength and fellowship, and thereby deny the ones in need of their freedom and personhood in illness, weakness, and loneliness. Rather than servants, we become manipulators. Service becomes self-serving. We say, in effect, "You will most fully exist for me when you have become—through my service to you—what my power enables you to become." When this happens, the one in need has become ours. We have bought the sufferer.

In addition to these problems, effectiveness as a criterion of service is unrealistic. There are, in fact, many situations in which what we wish to do for another simply cannot be done. Effectiveness requires too high a view of our own power, and too high a view of ourselves in relation to those whom we wish effectively to serve. In practice, we find this out. When we do, this knowledge can become an occasion for distance between ourselves and a sufferer. If service must be effective, then when we can no longer be effective we no longer have any reason to be there with and for the sufferer. The sufferer, by becoming an occasion for our effective use of power, becomes an object with which we can dispense when our power is seen to be ineffective.

The idea of service as the effective use of power is paradoxical at its center. Effectiveness requires the accumulation of power; but to be a servant involves a renunciation of power. This is why the discipline of service in the Gospels seems so foolish. It says there is a way of helping others by renouncing rather than by accumulating power. There is a service whose criterion is not effectiveness, but something else.

At the heart of service lies, not effectiveness, but *presence*. Service as presence means being *with* another. Christ's service to humankind was not effective in the sense that he brought an end to suffering and death, to illness, loneliness, weakness, social isolation, confusion, or political turmoil. Christ's service was his incarnation—his coming to be with us to take on our sufferings as his own, to stand with us and to go through with us whatever it is we are going through. When Jesus commanded the disciples to wash one another's feet saying, "I have given you an example that you also should do as I have done to you" (Jn 13:15), he was commanding them to be present to others as he was present to them.

Presence is a service of vulnerability. To be present to others is to put oneself in the position of being vulnerable to what they are vulnerable to, and of being vulnerable to them. It means being willing to suffer what the other suffers, and to go with the sufferer in his or her own suffering. This is different from trying to become the sufferer. Presence does not involve taking another's place. That would be demeaning. It would suggest, "I can take your suffering better than you can, so move aside; I will replace you." Instead, presence involves exposing oneself to what the sufferer is exposed to, and being with the other in that vulnerability.

The words "equality" and "justice" take on their most important meaning in this context. Presence demands equality and justice in the sense that it renounces the self-protection of power over the other and of whatever power could be summoned against the threats the sufferer endures. We do have power over others and power against threats to ourselves. Some people are stronger than other people: physically, intellectually, emotionally, socially, politically. Justice means refusing to use that power in order to avoid for oneself the position that another is condemned to. We are not born equal. Justice makes us equal. Service, presence, is not possible without it.

The sign of presence is compassion. When we are truly present to another our passions are linked. This is different from pity and even from empathy. Compassion is not feeling sorry for another. Nor is it just feeling inwardly in a way that corresponds to what the other feels. Our passions are the way we embody our life energies. In passion, what moves in us and through us shows in our faces, movements, and gestures. Compassion is allowing the life of another to move through me, to *move* me, so that I reveal, bodily, the impact of the other's life on me.

Vulnerability and justice make compassion possible. But compassion itself is the greatest service. When we are suffering, our deepest need is not the alleviation of our suffering but the knowledge that our suffering does not annihilate us. We know that we have not been overcome when we see our own life energies register in the face of another.

Finally, presence involves commitment. There are moments of particular vulnerability when equality makes compassion arise in especially striking ways. But such moments do not take place unless time has had its chance with us. We need to be with others over the long haul. Compassion demands that presence will not quit with the moment. It implies a future in which presence promises to be maintained. This is perhaps the feature of service that most makes it a discipline. Vulnerability for just a moment is not really vulnerability at all. Equality that threatens to turn quickly into inequality when the threats become too great is bogus. In order to serve, we must become servants and not just provide services.

Service, then, is a discipline of renouncing power in order to be present with others in vulnerability, equality, and compassion. Ironically, such service does help people. It is, in a kind of foolish way, effective. It repeatedly has the effect of providing space for other persons to tap their own resources and to gather their own energies. It also provides opportunity for a person in need to feed off of the powers of the servant. Here the one served draws power, freely and not under coercion. The one served is recognized as the person he or she is, and is not made into an object. The service of presence provides nourishment for body and spirit; it does not manipulate the flesh.

Those who have grieved over the death of a loved one know how this is true. The people who are most help to us in this situation are not the ones who try to do something for us. They are instead ones who suffer with us. They allow themselves to be vulnerable to what has happened to us and refuse to deny either the death or its pain. They do not place themselves at a distance from us but make themselves equals. They are the ones whose compassion expresses itself in the way they look at us and hold us. In them we see a natural reflection of our own selves, and not a forced pity. The sight of their faces illuminates our darkness and gives us a sense of life.

The discipline of service is a discipline through which care, concern, and aid are given by one person to another in a particular way, in a way that is shaped by presence—vulnerable, just, compassionate, and committed.[19] This discipline is integrally related to the disciplines of repentance and prayer. Just as prayer presupposes repentance but also deepens and refines it, so, too, does service presuppose, deepen, and refine repentance and prayer.

Service depends on a letting go of our self-protectiveness. The drive to establish and sustain ourselves is the main deterrent to vulnerability. To be both self-protective and vulnerable is a contradiction; they cannot both be maintained. Furthermore, the very dynamics of self-establishment and self-sustenance build up walls of injustice and inequality between people. We fatten our egos precisely by putting ourselves above and at a distance from others.

Likewise, service depends on prayer in both its explicit and implicit forms. We must be able to see people as they are, we must pay attention to them no matter their condition, before we can be in a position to be with them. And compassion and commitment require not only attention to another, but also the kind of energy that flows through us when our own life forces are purified by attention to God.

But service also affects the quality and degree of our repentance and prayer. In service, we recognize the limits of our own power and are made humble. In the experience of service, we realize more profoundly than in any other that all lives, not just our own, are established and sustained by a Power that lies outside of any of us. Through service our attention is drawn increasingly to that Power, and we find ourselves learning to pray in new and more obedient ways.

Worship as Paradigm

These three are the fundamental disciplines by which the moral lives of Christians grow. They are disciplines of discipleship, and through them we move more and more into a position where the mysteries of reality can be revealed to us. As we repent, pray, and serve, we ourselves are less and less central to our concern. We put ourselves out of the way so that God can do God's work in us. We get ourselves into a condition in which our imaginations may be transformed so that we can come to see, think, feel, value, and act as reformed selves.

Christians have a paradigm by which these disciplines are made known to us and acted out symbolically. That paradigm is worship. In worship our disciplines take on liturgical form, but they are the same disciplines nonetheless. When we come to worship, we come to put ourselves in a position to receive revelation. Worship is repentance, prayer, and service carried out in the context of a hearing of God's Word.

Our orders of worship reflect these disciplines. When we are called to worship, we are reminded of the presence of God and our attention is drawn to God. We come as repentant people, and our prayers of confession are our attempts to recognize ourselves as sinners in need and as ones who would turn from ourselves toward God. We come to pray: to

attend to God by singing hymns and saying prayers of praise, thanksgiving, intercession, and petition. We pray in a different form as we pay attention to God's Word in scripture, in preaching, and in the sacraments. And we do not come alone. We come with others who are there with us as equals and whose status or condition in the world is of no consequence. We are present with one another in God's presence, and present to one another as we receive each other in baptism and share with one another at Christ's table.

Of course, in worship we live through these disciplines symbolically, and the patterns of our living may not live up to the patterns of our liturgy. But worship is not "mere" symbol or ritual. These symbolic actions have a way of training us and shaping us at preconscious levels so that over time their order becomes imbedded in us. In worship, we see and sense who it is we are to be and how it is we are to move in order to become. Worship is an enactment of the core dynamics of the Christian life. This is why worship is its central and focusing activity. It is paradigmatic for all the rest of the Christian life.

The activity of worship is mandatory for those who would have their moral lives formed after the pattern of discipleship. In the ritual of worship we learn how the whole of our lives is to be shaped. To grow morally means, for Christians, to have one's whole life increasingly be conformed to the pattern of worship. To grow morally means to turn one's life into worship.

The Disciplines in the Life Cycle

From the way I have described the disciplines of the Christian moral life, it should be obvious that undertaking them in their fullness is an adult activity. These are not disciplines that children are capable of undertaking *as disciplines,* consciously and intentionally. Children are, however, capable of repentance, prayer, and service *as acts,* usually spontaneous and sporadic. I believe that repentance, prayer, and service are significant throughout the human life cycle, and that their relevance is not confined to adults.

This is not to argue that children can be morally mature. I want only to suggest that repentance, prayer, and service are possible at almost every age in the human life cycle. People can grow morally at every stage of human development. Moral growth takes place when whatever capacities we have are activated in repentance, prayer, and service. And, this can happen in some form at all but the earliest ages.

I have argued that moral growth per se is not developmental. But there is a connection between the movements of repentance, prayer, and service and the development of natural human capacities. As we develop, these movements become more complex. Human development opens broader and more complicated worlds to us. The forms that repentance, prayer, and service take will change in the light of this.

For example, the convergence in later adolescence of formal operational thinking (Piaget), the identity crisis (Erikson), and the capacity to organize the perspectives of other persons in a systematic way (Selman) opens up a significantly more complex world to pay attention to than the world of childhood. At adolescence, a more complicated and usually more insecure self must be given in repentance. Finally, the world to be served and the dynamics of service have dimensions to them that were previously hidden. Repentance, prayer, and service, then, become more difficult tasks in adolescence than they were in

childhood. The same is true, of course, in different ways in adulthood.

Natural human development on all registers places one in new situations, makes one conscious of hitherto unknown features of human experience, and makes possible increasing ability to communicate with others and to reflect systematically on one's condition. As a result, the range and complexity of moral experience, as well as the existential tensions generated by it, increase with development. This means that the movements of repentance, prayer, and service will themselves be significantly more complex and difficult to make, though perhaps more profoundly and maturely made when they are made.

Not only do the world and the movements become more complex, however. Our relationship to the world also becomes more intentional. As we become more mature developmentally, the movements of repentance, prayer, and service increasingly take on the character of disciplines. Less and less are they spontaneous and sporadic acts. We become more aware of what we are doing and more responsible for the shape of our lives. We come increasingly to choose or refuse to repent, pray, and serve.

The relation between moral growth and natural human development of physical, intellectual, psychological, and social capacities can be summarized, then, as follows: (1) Moral growth can take place within all of the developmental stages by the actualization of repentance, prayer, and service, using whatever capacities one has at that stage. Within each stage there is potential for moral growth or stagnation, depending on the degree to which these movements are made. (2) Natural development has the effect of increasing the range and complexity of moral experience, and, hence, the range and complexity of the movements of repentance, prayer, and service. (3)

Development brings with it increasing intentionality in and responsibility for these movements. They, therefore, increasingly take on the character of disciplines. (4) The fact that development takes place does not guarantee that repentance, prayer, and service will. Development does not ensure moral growth. At all stages of human development, moral egocentrism, lack of attention, and failure to serve are possible.

From Loved One to Stranger

The disciplines of the moral life are related not only to human development; they are also related to the contexts in which they are undertaken. We grow morally not only when the movements of repentance, prayer, and service are made in the more complex ways that human development demands. We grow also as we make these movements and undertake these disciplines in a broad variety of contexts. To be receptive, attentive, and of service to those closest to us—our loved ones, friends, and neighbors—is one thing. To do so with enemies and strangers is more difficult. But the moral life does not fully mature unless the latter is done.

We can try to live in a world surrounded by loved ones and friends, closing out others who as enemies threaten us or who as strangers are potential threats. But no matter how receptive, attentive, and serving we may be in such a world, life lived there alone is not morally mature. Until enemies and strangers are encountered in repentance, attention, and service, we simply do not know or have the opportunity to experience the depth at which these movements may be made. Loved ones and friends do not, by definition, present as deep and persistent a threat to our establish-

ment and sustainment as do enemies and, potentially, strangers. Unless, therefore, we encounter these, we have failed to make the movements at a level the term "maturity" connotes.

Furthermore, it is only when we come to face those who seem most alien to us that we are able to face what is most alien in those who are closest. It is often more difficult, for example, to allow ourselves to be vulnerable to and really see a friend's anger than it is to do so with the anger of an enemy. My spouse's loneliness is harder to take than the loneliness of a stranger, and I am more inclined in the first case to refuse to recognize it. The reason for this is simply that, with those closest to us, the threat and alienation strike more centrally into the core of our personhood. In these circumstances, our own selves are more deeply vulnerable. We may have to be receptive, attentive, and of service to strangers and enemies before we are able to be more deeply attentive to the most strange and threatening dimensions of our loved ones and neighbors.[20]

Encountering enemies and strangers is not just a matter of deepening disciplines, however. The moral life involves loving enemies and strangers. We are called to break down those barriers between ourselves and others that make us enemies and strangers. Repentance, attention, and service are initiatives we can take to bring those who were once enemies or strangers to us as friends and loved ones.[21]

The Church and Moral Growth

We grow morally as we repent, pray, and serve in the increasingly complex ways that human development requires and in the variety of contexts that range from relationships with loved ones to strangers. We cannot do this alone, however. We need to be in a community that supports us, guides us, and undertakes these disciplines with us. For Christians that community is the church.

The church is the worshiping community. We are that body of people who are learning together to repent, pray, and serve in the light of our history and an imagination that is teaching us to do so. The focus of our history and imagination is Jesus Christ, in whom we see what it means to live in repentance, prayer, and service. We seek to follow him, to be his disciples, and to undertake the disciplines that such a life requires.

As we follow him, we see that we cannot be the church and remain a closed system of intimate and exclusive social relationships through which we are protected from the world. To the extent that we actually are being transformed in repentance, prayer, and service, we find that we must continually strive to rupture our own boundaries. The church is just not the church except as it seeks to incorporate within its mutuality enemies and strangers. Its repentance, prayer, and service is for all people, for the world as such, and not just for others as Christians.[22] In the church we are impelled by the very dynamics of what it means to be the church to meet the enemies and strangers of our lives.

Most institutions are defined in terms of exclusion and care for their own. The church is not. This is why the church as a repenting, praying, and serving community is so significant for the shaping of the moral life. We can learn the disciplines of the moral life only in communities that provide resources for the breaking of self-securing, both personally and institutionally, and for attention and service to all the world. The church has such resources.

These are the resources on which we must draw as we educate for the moral life.

Notes

1. Diogenes Allen, *Between Two Worlds* (Atlanta: John Knox Press, 1977), pp. 14–15.
2. I began to consider these three disciplines as fundamental to the moral life of Christians in reflecting on Michael Foster's suggestions that the apprehension of mystery requires revelation and that revelation in turn presupposes repentance, the church, and prayer (*Mystery and Philosophy* [London: SCM Press, 1957], p. 82).
3. Jean Calvin, *The Institutes of the Christian Religion* III.3.5.
4. Donald Evans, *Struggle and Fulfillment* (Cleveland: William Collins Publishers, Inc., 1979), p. 21. See Introduction and Part One for Evans's full description of this struggle.
5. Ibid., p. 6.
6. Ibid. See Chapter Seven for a full discussion of this struggle.
7. Donald Evans, "Does Religious Faith Conflict with Moral Freedom?" in *Religion and Morality,* eds. G. Outka and J. P. Reeder, Jr. (Garden City, N.Y.: Anchor Books, 1973), p. 105.
8. Ibid., p. 358.
9. Iris Murdoch, *The Sovereignty of Good* (New York: Schocken Books, 1970), p. 55.
10. Ibid.
11. Ibid., p. 56.
12. This, of course, works both ways. Evil is just as able to absorb our attention as good, and can just as easily give us energy and claim our obedience. One of our great difficulties, unfortunately, is telling the difference between what is

good and what is not. Evil is often more attractive, dazzling, and compelling than good, which can often seem quite boring and mundane. See Allen, *Between Two Worlds,* pp. 17–18.

13. Ibid., p. 111.

14. Ibid., p. 130.

15. Murdoch, *Sovereignty of Good,* p. 101.

16. Ibid.

17. See Mt 20:20–28, Mt 23:11, Mk 9:33–35, Mk 10:35–44, and Lk 22:24–27.

18. See Hauerwas's discussion of this issue in his "The Politics of Charity," *Interpretation* 31 (1977): 251–62; reprinted in Hauerwas, *Truthfulness and Tragedy* (Notre Dame: University of Notre Dame Press, 1977), pp. 132–43.

19. In defining service in this way, I have put the emphasis on service as interpersonal. This has the significant disadvantage of implying that service is relevant only to one-on-one personal relationships, and has no relevance to our political or institutional life. This is a disadvantage because it is clear that service cannot be limited to dealing with the effects of evil forces on the limited number of persons whom we encounter. Service has a political and prophetic dimension that aims at structures of evil and the causes of human suffering. But in order to deal with this dimension, it would be necessary to indulge in at least as extensive an analysis as we have already taken up, and it is impossible to do this here.

The dilemma of the relation of power and effectiveness to service in political service is, however, even more entangled than it is with regard to personal service. In fact, many would maintain that the idea of service as presence is utterly irrelevant to political service since politics is by definition the manipulation of power. I believe, however, that an understand-ing of political service can be worked out in a coherent way that retains the dynamics of vulnerability, equality, and compassion at its center. Some beginnings in this direction can be found in Hauerwas, "The Politics of Charity," and in several works by John H. Yoder, including *The Christian Witness to the State* (Newton: Faith and Life Press, 1964) and *The Politics of Jesus* (Grand Rapids: Eerdmans, 1973).

20. This works two ways, however. We also need to have been receptive, attentive, and of service to our loved ones who are by definition more available to us and more supportive of us before we can assume the risk of these movements in more alien contexts. The situation is dialectical. The movements made in one context increase our resources for making them in the others.

21. Further discussion of this whole issue of contexts for the disciplines can be found in my "Christian Education and the Moral Life" (Ph.D. diss., Princeton Theological Seminary, 1978), pp. 203–20. Here these contexts are defined, their relationship to human development considered, and their bearing on one another more fully developed.

22. Edward Farley, in his *Ecclesial Man* (Philadelphia: Fortress Press, 1975), discusses "the transformed status of the stranger" in relation to the church. He puts the matter this way: "Insofar as the power of self-securing is broken and modified by freedom from the other and for the other, this power defines the very being of the participant of ecclesia. Thus, while the matrix of that power is ecclesia and its intersubjective structure, that toward which that power can be directed has no bounds. The new freedom is freedom for the other as such, not simply the other in ecclesia. The new obligation is for the other as such, not

simply the ecclesial other" (pp. 169–70). Farley goes on to point out that while being for others as such includes a desire for mutuality, it does not place conditions on that mutuality. The church does not require that others become just like them in order for this mutuality to take place. "In ecclesia the stranger is . . . not . . . one who, to be redeemed, must abandon his own home-world but [is] a potential participant in ecclesia simply because of his disrupted humanity. . . . Since interest, delight, and compassion for the other are marks of freedom for the other, the stranger's status is that of fellow-sufferer and potential participant in redemptive existence. . . . [E]cclesia adapts its social and institutional form to the home-world of the stranger and not vice versa" (p. 170).

Part 4

MAKING MORAL CHOICES: RESOURCES FOR REFLECTION

part 4

Making Moral Choices:
Resources for Reflection

Introduction

Traditionally, moral theologians have appealed to a variety of sources in their search for ethical wisdom—biblical materials, the tradition of the Christian community, the efforts of human reason, and experience. More recently, they are finding the empirical sciences to be an important dialogue partner. While some religious traditions have placed an emphasis upon one or another of these resources, Catholicism has maintained, at least in principle, that any satisfactory method in moral theology must draw upon them all. Each will be addressed by the essays in this section.

The first two selections are concerned with the ways that theologians use the Bible when doing ethics. William Spohn surveys a vast amount of theological literature on the subject and offers a typology of the diverse ways in which scripture is employed. Birch and Rasmussen discuss how the biblical materials can and ought to contribute to two essential tasks of Christian ethics—character formation and moral decision-making. Both essays underscore the complexity of the issue and the plurality of approaches used.

Roman Catholic moral theologians have a special concern, for since Catholics believe that pope and bishops have a responsibility to safeguard the faith and the teaching handed on by the community (tradition), moral theologians owe a certain respect to the teaching promulgated by the hierarchy of the Church. The question here is how tradition and official teaching in moral matters should be employed by theologians as they do their work, and how this "respect" (obsequium) for official teaching is to be understood.

The selection from Vatican II's *Lumen Gentium* contains the crucial conciliar position on the proper response to teachings of the magisterium. Avery Dulles' essay is a thoughtful treatment of how the teaching office can be understood in light of this conciliar statement. The brief but important selection from canon law is the juridical interpretation of the conciliar teaching, and the commentary on that canon by Ladislas Orsy offers an insightful and balanced interpretation of the law's meaning. As a whole, these selections are meant to provide an overview of the current debate on the authority of hierarchical teachings and the appropriate response due them.

Related to this issue is the relationship between theologians and bishops. While both share a common concern for truth, each has different responsibilities within the Christian community. Because of this, conflicts sometimes arise between the two over how truth is to be pursued, and how their respective roles as teachers is to be understood. We offer two perspectives on the nature of this relationship. The first is by Cardinal Ratzinger, who, as prefect of the Vatican Congregation for the Doctrine of the Faith, is responsible for overseeing the integrity of the faith and the work of theologians. The other is by Richard McCormick, an essay occasioned by the Vatican's investigation of moral theologian, Charles Curran.

At the center of much of the previously mentioned controversy is the matter of dissent from official church teaching. Under what conditions, if any, might a theologian disagree, privately and/or publicly, with a teaching of the magisterium? We include answers to that question by the American bishops, Charles Curran and William May.

Somewhat less controversial than the role of tradition in Catholic moral theology is the use of human reason in the discovery of truth. This approach is generally referred to as "natural law" and has long been a distinguishing feature of Catholic theological method. The debate occurring here has centered on how natural law is to be understood and whether it should play such a key role in moral method. Bruno Schüller, a German moral theologian, argues in his essay for the indispensable contribution of natural law to Christian ethics, while Columba Ryan offers an overview of various interpretations of natural law and how it might best be understood today. Finally, James Gustafson analyzes how the empirical sciences might be used in the work of theological ethics.

Throughout this section, the reader should bear in mind that the interest is primarily methodological. The selections deal with *how* these resources are to be used in Christian ethics, rather than with their *what,* their content.

23

What Are They Saying About Scripture and Ethics?

William Spohn, SJ

What are theologians saying about Scripture and ethics? All sorts of things—not all of which can be fit into one systematic approach. Six different ways of using Scripture for moral guidance emerge from reading the wide range of theological positions. This pluralism is a sign not of scholarly chaos but of the irreducible richness of Scripture itself. Believing that four Gospels are better than a single one, the Church welcomed pluralism even in its most central document. Both our moral life and the range of literary forms in the Bible are simply too rich to be reduced to a single moral system.

Let us briefly discuss our original question. We will look at *theologians* writing about *ethics*. The origin of theology and its practical test must always be rooted in the experience of believers. The task of theologians is to put lived experience of people of faith into organized terms. Ethics is the more organized and abstract expression of morality, our ordinary experience of discovering what is worth living for and trying to live for it. Morality and the life of faith are the actual lived experience; theology and ethics are the attempts to examine that experience and organize that experience in a more abstract way to enhance the moral life and the life of faith.

We will study the use of Scripture *in ethics,* a different task than that of studying the ethics in Scripture. The scholarly examination of the ethics of Paul's epistles or the influence of Judaism on the Sermon on the Mount must be presupposed here. What we are asking is what bearing the moral teaching of Paul has today on us as citizens. Does his advice in Romans 13:1–7 counsel us to adopt a passive attitude toward state authority because it is "ordained by God"? And for us. How many times do we read the Ten Commandments and omit the historical prologue that makes them a covenant response rather than a mere code of laws? The whole story of Sinai and the introductory

---

This article is excerpted from William Spohn, What Are They Saying About Scripture and Ethics? *(New York: Paulist Press, 1984) 3–17.*

words, "I, the Lord, am your God, who brought you out of the land of Egypt, that place of slavery" (Ex 20:2) precede the Decalogue's proclamation. The call of covenant morality rests on profound gratitude for an undeserved deliverance. Since that gratitude empowers faith-filled obedience, omitting the Exodus story impoverishes our response to the Decalogue.

Morality Is More Than Rules

Our own moral experience is also too rich to define morality as a simple set of rules, even if they do play an indispensable role in any morality that aims to be practical. How do we decide what to do when faced with a major decision in our lives? Rules are not the only sources of insight we have in deciding about a career change or the level of income to which we aspire. We gradually discover our way by sorting through our own remembered experiences, seeking advice from friends, looking to the example of people we admire, considering the commitments we have already made and the people who depend upon us, using our imaginations to envision the kind of people we would become in certain possible environments. We might also consider the state of the world today, a world of scarcity for some and surplus for others; we would probably spend some time quietly and prayerfully sorting out our reactions to possible courses of actions. We might consult the example of Jesus to see where the path of discipleship is leading. We might even discuss possible choices with some trusted and wise figures in the Church community. In a word, the voice of conscience is like a chord that unites a wide range of tones into a harmony. Merely asking "What must I do to keep the rules?" hardly does justice to

our rich moral experience. If God's Word is to speak to the complexity of this experience, it must have an equally rich number of avenues of expression. Hence, it is no wonder that an appreciation of Scripture for moral guidance will begin by admitting that the whole range of literary forms found in the canon addresses us morally.

Ironically, both fundamentalists and overly secularized Christians misuse Scripture by treating it only as a book of rules. Fundamentalists believe that the revelation of God is exactly the same in any part of the Bible; they thus claim to be able to take any verse and, without further interpretation, apply it as a moral guideline for today's Christians. Fundamentalism is a theology masquerading as an anti-theology. Lacking any critical awareness, it takes a particular form of nineteenth century American theology for granted and claims that this theology is actually the literal, plain sense of Scripture. When fundamentalism is not critical of its own presuppositions and methods, it often smuggles the values of bourgeois prosperity and nationalism into its use of Scripture. When it rules out any form of moral guidance for the Christian other than its own reading of the Bible, it is systematically immune to criticism. A modern example of this literal interpretation of the Bible and the resistance of fundamentalism to criticism is the racial prejudice that still exists in the South. Ordinary human decency and the consensus of the American judicial system cannot dissuade some colleges from forbidding interracial dating. At Bob Jones University, such a rule is not admitted as vestigial segregationist prejudice, but justified as the clear command of God from the Old Testament. Other preachers of the New Right assure us that supply-side economics is the plain will of God, invoking the New Testament's statement that those who do not work ought not to eat (see 2 Thes 3:10). Contrary to fundamentalist practices every scriptural passage needs interpretation, and every honest theology admits its method openly.

On the other side of the spectrum are those who contend that Scripture has no real authority for believers today. They argue that the cultural distance of our own society from societies that practiced holy war, child sacrifice, subjugation of women, or public execution by stoning is too vast to salvage any moral role for Scripture. If historical criticism has demonstrated how the various portions of Scripture were formed and reformed for particular communities, what possible lasting inspiration can the text offer us today? Instead of trying to interpret this outdated document, the Church should look elsewhere for insight on our own pressing issues, most of which were not even remotely anticipated by the authors of Scripture.

The preceding is in part an argument against authority, a theological matter that each of the six approaches to Scripture we will consider must explain. In general, we can say that Scripture is normative for Christians because the risen Lord of faith is identical to the person who was crucified, Jesus of Nazareth. Christians believe that the definitive, though not the exclusive, revelation of God occurred in the life of Jesus. Hence, the testimony of the first Christians to Jesus is the privileged revelation of the reality of God. God's intentions for human living are revealed through the whole of the canonical Scriptures, and not simply in archaic norms. Ironically enough, to reject the continuing moral authority of Scripture on the grounds that many of its moral rules are outdated is to err on the same grounds as the fundamentalists: both arguments treat the Bible primarily as a book of rules. In both cases, the prevalent wisdom of a particular culture becomes morally authoritative, unchallenged by the Gospel that cannot be cozily accommodated to any culture, liberal or conservative.

Within more mainstream Christianity, two further theological tendencies have restricted the use of Scripture in Christian ethics. The first is the Reformation warning on the role of morality in relation to salvation. Martin Luther and John Calvin detected the danger of legalism in paying excessive attention to morality. The second is Roman Catholic moral theology which has depended so heavily on natural law as the source of moral teaching that Scripture is either an afterthought or merely an ornament to a philosophical treatise. Before giving an overview of the six models, let us examine why both of the major branches of Western Christianity have been reluctant to use the Bible as a guide for life.

Legalism: The Problem of the Latent Pharisee

Part of Martin Luther's legacy to mainstream Protestantism is a suspicion of the Law in relation to faith. Luther saw in the self-concern of many Christians about their own perfection a dynamic that Paul had denounced. In his Letters to the Galatians and Romans, Paul insisted that the Law, though given by God, could never be salvific. The Law points out our transgressions but cannot save us from them. Its true function is to lead us to despair of trying to earn our salvation from God. The Gospel saves us from this self-centered preoccupation by relocating our trust in the gracious power of God, freely given in Christ. The Gospel is good news because it saves us from a commercial relationship with

God in which we try to oblige God to reward our moral accomplishments with his grace.

Law precedes Gospel in the experience of justification in Christ, but justification does not terminate Law in our experience. So long as we are both flesh and spirit, we will always know the temptation to "works' righteousness," the tendency to impress the Lord with our good deeds. In the spirit there is freedom, but in the letter of the Law we will find death. Hence, even faithful Christians are ambivalent toward moral norms. We need such norms to order society and point out transgression, but they appeal to the latent Pharisee of our flesh.

In his writings on the Decalogue Luther insists that the first command that calls us to faith is the indispensable precondition for keeping the other commandments. Unless our trust shifts from our own efforts to the grace of God, we will use each commandment as a rubric for our own righteousness. It will be too easy to claim that we have kept the Law only because we have not committed adultery or murdered anyone. Luther reinterprets the Decalogue to take away any grounds for boasting. He changes these norms into commands about virtuous attitudes and dispositions, which must continue to grow and can never rest in self-satisfaction. Commenting on the prohibition against killing, he writes,

> Not only he who directly does evil breaks this commandment, but also he who unnecessarily omits a service to his neighbor which he might render by anticipating and restraining, and by protecting and rescuing his fellow man from bodily harm and suffering. The chief design of God is that we permit no injury to befall any person, but that we show to everyone all kindness and love.[2]

We can never say, "I've loved enough; I've shown enough kindness." By turning the norm into a command regarding disposition, Luther removes from the Law its tendency to make us boast of our accomplishments before God.

This legacy has left many Lutherans ambivalent toward the issue of morality. The normative passages of Scripture become particularly difficult to interpret, since they seem to contain some threat of legalism. Even an appeal to follow the Sermon on the Mount or other explicit calls to discipleship runs the risk of presenting Jesus as a moral teacher rather than a bearer of God's free gift. John Calvin acknowledged a more constructive role for moral reflection in the Christian life; he saw it as a guide and source of encouragement in living out the grace of justification. Even the most morally earnest of Reformed Christians like the Puritans, for example, tended to translate scriptural guides for action into commands about dispositions of the heart.

Does Natural Law Need Scripture?

Roman Catholic moral theology has traditionally found its basis in natural law, a philosophical ethics, rather than in Scripture. According to such philosophy our ordinary human experience can instruct us on what we need to do and not do. Wherever human beings are found, certain necessary moral patterns rest on their common humanity; natural law is the reasonable expression of these common human necessities. As John Macquarrie states, "Natural law is foundational to morality. It is the inner drive toward authentic personhood and is presupposed in all particular ethical traditions, including the Christian one."[3] Our humanity is not a blank slate on which anything at all can be written; certain kinds of behavior lead to human flourishing while others lead to human frustration. This is true for all, Christians and non-Christians alike.

What can Scripture offer if morality is already established by nature? It cannot provide us with new content for morality, new information that human reason could not itself discover. Scripture could publicize to a fallen humanity what would otherwise be more difficult to know, and it could provide new motivation to do what is naturally right. However, in the actual instruction of moral theology and in the "manuals" or handbooks used in seminaries, Scripture played a minimal role. Even in the papal social encyclicals of the last hundred years, scriptural quotations are only occasional ornaments to supplement philosophical argument about the rights of labor or the duties of the state. Only after the Second Vatican Council do the official teachings of the Roman Catholic Church employ biblical imagery and themes. In a positive sense, this natural law tradition can speak to anybody of good will by appealing to the humanity that believers and non-believers alike possess. On the negative side, it does not nourish the moral reflections of believers on the profound realities of grace, freedom, and the person of Christ, which are the wellsprings of Christian commitment.

It is not surprising, therefore, that one of the Vatican Council's major requests in revising the training of priests should be a plea for a more biblical moral theology:

> Other theological disciplines should also be renewed by livelier contact with the mystery of Christ and the

history of salvation. Special attention needs to be given to the development of moral theology. Its scientific exposition should be more thoroughly nourished by scriptural teaching. It should show the nobility of the Christian vocation of the faithful, and their obligation to bring forth fruit in charity for the life of the world. . . .[4]

While Protestant moral reflection has stressed the realities of Christian conversion to the possible detriment of normative material, Roman Catholic moral theology has shown great confidence in applying moral rules to situations but neglected the transformation of heart that is central to New Testament moral teaching. Since Bernard Häring's landmark work, *The Law of Christ,* and Josef Fuchs' *Natural Law,* Catholic theologians have worked to redress this imbalance and show that Christian responsibility can be grounded in a biblically informed natural law.[5] Such Protestant theologians as James Gustafson, Paul Ramsey and others responded to the challenge of situation ethics by spelling out the necessary function of moral norms in Christian morality, but not by resting those norms on a natural law philosophical foundation.[6]

Let us now take a brief look at each of the six models for the use of Scripture in ethics. Naturally, these are not hermetically sealed compartments. While each model tends to concentrate on a specific form of biblical literature as the primary means God uses to reveal his moral intentions, all of the models refer to other forms of expression as well. Consequently, overlapping of the models is inevitable. This schema is intended as a pluralistic framework to highlight the pluralistic possibilities for using Scripture. The sixth model will present my views as a supplement to the previous positions, rather than as a refutation.

The Command of God

The first model, like each of the others, answers the basic moral question, "What ought I to do?" Its distinctive approach states: "Listen to the personal command of God directed to you and respond in obedient faith." This model focuses on those passages in Scripture that describe God's call to specific individuals and makes them the paradigm for all subsequent moral interaction.

With this approach, the Bible does not present us with general moral principles which we then apply to our situation. Any statements that seem to be general principles such as the Decalogue are actually mere summaries of God's call to specific individuals. At best they set the boundaries for the community of the covenant, the limits of life acceptable to God. They are like the white lines at the outer edge of a highway warning drivers to stay on the road. Like the lines, they cannot teach the motorists how to drive on the road. Life is guided within these boundaries by the direct, personal and specific inviting commands of God to individuals.

Just as Jesus called his disciples with a direct authority that could be met only by unquestioning obedience or disobedience, the demands of that same Lord call Christians of every age to become his disciples. The person who would stop and try to analyze philosophically that call to discipleship has already begun to hesitate and disobey. To have faith means to be obedient, and only those who do obey

the costly demands of the Lord actually have faith.

The obvious problem is how to recognize God's call. What dispositions of heart will enable us to discern the actual command of God? What qualities experienced by the listening believer indicate that a specific sense of obligation actually comes from God? Fundamentally, we turn to Christ for this discernment: only commands that witness to Christian freedom, which are calls rooted in the saving gift of Christ, can come from God. And only if we are guided by the Spirit of Christ can we obey with the joyful freedom of his disciples.

Scripture as Moral Reminder

This model is that espoused by modern proponents of natural law Christian ethics. What ought I to do? I must be human because the Lord has embraced that humanity in the incarnation. Scripture presupposes natural moral law and human ability to know what is right and wrong. God's intentions are already inscribed in our human nature in the dynamic drives to human flourishing and our intelligence, which orders those drives. Even though sin has clouded our motivations, it has not totally obscured our capacity to recognize the moral law.

As Thomas Aquinas taught, the New Law of Christ is primarily the gift of the Holy Spirit and secondarily the written letter of the Law.[7] Christ *does* bring a new dimension to the moral life, but it does not consist in new information about what it means to be human. It lies rather in this gift of the Spirit, which transforms our motivation so we can live the moral life with spontaneity and joy. In fact, any seemingly distinctive commands of Christian ethics, even if they are not always recognized as such, are already part of human morality at its deepest level.

For example, some people have asserted that the radically distinctive character of Christian ethics can be found in the commandment, "Love your enemy." They assume that at best, pure natural ethics could tolerate enemies out of consideration for their humanity. Josef Fuchs, however, points out that this command was always part of natural morality. If it were not, then it must be permissible for non-believers to hate their enemies![8] Rather than seeking new commands in the Bible, Christians should look for the witness to the fundamental reorientation of their basic intentions toward God. Only the grace of Christ can provide this radical conversion of heart.

Call to Liberation

From the experience of Latin American churches and the movements of human liberation, such as the civil rights movement and the feminist struggle, a third model for the use of Scripture emerges. Christians must join the oppressed in their struggle for liberation because only there can God be found. Scripture is used in a complex fashion here, combining some of the elements of the fourth and fifth models with an historical and economic analysis of the situation. The key symbol and event that reveals the God of Israel is the exodus from the slavery of Egypt. The Old Testament's historical and prophetic literature makes clear that God acts for the oppressed and demands the same commitment from those faithful to the covenant. Jesus confirms and deepens this liberating action of God by his own ministry, which challenged the oppressive, unjust structures of his own day.

Although liberation theology does not identify political liberation with the coming of God's Kingdom, it sees an indispensable connection between the struggle for justice and God's freeing us from sin. Since sin is embodied primarily in social structures, no real conversion can occur without first changing those dominant structures. All of the moral imperatives of the New Testament must be interpreted in light of this struggle. If my enemy is a military dictator, I can only "love my enemy" effectively if I struggle to remove the very power by which he oppresses other people. Hence, armed revolution cannot be ruled out by any literal appeal to the Sermon on the Mount.[9]

Response to Revelation

Our fourth model turns the moral question around. The Christian should ask "What is *God* doing in my life?" before asking the question "What ought I to do?" The basic imperative, therefore, is "Respond to the one God who is acting in everything that is happening to you." This approach presumes that God is intimately involved in the actual patterns of history and culture as well as the events of our personal lives. He does not direct everything that occurs, as in the old doctrine of predestination, but in a more complex way he judges, redeems and creates in history.

H. Richard Niebuhr, the American Protestant theologian, in the middle of the Second World War, asked: "What is God doing in the War?"[10] He searched the Bible for perspectives that would enable him to discern the hidden action of God in the present tragedy. He used the biblical symbols of judgment and the crucifixion to interpret the suffering of the innocent. Niebuhr did not claim any direct pipeline to the mind of God, but he did apply some basic patterns of God's action in biblical times to detect how God was acting in the war. These perspectives can help illuminate the present situation so that the believer may find the One who still acts in character today. Niebuhr concluded that God was endorsing neither side but was judging both the Allies and the Axis for their sins and calling all to repentance. The Bible continues to provide resources that allow us to discern God's present action and determine a fitting response.

Call to Discipleship

In our fifth model, moral questions are answered by referring directly to the New Testament story of Jesus Christ. To be disciples, Christians ought to embody their Master's distinctive way of life. The most important literary expressions here are story and parable. The story of Jesus claims to be the truth of our lives, so we either have to let it redefine our own identity or dismiss that claim as false. Prior to questions of action is the question of character. Do we have a coherent sense of self at the core of our identity? Unless the Gospel story redefines the person's character, he or she cannot follow the way of life proper to the disciple.

Letting the story of Jesus serve as the pattern for our own lives will conflict with the basic assumptions of our secular culture, which has its own story, one quite different from that which should be lived out in the Christian community.

For example, in Stanley Hauerwas' opinion, the abortion debate is like a spoken conversation between two deaf persons; neither side can enter the other's universe of discourse. Pro-life forces object to abortion on the basis of philosophical convictions rather than ex-

plicit Christian grounds. Pro-choice arguments are rooted in the secular story of our liberal culture, which maximizes choice and personal autonomy. The actual question the Church should pose is not whether the fetus is human, but whether the fetus is a child. Christians have to examine what kind of people we must be to welcome children into our communities as gifts, not threats.[11]

Responsive Love

This final summary position owes much to the previous models. It takes the new commandment of Jesus in John 15:12, "Love one another just as I have loved you," as the answer to the moral question. This mandate, spoken at the Last Supper after the washing of the feet, defines the Christian moral life as one of response and imitation. The love that Christ commands has a definite shape to it, a shape learned only from the experience of actually having been loved by Christ. The present experience of believers is normatively formed by the New Testament witness of Jesus and the whole story of God's dealings with Israel. Each virtue of the Christian life refers in some way to this pattern of God's love and finds as its motivation a grateful response to that enduring love.

This is an ethics of imitation, but not of the externals of Jesus' ministry. Rather, the locus of transformation is the heart of the Christian, where the fundamental dispositions and deep emotions that link conviction and action are shaped. The Spirit works to sanctify Christians by developing in them virtues and dispositions that correspond to those manifest in the historical Jesus who is the risen Lord. These cannot be abstracted from the biblical testimony. For example, when Paul exhorts the community at Philippi to consider each other's needs ahead of personal interest, he urges them to have the same attitude as Jesus. He then recounts in a beautiful hymn how Christ emptied himself even to the cross for us and how God raised him up. That faith memory provides not only the motivation for placing others first, it also shapes the content of true Christian altruism in community. Because the love that is at the core of all virtues of the Christian life has this same fundamental pattern, each of those virtues can be understood only in reference to the biblical testimony of how that distinctive love first appeared.

Some readers will find one of these six approaches more congenial than the others. The particular religious traditions that have influenced our interpretations of the Scripture may make some biblical literature more accessible to us than others. For other readers, several approaches described here will be familiar, which indicates that their own reading of biblical literature has already used several avenues of expression for moral reflection. Our aim is to place a fuller range of biblical material before all readers so that the discernment of the community will be enhanced by the richness of God's word.

Notes

1. John Howard Yoder, *The Politics of Jesus* (Grand Rapids: Wm. Eerdmans Publishing Co., 1972), p. 80.

2. Martin Luther, *The Large Catechism in Christian Ethics,* ed. by Waldo Beach and H. Richard Niebuhr, 2nd ed. (New York: John Wiley and Sons, 1973), p. 254.

3. John Macquarrie, *Three Issues in Ethics* (New York: Harper and Row, Publishers, 1970), p. 91.

4. "Decree on Priestly Formation," *The Documents of Vatican II,* ed. by Walter M. Abbott (New York: Guild Press, 1966), p. 452.

5. Bernard Häring, *The Law of Christ,* 3 vols. (Westminster: Newman Press, 1966); Josef Fuchs, S. J. *Natural Law: A Theological Investigation* (New York: Sheed and Ward, 1965).

6. See *Norm and Context in Christian Ethics* ed. by Gene H. Outka and Paul Ramsey (New York: Charles Scribner's Sons, 1968); Paul Ramsey, *Deeds and Rules in Christian Ethics* (New York: Charles Scribner's Sons, 1967).

7. Thomas Aquinas, *Summa Theologiae,* IIIae, q. 106, a. 1.

8. Josef Fuchs, *Human Values and Christian Morality* (Dublin: Gill and Macmillan Ltd., 1970), p. 122.

9. See Gustavo Gutierrez, *A Theology of Liberation* (Maryknoll: Orbis, 1973), p. 276.

10. H. Richard Niebuhr, "Is God in the War?" *Christian Century* 59 (1942): 953–55.

11. Stanley Hauerwas, *A Community of Character* (Notre Dame: Univ. of Notre Dame Press, 1981), pp. 212–29.

24

The Use of the Bible in
Christian Ethics

Bruce Birch and Larry Rasmussen

The project at hand is that of proposing the elements of a methodology, so we now ask how *can and ought* the Bible be used in Christian ethics. Answering that question will touch several bases: the kinds of uses of scripture, the kinds of materials used, the starting place for, and the range of, various uses. The general scheme for discussion will follow from the categories outlined above. Thus we shall address essentially two subjects, the Bible and character formation and the Bible and decision-making.

1. *The Bible and Character Formation.* Our contention is that the most effective and crucial impact of the Bible in Christian ethics is that of shaping the moral identity of the Christian and of the church. Until recently this has been discussed only sparingly in Christian ethics. The treatment of those biblical stories, symbols, images, paradigms, and beliefs expressly at the point of their shaping of moral character has found little systematic reflec-

tion. Indeed, Christian ethics in America has given too little attention to these forms of communication in general, an omission no doubt due to its preoccupation with decision-making and action on specific moral issues. The omission becomes a major one in light of the fact that despite the importance of explicit moral instruction in the moral life, rules, principles, and maxims are surely far less influential than dominating images and symbols, paradigmatic figures, rituals and stories. In all likelihood only a very small part of moral identity and conduct, Christian or otherwise, is the outcome of *explicitly* ethical discourse, even that well internalized in the form of moral instruction. A considerably larger part is the outcome of other forms of communication, much of which on the face of it has no obvious moral point at all.

What about the place of biblical materials in character formation? What might be said, even in exploratory fashion? At what points

---

This article is excerpted from The Bible and Ethics in Christian Life *(Minneapolis: Augsburg, 1976) 104–123.*

might these materials shape the kind of person the decision-maker is?

We begin with an illustration. It is perhaps too grand for the limited space available since it is that of the central paradigmatic figure in the Christian moral life. We cannot, of course, replay the New Testament accounts of Jesus' life, death, and resurrection. But we can imagine for illustrative purposes that a certain person has found in Jesus the object of her final loyalty, devotion and commitment and seeks to take from him the clues for her own way of being and doing. We can then ask what this implies regarding the role of the Bible.

She has a certain portrait of Jesus she regards as authentic. In that portrait Jesus identifies with the outcasts in society and trusts in God as Father, with apparently little or no anxiety about his own needs or his place and power in society. He also portrays compassion, a humble service, a willingness to endure unmerited suffering and face certain tragedy resolutely, a gentleness toward nature and a harshness about human arrogance.

We do not ask whether this person's portrait of Jesus is accurate. Rather we speculate about this: assuming such a portrait has become in fact a paradigm of Christian conduct for this person, at what points will it matter for morality? Putting aside the impact of other influences, biblical or non-biblical, her *perception, dispositions,* and *intentions* might be affected along something like the following lines.

Her general way of seeing life might become characterized by a set of acquired and nurtured moral sensitivities that search out those often invisible to many in society—the poor, the outcast, the ill, and infirm. She might come to possess a basic posture toward life that is more sensitive than most to human suffering and is at the same time unconcerned with her own needs. She might have a "feel" for where people hurt and be able to empathize deeply. She might acquire certain specific dispositions, such as an attitude of initial strong trust in people and a lack of suspicion and fear of strangers, an underlying hopefulness about improvement of the human lot, a deep appreciation for non-human life in the world of nature, and a severe impatience with people's claims to high and enduring achievement. There may be particular intentions present as well, all of them with plausible ties to the reigning example of Jesus in her life: to always seek non-violent resolution to conflict; to champion the causes of the oppressed; to seek the kingdom of God before all else.

What painted this compelling, exemplary figure for her? A collage of biblical materials. Perhaps the healing and feeding narratives; the parable of the Good Samaritan and the cycle of the lost sheep, coin, and son; the teachings on the mountain; Jesus' announcement of his ministry in Luke 4; and the events of Passion Week. Probably others as well. We list these few simply to register the possibility that a set of biblical materials has portrayed a paradigmatic figure who became for this person a chief source for her way of looking at the world and responding to it. The content of the paradigm helped "define what was real" for her; it generated a certain set of moral priorities rather than some other; and it disposed her to act and react in patterns that set her on one course instead of another. Her motives, attitudes, values, and intentions flowed from what she felt and hoped was in keeping with her model of the genuinely good life, that of Jesus.

Our choice of influential biblical materials might have been different and could, in any case, be extended almost indefinitely. We have chosen only one, that of an exemplary figure portrayed by scripture. (The particular one chosen has a special place, to be sure.) The contention is simply that the Bible can and ought to be a major force in molding perspectives, dispositions, and intentions.

It might be helpful to select an example less grand. For instance, how might a pictorial presentation from one of the parables affect character formation? The image of the Good Samaritan, if internalized as a major image, might evoke a general perspective that sees all humankind as a single family under God, and it might evoke the specific intention of helping to break down the barriers that in fact still separate "Jew" and "Samaritan," male and female, bond and free. Some particular dispositions might be engendered by this image: a readiness to respond to human need as such, whether that of perceived friend or perceived foe, or a consistent inclination to move toward rather than away from the stranger. Particular convictions might be elicited as well: keeping faith with God is aiding the neighbor; attending to human need is a compelling Christian duty; the gospel means banishing enmity and hostility.

Again the point is not *which* biblical materials generate *which* perspectives, attitudes, intentions and convictions, but *that* biblical materials *can and ought* to create a cast which has profound ramifications for character and conduct. Certain choices and actions would be eliminated from the outset, others affirmed, and a few never appear on the horizon as possibilities at all. In other words, if character is the chief architect of our conduct, *Christian* character might have its own major materials in the biblical resources.

We have no desire to oversimplify. We are aware both that many sources other than biblical ones have great influence on Christian moral identity and that among the biblical sources themselves there is great variety (this includes morally conflicting materials). A singular presentation of the Bible's meaning for Christian character is not possible, nor is a singular presentation of normative Christian character. We wish only to suggest that the role of the scriptures in the nurturing of a basic orientation and in the generating of particular attitudes and intentions is a central one.

The question arises, which materials are to be used? It is not evasive to say that for character formation the whole panorama of biblical materials is in view, from symbols and narratives to theological ruminations and devotional elements. The shaping of Christian identity engages them all in some way or another, at different moments in different settings for different purposes. Yet it is extremely difficult to say with any precision just which materials can and ought to be used for which times, places and purposes. Why?

The reason resides in the nature of moral development and the multi-faceted character of many biblical materials. Moral identity cannot at base be separated from the person's identity in general. It is a *dimension* of that identity rather than some self-contained piece of it. This gestalt nature of identity prohibits any easy directing of biblical materials (or any other) specifically and exclusively along lines of moral development.

What can be said with certainty about these materials and the formation of character is that Christian ethics needs to guard against every form of what might be called "genre reductionism." This is the effective selection, whether deliberate or not, of only certain kinds of biblical materials as the materials pertinent to ethics. Thus the wisdom sayings, moral teachings and prophetic injunctions are used, and the devotional materials, apocalyptic visions and miracle stories are not. The nature of character formation itself belies such apparently "obvious" distinctions for Christian ethics.

The nature of formation is not the only reason to avoid genre reductionism, however. A primary part of what it has meant historically to be a Christian is to place oneself into interaction with the *whole* scripture and its influence. To fractionize and reduce the canon has always been regarded as a *theological* heresy. For the sake of Christian *ethics,* it is to be resisted as well.

Of course the different materials may work in different ways. The theological discourses, those of Paul or the author of Job, for example, might be the source of certain reasoned convictions and beliefs of the faith. These then have their influence upon character in their own mode: what the person regards as propositional truth shapes who he or she is. The apocalyptic visions might be stimuli to a broader vision that in turn alters, even if ever so slightly, the way we see the world—some things come alive with meanings we did not discern before those strange images illumined them for us. The piety of the devotional materials might impress within us certain attitudes of mystery, humility, dependence and reverence that carry over into our moral habits. The nature psalms, for example, might move us toward a different response to the environment. The miracle stories, (the feeding of the five thousand, for example) might on one level of meaning carry over as the reinforcing of certain intentions (the resolution to feed the hungry in Jesus' name). At no point can we say on principle which biblical materials belong to those affecting the development of moral

character, and which do not. Thus Christian ethics, while it must seek to decipher what in fact the effects of different kinds of materials are, must not succumb to genre reductionism.

Another question arises. Where is the starting point for Christian ethics in its use of the Bible for character formation? Again it is not evasion if we say, "Almost anywhere, but usually not with the decision or issue at hand." The use of the Bible in the development of moral character is a matter of long-term nurture. Thus the attention of Christian ethics here is not to a currently provoking moral issue but to the ongoing worship and educational life of the church above all, and to the extensions and expressions of these in the family. The concern is to underline the moral importance of a continual immersion in biblical materials in worship and education. In a word, the starting point for moral identity is with the Bible in the life of the church as a gathered community.

The use of the Bible in the formation of character, through the recital of images, stories, historical narratives, rituals, and paradigms in the educational and worship life of the church, may not always draw on the world of biblical scholarship (in liturgical life, for example). Even when biblical scholarship *is* drawn upon for uses of the Bible directed to nurturing identity, through such as educational programs, the scholarship employed is not necessarily focused on Christian ethics directly. The situation is different, however, when Christian ethics turns to the use of the Bible for decision-making and action on particular moral issues. Here the attention to specific texts in order to come to terms with specific moral issues will entail much more of the indispensable critical work that biblical scholarship offers. Hence the dependence of

Christian ethics on biblical studies is a more direct one and its use of the Bible more closely tied to the work of biblical scholars. We must turn now to this topic of decision-making.

2. *The Bible and Decision-Making.* While the place of the Bible in decision-making and action on moral issues does not, in our judgment, match in significance its potential influence in character formation, there are nonetheless several important points of contact. The Bible's directness and degree of influence varies considerably among them, as we shall note.

The elements that consistently come to the fore in ethical decisions will serve as our framework.

a) The person's (or group's) analysis of the decision-situation and the understanding of the critical data and issues thrusts us immediately into a dual set of judgments about the place of scriptures. At certain points the biblical influence is negligible or non-existent. A thorough analysis of a moral issue and its setting will entail the use of certain data-gathering and analytical skills that are technical in nature and which have no significant relationship to any biblical materials at all. Many of the tools provided by the social sciences, life sciences, and natural sciences are of this kind and they play an indispensable role in Christian ethics. But even in the less formal analysis of many of our day-to-day decisions we employ a wide range of organizing and appraising skills we have learned as part of the culture's folk knowledge, skills with no perceptible connection to biblical materials. Here the Bible is of little import even though the task at hand is a critical one.

At other points, however, the impact of the Bible upon understanding and analysis may be considerable. What we regard as the significant data (necessarily a value judgment) and

the overriding moral issues in any given set of circumstances will reflect our perception of things, our angle of vision. Thus even basic apprehension is directly connected to that complex marriage of faith, character, and perception. In this way the internalizing of biblical materials in ways formative of our outlook may have its real, though indirect, impact.

The person mentioned in our earlier example can be brought to mind again. Her internalizing of that portrait of Jesus would sort the data and issues for her in a way that might yield a different analysis from that of someone living life by a contrasting paradigm.

b) The norms or standards brought to bear in decision-making may well show considerable influence from biblical materials. This influence may be *indirect* yet significant, as when the Bible has shaped widely held cultural norms. In this case those who may not grant the Bible any authority in their lives, indeed may openly reject it as an informing source for conduct, may yet employ moral norms that have, *via* a long history, some biblical roots. A certain notion of justice, a high regard for human life, a press toward equality, or basic moral rules in the form of civil law would be examples in many settings.

A more *direct* influence upon moral norms can take a variety of forms. The Bible might be regarded, as it has often been, as the source of a revealed norm of its own. Agapeic love is an example central in much of American Christian ethics in this century. The biblical notion of "shalom" has yet to be fully explored as another norm. The understanding of "righteousness" so rich throughout the Old Testament is a closely related one.

The biblical materials might directly supply norms in a somewhat different manner. The Bible might be, as it has often been, the major source of theological categories which encompass many moral norms. The terms of the theological framework become the terms for decision-making as these are worked out exegetically. Karl Barth, to cite one prominent example, first establishes exegetically the grand theological themes of creation and covenant. Then he uses these norm-laden themes for discussing several matters fraught with moral issues and choices—marriage and child-bearing, the functions of the state, economic life, abortion, euthanasia, capital punishment.[1] Here, and Barth is but one of many possible examples, biblical norms enter decision-making by way of theological motifs on the basis of which specific moral choices are rendered. The norms used are scriptural in origin and thus the Bible's influence remains direct.

Sometimes the biblical materials work differently, however. Rather than supplying a distinctive, revealed norm of their own, or a cluster of them, they work so as to transform the norms already common to the human enterprise. Thus an Augustine or an Aquinas was not simply accommodating or being hypocritical in affirming certain pagan norms and asserting their ethical integrity even while these norms needed transformation in light of biblical revelation. The norms, then, might originate in many quarters of the human experience. The biblical materials rank, illumine, and transform them.

Our contention is that the Bible can and ought to be a source of moral norms for the Christian life. At the same time, and for almost any given decision, it will not function as the sole source of norms. Nor should it.

The role of biblically influenced norms will be a double one. Negatively, some otherwise plausible norms will be ruled out. Positively, a different set will be confirmed or "authorized." An example of the former is ethical egoism. A case can be made for this. An individual's single basic obligation is to promote his or her own welfare as he or she defines that. Individual well-being, self-defined, when cast as *the* moral standard runs strongly counter to the biblical grain, however. Therefore *whatever* norm is considered must, at its base, be more other-regarding and self-denying than ethical egoism. Here, then, is a norm ruled out by the overwhelming testimony of the scriptures, even when a strong philosophical case might be made for it on other grounds. An example of a norm positively confirmed by the canon would be distributive justice, obliging people of similar abilities to make the same relative contributions and sacrifices in the communities they inhabit. Such a norm can summon biblical support that is not simply proof-texting or contorted theologizing from "well-chosen" materials. It would rally support from throughout the canon.

Thus, whether or not the biblical materials actually supply some of the norms for Christian ethics (and we assume they can and ought to), they influence the boundaries for all proposed norms from whatever sources. Some will be considered in bounds for Christian ethics, others out of bounds. Precisely which of the large number of remaining possibilities is most "faithful" for the Christian moral life is the subject of continuing debate in Christian ethics and in biblical studies. We cannot engage in that debate within the space available here. But we do need to parallel what was said about genre with the same for moral norms. It is methodologically erroneous to proceed with the assumption of a single biblical norm for Christian ethics. "Norm-reductionism" is to be combatted as vigorously as genre reductionism. This of course is not grounds for an utter norm relativism. Nor is it grounds for an indiscriminate pluralism. Any full discussion must face those tough questions about which norms should be the reigning ones in Christian ethics.

Do the biblical materials supply normative rules and principles for Christian ethics? Are there biblically rooted or influenced imperatives with the force of moral law? Our contention is, yes, there are. That affirmation doesn't answer a number of critical questions, however. How is the specific content determined? What would be the present fulfillment or "application" of the biblically grounded command? Are exceptions morally possible, and, if so, on what grounds? Are there biblical grounds for abrogating moral law as such under some circumstances? Without launching a discussion that would require a further volume, we can say some things which designate the way in which the Bible can properly be a source of moral rules and principles as norms in Christian ethics.

Any proposed rule or principle would need consistent backing throughout that corpus which defines the identity of the Christian and the church. In other words, a prescription of behavior that claimed to express authentic Christian identity would need to be able to demonstrate canonical integrity. The injunctions toward the poor are examples of imperatives with such backing.

The biblical materials might not only provide straight-forward prescriptions, however. They might also be the source of guidelines *for locating the burden of proof* on a given moral issue and choice.

War and revolution, for example, or even a case of assault on a normally peaceful neighborhood street, can force that moral turbulence which questions whether or not there is a justifiable taking of human life. In the heat of battle that question will be answered one way or another, with little or no reflection. But in a previous time of relative calm, or a later one, the person may ask for aid in making up his or her mind. The biblical materials can help locate the burden of proof. In this case, the scriptures mandate that the general rule be one against the taking of life. If there is any exception to be made that has moral integrity, then it must be one which at least begins with a non-violent bearing as the normal and normative one for the Christian. That is, the use of lethal violence is *not on the same level of choice* with non-violence, or even non-lethal violence. Its use, if allowed at all, requires a special justification. Further, that special justification itself would also need biblical warrants. Thus just war teachings in Christian ethics have sought scriptural grounds for an exceptional but morally permissible use of deadly violence. The point is that the biblical materials can function as the source of normative rules of rather specific content in Christian ethics—rules which set the terms for locating the burden of proof.

A closely related use is that of setting limits for morally permitted conduct, i.e., rules and principles that mark the edges, declaring what is out of bounds. The "shalt not's" of the Ten Commandments have functioned this way.

Rules and principles in Christian ethics may, then, be influenced by biblical materials in several ways:

• as the source for positive prescription in keeping with the basic identity of the Christian as Christian;

• as the source for establishing the boundaries of morally permissible behavior;

• as the source for locating where the burden of proof lies, or what the normal and normative bearing will be, and what kind of case constitutes a morally justified exception.

It should be added that the rules, principles, and other norms in Christian ethics may show considerable influence from biblical sources even when they are not *directly* taken from them. Indeed, norms often need to be "created." This is frequently the case when Christians face novel issues. Current biomedical technology has presented many such issues. A search for guidelines for fetal research is but one example. For the creation of new norms the course usually taken is to work from broader principles with biblical warrants, such as notions of the sanctity and the quality of life.

c) Any thorough treatment of the method of practical moral reasoning (or the steps for approaching and moving through a decision on a moral matter) entails more considerations than we can entertain here. In view of our major concerns several helpful statements can be made, however.

It is significant for Christian ethics that no single biblical way of making decisions exists. The scriptures give evidence of several modes. Thus an appeal by Christian ethics to the sources would not of itself settle the issue of the method to be preferred, even if the Bible were granted such authority in decision-making. Brevard Childs' observation is worth noting:

> It is of fundamental importance to recognize that at no point within the Bible is there ever spelled out a system or a technique by which one could move from the general imperatives of the law of God, such as found in the Decalogue, to the specific application within the concrete situation.[2]

At the same time, certain characteristics persist in the biblical materials in which decision-making is portrayed. These can be appropriated by Christian ethics as clues for its own determinations.

(1) The diversity in the Bible might itself suggest that singularity of method ought not be a matter of obsession in Christian ethics. The suggestion is that different decision-situations might legitimately be handled with different responses.[3] The application of agreed-upon principles through a form of casuistry might work very well in one instance, while a contextualist approach for highly contingent and unusual factors might better serve in another. Without further work this suggestion would beg the methodological question of determining which method is most appropriate when, and how one method might relate to another in an encompassing theory. But at least the biblical pluralism ought to give pause and stave off the methodological reductionism that can so easily characterizes Christian ethics.

(2) A biblically influenced method would have as one mark the community setting and community experience. Decision-making is overwhelmingly a community enterprise in the biblical materials. Whatever method or methods Christian ethics might choose as its own, the church would function as a major community of moral deliberation.

(3) In the biblical materials making decisions and taking stands appears to happen between two poles, that of a responsible sense of obligation to the community's standards and traditions on the one hand, and a creative or innovating freedom on the other. The burden of deciding and acting is never removed and the decision is always taken in freedom. Yet, it is never a rootless freedom or one without accountability to community precedent, experience and norms. A way of approaching and moving to and through a decision in Christian ethics would take account of these poles, again if the biblical materials are used as clues.

(4) Whatever the particular method, it would need to be in keeping with Christian

ethics as at root relational or response ethics. The touchstone for Israel's morality and that of the early church is always the faith-experience of God. All the elements used in determining which behavior is most fitting in a given set of circumstances take their form and function from this faith relationship. This means, to cite but one example, that rules, principles and other norms in the decision-making process are viewed as expressive of underlying relationships, indicating their kind, quality, and content. The rules, principles and other norms take their authority from the defining relationships, not the reverse. The Ten Commandments are never viewed or understood by Israel apart from the relationship-defining "preamble" that introduces them: "I am the Lord your God who brought you out of Egypt, out of the house of bondage." The biblical materials themselves indicate that whatever method of moral reasoning is used in Christian ethics, it needs to be in keeping with relational or response ethics. It needs to be a method that continually refers the decision-maker to the animating core of Christian morality in the living relationship with God.

d) We must turn now to questions of the kind of biblical materials used in decision-making and the proper starting point for their use.

The decision-situation and the provoking moral issue set the agenda for the conversation between the Bible and Christian ethics. One starts from the issue and its matrix and goes from there to the biblical materials, quite in contrast to the flow in character formation.

The starting point directly affects the biblical materials used. Whatever their genre, they will be sought because they address the particular issue at hand and/or illumine the situation. Thus a case engaging the moral issue of civil obedience and disobedience might turn to portions of scripture such as the admonitions of Peter and Paul to be subordinate to the ordained powers, or to the portrayal of the state as the beast in Revelation 13. Certain events in the life of Jesus might be consulted, such as those involving his relationship with the Zealots. These uncover a wrestling with the relevant issues of acquiring of political power and employing violence as a means. Note that even in this brief example several different forms of biblical literature are cited —moral admonition, apocalyptic vision, and historical account. But in contrast with the more generalized use of the Bible for character formation, here all are appropriated for a single, sharp focus upon a specific moral issue. Here, too, as mentioned earlier, the detailed work of biblical scholars on particular texts will be essential.

The focus on the particular does not mean, however, that only those materials *directly* addressing the issue are usable, or even the most important. For decision-making, as for moral development, there are virtually limitless possibilities in the rich symbols, accounts, images, and exemplary figures. There may be no clear and straightforward moral point in their textual presentation. Yet they may in one setting or another function as a source of decisive insight for the matter at hand. The symbols of bread and wine capture for some Christians a deep caring for the earth (among other meanings). The Eucharist generates and expresses for them a Christ-centered nature mysticism. In the face of actions oblivious to environmental welfare, these symbols illumine for these Christians the general direction of their action, even when no one particular policy is indicated. Or the Old Testament account of the Jubilee Year might for some enter into their dreams and choices for economic and political life, even when it does not do so by way of an "application" or "translation." It functions as a mind-expanding picture, a stimulus to creative vision.

Here we begin to wander into vaguely charted territory. It is the realm of the imagination in decision-making and the role of the Bible in provoking the imagination of the person in search of insight.

Imagination clearly plays a major role in making up our minds. Most of our decisions are not made by passing through tight syllogisms that have their top line in some general moral principle. Rather, an image or model or way of proceeding is brought from some other setting, often from some apparently unrelated body of knowledge, and is used "imaginatively" as illumination for what might be done.

The link with biblical materials is a vital one. They may serve as the source for the materials of imagination. Indeed, a too-easy insistence upon *directly* addressing specific moral issues often truncates severely what the Bible has to offer for decision-making. Often the best offered is precisely that which has no pertinence to the exigencies of the moment, *as we define them*. Instead, through those seemingly strange stories and images, allegories and parables, entered into by imagination, a different place to stand or a different angle of vision is acquired, a different world is inhabited. Often that is exactly what is needed. From there a constellation of resources may also be available, many of which may not be at hand in the decision-maker's own immediate cultural context. That, too, is often exactly what is needed.

What we are pointing to is exemplified by William Stringfellow's book, *An Ethic for Christians and Other Aliens in a Strange Land.* There a critique of America is played out between the 137th Psalm ("By the waters of

Babylon . . ."), the Book of Revelation, and Stringfellow's understanding of the last quarter century of American life. Stringfellow throughout links ancient imagery and present reality and uses scripture as the source of a different, informing perspective. His task, as he says,

> . . . is to treat the nation within the tradition of biblical politics—to understand America biblically—*not* the other way around, *not* (to put it in an appropriately awkward way) to construe the Bible Americanly.[4]

With this note on the Bible and imagination we have come full circle. The discussion has been that of the Bible's role in decision-making. But the nurturing of imagination so critical to decision-making turns out also to be of a piece with the formation of character. It is formative of both seeing and deciding. The starting point or occasion may be different—addressing the moral issue at hand in the one instance, participating in the ongoing life of the church as a worshiping, learning community in the other. Yet the different starting points represent only different points on the lines of influence. Seeing shapes decisions and actions. Decisions and actions form and alter perception. And in both, the same diverse biblical materials are used "imaginatively" to work the double influence. The uses of the Bible in identity formation and the uses of the Bible in decision-making play upon one another in a mutually animating way.[5]

Notes

1. Karl Barth, *Church Dogmatics* III/4 (Edinburgh: T. and T. Clark, 1961), trans. by A. T. Mackay, *et al., passim.*
2. Childs, 129.

3. The suggestion is that of Edward LeRoy Long Jr. in his *A Survey of Christian Ethics,* "A Prolegomena to Comprehensive Complementarity," 310ff.

4. William Stringfellow, *An Ethic for Christians and Other Aliens in a Strange Land* (Waco, Texas: Word Books, 1973), 13.

5. Much of the thrust of this chapter is captured in the musings of Undersecretary of State Chester Bowles recorded a month after the Bay of Pigs incident.

> The question which concerns me most about this new Administration is whether it lacks a genuine sense of conviction about what is right and what is wrong. I realize in posing the question I am raising an extremely serious point. Nevertheless I feel it must be faced.
>
> Anyone in public life who has strong convictions about the rights and wrongs of public morality, both domestic and international, has a very great advantage in times of strain, since his instincts on what to do are clear and immediate. Lacking such a framework of moral conviction or sense of what is right and what is wrong, he is forced to lean almost entirely upon his mental processes; he adds up the plusses and minuses of any question and comes up with a conclusion. Under normal conditions, when he is not tired or frustrated, this pragmatic approach should successfully bring him out on the right side of the question.
>
> What worries me are the conclusions that such an individual may reach when he is tired, angry, frustrated, or emotionally affected. The Cuban fiasco demonstrates how far astray a man as brilliant and well intentioned as Kennedy can go who lacks a basic moral reference point.

Cited from David Halberstam, *The Best and the Brightest* (Greenwich, Connecticut: Fawcett Publications, 1972), 88.

25

The Dogmatic Constitution on the Church

Vatican Council II

12. The holy People of God shares also in Christ's prophetic office: it spreads abroad a living witness to him, especially by a life of faith and love and by offering to God a sacrifice of praise, the fruit of lips praising his name (cf. Heb 13:15). The whole body of the faithful who have an anointing that comes from the holy one (cf. 1 Jn 2:20 and 27) cannot err in matters of belief. This characteristic is shown in the supernatural appreciation of the faith (*sensus fidei*)* of the whole people, when, "from the bishops to the last of the faithful"[1] they manifest a universal consent in matters of faith and morals. By this appreciation of the faith, aroused and sustained by the Spirit of truth, the People of God, guided by the sacred teaching authority (*magisterium*), and obeying it, receives not the mere word of men, but truly the word of God (cf. 1 Th 2:13), the faith

* (The *sensus fidei* refers to the instinctive sensitivity and discrimination which the members of the Church possess in matters of faith.—Translator.)

once for all delivered to the saints (cf. Jude 3). The People unfailingly adheres to this faith, penetrates it more deeply with right judgment, and applies it more fully in daily life.

It is not only through the sacraments and the ministrations of the Church that the Holy Spirit makes holy the People, leads them and enriches them with his virtues. Allotting his gifts according as he wills (cf. Cor 12:11), he also distributes special graces among the faithful of every rank. By these gifts he makes them fit and ready to undertake various tasks and offices for the renewal and building up of the Church, as it is written, "the manifestation of the Spirit is given to everyone for profit" (1 Cor 12:7). Whether these charisms be very remarkable or more simple and widely diffused, they are to be received with thanksgiving and consolation since they are fitting and useful for the needs of the Church. Extraordinary gifts are not to be rashly desired, nor is it from them that the fruits of apostolic labors are to be presumptuously expected. Those who have

---

This excerpt is taken from Austin Flannery, ed., Vatican II: The Conciliar and Post Conciliar Documents *(Grand Rapids: Eerdmans, 1975) par. 12 and 25.*

charge over the Church should judge the genuineness and proper use of these gifts, through their office not indeed to extinguish the Spirit, but to test all things and hold fast to what is good. (cf. Th. 5:12 and 19–21).

25. Among the more important duties of bishops that of preaching the Gospel has pride of place.[2] For the bishops and heralds of the faith, who draw new disciples to Christ; they are authentic teachers, that is, teachers endowed with the authority of Christ, who preach the faith to the people assigned to them, the faith which is destined to inform their thinking and direct their conduct; and under the light of the Holy Spirit they make that faith shine forth, drawing from the storehouse of revelation new things and old (cf. Mt 13:52); they make it bear fruit and with watchfulness they ward off whatever errors threaten their flock (cf. 2 Tim 4:14). Bishops who teach in communion with the Roman Pontiff are to be revered by all as witnesses of divine and Catholic truth; the faithful, for their part, are obliged to submit to their bishops' decision, made in the name of Christ, in matters of faith and morals, and to adhere to it with a ready and respectful allegiance of mind. This loyal submission of the will and intellect must be given, in a special way, to the authentic teaching authority of the Roman Pontiff, even when he does not speak *ex cathedra* in such wise, indeed, that his supreme teaching authority be acknowledged with respect, and that one sincerely adhere to decisions made by him, conformably with his manifest mind and intention, which is made known principally either by the character of the documents in question, or by the frequency with which a certain doctrine is proposed, or by the manner in which the doctrine is formulated.

Although the bishops, taken individually, do not enjoy the privilege of infallibility, they do, however, proclaim infallibly the doctrine of Christ on the following conditions: namely, when, even though dispersed throughout the world but preserving for all that amongst themselves and with Peter's successor the bond of communion, in their authoritative teaching concerning matters of faith and morals, they are in agreement that a particular teaching is to be held definitively and absolutely. This is still more clearly the case when, assembled in an ecumenical council, they are, for the universal Church, teachers of and judges in matters of faith and morals, whose decisions must be adhered to with the loyal and obedient assent of faith.[4]

This infallibility, however, with which the divine redeemer wished to endow his Church in defining doctrine pertaining to faith and morals, is co-extensive with the deposit of revelation, which must be religiously guarded and loyally and courageously expounded. The Roman Pontiff, head of the college of bishops, enjoys this infallibility in virtue of his office, when, as supreme pastor and teacher of all the faithful—who confirms his brethren in the faith (cf. Lk 22:32)—he proclaims in an absolute decision a doctrine pertaining to faith or morals.[5] For that reason his definitions are rightly said to be irreformable by their very nature and not by reason of the assent of the Church, is as much as they were made with the assistance of the Holy Spirit promised to him in the person of blessed Peter himself; and as a consequence they are in no way in need of the approval of others, and do not admit of appeal to any other tribunal. For in such a case the Roman Pontiff does not utter a pronouncement as a private person, but rather does he expound and defend the teaching of the Catholic faith as the supreme teacher of the universal Church, in whom the Church's charism of infallibility is present in a singular way.[6] The infallibility promised to the Church is also present in the body of bishops when, together with Peter's successor, they exercise the supreme teaching office. Now, the assent of the Church can never be lacking to such definitions on account of the same Holy Spirit's influence, through which Christ's whole flock is maintained in the unity of the faith and makes progress in it.[7]

Furthermore, when the Roman Pontiff, or the body of bishops together with him, define a doctrine, they make the definition in conformity with revelation itself, to which all are bound to adhere and to which they are obliged to submit; and this revelation is transmitted integrally either in written form or in oral tradition through the legitimate succession of bishops and above all through the watchful concern of the Roman Pontiff himself; and through the light of the Spirit of truth it is scrupulously preserved in the Church and unerringly explained.[8] The Roman Pontiff and the bishops, by reason of their office and the seriousness of the matter, apply themselves with zeal to the work of enquiring by every suitable means into this revelation and of giving apt expression to its contents;[9] they do not, however, admit any new public revelation as pertaining to the divine deposit of faith.[10]

Notes

1. See St. Augustine, *De Praed. Sanct.* 14, 27: *PL* 44, 980.
2. Cf. Council of Trent, *Decr. de reform.,* Session V, c. 2; n. 9, and Session XXIV, can. 4; *Conc. Oecr.* pp. 645 and 739.
3. Cf. Vatican Council I, Const. Dogm. *Dei Filius,* 3: *Denz.* 1712 (3011). Cf. the note added to schema I *de Eccl.* (taken from St. Rob. Bellarmine): Mansi 51, 579 C; also the revised schema of Const. II *de Ecclesia Christi,* with Kleutgen's commentary: Mansi 53, 313 AB. Pius IX, Letter *Tuas libenter: Denz.* 1683 (2879).
4. Code of Canon Law, c. 1322–1323.
5. Cf. Vatican Council I, Const. Dogm. *Pastor aeternus: Denz* 1839 (3074).
6. Cf. Gasser's explanation of Vatican Council I: Mansi 52, 1213 AC.
7. Gasser, ibid.: Mansi 1214 A.
8. Gasser, ibid.: Mansi 1215 CD, 1216–1217 A.
9. Gasser, ibid.: Mansi 1213.
10. Vatican Council I, Const. Dogm. *Pastor aeternus,* 4: *Denz.* 1836 (3070).

26

Doctrinal Authority for a Pilgrim Church

Avery Dulles, SJ

Enlightenment, according to Immanuel Kant, is the overcoming of self-caused immaturity. "Immaturity is the incapacity to use one's own intelligence without the guidance of another. The motto of the Enlightenment is 'sapere aude!'—have the courage to use your own intelligence."[1] Through laziness or cowardice, Kant goes on to say, a large portion of humankind gladly remains immature. It is more comfortable to be a minor, under the guardianship of others.

Kant recognized that in certain official functions one may take on an obligation to refrain from speaking according to one's own convictions and to abide by the teaching of an institution. For example, he notes, a pastor is obliged to teach his congregation according to the doctrine of the Church he serves. He has to state faithfully what the Church teaches, regardless of his own personal views. If he felt that the teaching of the Church were seriously wrong, he would no doubt have to resign his post. But as long as he is a priest he remains unfree, for he is executing the mandate of others.

Quite different, according to Kant, is the position of the scholar. He writes for the general public and in that capacity he is entitled, even obliged, to employ his own reason and to speak with complete candor.

Kant is typical of rationalism insofar as he presumes that reason is the best tool we have for getting at the truth, and that reason operates more effectively when unchecked by authority. Authority, he holds, is for the sake of the immature. It is only provisional. True personal conviction depends not upon authority but upon rational insight.

The rebellion against authority at the time of the Enlightenment was a time-conditioned reaction against the excesses of ecclesiastical authoritarianism, which was carried to unprecedented lengths in early modern times. When authority becomes oppressive and violates the integrity of honest inquiry and conscientious decision, it generates the kind of

This article is excerpted from The Resilient Church *(Garden City: Doubleday, 1977) 93–112.*

negative image reflected in the writers of the Enlightenment. The rejection of authority, however, is scarcely a sign of adulthood. Rather, it is a mark of adolescence. In practically all the affairs of daily living, mature persons rely upon authority in the sense that they depend on the advice of experienced and knowledgeable persons—those whom they have reason to regard as experts in the particular field. If we do this in law, in medicine, in history, and art criticism, why not in religion? In the case of a religion which, like Christianity, claims to rest on a definite revelation given in the past, belief is essentially linked with the acceptance of the testimony of those who, allegedly, were the prime recipients of the revelation. There is no way in which reason can prove by universally cogent arguments the truth of the interpretation that the New Testament and the creeds give to the figure of Jesus. If we antecedently refuse to take anything on authority, we cut ourselves off from the benefits of historical revelation. Christianity ceases to have any value except as a set of symbols for interpreting our own experience.

The acceptance of authority, as I understand it, does not mean the abandonment of reason. As I have explained more fully elsewhere, reason and authority are dialectically intertwined throughout the process of religious inquiry and the life of faith.[2] Reason is a necessary instrument for assessing the rival claims of various claimants to authority. Reason is also necessary to interpret authoritative statements, to judge whether the authority is speaking within its competence, and to reinterpret past statements to grasp their significance for new situations. Reason may at times detect false emphases or errors into which the authorities may have fallen. The critical thinking developed by Kant and the great philoso-

phers of the Enlightenment can thus be helpful in guarding against the absolutization of authority. Contemporary Christians are indebted to the Enlightenment for having developed defenses against an unhealthy authoritarianism.

While acknowledging the importance of relativizing authority, I would contend, against certain liberal theologians, that authority has a central place in the Christian religion. For the vitality of the faith it is essential that the authorities function properly. If the authorities fail to speak with truth and power, the whole community of faith is in danger of disintegrating. The right question for Christians is not whether to accept authority but rather how to identify and relate to the authorities. Many Christians make the mistake of overlooking some authorities and of absolutizing others.

The standard loci of authority in the Christian system are well known: the Bible, the pastoral office, the sense of the faithful, the judgment of theologians, and the testimony of prophetically gifted individuals. Certain groups of Christians have traditionally accented some of the instances as against others.

Classical Protestantism at one time coined the slogan, "The Bible alone."[3] The position was a protest against the teachings that had been cumulatively built up by the Scholastic theologians and the popes in the Middle Ages. The Reformation was, under one aspect, a radical call for simplification—for a return to primitive purity. The word "alone" in the formula has to be taken with a grain of salt, for no Protestants really ignored tradition. Luther and Calvin were scarcely less eager than the Roman Catholics to square their doctrine with the early ecumenical councils. In their controversies they drew heavily on the church Fathers and even, at times, on the medieval doctors. But they insisted that any Christian teaching—including that of councils and church Fathers—had to be aligned with Scripture. If anything could not be shown to agree with Scripture, it had for them no authority. Very many contemporary Protestants hold approximately this position.

From a Catholic point of view we may agree that the Bible, taken as a whole, is the word of God. It is the fundamental document of Israelite and Christian revelation. The Bible, we believe, is the fundamental touchstone of our faith. No teaching that contradicts the Bible, taken as whole, could be true.

On the other hand, the Catholic will have many difficulties against the catchword "Scripture alone." Let me put some of the familiar difficulties under three headings:

1. The Bible did not collect itself. It is a selection of Jewish and early Christian writings made in the early centuries by the Church—and more specifically by the leaders of the local and regional churches, and ultimately by councils. To put one's trust in the Bible, therefore, inevitably implies a certain trust in the Church that gathered up these writings and declared them to be authoritative for Christians. One cannot drive a wedge between the authority of the Church which canonized the Scriptures and that of the Scriptures which it canonized. To say "Bible alone" with the negative implication "not Church" is therefore unacceptable.

2. The Bible is not self-interpreting. It is a very complex collection of writings from different ages and situations. One can pick out sentences here and there that seem to teach error—things we know to be false from science, from history, or from faith. To gather up the meaning of the Scripture as a whole is an act of creative interpretation, in which all sorts of skills and funds of information are brought to bear. If the Bible is to speak to us today, its meaning must be mediated to us through other authorities—the exegete, the pastor, the believing community, or whatever. If the individual reader were handed a Bible outside of any ecclesial context, he would probably find it uninteresting, unintelligible, or seriously misleading.

3. According to the New Testament, Jesus has promised to remain forever present with his Church. The Holy Spirit, who previously "spoke by the prophets," remains at work in the Christian community to the end of time. Thus it may be presumed that Christians since biblical times have spoken with the special assistance of the Spirit. We should therefore make an effort to identify the occasions on which God may be judged to be speaking through persons who have lived since Christ and the apostles. To accept no authority but the Bible would be to reject, in part, the teaching of the Bible, which refers us to Christians who speak by the Spirit.

Among Catholics it is undisputed that the Holy Spirit who inspired the Scriptures is also at work in the Church, and therefore that there is living authority in the Church. But there are differences of opinion regarding the loci in which the presence of the Spirit is to be found: pastoral office, people of God, or a variety of charismatic leaders.

Since the Reformation, and especially since the eighteenth century, the Catholic emphasis has been upon the pastoral office and, more specifically, upon the papal and episcopal offices. In the Roman textbooks out of which most of the present clergy were taught in their seminary days, practically no other form of authority than that of the office-holder was acknowledged. The term "magisterium" came to be used to designate the teaching authority of popes and bishops—and the tendency was to reduce every other kind of theological authority to this one font.

According to the theory of apostolicity then prevalent—and still prevalent in some circles —the bishops and they alone were successors of the apostles. Apostolic succession was conceived as giving the bishops a special "charism of truth" proper to themselves. The pope, as head of the whole Church, was thought to have in himself as much authority as the entire body of bishops. Thus he was the supreme and universal teacher of all Christians, equipped with that infallibility with which Christ had endowed his Church.

This theory of authority, which may be called institutional or hierocratic, has real assets that should not be overlooked. For one thing it helps to safeguard the unity of the Church and its doctrinal continuity with the Church of apostolic times. If the Church is to cohere as a society, it must have ways of assembling a body of clearly identifiable, self-consistent, and certified teachings—qualities that are clearly fostered by the hierocratic model.

On the other hand, this model, taken in isolation, has certain liabilities.[4] By insisting as it does upon the formal and juridical aspects of authority, it encourages a kind of doctrinal extrinsicism, sometimes referred to as the "blank check" theory of assent. Furthermore, it does not sufficiently attend to the fact that the official teaching would not have power or credibility except that it emanates from a community of faith and is, so to speak, inscribed within this community. Official teaching has no force unless it somehow expresses the faith of the believing Church, and unless the teachers are bound by conviction to the community of believers. The doctrine of infallibility, in particular, becomes incredible if set

forth in an automatic or mechanistic way, without taking account of the human and Christian character of the process by which faith is gathered up and distilled into doctrine.

Some modern ecclesiologists, seeking the limitations of the hierocratic model, have attempted to substitute what may be called a democratic view of authority.[5] Without saying explicitly that the Church is a democracy, they lean in that direction. They speak of the common priesthood of all the faithful, and are uncomfortable with the idea that the priesthood, or authority, of the ordained would be essentially different from this. They would see the official teachers simply as those who publicly announce what is already the conviction of the faithful, or at least of a large majority of them. These democratic ecclesiologists strongly emphasize the "sense of the faithful" (*sensus fidelium*), which, according to Vatican II, is so assisted by the Holy Spirit that the people of God as a whole is infallible in its unanimous understanding of what constitutes a matter of faith.[6]

I am not sure whether any Catholic ecclesiologists go so far as to say that the pope can be bound by a majority vote of the bishops or that the bishops can be bound by a majority vote of the priests and faithful of their diocese. Such a view would be difficult to reconcile with Vatican I and with the whole tenor of the Catholic tradition. But because of the doctrine that the Holy Spirit is present in the whole Church as well as the rulers, majorities do have to be taken seriously. In actual practice, popes and bishops very rarely if ever seek to impose doctrines unless they believe those doctrines are already accepted by a large majority.

The attention given in modern theology to the active role of the faithful is in many ways a welcome development. It corrects certain exaggerations to which the hierocratic model is prone—especially the unhealthy concentration of all active power in the hands of a small ruling class, with the corresponding reduction of the lower classes in the Church to a state of passivity scarcely consonant with lively Christian commitment.

The main weakness of the democratic theory is that, like the hierocratic, it labors under a certain juridicism. Concerned with the formal aspects of authority, it overlooks the authority of the gospel or the content of revelation, which could conceivably be opposed to the drift of public opinion in the Church. Preoccupied with juridical structures, this theory leaves insufficient room for the inspirations and special graces bestowed by the Holy Spirit, who can raise up powerful voices of prophetic protest.

In contrast to some contemporary theologians of the Western world, I tend to be distrustful of majorities. I am fond of Kierkegaard's aphorism "The majority is always wrong." The *sensus fidelium,* as a theological font, should never be confused with the public-opinion poll. Not all in the Church are equally close to Christ and to the Holy Spirit. Many members of the Church are as much influenced by the mass media and the secular fashions of the day as they are by the gospel and Christian tradition. This does not mean, of course, that by taking power from the people and transferring it to a power elite one gets closer to the truth. The officials can easily make decisions in the light of their class interests and professional biases rather than the gospel itself. Where the teaching of the magisterium fails to resonate with the consciousness of the faithful at large, one has reason to suspect that the power of office has been incorrectly used.

In contradistinction to the hierocratic and democratic theories in their crude form, I should like to propose, as theologically more acceptable, a pluralistic theory of authority in the Church. The Church, I would maintain, depends for its health and vigor upon the coexistence of several distinct organs of authority, and hence on multiple groups of believers.[7] These authorities serve as mutual checks and balances. They exist in a state of natural tension and dialogue, and only when they spontaneously converge can authority make itself fully felt. The great French ecclesiologist Yves Congar has put the matter well:

> . . . if the question is to be considered theologically, it is impossible to restrict oneself to a *single* criterion, or to ancient texts without the "living magisterium," or to the living magisterium without the ancient texts, or to authority without the community, or to the latter without the former, or to the apostolicity of the ministry without the apostolicity of doctrine, or *vice versa,* or to the Roman Church separated from catholicity, or to the latter detached from the former. . . . All these criteria together should ensure a living faithfulness and identity in the full historicity of our lives and our knowledge. The fullness of the truth is associated with that of the means that God has given us to enable us to live by it; and with the totality of Christian existence.[8]

Among the authorities in the Church one must unquestionably include the documents which it recognizes as constitutive of its own beliefs. The canonical Scriptures, as we have said, serve as the basis and reference point of all Christian teaching. Anyone who seeks to impose beliefs and norms of conduct that evidently contravene the Scriptures will meet with deserved resistance. Even the magisterium of the Church, according to Vatican II, is not above the Word of God, but serves it.[9] A sound historicocritical approach, as cultivated by the community of biblical scholars, can prevent the Bible from being misused to support whatever anyone wants to maintain on nonbiblical grounds.

A second constitutive norm, which Catholics place on a par with the Bible, is sacred tradition. Tradition is known through various sedimentations, technically called the "monuments of tradition." They would include, most importantly, the solemn decisions of ecumenical councils. Unlike the Scriptures, these expressions of tradition, in Catholic theology, are not normally called the "word of God," but they bear witness to the word of God, and as such are authoritative.

Among the living voices that have authority in the Church I would mention, in the first place, the general sense of the faithful. This is to be obtained not simply by counting noses but by weighing opinions. The views of alert and committed Christians should be given more weight than those of indifferent or marginal Christians, but even the doubts of marginal persons should be attentively considered to see if they do not contain some prophetic message for the Church. The sense of the faithful should be seen not simply as a static index but as a process. If it becomes clear that large numbers of generous, intelligent, prayerful, and committed Christians who seriously study a given problem change their views in a certain direction, this may be evidence that the Holy Spirit is so inclining them. But there is need for caution and discernment to avoid mistaking the influences of secular fashion for the inspirations of divine grace.

In addition to the general community of the faithful, there are persons who by reason of their particular gifts or positions in the Church have special qualifications to speak with authority. Here I think one must consider three sets of factors: first, learning and other natural personal endowments, such as prudence and common sense; second, spiritual gifts such as faith and prophetic insight, attributable to prayerful intimacy with God; third, regular appointment to an office in the Church with the graces, concerns, and experiences that go with the office in question.

These three sets of qualifications can be brought into some kind of loose correspondence with three types of ministry that have been recognized in the Church since biblical times: the doctoral, the prophetic, and the pastoral. For the first, the human gifts of intelligence and learning are of chief importance; for the second, docility to the Holy Spirit; for the third, regular appointment to office. It would be a mistake to overlook the special authority of each of these three types of witness.

The three classifications of ministry are not, of course, mutually exclusive. A qualified teacher in the Church must be something more than an intelligent and learned person; he must be open to the movements of the Spirit and sensitive to pastoral concerns. So, likewise, the prophet may stand to gain if he is theologically educated and pastorally responsive. The pastor, finally, should be sensitive to the demands of sound doctrine and to the promptings of the Holy Spirit. It is possible for teachers and prophets, as well as pastors, to have a recognized office in the Church, as they would seem to have had in New Testament times, at least at Antioch. It would be a mistake, therefore, to identify the official Church exclusively with pastoral administration or to look upon prophecy and teaching as merely private charisms. The three types of ministry, while remaining distinct, should somewhat overlap and interpenetrate.

Is there a hierarchy of dignity among teachers, prophets, and pastors? To judge from the listings of charisms in the New Testament (1 Cor 12:27–31; Eph 4:11), one would conclude that the highest of the three in dignity are the prophets, who rank immediately after the apostles in both listings.[10] The administrators (*kybernēseis*) in First Corinthians rank not only after prophets and teachers, but after wonder-workers and healers. In Ephesians, however, the pastors (*poimenes*) rank after prophets and before teachers, or perhaps, according to another interpretation, the pastors in this text are the same persons as the teachers. The presbyters (*presbyteroi*) and bishops (*episkopoi*) do not appear in either list, but they are perhaps to be equated with the administrators and/or pastors. The New Testament *episkopoi* are the ancestors of the modern bishops, but are not identical.[11] They seem to have been something like an executive board of the presbyters, and combined in their persons some administrative and pastoral roles together with certain functions of proclaiming, teaching, and supervising doctrine. Like all the other officers, the *episkopoi* were subordinate to the apostles, so long as the apostles were still alive. Their authority, moreover, appears to have extended only to the local church.

Since biblical times the *episkopoi* have risen in status so as to occupy the highest rank in the ecclesiastical hierarchy. The term "successors of the apostles" is sometimes applied to the bishops and the bishops alone. This title could be misleading for three reasons: First, the apostles were founders of the Church, and as such they have no successors. Second the apostles, as wandering missionaries, did not have regular administrative responsibility for any particular local church. Third, we have no clear biblical or historical evidence that the apostles designated any particular class of persons in the Church to take over their transmissible functions. Still, the expression "successors of the apostles" can, if necessary, be defended.[12] For the bishops, in modern ecclesiastical polity, have a kind of general supervision, on the highest level, of all the functions of the Church, and in this way they resemble the New Testament *apostoloi,* at least as portrayed in the early chapters of Acts.

The precise reasons for the emergence of the *episkopoi* as a kind of ruling class in the Church need not concern us here. Presumably the power shift had something to do with the necessity of strong organizational structures to ward off heresies such as Gnosticism, Marcionism, and Montanism and to equip the Church to stand up under the pressures of persecution. It seems likely, too, that religious leaders imitated, consciously or unconsciously, the civil structure of government in the Roman Empire.

In the post-Tridentine Church, and in the Neo-Scholastic theology of the nineteenth and twentieth centuries, the dialectical tension between the charisms in the Church is virtually eliminated. All authentic teaching power is simply transferred to the episcopal order. The main disadvantage in this system is that the bishop is given an almost unbearable load of responsibility. He becomes in his diocese—at least theoretically—not only the highest administrator but also the chief priest and the supreme teacher. In this last capacity he is supposed to be in a position to settle intellectually all disputed doctrinal questions. To illustrate this awesome doctrinal responsibility, one may refer, for example, to the Ethical and Religious Directives for Catholic Health Facilities issued by the United States bishops in 1971, which state:

> The moral evaluation of new scientific developments and legitimately debated questions must be finally submitted to the teaching authority of the church in the person of the local bishop, who has the ultimate responsibility for teaching Catholic doctrine.[13]

In order to encourage the vigorous exercise of this responsibility, and to facilitate compliance with the bishop's doctrinal decisions, the authors strongly emphasize the grace of the episcopal office. They frequently quote St. Irenaeus to the effect that the bishops have the "sure charism of truth" (*charisma veritatis certum*).[14] But they neglect to mention that Irenaeus in this passage acknowledges that presbyters as well as bishops have this "charisma." Furthermore, according to many commentators, *charisma veritatis* in this passage signifies not a subjective grace for discerning the truth but the objective deposit of faith, "the precious and spiritual gift entrusted to the Church."[15] Irenaeus, speaking to the situation of his own time, was presumably referring to the fact that the apostles had thoroughly instructed the persons to whom they turned over the leadership of the apostolic churches.

The Neo-Scholastic theory, in my opinion, is very unconvincing. It fails to give a rationale for the kind of collaboration between bishops and theologians that has normally existed in the Church. There are ample resources for a better theory both in the New Testament and in the earlier theological tradition.

From the Acts and the Pauline letters, one has the impression that there was a special class of individuals in the early church recognized as having received from the Holy Spirit the gift of teaching Christian doctrine.[16] The *didaskaloi* could teach in their own right, and were not viewed as mere representatives of *episkopoi* or *presbyteroi*. The *episkopos* was primarily an administrator or, perhaps better, a pastor—a true shepherd of the flock. The presbyter-bishop was expected, among other things, to be "an apt teacher" (1 Tm 3:2; cf. Ti 1:9), but he was not expected to be a paragon of learning or to appropriate all doctrinal functions to himself. In many passages the *didaskaloi* are seen as a distinct class. According to Paul's ecclesiastical polity, as set forth in First Corinthians, the various ministries in the Church are bound together by mutual interdependence, as are the organs in a living body. Just as the eye and the ear cannot say to each other, "I have no need of you," so the teacher, the prophet, and the administrator must recognize their dependence upon one another for the sake of better service to the entire Christian community.

If this is true, it would seem to follow that those who have the specialization of teaching in the Church should have a voice in doctrinal decisions. In the words of a contemporary New Testament scholar:

> . . . if there is any group in the church which has the right to be heard when the church makes decisions it is that composed of those to whom the charism of teaching has been given, the *didaskaloi,* who, in the list of 1 Cor 12:28 rank third after the apostles and prophets. If this charism now exists in the

Church apart from the hierarchy—and to deny that it does is utterly arbitrary—it is surely possessed by the theologians. If the "whole church" is to have a part in the making of decisions, particularly in the making of decisions which bear upon the content of faith, the proper authority of the theologians must be given much more weight than is often the case in the present functioning of the church.[17]

In the early centuries the concentration of authority in the episcopal office did no great harm because the bishops of those times were less heavily burdened with administrative responsibilities than are their modern successors. Many of them were charismatic leaders and theologians. Irenaeus and Cyprian, Augustine and Leo, Athanasius and Chrysostom, Cyril of Jerusalem and Cyril of Alexandria, Gregory of Nyssa and Gregory of Nazianzus—these and many other great patristic theologians were also bishops.

In the Middle Ages, the doctoral function once again had a certain autonomy. As the cathedral schools outgrew the personal control of the bishops and evolved into universities with theological faculties, the *magistri* and *doctores* were seen as the primary teachers. Thomas Aquinas, for instance, makes a sharp distinction between the *officium praelationis* (prelacy), possessed by the bishop, and the *officium magisterii* (magisterium), which belongs to the professional theologian.[18] In one text he does speak of a magisterium of bishops, but only in a qualified sense; for he draws a distinction between the *magisterium cathedrae pastoralis* (pastoral magisterium), which belongs to the bishop, and the *magisterium cathedrae magistralis* (magisterial magisterium), which pertains to the theologian.[19] The former, he holds, is concerned with the regulation of preaching and public order in the church rather than with the intricacies of speculation.[20] The *magistri,* according to St. Thomas, teach by learning and argument rather than by appeal to their official status. The conclusions are no more valid than the evidence they are able to adduce. In this sense, therefore, the magisterium of the theologians is unauthoritative.[21]

In the course of the thirteenth century we see the beginnings of what Yves Congar calls a "magisterium of doctors" in the Church.[22] Over and above the task of scientific teaching, doctors and university faculties begin to acquire a certain decisive role, especially in judging cases of alleged heresy. The *studium* thus gradually takes its place as a third force in Christendom, alongside the *sacerdotium* and the *regnum.* By order of Pope Clement V, the decrees of the Council of Vienne (1311–12) were not made official until they had been submitted to the universities for approval. At a number of councils in the later Middle Ages, including Constance and Basel, the theologians were given a deliberative vote even though they were not bishops.[23] Facts such as these call into question the correctness of the statement, so often made in the past century, that theologians do not belong to the magisterium.

I recognize, of course, that theologians, whose energies are so often taken up with subtle speculative questions, are not always well suited to make decisions of a practical nature concerning the government and public preaching of the Church. It is necessary that there be pastoral authorities whose main concern is to supervise the mission and good order of the Church as a community of faith and witness. On the other hand, it is important that questions touching on the order of revelation and theology should not be settled without regard for the demands of truth and scholarship. In questions of a mixed nature, involving both pastoral and academic considerations, there is need for close collaboration between bishops, as holders of the chief pastoral power, and theologians.[24]

In making this recommendation I feel that I am merely articulating what is in practice developing. At Vatican II the theologians had considerable visibility, and in some cases it was well known that they were the real authors of certain speeches given by bishops and of certain sections of conciliar documents. Since the Council Pope Paul VI has set up an International Theological Commission that, even with limited autonomy, speaks in its own name. In the United States, as elsewhere, efforts are being made to establish regular working relationships between the bishops and learned societies such as the Catholic Theological Society of America, the Canon Law Society of America, and others. Groups of theologians collaborate closely with the National Conference of Catholic Bishops, especially through its Commission for Ecumenical and Interreligious Affairs. Both in the United States and abroad, it is common for consensus statements emanating from ecumenical dialogues to be signed by bishops and by theologians as coauthors. This practice might in the course of time be extended to other statements, more properly magisterial in character.

The tendencies represented by these new initiatives are in my opinion signs of closer collaboration, without confusion, between the scholarly and the pastoral functions in the Church. As this process continues, it may become possible for scholars to have a greater initiative in selecting their colleagues who are to be in contact with the pope and the bishops, lest those who do collaborate come to be

labeled "court theologians." I would hope also that there could be regular consultations in which theologians would have an appropriate input into the agenda.

The proper balance of authority demands that theologians should not be merely apologists for what the pastoral leaders decide, nor mere consultors to the pastors (though they may well be this *also*), but that they have a recognized voice in the Church, with a certain relative autonomy to develop their own positions by their own methodology and to seek to gain acceptance for these positions by the pastoral magisterium.

In speaking of the scholar's independence I am by no means returning to the position of Kant, rejected at the beginning of this chapter, but I am, I would hope, recognizing what is sound in the Kantian thesis. With Kant I would hold that it is possible and necessary to assess authoritative pronouncements in the light of rational criteria, but against him I am maintaining that theology is as much concerned with truth as are philosophy and the natural sciences. The theologian can be a true scholar—one who asks the hard questions and honestly expresses his real convictions—without on that account being less bound to the community of faith or less respectful toward the authorities recognized in the Church. In fact the Catholic Christian, reflecting on the faith, will find positive aids to truth in all the types of authority discussed in the preceding pages—the Bible, the "sense of the faithful," and the decisions reached in previous ages through interaction among pastors, prophets, and theologians. None of these instances, in my opinion, is a peremptory authority in isolation from the others, but in combination they afford the guidance needed for the sustenance of Christian faith and the progress of theology. Christian theology, as I understand the term, presupposes a commitment to the saving truth disclosed in the Christian sources.[25]

To give a somewhat practical turn to what I have been saying about teaching authority, I should like to conclude with some observations on dissent. This problem is, I suspect, one that will never cease to recur both in civil society and in the Church. There will always be painful conflicts between some who are sincerely convinced that certain ideas are intolerable within the community of faith and others who believe these same ideas are true or at least compatible with Christian commitment. I cannot propose a full solution, but pastors and theologians can, I think, fruitfully ponder together the sources of the difficulty and the best ways of treating conflicts so that they do not become destructive.

Dissent, in the sense in which we are using the term, is a matter internal to the society in which the opposite position is normative. Dissent in the Church means that a member of the Church takes exception to the position that has become official. Dissent therefore cannot be absolute. It occurs within the context of a larger agreement—namely, the acceptance of Christ as the supreme revelation of God and of the Church as the place where Christ is made specially present and accessible.

Generally speaking, dissent pertains not to fundamental articles of faith, which are regarded as constitutive of membership, but to relatively secondary teachings. Dissent can exist within the Church because it is not usual, nor would it be proper, to impose the supreme penalty of excommunication for views not infallibly proclaimed as pertaining to the very substance of the faith. Thus it is possible to be a Christian and a member of the Church even when one disagrees with certain official teachings.

The problem of dissent has always existed in the Church, but has not always been equally acute. In the "fortress Church" of the past several centuries, dissent was kept to a minimum. Catholics felt a strong obligation to stick together for the sake of survival, and were therefore willing to subject their personal judgment to that of the ruling authorities. The ecclesiology of nineteenth-century Neo-Scholasticism, with its heavy stress on "official charisms," tended to reinforce the authority structures. Dissent was handled by essentially the same moral principles as were applied to the case of an erroneous conscience, and thus insufficient consideration was given to the possibility that dissent might be a corrective force in the Church.[26]

The phenomenon of dissent has been intensified in recent years by all the factors that have tended to weaken the "hierocratic" view of authority and to substitute the kind of pluralistic or dialogic view I have attempted to sketch. Three aspects of the general climate of ideas may be singled out for special mention.

1. Under the influence of psychological and philosophical currents, our age has become particularly sensitive to the values of freedom and authenticity, and to the dignity of conscience as the ultimate norm for moral choice. Typical of our times is an abhorrence of laws and institutions that inhibit personal freedom, and a deep conviction that true religion should help its adherents to become mature, responsible persons. As previously explained, this does not mean a rejection of authority but it does involve a certain relativizing of authority.

2. Thanks to modern means of travel and communications, the believer almost inevitably lives in a pluralistic situation, at the intersection of many different cultures and traditions. This pluralism was sanctioned by

Vatican II, which invited the Church to seek out new forms of solidarity with the various cultures of humankind. There are increasingly few protected havens in which the mind of the faithful is predominantly formed by official Catholic teaching.

3. The Freudian and Marxist critiques of ideology, combined with evident abuses of power on the part of leaders in the political and economic world, have made us acutely aware that officeholders are under a constant temptation to employ their power to bolster up their position. When popes and bishops insist very heavily on apostolic succession, divine right, and the special graces attached to their office, they leave themselves open to the suspicion that ideology is at work.

Vatican II, in its formal discussion of the teaching authority of popes and bishops, did not directly challenge the reigning Neo-Scholastic theory. Article 25 of the Constitution on the Church may be interpreted as supporting the standard position of the day. It affirms the obligation to assent to the ordinary noninfallible teaching of the Roman pontiff without any explicit mention of the right to dissent. Several bishops at the Council submitted a proposal that allowance should be made for the case of an educated person who for solid reasons finds himself unable to assent internally to such teaching. To this the Doctrinal Commission replied that "approved theological explanations should be consulted."[27] Thus the Council in its formal teaching did not advance the discussion of dissent beyond where it had been in the previous generation.

Indirectly, however, the Council worked powerfully to undermine the authoritarian theory and to legitimate dissent in the Church. This it did in part by insisting on the necessary freedom of the act of faith and by attributing a primary role to personal conscience in the moral life. By contrast, the Neo-Scholastic doctrine of the magisterium, with its heavy accentuation of "blind obedience," minimizes the value of understanding and maturity in the life of faith.

Most importantly for our purposes, Vatican II quietly reversed the earlier positions of the Roman magisterium on a number of important issues. The obvious examples are well known. In biblical studies, for instance, the Constitution on Divine Revelation accepted a critical approach to the Bible, thus supporting the previous initiatives of Pius XII and delivering the Church once and for all from the incubus of the earlier decrees of the Biblical Commission. In the Decree on Ecumenism, the Council cordially greeted the ecumenical movement and involved the Catholic Church in the larger quest for Christian unity, thus putting an end to the hostility enshrined in Pius XII's *Mortalium animos*. In Church-state relations, the Declaration on Religious Freedom accepted the religiously neutral state, thus reversing the previously approved view that the state should formally profess the truth of Catholicism. In the theology of secular realities, the Pastoral Constitution on the Church in the Modern World adopted an evolutionary view of history and a modified optimism regarding secular systems of thought, thus terminating more than a century of vehement denunciations of modern civilization.[28]

As a result of these and other revisions, the Council rehabilitated many theologians who had suffered under severe restrictions with regard to their ability to teach and publish. The names of John Courtney Murray, Pierre Teilhard de Chardin, Henri de Lubac, and Yves Congar, all under a cloud of suspicion in the 1950s, suddenly became surrounded with a bright halo of enthusiasm.

By its actual practice of revision, the Council implicitly taught the legitimacy and even the value of dissent. In effect the Council said that the ordinary magisterium of the Roman pontiff had fallen into error and had unjustly harmed the careers of loyal and able scholars. Some of the thinkers who had resisted official teaching in the preconciliar period were among the principal precursors and architects of Vatican II.

As a result of the conciliar experience, together with the general climate of ideas previously alluded to, dissent is today perceived by many sophisticated Catholics as an inevitable and potentially beneficial phenomenon. Many would not wish to have a situation, even if it were possible, in which every Catholic agreed with every stated position of the hierarchy. On the other hand, dissent can be a source of confusion and discord; it is not something to be desired for its own sake. To alleviate the harmful effects of dissent, I would submit the following recommendations:

1. The pastoral magisterium should keep in close touch with the theologians and other intellectuals in the Church. Popes and bishops would do well not to act without benefit of the best available scholarship, as happened, to the detriment of the Church, when the Biblical Commission issued some of its less enlightened decrees. Conversely, scholars in the Church should try to cultivate greater sensitivity to pastoral considerations.

2. Generally speaking, the pastoral leaders should not speak in a binding way unless a relatively wide consensus has first been achieved. For authentic consensus to develop, there is need of free discussion. Only when it becomes clear through such discussion that the weight of responsible opinion decisively favors one side over the other can true consensus arise.

3. Where no such consensus exists, it is well to acknowledge publicly that good Christians do in fact disagree. Such disagreement will hardly be scandalous in our times, when open clashes of opinion are common in the scientific and political worlds. It would, however, be scandalous for the holders of pastoral power to suppress freedom of expression and debate on issues where there is as yet no agreed solution.

4. Even where there is no consensus, popes, bishops, and others in authority may clearly and candidly state their convictions on matters of pastoral importance and seek to win assent for their own positions by giving testimony and adducing arguments. If they do this without trying to impose their views by juridical pressures, they will generally meet with a favorable response on the part of the faithful who are hungry for pastoral leadership.

5. When members of the Church find themselves sincerely unable to give assent to a given teaching of the pastoral authorities, they should not feel that they are on that account disloyal or unfaithful. Noninfallible teaching, as Richard A. McCormick has pointed out, does not bring with it an immediate obligation to assent. Rather, it calls for "religious docility and deference—always on the assumption, of course, that authority has proceeded properly."[29] In view of such deference, the dissenter will be reluctant to conclude that the official teaching is clearly erroneous; he will carefully reassess his own position in the light of that teaching; and he will behave in a manner that fosters respect and support for the pastoral magisterium, even though he continues to strive for a revision of the current official teaching.

6. Provided that they speak with evident loyalty and respect for authority, dissenters should not be silenced. As already noted, ex-

perience has shown that in many cases those who dissent from church teaching in one generation are preparing the official positions of the Church in the future. Vatican II owes many of its successes to the very theologians who were under a cloud in the pontificate of Pius XII. The Church, like civil society, should cherish its "loyal opposition" as a precious asset.

These principles, although they seem quite evident in the light of the general ecclesiology governing this study, will be contested by some. There are still those who look upon the Church as an institution that must give oracular responses to all really important questions, and who consequently regard dissent as tantamount to disloyalty. My own point of view is governed by the vision of the Church as a pilgrim community renewing itself by creative interaction with its changing environment. The Church, "like a pilgrim in a foreign land," receives from the risen Lord not a clear vision of ultimate truth but the power "to show forth in the world the mystery of the Lord in a faithful though shadowed way, until at last it will be revealed in total splendor."[30] Thus the Church may in some sense be called a "Society of Explorers"—to borrow a term from Michael Polanyi's prescription for the scientific community.[31] The Church, like any other society, needs outside criticism, and depends on all the help that its thoughtful members can provide in the task of discerning the real meaning of the gospel for our time. Faith, then, is not simply a matter of accepting a fixed body of doctrine. More fundamentally, it is a committed and trustful participation in an ongoing process. In the course of responsible discussion, certain previously accepted doctrines will be modified. For progress to be achieved, there must be discussion, and for there to be discussion, all must be assured of

their "lawful freedom of inquiry and of thought, and of the freedom to express their minds humbly and courageously about those matters in which they enjoy competence."[32] Without such freedom, and thus without the possibility of dissent, the Church would be deprived of that creative interaction which, as we have seen, is the key to authentic renewal.

Notes

1. I. Kant, "What is Enlightenment?" in C. J. Friedrich, ed., *Kant's Moral and Political Writings* (New York: Modern Library, 1949), pp. 132–39.
2. See A. Dulles, *The Survival of Dogma* (Garden City: Doubleday, 1971; Image Books, 1973), esp. chap. 2 and 3.
3. William Chillingworth gave this principle its sharpest formulation: "The BIBLE, I say, the BIBLE only, is the Religion of Protestants" (*The Religion of Protestants, A Safe Way to Salvation*, published 1638). The so-called "material principle" of the Reformation, "Scripture alone," is ably criticized by Wolfhart Pannenberg in his essay "The Crisis of the Scripture Principle," *Basic Questions in Theology*, 1 (Philadelphia: Fortress, 1970), 1–14. But Pannenberg, here and elsewhere, tends to exalt the role of reason to the detriment of authority. His positions are best understood as a reaction against the excesses of the "theology of the word" in some sections of contemporary European Protestantism.
4. For a critique, see K. Rahner, "The Teaching Office of the Church in the Present-day Crisis of Authority," *Theological Investigations*, 12 (New York: Seabury, 1974), 3–30.
5. See Alois Müller, ed., *Democratization of the Church*, Concilium vol. 63 (New

York: Herder and Herder, 1971). A nuanced presentation of the problem is given by Patrick Granfield in his *Ecclesial Cybernetics: A Study of Democracy in the Church* (New York: Macmillan, 1973). While holding that the Catholic Church neither is nor should be a democracy (p. 186), Granfield contends that it is in need of "cybernetic reform through democratization" (p. 211). As a correction to the hierocratic model, this cybernetic model makes an important contribution.

6. *Lumen gentium,* § 12, in W. M. Abbott, ed., *The Documents of Vatican II* (New York: America Press, 1966), p. 29.

7. For a fuller statement of my position on this point see Dulles, *The Survival of Dogma,* chap. 5.

8. Y. Congar, "Norms of Christian Allegiance and Identity in the History of the Church," in E. Schillebeeckx, ed., *Truth and Certainty,* Concilium vol. 83 (New York: Herder and Herder, 1973), pp. 24–25.

9. *Dei Verbum,* § 10, in Abbott, p. 118.

10. See J. L. McKenzie, *Authority in the Church* (New York: Sheed and Ward, 1966), chap. 5.

11. A brief but very helpful study of the New Testament *episkopoi* may be found in R. E. Brown, *Priest and Bishop: Biblical Reflections* (New York: Paulist Press, 1970), esp. pp. 34–40.

12. See the paper drawn up by the International Theological Commission, "Apostolic Succession: A Clarification," *Origins,* 4, no. 13 (Sept. 19, 1974), 193–200.

13. Text in John Dedek, *Contemporary Medical Ethics* (New York: Sheed and Ward, 1975), p. 208.

14. Irenaeus, *Adversus haereses* 4.26.2, in *Patrologia Graeca* 7:1053; Eng. trans. in *The Ante-Nicene Fathers* (New York: Scribner's, 1899), vol. 1, p. 497.

15. Y. Congar, *Tradition and Traditions* (New York: Macmillan, 1967), p. 177. Congar is here following the view of K. Müller and D. van den Eynde. For an alternative interpretation see Louis Ligier, "*Le charisma veritatis certum des évêques,*" in *L'Homme devant Dieu: Mélanges offerts au Père Henri de Lubac* (Paris: Aubier, 1963), vol. 1, pp. 247–68; also Norbert Brox, "*Charisma veritatis certum,*" *Zeitschrift für Kirchengeschichte,* 75 (1964), 327–31.

16. On teaching authority in the Church of the apostolic age, see McKenzie, *Authority in the Church,* chaps. 5 and 6.

17. Myles M. Bourke, "Collegial Decision-making in the New Testament," in J. A. Coriden, ed., *Who Decides for the Church?* (Hartford: Canon Law Society of America, 1971), p. 13.

18. Thomas Aquinas, *In 4 Sent.,* Dist. 19, q. 2, a. 2, qua. 2, ad 4 (Parma ed., vol. 7, p. 852).

19. Thomas Aquinas, *Quodlibet* 3, qu. 4, art. 1 (Parma ed., vol. 9, p. 490).

20. See also Thomas Aquinas, *Contra Impugnantes Dei cultum et religionem,* chap. 2 (Parma ed., vol. 15, p. 7).

21. M. D. Chenu, " 'Authentica' et 'magistralia.' Deux lieux théologiques aux XII–XIII siècles," *Divus Thomas* (Piacenza), 28 (1925), 257–85. Cf. Chenu, *La théologie au douzième siècle,* 2nd ed. (Paris: Vrin, 1966), pp. 351–65.

22. Y. Congar, "Bref Histoire des Formes du 'Magistère' et ses relations avec les docteurs," *Rev. des sciences phil. et theol.,* 60 (1976), 104.

23. For some brief historical indications with further references see Dulles, *The Survival of Dogma,* chap. 6.

24. Collegial association of the members of the hierarchical magisterium and individual theologians is called for by the International Theological Commission in the fourth of its *Theses on the Relationship*

Between the Ecclesiastical Magisterium and Theology (Washington, D.C.: USCC, 1977), p. 3. An excellent discussion of current relationships may be found in A. L. Descamps, "Théologie et magistère," *Ephemerides theologicae lovanienses*, 52, no. 1 (June 1976), 82–133. In discussing the relations between bishops and theologians, one should not lose sight of what has been said earlier in this chapter about the authority of the whole body of the faithful. It goes without saying that both pastors and theologians should seek to maintain close contact with the laity, upon whom rests the chief burden of living out the faith in the circumstances of today's world.

25. I thus differ from those who hold that the Christian theologian need not write from the perspective of Christian belief and that the Christian texts should not function as norms for theology. David Tracy, in his *Blessed Rage for Order* (New York: Seabury Press, 1975), argues that the theologian's commitment should be to the "faith of secularity" which is shared in common by the secularist and the modern Christian (p. 8), and that the fundamental loyalty of the theologian should be to "that morality of scientific knowledge which he shares with his colleagues, the philosophers, historians, and social scientists" (p. 7). Tracy accordingly contends that the traditional Christian beliefs may not serve as warrants for theological arguments (ibid). Richard P. McBrien, in his review, rightly points out that Tracy's position apparently rests on a positivistic conception of "the Christian fact" and that it "seems to erase the difference between theology and philosophy" (*Com-*

monweal, 103, no. 25 [Dec. 3, 1976], 797–98). For a discussion of possible differences between Tracy and myself I refer again to my review article, "Method in Fundamental Theology," *Theological Studies,* 37 (1976), 304–16.

26. A brief catena of quotations from typical manualists and other "approved authors" of the period between the two Vatican Councils may be found in H. J. McSorley, "Some Ecclesiological Reflections on *Humanae vitae,*" *Bijdragen,* 30 (1969), 3–8. For a fuller discussion of the same theme see J. A. Komonchak, "Ordinary Papal Magisterium and Religious Assent," in C. E. Curran, ed., *Contraception: Authority and Dissent* (New York: Herder and Herder, 1969), pp. 101–26.

27. See "Some Ecclesiological Reflections on *Humanae vitae,*" McSorley, p. 3; Komonchak, "Ordinary Papal Magisterium and Religious Assent," pp. 104–5.

28. For some prudent reservations with regard to this last assertion, see L. J. O'Donovan, "Was Vatican II Evolutionary?" *Theological Studies,* 36 (1975), 493–502.

29. R. A. McCormick, "The Magisterium: A New Model," *America,* 122, no. 25 (June 27, 1970), 675. See also McCormick's fuller discussions of the magisterium and dissent in *Theological Studies,* 29 (1968), 714–18; 30 (1969), 644–68; and 38 (1977), 84–100; and in *Proceedings of the Catholic Theological Society of America,* 24 (1969), 239–54.

30. *Lumen gentium,* § 8, in Abbott, p. 24.

31. M. Polanyi, *The Tacit Dimension* (Garden City: Doubleday Anchor Books, 1967), pp. 53–92.

32. *Gaudium et spes,* § 62, in Abbott, p. 270.

27

Canon 752

A religious respect of intellect and will, even if not the assent of faith, is to be paid to the teaching which the Supreme Pontiff or the college of bishops enunciate on faith or morals when they exercise the authentic magisterium even if they do not intend to proclaim it with a definitive act; therefore the Christian faithful are to take care to avoid whatever is not in harmony with that teaching.

The text of canon 752 is reprinted from The Code of Canon Law: A Text and Commentary, *ed. J. Coriden, T. Green, D. Heintschel (New York: Paulist Press, 1986).*

28

Reflections on a Canon

Ladislas Orsy, SJ

In the Code of Canon Law, promulgated in 1983, there is a special section—entitled "The Teaching Office of the Church"—with several new canons in it. This article will focus on one of them. As always, new rules reflect new problems in the church; they are responses to emerging needs.

The problem of religious respect or submission to noninfallible teaching is with us more than ever before in history. Many factors have contributed to this situation. The progress in understanding and defining the scope and limits of the infallibility of the church, and of the role of the pope and of the episcopal college in exercising it, led to questions about the significance of their noninfallible pronouncements. Further, our age has produced many new questions concerning faith and morals to which there are no obvious answers in Christian tradition. The church itself must reflect and search, even make provisional statements, before it can come to a definitive judgment. Also, particularly since the 19th century, there has been a shift in the exercise of the teaching office of the See of Rome; besides acting as

judges in doctrinal disputes, the popes have assumed a greater initiative in clarifying Christian traditions in relation to new questions, which understandably has led to an expansion of noninfallible teaching.

In approaching the problem, history—and very recent history at that—has taught us to be cautious. Within living memory we have seen how some theologians, once silenced and penalized, have come to play a major role at Vatican II; we have seen also how noninfallible positions and pronouncements have been quietly reversed by the same council. Be that as it may, the problem of how to respond to noninfallible teaching is with us, and will remain so for a long time to come. New questions concerning faith and morals will continue to be addressed to the church. The church, not having the gift of sudden enlightenment, will seek answers as it can—through any honest means or method that faith and reason can find, such as prayer, reflection, disputes or debates. This is a complex and unique process in which every member of the social body must play its own proper part. It is

---

This article is reprinted from America *154 (May 17, 1986): 396–399.*

not to be compared to any kind of political operation; it is the way the living body of Christ on earth seeks understanding.

The purpose of this article is not to describe that process in all its details; far from it. It merely wants to point toward the complexity of the process, and does so on the basis of somewhat limited but still authentic information taken from the new Code of Canon Law.

Canon 752 is concerned with this specific issue: "When the pope or the episcopal college in the exercise of their authentic teaching office [*magisterium*] affirm [declare, enunciate] a doctrine concerning faith or morals without intending to proclaim it with a definitive act, [on the part of the faithful] no assent of faith but religious respect [in Latin: *obsequium;* compliance? submission?] of mind and will is due. The faithful, therefore, should avoid what is not congruent [*non congruit*] with such a doctrine."

The canon draws a sharp distinction between a doctrine that has been proclaimed with a definitive act, and a doctrine that has not been so affirmed. The former is really part of the profession of the faith of the church, even if it is not explicitly in any creed; the latter is not, although it is not lightly spoken. In the first case, the church has committed itself with a certainty that only faith can give; in the second case, it is still on the way toward such a certainty.

Accordingly, the canon says, the faithful must exercise discretion. If the church has committed itself, they too, in order to be one with the church, must do the same with an assent of faith. Such an assent is a surrender to God, revealing Himself and His kingdom to us—a surrender ultimately on the testimony of the Spirit, not on the strength of any argument.

If the church has not committed itself with an act of faith, the faithful, to be one with the church, must not do it either. Their response to the words of the teaching authority must be religious *obsequium*—a term that I provisionally translate as "respect" with the warning that its meaning certainly goes beyond a simple respect for another opinion, as we shall see later. Such a "respect," however, is not, and cannot be, a surrender to God speaking; it is a response to the church searching. Since there is a human element in this search, there must be one in the response, too. Arguments given by the teaching authority play their role.

In concrete cases, the distinction between the two types of doctrine, and consequently between the two types of response, may not be so clear as the canon makes it (law has a genius for simplifying issues in view of action); but the theoretical soundness of the distinction is not canceled out by the practical problems of its application.

At any rate, it is clear that the law asks for religious *obsequium* in response to noninfallible teaching, but it is not clear as yet what exactly this *obsequium* means. Since it is a response to noninfallible teaching, we should go beyond the field of law to have a better understanding of it, and see what the church is doing in so teaching.

Noninfallible teaching is intimately connected with the church's search for a better understanding of the evangelical message. John the Evangelist reports that Jesus said at His last supper: "I have yet many things to say to you but you cannot bear them now. When the Spirit of truth comes, he will guide you into all the truth" (Jn 16:13). That is, the Lord did not give the full understanding of the truth to the apostles, or to the primitive church. Rather, He set the believing community on the path toward it where it has remained ever since, searching, struggling, articulating: faith seeking understanding.

There is the paradox of the church: It is

endowed with divine gifts and it is subject to human limitations; it is in possession of the truth and it has to seek the truth.

This search is the task of the whole church. Vatican II could not have been more explicit about it: "The body of the faithful as a whole, anointed as they are by the Holy One (cf. Jn 2:20,27), cannot err in matters of belief. Thanks to a supernatural sense of the faith that characterizes the People as a whole, it manifests this unerring quality when 'from the bishops down to the last member of the laity,' it shows universal agreement in matters of faith and morals. For, by this sense of faith which is aroused and sustained by the Spirit of truth, God's People accepts not the word of men but the very Word of God (cf. 1 Th 2:13). It clings without fail to the faith once delivered to the saints (cf. Jude 3), penetrates it more deeply by accurate insights and applies it more thoroughly to life. All this it does under the lead of a sacred teaching authority to which it loyally defers" (Dogmatic Constitution on the Church, No. 12).

The search belongs to the whole body; all, head and members, should take part in it; all together, they should arrive at a fuller understanding of the mystery. In this process, a delicate and complex pattern of rights and duties arises. They are not juridical relations, but they are no less real for that.

The faithful have a right to be informed correctly, as far as possible, concerning what point of doctrine belongs to the core of our Christian beliefs and what does not. In the first case, their response ought to be a surrender to the Word of God, alive in the church. In the second case, it must be a religious *obsequium,* an attitude essentially different from an act of faith. This distinction is vital. If there is no surrender to God's invitation to believe, the "sacrament" of the Word of God cannot come alive in the life of the hearer; if there is an assent of faith when it is not due, a serious crisis of faith may arise later if the doctrine stated needs to be corrected, completed or perhaps abandoned. Many of the faithful experienced such a "crisis of faith" after Vatican II because "the teaching of the church has changed." In truth, our faith has not changed. The root of the crisis was in earlier misinformation. Points of doctrine that required an assent of faith and theological opinions that did not were indiscriminately proposed by less than well informed preachers as "the teaching of the church," and when the council reaffirmed the essential doctrines and modified or abandoned other theological opinions, the crisis followed inevitably.

Further, if the faithful have the capacity to penetrate the mysteries by accurate insights, and to apply the evangelical teaching more thoroughly to their lives on the strength of their baptismal consecration, they must have the right, not only to reflect in silence, but also to discuss their insights in the community. In this process, those who have the mandate to teach authentically also have the duty to listen; the episcopal college with the pope presiding can indeed be enlightened by the rest of the faithful. This duty to listen does not take away their right to be judges of the authenticity of the insights and applications proposed; for this, they have the assistance of the Spirit through their ordination. They can bring the search to a close, but as long as they have not done so, the search should go on.

The process of "faith seeking understanding" must be marked by truth and freedom. By truth: As far as possible, all preaching and teaching should carefully distinguish between doctrine to which the assent of faith is due and doctrine that must be "respectfully received" but without such an assent. By freedom: The capacity to penetrate the mysteries with deeper insights and apply them more thoroughly to life was given to the whole church. Hence, as far as it is possible, all should have the opportunity to contribute to the process. But this should be "under the lead of a sacred teaching authority," that is, under the successors of Peter and of the other apostles. Their insights have a special standing, due to the gentle assistance of the Spirit, even while they are searching. To confine this help only to the moment of their final judgment would be incorrect. Yet, the divine assistance in the searching stage is not so strong that their insights could not be completed or corrected.

This brings us to a better understanding of the text of the canon that speaks of a religious respect, *obsequium* of mind and will. The word cannot be given an easy and standard meaning. When the search for understanding is at its very beginning and the statements of the teaching authority are somewhat tentative (as they were, no doubt, in the case of the earliest declarations of the Biblical Commission), *obsequium* may not mean more than respectful listening and reflection on what has been "officially" stated—knowing that the church as a whole is still far from a final commitment. The scope for freedom must be great at that stage. When the search for a full understanding comes close to a clear vision and the minds and hearts in the church converge "from the bishops down to the last member of the laity," religious respect may well mean submission since the community is on the threshold of a surrender in faith.

We are in a better position now to raise the question about the meaning of "dissent" from noninfallible teaching. I wish that word "dissent" had never been used! It is too simple to carry the shades of meaning that a complex reality postulates. After all, as long as the pope and bishops have not committed themselves

and consequently have not bound the rest of the church, all are on the way toward the full truth. If "to dissent" means to offer at that stage particular insights that are different from the insights of those who are exercising teaching authority, we are not talking so much of dissent as of contribution toward a common assent that should eventually emerge from the search for "all the truth." Should the "dissenter" claim that he alone has the light, he would deny the communitarian nature of the search. Should the dissenter be unduly silenced, his valuable contribution may be lost.

Now it is easier to understand the last clause of the canon: "The faithful, therefore, should avoid what is not congruent with such a doctrine." Undoubtedly, it is not a call for an assent of faith. It is a call for *obsequium,* as it is fitting and due according to the nature of the case. At times, the voicing of a different opinion can be most congruent because it advances the search and thus helps to clarify the doctrine further; it would not be difficult to show that some of the writings of Cardinal Newman would fall into this category. At times it can be incongruent because it has little positive to offer and it disrupts the church; Archbishop Marcel Lefebvre's "dissent" from the noninfallible teaching of Vatican II would be a good example of this.

Two more ambiguities should be cleared up here: one is about "ordinary magisterium," another about "official teaching."

"Ordinary magisterium" had been used originally, especially in theological textbooks published before Vatican II, to describe infallible teaching by ordinary means; that is, not through an ecumenical council or solemn papal definition, but through constant affirmations over a long period of time. The response of the faithful to such "ordinary magisterium" ought to be an assent of faith. The mystery of the Assumption could be singled out as having been taught in this way before its solemn definition.

In more recent times, however, "ordinary magisterium" has acquired a new significance and an essentially different one at that. It is used more and more to mean noninfallible teaching as described in the second part of this canon: authentic but not definitive. The response can be only "religious respect."

Admittedly, in concrete cases the dividing line between the two meanings can be blurred, but it can be clear as well. Not to perceive this distinction may easily lead to an incorrect response.

"Official teaching" is a somewhat vague and all-embracing expression. It can mean a formal definition by an ecumenical council just as much as it can refer to an instruction by a Roman congregation. There is no way of saying what in a precise case the response to a piece of "official teaching" should be without a close examination of the source of the teaching and of its content.

That much for theory. Now some practical consequences can be drawn.

Simple statements—such as "a noninfallible statement can never bind" or "the official teaching always binds, infallible or not"—should be avoided. They do not do justice to a complex process. The particular importance of an issue, the progress already made, the weight of the reasons offered for a response—all such elements should be taken into consideration before the nature of a response to a particular point of teaching can be determined. While no "assent of faith" is ever due before a definitive proclamation, religious *obsequium* should be given, but in a degree that cannot be defined a priori; it may bind us to a respectful consideration of the teaching in one case, to readiness for submission in another case.

There should be an effort on the part of the church to educate the faithful in the understanding of these admittedly complicated matters. It can be done best by steadily explaining the nature of the church: a human community endowed with divine gifts, in possession of the truth and in the process of searching for a better understanding of it. To know and to love the church, the faithful must grasp, not only that it is of divine foundation, but that it is operating under human limitations. The Word of God has been handed over to human beings. No one should say that all this is too sophisticated for the ordinary faithful. They see the human side of the church anyway; the teachers' and preachers' task is to bring sense into what often appears as "not fitting for the church."

There should be no undue dichotomy between theory and practice. If the highest teaching authority, be it an ecumenical council, or the college of bishops, or the pope, has not committed itself with an act of faith to a particular belief, the faithful should not be compelled to do so either in the practical order. This may happen if a noninfallible doctrine is enforced by heavy disciplinary measures, or by an exclusion from offices, or by the denial of the sacraments to those who respect, but as yet have not adopted, the official position. Any such action would mean requiring an assent of faith in practice when it is not due in theory.

There are two ways of sinning against the teaching authority of the church: by downgrading it, or by upgrading it. To downgrade it means to deny the weight of authority that is present in a proclamation; to upgrade it means to project a strength into an official affirmation that the teacher himself has not put there.

For instance, if someone said that the council's Dogmatic Constitution on the Church is a mere exhortation, he would sin by downgrading an important conciliar document; or if someone said that the *Syllabus of Errors* of Pope Pius IX consists of dogmatic definitions, he would sin by upgrading the theological value of the statements contained in it. There is no virtue in either of these excesses; there is, however, an infidelity to the intention of the respective authors in both cases. In other terms, we are bound to give to every point of doctrine as much authority as the church has granted to it; neither less, nor more. Then, and then only, are we rooted in truth.

Finally, a most important conclusion that puts everything that has been said in this article into the right context: In the canon we examined, both the "assent of faith" and the "religious *obsequium*" appear as if they were legal obligations. In truth, they are the gifts of the Spirit. No one can surrender to God unless moved to do so by the Spirit. No one can responsibly participate in the church's search for a deeper understanding of the mysteries unless prompted to do so by the Spirit. The canon describes rather than prescribes the manifold gifts that enable the Christian community to respond to God's unfolding revelation.

29

Bishops, Theologians and Morality

Josef Ratzinger

The word "moral" is slowly beginning to regain a place of honor. For it is becoming ever more clear that we should not do everything we can do. It is becoming ever more evident that the peculiar sickness of the modern world is its failings in morality.

Recently a Russian author has said:

"Mankind today, with his dread of missiles, is like a man who lives in continual fear that his house will be burned down. He can think of nothing else but how to prevent the arson. In so doing, he does not notice that he has cancer. He will not die of arson, but by the inner decomposition of his body brought on by the alien organism of the cancer."

So mankind today, says this author, is in danger of being ruined from within, by his own moral decay. But instead of struggling against this life-threatening disease, he stares as though hypnotized at the external danger, which is only a byproduct of his own inner moral disease.

Still, it has become a rather common observation that the value placed upon technical expertise is out of all proportion when compared to the scant attention paid to moral development. Today we seem to know more about how to build bombs than how to judge whether it is moral to use them. This lack of proportion paid to morality is the key question of our day. Therefore, the renewal of morality is not just some rearguard action of a zealot opposed to progress, but the critical question upon which any real progress will depend.

Thus, during these days we will not be dealing with disputed points of interest only to the church, but rather we are standing at the very point where the church goes beyond herself. It is precisely when we look at her moral message that we can see that the church is not some kind of club for the satisfaction of social or even personal ideal needs. Rather, we see that she performs an essential service right in the midst of the turmoil which society is going through. She is not, in the first place, some kind of "moral institution." That is how they tried to describe her and to justify her

This article originally appeared in Origins 13 (March 15, 1984): 657, 659–666.

existence in the period of the Enlightenment. Nevertheless, she does have something to do with the moral resources of humanity. We could call these moral resources the most important raw material we have for human existence now and for making possible a future in which it will still be worthwhile to be a person.

The question which is posed by my theme might be formulated like this: What contribution can the church make toward forging a balance between external progress and morality? What can she do, not just to keep herself in existence, but to open up once again the moral resources of humanity? One might go so far as to say the church will survive only if she is in a position to help mankind overcome this hour of trial. In order to do this she must show herself as a moral power. And she must do this in two ways: She must set standards, and she must awaken both the will and the power of people to respond to these standards. In this context the question takes on a particular shape, namely, how can bishops work together with theologians, the bishops being charged with the transmission of the faith and the theologians being charged with the dialogue between the world of faith and the mind-set of the world at large?

It would be too facile to answer these questions with a few tactical formulas to produce a satisfactory agreement between those who are responsible for the decisions and the experts, even though it is so important to work out and make use of such practical rules. But it is not at all so easy to reproduce mechanically the general structural relationship between the competence to make decisions and expert knowledge. Each maintains its own form through the particular character of the matter involved. So it is necessary before searching for rules for collaboration between bishops

and moral theologians, first of all, to reflect— at least in very general outline—on the question of the sources and the method of moral knowledge. How can we arrive at moral knowledge at all? How do we arrive at correct moral judgments?

I. The Four Sources of Moral Knowledge and Their Problems

1. Reduction to "Objectivity"

When we come now to the question we have posed for ourselves concerning the method of moral knowledge, we see very clearly the poverty of the modern world about which we have already spoken: its lack of ideas when faced with the moral problem, the underdevelopment of moral reason as compared with calculating reason. A mark of modern society is specialization, which also includes a division of labor. This results in competence to acquire knowledge: In the individual fields of human knowledge and action the particular specialist is competent who, in the process of our ever-expanding and precise knowledge, manages to get an overview and an experience of a specific sector. But are there specialists in the field of morality, which does not admit of division of labor, when they all proceed each in his own way?

A division of labor in the area of knowledge presumes a quantification of the object of knowledge. One might think here of Henry Ford's famous assembly line. Every worker performs a specific task in the overall construction of the Model T. No one worker can build a whole car, much less design one, or even know how the mechanism functions.

One can divide and distribute only that which has become quantity. The success of modern science is based on the translation of the reality we encounter into quantitative measures. In this way the world becomes measurable and technologically exploitable. But could we not say that the crisis of humanity in our times finds its roots in this method and in its increasing domination in all aspects of human life? Calculation, which in turn is subject to what is quantitative, is the method of what is not free. It works when we are dealing with what can be calculated, ordered and necessary. It is good for building cars.

If morality, however, is the area of freedom and if its norms are laws of freedom, then inevitably these laws will not be sufficient for us: They must leave us perplexed in the face of that which is truly human. A simple answer suggests itself here. Perhaps freedom is only an illusion, the remains of an old dream of humanity from which, for better or for worse, we must separate ourselves. Does not everything point to the fact that man, caught up in the physical and biological net of reality, is thoroughly determined? Must not a complete enlightenment lead to a situation in which even in mankind morality will be replaced by technique, that is, by a correct ordering and combination of predetermined elements which will then yield the desired result?

And so there emerges the thought of calculating human behavior to analyze the predetermined state which is proper and fundamental to man and so to discover a formula for happiness and survival. Statistics and planning together provide the new "morality" with which man prepares his way into the future. All moral rules, which man could then calculate, would thus be directed to those ends which man himself has in mind for humanity. Just as man designs technical tools for his own purposes, so in the area of morality he imposes his own goals on the laws of nature.

But here the decisive question remains open: Who determines the goals? Who plans the future of man? Granted there are many who are powerful who would gladly arrogate this right to themselves, no one of us has the right to do so. Who then could have the right to oblige all men to pursue one particular goal or another? At this point we must postpone attempts to answer the question of the sources of morality, but this is not to imply that it is either resolved or unessential.

A second question now emerges: If there are ends which man must pursue, how does he know them? It should be clear that we cannot reduce moral knowledge to some model of knowledge in general, understood as the calculation and combination of known measures which are demonstrable because of their repetition.

Obviously it cannot be disputed that a good amount of useful data about mankind and the world can, nevertheless, be gathered in this way. But since human behavior is not at all so easy to repeat or reproduce identically in others, any attempt to subject human behavior to a purely scientific analysis encounters sooner or later an insurmountable limitation: namely, the limitations of humanity itself, which is after all what we are discussing.

Only at the price of ignoring what is precisely human could the question of morality be analyzed in the ordinary way of human knowing. The fact that this is actually being attempted in various quarters today is the great inner threat to mankind today. The tree of knowledge from which man eats in this case does not give the knowledge of good and evil, but rather blinds man to discerning the difference between them. Man will not return to paradise through such blindness, because it is not based on a purer humanity, but on the rejection of humanity.

2. Subjectivity and Conscience

We see then that in the question of morality there cannot be experts in the same way as there can be in microelectronics or computer science. Plato realized that when he said that a person cannot express "with scholastic words" what the word "good" means. But in what other way can we learn it?

There are a number of suggestions here which must be examined in order, but briefly. It is only in the convergence of the various ways that we can find the way itself.

To begin with, there is today a broadly accepted alternative to the complete objectification of moral knowledge, whose shortcomings we have just seen. In one sector of modern thinking we have the strange situation where man, faced with both the greatness and the limitations of quantitative analysis, tries to overcome the distinction between the subject and object. We can calculate the world since and to the extent that we make it an "object." Opposed to this "objective," which is what can be studied by science, there remains the "subjective," the world of the incalculable and the free. In this division of the world, religion and morality are relegated to the world of the subjective. They are subjective in the sense that they cannot be analyzed by science nor placed within the generally valid criteria of ordinary knowledge. In this view the subjective really does exist, though the ultimate analysis of it is up to the individual's imagination to decide.

Obviously in such a reduction of morality to the subjective it becomes impossible to address the objective concerns of our day which demand a moral answer. To that extent, this approach to the problem is losing favor today. Still, in practical life and especially in the discussion within the church itself, it still plays an important role, insofar as here the subjection of morality to the area of the subjective has become linked with the long Christian tradition of the teaching on conscience.

Conscience is understood by many as a sort of deification of subjectivity, a rock of bronze on which even the magisterium is shattered. It is said that in light of the conscience, no other cases apply. Conscience appears finally as subjectivity raised to the ultimate standard.

We will have to examine this question in closer detail, as it already touches directly the precise theme of my talk. For the moment, however, I note that conscience is presented as one source of moral knowledge, that is to say, a personal, primitive knowledge of good and evil which appears in the individual man as a source of his ability to make moral judgments.

3. The Will of God and His Revelation

If we follow a little further the pathway of conscience as we find it in the tradition, then we encounter another fundamental element in the moral area. The idea of conscience cannot be separated in its history from the idea of the responsibility of man before God.

To a great extent it expresses the thought of a kind of co-knowledge of man with God, and precisely from here there emerges the absoluteness with which conscience asserts its superiority over any and all authorities. The history of morality is inseparably linked with the history of thought about God. As far as the fixed character of the natural laws is concerned, morality means the free "yes" given by one will to another, in this case, the conformity of man to the will of God and the consequent correct perception of things as they really are. As an ultimate source of morality, then, we have to take into consideration the process of how God makes his desires for mankind known, how one acquires knowledge of the divine commandments in which the special ends of man and the world become clear. If such objective morality is based on revelation, then immediately the next question arises: How can one know revelation as revelation? How can revelation be identified as such?

4. The Community as a Source of Morality

Here we meet with another factor which has played and still plays an extremely important role in the working out of various moral theories. The Latin word *mores* without any distinction contains meanings which we have learned to distinguish carefully: Mores are the habits, customs and lifestyle of a people, practically what we would call today "the American way of life" or the "California style." At the same time, alongside the totality of life habits, the word also has a specifically moral meaning.

When St. Augustine, for example, wrote *De Moribus Ecclesiae et de moribus Manichaeorum,* it was not a question of comparative morality in today's sense. Rather, in making a comparison between the form of life of the Catholic Church, her total lifestyle, and that of the Manicheans, he goes on to distinguish two distinct types of morality within the broader context of lifestyle. Likewise, in the language of the Council of Trent the formula *fides et mores* does not simply mean faith and morals in today's sense of the terms, but rather in the broader sense in which the customs of the life of the church, including moral order in the strict sense, are understood.

In this use of language something very important appears: "Morality" is not an abstract code of norms for behavior, but it presupposes a community way of life within which morality itself is clarified and is able to be observed. Historically considered, morality does not belong to the area of subjectivity, but is guaranteed by the community and has a reference to the community. In the lifestyle of a community the experience of generations is stored up: experiences of things which can build up a society or tear it down, how the happiness of an individual and the continuity of the community as a whole can be brought together in a balanced way and how that equilibrium can be maintained.

Every morality needs its "we," with its prerational and suprarational experiences, in which not only the analysis of the present moment speaks, but rather in which the wisdom of the generations converges.

A crisis in morality occurs in a community when new areas of knowledge emerge which the current life patterns cannot cope with, to the point that what up until then appeared as supportive and proven appears now as insufficient, or indeed as contradictory or as an obstacle to the new knowledge and reality. Then the question arises, how can the community find a new way of life which will once more make possible a common moral existence for life and for the world itself. It remains true that morality needs a "we" and that it requires a link with the experience of past generations and with the primitive wisdom of humanity.

And so we return to the question from which we began, namely, the problem of revelation. We can make this assertion: The various concrete community experiences of different races and peoples are valuable as signposts for human behavior, but by themselves cannot be considered sources for morality. It is impossible in the long run to have a society which lives, as it were, only as a reaction from what is negative and evil. If a society wishes to survive, it must to a certain extent return to the primitive virtues, to the basic standard models of humanity.

Still, it is certainly possible for important areas of life in a society to become corrupt, so that the predominant custom of men and women does not guide but seduces. A society with the custom of cannibalism, slavery or dependence on drugs. An individual can rely on his own experience and on the common historical experiences only to a limited degree. In history, therefore, morality was never based exclusively on experience and custom. Its unconditional character could not be understood except in reference to the unconditional character of God's will: In the last analysis, morality was founded on a divine revelation of will, out of which alone a community could emerge and in accord with which the survival of the community as such was guaranteed.

I must leave aside at this point a series of questions which really ought to be asked, so that I can return to my particular theme. Despite the fragmentary nature of these reflections so far, we can nevertheless see that the faith of the church is in agreement with the fundamental traditions of humanity on several points. Christian faith is also convinced that God alone can be the measure of man and that only the divine will can unconditionally oblige man. Christian faith is further convinced that revelation situates us in the community life model of a "we" whose nature and direction cannot be explained simply in terms of the human will alone.

Clearly the Christian looks at this "we," whose customs constitute the proximate source of moral knowledge, not simply in terms of his own local society, but in terms of a new society which can be explained only through revelation and which transcends all local societies (it is "catholic") and which subordinates them to the dictates of the divine will which are addressed to them all.

With this as a context, one can experience what morality is by seeking in the first place the *mores ecclesiae*: Thus the person who is by virtue of his office responsible for the form of life of the church—the bishop—in Catholic tradition bears the principal responsibility for teaching Christians morals as well as faith. It also means that in the area of morality those who have the greatest right to speak are those who live according to the deepest essence of the church to the most profound degree—the saints. But with these remarks I have moved on too quickly. I simply wanted to note the fact that we are still working toward our theme, even though it may seem that our aim has disappeared in the individual points of this reflection. Perhaps it would be good at this point to sum up what we have seen, so that then, as far as we can, we can move on to the concrete implications of all of this.

We have located four sources of morality. If taken in isolation from each other, each leaves several questions unanswered.

But when they are taken in combination, then the path of moral knowledge opens up before us. If on one hand we have to conclude that authentic morality cannot be constructed on the basis of an examination of the concrete world alone, still morality must be concerned with objective morality since moral behavior must do justice to truth. It is in this way that reality—and reason which knows and explains reality—is without a doubt an irreplaceable source of morality.

As a second source, we spoke of conscience.

The wisdom of tradition is a third source, embodied in a living "we," an active community which for the Christian is concretely realized in the new community of the church. Finally we saw that all these sources lead to true morality when the will of God is present. For in the final analysis, only the will of God can establish the boundary between good and evil, which is something different from the boundary between what is useful or not or what is proven and what is unknown. The Catholic Church sees an important confirmation of her teaching in the fact that within her these elements interpenetrate and illumine each other. Her teaching brings conscience to expression. Conscience is seen to be valid precisely because it incorporates the inner truth of things in accord with reality, which is after all the voice of the Creator.

These three things, objectivity, tradition and conscience, in turn point to the divine commandments.

These commandments on one hand constitute the basis of the church's teaching, they form consciences and make reality intelligible. On the other hand, because they correspond to reality as perceived by conscience, they are for their part able to be confirmed as true revelations of the divine will.

II. Second Principal Problem: Conscience and Objectivity

No doubt it might be observed that what I have just said is an idealization of a reality which in fact is not all that harmonious. A number of nuances would have to be added in order to be more realistic. Two main objections, related to the first two of the four sources of morality, tend now to arise.

There is the rather common impression that the church is not in a position to respond in a correct manner to reality in today's world. In-

stead of listening to the language of reality, she is immovably chained to antiquated points of view which she tries to impose on men. Right here a conflict arises between the bishop and the expert. In many ways this conflict appears to be a conflict between a doctrine which is distant from reality and an exact understanding of current reality.

The second objection comes from the area of conscience: The consciences of many Christians are by no means in harmony with many expressions of the church's magisterium. Indeed it often seems that the conscience is that which gives dissent some legitimacy.

So then if we wish to arrive at a clear position as regards the function of the bishop as teacher of morality and his relationship to the experts in moral theology, then it is necessary, if only in rough outline, to look into the two questions which have arisen: What is conscience? And how can one learn which form of behavior corresponds to things as they really are, to reality, and is thus moral behavior in the meaningful sense of the term?

1. What Is Conscience and How Does It Speak?

When one speaks of conscience today, three principal streams of thought come to mind. We have already touched on the first of these. For conscience asserts the right of subjectivity which can in no way be measured objectively. But in response there immediately arises the objection: Who establishes such an absolute right of subjectivity? It may indeed have a relative right, but in really important cases must not that right be sacrificed to an objective common good of the highest level?

It is strange that some theologians have difficulty accepting the precise and limited doctrine of papal infallibility, but see no problem in granting *de facto* infallibility to everyone who has a conscience.

In fact it is not possible to assert an absolute right for subjectivity as such.

Conscience also signifies in some way the voice of God within us.

With this notion the completely inviolable character of the conscience is established: In conscience we have a case which would be above any human law. The fact of such a direct bond between God and man gives man an absolute dignity. But then the question arises, does God speak to men in a contradictory manner? Does he contradict himself? Does he forbid one person, even to the point of martyrdom, to do something which he allows or even requires from another?

It is clear that it is not possible to justify the equation of the individual judgments of conscience with the voice of God. Conscience is not an oracle.

We now encounter a third meaning: Conscience is the superego, the internalization of the will and the convictions of others who have formed us and have so impressed their will on us that it no longer speaks to us externally, but rather from deep within our inner self. In this situation conscience would not be a real source of morality at all, but only the reflection of the will of another, an alien guide within ourselves. Conscience would not then be an organ of freedom, but an internalized slavery from which man would logically have to free himself in order to discover the breadth of his real freedom.

Even though one might explain many individual expressions of conscience in this way, this theory cannot stand completely.

On one hand we find children, before they are formally educated, who react spontaneously against injustice. They give a spontaneous "yes" to what is good and true which precedes any educational interventions, which often enough only darken them or crush them rather than let them grow. On the other hand, there are mature men and women in whom one finds a freedom and an alertness of conscience which sets itself against what has been learned or what is commonly done. Such a conscience has become an inner sense of what is good, a kind of remote control to guide him through what he has been taught.

What is the real position of conscience? Conscience is an organ, not an oracle. It is an organ because it is something which for us is a given, which belongs to our essence and not something which has been made outside of us. But because it is an organ, it requires growth, training and practice. I find the comparison with speech is very fitting in this case. Why do we speak? We speak because we have learned to speak from our parents. We speak the language which they taught us, though we realize there are other languages which we cannot speak or understand. The person who has never learned to speak is mute. And yet language is not an external conditioning which we have internalized, but rather something which is properly internal to us.

It is formed from outside, but this formation responds to the given of our own nature, that we can express ourselves in language. Man is as such a speaking essence, but he becomes so only insofar as he learns speech from others. In this way we encounter the fundamental notion of what it means to be a man: Man is "a being who needs the help of others to become what he is in himself" (R. Spaemann).

We see this fundamental anthropological structure once again in conscience. Man is in himself a being who has an organ of internal knowledge about good and evil. But for it to become what it is, it needs the help of others. Conscience requires formation and education. It can become stunted, it can be stamped out, it can be falsified so that it can only speak in a stunted or distorted way. The silence of conscience can become a deadly sickness for an entire civilization.

In the Psalms we meet from time to time the prayer that God should free man from his hidden sins. The psalmist sees as his greatest danger the fact that he no longer recognizes them as sins and thus falls into them in apparently good conscience. Not being able to have a guilty conscience is a sickness, just as not being able to experience pain is a sickness. And thus one cannot approve the maxim that everyone may always do what his conscience allows him to do: In that case the person without a conscience would be permitted to do anything. In truth it is his fault that his conscience is so broken that he no longer sees what he as a man should see.

In other words, included in the concept of conscience is an obligation, namely, the obligation to care for it, to form it and educate it. Conscience has a right to respect and obedience in the measure in which the person himself respects it and gives it the care which its dignity deserves. The right of conscience is the obligation of the formation of conscience. Just as we try to develop our use of language and we try to rule our use of rules, so must we also seek the true measure of conscience so that finally the inner word of conscience can arrive at its validity.

For us this means that the church's magisterium bears the responsibility for correct formation. It makes an appeal, one can say, to the inner vibrations its word causes in the process of the maturing of conscience. It is thus an oversimplification to put a statement of the magisterium in opposition to conscience. In such a case I must ask myself much more. What is it in me which contradicts this word of the magisterium? Is it perhaps only my comfort? My obstinance? Or is it an estrange-

ment through some way of life which allows me something which the magisterium forbids and which appears to me to be better motivated or more suitable simply because society considers it reasonable? It is only in the context of this kind of struggle that the conscience can be trained and the magisterium has the right to expect that the conscience will be open to it in a manner befitting the seriousness of the matter.

If I believe that the church has its origins in the Lord, then the teaching office in the church has a right to expect that it, as it authentically develops, will be accepted as a priority factor in the formation of conscience. There corresponds to this then an obligation of the magisterium to speak its word in such a way that it will be understood in the midst of conflicts of values and orientations. It must express itself in such a way that an inner resonance of its word may be possible within the conscience, and this means more than just an occasional declaration of the highest level. Here we need what Plato was referring to when he said the good cannot be known scholastically, but only after regular familial discussion can the notion of the good spring into the soul like light springing from a small spark (Seventh Letter). This constant "familial discussion" within the church must build up the community conscience—those who try to express their word in the teaching office, as well as those who wish to learn that word from within themselves.

2. *Nature, Reason and Objectivity*

Thus we have already arrived at the other point which I want to touch on: The word of the magisterium is for many Christians today no longer plausible because its reasonableness and objectivity are no longer transparent. The magisterium is accused of setting out from an outdated understanding of reality. Like the old Stoics, the magisterium argues from "nature." But this expression "nature" has been completely surpassed with the entire metaphysical age.

At first, this so-called naturalism of the magisterial tradition was seen in opposition to the personalism of the Bible. The opposition of nature and person as a basic pattern for argumentation was at the same time seen as an opposition between philosophical and biblical tradition. Still it has now long been recognized that there is no such thing as a pure "biblicism" and that even "personalism" has its own philosophical aspects. Today we see almost the direct opposite movement: The Bible has to a great extent vanished from the modern works in moral theology. In its place a tendency toward a particularly strong rational analysis has become dominant, together with the assertion of the autonomy of morals, which is based neither on nature nor on the person, but on historicity and future-oriented models of social behavior.

One must try to discover what is socially compatible and what serves the building of a future human society. The "reality" on which "objectivity" is based is seen no longer as a nature which precedes man, but rather in the world which he himself has structured, which one may now simply analyze and from which one may extrapolate what the future will bring. Here we come up against the real reason why Christianity today, not only in the area of the moral, to a great extent lacks direct plausibility. As we have already seen, as a result of the philosophical change introduced by Kant, the division of reality into subjective and objective has become dominant.

The objective is not simply reality in itself, but reality only inasmuch as it is the object of our thought and is thus measurable and can be calculated. The subjective, for its part, eludes "objective" explanation. This means, however, that the reality we encounter speaks only the language of human calculation, but has within itself no moral expression. The constantly expanding radical forms of the theory of evolution lead to the same conclusion, though from a different starting point: The world presupposes no reason; what is reasonable in it is the result of a combination of accidents whose ongoing accumulation then developed a kind of necessity.

According to such a viewpoint, the world contains no meaning, but only goals, which are posited by evolution itself. If the world is thus a montage of static appearances, then the highest moral directive it can then give to man is that he himself should be engaged in some kind of montage of the future and that he himself should direct everything according to what he reckons is useful. The norm thus lies always in the future: In this view the greatest possible betterment of the world is the only moral commandment.

In contrast, the church believes that in the beginning was the *Logos* and that therefore being itself bears the language of the *Logos,* not just mathematical, but also aesthetical and moral reason. This is what is meant when the church insists that "nature" has a moral expression. No one is saying that biologism should become the standard of man. That viewpoint has been recommended only by some behavioral scientists.

The church professes herself the advocate of the reason of creation and practices what she means when she says: I believe in God, the Creator of Heaven and Earth. There is a reason for being, and when man separates himself from it totally and recognizes the reason only of what he himself has made, then he abandons what is precisely moral in the strict sense.

In some way or another we are beginning to realize that materiality contains a spiritual expression and that it is not simply for calculation and use. In some way we see that there is a reason which precedes us which alone can keep our reason in balance and can keep us from falling into external unreason.

In the last analysis, the language of being, the language of nature, is identical with the language of conscience. But in order to hear that language it is necessary, as with all language, to practice it. The organ for this, however, has become deadened in our technical world. This is why there is a lack of plausibility here. The church would betray not only her own message, but the destiny of humanity if she were to renounce being the guardian of being and its moral message. In this sense she may be opposed to what is "plausible," but at the same time she stands for the most profound claims of reason. It becomes obvious here that reason also is an organ and not an oracle. And reason too requires training and community.

Whether a person is able to attribute reason to being and to decipher his own moral dimension depends on whether he answers the question about God. If the *Logos* of the beginning does not exist, neither can there be any *Logos* in things. What Kolakowski recently discovers then becomes emphatically true: When there is no God, there is no morality and in fact no mankind either. In this sense, in the deeper analysis, everything depends on God, on a God who is Creator and on a God who has revealed himself. For this reason, once again, we need the community which can guarantee God, who no one on his own could dare bring into his life.

Even Abraham, our father in faith, was not being completely innovative when he introduced monotheism 2,000 years before Christ. Even that primitive society already cherished its belief in the divine.

The question of God, which is the central point, is not a question for specialists. The perception of God is precisely that simplicity which the specialists can never monopolize, but rather which can be perceived only by maintaining a simplicity of vision. Perhaps we find it so difficult today to deal with the essence of humanity because we have ceased being capable of simplicity.

Therefore, morality requires not the specialist, but the witness. The position of the bishop as teacher rests on this: He teaches not what he himself has discovered.

But he witnesses to the life wisdom of faith in which the primitive wisdom of humanity is cleansed, maintained, deepened. Through contact with God, depending on how perceptive the conscience is, this primitive human knowledge becomes a real vehicle of communication with truth by means of the communion it shares with the conscience of the saints and with the knowledge of Jesus Christ.

Naturally it does not follow from this that scientific work regarding the criteria of morality and specialized knowledge in this area have become unnecessary. Since conscience requires training, since tradition must be lived and must develop in times of change and since moral behavior is a response to reality and therefore requires a knowledge of reality, for all these reasons the observation and study of reality as well as the traditions of moral thought are important. To put it another way, to seek a thorough knowledge of reality is a fundamental commandment of morality. It was not without reason that the ancients placed prudence as the first cardinal virtue: They understood it to mean the willingness and the capacity to perceive reality and to respond to it in an objective manner.

III. Applications

Now that we have considered all of this, we can formulate the essential tasks of both bishop and specialized theologian in moral questions and from this will automatically emerge the rules for their working together in a correct manner.

1. The Bishop as Teacher of Morality

a) The bishop is a witness to the *mores Ecclesiae Catholicae,* to those rules of life which have grown up in the common experience of the believing conscience in the struggle with God and with historical reality. As a witness the bishop must in the first place know this tradition in its foundations, its content and its various stages. One can only bear witness to what one knows. The knowledge of the essential moral tradition of the faith is therefore a fundamental demand of the episcopal office.

b) Since it is a question of a tradition which comes from conscience and speaks to conscience, the bishop himself must be a man of a seeing and listening conscience. He must strive, in living the *mores Ecclesiae Catholicae,* to see that his own personal conscience is sharpened. He must know morality not second, but firsthand. He must not simply pass on a tradition, but bear witness to what has become for himself a credible and proven lifestyle.

c) Setting out from such a personal knowledge of the moral word of the church, he must attempt to remain in discussion with those experts who seek the correct application of the simple words of faith to the complicated reality of a particular time. He must therefore be prepared to become a learner and a critical partner of the experts. He must learn to see

where it is a question of the knowledge of new realities, new problems, new possibilities for understanding and so for maturing and cleansing the moral heritage. He must be critical when expert science forgets its own boundaries or reduces morality to a simple specialization.

2. The Tasks of the Moral Theologian

On the basis of our reflections so far, we might define the tasks of the moral theologian in the following manner:

a) As a theologian, the moral theologian also finds his starting point in the *mores Ecclesiae Catholicae* which he researches and which, in their essential link with what is Catholic, he distinguishes. And so he also tries to recognize in the mores that which is specifically moral and constant and to understand them in a unified way in the total context of the faith. He seeks the *ratio fidei.*

b) He then brings this reason of faith in a critical way into dialogue with the reason and the plausibility of the particular time. He helps toward the understanding of the moral demands of the Gospel in the particular conditions of his day and so serves the formation of conscience. In this way he serves also the development, purification and deepening of the moral message of the church.

c) Above all, the moral theologian will also take up the new questions which new developments and relationships pose for the traditional norms. He will attempt to know precisely the objective components of such discussions (for example, the technology of armaments, economic problems, medical developments, etc.) in order to work out the best way to pose the questions and so to arrive at the relationship with the constants of the moral tradition of the faith.

In this sense he stands in critical dialogue with the moral evaluations of society and in all this he helps the teaching office of the church to present its moral message in the particular time.

3. *The Relationship Between Bishop and Theologian*

From our reflections on the individual tasks it is now possible to derive the fundamental rules for the relationship between teaching office and expert.

a) The teaching office depends on the specialized knowledge of the experts and must let itself be thoroughly informed by them about the content of the matter in question before making an utterance regarding new problems. The teaching office must therefore not be too hasty in taking up a position regarding questions that are not yet clarified nor must it apply its binding statements beyond what the principles of tradition permit.

On the other hand, the teaching office of the church must defend man against himself to prevent his destruction even if this means opposing the philosophy of an entire epoch. For example, in a period in which the world thinks of itself only as a product and as an end, the teaching office of the church must continually try to get nature to be recognized as creation in its defense of the unborn. There is an obligation to information, an obligation to respect the boundaries of universally binding moral statements and an obligation to witness. The moral catechesis must go beyond that which can be determined with certainty and should offer models of behavior in concrete circumstances (casuistry).

But it seems important to me clearly to distinguish between these cases and the specific moral teaching. I have the impression that the regular and unnuanced introduction of cases into the specific moral statement or likewise the failure to distinguish between them has contributed to discrediting the moral teaching of the church in our century in a substantial way.

b) But the task of the moral theologian is not simply being in service to the teaching office. It also stands in dialogue with the ethical questions of the time and contributes, through the development of models of behavior, to the process of the formation of conscience. As regards the magisterium, his task is to precede it: He goes before it, noticing new questions, gathering knowledge of their objective content and preparing answers. The moral theologian likewise accompanies the magisterium and follows it, bringing its pronouncements into the dialogue of his time and relating the basic lines of the discussion to concrete situations.

4. *Criticism of the Magisterium: Its Rules and Limits*

Today interest in the relationship between the episcopal magisterium and scientific theology is concentrated above all on the question: Can the moral theologian criticize the teaching office?

After what we have said about the structure of moral expression and about its relationship to specialized science, we must distinguish:

a) First of all, we must apply here what the Second Vatican Council said about the steps of assent and in like manner the stages of criticism with regard to church teaching. Criticism may be framed according to the level and demands of the magisterial teaching. It will be all the more helpful when it fills in a lack of information, clarifies shortcomings of the linguistic or conceptual presentation and at the same time deepens the insight into the limits and range of the particular teaching.

b) In the light of our reflection, on the other hand, we see that it is not for the expert himself to draw up norms or to annul the norms, perhaps by setting up factions or pressure groups. As we have seen, norms can only be witnessed to, but not produced or annulled by some calculated analysis. When this happens the peculiar nature of morality itself is misunderstood. Therefore, dissent can only have meaning in the area of casuistry, not in the specific area of norms. The most important thing in the relationship between the magisterium and moral theology appears to me, in the last analysis, to lie in what Plato recommends as the path to moral knowledge, in "regular familial discussion," a discussion in which we must all learn to become more and more hearers of the biblical word, vitally addressed and directed to the *mores Ecclesiae Catholicae.*

30

The Search for Truth in a
Catholic Context

Richard A. McCormick, SJ

The Sept. 27, 1986, issue of The New York
Times headlined an article, "The Vatican and
Dissent in America." The Chicago Sun Times
of Sept. 28 featured a long report with the title
"Catholics in Conflict: Papal Crackdown Ex-
poses Bitter Split in the U.S. Church." The
Sept. 28 Chicago Tribune carried an article on
Archbishop Rembert G. Weakland of Mil-
waukee entitled "Archbishop Asks Rome to
Ease Up." The Sept. 28 New York Times pre-
sented this headline: "Two Bishops Weighing
Vatican Trip to Tell of Turmoil in Seattle
Area."

And so it goes across the country. Because
the ink has flowed so freely in recent weeks, it
is safe to say that most people are at least
passingly aware of the dramatis personae and
the storyline. The actors are chiefly three: the
Vatican, the Catholic University theologian
Charles E. Curran and Seattle Archbishop
Raymond G. Hunthausen. The bare facts of
the storyline: Father Curran was stripped of
his "canonical mission" (his juridical approval

to teach as a Catholic theologian), and Archbishop Hunthausen's episcopal authority in
five important areas (marriage tribunal, moral
issues involving homosexuals and health care
institutions, liturgy and worship, seminary and
clergy formation, and the departure of priests)
was transferred to recently appointed Auxiliary Bishop Donald W. Wuerl.

To view these incidents as isolated and
unrelated because they concern individuals in
distinct places and areas of concern would be
tempting but shortsighted. I am not referring
to an orchestrated brush-up of the American
church. I am referring to these interventions in
terms of their implications and fallout. From
this perspective they raise issues of the first
magnitude for the American church. The basic
question they pose is: "How is the search for
truth to be conducted in the Catholic context?" By "truth" I mean especially moral
truths, because they are the chief concerns.
The fact that Archbishop Hunthausen acts
largely at the pastoral level and Father Curran

This article originally appeared in America 155 (*November 8, 1986): 276–281.*

at the theological should not distract us from the coincidence of concerns raised by their distinct searches. As Roberto Suro worded it: "The concern most often raised by Vatican officials involves the leadership of the church in the United States, and both the Archbishop Hunthausen and Father Curran matters fall into this realm" (The New York Times, Sept. 27). The questioned leadership is heavily in the moral sphere.

Both Father Curran and Archbishop Hunthausen have provided their own answers to this question in their respective spheres. Father Curran has said that public theological dissent is essential to that search. The matter is less clear in Archbishop Hunthausen's case because the indictments remain fuzzy. But unless I am badly mistaken, Archbishop Hunthausen has been saying by his pastoral procedures that some of the following are essential to the search: compassionate understanding of human weakness and failure, patient and attentive listening, trusting proportionate responsibility to others, playing it loose as things work out and making bold, symbolic protest in some instances. The trouble is, or seems to be, that these responses are read by some as laxness on doctrine.

Let me say at the outset that I agree in principle with Father Curran and Archbishop Hunthausen—"in principle" because both not only tolerate but encourage debate about details and particulars as part of their search. Because the issues are of such gravity for the American church, and because they are dominantly theological, I want to list 10 points that structure my own agreement with Father Curran and Archbishop Hunthausen, as well as my profound disappointment at the silence of most bishops on these matters—notable exceptions are Archbishop Weakland, Bishop Matthew H. Clark of Rochester, N.Y., and

Thomas J. Gumbleton, Auxiliary Bishop of Detroit. It would be highly imaginative to expect agreement on all of these points. But if they provoke more precise and enlightened disagreement, they will have served a useful purpose.

The search for truth does have a "Catholic context." This point might seem quaintly parochial. Truth is, after all, truth. There are well-accepted canons for its pursuit in the scientific community at all levels—historical, scientific, literary, philosophical, theological. Furthermore, earthly realities enjoy their own autonomy, as Vatican II expressly insisted. How, then, does the "Catholic context" make any difference in the search for truth?

The "Catholic context" makes a difference because theology is precisely theology. It is reflection on faith and its behavioral implications. In this sense, theology differs from other disciplines. The facts (truths) that found and energize the believing community and influence its moral behavior are not like data from other disciplines. They concern God's nature, intentions and actions as experienced and interpreted by a historical religious community.

Catholics believe that Christ established His church with teaching authority as a protection against the opaqueness, weakness and other vulnerabilities of the human spirit. This authority roots in the conviction about the presence of the Spirit to the whole church, but it is thought to be enjoyed in a special way by its pastors. One classic way of stating the claims of the hierarchy's ordinary use of this authority (and by "ordinary" I mean without the claim of infallibility, which is the way of most church teaching, certainly moral teaching) is to say that it enjoys the presumption of the truth. This presumption in turn generates a particular response from Catholics. It is a type of respect that most often translates factually into assent or acceptance. To deny this presumption is evidently to deny the authority itself. This authoritative teaching dimension is the chief reason for speaking of the "Catholic context" in the search for moral truth. To reject such a context is to misunderstand either theology and/or its Catholic specification.

But there the consensus ends and the face-off begins. My following nine points will touch dimensions of these disagreements. It must suffice here to underline the term "presumption" in the phrase "presumption of truth." Presumptions are not carved in granite. Presumptions can be and have been undermined by further consideration, changed facts, the presence of human folly and other factors. In a word, so-called official teaching enjoys this presumption to the extent that the undermining factors have been avoided insofar as is humanly possible. This is especially the case in the moral realm, where human experience and reflection are so vital in discerning the morally right and wrong. More specifically, the pastors of the church enjoy this presumption only insofar as they have appropriately tapped the available sources of human understanding, as the late Karl Rahner, S.J., so often insisted. When they short-circuit these processes—whether by haste, hubris, pressure, political purpose or whatever—the presumption is correspondingly weakened. I say this for one simple reason: It is not often said. The terms "authentic" and "official" are often pressed on the noun "teaching" as if they were simply convertible with absolute certainty. When this happens we have corrupted a presumption of truth into presumptuousness.

There are limits to this teaching competence. This is a further specification of the point just made. The specification is necessary because, quite frankly, certain Catholic fundamentalists speak and act as if there were no distinctions or limits. This tendency was noted by the great French Dominican Yves Congar when he stated that the ordinary magisterium "has been almost assimilated, in current opinion, to the prerogatives of the extraordinary magisterium." Thus we have what is known as "creeping infallibilism."

Human hankerings after simplicity and certainty have conscripted two theological supports for this creeping. One is the sprawling usage (by the Councils of Trent, Vatican I and II) of "faith and morals," sprawling because it fails to distinguish the deposit of faith from matters outside of it or not essential to it.

The church's teaching competence is different when it deals with matters not of the deposit or not essential to it. Thus, traditional theology insists that the church's teaching competence is analogous. That is, it means different things and makes different claims depending on the subject matter. Briefly, it can be infallibly competent or noninfallibly competent (which is not to be equated with "certainly true" and "probably erroneous"). The response of the believer is remarkably different in the two cases. In the first case it is an act of faith. In the second it is not, although "creeping infallibilists" would have us think so as they divide the world simplistically into orthodox and unorthodox, loyalists and dissenters (note the assumptions in that asymmetry). "Faith and morals" is often the vehicle of this simplicism, as if everything authoritatively proposed in the moral sphere pertained to the deposit of faith and is therefore "almost infallibly" taught. There is virtual theological unanimity that concrete moral norms do not pertain to the church's infallible teaching competence.

The other support for "creeping infallibilism" is appeal to the "special assistance of the Holy Spirit" where ordinary moral teaching is involved. Pope Paul VI, in *Humanae vitae*, referred to this when he stated that "that respect [*obsequium*] . . . obliges not only because of the reasons adduced, but rather because of the light of the Holy Spirit which is given in a particular way to the pastors of the church in order that they may illustrate the truth" (No. 28).

The distinction of the church's teaching competence into infallible and noninfallible means, of course, that the assistance of the Holy Spirit is an analogous notion. That assistance can guarantee a teaching. If, however, the teaching is not presented in a final and definitive way, the assistance of the Spirit must be understood in a different (that is, analogous) way.

Further discussion of this point is unnecessary. The point I am making is that certain theological appeals ("faith and morals," "assistance of the Holy Spirit") can be and have been expanded uncritically in a way that removes any limits on the church's teaching competence and caricatures the search for truth in the Catholic context.

Theology has a necessary but limited contribution to make. When people reflect on their faith and its behavioral implications, theology begins. And clearly, such reflection occurs at different historical times, with different circumstances and needs, different problems and challenges, different cultures. In other words, the faith must be appropriated over and over again. We must wrestle to own it and deepen it for ourselves in our times, as others in the past did. The past is instructive. It is not imprisoning. This means that new symbols and new formulations must be discovered. Theology attempts to lead and coordinate this effort. Without such exploratory struggles, we will be dealing with faith-in-formaldehyde, what the ecclesiastical historian Jaroslav Pelikan called the "dead faith of the living." Almost everyone admits this creative and innovative role to be among theology's most important. Therefore, not much more need be said.

But important as it is, theology's role is limited. Certain limitations are obvious. We all see darkly, make false starts, succumb to our enthusiasms, construct wobbly analyses and resist criticism. I do not refer to such limitations here. Rather, I refer to the fact that theology is a scientific discipline in the service of the faith. Whether this service is an aid to the continuing daily reappropriation and deepening of the faith in our times is a heavy charge laid upon the pastors of the church. In other words, theologians cannot speak for the whole church. Only the Pope and the bishops with the Pope can do that.

Thus within the believing community, the magisterium and theology have two different but closely related tasks that call for what the Most Rev. John S. Cummins, Bishop of Oakland, Calif., calls "respectful mutuality." Bishop Cummins rightly states that both theology and the episcopate "exist within that community of believers and are meaningful only in relation to it." To treat theologians— and their analyses and conclusions—as if they were bishops is to mistreat them.

It seems to me that this is at the heart of the nervous worry about public dissent. Dissent quickly gets popularized, trickles down and comes to be viewed by the unwary as equally valid pastorally as official teaching. If that is the case, theologians are threatened by being taken for what they are not. But the answer lies in education, not execution.

Theology is a public enterprise. This might seem to have the bite of a harmless truism. But in the present circumstances it is crucial to emphasize this concept. Theology is not a closed society of arcane theory-spinners. It is a reflection *on the faith of the church,* and therefore should flourish wherever that faith is found. Theological research examines, draws upon, challenges, deepens the faith of people —and therefore must interplay with, be available to, be tested by, make sense to those whose faith is involved. Briefly, since it is of the public, with the public and for the public, it must be done in public. Presumably Vatican II had something like this in mind when it stated that all the faithful possess "lawful freedom of inquiry and of thought, and the freedom to express their minds humbly and courageously about those matters in which they enjoy competence" ("Pastoral Constitution on the Church in the Modern World," No. 62).

Theology has an essential critical role. The church is a pilgrim church. It is *in via* (on the way). That means that its formulations of its moral convictions are also *in via,* never finished and always in need of improvement, updating and adjustment to changing circumstances. Not only are moral and doctrinal formulations the product of limited minds, with limited insight, concepts and language; they are historically conditioned by the circumstances in which they were drafted. The Congregation for the Doctrine of the Faith acknowledged a fourfold historical conditioning (*Mysterium ecclesiae,* 1973). Statements of the faith are affected by the presuppositions, the concerns ("the intention of solving certain questions"), the thought categories ("the changeable conceptions of a given epoch") and the available vocabulary of the times.

Vatican II expressly adverted to this conditioning when it distinguished between the substance of the faith and its formulation. It stated: "The deposit of faith or revealed truths are one thing; the manner in which they are formulated without violence to their meaning and significance is another" ("The Pastoral Constitution on the Church in the Modern World," No. 62).

This means that one of theology's most important roles is a critical one, a distancing from past formulations and the proposal of new ones more adequate to the circumstances and insights of the time. This distancing and reformation can be called critical evaluation or dissent. Without the fulfillment of this task—under whatever name—there is no doctrinal development. The church's teaching gets frozen into the last official formulation. Critical evaluation is, then, only common sense.

The problem of the church, then, is not precisely dissent. That we have always had. Indeed it is essential to the health of a living community, as the present Holy Father himself has persuasively argued (*The Acting Person*). He called it "opposition." But whatever its name—whether opposition, dissent, disgreement, critical evaluation—a community without it is a community in comfortable stagnation. It is a community ripe for the picking by any ideologues—fascists, Communists, left-wingers, right-wingers, nationalists and, let it be said softly, curialists.

The problem of the church, then, is not dissent, but how to use it constructively, how to learn from it, how to profit by it. Every magazine editor knows this. Every public servant in a democracy knows it, too. Yes, yes, of course the church is not a democracy. Left unsaid in that sweeping put-down is that the nondemocratic church would have inflicted far fewer self-wounds had it made use of some democratic procedures in its teaching-learning processes. Americans know this down to their pulses. Vatican II learned it and asserted it in principle over and over again. The only remaining problem is to convince some Catholics that dissent is not a threat—unless they conceive the church as an isolated fortress—but an invigorating contribution to continued life and growth. Dissent is an anathema only or especially to those who claim to have captured—really imprisoned—God and God's purposes in their own conceptual fortress.

In summary, since theology is both public and critical, public critical evaluation, or dissent, is part of its task. I am astonished at—and at some point deeply afraid of—those who question this or are threatened by it. Their agenda is showing.

To acknowledge the public and critical role of theology is not to espouse two magisteria. This statement is meant to meet head-on those who reject any public dissent as equivalent to espousing a second magisterium. That is, with all due respect, a red herring. Two different competences do not two magisteria make. Both competences—scholars and the magisterium—must relate healthily, even if not without tension, if the church's teaching office is to be credible and effective.

So there is no question of the Pope vs. theologians, or bishops vs. theologians. Theologians will never be able to speak for the church as the Pope can. That juridical point is not the issue. The issue is: What must the church do to insure that its teaching is the soundest reflection of the Gospel at a particular time? Does the "certain charism of truth" traditionally and rightly attributed to the Pope and hierarchy exempt them from listening to the voice of experience and theological reflection? If the church is intolerant of dissent, is it not excluding a possible source of correction and improvement, as well as of error? Is not public exchange the risk it must run if it is to be open to all sources of knowledge? What notion of church and church teaching is im-

plied in the silencing of dissent? These are the true issues. To state them in terms of two competitive magisteria is utterly to juridicize such issues. If scholars present their views as if they were the last word ("authentic teaching"), then they are wrong, and that should be clearly pointed out. If, however, that "pointing out" takes the form of negating theology's essential critical role, then that error, too, must be identified for what it is—overkill.

The point can be made—how persuasively I leave to others—that the "confusion of the faithful" is not rooted exclusively or even primarily in theological dissent at all, but in the failure of authorities to listen in any meaningful way to the "sense of the faithful" and theological analyses that draw upon it. When traditional formulations are simply repeated in the face of competent challenges to them, teaching is reduced to ecclesiastical muscle-flexing. That *is* confusing, and it ought to be.

Dissent has its limits. Such limits are both pastoral and doctrinal. At the pastoral level, a prudent (I did not say pusillanimous) scholar will always view the value of his own opinions in the light of a larger whole—the good of the church. This is but Christian realism. Sometimes the time is just not ripe for saying or doing what one thinks ought to be said or done. To act as if it were is to waft theology into an unreal world and exempt it from any accountability based in the messiness of reality.

As for doctrinal limits, Father Curran has argued that he dissents from no infallibly proposed teachings and follows the criteria for dissent established by the American bishops and therefore is within the limits of legitimate dissent. This has been rejected from two sources.

Cardinal Josef Ratzinger's is the first rejection. "The church," he said in a letter to Father Curran, dated July 25, 1986, "does not build its life upon the infallible magisterium alone but on the teaching of its authentic, ordinary magisterium as well." True enough. But the implications of this statement are startling. The equivalent argument is that those teachings upon which the church builds its life are removed from critical evaluation, or dissent. Even recent history would be harsh on that statement. Was not the rejection of common worship with other Christians a part of the church's life prior to Vatican II? The same for rejection of religious liberty? The same for tolerance of slavery for so many centuries? Was not procreation as the primary end of marriage part of the church's thought and life prior to Vatican II? And so on.

The second rejection is that of The Most Rev. James A. Hickey, Archbishop of Washington, D.C. He states that the norms for dissent established by the American bishops "are simply not workable." What does "not workable" mean? What are the criteria for workability? Who is to blame and why if any public dissent is "not workable"? And who decides these things? It may be comfortably left to the American bishops to decide whether a single member of the hierarchy can abrogate policies they have established for the entire U.S. church.

Finally, it has been urged (by both Cardinal Ratzinger and Archbishop Hickey) that the church has the right to have its doctrine taught faithfully and clearly, and to certify only those professors who will do so. That is certainly true, but it is certainly not all of the truth. Does it mean that after the official teaching is presented, no critical evaluation of it is ever called for, is ever permissible? Does that not imply that no criticism is *possible?* And if no criticism is possible, what has happened to the historically conditioned character of church utterances clearly admitted by the Congregation for the Doctrine of the Faith? What has happened to doctrinal development? Indeed, what has happened to the distinction between infallible and noninfallible? And what has happened to our historical memories? The person who excludes dissent in principle from the role of the Catholic teacher, especially at the level of higher education, has confused teaching with indoctrination.

There are reasonable criteria for public dissent. This statement flows from the previous one. If there are limits to *what* may be the object of dissent, these limits themselves clearly act as criteria. Here I am underlining the quality of respect that ought to accompany dissent. This is one of three conditions (the others being absence of scandal and serious reasons) proposed by the American bishops for the legitimate expression of dissent. Such respect is not an assumed public politesse. It flows spontaneously from the conviction that the pastors of the church have a unique, if not the only, voice in our moral guidance. Such respect will translate effortlessly into 1) respect for the office of the teacher; 2) critical reassessment of one's own conclusions; 3) a reluctance (and only that) to conclude to error because one knows that the wisdom of the entire church (see above on the notion of presumption) has gone into the teaching in question, and 4) conduct in the public forum that fosters respect for the teaching office of the church.

I would be dishonest if I omitted a gloss on No. 3 above. It is my unavoidable impression that much dissent in the church is related to the suspicion that the wisdom resident in the entire church has *not* gone into some teachings. More directly, bishops, theologians, priests and other competent Catholics have told me repeatedly that *in certain areas* Rome will say only what Rome has said. Why sexuality and authority are indissolubly wed in this way I shall leave to others.

To suppress dissent is counterproductive. One good reason for saying this is that disciplinary suppression is unnecessary. If Rome disagrees with the theology of Father Curran or the pastoral procedures of Archbishop Hunthausen, it could easily say so—*urbi et orbi.* But why remove a bishop's jurisdiction or a theologian's canonical mission to teach as a Catholic theologian? Why intimidate all bishops and all theologians in the process? Why undermine the very credibility of the magisterium in the process?

Another good reason for the counterproductivity of dissent-suppression is historical. Archbishop Weakland, in a refreshingly courageous analysis, reminded his diocese, and really all of us, that suppression of dissent leads to the comfort—and vitality—of the tomb. Roman interventions at the beginning of this century led to 50 years of theological ossification in the United States. Is that what we want when the world is being challenged as never before by scientific, technological and cultural sea-changes?

The solution lies in education of Catholics. Education to what? A host of things: history; the role of bishops and theologians in the church; the fact that God writes with crooked lines, and among those crooked lines are all of us; the real meaning of Catholic education, and so forth. The task is huge and the shortcuts tempting. But in the long haul there are no shortcuts.

How is the search for truth to be conducted in the Catholic context? The American bishops have provided us with a powerful example in the open and revisionary process used in the development of their recent pastoral letters on peace and on the economy. They have welcomed all points of view, even dissenting ones. A similar example can be provided by Catholic colleges and universities. The word "campus" is really the Latin word (*campus*) meaning field. It designates the arena where armies settled disputes with lance and sword. College campuses exist in part to render such incivility obsolete. The vigorous exchange of ideas by the open-minded in the university setting is the way to reconcile our differences. That is why colleges have campuses, open forums for the discussion and clash of ideas. The word "campus" should stand as a reminder that the clash of swords, the targeting of missiles and any use of force represent human failure, that vigorous but civil exchange is a form of loyalty to and protection of our humanity.

Suppression of dissent is a use of force. Can the Catholic Church learn a small lesson from the American bishops and its own universities on how the search for truth is to be conducted in the Catholic context? The question is far larger than the issues of Father Curran and Archbishop Hunthausen.

31

Norms of Licit Theological Dissent

National Conference of Catholic Bishops

There exist in the Church a lawful freedom of inquiry and of thought and also general norms of licit dissent. This is particularly true in the area of legitimate theological speculation and research. When conclusions reached by such professional theological work prompt a scholar to dissent from noninfallible received teaching, the norms of licit dissent come into play. They require of him careful respect for the consciences of those who lack his special competence or opportunity for judicious investigation. These norms also require setting forth his dissent with propriety and with regard for the gravity of the matter and the deference due the authority which has pronounced on it.

50. The reverence due all sacred matters, particularly questions which touch on salvation, will not necessarily require the responsible scholar to relinquish his opinion but certainly to propose it with prudence born of intellectual grace and a Christian confidence that the truth is great and will prevail.

51. When there is question of theological dissent from noninfallible doctrine, we must recall that there is always a presumption in favor of the magisterium. Even noninfallible authentic doctrine, though it may admit of development or call for clarification or revision, remains binding and carries with it a moral certitude, especially when it is addressed to the Universal Church, without ambiguity, in response to urgent questions bound up with faith and crucial to morals. The expression of theological dissent from the magisterium is in order only if the reasons are serious and well-founded, if the manner of the dissent does not question or impugn the teaching authority of the Church and is such as not to give scandal.

52. Since our age is characterized by popular interest in theological debate, and given the realities of modern mass media, the ways in which theological dissent may be effectively expressed, in a manner consistent with pastoral solicitude, should become the object of

This selection is excerpted from Human Life in Our Day *(Washington, D.C.: U.S. Catholic Conference, 1968) par. 49–54.*

fruitful dialogue between bishops and theologians. These have their diverse ministries in the Church, their distinct responsibilities to the faith, and their respective charisms.

53. Even responsible dissent does not excuse one from faithful presentation of the authentic doctrine of the Church when one is performing a pastoral ministry in her name.

54. We count on priests, the counsellors of persons and families, to heed the appeal of Pope Paul that they "expound the Church's teaching on marriage without ambiguity"; that they "diminish in no way the saving teaching of Christ," but "teach married couples the indispensable way of prayer . . . without ever allowing them to be discouraged by their weakness" (*Humanae Vitae,* 29). We commend to confessors, as does Pope Paul, the example of the Lord Himself, Who was indeed intransigent with evil, but merciful towards individuals.

32

Public Dissent in the Church

Charles E. Curran

In the fall of 1985 I agreed to accept the kind invitation of our convention program committee to give this plenary session on the topic: "Authority and Structure in the Churches: Perspective of a Catholic Theologian." Since that time there has been some water over the dam. The Vatican Congregation for the Doctrine of the Faith has urged me to "reconsider and to retract those positions which violate the conditions for a professor to be called a Catholic theologian." According to Cardinal Ratzinger, the prefect of the congregation, there is an inherent contradiction if "one who is to teach in the name of the church in fact denies her teaching."

This paper will attempt to be faithful to the original topic by focusing on the pertinent issues and aspects involved in my present case. From the very beginning I am conscious of my own prejudices and biases. This paper is presented from my own perspective and therefore is bound to serve as an apologetic or defense of my position. However, at the same time I have the broader intention of using this case

to raise up the important issues which the theological community, the hierarchical teaching office in the Roman Catholic Church and the total people of God need to address.

The subject of this paper will thus be specifically Roman Catholic, dealing with the role of the theologian in the Roman Catholic Church. However, the questions raised and the issues discussed have not only an indirect interest for other Christian churches and other Christian theologians, but they also deal directly with many of the same issues which arise for all Christian churches and all their theologians. Before pointing out and discussing the more specific issues involved in this case, it is important to recognize the context and presuppositions for the discussion.

Context and Presuppositions

The general context for this paper and for the entire case is that of the Roman Catholic Church and Catholic theology. I have made it

---

This article originally appeared in Origins 16 (1986): 174–184.

very clear that I am a believing Catholic and intend to do Catholic theology. Despite my intentions, I still might be wrong; but I maintain that my positions are totally acceptable for a Catholic theologian who is a believing Roman Catholic.

The mission of the entire church is to be faithful to the word and work of Jesus. God's revelation has been handed over and entrusted to the church, which faithfully hands this down from generation to generation through the assistance of the Holy Spirit. Roman Catholicism recognizes that revelation was closed at the end of apostolic times, but revelation itself develops and is understood in the light of the different historical and cultural circumstances of the hearers and doers of the Word.

Roman Catholic faith and theology have strongly disagreed with the emphasis on the Scripture alone. The Scripture must always be understood in light of the thought patterns of our own time. The Catholic insistence on the Scripture and tradition recognized the need to develop and understand God's revelation in Jesus Christ in the light of the contemporary circumstances. The early councils of the fourth, fifth and subsequent centuries illustrate how in matters touching the very heart of faith—the understanding of God and of Jesus Christ—the living church felt the need to go beyond the words of the Scripture, to understand better and more adequately the revelation of God. Thus, the Christian church taught there are three persons in God and two natures in Jesus. Fidelity to the tradition does not mean merely repeating the very words of the Scripture or of older church teaching. The Christian tradition is a living tradition, and fidelity involves a creative fidelity which seeks to preserve in its own time and place the incarnational principle. Creative fidelity is the task of the church in bearing witness to the word and work of Jesus.

In carrying out its call to creative fidelity to the word and work of Jesus, the church is helped by the papal and episcopal roles in the church. The existence of this pastoral teaching function of pope and bishops in the church must be recognized by all. However, there has been much development in the understanding of the exact nature of that teaching office, how it is exercised and what is its relationship to the other functions connected with the office of pope and bishops in the church. Much of the following discussion will center on what is often called today the ordinary magisterium of the papal office. This term *ordinary magisterium* understood in this present sense has only been in use since the 19th century. A Catholic must recognize the pastoral office of teaching given to the pope and bishops, but also to realize that this teaching function has been exercised in different ways over the years.

These aspects briefly mentioned in this opening section are very important and could be developed at much greater length and depth. However, in this paper they are being recalled as the necessary context and presuppositions for the discussion of the issues raised by the case involving the Congregation for the Doctrine of the Faith and myself. I understand myself to be a Catholic theologian and a Catholic believer who recognizes the call of the church to be faithful in a creative way to the word and work of Jesus and gratefully and loyally accepts the papal and episcopal functions in the church.

This paper will now focus on what in my judgment are the primary issues involved in my case. In the process I will state briefly my own position on these issues, but the primary purpose is to raise up for discussion the primary issues which are involved. Five issues will be considered: the role of the theologian, the possibility of public theological dissent from some non-infallible hierarchical church teachings, the possibility and right of dissent by the Christian faithful, the justice and fairness of the process, and academic freedom for theology and Catholic institutions of higher learning.

The Sept. 17 letter from Cardinal Ratzinger calls upon me to retract my positions in the following specific areas: contraception and sterilization; abortion and euthanasia; masturbation, premarital intercourse and homosexual acts; the indissolubility of marriage. However, as Richard McCormick perceptively points out, these issues and agreement with my positions on these issues do not constitute the major points of contention in the dispute between the congregation and myself. These are important topics, but they are primarily illustrative of the more fundamental issues involved. However, it is necessary to point out that in all these issues my position is quite nuanced.

Role of the Theologian

There has been much written on the role of the theologian and the relationship between the function of bishops and theologians in the church. It is impossible to add to this discussion in this short space, but rather the purpose is to raise up the underlying issues involved in the present controversy. Many and probably the majority of Catholic theologians writing today see the role of the Catholic theologian as somewhat independent and cooperative in relationship to the hierarchical office and not delegated or derivative from the role of pope and bishops. The theologian is a scholar who

studies critically, thematically and systematically Christian faith and action. Such a scholar must theologize within the Catholic faith context and must give due importance to all the *loci theologici,* including the teaching of the hierarchical magisterium. The Catholic theologian to be such must give the required assent to official church teaching, but the theologian does not derive his or her theological office from delegation by the hierarchical officeholders. Likewise the teaching function of pope and bishops uses an entirely different methodology from the teaching function of theologians. Note that I have described this understanding of the Catholic theologian as somewhat independent and cooperative with regard to the hierarchical role in the church. The above paragraph has tried to explain concisely in what the independence consists and how that independence is modified by the call of the theologian and all believers to give due assent to the pastoral teaching role of bishops and pope.

However, there is a very different understanding of the role of the theologian found in more recent church legislation. The new Code of Canon Law, which came into effect in the fall of 1983, and the apostolic constitution for ecclesiastical faculties and universities, *Sapientia Christiana,* understand the role of the theologian as primarily derived from the hierarchical teaching office and functioning by reason of delegation given by the hierarchical teaching office. A good illustration of this understanding of the theologian as delegate and representative of the hierarchical teaching office is found in Canon 812 of the new Code of Canon Law: "Those who teach theological subjects in any institution of higher studies must have a mandate from the competent ecclesiastical authority."

According to the code, this mandate is required for all those who teach theology in any Catholic institution of higher learning. Earlier versions of the code spoke of a "canonical mission" instead of a mandate. *Sapientia Christiana,* the apostolic constitution governing ecclesiastical faculties, requires a canonical mission from the chancellor for those teaching disciplines concerning faith or morals. The final version of the code uses the word *mandate* and not canonical mission because canonical mission appears to imply the assignment of a person to an ecclesiastical office. The implication of this new canon and of other recent legislation is that the Catholic theologian in a Catholic institution officially exercises the function of teaching in that school through a delegation from the bishop. The role of the Catholic theologian is thus derived from the hierarchical teaching function and juridically depends upon it.

It seems there has been an interesting, even contradictory, development in Catholic documents within the last few years. The more theoretical documents seem to indicate a recognition for a somewhat independent and cooperative role for theologians, whereas the legislative documents understand the theological role as derivative and delegated from the hierarchical teaching office.

There is no doubt that from the 19th century until recent times the role of the theologian was seen as subordinate to and derivative from the hierarchical teaching office. However, Vatican Council II in its general ecclesiology and in its understanding of theologians can be interpreted to adopt a more cooperative and somewhat independent understanding of the role of theologians vis-a-vis the hierarchical magisterium. The cooperative model does not deny the official role of the hierarchical office in protecting and proclaiming the faith, but theology is a scholarly discipline distinct from but related to the proclamation of the faith by the hierarchical teaching office.

However, canonists recognize that recent canonical legislation, including the new Code of Canon Law, understands the theological function as derivative from the hierarchical teaching function. Newer legislation and its interpretation by canonists indicate that the development has been moving very much in this direction. In the older Code of Canon Law there was no requirement for theologians in Catholic institutions to have a canonical mandate or mission to teach theology. The older code saw the role of the ordinary or diocesan bishop in terms of negative vigilance with regard to individual teachers of theology and not one of positive deputation.

There can be no doubt that present church legislation tends to see the theological function as derivative from the hierarchical teaching function. However, very many Catholic theologians today appeal to more recent developments in Catholic understanding to substantiate a somewhat cooperative and independent understanding of the theological role vis-a-vis the hierarchical role. History indicates that the derivative understanding really began only in the 19th century. In this section I have purposely and consciously used the expression hierarchical teaching office or function to indicate that the teaching function and role of the total church and of others in the church cannot be totally reduced to the hierarchical teaching office.

The correspondence between the Congregation for the Doctrine of the Faith and myself never explicitly goes into this question as such, but the congregation is operating out of a derivative understanding of the role of the theologian while I adopt the somewhat independent and cooperative understanding.

Public Theological Dissent from Some Non-Infallible Hierarchical Church Teachings

The correspondence from the congregation indicates that the problem is public dissent and not just private dissent. However, the meaning of public is never developed. The entire investigation centers on my theological writings, so the only logical conclusion is that *public* here refers to theological writings. Private dissent apparently means something that is not written and is not spoken publicly.

In 1979, after receiving the first set of observations from the congregation, I had the feeling that the investigation would soon focus clearly on the public aspect of dissent and on the manner and mode of dissent. Past experience was the basis for this judgment.

In 1968 I acted as the spokesperson for a group of theologians who ultimately numbered over 600 and issued a public statement at a press conference which concluded that Catholic spouses may responsibly decide according to their conscience that artificial contraception in some circumstances is permissible and even necessary to preserve and foster the values and sacredness of marriage. In response to this statement, the trustees of The Catholic University of America on Sept. 5, 1969, mandated an inquiry in accord with academic due process to determine if the Catholic University professors involved in this dissent had violated by their declarations and actions their responsibilities to the university.

A few months later the object of the inquiry had definitely changed. "Hence the focus of the present inquiry is on the style and method whereby some faculty members expressed personal dissent from papal teaching" and apparently helped organize additional public dissent to such teaching. The board of trustees did not question the right of a scholar to have or hold private dissent from non-infallible church teaching. In the context of the inquiry it became clear that public and organized dissent referred primarily to holding a press conference and to actively soliciting other theologians to sign the original statement. The primary question of public dissent thus was not regular theological publication but the use of the more popular media.

In response to this new focus of the inquiry, the subject professors at Catholic University, through their counsel, pointed out the changed focus but went on to show that such public and organized dissent in the popular media was a responsible action by Catholic theologians. The shift in the focus of the inquiry seemed to come from the fact that the trustees, including the bishops on the board of trustees, were willing to recognize the possibility of even public dissent in theological journals as being legitimate, but objected to the use of the popular media. The faculty inquiry committee fully agreed with the thrust of the argument proposed by the professors, and the professors were exonerated in this hearing.

However, to my surprise, the investigation from the congregation never moved explicitly into the direction of the manner and mode of dissent and even at times the use of popular media. The conclusion logically follows from the position taken by the congregation that the only acceptable form of dissent on these issues is that which is neither written nor spoken publicly. At most the theologian can think in a dissenting way, perhaps even discuss the matter in private and write private letters to the proper authorities explaining the reasons for one's dissent. It is safe to say that the vast majority of Catholic theologians writing today explicitly disagree with the position of the congregation. For this reason I have remained

surprised even to the present day that the
Congregation for the Doctrine of the Faith
was proposing such a restricted notion of legitimate theological dissent from such non-infallible teaching. In principle, they seem to
allow for no public theological dissent even in
theological journals on non-infallible church
teaching.

The central point at issue in the controversy
is the possibility of public theological dissent
from some non-infallible teaching. I have
always pointed out in the correspondence that
I have been dealing with the non-infallible hierarchical teaching office. This position was
accepted by the congregation in all of the correspondence prior to the Sept. 17, 1985, letter
to me from Cardinal Ratzinger. A very few
Catholic theologians have maintained that the
teaching on artificial contraception is infallible
from the ordinary teaching of pope and bishops throughout the world. However, this position is not held by the vast majority of
theologians and has not been proposed or defended by the congregation. One could also
maintain that the Catholic teaching on divorce
is infallible by reason of the teaching of the
Council of Trent. However, the phrasing of
the canons with regard to the indissolubility
of marriage, the attempt not to condemn the
practice of *economia* of the Greek church and
the somewhat broad understanding of *anathema sit* at that time of Trent argue against the
infallible nature of the Catholic Church's
teaching on the indissolubility of marriage.
Accepted standard textbooks, such as that of
Adnes, recognize that the teaching on absolute intrinsic indissolubility is not infallible.
Thus my position all along has been that I have
never denied an infallible teaching of the
church.

However, in the Sept. 17 letter Cardinal
Ratzinger seems to claim that the assent of

faith is somehow involved in my case. I have
strenuously maintained that the assent of faith
is not involved and we are dealing with the
obsequium religiosum which is due in cases of
non-infallible teaching. I assume as a result of
my meeting with Cardinal Ratzinger in Rome
on March 8 that we are in no way involved
with the assent of faith. However, it is very
clear that the congregation maintains that the
obsequium religiosum due to non-infallible
teaching does not allow the theologian to dissent publicly in these cases.

Cardinal Ratzinger himself has called the
distinction between infallible and non-infallible teaching "legalistic." Only in this century
have theologians made this distinction in such
a sharp way. "When one affirms that non-infallible doctrines, even though they make up
part of the teaching of the church, can be
legitimately contested, one ends up by destroying the practice of the Christian life and
reduces the faith to a collection of doctrines."
Ratzinger de-emphasizes the distinction between infallible and non-infallible teaching to
help support his position that a theologian
cannot dissent publicly from non-infallible
church teaching. What is to be said about
Ratzinger's understanding?

It is true that the sharp distinction between
infallible and non-infallible teaching is recent,
for it became prevalent only at the time of the
First Vatican Council (1870), which defended
the infallibility of the pope. After that time,
theologians quite rightly distinguished the two
levels of teaching and the two different assents
which are due to such teachings. All the faithful owe the assent of faith to infallible teaching and the *obsequium religiosum* of intellect
and will to authoritative or authentic, non-infallible teaching.

The distinction became well entrenched in
the theology manuals of the 20th century be-

fore Vatican II. Such a distinction helped to explain that official teaching on some issues had been wrong and had subsequently been corrected (e.g., the condemnation of interest taking, the need for the intention of procreation to justify conjugal relations). At the time of Vatican Council I and later it was also pointed out that Popes Liberius (d. 366), Vigilius (d. 555) and Honorius (d. 638) all proposed erroneous teachings which were subsequently rejected through theological dissent.

Vatican Council II changed many earlier teachings such as those on religious freedom and the relationship of the Roman Catholic Church to other Christian churches and to the true church of Jesus Christ. Scripture scholars for the last generation or so have publicly disagreed with the teachings that were proposed by the biblical commission in the first two decades of this century. The theologians thus recognized the distinction between infallible and non-infallible teaching and used it, among other purposes, to explain why certain earlier errors in church teaching did not refute the Vatican I teaching on papal infallibility. These theologians likewise recognized the possibility of dissent from such non-infallible teaching at times, but did not explicitly justify public dissent.

The theologians are not the only ones to use this distinction. *Lumen Gentium,* the Constitution on the Church of the Second Vatican Council, recognizes this distinction between infallible and non-infallible teaching and the two different types of assent which are due (No. 25). The new Code of Canon Law clearly distinguishes between the assent of faith and the *obsequium religiosum* of intellect and will which is due to the authoritative teaching of the pope and college of bishops even when they do not intend to proclaim that doctrine

by a definitive act (Canon 752). This distinction is thus not only accepted by theologians but also by official documents and by the new Code of Canon Law.

Some theological manuals and many contemporary theologians understand the *obsequium religiosum* owed to authoritative, non-infallible teaching to justify at times the possibility of theological dissent and, at the present time, even public dissent. Some bishops' conferences explicitly recognized the legitimacy of dissent from the papal encyclical *Humanae Vitae* issued in 1968. Also documents from bishops conferences have recognized the possibility of public theological dissent from some non-infallible church teaching. The U.S. bishops in their 1968 pastoral letter "Human Life in Our Day" pinpoint that in non-infallible teaching there is always a presumption in favor of the magisterium—a position held by most theologians. However, the pastoral letter also recognizes the legitimacy of public theological dissent from such teaching if the reasons are serious and well-founded, if the manner of the dissent does not question or impugn the teaching authority of the church and if the dissent is such as not to give scandal. Since I have developed at great length in my correspondence with the congregation both the arguments justifying the possibility of public dissent and the many theologians and others in the church who recognize such a possibility, there is no need to repeat this here.

One significant aspect of the question deserves mention here because of some recent developments—the understanding and translation of *obsequium religiosum*. *Obsequium* has often been translated as submission or obedience. Bishop Christopher Butler was, to my knowledge, the first to translate the word *obsequium* as respect. Francis Sullivan, in his book on magisterium, rejects the translation of "due respect," but still allows the possibility of legitimate public theological dissent from non-infallible church teaching.

Sullivan claims that "submission" and not "due respect" is the proper translation of *obsequium,* but the Gregorian University professor still recognizes the possibility and legitimacy of public dissent from authoritative, non-infallible teaching.

The English text of the Code of Canon Law found in the commentary commissioned by the Canon Law Society of America and authorized by the executive committee of the National Conference of Catholic Bishops in the United States translates *obsequium* as respect. Ladislas Orsy, in a recent commentary on Canon 752, recognizes difficulties in translating *obsequium* but opts for respect. Orsy also recognizes the possibility of legitimate public dissent from some authoritative, non-infallible teaching. The discussion over the proper understanding and translation of *obsequium* has been an occasion for many to recognize the possibility of legitimate public dissent from some non-infallible church teaching.

There can be no doubt that church documents, the Code of Canon Law, theologians in general and canonists in general have accepted the importance of the distinction between infallible and non-infallible hierarchical teaching. Although I believe the distinction between infallible and non-infallible teaching is very important and necessary, there is a need to say more in dealing with the possibility of public dissent. I disagree with Cardinal Ratzinger's attempt to smooth over somewhat the clear distinction between fallible and non-infallible teaching, but his remarks show the need to say something in addition to the distinction between infallible and non-infallible

teaching. What about the danger of reducing the Christian faith in practice to a small, abstract core?

In my own comments about this case, I have been careful not only to use the distinction between infallible and non-infallible teaching but also to talk about what is core and central to the faith as distinguished from those things that are more removed and peripheral. Also I have consistently spoken about the right to dissent publicly from *some* non-infallible church teaching. The distinction between infallible and non-infallible church teaching is absolutely necessary, but not sufficient. The older theology tries to deal with questions of the relationship of church teaching to the core of faith through the use of theological notes. These notes and their opposites, in terms of censures, attempted to recognize the complexity by categorizing many different types of non-infallible teaching. In a true sense there is a need today to redevelop the concept of theological notes in the light of the realities of the present time.

As important as the concept of infallible teaching is, there are some very significant limitations involved in it. Infallible teaching, especially of the extraordinary type by pope or council, has usually come in response to an attack on or a denial of something central to the faith. However, some points which have never been attacked, such as the existence of God, have never been defined by the extraordinary hierarchical teaching office. On the other hand, the limits and imperfections of any infallible teaching have been rightly recognized. Infallible teaching itself is always open to development, better understanding and even purification. Thus, one must be careful when speaking about infallible teaching both because some things might pertain to the core of faith which have at least not been infallibly taught by the extraordinary teaching function of the pope and bishops, and because even infallible teaching itself is open to development and further interpretation. However, in the present discussion the distinction between infallible and non-infallible is very important. It allows me to deal with a limited area—the area of non-infallible teaching. I am in no way questioning what is an essential matter of Catholic faith.

Within this large area of what is non-infallible and not central to the Christian faith, it is necessary to recognize various degrees and levels of relationship to faith. Here an updating of the older theological notes would be very useful. I have recognized this fact by consciously referring to dissent from *some* non-infallible teachings which are somewhat removed from the core and central faith realities. It is true that I have not attempted to develop all the distinctions involved in non-infallible teaching, but in the light of the purposes of the present discussion I have tried to show that the particular issues under discussion are removed from the central realities of Christian faith.

The Catholic tradition in moral theology has insisted that its moral teaching is based primarily on natural law and not primarily on faith or the Scripture. The natural law is understood to be human reason reflecting on human nature. Even those teachings which have some basis in Scripture (e.g., the indissolubility of marriage, homosexuality) were also said to be based on natural law. This insistence on the rational nature of Catholic moral teaching recognizes such teaching can and should be shared by all human beings of all faiths and of no faith. Such teachings are thus somewhat removed from the core of Catholic

faith as such. The distance of these teachings from the core of faith and the central realities of faith grounds the possibility of legitimate dissent.

In addition, the issues under discussion are specific, concrete, universal moral norms existing in the midst of complex reality. Logic demands that the more specific and complex the reality, the less is the possibility of certitude. Moral norms, in my judgment, are not the primary, or the only, or the most important concern of moral teaching and of moral theology. Moral teaching deals with general perspectives, values, attitudes, and dispositions as well as norms. Values, attitudes and dispositions are much more important and far-reaching for the moral life than are norms. These values and dispositions by their very nature are somewhat more general and can be more universally accepted as necessary for Christian and human life.

Within the church all can and should agree that the disciples of Jesus are called to be loving, faithful, hopeful, caring people who strive to live out the reality of the paschal mystery. Disrespect for persons, cheating, slavery, dishonesty and injustice are always wrong. However, the universal binding force of specific concrete material norms cannot enjoy the same degree or level of certitude. Norms exist to protect and promote values, but in practice conflicts often arise in the midst of the complexity and specificity involved. Thus the issues under consideration in this case are quite far removed from the core of faith and exist at such a level of complexity and specificity that one has to recognize some possibility of dissent.

It is also necessary to recognize the necessary distinction between the possibility of dissent and the legitimacy of dissent on particular questions. Reasons must be given which are convincing in order to justify the dissent in practice. The central issue involved in the controversy between the Congregation for the Doctrine of the Faith and myself is the possibility of public theological dissent from some non-infallible teaching which is quite remote from the core of faith, heavily dependent on support from human reason, and involved in such complexity and specificity that logically one cannot claim absolute certitude.

There is a further question which has not received much discussion from the Catholic theological community but which should at least be raised. We have generally talked about the responsibilities and rights of Catholic theologians in general. Are there any distinctions that must be made concerning theologians? Are the rights and responsibilities of Catholic theologians and the particular right to dissent in these areas the same for all Catholic theologians? Is there a difference between the theologian as teacher and as researcher and writer? Is there a difference if the theologian teaches in a seminary, a college or a university? In the particular cases under discussion, I would develop the thesis that these differences do not affect the possibility and legitimacy of public theological dissent. All of us can agree on the need to explore this question in much greater depth. In addition, more attention must be given to the limits of legitimate dissent.

The Christian Faithful and Dissent

There is a third aspect or issue which has not received the attention it needs—the possibility and legitimacy of dissent on the part of the members of the church. In a very true sense my present controversy involves more than just the role of theologians in the church.

There can be no doubt that much of the friction between theologians and the hierarchical magisterium has occurred on more practical questions, including moral issues touching on sexuality. The issues are not just abstract questions about which people speculate, but they involve concrete decisions about specific actions which are to be done. Problems arise in these areas precisely because they involve more than speculation. Here the position proposed by theologians might have some practical bearing on how people live. All must recognize that the distinction between the roles of bishops and theologians would be much clearer if the role of theologians were restricted to the realm of speculation, with no effect on what people do in practice. However, life is not so easily compartmentalized.

Elsewhere I have defended the fact that on some issues a loyal Catholic may disagree in theory and in practice with the church's non-infallible teaching and still consider oneself a loyal and good Roman Catholic. In a sense, under certain conditions one can speak of a right of the Catholic faithful to dissent from certain non-infallible teachings. In the aftermath of *Humanae Vitae* in 1968 some bishops' conferences recognized that dissent in practice from the encyclical's teaching condemning artificial contraception could be legitimate and did not cut one off from the body of the faithful. The congregation, in its correspondence with me, has not gone into this issue. Those who deny the legitimacy of such dissent in practice would seem to face a difficult ecclesiological problem when confronted with the fact that the vast majority of fertile Catholic spouses use artificial contraception. What is the relationship of these spouses to the Roman Catholic Church?

The importance of recognizing this possibility and even right on the part of the faithful greatly affects how the theologian functions. If there is such a possibility, then the individual members of the Catholic Church have a right to know about it. I hasten to add that the individual members also have a right to know what is the official teaching of the church and should be conscious of the dangers of finitude and sin that can skewer any human decision. Public dissent by a Catholic theologian would then be called for not only because theologians must discuss with one another in the attempt to understand better God's word and to arrive at truth, but also because the people of God need this information to make their own moral decisions. Thus, for example, in the light of the situation present at the time of the issuance of the encyclical *Humanae Vitae* in 1968, it was important for Roman Catholic spouses to know that they did not have to make a choice between using artificial contraception under some conditions and ceasing to be members of the Roman Catholic Church. The Catholic theologian, among others, had an obligation to tell this to Catholic spouses.

The possibility for legitimate dissent in practice by the faithful also affects the matter of scandal. The U.S. bishops in their 1968 letter proposed three conditions under which public theological dissent is in order. One of these conditions is that the dissent be such as not to give scandal. In my correspondence with the congregation I repeatedly asked them for criteria which should govern public dissent in the church. No developed criteria were ever forthcoming. However, in the April 1983 observations from the congregation, it was mentioned briefly that to dissent publicly and to encourage dissent in others runs the risk of causing scandal.

Scandal in the strict sense is an action or omission which provides another the occasion of sinning. In the broad sense, scandal is the wonderment and confusion which are caused by a certain action or omission. Richard McCormick has already discussed the issue of scandal understood in the strict sense. What about scandal as the wonderment and confusion caused among the faithful by public theological dissent?

There can be no doubt that in the past there has been a strong tendency on the part of the hierarchical leaders of the church to look upon the faithful as poor and ignorant sheep who had to be protected and helped. This same vision and understanding of the ordinary common people also lay behind an older Catholic justification of monarchy and government from above. Catholic social teaching itself has changed in the 20th century and accepted the need for and importance of democratic political institutions. No longer are the citizens the poor sheep or the "ignorant multitude," to use the phrase employed by Pope Leo XIII. So too the members of the church can no longer be considered as poor sheep; but greater importance must be given to their increased education and rights in all areas, including religion.

Perhaps at times theologians, who often associate with people who are well-educated, will fail to give enough importance to the danger of disturbing some of the faithful with their teachings. However, in this day and age it seems many more Catholic lay people would be scandalized if theologians were forbidden to discuss publicly important topics of the day such as contraception, divorce, abortion and homosexuality. These issues are being discussed at great length and in all places today, and theologians must be able to enter into the discussion even to the point of dissenting from some official Catholic teaching. In addition, if the faithful can at times dissent in practice and remain loyal Roman Catholics, then they have the right to know what theologians are discussing.

In this entire discussion it would ultimately be erroneous to confine the question just to the possibility and right of theologians to dissent publicly from some non-infallible teachings. This present discussion is complicated by the fact that the dissent is not just speculative but is also practical. There is need for further development and nuancing, but on all the moral issues under consideration I have carefully tried to indicate what the legitimate possibilities are for the faithful in practice. The right of the faithful in this matter definitely colors one's approach to public theological dissent and to the dangers of scandal brought about by such dissent or the lack of it.

Justice and Fairness of the Process

Catholic theology has always emphasized the incarnational principle with its emphasis on visible human structures. Catholic ecclesiology well illustrates this approach by insisting on the church as a visible human community—the people of God with a hierarchical office. The visible church strives to be a sacrament or sign of the presence of God in the world, in and through this visible community.

Within the community there are bound to be tensions involving the role of bishops and the role of theologians. Both strive to work for the good of the church, but there will always be tensions. To claim there is no tension would be illusionary and ultimately would deny that the church is a living, pilgrim community. The church is ways striving to know and live better the word and work of Jesus in the particular historical and cultural circumstances of time and place.

The role of the theologian by definition will often be that of probing, pushing and tentatively pushing the boundaries forward. The hierarchical teaching office must promote such creative and faithful theological activity, while at the same time it must rightly wait until these newer developments emerge more clearly. The church, in justice, must find ways to deal with this tension in the relationship between theologians and the hierarchical teaching office. The good of the church, the credibility of its teaching office and the need to protect the rights of all concerned call for just ways of dealing with these inevitable tensions.

The present case raises questions of justice and of the credibility of the teaching office in the church. It is recognized by all that there are many Catholic theologians who publicly dissent from some non-infallible teachings. Likewise there are many Catholic theologians who hold similar positions and even more radical positions on the moral issues involved in the present case. However, the issues of justice and credibility go much deeper.

First, it is necessary for the congregation to state its position on public theological dissent from non-infallible teaching. Is such dissent ever allowed? If so, under what conditions or criteria? From the correspondence, it would seem that the congregation is claiming that all public theological dissent is wrong or at least public dissent on these particular issues is wrong. Does the congregation truly hold such a position?

As mentioned earlier, the U.S. bishops in 1968, in the light of the controversy engendered by *Humanae Vitae,* proposed three conditions for justifying public dissent from non-infallible teaching. The three conditions are: The reasons must be serious and well-founded; the manner of the dissent must not question or impugn the teaching authority of the church; and it must not give scandal. I have consistently maintained that my dissent has been in accord with these norms. The congregation was unwilling to accept these norms. Does the congregation disagree with the U.S. bishops and with the vast majority of Catholic theologians?

Archbishop John Quinn, then of Oklahoma City, at the Synod of Bishops in 1974 pointed out the real need to arrive at some consensus and understanding about dissent and urged discussion between representatives of the Holy See and representatives of theologians to arrive at acceptable guidelines governing theological dissent in the church (Origins 4, 1974–5, 319–320). Archbishop Quinn brought up the same problem again at the Synod of Bishops in 1980. For the good of the church there continues to be a "real need" to arrive at some guidelines in this area.

In addition, there is need for juridical structures which better safeguard justice and the rights of all concerned. Some of the problems with the present procedures of the congregation have already been pointed out in the correspondence. The congregation, in a letter to me, has defended its procedures because the *ratio agendi* is not a trial, but rather a procedure designed to generate a careful and accurate examination of the contents of published writings by the author. However, since the process can result in severe punishment for the person involved, it seems that such a process should incorporate the contemporary standards of justice found in other juridical proceedings.

One set of problems stems from the fact that the congregation is the prosecutor, the judge and jury. Some people have objected

strongly to the fact that the cardinal-prefect has commented publicly on the present case and disagreed in the public media with my position while the case has been in progress. Problems have also been raised against the existing procedures from the viewpoints of the secrecy of the first part of the process, the failure to allow the one being investigated to have counsel, the failure to disclose the accusers and the total record to the accused, and the lack of any substantive appeal process (Granfield, 131f).

There have been many suggestions made for improvements in the procedures. The German bishops have adopted procedures for use in Germany. Cardinal Ratzinger in 1984 admitted that there has been a decree of the plenary session of the congregation in favor of a revision of the current procedures of the congregation. The proposals made by the German conference of bishops have been accepted in principle. However, because of the workload and time constraints, the decree has not been put into effect (National Catholic Reporter, Aug. 12, 1984, p. 6).

In 1980 a joint committee of the Catholic Theological Society of America and the Canon Law Society of America was formed to address the question of cooperation between theologians and the hierarchical magisterium in the United States, with a view toward developing norms that could be used in settling disputes. The committee prepared a detailed set of procedures in 1983, but they are still under study by the U.S. bishops.

In the meantime there has been one case involving the investigation of a theologian's writings by the doctrinal committee of the U.S. bishops. Little is known about the process itself, but the final statement from the committee indicates that the dialogue was fruitful and that the theologian in question,

Richard McBrien, had the right to call other theologians to defend and explain his positions. Perhaps the process used in this case might prove helpful in other similar cases. A detailed discussion of proposed guidelines lies beyond the scope of this present paper.

The major points made here are that justice and the credibility of the church's teaching office call for a recognition of the norms or criteria governing public dissent in the church, the equitable application of these norms and the review of existing procedures to incorporate the safeguards of contemporary justice in the process of examining theologians. The call for these changes has been repeatedly made in the past. The need is even more urgent today.

33

Conscience Formation and the Teaching of the Church

William E. May

In the final chapter of his massive and important work on fundamental moral theology[1] Germain Grisez calls attention to some significant remarks by Karl Rahner, made in a book published in English translation in 1963, on the subject of a "Catholic" conscience.[2] Because Rahner, in this passage, so ably summarized the received teaching on conscience formation and the teaching of the Church, it will be worth our while to set forth his thought on this subject in some detail.

Rahner began by noting that conscience is the proximate source of moral obligation, and as such must be followed even when it is mistaken. Nonetheless, one must form one's conscience rightly and avoid confusing it with mere subjective inclination. Thus, Rahner insisted,

> Man has a duty to do everything he can to conform his conscience to the objective moral law, to inform himself and let himself be taught and make himself prepared to accept

(how difficult this often is!) instruction from the word of God, the magisterium of the Church, and every just authority in its own sphere.[3]

Rahner continued by saying that moral maturity means keeping the commandments given to us by God and proclaimed by the Church. He insisted that

> the Church teaches these commandments with divine authority exactly as she teaches the other "truths of the faith," either through her "ordinary" magisterium or through an act of her "extraordinary" magisterium in ex cathedra definitions of the Pope or a general council. But also through her ordinary magisterium, that is, in the normal teaching of the faith to the faithful in schools, sermons, and all the other kinds of instruction. In the nature of the case this will be the normal way in which

---

This article originally appeared in Homiletic and Pastoral Review 87 (October 1986): 11–20.

moral norms are taught, and definitions by Pope or general council the
exception; but it is binding on the
faithful in conscience just as the
teaching through the extraordinary
magisterium is. It is therefore quite
untrue that only those moral norms
for which there is a solemn definition . . . are binding in the faith on
the Christian as revealed by God,
and must be accepted by him as the
rule for his own behavior. . . .
When the whole Church in her everyday teaching does in fact teach a
moral rule everywhere in the whole
world as a commandment of God,
she is preserved from error by the
assistance of the Holy Ghost, and
this rule is therefore really the will of
God and is binding on the faithful in
conscience, even before it has been
expressly confirmed by a solemn
definition.[4]

Although an individual conscience can err
guiltlessly, one must never, Rahner held, appeal from a norm taught by the Church to
one's personal conscience to make an exception for oneself. On this matter Rahner was
quite eloquent and forceful, for he wrote:

If we Christians, when faced with a
moral decision, really realized that
the world is under the Cross on
which God himself hung nailed and
pierced, that obedience to God's law
also entails man's death, that we may
not do evil in order that good may
come of it, that it is an error and
heresy of this eudaemonic modern
age to hold that the morally right
thing can never lead to a tragic situation from which in this world there
is no way out; if we really realized
that as Christians we must expect al-

most to take for granted that at
some time in our life our Christianity
will involve us in a situation in which
we must either sacrifice everything
or lose our soul . . . then there
would indeed be fewer Christians
who think that their situation requires a special ruling which is not so
harsh as the laws proclaimed as
God's laws by the Church, then
there would be fewer confessors and
spiritual advisors who, for fear of
telling their penitent how strict is
God's law, fail in their duty and tell
him instead to follow his own conscience, as he had not asked.[5]

Rahner concluded his essay by observing
that in a sinful world God's law seems unrealistic, but the trouble is not with God's law but
with the sinful world. The requirements of
God's law in no way diminish the freedom of
God's children; nor are they in any way opposed to the movements of his Spirit, for one
who lives by the Spirit fulfills the commandments in a surpassingly marvelous way and
does not violate them. In short, God's commandments expressed in Jesus are still spoken
to us today by the mouth of the Church, and
our obedience is required whenever we are
tempted to disobey.

Thus did Rahner write in an essay composed shortly before Vatican Council II. After
the Council, in the aftermath of *Humanae
Vitae* Rahner himself explicitly supported dissent from magisterial teaching on moral questions.[6] Again, after the Council, and again
after Pope Paul VI's encyclical on marriage
and the proper regulation of conception, a
group of American theologians asserted that
"it is common teaching in the Church that
Catholics may dissent from authoritive, non-
infallible teachings of the magisterium when

sufficient reasons for doing so exist."[7] In 1978 one of those theologians, Charles E. Curran, had formulated as a general thesis the proposition that dissent can be legitimate with respect to ANY specific moral teaching proposed by the magisterium, and among the specific issues on which dissent from "official teaching" is legitimate, he claimed, are contraception, abortion, sterilization, euthanasia, remarriage after divorce.[8]

Avoid Subjective Inclinations

It is accurate, in my opinion, to say that the thesis set forth by Curran in 1978 is shared by many contemporary Catholic moral theologians and laypersons. It is also accurate, in my opinion, to say that this thesis is irreconcilable with the position articulated by Rahner prior to Vatican Council II. Some may conclude that this simply shows that Rahner's earlier position—remember, he himself rejected it later—reflects a "pre-Vatican II mentality," and that Rahner's later view and Curran's thesis are rooted in the teaching of Vatican Council II. This conclusion, however, is far from being self evident; it is possible that it may be quite incorrect. To determine whether or not it can be supported by the teaching of Vatican Council II it is first necessary to examine relevant material from the Council documents.

Here I propose to examine the teaching of Vatican Council II on (1) the relationship between personal conscience and the natural law or objective morality, (2) the authority of the Church to teach on moral questions, (3) some very specific moral teachings firmly set forth by the Council, and (4) the insistence of Vatican Council II on the magisterium's authority to propose truths of both faith and morals

infallibly and to bind the consciences of the faithful even when the teachings it proposes are not proposed infallibly.

1. Conscience, the Natural Law, and Objective Morality

The Council respected the dignity of human persons and of personal conscience. Emphasizing this dignity, it declared:

> In the depths of his conscience man detects a law which he does not impose upon himself but which holds him to obedience. Always summoning him to love good and avoid evil, the voice of this law can when necessary speak to his heart more specifically: do this, shun that. For man has in his heart a law written by God. To obey it is the very dignity of man: according to it he will be judged (*Gaudium et Spes*, n. 16).

The law mentioned here is called "natural law" in the Catholic tradition, and in another context the Council taught that the natural law is our participation as intelligent beings in God's divine, eternal law:

> The highest norm of human life is the divine law—eternal, objective, and universal—whereby God orders, directs, and governs the whole world and the ways of the human community according to a plan of his wisdom and love. God makes man a sharer in this his law so that, by divine providence's sweet disposing, man can recognize more and more the unchanging truth (*Dignitatis Humanae*, n. 3).

That the Council Fathers were here invoking the long Catholic tradition on the natural law is unmistakably clear, for at this point they provide a footnote to three texts of St. Thomas Aquinas,[9] including this: "The eternal law is unchanging truth; and everyone somehow knows the truth, at least the general principles of the natural law, even though in other matters some people share more and some less in the knowledge of truth".[10]

Thus there was nothing startling in the Council's teaching that human persons share in the eternal law, and it clearly made its own the Angelic Doctor's view that the natural law is "the participation of the eternal law in the rational creature," who is subject to divine providence in a more excellent way than other creatures insofar as the rational or intelligent creature provides for himself and others and thus shares in divine providence itself.[11]

It is this law that conscience discovers. Conscience is the witness to this law, and through the mediation of conscience, the Council taught, human persons come to know "the dictates of the divine law" and in this way deepen their participation in it.[12]

Continuing its exposition of conscience, Vatican Council II describes it metaphorically in a way earlier adopted by Pope Pius XII.[13] "Conscience is the most secret core and sanctuary of a man. There he is alone with God, whose voice echoes in his depths. In a wonderful way conscience reveals that law which is fulfilled by love of God and neighbor" (*Gaudium et Spes*, n. 16).

Humans Participate

At this point, the Council refers to the precept of love found in the New Testament (cf. Mt 22:37–40; Gal 5:14). Implicit is the teaching that the law which Christian love fulfills and must fulfill is the natural law.

Since conscience expresses the natural law, which can be known, at least to some degree, by everyone, and since this law is objective, the Council Fathers affirmed that

> in fidelity to conscience Christians are joined with the rest of mankind in the search for truth, and for the genuine solution to the numerous problems which arise in the life of individuals and from social relationships. Hence the more that a correct conscience holds sway, the more persons and groups turn away from blind choice and strive to be guided by objective norms of morality. (*Gaudium et Spes*, n. 16).

Note that here the Council Fathers speak of a "correct" conscience. When correct, conscience demands that one be reasonable, not arbitrary; that one conform to objective or true norms, not to subjective opinions arbitrarily chosen. But conscience is not infallible. As the Council Fathers observed, "conscience frequently errs from invincible ignorance without losing its dignity." But, they continued, "the same cannot be said of a man who cares little for truth and goodness, or a conscience which by degrees grows practically sightless as a result of habitual sin" (*Gaudium et Spes*, n. 16).

Conscience Witnesses

From these texts it is evident that the Council respected the dignity of moral conscience. Yet it specified the nature of this dignity: the dignity of conscience consists in its capacity to disclose the objective truth about what is to be done, both in particular assessments and in general norms. Through the mediation of conscience we can come to know objective moral norms whose truth is a living image of the unchanging truth of God. This teaching of the Council corresponds to and is indeed an explicitation of an equally unwavering and even more frequently repeated conciliar teaching, namely, that human dignity consists in the capacity to understand, to some extent, what God expects of us, and then to choose freely to shape our choices and actions according to that understanding and thereby to relate ourselves to God in faith, hope, and love.

2. The Authority of the Church to Propose Objective Moral Norms

It has already been noted that moral conscience, our capacity to come to know what God requires of us, can be mistaken. Thus it is necessary for us to instruct or form our conscience, to seek the truth. In short, if we are to carry out responsibly our obligation in conscience to seek the truth we have an obligation in conscience to look for the truth where we can reasonably expect to find it. And obviously, as Catholics, who believe that the Catholic Church is the living body of Christ; we regard the Church as the LUMEN GENTIUM, God's light to the people of the world. Thus its teachings on moral questions is obviously one major source where the Catholic will look in order to shape and instruct his conscience. And Vatican Council II was quite insistent and clear on this point, for it taught the following:

> In forming their conscience the faithful will pay careful attention to the sacred and certain teaching of the Church. For the Catholic Church is by will of Christ the teacher of truth. It is her duty to proclaim and teach with authority

the truth which is Christ and, at the same time, to declare and confirm by her authority the principles of the moral order which spring from human nature itself (*Dignitatis Humanae,* n. 14).

The Council, moreover, is very clear in specifying who has the authority, given by Christ, to teach in his name. It makes its own the doctrine firmly set forth at Vatican Council I[14] that the Roman Pontiff, by the institution of Jesus himself, is the successor to Peter as head of the Church (*Lumen Gentium,* n. 18), and it adds to this teaching by saying:

> Just as the role that the Lord gave individually to Peter, the first among the apostles, is permanent and was meant to be transmitted to his successors, so also the apostles' office of nurturing the Church is permanent, and was meant to be exercised without interruption by the sacred order of bishops. Therefore, this sacred Synod teaches that by divine institution bishops have succeeded to the place of the apostles as shepherds of the Church and that he who hears them hears Christ, while he who rejects them rejects Christ and him who sent Christ (*Lumen Gentium* n. 20).

There can then be no question who is authorized to speak in behalf of the whole Church. The authority of Christ himself has been vested in his vicar, the Roman Pontiff, and in the bishops throughout the world when they speak in union with and under the headship of the Pope.

More texts from Vatican Council II could be cited to support what has already been said in this section (cf. e.g., *Dei Verbum,* n. 10), but the passages already cited and referred to suffice to show how firmly Vatican Council II proposes as a doctrine of Catholic faith the truth that Jesus himself has entrusted to the Pope and to bishops in communion with him his own teaching authority, an authority to which the Catholic faithful, including theologians and bishops and popes as members of the Church, must in conscience defer in settling issues of faith and morals.

3. Specific Moral Teaching of Vatican Council II

Moreover, it is evident from an examination of the texts of the Council that the authority of the Church on moral questions is not limited to the articulation of very general norms of the divine and natural laws—norms that people everywhere can grasp for themselves, such as that good is to be done and pursued and evil is to be avoided.[15] The authority of the Church, i.e., of its divinely instituted magisterium or teaching office, extends to specific questions of morality.

Binding Force of Natural Law

Thus, in speaking of the terrible problem of war, the Council Fathers found it necessary to specify the limits of what one can rightly choose to do in protecting human rights. The Council Fathers first called to the attention of all "the permanent binding force of universal natural law and it all-embracing principles. Man's conscience," the Fathers declared, "itself gives ever more emphatic voice to these principles" (*Gaudium et Spes*, n. 79). Here the Council called attention to general principles or norms of the natural law, principles known to all men through the mediation of conscience. But the Fathers then continued:

"Therefore, actions which deliberately conflict with these same principles, as well as orders commanding such actions, are criminal" (*ibid.*). They then specified actions "deliberately opposed" to the universally binding norms of the natural law, namely, "those actions which by intention exterminate a whole people, nation, or ethnic minority" (*ibid.*) and "every warlike act which tends indiscriminately to the destruction of entire cities or of extensive areas along with their populations" (*ibid.*, n. 80).

Here the council Fathers are teaching that from the universally binding PRINCIPLES of the natural and divine law one can derive universally binding specific NORMS of morality, norms absolutely proscribing specifiable sorts of human choices and actions. The Council is here clearly teaching that the following specific norm is absolutely binding,[16] with no possible exceptions, namely, ONE OUGHT NEVER INTEND TO KILL NONCOMBATANT POPULATIONS, EVEN IN THE WAGING OF A WAR TO DEFEND HUMAN RIGHTS.

Again, in a context dealing with the inestimable dignity of the human person and the absolutely inviolable rights of human persons (*Gaudium et Spes*, n. 26), the Council Fathers unequivocally declared:

> Whatever is opposed to life itself, such as any sort of homocide, genocide, abortion, euthanasia, and wilful suicide . . . all these and others of their like are indeed shameful. While they poison human civilization they degrade those who act more than those who suffer the injury (*Gaudium et Spes*, n. 27).

Here several moral absolutes, i.e., non-defeasible specific moral norms, are clearly proposed by the Council. In the judgment of the Council Fathers it is absolutely wrong and contrary to the divine and natural law to choose to kill unborn children, suffering individuals whether dying or nondying, and oneself.

From these texts we can see that the Fathers of Vatican Council II not only taught that there are general moral principles binding all persons but also very specific moral norms derived from these principles that are universally valid and binding on the consciences of all. Nor was this teaching of the Council regarded as surprising when it was given, for the Council Fathers were simply reaffirming longstanding Catholic tradition.

4. The Magisterium's Authority to Propose Moral Truths Infallibly and the Binding Force of Noninfallibly Proposed Moral Norms

Here it is useful to recall that Rahner had insisted that the Church proposes moral norms infallibly through the "ordinary magisterium." He said that, with respect to moral norms, this would generally be the way in which such truths were taught. A central passage in *Lumen Gentium* makes the very same point, it seems to me. In fact, the passage is almost a paraphrase of the material from Rahner cited at the beginning of this essay. It reads as follows:

> Although the bishops, taken individually, do not enjoy the privilege of infallibility, they do, however, proclaim infallibly the doctrine of Christ on the following conditions: namely, when, even though dispersed throughout the world but preserving for all that amongst themselves and with Peter's successor the bond of communion, in their authoritative teaching concerning matters of faith and morals, they are in agreement that a particular teach-

ing is to be held definitively and absolutely (*Lumen Gentium,* n. 25).

As this passage makes clear (and as Rahner had made clear earlier), it is not necessary for there to be a solemn definition on the part of the magisterium in order for its teachings on faith AND MORALS to be infallibly proposed. So long as the teachings of the magisterium are proposed in such a way that they meet the criteria set forth in this passage, they are infallibly proposed.

If we examine specific moral teachings of the magisterium and apply to them these criteria we shall, I am convinced, discover that the substantive core of Catholic teaching on moral issues has been infallibly taught (e.g., the moral norms set forth in Decalogue, as this has been constantly understood by the Church, i.e., as holding as absolutely immoral the killing of the innocent, adultery [or sexual union by a married person with some one other than his or her spouse], fornication, perjury). In 1978 Germain G. Grisez and John Ford, S.J., provided massive evidence that the Church's teaching on the immorality of contraception (an immorality that Pope John Paul II has subsequently sought to show is intimately linked to divine revelation[17]) has been infallibly proposed.[18] Francis Sullivan, S.J., sought to call the analysis of Grisez and Ford into question in a work he authored on the magisterium of the Church,[19] but the weaknesses in Sullivan's presentation have been clearly exposed by Grisez in a patient and painstaking review of Sullivan's work.[20]

Solemn Definition NOT Required

Moreover, it is instructive, in my judgment, to note what the American bishops said in their pastoral on peace and war, *The Challenge of Peace.* While noting that in some places (e.g., no first use of nuclear weapons) they were presenting their own considered prudential judgments from which Catholics might, in conscience, disagree, they insisted that in other places they were merely reaffirming the constant, firm teaching of the Church (e.g., the absolute immunity of noncombatants from direct attack, the absolute immorality of killing the innocent), and that such teaching was absolutely binding.[21] They evidently thought that on the issue of innocent human life they were reaffirming what is taught definitively and decisively, i.e., infallibly, by the Church. They evidently concurred with Rahner's judgment that on this matter they were simply teaching what the Church "in her everyday teaching does in fact teach . . . as a commandment of God," and that the Church, by so teaching, is preserved from error by the assistance of the Holy Spirit.

Thus, in my judgment, a very strong case can be (and has been) made that the central core of the Church's teaching on moral questions has been infallibly proposed. Not only was it universally taught from the time of the *Didache* on that abortion, infanticide, adultery, and fornication were absolutely incompatible with Christian moral life, the teaching on the absolute inviolability of human life from direct attack, on the immorality of adultery, and on fornication was clearly set forth in *The Catechism of the Council of Trent*, a catechism prepared to help implement that Council's reform of Catholic life and one used either directly or as a source for catechetical instruction for over 400 years. Thus these moral norms were proposed, and proposed definitively in the "everyday" teaching of the Church throughout the world.

Moreover, Vatican Council II insisted that Catholics are to adhere to the teachings of their bishops on matters of faith and morals even when the teaching proposed by the bishops is not proposed infallibly. The council stressed that "this loyal submission of the will and intellect must be given, in a special way, to the authentic teaching authority of the Roman Pontiff, even when he does not speak ex cathedra" (*Lumen Gentium*, n. 25). Surely new questions of moral import do arise. For instance, today there is the question of artificial insemination by a husband and of in vitro fertilization. There is not, of course, a long-standing Catholic tradition on these issues. But the Roman Pontiffs, in particular Pope Pius XII, have provided clear teaching on these questions, judging that such modes of generating human life are not in conformity with God's intelligent plan for human existence. I believe that this teaching of the Roman Pontiffs can be shown to be true and I have tried to show why in several articles.[22] But perhaps this teaching has not been proposed in a way that meets the criteria for infallibly proposed teaching as these criteria are set forth in *Lumen Gentium*. Yet it is still authentic teaching of the magisterium of the Church and, as such, a teaching that ought to be given assent by Catholics. Still, it may be that this teaching is not clearly seen to be true in all cases by some. What, then, are they to do? According to approved authors (prior to the Council), individuals might provisionally withhold assent from such teachings when there are sufficient reasons to do so.[23] But withholding assent, while continuing to study the matter with a willingness to accept the magisterial teaching in question, is quite different from actively dissenting.

Authentic Teaching Authority

This paper began by citing extensively from an important essay by Karl Rahner on the formation of a Catholic conscience. His observations on the obligation of Catholics to form their consciences in accordance with the teaching of the Church were simply an exceptionally well articulated presentation of what was, at the time, "received teaching." It clearly recognized that the Church has infallibly proposed specific moral norms and that Catholics are bound, in faith, to accept these as true.

While some contemporary theologians assert that the position set forth by Rahner in a work written prior to the Council reflects a pre-Vatican II mentality and while some contemporary theologians assert that NO specific teachings of the Church on moral questions have been infallibly proposed, no contemporary theologians have been able to show that Vatican Council II repudiated the position taken by Rahner. I believe that I have shown that this Council, far from repudiating that position, made it its own.

In our struggle to come to know what we are to do if we are to be the beings God wills us to be we need help. God is our best and greatest friend and he has come to our help. For he has, through his Son, given to us the Church in which his Spirit dwells. It is the house of truth, the light to the nations, the guide for our consciences.

Notes

1. Germain G. Grisez, *The Way of Our Lord Jesus Christ,* Vol. 1, *Christian Moral Principles* (Chicago: Franciscan Herald Press, 1984), p. 878.

2. Karl Rahner, S.J., *Nature and Grace: Dilemmas in the Modern Church* (London: Sheed & Ward, Inc., 1963), pp. 49–69. The title of the relevant essay is "An Appeal to Conscience," and it is found in a part of the book subtitled, "Dangers to Catholicism Today."

3. *Ibid.,* p. 50.

4. *Ibid.,* pp. 51–53.

5. *Ibid.,* pp. 55–56.

6. See, for instance, Rahner's "Theology and the Magisterium," *Theology Digest* 29.3 (1981), p. 261. A perceptive essay on the "later" Rahner and the harm that dissenting theologians are doing and how to remedy the matter is that of Ralph McInerny, "Whither the Roman Catholic Theologians?," *Center Journal* 1.2 (1982) 85–102.

7. Charles E. Curran, Robert E. Hunt, and the "Subject Professors," with John F. Hunt and Terrence E. Connelly, *Dissent in and for the Church: Theologians and Humanae Vitae* (New York: Sheed & Ward, Inc., 1969), p. 26.

8. Charles E. Curran, "Ten Years Later," *Commonweal* 105 (July 7, 1978), p. 429. See also his *New Perspectives in Moral Theology* (Notre Dame, In: University of Notre Dame Press, 1974), pp. 19–22, 41–42, 192–193, 211, 271–276.

9. The three texts of Aquinas to which reference is made are *Summa Theologiae,* 1–2, q. 91, a. 1; q. 93, a. 1; and q. 93, a. 2.

10. *Summa Theologiae,* 1–2, q. 93, a. 2.

11. See *Dignitatis Humanae,* n. 3, and *Summa Theologiae,* 1–2, q. 91, a. 2.

12. For an excellent analysis of this entire subject see John M. Finnis, "The Natural Law, Objective Morality, and Vatican II," in *Principles of Catholic Moral Life,* ed. William E. May (Chicago: Franciscan Herald Press, 1981), pp. 113–150.

13. Pius XII, radio message on rightly forming the Christian conscience in youth, 23 March 1952. AAS 44 (1952) 271.

14. *Enchiridion Symbolorum,* ed. Henricus Denzinger and Adolphus Schoenmetzer (32nd. ed. Barcelona: Herder, 1963), n. 3058.

15. See *Summa Theologiae,* 1–2, q. 94, a. 2.

16. Dissenting moral theologians, such as Curran, Richard McCormick, Philip Keane, Timothy O'Connell and others, hold that no specific concrete norms are

absolutely true. At most they are "virtually exceptionless." For a critique of this view, see Grisez, *Christian Moral Principles,* ch. 6.

17. Pope John Paul II, *Reflections on 'Humanae Vitae'* (Boston: St. Paul Editions, 1984).

18. Germain G. Grisez and John C. Ford, S.J., "Contraception and the Infallibility of the Ordinary Magisterium," *Theological Studies* 39 (1978) 258–312.

19. Francis J. Sullivan, S.J., *Magisterium* (New York: Paulist Press, 1984).

20. Germain G. Grisez, "Infallibility and Specific Moral Norms: A Review Discussion," *Thomist* 49 (1985) 248–287.

21. *The Challenge of Peace,* A Pastoral Letter of the Bishops of the United States (Washington, D.C.: United States Catholic Conference, 1983), nn. 9, 104.

22. For instance, in " 'Begotten, Not Made': Reflections on the Laboratory Generation of Human Life," in *Pope John Paul II Lectures in Bioethics,* Vol. 1, *Perspectives in Biothics,* ed. Francis J. Lescoe and David Q. Liptak (Cromwell, Ct.: Pope John Paul II Center, 1983), pp. 31–63.

23. On this see Franciscus A. Sullivan, S.J., *De Ecclesia* (Romae: Apud Aedes Universitatis Gregorianae, 1963), p. 354; L. Salaverri, S.J. *De Ecclesia Christi,* in *Sacrae Theologiae Summa,* vol. 1, *Theologia Fundamentalis,* ed. 5 (Matriti: Biblioteca de Autores Cristianos, 1952), p. 708, n. 669.

34

Can Moral Theology Ignore Natural Law?

Bruno Schüller, SJ

The doctrine of natural law has lost considerable ground among Catholic theologians in recent years. Attempts to solve moral questions by appeals to natural law frequently meet with scepticism. The old optimism of quick sure solutions in all matters has turned to disappointment in the face of problems presented by capital punishment, atomic war, and contraception. Many ask if the very process of natural law thinking has not led us to a dead end.

This scepticism is caused by a new awareness of historical development in relation to a natural law which seems to stem from a static conception of man. Philosophy is not so readily admitted to the realm of theology today and natural law seems to be merely the result of philosophical reflection. Men feel that theology should be learned from history and that many distortions of Christian faith were introduced by reliance on philosophical concepts and categories. For the task of theology is to listen to the word of God in Scripture and tradition but not to the word of some philosopher.

Do these men then deny the existence of a *lex naturae?* Hardly, at least no Catholic theologian would. Scripture, tradition and the magisterium all guarantee it. What they do challenge is whether moral theology has to rely so heavily on natural law reasoning as it has till now. Once acknowledged, cannot the *lex naturae* simply be set aside by the Christian who has a much clearer awareness of God's will in the words and deeds of Christ?

First we will try to answer this last question and then examine how well natural law meets the demand for a historical interpretation of human morality. Finally we will consider some of the difficulties in moral understanding and moral-theological proofs which really seem to be the problem at the root of much of the present scepticism.

Law of Nature Defined

We will make no distinction between natural right, natural moral code, and *lex naturae*. From the side of the knowing subject natural

This article originally appeared in Theology Digest 15 (Summer 1967): 94–99.

law can be defined as the complexus of all those moral (and legal) norms of behavior knowable to man by reason independently of God's revelation. For without access to revelation man can only rely on the natural humanity of mankind for the validity and meaning of moral commands. Opposed to this is the *lex gratiae* or those divine commands which refer to the Christian in so far as he is a "new creation" in Christ. This *lex gratiae* is only knowable by faith.

The classic NT scripture proof for the *lex naturae* occurs in the first two chapters of Romans. Why does Paul bother at this point to mention that the pagans know the moral demands of God without the Torah? This simply clarifies his larger theme in the first four chapters of Romans: Justification is not by the power of the law but by faith in Christ Jesus (1:16ff). Although justification is by observance of the law (2:13), since original sin neither Jew nor pagan has observed the law (3:10–12). "All have sinned and fall short of the glory of God;" they can only hope for justification by God's grace through the redemption of Christ (3:23–24).

The gospel of justification by faith can only be understood if we first see the guilt of all mankind. The Jews are guilty by the Torah, which they have not followed; the pagans are guilty by the moral demands of God known as their creator, which they have ignored, "and so they" too "are without excuse" (1:20). *This question of the natural moral law arises only in so far as it is provoked by the gospel and helps toward understanding the gospel.* Here then is the formula by which alone theology as such can speak of the natural moral law: beginning from the gospel and leading back to it again.

This insight, however, does not tell us whether Christians, to whom the Lord himself revealed God's will, are also directed to natural law to learn God's will at times. Suppose that the primitive Christian community had accepted, directly or indirectly, certain rules of moral behavior from their pagan surroundings. This would be a recognition that norms outside the Judaeo-Christian revelation apply to Christians and also reveal God's will to them.

Why Look Outside?

But why should the primitive community do this? Because Jesus did not leave a code of prescriptions for every possible situation in life. They always looked first to the words of Jesus, but very soon found situations demanding moral judgment which went beyond Jesus' commands. In 1 Cor 7 Paul rejects divorce saying, "I give charge, not I but the Lord." Then concerning mixed marriage he says, "to the rest I say, not the Lord."

How does Paul try to learn God's will in cases where he knows no express command of the Lord? Paul takes over the norms developed by the Jews of the diaspora. They did not bring their legal disputes before pagan judges; so Paul forbids the Corinthians to do it (1 Cor 6:1–7). They made it a duty to obey pagan authority, and so Paul advocates loyalty. There is nothing specifically Christian about the motivation, even in the famous passage of Rom 13:1–7.

Taken From Hellenism

Significantly, Paul takes over from Hellenistic Jewry catalogues of virtues and vices which show the influence of popular Stoic philosophy outside the sphere of revelation of the word. The moral concepts in Phlp 1:4–8 are characteristic of the moral philosophy of Hellenism. Another example of this influence is the domestic admonitions in Col 3:18–41; Eph 5:22–26; Ti 2:1–10. They follow the same scheme as those of Stoic moral philosophy: duties of spouses, duties of parents and children, duties of masters and slaves. Of course Paul obtained these admonitions indirectly through Hellenic Jewry. In the NT they have Christian motivation, but only slightly so in Col 3:18–41, though more distinctly in Eph 5:22–33 and 1 Pt 2:13ff. Even Paul's theology of conjugal obedience (Col 3:18) and Christian marriage (Eph 5:22–23) introduces no new duties or moral commands which were not part of the domestic admonitions of the times, namely that husbands love their wives and wives be subject to their husbands.

From the foregoing one point is certain: The apostolic parenesis contains moral directions stemming from the natural moral law as known outside the sphere of the revelation of the word. So moral theology cannot be denied the use of moral insights of philosophical origin. Can moral theology then ignore these insights? The procedure of the primitive community would lead one to suspect that Christians are directed to the *lex naturae* when the express commands of Christ and the apostles do not suffice for the moral evaluation of a life situation. But this question cannot be answered by Scripture alone; it calls for theological reflection as well.

Perception of moral values is a sort of intuition. Hence the validity of a moral value cannot be strictly proven but only pointed to. Good and evil, merit and guilt, and so on can only be phenomenologically described, not strictly defined. Faith in revelation cannot be the way such values are logically and primarily perceived, since the knowledge attained by faith is not by means of intuition but is transmitted through signs. Christian faith is a knowledge based on God's authority. The encounter between believing man and revealing God takes place by means of language. In God's use of man's language, the moral "vocabulary" extends as far as the natural moral experience of man. If this is so, it seems that God can reveal only those moral insights which man knows or could know through his natural moral experience.

Lex Gratiae Communicable

Such a conclusion would be hasty. Since men's natural existence images God, his language must be capable of being a sign of a divine reality. The NT moral message (*lex gratiae*) is new and not deducible from the *lex naturae*, since it appears to man as a "new creation" in Christ. Christ's grace is task as well as gift. Yet this demand can be communicated to man since grace has its analogous image in nature. The moral conception corresponding to the *lex naturae* can point to the supernatural reality of the *lex gratiae*. A believer can only hear and understand the message of Christ because he understands and expresses himself as a moral being prior to God's words of revelation. The creator first confronts man with his will in the *lex naturae*, thus making man a possible "hearer of the word." Natural moral law is man's *potentia oboedientialis* for the *lex gratiae*.

Is the Christian free to seek God's will either in the message of Christ or in the *lex naturae*? These are not really alternatives; for whoever earnestly turns to Christ for direction thereby proves (prior to Christ's answer) that he knows he is called as a moral being to direct his life by God's will. When in faith he understands Christ's answer expressed in human speech, Christ's word makes the natural law more accessible to him. Otherwise he could not understand the law of Christ, for man grasps this only insofar as it is mirrored in natural law.

This leads to the much-discussed question: Does the NT contain substantially new commands not belonging to natural law? Historically speaking, have men who had no direct contact with Judeo-Christian revelation come to the insight that morality equals love of God, neighbor, and enemy? Even supposing that history answers affirmatively, there still is no proof that Christ's grace was not responsible. If history's answer is negative, one comes to no information about the true content of natural law since original sin could have caused the failure.

The answer must come from an ethical reflexion on the ontological level. Since without faith man knows nothing of his supernatural vocation, as soon as a moral norm becomes clear without faith as its basis, then its content is part of natural law. The commandments of love of God, neighbor, enemy, of humility and faith and hope, usually called specifically Christian, can all become clear from analysis of human existence. These are precepts enjoined on man because as God's creature he exists with others like himself.

Faith is a good example since it is most easily objected to as a *natural* precept. According to K. Rahner, man is by nature that being who can be called to believe in God's word and who understands himself most deeply as this possibility. Man would not be able to grasp or relate to himself Christ's call to faith, unless he knew immediately from his natural understanding of existence what faith means as man's answer to God's word.

The *newness* in the law of Christ is not the content of what is required, but the new *kind*

of love, hope, and humility demanded. Because he is "a new creation in Christ," the gift of supernatural grace transforms all areas of the Christian's life. For Christians the precepts of the *lex naturae* are also those of the *lex gratiae,* but not as if they were simply identical, but because we can formulate them only with the same words and concepts. The Christian who does all things "in the Lord" not only fulfills the natural law but also the law of Christ. In areas such as economics and politics Scripture only partially expresses the content of the law of Christ. Recognition of the law of nature here is ipso facto recognition of the law of Christ.

In short understanding in faith the ethical message of Christ entails as its (transcendental) presupposition natural understanding of the *lex naturae*. Natural insight into the *lex naturae* necessarily translates itself for the believing Christian into knowledge of the *lex Christi*. This is the reason moral theology cannot omit natural law from its methodical reflexion. The better a moral theologian understands the law of nature, the better his position to hear and grasp the law of Christ without distortion.

Being Grounds *Ought*

How can man by understanding himself in his natural being become aware of a divine law? Catholic natural law doctrine answers that obligation is grounded in being. In grasping what he is, man also grasps what he is to become by his free self-determination. In man every gift is also task. Man's being is a continual free gift of God, man's sole task as person is to freely accept what as God's creature he is.

Scripture makes the same point. Once darkness, Christians *are* now light in the Lord and *should* act as children of the light (Eph 5:8–11). Christ's grace is always both gift and command, but first of all gift. In the reflex grounding of moral precepts, moral theology and philosophical ethics ought to have the same formal guiding principle, the interpretation of the demands of our God-given being. Moral theology can be defined as theological anthropology translated from the indicative to the imperative.

Room for Change?

Since there are elements of continuity and change in man's being, a distinction must be made between moral norms based on man's unchangeable metaphysical nature and those grounded in man's changing historicity. The questionable restriction of natural law norms to those based on the unchangeable metaphysical nature of man seems to stem from a fear of relativism and an attempt to avoid its dangers by estimating what is historically changeable in man as narrowly as possible.

But the *ought's* ground in being leaves room for change, since it only states the correlation between them. The extent to which man remains the same through historical change is a problem for metaphysical anthropology, not ethics. Precisely to the extent that man's being changes with time must the applicable ethical norm also change in every case.

Some examples will clarify this concretely. Children owe their parents love, reverence, and obedience until they come of age—then the duty to obey ceases. Put abstractly, because the growing person's being changes, the obligations demanded of him also change. Or what of the NT admonition that wives be subject to their husbands in all things? This obviously presupposes a lack of "age" on the

wife's part no longer valid—at least for most of the Western world. Today the model for the relation of husband and wife is rather one of equal partners with no one-sided superiority or subjection. There is no problem with relativism, for the husband/wife relationship has objectively changed and with it the ethical precepts appropriate for them.

How can one tell if traditional moral precepts still contain God's will today? The more general and abstract the moral principles, the more reason there is to think they have a timeless validity. One cannot doubt that Christians of all times have to prove their authentic faith by their love of neighbor. But there is more reason to consider concrete and detailed prescriptions timebound and to re-examine their demands. Since every moral precept is justified by the God-given being of man, here and now its continuing validity must in principle be able to be perceived from that given reality.

Even moral precepts in the NT must be checked since they were directed to Judeans, Corinthians, and Philippians, and in the twentieth century we are simply not the same men they were. The difficulties of a natural law grounding of moral precepts cannot be avoided by recourse to Scripture, since its own ethical message must be interpreted. Interpretation that depends on the movement from *is* to *ought* is difficult because of the character of ethical knowledge and proof.

A Problem of Proof

There are peculiar difficulties in ethical proof. The understanding grounding the *ought* must penetrate to the essential character of human existence and not remain in the merely empirical or factual area. The latter is precisely the contingent, the non-necessary, and cannot ground the absolute necessity of moral law. For example, the growth of male facial hair cannot ground a prohibition to shave. Man can interpret his being as an *ought* that concerns him absolutely only because he understands that being as a meaningful absolute value. Since moral values are primary, perceptible only by a kind of intuition, the moral value of truthfulness, for example, cannot be demonstrated "conclusively" like a mathematical proposition. All that can be done is to turn another's attention in the direction where he must look to perceive the value of honesty. Because of their being underived, primary character, ethical precepts can only be exhibited phenomenologically.

Moral theologians and ethicians often do not take trouble to investigate phenomenologically those areas of life which are judged morally. For example, the venial seriousness of lying is based on the meaning of speech, where speech is understood as a medium for communicating thought. But closer analysis shows that speech can also be a means of self-communication and of personal encounter. A falsification of this personal relationship is much more serious than mere false information.

Insight into moral values depends not only on my intellectual clarity and penetration, but on the right attitude of my will and affective life, my early childhood experiences, and the cultural, social, and historical factors of the milieu. To indicate the objective validity of moral norms and values, moralists must incorporate knowledge from modern sociology and psychology—a task hardly begun. Nor does it further moral theology to exclude philosophical reflection on the natural law. All these factors, philosophy included, help achieve a competent moral theology.

35

The Traditional Concept of
Natural Law:
An Interpretation

Columba Ryan, OP

In a short essay on the traditional concept of natural law it is hardly possible to go into the complicated story of its historical development. This history has often been written,[1] and it contains chapters about which there is little agreement among scholars. But without entering into these difficult questions, it may be useful to remind the reader of some of the strands that went to the making of the idea before it was given a certain coherence and consistency by St Thomas Aquinas and so inherited as a central concept in Catholic thought. For it is when we see something of its complexity, not to say its inherent tensions and conflicts, that we may appreciate that the traditional synthesis may still stand in need of elaboration or even qualification. The development of a complex idea is seldom absolutely finalized.

"The origin of the idea of natural law may be ascribed to an old and indefeasible movement of the human mind (we may trace it already in the *Antigone* of Sophocles) which impels it towards the notion of an eternal and immutable justice; a justice which human authority expresses, or ought to express—but does not make."[2] Sir Ernest Barker had in mind, of course, the often quoted lines of Sophocles, where Antigone defends herself before Creon for burying Polynices in defiance of a positive edict:

> That order did not come from God.
> Justice that dwells with the gods below,
> knows no such law.
> I did not think your edicts strong enough
> To over-rule the unwritten,
> unalterable laws of God and heaven,
> you being only a man.
> They are not of yesterday or today, but
> everlasting

This article originally appeared in Illtud Evans, ed. Light on Natural Law (London: Burns and Oates, 1965) 13–37.

Though where they come from, none of us can tell.[3]

Such a passage may seem to us a fairly clear appeal from the tyranny of man-made positive law to a higher law, eternal and unchallengeable, by which positive law may be judged. And one might buttress such an interpretation by fragments from some of the pre-Socratic philosophers; Xenophanes speaks of "things that are shameful and a reproach among men: theft, adultery, and mutual deception",[4] and Heraclitus of a law which, however much disregarded, is nevertheless binding and universal: "One must follow that which is common to all. But although the law is universal the majority live as if they had understanding peculiar to themselves."[5] For Heraclitus this is a matter of reason: "If we speak with intelligence, we must base our strength on that which is common to all" and "The thinking faculty is common to all",[6] but for others it is perhaps seen to be rather a matter of "nature"; Philolaus of Tarentum has left us the tantalizingly brief remark, "By nature, not by convention",[7] a contrast that may be at work in the Sophist Antiphon when he writes: "The edicts of the laws are imposed artificially, but those of nature are compulsory. . . . If a man who transgresses the legal code evades those who have agreed to these edicts, he avoids both disgrace and penalty. . . . But if a man violates . . . any of the laws which are implanted in nature, even if he evades all men's detection, the ill is no less, and even if all see, it is no greater. For he is not hurt on account of an opinion, but because of truth."[8]

It is easy to interpret such passages as if "nature" and "truth" had some higher values than "convention" and "opinion"; but to do so may in fact be to read back our own ideas into these early authors. It is by no means clear that "nature" and "truth" do not rather represent what we should think of nowadays as a kind of blind, compelling instinct in contrast with the cooler calculations of human reason. Perhaps the natural law to which Antigone appeals is not so much something ethically superior as naturally ineluctable—the instinct of nature which excuses and explains her action without making it morally defensible. Such a concept, at any rate, of law, if law it may be called, is to be found in Democritus: "For human beings it is one of the necessities of life to have children, arising from nature and primeval law. This is obvious in other animals too; they all have offspring by nature, and not for the sake of profit."[9]

So we may detect already two possible strands in the concept of natural law: the idea that it represents some higher ideal of justice to which appeal may be made, and the idea that it is a compulsively blind instinct of nature. The two ideas set up a tension and conflict within the notion of natural law that may be traced much later in its development, and that may be found still confusing discussions of the subject today. When Cicero (whose writings were so influential in the development of the medieval concept) wrote of "true law which is right reason in agreement with nature, of universal application, unchanging and everlasting", he was seeing it as an ideal of justice; for he continued: "It is a sin to try to alter this law, nor is it allowable to repeal any part of it, and it is impossible to abolish it entirely. . . . There will not be a different law at Rome and at Athens, a different law now and in the future, but one eternal and unchangeable law for all nations and for all times."[10] But another approach to the natural law is to be found in a famous definition, well known and influential in the Middle Ages, given by Ulpian (*c.* A.D. 220) in his *Institutes*, or at least attributed to him in Justinian's *Digest:* "Natural law is that which nature has taught all animals; this law indeed is not peculiar to the human race, but belongs to all animals."[11] Here the natural law seems to come much closer to the idea of animal instinct. Even today when people speak of the natural law they may sometimes be found to be supposing that it refers to what is natural in the sense of instinctual in us as against what may be thought of as planned and regulated and artificial; and when this happens they are at cross-purposes with others (and even with themselves in other phases of their arguments) who think of it essentially as the ideal and the reasonable.

Besides these two strands in the concept we may note much more briefly others also. When Ulpian gave the definition just mentioned, it was within a tripartite division of law into natural law (*ius naturale*), the law of nations (*ius gentium*), and the law of the city (*ius civile*); he therefore contrasted natural law with *ius gentium*. But Gaius before him had identified these two laws, and his account too was incorporated into Justinian's compilation, with the result that there entered into the traditional concept of natural law in the whole complex notion of the *ius gentium*.[12] It is not part of this essay to investigate what this involves nor to decide whether the origins of *ius gentium* lie in an empirically established lowest common denominator of the laws recognized by the peoples subject to Rome or in the more abstract consideration of a *ius* common to all men because founded upon "natural reason".[13] It is sufficient to have called attention to this further strand in the evolution of the idea of natural law.

Yet another confusing element is to be found in the widely used definition given by the twelfth-century Italian monk and canonist, Gratian. "Mankind", he says, "is ruled by two laws: natural law and custom. Natural law is that which is contained in the Scriptures and the Gospel."[14] Taken at its face value this might seem to make natural law dependent upon Revelation, and though such a view can hardly be attributed to Gratian himself[15] a certain conjugation of the concept with the Decalogue and with Christian ethics is henceforward fairly well in evidence; the natural law is thought of as "divine" without its always being clear in what sense this is to be understood.

In mentioning these various strands in the making of the concept it has not been my intention to be either exhaustive or to make them appear to be completely distinct one from the other. The different strands overlap one with the other, but they also introduce tensions and even contradictions within the concept, which it is necessary at least to be aware of in any attempt to handle the subject.

As for the developments of the concept after the Middle Ages—the ideas of natural law, for example, that lie behind the revolutionary movement of the eighteenth century —I make no attempt to trace these. This is not because they are not important in themselves, but simply because I am concerned only to give some account of the concept as it has entered the traditional teaching of the Catholic Church; and in this teaching the seminal influence has been that of St Thomas Aquinas.

I do not however propose to set out in any formal manner the teaching of Aquinas. Rather, I shall take him as a kind of guide and mentor in proposing what will be a personal statement of the concept of natural law that may be at once faithful to the role it plays in the Catholic tradition on this matter, and of relevance to the issues in which it is today customarily invoked in Catholic moral teaching. That it is a matter of some importance to understand the concept can hardly be gainsaid when one hears it so constantly invoked in arguments about contraception, nuclear warfare, religious freedom and so forth. And quite apart from these applications, the concept has been given renewed attention as the result of the need to have some theory which will justify the rejection of unjust legislation. It may seem to many, and as I think rightly, that without an appeal to something like natural law, such proceedings as the Nuremberg trial have no rational basis. The importance of the theory of natural law is that it affords the possibility of rebellion; it provides a court of appeal, and without it there is no court of appeal beyond the edicts of men.

It is true that, merely because one law within a given legal system may be criticized by reference to other laws within the system, it cannot be argued that there must be some criterion outside the whole system whereby the totality of the laws may be criticized. This would involve the logical fallacy that because all the laws can be referred to some criterion, there is one criterion for all laws. But what I should wish to say is that the very possibility of any law being referred to any criterion, even within a legal system, implies that there is, within the legal system, a structure which makes possible critical scrutiny. Or, more simply, the calling in question of the obligatory character of any given law raises the whole problem of the obligatory character of law, and this obligatory character within a legal system constitutes the kernel of the concept of natural law.

This leads to an observation of some importance. The fact that we use the word "law" in speaking both of natural law and positive law may easily lead us to suppose that such "laws" are in every respect the same sort of thing, laws standing side by side. The temptation then is to look for a natural law which functions in the same way as positive law (to look for a kind of written code "in the heavens" or "in men's hearts" and so on), and upon finding that there is no such thing, and that, by comparison with positive laws, the natural law is vague and the subject of endless disagreement, to conclude that it simply does not exist. But this would be a simple mistake, the result of a systematically misleading expression. For in fact to speak of both the natural law and positive law as "laws" is to do the same kind of thing as to speak of tables and chairs as objects or beings or things, and to speak of God likewise. If this leads us to think of God as one more thing alongside of and beyond things like tables and chairs, we are being systematically misled by the expression "object" or "being" or "thing". This is a "category mistake". Instead we should understand that God is interior to, and the very ground of possibility of, every "thing" that is. Likewise, in speaking of natural law as "law" we should think of it not as lying alongside of, and somehow superior to, all other laws, but as that which is at the heart of, and constitutes the possibility, indeed the obligatory character, of every other law. In other words when we are speaking of natural law, we are in the field of ethics or morality rather than in that of legality in a narrow sense.

It is important to have made this observation for it goes some way to meeting the objection commonly made that natural law is so vague and so much the matter of endless controversy as to be useless in the practical business of reaching legal decisions or agreement on disputed points. The assumption from which this objection springs is that natural law is to fulfil the functions of positive law, only "more so" or in a higher order of justice; it is the objection of practical lawyers concerned with getting things settled.[16] But in fact this is not the function of natural law as such; for though the natural law may be embodied in directives of a more or less general kind, as we shall see, the point of describing such directives as belonging to natural law is not so much to call attention to their content as to the moral character of their obligatory force. The theory of natural law is a theory of what makes laws laws, not an easy substitute for making laws, for legislating.

Before going on to a positive description of what is meant in the Catholic tradition by natural law, it may help to avoid certain misunderstandings if we begin with certain disavowals.

First, though it is in some sense the law of God, and is often so referred to in Catholic documents,[17] the natural law is not divine law in the sense that it is dependent, in any necessary way, upon a special divine revelation.

Second, it is not the result simply of the will of God, in such manner that had God willed otherwise the law might have been quite different and opposite to what it is. This is, of course, to take up an attitude to the whole character of law and to deny that in the last resort it derives from an exercise of sheer sovereignty. It is to reject, for example, the definition of law by Austin (and earlier by Ockham and Gerson) as simply the command or imperative of authority.

Thirdly, I believe it true to say that the concept of natural law is not dependent upon belief in God's existence. *Etiamsi daremus non esse Deum,* even if we were to allow that God is not, as Grotius observed, the natural law would retain its validity; and, though I know of no passage where St Thomas entertains this hypothesis, Grotius had his medieval forerunners in making such an assertion; nor

were they, in my opinion, out of step with Aquinas' conception of the natural law in so doing. Admittedly, the status of the natural law would in that hypothesis be considerably altered, for it would then have an ultimacy which, given the existence of God, it does not have; but its character as law would not be changed.

Fourthly, it is no part of natural law theory to hold that there is a whole range of human conduct which can be seen, with only a little good will, to be right. The dictates of the natural law may be, are, and may be expected to be a matter about which there is the utmost confusion and disagreement.

Finally, not everything which can be said to be in one sense or another "unnatural" is against the natural law. Most human activity is artificial and yet may be required by natural law; and it is, in one of the commonest uses of that most ambiguous word "natural", very natural indeed to offend against the natural law.

If these disavowals appear sweepingly dogmatic, I must plead that I am not here concerned to prove them. I am only concerned to say that none of the things denied are necessarily implied by any and every theory of the natural law. That this is so I hope will become apparent from the account that we must now go on to give. For the moment I have been concerned simply to remove obstacles to understanding this account which might arise from *a priori* anticipations of what it must imply.

By way of beginning, at last, a more constructive account, I shall use an extremely crude analogy, but one that, because of its simplicity, may do more than a more sophisticated account to make its point.

Manufactured products, whether simple or more complicated, are as often as not accompanied, when they are bought, by the maker's instructions or rules of how to use them. These rules are not arbitrary fiats of the manufacturer which might be entirely different from what they are. They tell the buyer how to get the best out of the product; if it is used in such and such a way, it will last, and perform its function well; if used in some other way, it will be broken, or give indifferent service.

What the manufacturer is doing is to tell the buyer what he knows of the nature of his product. Admittedly, we have here to do with an artifact, and the maker's knowledge is based on his having designed the product for a purpose. But his rules do not reflect this knowledge alone; they are to some extent based also on the knowledge he has of the materials used—they will stand up to certain usages while to others they will not.

There is some sense in which the rules listed by the maker are not simply written on his paper list of instructions. They reflect what may be said to be built into the products. In this sense they are the "rules" or "laws" of its very make-up; the "rules" of its nature. Nor is it even necessary that a list of instructions should be provided. It would theoretically be possible for the buyer to examine the thing, take it to pieces and reassemble it, and arrive at the same set of rules; he would then have read them off the product itself.

All this provides an analogy, though only a partial one, to natural law. Instead of manufacturers' products, we have to do with human beings. There could, theoretically, be issued with every human baby rules for his proper "use"—describing the way he is to be used to get the best out of him, to see that, as a human being, he finds proper fulfilment. But in fact, of course, no list of rules is issued. It is left for men to discover for themselves the "rules" built into their nature as human beings, to discover how to use themselves if they are to get the best out of themselves and find their proper human fulfilment. And by natural law is meant not these "rules" as built into them (my use throughout of inverted commas has been intentional, to call attention to the fact that such "rules" are scarcely properly so called) but these "rules" as recognized by men on reflection upon what it is to be human and to find human fulfilment.

Here it is important to insist that "to be human" must be understood in the total human context. Arguments for something's being in accordance with or against the natural law often enough appear to forget this. One example may illustrate this point. What Dr. Rock[18] cites as "a typical statement of the conventional Catholic position" runs as follows: "The reason why the artificial practice of birth control is immoral is written into the very nature of the sexual organs and the marital act itself. The sex organs were made by God to reproduce the human race. Only when husband and wife unite naturally is the union of sperm possible. Therefore the primary purpose of the marital act is the conception of human life."[19] Apart from a good many things wrong with this argument as it stands, and the fact that if it proves anything it proves too much for it would be equally applicable to birth control applied to animals, the whole approach appears to me wrong. For it seems to suppose that by a simple inspection of physical organs, rules can be reached for human behaviour. But man is not simply a complex of organs. "Human beings define themselves in relation to the world, and in relation to those around them."[20] To discover what it is to be human and to achieve properly human fulfilment, account must be taken of man not simply as a biological object, not even simply biologically (which would introduce a whole consideration of his ecology), but in the specifically human dimension in which he enters into communication with others at a human level. That is "natural" to man which constitutes him not merely in isolation, but in relation to the whole world-for-man which he creates around him (the highly artificial world of civilization), and in relation to other persons who stand not simply as objects but as other subjects around him. This is a point to which we shall have occasion later to return. It needs here to be made very forcefully because of the frequency with which it is overlooked in natural law arguments.

When we insisted earlier that the natural law is not to be taken as referring to the "rules" built into a man's make-up, but to his recognition of these "rules", we touched, in fact, upon the difference between the natural law and what may be called "the laws of nature" (if we may use the latter expression in a rather restricted sense). We may say that the "rules" built into the make-up of things—whether of inanimate objects, plants, animals, human beings—constitute in each the "law" of their nature. But only in man, with his capacity to reflect upon and know himself, can there be any question of natural law, the recognition for himself of how he is to act; and only in his case, with his freedom of action, can there be a responsible following or deviation from the "rules" of his nature (and even this only to a limited extent).

It will now be seen more clearly why it was possible to say that the concept of natural law is not dependent on the existence of God. For whether man comes from the hand of a Creator or not he must be said to have some particular make-up. It will also be seen in what sense, and in what sense alone, the natural law is the law of God. It is only to the extent that God has made the creature, and made it carrying within itself the "rules" of its make-up. So far as the natural law is a faithful recognition of these rules, it is the faithful reflection of the designs of God, or, as Aquinas says, a participation in the eternal law, which is the ordering wisdom of God.[21]

The analogy so far pursued is however a very insufficient one. We must now take account of two objections that may be made to it. The first is that it would be very odd to say that a maker's instructions were in any usual sense obligatory. However minatory the form of words he may use (DON'T do this, Do this, etc.), all they amount to is this: *if* you wish to get the best service out of this product, act in such and such a way. Such rules are, in the last analysis, descriptive rather than prescriptive.

The second objection to the account of natural law so far given is that whereas the natural law has traditionally been taken to be permanent and immutable, it may very plausibly be argued that man's nature (prescinding anyway from the difficulty that the concept of nature presents to the contemporary mind) is in constant process of development according to his cultural evolution.

I can do no more than sketch an outline of an answer to these objections. Certainly, in regard to the first, I do not wish to say that the natural law for man is simply to take the form: if you wish to get the best out of yourself, act thus. To say this would be in fact to reduce "ought" to "is", the moral judgment to a matter of fact.

When St Thomas Aquinas speaks of law, he speaks of it as a *dictamen practicae rationis,* a dictate of the practical reason. And he constantly draws a parallel between the working of the practical reason and that of the theoretic or speculative reason. As in theoretical reasoning we reach conclusions from premises, or what he calls first principles, so do we reach by practical reason conclusions from first principles. The conclusions of practical reasoning are for him decision as to action;[22] the first principles by which we reach such conclusions constitute for him the natural law, or the precepts of the natural law.[23] Now, though this parallel is in many ways illuminating, it may be misleading if we draw it too closely. It is tempting to think of the process of practical reason going roughly as follows: the good is always to be done; but such and such is good; therefore such and such is to be done. But where this, I think, is mistaken is that it turns practical reasoning into just another piece of theory. And from this we can be saved if we notice that Aquinas elsewhere refers to the "conclusions" of the practical reason as actions—not just as decisions to act, still less as conclusions about what ought to be done. He speaks, also, of the first principle of practical reasoning, as the end (*finis*) itself.[24] What I wish to suggest is that if we are to understand him aright, the process of practical reasoning is *not simply* a parallel to theoretic reasoning with only the difference that it is concerned with things to be done. Rather, to put it extravagantly, it is "a piece of doing" —the outcome is action, the initial principle is the bent of the will to the good, to its end or *finis*. We do not start upon this process by a theoretic statement that the good is to be done, but by the will's "going for" the good. It is true that the "bent" of the will to the good is within the perspective of a cognitive recognition, for it is not a blind impulse but consciously orientated to the good recognized as such; and it is true that given this conscious bent, the reason further intervenes to intimate that such and such conduct is in fact recognizably good.[25] But the initial dynamism of the will's "bent" to the good carries right through

the process. Thus the "conclusion" is not a theoretic conclusion about what is to be done; rather that initial "bent" of the will to good, instructed by the reason's intimation of what is good, carries through then and there to action, or at the least to a decision which is to be understood as already an inception of action rather than a piece of theory.

Now what this implies is that the "ought" judgment never reduces to a simple "is" assertion, and that basically there is an initial obligation arising from our natural bent to good (natural not in any sense contrasted with rational, for it is not blindly impulsive, but natural in the sense of being an ineluctable tendency of our human make-up). And, in fact, Aquinas does insist that though the precepts of natural law are matters of reason, they take place always within the dynamism of the will and are shot through with its force.[26]

This is why the "rules" built into a man's nature, unlike those in any other being, provide the basis for the obligatory character of natural law. It is not a question of "if you will achieve your end, you should do this", but "you are bent necessarily upon your end, and this you must do as the means you recognize".

The parallel that we have been discussing between the principles of reasoning in the theoretic order and those in the practical order lends itself to another observation.

When Aquinas speaks of principles in the theoretic order he does so with considerable ambiguity. At times he speaks as if such principles were the premises in a piece of reasoning. But at other times his first principles are such as the principle of contradiction, of excluded middle, etc. Now from such principles it is impossible to derive any argument. The truth is that by first principles he may mean the fundamental axioms in any given field of enquiry. But at other times he means principles immanent to the whole process of reasoning —not premises in an argument, but the structure without which no argument would be coherent—not axioms but rules of thought.

Now rules one cannot get on without, and, to the extent that one is rational, one cannot be without. But the principles which constitute the premises of an argument, axioms, are a matter either of prescription or of notification from experience.

There is a parallel to this ambiguity in Aquinas' account of natural law in terms of practical reasoning. When he speaks of it as constituting the first principles of practical reasoning he seems at times to think of it as comprising the rules without which no such "reasoning", or, in the light of what we have said, no such piece of action, can get under weigh—the purely formal rules therein involved. It is in this sense that the first principle of all is that the good is to be done, evil avoided (and in all that follows it is necessary to take these rather intellectualist expressions as referring not to a theoretic judgment, but a shorthand expression to refer to the dynamic bent of the will under the guidance of understanding to which we have already referred). Thus it is that Aquinas can speak of "the light of natural reason, by which we distinguish good and evil (*qui discernimus quid sit bonum et malum*), which belongs to natural law",[27] and can write, "The first principle of practical reason is founded on the notion of the good, the notion which is that the good is that which all have an inclination to (*appetunt*). The first precept of the law is therefore this: the good is to be done and pursued, the evil avoided."[28] In other words, the basic rule of morality consists in the discrimination of good from evil; and without this there can be no decisions as to conduct nor any obligation attaching to them, any more than in the theoretic order

there can be any possibility of reaching conclusions without accepting the rules of reasoning. At this basic level it makes sense to say that no man can be without knowledge of the natural law. It is highly doubtful whether any human being (whatever his outward profession) can ever be denuded of this radical sense of right and wrong, or devoid of the urge to pursue that which presents itself to him in the guise of good, or avoid that which appears as evil. And if there were such a person, he would forfeit his claim to being human, and be, in the moral order, what in the order of theoretic truth is a lunatic, or an infant (and even lunatics and infants have at least the radical capacity for, in the one case, acceptance of the rules of reasoning, and in the other, discrimination between good and evil).

But so far we remain at the purely formal level; from the rules of reasoning, or the rules of morality, no conclusions and no decisions can be elicited. These rules need to operate in a given content, and the most general content is supplied by "first principles" taken in the sense of axioms. Such axioms, apart from the case of purely formal sciences where they may be prescribed, are discovered in experience. And thus it is that Aquinas will speak of the natural law as comprising, besides its purely formal rules, the broad recognition, based upon experience (of the most general sort) of particular heads of goods. Such recognition constitutes the principles of natural law in the second sense of "first principles". These primitive recognitions of, and urges to, particular goods he classifies under three heads which we may call the good of individual survival, biological good, and the good of human communication. "First, there is in man an inclination to good according to the nature which he has in common with all substances . . . in accordance with this inclination everything by which the life of a man is preserved, and its opposite held in check, pertains to the natural law. Second, there is in man an inclination to things which concern him more specifically according to the nature which he shares with other animals: and it is in virtue of this inclination that those things which nature has taught to all animals are said to be of the natural law; such as the intercourse of male and female, the education of offspring, and so on. Thirdly, there is in man an inclination to good according to the nature of reason, which is special to him; thus man has a natural inclination to know the truth, and to live in society: and so whatever pertains to this inclination pertains to the natural law."[29] Upon these urges or primary recognitions of quite general goods in the concrete, the good is now no longer apprehended purely formally), one cannot, I think, immediately base principles such as "Thou shalt not commit suicide", "Thou shalt not practice birth control", "Thou shalt not lie", and so on, but rather upon principles of the form "some arrangements should be made for the preservation of life", "some for the organization of the family", "some for the organization of society", in each case leaving it open to further experience and enquiry *what* the arrangements are to be. Or, as Eric d'Arcy puts it,[30] the primary precepts of the natural law are not of the form "adultery is wrong, murder is wrong", but of the form "sexuality demands some form of regulation", "there is a difference between killing a rabbit and killing a man". And when this is understood, it becomes much more plausible to say that such primary precepts of the natural law "are everywhere identical, immutable and ineradicable".[31]

But if this is the only content of the natural law, it provides us with singularly little guidance in human conduct, even though already what it does is not negligible, since it provides us in principle with the basic possibility of examining and justifying human decisions and conduct instead of leaving us to suppose that they are matters about which there can be no argument, and for which there can be no criterion of obligation. However, St Thomas goes further than this. He thinks that from these quite general precepts we may derive others by way of conclusions.[32] And if it seems that we have lost sight, now, of his description of the natural law as consisting of the *principles* of practical reasoning to exchange it for something that comprises also conclusions, we should remember that principles have to be thought of relatively to conclusions, as it were on a sliding scale. What is a conclusion in relation to higher principles may be itself a principle in relation to conclusions to be drawn from it. The natural law has different levels; basically it consists of those highest principles which are simply given and indemonstrable—whether as the rules of moral conduct or as the primary axioms of an entirely general moral awareness; but it comprises also anything which may be derived, by way of conclusion, from such axioms, and which may serve in turn as principles in reaching individual decisions as to conduct. In this way, the natural law is indefinitely extendable, as we come into fuller and fuller possession of what we see to be derivable from the original premises. But, and it is important to notice this, such development is not to be had without constant reference to a wider and more sensitive assessment of experience; nor is it to be had without danger of making mistakes, and without exacting enquiry. The process of practical reasoning is no more infallible, and no surer of its results, nor is it any more ready-made, than the parallel process of theoretic reasoning whereby we attempt to reach speculative truths. If, in pursuing more and more detailed conclusions within the body of natural law, we find greater and greater confusion and disagreement, we should be no more disconcerted at this than we are when we find ourselves beset by perplexities in the pursuit of truth. But, just as our pursuit of truth is not to be abandoned as an impossibility and a futile waste of time merely because we find it difficult to establish what is the truth, so our accommodation to the requirements of natural law is not to be given up or seen as useless merely because we find it impossible in practice to reach agreement. Truth is not less truth, and an ideal to be sought, for its not being adequately found; and the natural law is not less the law, and a court of appeal, for its not being adequately agreed.

In relation to the conclusions to be drawn from the primary principles of practical reasoning the parallel with those drawn in the theoretic order may again however be misleading. Here St Thomas himself puts us on our guard: "There is a difference between theoretic and practical reason. Theoretic reason is concerned with what is necessary, with what cannot be otherwise: truth is discovered in its special conclusions without exceptions, as it is also in its general principles. But practical reason, being concerned with human conduct, has to do with the contingent. And so, though there is a certain necessity about its general principles, the further it descends into detail, the more it may encounter exceptions. Thus in the theoretic order there is the same truth for everyone, though it may not be equally recognized by all except in its very general principles. But in the practical order there is not the same truth or practical rightness for everybody, as far as detail is concerned, but only in general principles (and even in those for whom there is the same rightness it may not be equally recognized by all). . . . It is right for all to act according to reason. And from this it follows in detail that things borrowed should be returned to their owner. This is right for the most part (*ut in pluribus*), but it can in some cases be harmful, and so against reason, as for example if what is returned comes to be used treasonably. . . . And the further one descends into details, the more does this happen. Thus the natural law in its first general principles is the same for all both as to what is right and in their recognition of it. But in relation to details which come as conclusions from those general principles, it is the same for all for the most part (both as to what is right and in their knowledge of it), but may, in some cases, admit of exception as to what is right because of particular circumstances as well as not being known to all."[33]

There are two important admissions made here. First, that to maintain a theory of natural law is not to be committed to the view that everything in it must be clearly recognized by all men. St Thomas envisages failure to recognize the more detailed requirements of the law as coming not only from inability to argue straight, but also from the effects of passion, lack of culture, and bad habits.[34] Secondly, that what is laid down by the law has not a rigidly universal application.

All this prepares the way to our considering the second objection that we raised in connection with the analogy of the manufacturer's list of rules. Is it not the case that human nature, upon which the whole elaborate fabric of the natural law is based, may change and develop? And may we not then say that what was once right, in changed circumstances no longer has application? I think this question has to be given rather more sympathetic consideration than Catholic tradition has been inclined to give it in the past. I have already insisted that when we consider human nature, consider what it is to be human and find human fulfilment, we must take human nature in its total dimensions. To be human involves being in a world-for-man which is very largely of man's own making; it is to be engaged in a world of communication, taking communication in the broadest of senses to refer not only to linguistic communication but the whole network of artificial transactions and conventions that man in society creates about him. Human fulfilment is to be judged not simply in biological terms, but in terms of the full realization of a man's personality in relation with other persons against the background of this network of communications. That will be right for him which enables him to fulfil himself in this dimension, and that wrong which does not. There is a sense in which the existentialist affirmation that man creates his essence by the decisions he takes rather than comes into the world with a ready-made essence represents a profound insight. To be forever progressing is a characteristic of man; the world around him is *his* world, the world for *him,* the world of his own ceaseless making and realization.[35] And this seems to mean two things: first, that he has ever new conclusions to draw from the general principles of the natural law, as he is confronted by new situations of his own invention; and secondly that conclusions earlier drawn may, in the changed circumstances, have no further application, or only a modified application. It is not that the basic principles of natural law are subject to change; but that there can and must be new applications in detail, and that some applications that held in particular circumstances in new circumstances may no longer hold.

St Thomas himself seems, in spite of the weight of tradition in favour of the absolute immutability of natural law, to have adumbrated some such possibility of development: "In one sense there is nothing to prevent change in the natural law; for much is added to it which is useful to human life, both by divine law and by the laws of men. . . . And there may be change in the sense that something ceases to be of natural law which formerly was so. As far as its first principles are concerned it is entirely immutable; but as far as subsequent precepts are concerned, in respect of those which we have said to be closely related to the first principles as conclusions to premises, the natural law does not change as if what was right for the most part were not always so; still, it may change in some particular, and in some cases because of special causes hindering the observance of these precepts."[36] St Thomas admittedly has in mind only individual cases of exception; but it may be asked whether, in principle, his ideas may not be enlarged to cover wider "exceptions". This is a question that should at least be further explored.

At the end of this perhaps too personal statement of the traditional concept of natural law, it may be asked whether I have not so diminished it as to make it of little value. I have argued that it is not "law" in the same sense as positive law; that its primary injunctions are purely formal, amounting to little more than discrimination between good and evil; that its derivative precepts are either so general as to provide little guidance to conduct or else so disputable as to win no general consent; and that in its more detailed applications it may be subject to change and exception. Is there anything left? I think the suggestion that there is not comes from asking and expecting too much of the natural law (as sometimes men ask too much of the existence of God, as if he were there to be a *deus ex machina* to solve all problems). The natural law does not provide a ready-made yardstick by which to measure other laws; it is not an alternative code which may be consulted to find whether it contains the laws made by men. If it were, there would be no need for the laws of men, except in those matters left open by nature and upon which some determining decision by authority is required. But it does provide the moral background or rather the immanent structure whereby good laws may be seen to be good laws, in their making and in their acceptance; it represents the pattern of law as law, discoverable, as patterns are, by those who enquire diligently; it might even be described as the special logic of law, as ever present and necessary to law as logic is to argument, but as little obvious to those who are not trained in it (even when they use it) as logic is to most men when they are engaged in argument. And as we may justify or invalidate an argument by appeal to logic, so we may justify or invalidate the laws of men by appeal to the natural law.

One final point may be suggested. The Catholic Church is accustomed to invoke the natural law in her moral teaching. It is often enough supposed that when this is done it is by way of appeal to evidence. But if my interpretation is correct, this is an appeal to evidence about which there is practically no agreement; and it is not to be wondered at, therefore, that it makes little impression on those outside her fold. What I should suggest instead is this: when the Church invokes the natural law, it is not by way of appeal so much as by way of affirmation. The Church, guided by the Holy Spirit, is charged with the guidance of men to salvation; this involves a teaching of morals. But as, in the field of doctrinal truth, the Church does not confine herself to matters which can be known from divine revelation alone, but affirms others too which she herself insists may be known, in principle, by human reason (as when she affirms the existence of God), so in her moral teaching she affirms that certain conduct is not only right and necessary for salvation, but is at the same time in keeping with human nature, is a matter of natural law.[37] The effect of such affirmation is not to provide an argument, still less to exonerate men from the difficult enquiry into what is right and in keeping with the natural law, but simply to assert, with her divine authority, that what she so teaches is incumbent upon all men quite apart from the extra demands of their supernatural destiny, incumbent upon them if they would truly fulfil themselves as men. It is left to philosophers and theologians, to sociologists and statesmen, to discover the why and the wherefore.

Notes

1. See, for example, the general treatment by C. J. Friedrich, *The Philosophy of Law in Historical Perspective* (University of Chicago Press, 1958; 2nd ed. 1963); or the more specialized studies of H. E. Jolowicz, *Historical Introduction to the Study of Roman Law* (Cambridge U.P., 1939), Otto Gierke, *Political Theories of the Middle Ages* (tr. F. W. Maitland, Cambridge, 1900) and *Natural Law and the Theory of Society, 1500 to 1800* (tr. Ernest Barker, Cambridge, 1934); and the short, but suggestive, sketch by Prof. A. P. d'Entrèves, *Natural Law, an Introduction to Legal Philosophy* (Hutchinson, 1951). In relation to the thought particularly of Aquinas, see P. M. Farrell, "Sources of St Thomas' Conception of Natural Law", in *The Thomist*, XX

(1957), 237–94, and for the medieval background, O. Lottin, *Le Droit Naturel chez St Thomas d'Aquin et ses prédécesseurs* (Bruges, 1931) and more briefly "La Loi naturelle depuis le début du XII siècle" in his *Psychologie et Morale aux XII et XIII Siècles,* t. II, 3 (Louvain, 1948).

2. Sir Ernest Barker, *Traditions of Civility* (Cambridge U.P., 1948), p. 312, quoted by d'Entrèves, *op. cit.,* p. 8.

3. Sophocles, *Antigone* (Penguin, trans. E. F. Watling, p. 138), lines 450–7; cf. *Oedipus Tyrannus,* lines 863–71.

4. Diels, *Fragmente der Vorsokratiker* (5th ed.), 21, B. fragm. 10; translation Kathleen Freeman, *Ancilla to the Pre-Socratic Philosophers* (Basil Blackwell, 1956), p. 22.

5. Diels, 22, B, fr. 2; Freeman, p. 24.

6. Diels, 22, B, fr. 114, 113; Freeman, p. 32.

7. Diels, 44, B, fr. 9; Freeman, p. 74.

8. Diels, 87, B, fr. 44; Freeman, p. 147.

9. That there may be a conception of the natural law that does not entail its being ethically superior to human law may be suggested by the words of Antiphon in the same fragment (fr. 44A col. 2 and col. 4): "The majority of just acts according to law are prescribed contrary to nature . . . the advantages laid down by the laws are chains upon nature, but those laid down by nature are free." It is interesting to note that Professor d'Entrèves (*op. cit.,* pp. 30 ff.) argues that the Roman, as opposed to the medieval and later conception of natural law, does not involve "an assertion of the superiority of natural to positive law, in the sense that, in case of conflict, the one should overrule the other".

10. Cicero, *De Republica,* lib. iii, c. xxii, 33.

11. Justinian, *Digest,* lib. I, tit. i. 1.

12. Gaius, *Institutes,* lib. I, i; Justinian, *Institutes,* lib. I, tit. ii, 1; cf. St. Thomas, *Summa Theol.,* II–II, Q. 57, a. 3.

13. For a discussion of the question of the origins of the *ius gentium* see Farrell, *art. cit.,* pp. 264–7, and Jolowicz, *op. cit.,* pp. 102 f.

14. Gratian, *Decretum,* I pars, dist. I, proem.

15. Gratian's view seems to be that the natural law is confirmed by Revelation; in itself "it came into existence with the very creation of man as a rational being, nor does it vary in time but remains unchangeable" (*Decretum,* I pars, dist. V. 1. §1).

16. See for example the remarks made by Professor Dennis Lloyd in his recent book *The Idea of Law* (Pelican Books, 1964, pp. 103–4).

17. E.g., Pius XI's encyclical *Casti Connubii* where expressions abound such as "natura Deoque iubentibus", "ipso Creatore ipsaque naturae lege iubentibus", "ad Dei naturaeque legis normam". (A.A.S., XXII [1930], pp. 545, 546, 547. These passages may be found in Denzinger (ed. 31), No. 2230, 2231.)

18. John Rock, *The Time has Come* (New York, 1963), p. 53.

19. The passage is quoted by Dr. Rock, *loc. cit.,* from Mgr G. A. Kelly, *The Catholic Marriage Manual.*

20. Marc Oraison in *The Catholic Viewpoint on the Liège Trial* (Mercier Press, 1964), p. 53.

21. "The natural law is simply a participation in the eternal law by a creature endowed with reason" (*Summa Theol.,* I–II, Q. 91, a. 1).

22. E.g., *Summa Theol.,* I–II, Q. 76, a. 1; I–II, 13, Q. 13, a. 3.

23. E.g., *ibid.,* I–II, Q. 90, a. 1 ad 2um; I–II, Q. 94, a. 2; cf. Q. 94, a. 1 ad 2um.

24. E.g., *ibid.,* I–II, Q. 13, a. 3, for the first principle regarded as end (*finis*). For the conclusions referred to as actions, see I–II, Q. 76, a. 1; cf. also I–II, Q. 90, a. 1 ad 2um. The precise relationship between the roles of the reason and the will

in the practical decision or "*electio*" is discussed in I–II, Q. 13, a. 1; and more generally in Q. 17, a. 1.

25. Cf. *ibid.*, I–II, Q. 9, a. 1 (especially ad 3um); and Q. 17, a. 1 where Aquinas uses the word "*intimatio*" of the reason.

26. Cf. *ibid.*, I–II, Q. 90, a. 1 ad 3um.

27. *Ibid.*, I–II, Q. 91, a. 2.

28. *Ibid.*, I–II, Q. 94, a. 2.

29. *Ibid.*, I–II, Q. 94, a. 2.

30. Eric d'Arcy, *Conscience and its Right to Freedom* (Sheed and Ward, 1961), pp. 64–5.

31. This phrase is sometimes offered as a summary of the doctrine of *Summa Theol.*, I–II, Q. 94, articles 4, 5, and 6. But in fact the doctrine there is a good deal more supple than such a summary would suggest.

32. *Summa Theol.*, I–II, Q. 94, a. 2 and a. 6; cf. Q. 90, a. 3, and Q. 95, a. 2.

33. *Ibid.*, I–II, Q. 94, a. 4.

34. *Ibid.*, I–II, Q. 94, a. 6.

35. I am indebted for this remark to Fr M. B. Crowe, "Human Nature—Immutable or Mutable", in *The Irish Theological Quarterly*, XXX (1963), p. 204.

36. *Summa Theol.*, I–II, Q. 94, a. 5. Fr Crowe, in the article referred to in the previous note, calls attention to several passages in which St Thomas speaks of human nature itself being subject to change (II–II, Q. 57, a. 2 ad 1um) and of the *ius naturale* itself being consequently variable (*Summa Theol.*, Supplement, Q. 41, a. 1 ad 3um).

37. This parallel between the declaration by the Church of what may be known by reason and her declaration of the natural law is suggested to me by a comparison of *Summa Theol.*, I, Q. 1, a. 1 with I–II, Q. 91, a. 4.

36

The Relationship of
Empirical Science to Moral Thought

James M. Gustafson

The extensive development of empirical sciences in the United States and abroad has had several consequences for moral thought, particularly for practical moral theology and ethics. The range of empirical sciences that impinge upon moral thought is almost as extensive as the range of actual problems that are discussed. Moral theologians have become intrigued with the rapid development of the social and/or behavioral sciences. It is no longer possible to discuss economic ethics, for example, at the level of generalization used in the great social encyclicals. Now one must have technical knowledge of the gross national product, the economics of development, the function of monetary and fiscal policies, etc. Nor is it possible to discuss political ethics without awareness of the structure and the functions of various political systems, the ways in which they operate in relation to law and constitutions, and even the behavior of voters. Sociology provides a basis for the critiques of moral thought itself, as one finds in

Karl Mannheim's essays in sociology of knowledge, and particularly, for example, in his essay, "Conservative Thought."[1] Sociology also provides concepts and data about social behavior, institutions, and class structures. Psychology is used to understand the nature of moral agents, and also increasingly to assist in the definition of moral norms of fulfillment, happiness and well-being.

The harder data of the biological and physical sciences impinge on other areas of concern to moral theologians. The science of fetology bears in many ways upon the ethical arguments about abortion. The technology developing from the science of genetics has attracted the attentions not only of moral theologians such as Paul Ramsey, but also of the dogmatic theologian Karl Rahner.[2]

Further suggestions about the general impingements of the empirical sciences on moral thought are not necessary. In this paper I shall address several foci of the relationship. The assigned task is a large one, and thus the paper

This article originally appeared in Proceedings of the Catholic Theological Society of America 26 (1971): 122–137.

is more an exercise in clarification and exploration than a thorough study. The relevant literature is relatively sparse.[3] Philosophical issues whose development requires more intensive development than is possible in this paper will be alluded to.

The order of discussion in this paper is as follows: A) The areas of moral thought in which one finds significant use of empirical sciences. These are 1) the understanding of the nature of persons as moral agents, 2) the understanding of the circumstances in which decisions and actions occur, 3) the prediction of potential consequences of various courses of action, and 4) the development of moral norms. B) Major problems involved in the use of empirical sciences in moral thought. These all affect the selection of empirical materials: 1) the judgment about what data and concepts are relevant to the moral issue involved; 2) this first raises the issues of the principles of interpretation in the empirical studies, of what are involved in the selection and significance of the data used; and 3) it secondly raises the issue of the normative biases built into the empirical studies.

A. Use of Empirical Sciences in Moral Thought

1. Psychological, sociological and anthropological studies have had a very significant impact in recent decades on the *understanding of persons*. The question to which these sciences have offered tentative answers is this: How can the behavior of persons be explained? Included in human behavior is moral action. Explanations are offered not only to account for particular acts, but also for the kind of person an individual has become, which in turn conditions, if not determines

what one does. The central concern that erupts in these accounts is the degree of answerability that agents have for their conduct. It is not as if the question of free will and determinism is raised for the first time with the development of social and behavioral sciences in recent decades. The question has been answered by philosophers and theologians in different ways throughout the history of Western thought. But the discussion of answers has shifted from the realm of metaphysics to the realm of descriptive and analytical accounts of human persons and their behavior. Indeed, one might begin such an account at the pre-social level of the genotypes of individuals, which have some determinative significance on their capacities to become and to act.

Another concern that emerges from these accounts is the extent to which individual differences between persons have to be taken into account in moral judgments. One can ask whether on the basis of empirical accounts of individual differences, whether one does not have to make moral judgments about actions with reference to the specific persons who have acted, rather than to a class of actions. For example would we morally excuse one person for committing adultery, while morally blaming another?

In general it is clear that the persuasive power of scientific accounts of the development of persons, and explanations of their actions has deeply affected moral thought with regard to these two concerns. There has been a major trend toward the willingness to excuse persons from moral accountability for their actions in the light of knowledge we have about their relationships with their parents, about the moral values of the communities in which they grew up, and the social circumstances in which they have been nurtured. In the arena of legal accountability one sees that psychiatric data are used to warrant an excusing condition. Data and concepts from psychiatry (or other fields) are used to make a case for the limitations of answerability. Men are not as prone to believe that an agent has "free will" in the strong sense that they once believed, and thus in some circles there is an erosion of the notion of moral responsibility itself. Although the concept of causality employed in the social scientific account of behavior has been subject to rigorous philosophical criticism in recent decades, partially in the interests of retaining a meaningful concept of moral responsibility, "blame" is often laid for moral faults not so much on the agent, as on the conditions over which he presumably has no control.

The accounts given of the formation of persons and of their actions also, quite consistently, has led to a trend to make judgments of moral actions increasingly specific with reference to the individuals who engaged in them. While this trend is ambiguous, it is nonetheless present: there are moralists who would suggest, for example, that adultery is morally indifferent, if not approvable, for two individuals who have particular needs under particular circumstances, while it is morally wrong for other individuals with other needs in other circumstances.

Thus far we have assumed that there is a vague and general agreement among the empirical sciences about the determination of human persons and behavior. It would appear at this point that one could speak of "the contemporary scientific understanding of man."[4] That such a generalization is not warranted is apparent to the critical reader of psychology, sociology, and other fields. Thus our later discussion of critical problems in the employment of empirical sciences can be an-

ticipated here by indicating that any moral theologian chooses from a number of renderings of the explanation of persons and behavior. Let us hypothetically suggest that he has read Freud, B. F. Skinner, and Rollo May, and has thought about the implications of the writings of each of these three persons for understanding the moral agent. The critical questions are which one should he choose, and why choose the one he does. It is likely that the moralist will choose the one whose interpretation is most in accord with his philosophical, moral, or theological predilections. If this is the case, one can ask whether he can claim "scientific" authority for the view of the agent that he adopts. If he chooses to claim such authority, he obviously has to make his case on scientific grounds, which implies that he will have to adjudicate between the scientific claims made by each of his three authors. The moral theologian could, however, make a weaker claim for one or more of the authors, namely that the authors are sources of "insight" into the nature of persons and into human behavior. If such a claim is made, he bears his own authority for the way in which he combines or uses the insights he gleans from one or more of the authors. He might take recourse to the justification that his own combination of insights "makes sense" to him, and hopefully to others—a justification which has its own implicit empirical references, but which does not rely upon the sorts of scientific evidences offered by Freud, Skinner, and May.

The choice actually is more difficult than we have thus far suggested, for it involves not only some selection of empirical data, but also the selection of certain concepts and principles of explanation. In each of the authors the data, concepts, and principles of explanation have been systematized to the degree that there is coherence in the overall position. Thus, as we shall note more extensively, the concepts and principles of explanation are already involved in the isolation of certain data about persons and behavior as being significant, and the ruling out of other data.

Enough has been said to rule out the simple use of a simple notion, namely "the contemporary scientific understanding of man" in developing a view of the moral agent. Here we only note the complexity of the issues involved in the use of empirical sciences in this area of moral thought.

2. The social and other sciences are often used to get a more precise and complete *understanding of the circumstances* in which a moral problem occurs, and thus in defining both the causes and options for action. This has been clear for a long time in the arena of medical ethics. For example, Catholic moralists have long been schooled in the biological processes of conception, and birth, and have argued their moral cases using the best available scientific data that pertain to the related moral issues. In areas of social morality some Protestants and Catholics have been operating in a similar way.

Let us take the interest in developing a social ethics for urban problems as a general instance in which empirical sciences would pertain. All ethicians would readily admit that a study of the history of cities would not provide sufficiently accurate and insightful information for understanding contemporary urban existence, though Lewis Mumford's *The City in History* might provide insight and perspective.[5] All would also admit that cities are much too complex for any one person to have a full range of experience of their life; each person is likely to have a partial experience of urban existence, as a participant in its productive economy, a resident of a particular neighborhood, a driver on its expressways, etc. Thus some supplemental information, some concepts for ordering it, and some principles for interpreting its significance are necessary beyond reliance on the knowledge of history and personal experience.

Among other things, one needs to know something of the structure and dynamics of the social order, the political order, and the economic order, to name but three factors. On the face of it, to turn to the social sciences makes sense. When one does, however, he is faced with choices comparable in principle to those above between Freud, Skinner, and Rollo May. Let us confine ourselves simply to the question of how best to understand the distribution of power in the city. A few years ago, for example, the social ethician had choices to make between the model of *The Power Elite,* described by C. Wright Mills with reference to the nation as a whole, which had structural similarities to Floyd Hunter's *Community Power Structure,* a study of Atlanta, on the one hand, and on the other hand, Robert A. Dahl's widely acclaimed study of New Haven, *Who Governs?*[6] Hunter and Mills found evidence for the existence of interlocking elites who by virtue of social and familial connections, responsibilities in industrial, political, military and other institutions, seemed to be in control of what was going on in American urban life. Dahl explicitly challenged this interpretation with evidences he gathered for the existence of much greater diversity of centers of power in a city. (The issue of locus and distribution of power is complicated even more by the shifts that are rapidly taking place; all of the books I refer to were written before the emergence of black power, chicano power, and other ethnic developments in American cities.)

How would the moralist decide between

the option of Hunter and Dahl? First, he might review the evidences of each author, and seek to determine what evidences were omitted. He might assess the methods of research that were used, and judge which has the greater degree of sufficiency for the study of urban power structures. If he finds one to be a superior scientific study, he might use its authority for his work precisely on those grounds. But second, he might probe behind the scientific work to inquire into the concepts, the principles of interpretation, and indeed, the basic assumptions about the political and social process that inform each of the studies. Are there reasons why Hunter is pre-disposed to a power elite model of analysis? Is there a view of man involved in his choice? One which, in a sense, sees men as power-seeking (in a quiet conspiratorial sort of way) in their efforts to retain control of urban institutions for their own class interests? Are there reasons why Dahl is pre-disposed to an analysis which finds power more widely dispersed? Does Dahl's empirical work rest on confidence in the liberal democratic process, and does this confidence affect his analysis in crucial ways? Does it shade his awareness of power elites? Does it heighten his awareness of pluralism? If the moralist finds answers to these questions, he makes not simply a choice of the best scientific study, but a choice of a point of view that involves philosophical commitments, and that leads to certain pre-dispositions in the area of morality. The choice of model will have a significant influence on the kinds of social ethical policies he develops and supports; if these policies inform institutions and programs, they will in turn affect actions and their consequences.

3. Max Weber, in his sophisticated studies of the methodology of the social sciences, long ago indicated that one of the functions of such research for moral and policy choices is to assist one in *predicting the consequences of certain choices.*[7] His argument is part of a larger concern, namely one that attempts to limit the value biases in social sciences. Whatever one thinks of the total effort in this regard, one would have to admit that social and other empirical research can make the prediction of consequences more accurate. The point is this: if on moral grounds you choose course of action *a* under the known circumstances, then consequences *l*, *m*, and *n* are likely to occur; but if you choose course of action *b*, consequences *o*, *p*, and *q* are likely to occur.

The arena in which the moral choices are made is significant for the degree of accuracy in prediction. In the situation of a dying patient, predictions can have a high degree of accuracy. If a physician decides that patient *x* no longer has any right to use artificial life support systems, there is no question that by "pulling the plug" one creates the circumstances in which he will die. In the arena of social problems, however, the accuracy of predictions is not as precise. (I once read an article which indicated that the Ford Motor Company developed the Edsel on the basis of potential markets that were indicated by social research. As I recall, the research suggested that persons who moved from lower to higher priced cars tended to stay in the same automobile "family." Thus it was predicted that by building a car in the Ford family that was more elaborate than the Ford, the company could increase its share of the total auto market. The illustration is trivial, but it makes the point.)

The moralist can make certain maximalist or minimalist claims for the authority of empirical research in the prediction of consequences for moral action. Hypothetically, he might establish a set of ends to be "good," and on the basis of social research define the policies and actions that would guarantee the achievement of those ends. (Max Millikan, in his essay on the uses of research in policy, in Daniel Lerner's, *The Human Meaning of the Social Sciences* indicates that researchers are often frustrated because persons who formulate policy and engage in the exercise of power rarely simply follow recommendations of the research. Millikan argues that policy makers have other matters to bring to bear than those in the purview of the researcher, and that the contribution of research is "to deepen, broaden, and extend the policy-maker's capacity for judgment—not to provide him with answers."[8]) The moralist, however, is not likely to have so mechanistic a view of social developments that research would permit him to function as a social technocrat or engineer who can control events to guarantee their outcome.

A more modest claim is likely. In the light of empirical research the moralist is likely to gain insight into the potential consequences of various courses of morally determined action. Insofar as the consequences of action have moral weight, that is, insofar as they can be judged to be morally good or better, evil or less evil, calculation of consequences is of major importance. In this regard social research can fulfill an important role in more precise calculation. This is possible without accepting a view of absolute determinism; what one accepts is at least the degree of determinism that is assumed in all views of human action, namely that to initiate an act is to intend certain consequences and to exercise such powers as one has to make those consequences most likely to occur.

4. The more problematic use of the empirical sciences is in the *development of moral norms*. It is problematic because it raises the philosophical questions of the relations of fact to value, of the *is* to the *ought*. Our concern is

not to rehearse that question in terms of the logical problems involved, or to review the hundreds of pages of discussion about it in the past seventy years. Rather we shall indicate some of the problems involved in the relation of empirical sciences to moral norms. Since the range of such sciences is so wide, and the applicability so multiple, our investigation takes on even more of an outline form at this point.

First, let us examine the possibility that the moral norms for economic justice might arise out of economic science, out of economic data. In the introduction I indicated that one no longer finds the level of generality of the great social encyclicals to be satisfactory for social ethics. Thus it is clear that I am positive about the contribution of economic science to economic ethics. But one immediately is pressed to ask: what are the principles used to judge a "good" economic system from the standpoint of economics? Not being well versed in economics, I can only indicate some hunches in this area; but it does not take much reading to find out that there are differences of opinion about what constitutes a good economic system. Clearly the science seeks *to minimize radical instability* in the economic system when economic knowledge is applied to policy. However, there are differences of opinion about how much instability is tolerable, and at what costs to whom in the society. Certainly *growth* has been a factor in recent decades in judging a "good" economic system. Growth clearly affects stability, and depending on where the growth is, it affects some persons adversely and other persons advantageously.

The more clearly ethical questions emerge when a word like *distribution* is introduced into the discourse, for it immediately evokes tones of justice. But it also calls attention to differences of opinion within the science itself. For example, I believe there was a strong opinion a few years ago that the way in which the economy might best grow would be for some persons to have sufficient resources beyond their needs in order to plow the surplus back into the economy in the form of capital investments. There was alongside of that the opinion that the pump should be primed at the other end, that is, by increasing the consumer power of the masses sufficiently to create increased demands which in turn would call forth increased capital investment. (I do not mean to suggest that these two opinions were not reconcilable at some levels.) My point is to suggest that the question of how wealth should be distributed is a factor within the development of the system, and does not necessarily, from the standpoint of the economist, immediately raise the questions of justice. But the question of distributive justice with all of its ramifications does enter rather quickly into a critical discussion. If one takes either of two famous formulas, "To each his due," and "Equals shall be treated equally," one quickly sees that economic science alone cannot determine what is due to each person, or who are the equals who ought to be treated equally, except on the assumption that the free market system takes care of the question of justice—that is, in a free market system persons would receive what was due them, and if they did not receive much they were not due much.

I hope it does not enlarge issues too swiftly or too much to suggest that when economists address policy questions (and the purpose of their science is in large part to contribute to policy and the direction of society), the themes of liberty, justice, and power are always latent. Indeed, one difference between state controlled economies, such as that of the Soviet Union, and freer economies, such as that of the United States, is the difference between the allocations of liberty, justice, and power. One might argue, I suppose, that from an economic standpoint one reaches decisions about these distributions; that is, one might develop norms for the distribution of liberty, justice, and power out of assessments about what it takes to make the economy function with a minimum basis of instability and a necessary rate of growth. Yet, what might be judged to be best for the economic system to function as a system does not from various moral points of view satisfy, for example, the concern for distributive justice. What determines the norms of justice are non-economic judgments about whether persons are to be rewarded according to need, or according to productive contribution or other criteria of merit, or according to ascribed status due to inherited social class. Clearly, if need were the criterion, it would have significant consequences on the allocations of power and liberty in the society. These would be different from the consequences that occur if one or several criteria of merit were used, or if there were a mixture of need and merit. The moral norm of distributive justice does not arise from economic science, but is independent of it.

When one is addressing questions of economic *policy,* one is in an arena in which ethical considerations and economic science interact with each other. At this level a case might be made that policy norms, used to determine the exercise of economic power, take on a character that is both empirically and ethically informed. (In a sense, the encyclicals have not been policy statements, but guides for policy; the policies illumined or directed by them had to be worked out under particular economic, not to mention political and other social conditions). Yet even at the level of economic policy it is not possible to say that good economics is good ethics, since the references of the word good in each case is different. Good economics usually refers to the successful functioning of an economic system as this is interpreted from a particular point of view in that science, and not to concepts such as distributive justice. Policy norms are informed by economic science, and refer to a given set of conditions in which the ends of human and moral values are sought, but policy norms are not in a restrictive sense purely moral norms.

In the area of obligations to keep life alive, at certain points the statistically human functions to establish the moral norm. These points pertain to birth defects. Birth anomalies of the grossest order are often called "monstrosities," and no moralist questions whether an obstetrician has the right not to sustain such living matter. Such monstrosities deviate so significantly from the statistical norm of the physically human that they are not judged morally to be human. At the other end of the spectrum are the "normal" infants, who are within the statistical range of the descriptively human, and here there is no argument about the obligations of obstetricians to sustain the life of such infants. Increasingly, questions are being raised about genetically defective fetuses, and about the relation of the statistical norm to the moral norm, or put in the form of a question, how defective (statistically deviant from the norm) does a fetus have to be before it is judged not to be normatively human from a moral point of view? Is the mongoloid fetus to be so judged? Is the fetus that has the dreaded Tay-Sachs disease? It is clear that the statistical norm refers not only to individual humans in such cases, but also to a normative conception of the human gene pool. A judgment about the benefits or cost to the future of the human race is based upon statistical extrapolations.

Clearly in the cases purported to be ambiguous the moral norm of the right to life is determined not merely by empirical evidence, but also by what the human community values as normatively human. There are appeals to moral values which are not imbedded in the empirically (physically) normative in all the instances in which the moralist would insist upon the right to life of fetuses or infants who deviate. Yet it should be clear that by permitting a judgment in cases of gross deformities that is based on empirical evidence alone, the moralist has opened the door to the use of such evidence in other cases as well. There might be several responses to this dilemma. One, it could be argued that even in the cases of gross deformities there are appeals to moral values which enter into the judgment, and these support the contention that there is no obligation to sustain the living matter. Another might be an elaboration of the first, namely that there is a dialectic between the empirical and the ethical, and that this must be worked out with references to particular instances, or to classes of instances. If this is granted, however, one must accept a degree of necessary uncertitude of moral judgment, for one would be appealing both to "facts" and to "values" which do not cohere perfectly.[9]

B. Major Problems Involved in the Use of Empirical Sciences

The purpose of this part of the paper is to specify some of the issues previously suggested. This can be done by formulating three major questions.

1. What data and concepts are relevant to the moral issue under discussion?

The answers to this question involve a number of difficult considerations. First, responses to "moral" problems are made in terms of the delineations of what empirically is the issue; such delineations are made in terms of experiential or empirical data. Thus what is included and excluded is crucial to what the actual moral issue is. One simple example will make the point clear. What is the situation of a dying patient? One has a different definition of the moral issues if the financial circumstances of his family is included in the situation than if it is excluded. If the use of artificial life support systems is draining the family resources, is this a relevant consideration in the determination? From some moral points of view it is not, from others it is. To include such information reflects a moral point of view; at the same time the exclusion of the information would state the moral issues in a different way.

Second, in many instances the empirical studies used in moral theology and social ethics were not designed to help the moralist answer his questions; the studies were not done to resolve the moral questions. Thus the studies are in a profound sense "translated" from their own arena of purpose to another. Certain information which is crucial for the moralist might not have been crucial for another purpose. Great care must be taken in acknowledging the limitations and difficulties of this translation process, for it might not only distort the data used, but also require a reformulation of the moral questions in such a way that crucial aspects from an ethician's point of view are ignored.

Third, it is possible that a pre-determination of which data and concepts are relevant to the moral issue might foreclose awareness of other studies, points of view, and information that are in the end of equal, if not greater relevance. For example, as one proceeds with

a question of economic ethics, he might foreclose it if he is not aware that political and social issues studied by other sciences are at least as significant, if not more so, in coming to a resolution. The ethician clearly needs to be open to a wide range of studies that might possibly pertain to the issues he is specifically attending to. The peril of openness should also be noted: since most human problems defy the boundaries within which research is conducted, it is possible to develop a degree of complexity of information and concepts that makes thinking unmanageable, and resolution impossible.

2. What interpretation of a field should be accepted? And on what grounds?

This question has been addressed at several points previously, and the considerations need only to be summarized here. If the moralist accepts an interpretation on its "scientific" adequacy, he has the burden of making his case for his choice on scientific grounds. Clearly most moralists are in no position to do that. Yet a counsel of despair is out of order. There are ways available to the moralist for determining which scholars are more reliable, and which interpretations are at least most questionable. The moralist clearly needs to be in communication with scholars in the areas from which he borrows in order to avoid horrendous mistakes of judgment, but he has to accept responsibility for making choices within the best of his knowledge.

If he chooses those studies that have an affinity with his own philosophical or theological point of view, he must be prepared to defend such decisions. In such an instance he would argue for the researcher's philosophical point of view as being more adequate, accurate, or at least plausible with reference to the understanding of man and society. For example, if he has a preference for social research that maximally takes into account man's capacity to choose, decide and act (in short, a high measure of free will), he is in a sense not only under obligation to defend that philosophically, but also to argue that studies done from such a position are more likely to be empirically adequate.

The moralist's third possibility is more eclectic, namely to use empirical research for sources of "insight" into the nature of man and society. Here he takes full responsibility to be his own thinker, and not to borrow authority from the research. To defend such use he will probably make claims for interpretations and data on the basis of the "sense" that they make to him, and to his purposes. His uses are subject to critical judgment and to revision when the insights appear to be inadequate or the data invalid.

3. How does the moralist deal with the value biases of the studies that he uses?

If it is conceded that value preferences are involved in many dimensions of empirical research, this question can be difficult to answer. The researcher's choice of an area of study at least refers to his interests, if not to what he values as being significant for the human good. Thus there is a reference to value in the choice of what to study. In addition, his preference for certain values is likely to have a considerable measure of effect on how he defines his research problem, what he is looking for, and what he consequently sees. This has become clear in the conflicts within some of the social sciences between those who have revolutionary tendencies and those who are "liberal reformers."

Again, a counsel of despair is out of order, for while the post-empirical and even post-ethical (in the sense of decisions about values or ways of life that can never be fully defended on rational grounds alone) are at work, there are canons of evaluation about good research which mitigate some of the potential idiosyncratic consequences of these assumptions. As empirical sciences become more sophisticated about these matters, there is greater articulation of them by the researchers, and this facilitates the moralists' discourse.

The moralist has to accept responsibility for his own way of answering all three of these questions. He is, after all, finite. He can, after all, only do what he has the capacities to do. Within awareness of these questions, he is more likely to be a better moralist by being widely and deeply informed from the side of empirical research. But empirical research will never replace ethical arguments in the resolution of moral issues.

Notes

1. Karl Mannheim, "Conservative Thought," in *Essays in Sociology and Social Psychology,* (London: Routledge and Kegan Paul, 1953), pp. 74–164.

2. Paul Ramsey, *Fabricated Man* (New Haven: Yale University Press, 1970); Karl Rahner, "Experiment Mensch" *Schriften zur Theologie,* VIII, (Einsiedeln: Benziger Verlag, 1967), 260–85; "Zum Problem der Gentischen Manipulation." *Ibid.,* 286–321. The first Rahner article is digested in "Experiment: Man," *Theology Digest,* Sesquicentennial Issue, 1968, pp. 57–69.

3. See Gibson Winter, *Elements for a Social Ethic* (New York: Macmillan, 1966), pp 3–82; Max Stackhouse, "Technical Data and Ethical Norms," *Journal for the Scientific Study of Religion,* 5, pp. 191–203; and Wilhelm Koyff, "Empirical Social Study and Ethics," *Concilium,* 5, No. 4, pp. 5–13.

4. John Giles Milhaven, *Toward a New*

Catholic Morality (Garden City: Doubleday, 1970). p. 118. This paper is in general a critical, but sympathetic, response to Milhaven's chapter, "The Behavioral Sciences," and to essays of Robert Springer, S.J.

5. Lewis Mumford, *The City in History* (New York: Harcourt, Brace and World, 1961). See also Max Weber's classic study, *The City* (Glencoe, Ill.: The Free Press, 1958).

6. C. Wright Mills, *The Power Elite* (New York: Oxford Univ. Press, 1956). Floyd Hunter, *Community Power Structure* (Chapel Hill: Univ. of North Carolina Press, 1953). Robert A. Dahl, *Who Governs?* (New Haven: Yale Univ. Press, 1961).

7. Max Weber, *The Methodology of the Social Sciences* (Glencoe, Ill.: The Free Press, 1949). The essays in this volume were first published between 1903 and 1917 during the "method controversies" going on in German scholarship about the natural and "human" sciences. They, together with other literature of that struggle, are still worth serious study today.

8. Max F. Millikan. "Inquiry and Policy: The Relation of Knowledge to Action," in Daniel Lerner, ed., *The Human Meaning of the Social Sciences* (New York: Meridian Books, 1959), p. 167.

9. The choice of both the previous example from economics and this one from medicine is intended to respond to John Giles Milhaven's statements in his "Exit for Ethicists," *Commonweal*, 91 (Oct. 31, 1969), 139. "Thus the ethical question can be purely a question of economics and an economics course appropriately replace the encyclicals." "Good medicine was good morality, and vice versa. . . ."

Part 5

THE VOICE OF EXPERIENCE: THE NATURE, USE AND LIMITS OF MORAL NORMS

part 5

The Voice of Experience:
The Nature, Use and Limits
of Moral Norms

Introduction

Moral reflection and moral discourse do not occur in a vacuum. Nor do moral decisions drop out of thin air. They all rely, as we saw in Part 4, on a number of sources. Some provide factual data, while others contribute human, ethical and religious insight.

Another extremely valuable source of ethical wisdom is moral norms. These can be seen as summaries of human moral experience over the centuries. They promote the values and behaviors that enhance human well-being, while prohibiting those which seem destructive. Norms offer short-cuts to the values and behaviors consistent or not consistent with a Christian style of life. While they don't resolve all moral dilemmas, they do provide the moral agent with guidance—in some instances very general ("be just"), in others more specific ("euthanasia is wrong"). These specific or concrete moral norms have been and continue to be cause for a lively debate, particularly among Roman Catholic moral theologians.

Some want to hold to the exceptionless nature of such behavioral norms as "abortion is wrong" and "sexual intercourse outside of marriage is immoral." Others, however, referred to as "proportionalists," maintain that some behaviors, which may seem to be absolutely immoral, can be morally justified under certain conditions.

This new direction results largely from a more historically conscious approach to moral theology. If more attention is given to the concrete situation, to the situational uniqueness of persons and communities, and to the developmental nature of all reality, can one still speak of universal, exceptionless moral norms?

Denis O'Callaghan provides a fine overview of the origin and nature of moral principles and their use in the moral lives of the individual and the community. He also explores the possibility of exceptions to moral norms, moving us into the current debate. Philip Keane surveys the various positions in the debate surrounding the absoluteness of moral norms. He situates this controversy in the broader context of moral objectivity, looks at current arguments pro and con, and in a balanced way points out certain dangers and areas needing further development in the newer approaches.

Richard Gula offers a closer look at some of the major players on the proportionalist side of the debate. Among these is the German moral theologian, Josef Fuchs. His treatment of the absoluteness of behavioral moral norms, which is considered a classic, serves as an example of some of the foundational work being done by so-called proportionalists. It is included here as a more scholarly and in-depth discussion of the issue. Finally, John Connery provides an opposing view, a balanced and respectful critique of proportionalism. He raises the objections and concerns of those who hold for the exceptionless nature of behavioral norms.

37

The Meaning of Moral Principle

Denis F. O'Callaghan

What function do moral principles serve in man's life and action? On investigation one discovers that they fulfil, or are expected to fulfil, a much more complex role than that explicitly attributed to them in the typical pattern of moral decision making. Here moral principles present themselves as criteria for distinguishing right from wrong in particular situations. But, viewed in another way, moral principle plays a much larger role than this in the life of the individual and in the moral welfare of the community.

The individual must find in his moral principles growth points and incentives for moral development. The moral principles implied here are not just those which serve to identify certain actions as right or wrong but those which give moral colour and direction to one's life. In fact, the description moral attaches more immediately to person than to behaviour. Aristotle remarked that the just man is he who acts from a sense of justice, not he who happens to perform just actions. Principles which measure the moral content of particular actions derive from a more static or code morality, whereas those which orientate life derive from a more dynamic or ideal morality. The former are a matter of means to be employed, the latter are a matter of ends to be attained. The former provide the moralist's material, the latter headline the prophet's message.

In his moral ideals the person lays down once for all a moral policy according to which or towards which he wills to direct his life. They are *his* principles, they are the conscience he has formed for himself. These principles introduce order and pattern into his moral life and correct arbitrariness and the tendency to bend with expediency or self-interest. But they do more than this. They act as a beacon drawing him forward to become the person he should be. His principles identify the moral individual; they constitute his moral personality. It does not matter that other people hold different standards in regard to business dealings, political integrity, pre-marital sex or whatever. True, this kind of conviction

These articles originally appeared in The Furrow 22 (1971): 555–563, 687–696.

could make for Pharisaic self-satisfaction, but such an attitude just cannot be part of the make-up of the person who is genuinely moral in the sense outlined above. In fact he will tend to make allowances and excuses for others and to be severely critical of self. Himself he knows from within, others he sees from outside.

In speaking of the morality of the individual one just cannot separate him from the community of which he forms part. In every-day life one notes that the moral standards of the individual tend to reflect the moral standards current in his community, and in turn his ideals and the way in which he lives out his ideals affects the community. This underlines the task of educators and moral leaders. Their role is to inspire ever higher moral ideals in their communities. The cloak of the prophet has fallen on them and they fail their responsibility when they preach a grey innocuous morality without life or challenge.

It is the man of principle who teaches moral ideals. Experience shows that men cannot ignore him or be neutral in regard to him no more than they could ignore or be neutral in regard to Christ. The selfish and materially minded whom he makes uncomfortable may deride him but such derision is itself a grudging praise. This man of principle is the just man of the Psalms and Wisdom literature. For him the overriding concern in life is to live out his moral convictions before the Lord.

If the day comes when the community fails to honour such people it will be an undeniable sign of general moral decadence. If the day comes when moral leaders choose to employ casuistry (which might be legitimate in some private capacity) rather than stand by principle then morality will certainly suffer.

It is evident that there is a world of difference between the kind of moral principle of which we have been speaking in the previous pages and the type of moral principle which is familiar to us in the casuist tradition. In the first case principle is something to be lived and died for, in the second it is something to be pared down and maybe got around. One kind of principle scorns self-interest, the other comes to terms with it. Christ and the gospels present us with one kind of principle, the moral manuals present us with the other. It is a daunting task to hold the balance between the two, but the ultimate in confusion is reached when one fails to recognize that there is a difference. This happens, for instance, when one attempts to read Christ's Sermon on the Mount as a code of morals and apply criteria to it which are quite alien to it. As a concrete example one has only to see how Christ's teaching on the indissolubility of marriage has been interpreted in the moral and legal traditions.

In the casuist moral scheme principles have been given the more limited role of informing conscience with a view to particular actions. In the process of informing conscience one may distinguish two levels of operation. Firstly there is the *factual* level, the level of objective observation, in which the person takes all measures necessary to acquaint himself with the facts of the situation and with the consequences which may or will result from a certain line of action. This preliminary step is itself a duty of prudence because the person is accountable in conscience for the full reality of his action, not only for what he intends to do but for all the foreseeable consequences as well. The amount of prior reflection and consultation required here will depend on the importance of the matter in hand. Next there comes the *critical* level, the level of moral judgment, where the person assesses different courses of action from the viewpoint of morality as distinct from that of expediency or mere practicality. It is here that moral principles find their usual role. It is suggested that the task of conscience is to apply general principles to particular situations, and informing one's conscience in this sense may mean no more than identifying the relevant moral principle and applying it rigorously. In fact, some strands of the casuist tradition makes one feel that the ideal scheme is when conscience is at a minimum or short-circuited by principle.

This raises the fundamental question: Where does one get one's principles? How are they formulated? These are the questions which come up for discussion again and again in our times. The authority crisis is at its most strident and emotional here. One fact is certain—there is no way of by-passing this question. Emphatic re-assertions of traditional formulae and suggestions that those who raise the questions are seeking to justify laxer moral attitudes and behaviour are counter-productive. Some moral leaders may still read their duty in these terms but far from achieving any positive result this tends to lose the genuine moral case and alienate the searching conscience. The person who questions a particular moral principle or a particular formulation of a moral principle is not thereby questioning the existence of an objective morality. He may indeed be doing just this, but more likely than not—and almost certainly if he is a Christian —he is asking whether a given principle or a particular formulation of a principle corresponds to objective morality. He does accept that there is a right moral solution in any given moral situation and that there is an absolute obligation to act in accordance with this solution. He will state that God always knows what this solution is whereas man often can only surmise what it is. To this way of thinking the charge that one is denying objective

morality when one questions a given formulation of principle appears particularly inept and uncomprehending. All this may be labouring a pretty obvious point, but it is the source of a lot of confusion and of some ill-will.

Where does one discover principles for moral action, and how does one formulate them? It would be too much to expect that one could answer this question to everyone's satisfaction, but at least there should be agreement on some basic points.

The first point is that moral values are primary whereas moral principles are derived. Conscience perceives or recognizes values, it works out or formulates principles. Typical values are respect for the person; respect for his life, his freedom, his property; respect for truth and privacy. These are the traditional natural law values. It is on the basis of such values that one establishes principles. For instance, one does not read off directly a blueprint for marriage (monogamous, permanent, etc.) as a statement of natural law. One concludes to a marriage structure from analysis of the values which marriage serves in regard to the child, partners, community.

Where moral values are abstract and general, principles are concrete and particular. Principles are guidelines for action, directives which bring moral values to bear on specific situations. Moral values are more readily appreciated, principles are more often questioned. They are questionable because they interact with the varying situations of life. They are questionable also because the very manner in which they come to be formulated. Where number of values intersect in a situation the resulting principle will be more complex and more open to question and further development. Even though many people would seem to welcome there cannot be a simple rule of thumb for solving the complex human situations which one meets with in business and medical ethics and in responsibilities of community living. Moreover precisely because principles undertake to relate perennial values to the myriad circumstances of life it should surprise no one that they come to be formulated in different ways as time goes on.

It is this suggestion of development or of change in moral principle which tends to raise hackles and turn theological discussion into controversy. The painstaking research into the history of morality which recent years have brought about has provided a corrective to the rather over-simplified picture which the textbooks sometimes presented. It is evident that change may come about because of a more enlightened understanding of what a given moral value entails. This is simply the progress of moral civilization. Change may also come about because of some alteration in the general situation to which the moral value relates or, more often than not, the two kinds of change may combine their forces in a given case.

As an example of the first kind of change one may cite Christian attitudes to slavery. St Paul accepts slavery as a social structure of his time and integrates it into Christian morality urging masters to be kind to their slaves and slaves to be loyal and obedient to their masters. It was only later that the whole institution of slavery was called in question morally and judged discriminatory and unjust in that it deprived a whole class of persons of basic human rights. St Paul's domestic ethic, his attitude to the female sex, is similarly coloured by contemporary mores. An example of the second kind of change is encountered in the moral principle on usury. In the primitive human condition money made its appearance as a means of barter. It had mere exchange value, was simply non-productive and so there was no title to any interest on a loan. With the

rise of commerce money came to play a different role in the community. It now had an investment function. Actual ready money had a potential value over and above its face value, and so there was a title of interest. It is salutary to recall that moral teachers continued to work with the antiquated definition of money for centuries and centuries after the change in the situation had come about. An example which combines the two kinds of change mentioned above is capital punishment or, in much the same kind of way, war. The institution of capital punishment was inspired by a number of theological, philosophical and practical considerations. At the practical level it was proposed as a measure for neutralizing criminals who would otherwise pose a threat to the community and as a deterrent to potential wrongdoers. At the philosophical level it represented a view of retributive justice which demanded life for life. On the theological level it presupposed that God had delegated to civil authority some of his power over life and death. In contemporary thinking these considerations no longer prove so convincing and the moral sense of the community is coming to see that capital punishment is a degrading experience of collective revenge in a civilized community, which anyway has other ways of remedying the evils which capital punishment set out to combat.

From the point of view of the development of moral principle the Bible is instructive. The Decalogue itself is a very primitive moral code. But apart from this we can read in Exodus, Leviticus and Deuteronomy regulations which must be regarded as the institutionalization of prejudice and taboo into moral principles. Here we find moral directives in regard to food and drink, marriage, slavery, sexual uncleanness, rising damp in houses etc. which ring very strange to our ears. 'A woman shall not wear an article proper to a man, nor shall a man wear woman's dress; for anyone who does such things is an abomination to the Lord' (Dt 22:5). 'You shall not plough with an ox and an ass harnessed together. You shall not wear cloth or two threads, wool and linen woven together' (Dt 22:10). Admittedly, it is difficult to tease out the various strands in many of these directives because the Pentateuch lumps together in its moral teaching regulations which belong more properly to civil and criminal law.

The admission of development in moral principle is simply a sign that our moral thinking is human also. It would be conceit to think that any age had all the answers and that it had summed up the moral situation accurately for all time, or that a change in the human situation may not involve some modification in principles. Aristotle had one kind of change in mind when he said that the accuracy of mathematical science is not to be expected in moral argumentation and formulation. St Thomas had another kind in mind when he distinguished between primary and secondary principles of natural law and between man's ontological and historical nature. The secondary principles are those liable to dispensation the principles of man's historical nature are those subject to variation with changing circumstances. The pity is that lesser minds have come to speak of natural law as if it were a detailed chart written in human nature, a maker's handbook which the professional moralist is trained to read. If there is any sure way of losing the moral case it is by overstating it. Even the very phrase 'right reason' can suggest that the elaboration of moral principles is primarily an intellectual exercise, whereas the experience of moral living in a community is the vital and most important part of the process.

For the person who accepts that Christ's message is a message from God and that he established a teaching authority to perpetuate his mission the question of guidance in moral life takes on a different colouring. He will accept that the Church which is inspired by the Spirit of Truth and which incorporates the magisterium or teaching authority of Christ has the right and responsibility to propose moral guidelines which bind the Christian in conscience. The Church has played this role from the very beginning of its history. St Paul sees that his function as apostle teaching in Christ's name implies moral direction as part of his ministry. The First Council of Jerusalem presided over by St Peter discussed certain moral questions which were causing friction between Jews and non-Jews and came to its decision with the preface: 'It has appeared good to the Holy Spirit and to us'. This has been the role of the Church all down the centuries in Councils' statements, in papal pronouncements, in the teaching of the bishops throughout the world.

In these moral decisions the Church does not set out to solve theoretically certain questions of morality for all time. It sets out to explain the force of Christ's teaching and to provide practical moral guidelines for various areas of Christian life. These directives, though not definitive, constitute a safe and secure guide for conscience, and the believer must listen to them and accept them. To require that they be infallible before they can claim one's allegiance really shows that one has little knowledge of the nature of moral principle and of the limitations which man's life and insights presuppose.

This act of faith in the Church does not mean that one is disconcerted when one learns that it has modified its moral teaching down the ages whether this be in regard to usury, freedom of religion, or whatever. In fact, this readiness to take new insights and new circumstances into account is a sign of integrity and vitality and makes the Church all the more convincing as a moral teacher. Neither should one expect that the Church should have an answer to every question. Such omni-competence would be quite artificial and would make moral teaching into pure formalism. In the days of Pius XII some people came to expect this kind of service from the Pope. Many of his allocutions now read coldly moralistic, apart altogether from the fact that some of the decisions were premature even on the scientific evidence available.

Against the general background which we have tried to map out in this article the topic of moral principle raises other questions of a more technical nature—Are there intrinsically evil actions? Do moral principles admit of exceptions?

Moral Principle and Exception

The possibility of exception is, by the very nature of the case, built into moral principle. The onus of proof is on the person who states that a given moral principle admits of no exception. This seems a very obvious point, and it is borne out by the fact that traditional morality proposed so very few principles as absolute. Given the various forms moral principles may take, the matter of exception becomes crucial only in principles which propose to lay down minimal moral requirements, principles typically introduced by a 'Thou shalt not'. Once the nature of moral principle in its various forms is appreciated this statement is self-explanatory.

Where principles propose ideals for the person, ideals which represent a challenge towards ever more demanding moral growth, the factor of varied response is taken for granted. One person, because of his awareness of the moral call, because of the generosity of his nature, because of the opportunities which life puts in his way advances further towards making the ideal operative in his life and action. Another because of the limitations imposed upon him by nature and circumstance will not have the same moral sensitivity and will not make the same moral progress. In similar vein but with reference to more material advancement Juvenal remarked: *Haud facile emergunt quos obstant res angustae domi*. The moral principles we deal with here are formulated along the lines of Christ's Sermon on the Mount. The ideals set out in such principles can never be satisfied. As in Bunyan's *Pilgrim's Progress* the Christian can never rest content with his moral achievement. But no one is expected to make the full journey at one step nor is surprise expressed that different people make different distances on the way. Short-fall or, if you wish, 'exception' is taken for granted at this level of moral principle.

Where moral principles establish minimal demands for moral action in specific areas the matter of exception raises more difficult questions. This form of principle typically belongs to code morality. We are familiar with it in the Decalogue. There should be no tension between this principle, which prescribes certain requirements for moral action as basic and universal, and that other kind of principle, which sets out moral ideals which each individual is called on to fulfil as generously as possible. One marks out the lower boundaries of morals, the limits between morality and immorality, the other sketches the heights to which conscientious man should strain. Traditionally the moralist has devoted a great deal of attention to this minimal level of morality, the high-water mark of sin. Here he recognized 'obligation' and 'moral law' and tended to dismiss the rest rather cavalierly as 'counsel' and 'evangelical perfection'. He tended to stay with Moses rather than go on to Christ. To some extent Christ's words applied to him: 'You pay tithes on mint and anise and cummin, and have neglected the weightier things of the law justice and mercy and faith, these you ought to have done without neglecting the others'.[1]

Going on to Christ does not mean setting minimal morality aside. The fact that certain principles mark the low points of the moral graph does not take from their binding force. Their purpose is to lay the foundations essential for any morality. The early Church had its problems here. Peter had to warn Christians: 'Live as free men, yet without using your freedom as a pretext for evil'.[2] Paul had similar remarks on those who took his teaching on the Christian as born into freedom and the Decalogue as superseded to mean that the moral law of the old dispensation could now be ignored. He did say: 'But now we are discharged from the law, dead to that which held us captive, so that we serve not under the old written code but in the new life of the Spirit',[3] but he had to correct the resulting misunderstanding of this new freedom: ' "All things are lawful for me", but I am not going to let anything dominate me. . . . The body is not meant for fornication; it is for the Lord. . . . Keep away from fornication'.[4] The lists of sins which are so familiar to us in the Pauline writings bear out this point of universally identifiable immorality at the lower end of the moral scale.

The typical lower case moral principle takes a negative form—*Thou shalt not kill, steal, commit adultery.*—The purpose of this kind of principle is to outlaw for everybody particular actions as incompatible with moral living. The negative gives added force and definition, a 'No Road' sign. Sometimes a principle of code morality may be stated in positive terms —'Honour your father and your mother'. This crosses the line into the sphere of open-ended or dynamic morality spoken of above. Precisely because the obligation is of this kind it cannot be easily pinned down or delimited, and so the factor of varied response or shortfall is admitted. The manual tradition had a maxim for this: *Praecepta positiva non obligant cum nimio incommodo,* positive precepts give way in face of disproportionate inconvenience. However, if one scratches a positive precept of this kind one finds a negative very close to the surface. 'Honour your father and your mother' = 'You shall not dishonour your father and your mother'. Acts of dishonour are more readily defined than the duties of honour. 'Whoever strikes his father or mother . . . or curses his father or mother shall be put to death'.[5] The negative admitted no parley and the manuals had a neat maxim: *Praecepta negativa obligant semper pro semper,* negative precepts always impose an obligation.

The reader may suspect that sometimes this interplay of positive and negative formulation is little more than a question of grammar and an attachment to definiteness on the part of the legal mind. Sometimes, however, there is much more at stake than grammar, and this brings us to the nub of our problem. We refer here to those principles which outlaw certain kinds of action as 'intrinsically evil'. On this title they admit no exception to their ruling. In traditional moral discussion the mark of 'intrinsic evil' means that a certain action is branded as wrong in all conceivable circumstances. No motive can justify it. The relevant maxim is: *Malum non est faciendum ut bonum eveniat,* one may never do evil to achieve a good purpose. All negative principles do not have this force. For instance, the precept 'Thou shalt not steal' admits that one may take or commandeer another's property in case of extreme need. Traditionally principles of intrinsic evil occur only in the sphere of sex (masturbation, pre-marital sex, homosexuality, contraception, etc.), and in the case of the lie and the killing of the innocent.

What does one really say in the statement: 'A lie is always wrong', 'Murder/suicide is always wrong'? Taken at face value these statements are platitudes since the terms lie, murder, suicide incorporate in their very use a foregone verdict of moral disapproval. One has no choice but agree that 'Unjustifiable or unlawful killing is always wrong' just as 'character assassination is always wrong'. If one wishes to say anything one must ask: What is a lie? What is murder? What is suicide? One must define these words in neutral terms, in terms which do not have a moral charge. Here traditional morality finds itself in difficulty. For instance, an obvious definition of lying is 'saying what one knows to be untrue', but this would outlaw the mental reservation 'Not at home' or 'Do not know', which convention found necessary and morality found acceptable. This suggested other definitions: 'Lying is the intentional deception of another', 'Lying is deceiving someone who has a right to the truth'. In other words one tailored the definition to allow for the exceptional case. Similarly in the case of murder. Murder came to be defined as the 'direct killing of the innocent person' to allow for cases where the killing was the indirect or side-effect of some otherwise necessary procedure (for instance, the doing to death of the foetus in the removal of a cancerous pregnant uterus) and where the killing affected someone who had abdicated

his right to live (capital punishment of the lawfully condemned criminal). But here the question must arise: Perhaps there are further sub-distinctions and exceptions?

From all this it is clear that the person who sets out to prove a moral absolute, to establish that a given action is intrinsically evil, is taking on a Herculean task. Proving a negative is the most awesome undertaking in logic. It is here that one feels most unhappy with traditional moralizing. The moralists show so little awareness of what they are taking on when they set out to give proof from reason or from 'the nature of things'. These proofs are frequently so threadbare that one suspects that the author did not depend on them to carry conviction. The reason for this is that he and his readers had already accepted the conclusion on authority and so 'proof' was purely by the way. This is a very significant point in regard to traditional moral absolutes—it is not so much that they *are* absolutes as that the magisterium or teaching authority *makes* them absolutes. The suggestion that authority can supply for or top up the deficiency of reason in establishing the morality of concrete moral problems is open to serious question: An authority which incorporates the inspiration of the gospel can certainly bring an over-all perspective into morality, but this does not imply a special charism for reading off the small print of natural law. It seems better to approach the role of authority in a different way. The concern of a teaching authority with responsibility for the moral quality of individual and community life is more than a concern with ontology (intrinsic evil, the nature of things); it is a concern above all with what best serves the moral welfare of the person and of the community. Consequently, the moral norms which it proposes are not just a matter of logic, but of life as well. It employs an absolute form of principle where crucial values are at stake, for instance, such values as the right to life of the innocent and the helpless or the stability of family life. Hence it outlaws absolutely abortion, euthanasia or civil divorce. It formulates its principles in this absolute manner because there is no other effective way of safe-guarding the important values at stake. Exception would mean precedent and experience teaches how precedent tends to ladder in some areas of life.

Authority, then, can establish moral absolutes, but it cannot make actions intrinsically evil. We now come to the matter of putting these absolutes into practice. Does the intractability of the human situation affect them in any way? It is here that casuistry makes its contribution. Casuistry has had a very bad press in recent times. To many people it suggests chicanery and dishonesty, hairsplitting and word juggling, arbitrary rules for breaking the rules. It trails behind it associations which reach back to Christ's strictures on the Pharisees, who emptied God's word of meaning for the sake of their system and who through legal exaggeration laid very heavy burdens on their people.[6] Admittedly, casuistry can become all this, but does the method merit such blanket condemnation? Casuistry as a responsible moral system is the strategy by which love and mercy find a way. 'The fruit of the Spirit is love, joy, peace, patience, kindness, goodness, faithfulness, gentleness, self-control; against such there is no law'.[7] The harshness of *Fiat justitia ruat coelum* was never found in casuist morality. It will be instructive to show how traditional casuistry managed when intractable situation encountered absolute principle. We have seen how the mental reservation was invoked as a way out of the moral perplexity

occasioned by the conflict of concealing the truth and still not telling a lie. Suicide (direct killing of self) was declared to be intrinsically evil, but self-sacrifice (indirect killing of self) was admitted where a value more sacred than life was at stake. So the casuist would exercise his ingenuity to show that the death of the patriot on hunger-strike or the death of the girl who jumped from a high flat to avoid a would-be rapist were cases of lawful self-sacrifice or indirect killing. Contraception was declared intrinsically evil, but the casuist did succeed in making a case for the woman who was at risk of rape on the plea that contraception had reference to *voluntary* sexual intercourse. Direct abortion was declared to be intrinsically evil. In the days before aseptic Caeserean section what of the case of difficult birth where mother and child were both doomed? In 1884 the Holy Office stated that one could not safely teach (*tuto doceri non potest*) that in this case a doctor might perform craniotomy on the child. Many casuists read ambiguity into this statement; if the Holy Office had intended to outlaw the operation it would have used the clear words *Praxim non licere* (The procedure is not lawful).

It is all too easy to pillory the shortcomings of the methods used in casuistry, which strove to operate in the no man's land between law and life. The fact is that these methods have proved themselves and survived the test of experience, which is more than can be said for any of the systems that pass under the name of New Morality. The principles of traditional morality upheld the just and the right against human arbitrariness and self-indulgence. They stood definitely for the good life as against the good time. One may question the legal formulation in which these principles were cast, but in the ordinary course of life the actions which fell under them would be judged immoral in any responsible moral system. In the borderline cases where the application of a rigid principle outraged common and moral sense casuistry came to the rescue. No doubt some moralists of a rigid legal cast of mind— good men in the worst sense of the word, as Mark Twain called them—refused to see anything beyond the bald formulation of the principle and its slide-rule application. Fortunately, the system of probabilism saved moral decision from becoming any one man's preserve.

The casuist method of meeting the obstinacy of the human situation may not appeal to everyone. Some may be more attracted to the system of condescension (*synkatabasis*) or *epicheia* which is found in the Greek tradition. This system of moral sensitivity in tolerating shortcomings, of tempering the wind to the shorn lamb, is very Scriptural in inspiration. In Isaiah 42:3 the Servant of Yahweh is described as one who 'does not break the crushed reed, nor quench the wavering flame,' a description which Matthew refers to Christ. The traditional attitude to divorce and remarriage in the Greek Church is typical of this epicheia. In Mt 19:8 Jesus says that Moses allowed divorce to the Israelites because of their 'hardness of heart' (*sklerokardia*), their unteachable and morally insensitive nature. He did not condemn Moses for introducing this compromise. It was forced upon him by events, by the need to bring some order into what had come to be an irresponsible situation. In other words, divorce on certain stated conditions was the lesser of two evils. The Church can also find itself face to face with *sklerokardia,* the intractable circumstances of human life and nature. This explains why it too has introduced a procedure for dissolving marriage. We can see this originally in the Pauline Privilege as interpreted by Church usage, but it is very questionable whether Paul himself in 1 Cor 7:12–16 contemplated anything more than separation without remarriage. In the Greek Church one does not find the attitude which goes with the more legal pattern of divorce in the Western Church. Here once a dispensation has been granted the legal bond is no more and the 'lucky' man or woman feels quite free and justified in re-marrying. In the Greek tradition the sense of failure remains. The principle of indissolubility still continues to exert a force over those who have failed to measure up to it. All this may seem alien enough to us, but it is interesting to discover that in the crisis occasioned by *Humanae Vitae* many episcopal conferences have employed something very like the Greek tradition of 'condescension'.[8]

In the above article we have shown that the question of moral principle and exception is perennial in every tradition of moral theology. The Latin casuist tradition solved it in one way, the Greek tradition of epicheia solved it in another. Today there is renewed search for a better and more consistent way of answering the question. It is seen that exception is not something that one introduces artificially and from outside into a moral principle. The very human way in which moral principle comes to be formulated always allows for further development and may admit of interim exception. In all honesty it must be said that those who condemn this search have not understood what the reliance on casuistic method in traditional morality was about. The search is not a question of denying an objective morality; it is a matter of discovering it as well as human resources can do so at a particular moment in human history. Believing in God means that one searches out the divine will in place of asserting one's own. The conviction that one's judgment is based on the best way of ascertaining this will is the determinant of a good conscience in the believer.

Notes

1. Mat 23:23.
2. 1 Peter 2:16.
3. 2 Cor 3:6–17.
4. 1 Cor 6:12–20.
5. Exodus 21:15, 17.
6. Mat 15:3–20; 23:13–32.
7. Gal 5:22.
8. I have examined this approach in 'Humanae Vitae in Perspective: Survey of Recent French Writing' in *ITQ*, October 1970, pp. 309–321.

38

The Objective Moral Order: Reflections on Recent Research

Philip S. Keane, SS

In fundamental moral theology, probably no theme, with the possible exception of fundamental option, has been more discussed in recent years than objective morality. This essay reports and reflects upon the current state of the discussion. The essay contains five sections: Catholic principles concerning moral objectivity, twentieth-century Catholic philosophy and the rethinking of moral objectivity, the premoral-goods-and-evils plus proportionate-reason approach to moral objectivity, possible problems and difficulties with this approach, and questions which need further discussion.

Basic Catholic Principles

As a starting point, it seems helpful to review the basic Catholic principles concerning moral objectivity which are held in official Catholic teaching and by Catholic scholars committed to the natural-law tradition.[1] Four principles can be stated here. First, there exists an objective moral order in which some actions are right and other actions are wrong; the moral order is not fleeting or capricious; it is not something we can make up at will,[2] granted, of course, that throughout history we continually gain insights into the exact nature of the moral order. Once we accept an objective moral order, we can say that if an action is in fact objectively immoral, no circumstances or intentions can make it objectively moral. To say otherwise would be to move into a strong form of situation ethics rather than to remain with the natural-law tradition.

The second principle states not only that the objective moral order exists but also that the human person (by reason even without the aid of faith) is able to know this order and understand that he or she ought to do what is objectively morally good and avoid doing what is objectively morally evil.[3] Without this principle the existence of the objective moral order would be meaningless for human persons. But with this principle the human ability to know the moral order and the human obli-

This article originally appeared in Theological Studies 43 *(March 1982): 260–278.*

gation to act on this knowledge are clearly affirmed. The second principle does not assert that the person has moral knowledge and understands his or her obligation in every concrete case, but it states clearly our fundamental ability to know the moral order and our obligation to act on this knowledge.

The third principle: once the human person and community come to objective moral knowledge, that knowledge is universalizable. If an action is objectively morally evil, the very same action is always objectively morally evil. Usually moral knowledge is said to be universalizable on two levels, the formal and the material. On the formal level, universalizability means that whenever an abstracted intellectual notion of immorality is present in an action, that action is morally evil. On the material level, universalizability means that whenever a concrete human behavior containing an abstracted or formal notion of moral evil is present, that behavior is objectively morally evil.

The fourth basic principle deals with a theme cited earlier: human persons do not always actualize their fundamental ability to know the objective moral order. Sometimes, either with or without fault or culpability, the human person will fail to know the objective moral order on a given point or fail to be free enough to act on his or her knowledge. This failure, while it cannot be ignored, and while it may render the person less guilty or not guilty of sin, does not change the objective moral order. In particular, this failure does not allow the community to weaken its moral norms. Neither does it prevent the community from taking appropriate actions to enforce objective moral norms. For example, not all the unjust killings of human persons (i.e., murders) may be committed by culpable human agents. But the community has just as

much right to seek to prevent the murder done by the maniac as the murder by the person who has full knowledge and deliberation. Of course, the community, in a spirit of humility, must keep on examining its moral norms to make sure they are articulated as adequately as possible.

The fourth principle also requires that the community be as sensitive as possible in dealing with those individuals in whose cases there is a strong likelihood of nonculpability. The tradition of care and compassion towards the nonculpable has a very long standing in the Roman Catholic view of life.[4] It is found both in the Scriptures (e.g., "Judge not, that you not be judged"[5]) and in traditional moral theology (e.g., in the manuals' treatment of the various impediments to human liberty[6]). It is often called pastoral sensitivity.

Rethinking Moral Objectivity

On the four principles just described, I see no basic disagreement among Catholic natural-law thinkers,[7] and certainly the Roman magisterium supports the principles. At the same time it is clear that, among Catholic moral theologians of our era, there is an ongoing debate about moral objectivity and universal moral norms. What are the issues under discussion? Why has the debate on moral objectivity surfaced?

In my judgment, contemporary Catholic philosophy is the most important single source for today's debates about moral objectivity. Of the many important philosophies now in circulation in Roman Catholicism, two strands are of greatest prominence, Neo-Thomism and transcendental Thomism. Both have contributed much to Catholic theology. In the Vatican II and post-Vatican II period, however, transcendental Thomism has come to have an increasingly important influence.[8] One fairly outspoken critic of transcendental Thomism has conceded that almost every significant theological advance made at Vatican II can be attributed to it.[9]

Many significant elements make up transcendental Thomism. Two of these, its anthropology and its epistemology, are particularly pertinent. As an anthropology (in Rahner, for instance), transcendental Thomism holds that the human person is a complex being, multileveled or multilayered.[10] Because of this complexity, I can never fully catch up with myself, never fully reflect on my actions. This is not a new notion: the complexity of the human person and the difficulty of analyzing human actions can be found in traditional sources and is even implied in the Council of Trent.[11] It should be emphasized that transcendental Thomist anthropology does not assert that human persons and human actions are so mysterious that knowledge of the objective moral order becomes impossible. But its insight into human complexity does raise questions about exactly how we are to grasp objective moral truth.

From the epistemological viewpoint (perhaps best exemplified in the works of Lonergan), transcendental Thomism points out that all our learning has about it a heuristic or processive character. We know the truth, but our knowledge of it is constantly unfolding itself, constantly projecting itself into the future through the recurrent operations of experiencing, understanding, judging, and deciding.[12] Ultimately the term of our knowing is the holy mystery of God, who is the ground of our existence, the ground whose reality we will never fully grasp.

To fit the insights of transcendental Thomist anthropology and epistemology into traditional categories, it can be said that these insights exclude the possibility of a metaphysical certitude about moral matters. But moral certitude on specific moral matters is possible, and on such matters moral certitude is enough.[13]

All this brings to the fore the key question raised by transcendental Thomist philosophy: How do we know the objective moral order?[14] What sort of data do we need? If the proper subject matter of traditional moral theology is human nature adequately considered, how do we adequately consider human nature? What needs to be included in an adequate consideration?

To answer such questions, a number of prominent Catholic moralists, relying on the philosophy just described, have called for a more exact analysis of the human person and human actions. If the human person is as complex as transcendental Thomism says that she or he is, does a relatively external picture of persons and actions suffice for our knowledge of the objective moral order? Or should we go farther in our search? Should we include in our description of objective moral actions more internal, more concrete, and more specific features of these actions? Surely it would be wrong to include mere subjective bias in our description. But is all the knowledge we possess about human persons and the interior structure of their actions merely subjective knowledge? Is not some of this knowledge objectively true knowledge which deserves to be included in an adequate description of the objective moral order? For instance, is not our knowledge of the growth traumas undergone by teenagers an objective knowledge which might legitimately be included in a description of the objective moral actions in which they engage?

The moralists who follow such lines of thinking ultimately come to a key point. If the external or exterior structure of an action does not give a sufficient picture from which to grasp the moral object of the action, might it be possible for two actions which have the same external structure to be objectively morally different when they are considered adequately, i.e., in their human wholeness? For example, would it be possible for the act of masturbation performed by the teen-ager to have an objectively different moral formality than the act of masturbation performed by a mature adult? Would it be possible for the homosexual action performed by someone in whom the homosexual orientation is unconquerable to have a different moral objectivity than a homosexual action performed by someone who is heterosexually oriented?

Those moralists who root their research in transcendental Thomist anthropology and epistemology are often inclined to answer the preceding questions affirmatively, i.e., to argue that identity of external structure does not always mean that two actions have the same moral object. Moralists working out of other philosophical backgrounds might well make similar arguments,[15] but transcendental Thomism seems to have had the most powerful impact on the major Catholic figures who are reassessing the question of moral objectivity.

A distinction between the exterior structure of actions and their moral object is not new. It is implied in a traditional phrase: the object of morality is human nature adequately considered.[16] In many moral issues which were discussed in traditional sources, this distinction was operative. Adultery, premarital sexual intercourse, and conjugal intercourse all have the same external structure; they would look the same if photographed. But we have traditionally understood that these three actions have different moral objects and that only one of them is objectively morally good. The basic question of moral objectivity, therefore, is not

whether external structure always yields the same moral object. The question is how much about the person and his or her action must be taken into account in order to grasp adequately the moral object of an act. The thrust of the moralists referred to above is that a more complete analysis of human persons and their actions is necessary before an adequate account of moral objectivity is possible.

Premoral/Nonmoral/Ontic Plus Proportionate-Reason Thought Pattern

There are, of course, many possible patterns for accomplishing this more complete analysis. Since about 1965, however, one pattern has become especially prominent among some well-known Roman Catholic moralists: the premoral/nonmoral/ontic plus proportionate-reason thought pattern.[17] It is worth serious study because it has significantly influenced the debate on moral objectivity.

The authors who use this pattern begin by pointing out that because we live in a finite and sinful world in which infinite goodness cannot be achieved in single actions, all our actions, even before we consider their morality, contain features which open up or enhance our humanity and features which close or restrict it. It is precisely these openness-oriented and closure-oriented features of our actions that some moralists are using as a basis for a more complete approach to moral objectivity.

The terminology used to describe these features varies. Josef Fuchs refers to the premoral evils in an action,[18] Richard McCormick and Bruno Schüller to the nonmoral evils,[19] Louis Janssens to the ontic evils,[20] Peter Knauer (early in the debate) to the physical evils.[21]

These authors are interested in distinguishing the premoral/nonmoral/ontic (or physical) evil in an action from the level of moral evil, thus explaining why they often speak about premoral etc. evil. But surely it is legitimate to speak of the premoral/nonmoral/ontic goods in an action as well as of the premoral/nonmoral/ontic evils. Some recent writing has described the premoral etc. level as the level of values and disvalues in an action.[22]

The notion underlying premoral as distinguished from moral goods and evils is not new. *Malum physicum* and *malum morale* are traditional terms. Even more significantly, the distinction between the premoral etc. level and the moral level of an action is very closely related to the basic scholastic distinction between primary matter and substantial form. The premorally good and evil features of an action are its matter, its material. The objective morality of an action is the action's substantial form, its meaning or intelligibility. The knowing human person must grasp the objective morality or formal intelligibility from the matter of the action. The person cannot draw from the action a form or intelligibility which is not capable of truly being found in its matter. Neither can the person draw a form or moral objectivity from the matter in a way which is not coherent with what we know about how we know.

This brings us to the key question: how to determine whether an action which contains both premoral good and premoral evil (as all finite actions inevitably do) is morally good or evil. The authors cited above have tackled this question especially by an analysis of the double-effect principle. They have noted that in the standard approach to double-effect situations (quite similar to premoral good and evil situations) there are two key rules[23] for determining whether an act containing both premorally good and premorally evil aspects is a morally good or morally evil act. The first rule (which traditionally has been decisive in dealing with many issues[24]) addresses the question of the structural relationship of the good and evil aspects of the action. How are the premorally good and evil aspects related to each other? As collateral results of some third aspect of the act? Or with the premorally evil aspect causing the premorally good aspect? Or vice versa? Similarly, how is the premorally evil aspect of the act related to the will of the person doing the act? Does the person want this premoral evil for itself? Does he or she want it as a means to an end? Or is the premoral evil simply the result of something else the person wills?

This rule concerning the structural relationship of the premoral good and evil in an action gives us much valuable insight. It tells us that we can never intend even premoral evil for its own sake; that if we already know an action is objectively immoral, we may never use it as a means to any end; that our will is more distant from a premoral evil which is only the result of something else we do, so that there is greater possibility that it might be morally good to do an action from which premoral evil comes about as an aftereffect. Hence we must always pay attention to the structural relationship of the premoral good and evil in our actions.

Structural relationship does not, however, give us a sufficiently precise definition of moral good and evil. From structural relationship we know that while we may sometimes use a premoral evil to achieve a good end (e.g., a just war, an amputation of a diseased limb), we may never use moral evil for a good end. But we do not know what exactly distinguishes a premoral evil from a moral evil. Thus some contemporary moralists have asserted that while we cannot ignore the structure of an act, double effect's second key rule, proportionate reason, is the decisive criterion for distinguishing premoral from moral evil.

The principle of proportionate reason asks: What is the fundamental reality found in the totality of the objective action? Is the doing of the action truly proportionate or coherent when all the aspects of the action are considered? What is the *ratio* or defining meaning of the action?

In explaining proportionate reason we must carefully discern exactly what it means. In many modern languages the first notion suggested by the word "proportion" is a mathematical or weighing notion. Proportion understood in this sense suggests that we should calculate the relative weights of the harms and benefits the action brings about: if there is a greater amount of harm, the action is morally evil; if there is a greater amount of benefit, the action is morally good.

Weighing or calculating of harms and benefits may often be helpful in moral reflection and analysis. It may open up the proportionality or proportionate reason the action contains. However, the weighing notion is not an adequate theological notion of proportionate reason; it does not reflect what theology has in mind when it uses phrases such as *recta ratio* and *recta ratio agibilium*. A more adequate theology of proportionate reason asks what defines an action, what gives the action its meaning or *ratio*. It seeks after the intelligibility which informs the material elements of the action. If we simply add up the harms and benefits, we may fail to notice that a feature of the action which is mathematically on the smaller side of the scale is actually more central to the action, more definitive of what the action is. With this in mind we can see that if it is to be the decisive criterion in defining moral good and evil, proportionate reason cannot forget how the action is done, how the person wills it, or any other aspect of the action.

The themes just reviewed indicate that the approach of some contemporary Catholic theologians to moral objectivity consists in two main steps. First, this approach seeks to reflect more completely on an action by bringing to consciousness the premorally (or nonmorally or ontically) good and evil features of the action. Second, this approach, without dismissing other criteria, uses proportionate reason as the decisive criterion in moving from the premoral level to the level of objective moral goodness or evil.

Since this summary has drawn upon and tried to synthesize the approaches of several different authors, we should note that each of them has approached the question in a particular and nuanced way. Two important distinctions can be mentioned here. First, some of the authors, such as Fuchs, rely fairly explicitly on transcendental Thomism's viewpoints about epistemology and anthropology. Others, such as McCormick, refer more rarely to such viewpoints. But in all the authors these viewpoints are an important background context, at least implicitly.[25]

Second, some of these authors are more theoretical in their approaches, leaving to others the task of testing the theoretical position by applying it to specific cases. But some have both developed the theory and applied it to specific moral cases.[26] My opinion is that both the theoretical work and the specific applications have helped to provide a basis from which the pros and cons of this pattern can be assessed.

Possible Problems and Difficulties

The current developments on premoral good and evil as joined to proportionate reason are only about fifteen years old. Hence it is not surprising that a variety of questions have arisen on these developments. While the premoral/proportionate-reason pattern has the support of some significant theologians, others have serious reservations about it.[27] In this section I shall review some of the major questions about the pattern and then assess its possible prospects. Six problematic areas will be reviewed.

First, there is concern that the premoral/ proportionate-reason approach denies the existence of intrinsic moral evil. The approach does insist that intrinsic moral evil does not exist on the premoral/nonmoral/ontic level (where intelligibility or substantial form in the moral sphere is not yet the question) but only on the objective moral level. This approach, therefore, does not speak of intrinsic moral evil until its requirement for a fuller and more concrete analysis of the moral object of an act has been met. However, once an action has been determined to be objectively morally evil, the premoral/proportionate-reason approach has no problem with calling an objectively immoral action intrinsically evil. No extrinsic circumstances can alter the moral evil of such an action. Thus it does not seem fully accurate to assert that the premoral/proportionate-reason approach denies the existence of intrinsic moral evil. It is true that the approach defines intrinsic moral evils more concretely than some systems, based on its more complete process of grasping objective moral good and evil.[28] Thus the precise question concerning intrinsic evil is not the matter of intrinsic evil per se; it is the question of the adequacy, in the first place, of the premoral/ proportionate-reason pattern in its description of moral objectivity.

Second, there is concern that the premoral/proportionate-reason approach does not allow for the teaching of concrete universal moral norms. The approach has no quarrel with the basic principle of universalizability in moral theology: once an action is understood to be objectively morally evil, it will be so whenever and wherever it occurs. Of course, the approach insists on its more careful and more specific process of determining whether an action is objectively immoral in the first place. It also insists on finding the same degree of specificity in other actions before they would fall under a universal moral norm. It holds that universal moral norms of a concrete sort may not apply to quite so many specific acts as would be the case in thought systems which accept a less complete and sometimes more external view of an action as a sufficient basis for arriving at the action's moral objectivity. So, as with the first concern, the precise issue for the second concern is not universal concrete norms per se; the issue is how we arrive at moral objectivity, how we recognize this objectivity in a manner consistent with what we know about how we know.[29]

Third, there is a high degree of concern that the premoral/proportionate-reason pattern leads to consequentialism or utilitarianism.[30] This is an important concern, since consequences alone ought not to be the basis for moral decision-making. As was stated earlier, the term "proportionate reason" can be used and interpreted consequentially, i.e., in a utilitarian fashion.[31] If all we think about when we say "proportionate reason" is the weighing of the good and bad results of an act, proportionate reason does lead to consequentialism. However, if we grasp the notion of proportionate reason more completely (along the lines suggested earlier in this essay), the notion includes much more than consequences. It includes norms and principles; it strives towards that which gives an act its basic meaning or definition. Thus it does seem possible to apply the notion of proportionate reason in a manner which avoids a one-sided consequentia-lism.[32]

Fourth, there is concern over whether the premoral/proportionate-reason pattern is too subjective or individualistic, too little concerned about the community with its responsibility to discern and maintain moral norms. The pattern strongly emphasizes the mystery of the human person. It does attend to important basic facts about human subjects and human knowing in its account of the human achievement of moral objectivity. Uses of the pattern which ignore community norms could slip into a subjectivism or individualism. At its heart, however, the premoral/proportionate-reason pattern insists on an objective moral order and refuses to accept a form or intelligibility which cannot genuinely be found in the matter or premoral level of an action. An action does not become moral merely because someone thinks it is moral.[33] The priority of the community and its objective moral judgments remains in place. While the fourth concern points to possible difficulties of interpretation, the premoral/proportionate-reason thought pattern is not inherently subjectivistic.

Fifth, there is concern that the notion of premoral etc. evil is too vague, too nonspecific. Since virtually every action in life contains both premorally good and premorally evil elements, how do we know which elements determine the moral objectivity of the action? How do we discern which elements of premoral good and evil are truly definitive of the action, and which elements are more peripheral and less worthy of consideration in describing the core of the action? In my judgment, of all the concerns so far discussed, this concern is most in need of additional study and reflection.[34] As with some of the previous concerns, the heart of this concern seems to be the understanding of proportionate reason. If a more precise consensus could be achieved on the meaning of proportionate reason, we would have a more sufficient basis from which to decide which premorally good and evil aspects in an action are significant in the epistemological process of discerning the objective morality of the action.

Sixth, there is a concern that we as a people are not wise enough or mature enough to use the premoral/proportionate-reason approach. Once we grant that proportionate reason cannot be arrived at mathematically, it can be quite difficult to interrelate the various values which form a specific action. Thus there is concern that proportionate reason may cause confusion on moral matters, especially if oversimplified versions of it are applied to concrete cases. This concern is often called the pastoral-suitability or pastoral-acceptability concern.[35] It has been raised or alluded to not only by Roman Catholics but also by some leading Protestant scholars.[36]

This pastoral-suitability concern has highly significant ramifications for the teaching office of the Church. In particular, the Roman Catholic Church, with its strong emphasis on the need for pastorally suitable moral teaching, will want to study carefully the pastoral-suitability of the premoral/proportionate-reason approach.

I have placed this pastoral concern last because it depends in many respects on the judgments to be made about the five previous concerns. If satisfactory ways to address the other concerns can be found, the evidence will point more towards the pastoral acceptability of the premoral/proportionate-reason approach.[37] But if satisfactory answers to the previous concerns cannot be found, the pastoral objections to the approach will become more decisive.

Above I have used a theory-to-practice approach to pastoral suitability, suggesting that if the more theoretical concerns about the premoral/proportionate-reason thought pattern could be satisfactorily resolved, the pattern would prove pastorally suitable. However, since we are now more aware of the real-life experience of people as a *locus theologicus,* a practice-to-theory approach also has validity. Thus it might be said that the more that people find the premoral/proportionate-reason pattern to be valuable in dealing with real-life experiences, the more seriously are scholars challenged to find adequate answers to the theoretical concerns about the pattern.

In view of the six concerns, what can be said about the state of the question under discussion? For the present, two key points can be made. First, none of these concerns has proven strong enough to keep the pattern from winning significant theological support from scholars who find it theoretically and pastorally sound. Therefore the pattern must be taken seriously. There is not at this time sufficient evidence for definitively rejecting it.

Second, in light of the concerns, the premoral/proportionate-reason pattern is not a completed pattern totally acceptable in all respects. It is a developing pattern which calls for further study and evaluation.[38] There is not sufficient evidence for a definitive acceptance of it. Scholars coming from a wide variety of approaches have questioned the pattern;[39] their questions cannot be ignored.

For the future, two major directions seem possible. First, through ongoing discussion the premoral/proportionate-reason pattern may prove increasingly acceptable as an approach to moral objectivity. I myself find this possible direction to be more likely, since reasonable answers for the six areas of concern appear possible.

The second direction is that in the light of continuing discussion doubts about the premoral-evil and proportionate-reason pattern may continue or even increase, so that the pattern ultimately proves inadequate. If this happens, it seems likely that other theological approaches will appear as part of the effort to come to the more complete account of moral objectivity called for by transcendental Thomism and other philosophies. It is important to remember that the premoral/proportionate-reason approach is essentially a means of raising a deeper issue: how the human mind arrives at moral objectivity in specific cases. Regardless of what happens in the current debate, that issue will remain crucial. Even if transcendental Thomism wanes in importance, the perennial question about how to understand moral objectivity will continue to persist.

Questions Calling for Further Study

Clearly, the concerns raised in the preceding section point to many questions which need further study. Here four such questions will be singled out.

The first has to do with finding a better way to determine which premoral features of an action are of such significance that they more readily lead toward an adequate moral description of the action. Which features more truly contribute to the objectivity of the act and which are more accurately understood as extrinsic circumstances? Should the closeness with which the different features of an action are intertwined lead to a different assessment of these features? Does it matter that some premorally evil features in an action originate from human finitude while others originate from human sinfulness?[40]

This question has a special importance relative to the type of freedom and knowledge present or lacking in the composition of the act. If an action with significant premorally evil features springs from a lack of due freedom or knowledge, there would seem to be a strong argument for calling the action objectively immoral, even if the person is not culpable for the lack of freedom or knowledge in the particular case. But if the person is lacking a freedom or knowledge which in the light of community standards is not due her or him (though it may be due others), the premoral evil which springs therefrom might perhaps not be a moral evil.[41] For example, on a given type of issue, a teen-ager might not be reasonably expected to have the same level of freedom or knowledge we would expect of a mature adult. Might the teen-ager's behavior in this case deserve a different objective moral evaluation than the behavior of the adult? These thoughts are tentative and probing. They stem from the insight that the nature of human knowing and choosing must be part of the way in which we account for the objective moral order.

A second issue needing study is the exact meaning of proportionate reason. The soundness of the premoral/proportionate-reason pattern in dealing with problems such as consequentialism depends very much on the development of an adequate understanding of proportionate reason. Authors such as Knauer and McCormick have given careful articulation to the notion,[42] but more work needs to be done. One theme is the relationship between proportionate reason and human intending in the moral sphere. When a truly proportionate reason is present in an action so that the action is morally good, the human will is clearly not morally intending the premoral evil in the action, even if the premoral evil

must be done as a means to the premoral good. Hence proportionate reason is ultimately a more accurate indicator of what the person is actually doing in a complex human action than is the external structural relationship of the various premoral aspects of the action.[43]

This suggests that a dynamic interrelationship exists between proportionate reason and the human intending will, that an interaction between proportionate reason and intelligent human intending is a factor in the breakthrough to genuine moral objectivity.[44] Our past tradition's concern to see subjective culpability and nonculpability as issues distinct from moral objectivity is legitimate. But it may be that some past theologies made too great a separation between the meaning-giving human subject and the realm of moral objectivity. Further exploration of the relationship between proportionate reason and human intending might avoid separating them unduly.

Recall our comparison of premoral good/evil and proportionate reason to the concepts of primary matter and substantial form. Objective morality consists in drawing substantial form from the primary matter or premoral good/evil, in drawing intelligibility from the matter. The decisive question to proportionate-reason theory is whether the form or intelligibility which the reflecting human subject draws from the matter is really in the matter, really drawable from the matter. If the form is not coherent with the matter, the action lacks proportionate reason and the person's intention becomes sheer nominalism. But can we make this decisive test of proportionality based on the matter (premoral good and evil) alone? Must we not interrelate both the matter and the intentionality of an action so as to get at the action's proportionate reason? Should we not compare the individual's intention over the matter with the intentionality or meaning which the community finds in the same matter? Answers to these difficult questions might significantly enhance our understanding of moral objectivity.

A third area calling for study is the question of a more exact understanding of universal moral norms. The premoral/proportionate-reason pattern has no quarrel with the universalizability principle: if something is true, it is always true, either in the formal or the material order. But precisely how does the universalizability principle apply to concrete human behaviors with all their complexity, historicity, etc.?

Karl Rahner suggests that our knowledge of moral objectivity in concrete cases is never simply a deduction from universal principles.[45] For Rahner, human creativity, human learning, and human reflection are always part of the process of grasping objective moral truth in concrete cases. Sometimes our grasp of the objective morality or immorality of an action comes about so instinctively that we do not become explicitly aware of the creativity and abstraction from the concrete which are taking place. But the creativity and abstraction are always there. Thus, might it not be true that the distinction between formal and material norms needs to be made less rigid? Might not even the most formal of our norms always contain an implicit reference to specific material actions, especially since all human knowing has concrete knowledge at its root?[46] Might it not also be true that our more specific and material moral norms always contain a formal element whose presence must be epistemologically evaluated as existing in the new concrete actions to which we are applying the material universal norms? To answer these questions negatively would ultimately be to assert that moral choice can be made without thinking. If there is no thinking, one wonders whether moral choice could be either moral or human.

This recalls our central point: the discernment of moral objectivity is the achievement of thinking human beings, of the thinking and knowing human community. Our account of the human, natural-law-based achievement of moral objectivity must take into account the way human beings think and come to know truth. Lonergan has noted that reality is more than the "already out there now."[47] We cannot humanly or rationally propose an account of moral objectivity which is not consistent with the metaphysics and epistemology of human knowing.

One more brief note on the ongoing study of moral norms. Without committing ourselves to the specific terms, might not the proposed insight about the need for a less rigid distinction between material and formal norms be the reason why a few authors have proposed terms such as "practical absolutes" or "virtually exceptionless moral norms"?[48] Some have criticized these terms, but the question they raise needs to be asked.

A fourth question calls for further study: finding an appropriate context in which to carry on the discussion of the difficult problem of moral objectivity.[49] The magisterium is legitimately concerned that the presumption in its favor be respected by theologians and by believers in general. The magisterium also wishes to avoid unproductive confusion on moral matters. Theologians, on the other hand, need an adequate sphere of freedom to discuss moral objectivity, and, as *Gaudium et spes* noted,[50] all believers have a freedom to inquire in accord with their capabilities. Ongoing dialogue is much needed to foster the rights of all the parties involved in the discussion of moral objectivity. Such dialogue about proper discussion contexts is also needed on many other issues besides moral objectivity.[51]

One suggestion is in order on how the discussion about moral objectivity might become less problematic in the pastoral sphere while the inquiry continues. For those who do not understand technical theological language, a contemporary formula on the objective morality of an act, a formula such as "containing a morally significant degree of ontic evil, but perhaps without objective moral evil," is rather meaningless. The underlying notion will have to be conveyed in nontechnical language. The same holds true for a more traditional formula such as "objectively gravely morally evil, but perhaps without subjective culpability," relatively meaningless to some persons.

With this in mind, might it not be possible for pastoral ministers, whatever technical position they hold on the metaphysics of moral objectivity, to use the same kind of nontechnical language when they deal with persons for whom technical theological terms are unclear? Both of the formulas mentioned above have two ultimate purposes. First, they aim to lead persons to higher degrees of freedom of action. Even if freedom is not due a person at a given time, the challenge remains to make that freedom due at a later time. Whatever one thinks about moral objectivity, persons are to be challenged to keep trying to eliminate all forms of evil from their behavior. Second, both formulas point out that persons need to be shown care and compassion. Neither refuses to accept persons' limitations or expects them to accomplish the here and now impossible. Both formulas are compassionate, as has always been the case with the Church's moral tradition.

If these two points—challenging confrontation and caring compassion—can always be present in pastoral situations, I think the needs of all believers can be reasonably well met while the crucial discussion of moral objectivity continues as it must.

Notes

1. What follows is only a brief summary of key themes in natural-law thinking. For a more complete treatment, cf. Eric Darcy, "Natural Law," *Encyclopedia of Bioethics* 3 (New York: Macmillan and Free Press, 1979) 1131–37, with an extensive bibliography.

2. On this matter of our making up morality by naming things whatever we want them to mean, cf. Karl Rahner's description of situation ethics as "massive nominalism": "On the Question of a Formal Existential Ethics," *Theological Investigations* 2 (Baltimore: Helicon, 1963) 219.

3. The traditional Protestant opposition to natural law is usually an opposition to the epistemological rather than to the ontological principle. For an example of the Protestant opposition to natural law, cf. Karl Barth, *Community, State, and Church: Three Essays* (Garden City, N.Y.: Doubleday, 1960) esp. 49. For the more recent Protestant openness to natural law, cf. James Gustafson, *Protestant and Roman Catholic Ethics: Prospects for Rapprochement* (Chicago: Univ. of Chicago, 1978) esp. 80–94.

4. For an explanation of pastoral sensitivity in moral matters, cf. Bernard Häring, "A Theological Evaluation," in *The Morality of Abortion,* ed. John T. Noonan (Cambridge, Mass.: Harvard Univ., 1970) 139–42.

5. Lk 6:37.

6. E.g., B. H. Merkelbach, *Summa theologiae moralis* 1 (11th ed.; Bruges: Desclée de Brouwer, 1962) 71–101.

7. Within the basic agreement there are diverse emphases among Catholic natural-law scholars. Diverse approaches to epistemology are foundational to many of the debates to be considered here.

8. Major transcendental Thomist works include Joseph Maréchal, *Le point de*

départ de la métaphysique (3rd ed.; Paris: Desclée de Brouwer, 1944–49); Karl Rahner, *Geist in Welt* (2nd ed.; Munich: Kösel, 1957); Bernard J. F. Lonergan, *Insight: A Study of Human Understanding* (rev. ed.; London: Longmans, Green, 1958); Emerich Coreth, *Metaphysik: Eine methodischsystematische Grundlegung* (Innsbruck: Tyrolia, 1961).

9. Cf. Leslie Dewart, "On Transcendental Thomism," *Continuum* 6 (1968) 390.

10. This multileveled anthropology is summarized, with references to Rahner, in John W. Glaser, "Transition between Grace and Sin: Fresh Perspectives," *TS* 29 (1968) 261–74.

11. I refer to Trent's position that we are never fully sure of our salvation—which is thus not a simple deduction from our external acts; cf. Decree on Justification (DS 1540, 1565).

12. Cf. Bernard Lonergan, "Cognitional Structure," *Collection: Papers by Bernard Lonergan* (New York: Herder and Herder, 1967) 221–39.

13. Cf. Josef Fuchs, "The Absoluteness of Moral Terms," *Greg* 52 (1971) 457.

14. In asking this question from the natural-law viewpoint, I have no intention of ignoring the moral guidance the believer can gain from revelation and the magisterium. Still, our tradition has strongly insisted that we know the moral order naturally, and thus we must account for how we know it naturally. Since the magisterium tends not to speak infallibly on concrete moral dilemmas, it too is concerned for an adequate natural-law approach to moral objectivity.

15. Other current systems which might seek a new approach to moral objectivity include existential phenomenology, language philosophy, historical criticism, and hermeneutical inquiry.

16. Thus it is inaccurate to say that the essence of traditional Roman Catholic moral theology was one-sidedly physical in its approach to human actions. But there were clear problems of physicalism in the way in which particular authors and manuals dealt with some moral issues.

17. Important works which have developed the pattern include Peter Knauer, "The Hermeneutic Function of the Principle of Double Effect," *Natural Law Forum* 12 (1967) 132–61; idem, "Fundamentalethik: Teleologische als deontologische Normenbegründung," *TP* 55 (1980) 321–60; Josef Fuchs, "The Absoluteness of Moral Terms," *Greg* 52 (1971) 415–57; Bruno Schüller, "Direkte Tötung—indirekte Tötung," *TP* 47 (1972) 341–57; Louis Janssens, "Ontic and Moral Evil," *Louvain Studies* 4 (1972) 115–56; Richard A. McCormick, *Ambiguity in Moral Choice* (Milwaukee: Marquette Univ., 1973). The first article by Knauer and the articles by Fuchs, Janssens, and Schüller (in translation) are reprinted in *Readings in Moral Theology No. 1: Moral Norms and Catholic Tradition* (hereafter *RMT*), ed. Charles E. Curran and Richard A. McCormick (New York: Paulist, 1979). *Ambiguity in Moral Choice* has been reprinted with a series of commentaries and a response in *Doing Evil to Achieve Good: Moral Choice in Conflict Situations* (hereafter *DEAG*), ed. Paul Ramsey and Richard A. McCormick (Chicago: Loyola Univ., 1978). Subsequent references will be to these anthologies.

18. Fuchs, *RMT* 119–22.

19. McCormick, *DEAG* 31, 37; Schüller, *RMT* 142–44.

20. Janssens, *RMT* 60–87.

21. Knauer, *RMT* 2–3.

22. For a sharp critique of this language, cf. Paul M. Quay, "Morality by Calculation of Values," *RMT* 309–15.

23. There are four rules in the double-effect principle, but the key is how to relate the two rules described above.

24. The tradition always recognized that in some cases the good and bad effects stemmed from some other good or indifferent actions. In such cases the structural relationship of the effects was not an adequate criterion, and proportionate reason had to be decisive.

25. One limitation of Lisa Sowle Cahill's recent excellent article "Teleology, Utilitarianism, and Christian Ethics," *TS* 42 (1981) 601–29, is that the article, which concentrates mostly on McCormick, may treat the Catholic authors who are reinterpreting double effect too much as a univocal or monolithic group. For an example of Fuchs's more explicit interest in a transcendental anthropology, cf. *RMT* 105–6. For an occasion when McCormick does use a Rahnerian perspective, cf. "Reproductive Technologies: Ethical Issues," *Encyclopedia of Bioethics* 4, 1459–60. It would be worth comparing in detail the anthropologies and epistemologies of the proponents and opponents of the premoral/proportionate-reason pattern. Such a comparison might help resolve the concerns about objectivity, intentionality, and consequentialism which we will discuss later.

26. On careful examination it can be seen that several major theoreticians of the reinterpreted double-effect principle have applied it, either explicitly or implicitly, to specific and controversial issues, such as contraception and sterilization; cf. P. Knauer, *RMT* 29–35; R. McCormick, "Medical Moral Opinions: Vasectomy and Sterilization," *Linacre Quarterly* 38 (1971) 9–10; idem, "Notes on Moral Theology," *TS* 39 (1978) 96–97. The distinction between theory and practice, however, remains valid and important. One might accept the theoretical reinterpretation of the double-effect principle and still insist that proportionate reasons can never be found in favor of masturbation, homosexual acts, etc. Critiques of the various specific applications of the premoral/proportionate-reason pattern are not possible in this essay. But clearly, all the nuances I make should be part of the way we apply the pattern to specific cases, e.g., to the cases treated in my *Sexual Morality: A Catholic Perspective* (New York: Paulist, 1977).

27. Prominent critics of the thought pattern include Paul Ramsey, Frederick Carney, John Connery, and William E. May; cf. Ramsey, "Incommensurability and Indeterminancy in Moral Choice," *DEAG* 69–144; Carney, "On McCormick and Teleological Morality," *JRE* 6 (1978) 81–107; Connery, "Morality of Consequences: A Critical Appraisal," *RMT* 244–66; idem, "Catholic Ethics: Has the Norm for Rule-Making Changed?" *TS* 42 (1981) 232–50; May, "The Moral Meaning of Human Acts," *Homiletic and Pastoral Review* 79 (1978) 10–21; idem, ed., *Principles of Catholic Moral Life* (Chicago: Franciscan Herald, 1980). Works more in the nature of commentaries on the discussion include John Langan, "Direct and Indirect: Some Recent Exchanges between Paul Ramsey and Richard McCormick," *Religious Studies Review* 5 (1979) 95–101, and Paul E. McKeever, "Proportionalism as a Methodology in Catholic Moral Theology," *Human Sexuality and Personhood* (St. Louis: Pope John XXIII Center, 1981) 211–22. It is important that the serious and necessary dialogue on this matter be rigorous and accurate. In *Sexual Morality* I described the position of a group of authors as "usually perceptive" (228). A recent critical article directly quotes me as finding the group of authors to be "unusually perceptive," a clear alteration of my actual text. Cf. *Australasian Catholic Record* 57 (1980) 402.

28. In view of this different understanding, opinions vary on what to do with the specific term "intrinsic evil." Knauer (*RMT* 7) seems to want to keep the term, but clearly with a broader focus. Fuchs (*RMT* 125) rejects the term as defined in a narrow sense. Albert Di Ianni, "The Direct/Indirect Distinction in Morals," (*RMT* 223–25), distinguishes between a strong sense (which he rejects) and a weak sense of intrinsic evil (which he accepts). Di Ianni's weak intrinsic evil seems to have some similarities to my concern for being more precise about the significance of various types of premoral evil and to my proposal for terms such as "morally significant ontic evils" (cf. n. 34 below). McCormick (*RMT* 329) would seem to prefer dropping the term "intrinsic evil."

29. Here again is the epistemological-anthropological foundation on which the whole development of a new approach to moral objectivity is based.

30. For reflections on the relationship of the long-standing debate on utilitarianism to the present Roman Catholic debate on double effect, cf. Charles E. Curran, "Utilitarianism and Contemporary Roman Catholic Theology: Situating the Debates," *RMT* 341–62, and Cahill (n. 25 above, 601–29).

31. In this context it is interesting to note that the English-language term "ratio" has a much more mathematical or balancing connotation than does its Latin cognate *ratio*.

32. Cahill makes this point very well (n. 25 above, esp. 627–29). Consequences can, of course, be part of an approach to proportionate reason. Thus it is not a question of avoiding all use of consequences in moral reasoning, but rather of avoiding a one-sided or overly exclusive emphasis on consequences.

33. An objectively moral or immoral action must have intelligibility. But the material in the action must be apt to sustain the intelligibility which the person seeks to draw from it. We cannot twist the material to make it mean anything we want it to mean.

34. In my own writing (cf. *Sexual Morality* 49, 200) I have found it necessary to use such terms as "significant degrees of ontic evil" and "morally significant ontic evils" in the struggle to be more precise about which premoral evils are deserving of consideration and which are not.

35. In *Sexual Morality* I wrote at length on possible applications of the premoral/proportionate-reason thought pattern in the area of human sexuality. I developed the possible applications at length and with consistency precisely as a means of further testing in a scholarly context the validity and coherence of the thought pattern. Such scholarly inquiry is an important part of theological work. I do not believe that such inquiry in itself violates the pastoral-suitability concern.

36. Paul Ramsey's insistence that the premoral/proportionate-reason thought pattern forces us to measure things which are immeasurable seems to have overtones of concern for pastoral sensitivity (cf. his comparison of McCormick and Daniel Maguire on euthanasia in *DEAG* 130–31.) See also Frederick S. Carney, "On McCormick and Teleological Methodology," *JRE* 6 (1978) 104.

37. In suggesting that this thought pattern might move towards a wider pastoral suitability, I am not implying that the technical terms used in the scholarly discussion should ever have widespread application at the pastoral level. If the pattern were to prove more suitable pastorally, other, less technical terminology would have to be developed. A suggestion on such terminology will be made below.

38. In an address to a large group of American and Canadian Catholic bishops in February 1981, Paul E. McKeever ("Proportionalism as a Methodology in Catholic Moral Theology," n. 27 above, esp. 219–21) offers a similar and well-articulated conclusion on the status of the premoral/proportionate-reason thought pattern.

39. An example of a more progressive Roman Catholic moralist who has some reservations about the premoral/proportionate-reason thought pattern is Charles E. Curran ("The Principle of Double Effect," *Ongoing Revision: Studies in Moral Theology* [Notre Dame, Indiana: Fides, 1975] 173–209).

40. For an important recent contribution on this point, cf. Josef Fuchs, "The Sin of the World and Normative Morality," *Greg* 61 (1980) 51–76.

41. There is more here than the mere fact that the individual lacks freedom (which would only argue to subjective nonculpability). The point is that the freedom is not expected. Should this fact lead to a different objective or community judgment?

42. Knauer, *RMT* 10–14; McCormick, *DEAG* 45–50.

43. Part of the issue here is whether psychological intention is to be distinguished from moral intention. Surely a doctor who amputates a limb to save a person's life has to intend to remove the limb. But does he or she morally intend the evil in the amputation?

44. This suggestion harks back to one of the basic themes of all realistic philosophies: an immediate and dynamic union of knower and known. The suggestion especially reminds us of Joseph Maréchal's concern with what the dynamic union of knower and known reveals about human knowing; cf. *A Maréchal Reader* (New York: Herder and Herder, 1970) 82–86.

45. Karl Rahner, "On the Question of a Formal Existential Ethics," *Theological Investigations* 2, esp. 222–31.

46. Cf. Rahner's theme that abstraction and conversion to the phantasm are intrinsic moments of each other (*Spirit in the World* [New York: Herder and Herder, 1968] 230–36). A contemporary exploration of the same theme (abstraction and fidelity to experience) can be found in David W. Tracy, *The Analogical Imagination* (New York: Crossroad, 1981) esp. 198.

47. Lonergan, *Insight*, 251–54, 385–89, and throughout.

48. Josef Fuchs, *RMT* 126; Albert Di Ianni, *RMT* 229.

49. It seems reasonable to make a distinction between the basic task and mission of the magisterium (which must be upheld by all Catholics) and specific questions about how the magisterium might best function to serve out its mission to the gospel and the Church. The issue of the most appropriate context for the discussion of controverted, noninfallible theological questions is a question about the function of theology and the magisterium rather than about the basic mission and purpose of the magisterium.

50. *Gaudium et spes* 62.

51. Much more would have to be said for an adequate treatment of the magisterium. Significant recent source materials include *Chicago Studies* 17, no. 2 (Summer 1978; a special issue on the topic); Karl Rahner, "Theologie und Lehramt," *Stimmen der Zeit* 198 (1980) 363–75; Richard A. McCormick, "Notes on Moral Theology," *TS* 42 (1981) 78–80, 115–21; and the statement of the German-speaking Society of Dogmatic and Fundamental Theologians, *Origins* 10, no. 36 (Feb. 19, 1981) 568–69.

39

The Meaning and Limits of Moral Norms

Richard Gula

After this long route by way of context and sources, we come to the meaning and limits of moral norms. According to Daniel C. Maguire, moral norms preserve in propositional form the insights of the human experience of value, the experience of what helps or hinders the well-being of persons and of all creation.[1] Moral norms are not recipes for moral action, nor are they the blueprint for present or future moral structures. However, they do enable us to bring some depth and breadth to moral judgment. They also provide some consistency and stability in the moral life. They provide illuminating patterns and common denominators which help us make our way through potential or real moral dilemmas. Moral norms, while never taking the place of our freedom, can help us discern what is right and good.

Moral norms can be positive (give to each his/her due) or negative (do not kill); very general (be good) or quite particular (do not speak a falsehood). Moral theology is interested in both the sorts of persons we ought to be

(character) and the sorts of actions we ought to perform (action). Moral theology distinguishes two categories of norms depending on whether they relate to character or action. *Formal* (or general) norms relate to character. *Material* (or particular) norms, also called concrete, behavioral norms, relate to action. We will look at the meaning and limits of each type.

Formal Norms

Many people often ask if there are any absolutes in contemporary morality. Are there permanent and enduring moral norms? Yes, there are. The Roman Catholic Church has frequently witnessed to these absolutes in official teaching. Of the many examples that can be given of this witness, this statement from *Persona Humana* (the "Declaration on Certain Questions Concerning Sexual Ethics") of 1975 is typical:

This article is excerpted from What Are They Saying About Moral Norms? *(New York: Paulist, 1982) 54–60, 61–79.*

Now in fact the Church throughout her history has always considered a certain number of precepts of the natural law as having an absolute and immutable value, and in their transgression she has seen a contradiction of the teaching and spirit of the Gospel (n. 4).

Many theologians today interpret these kinds of norms as formal norms. These permanent and enduring norms reflect fixed points to divine revelation (like Jesus, the kingdom, conversion, the commandment of love, openness to the poor, etc.) and what is universal to humankind (like basic needs of security, acceptance, affection, etc., and basic goods like life, freedom, etc.). The origin of such norms reaches below the permutations of culture and different ages. As *Persona Humana* maintains:

These principles and norms [which pertain to certain fundamental values of human and Christian life] in no way owe their origin to a certain type of culture, but rather to knowledge of the divine law and of human nature (n. 5).

Yet the concrete expression of these norms and the fundamental values which they express partake of particular cultures and historical epochs. Timothy O'Connell explains this well when he says formal norms express values which are universal among humankind. While the way of expressing these values may differ among persons and groups, the affirmation of them as constitutive of what it means to be human is universally accepted.[2] Louis Janssens speaks of the implications of the character of formal norms as absolute this way:

For instance, it will remain true that, always and in all circumstances, we must be just: we ought to be so disposed as to be concerned with the growth of truly human social relationships and structures as well as with the promotion of the possibilities for that purpose.[3]

What these theologians seem to be saying is that while we can and must speak of some moral norms as absolute, these same norms are nonetheless limited by nothing less than the absolute par excellence of Christian faith —the incarnational principle itself.

Many theologians further relate formal norms to the sorts of persons we ought to be. As Louis Janssens puts it, formal norms "assert what our dispositions ought to be."[4] This means that formal norms point to what the animating element of our moral life ought to be. For Timothy O'Connell, they "articulate the inner value-dynamic of the human person."[5] This means that formal norms do not tell us what we ought to do, but bring to a focus the sorts of persons we ought to become, and they exhort, challenge, and encourage us to become that way.[6]

What are some examples of formal norms? The great commandment: love God and love your neighbor as yourself (Mt 22:37–40; cf. Mk 12:29–34; Lk 10:27) and the golden rule: "Whatever you wish others to do to you, do so to them" (Mt 7:12; Lk 6:31) are formal norms. Other examples are do good and avoid evil, respect life, be honest, be just, be chaste, be grateful, be humble, be prudent, be reasonable, etc.; expressed negatively, do not be selfish, vain, promiscuous, proud, stingy, merciless, foolish, etc.

These examples of formal norms are expressed in the language of traditional moral virtues when expressed positively, or vices when expressed negatively. There are other expressions of formal norms which are a little more puzzling than these. The more puzzling kinds of formal norms are those which include such terms as: murder, lying, stealing, adultery, blasphemy, genocide, euthanasia, slavery, etc. What makes these kinds of formal norms somewhat puzzling is that they are expressed with "synthetic" terms.

What is the meaning of synthetic terms? Louis Janssens describes synthetic terms as words "which refer to the material content of an action but at the same time formulate a moral judgment."[7] This means that synthetic terms are compact value terms, not simply descriptive terms; that is, they already bear as part of their meaning a moral qualification. For example, "murder" is a morally qualifying term affirming that a killing (a descriptive term) is unjust (an evaluative term); "lie" is a morally qualifying term affirming that a falsehood (a descriptive term) is immoral (an evaluative term); "adultery" is a morally qualifying term affirming that an act of sexual intercourse (a descriptive term) is with the wrong person and for the wrong reasons (evaluative terms).[8]

Therefore, formal norms that use synthetic terms *not only* identify material action, *but also* bear moral evaluation of that action. When an action is finally designated as "murder," "adultery," "genocide," etc., nothing can ever justify the action to make it morally right. This makes norms which use these terms, norms like "do not lie," "do not steal," "do not commit adultery," absolute. These are absolute because they are tautological; that is, they simply tell us that immoral behavior is immoral. Once an action is designated as immoral, it can never be justified. These norms which use synthetic terms do not give us any new information. They simply affirm what we already know. The real issue that

remains for the moral person is not to determine whether murder, lying, stealing, adultery, blasphemy, or the like could ever be justified. They cannot. The real issue is how intention and circumstances must be weighed and related in order to count this material act (killing) as immoral (murder). We cannot know which act of killing is murder until we have considered the whole action. Once an act of killing can rightly be defined by the synthetic term "murder," the action is taken as a whole and no further intention or circumstances can justify it. But the proper proportion of the action, intention, and circumstances must be determined before this judgment can be made.[9]

Formal norms, whether expressing ways of being in the language of virtue or with synthetic terms, are limited in that they do not determine the concrete content of what we ought to do. The formal norm "be chaste," for example, describes an inner attitude of ordering our sexuality in such a way that we respect ourselves, others, and the demands of social life. This norm does not, however, tell us which actions embody a chaste disposition in every instance. In like manner, the formal norm "do not murder" does not give us new information about the action of killing. It simply reminds us of what we already know (unjust killing is unjust) and urges us to act on this knowledge.

Even though formal norms do not tell us what to do, they are still quite useful. Timothy O'Connell and Louis Janssens have been emphatic on the importance of formal norms to provide motivation, exhortation, and challenge to do what we already know to be right and good.[10] Timothy O'Connell says it well:

> I do not need only the data, I also
> need encouragement. I need formu-

lations of my own values, formulations which in their conciseness and directness help me remain faithful to those values. And here is the specific (and very important) function of formal norms. They take the meaning of humanity, with its challenge of intellect and freedom. They apply that meaning to a particular area of human life (for example, property rights). And they declare, in pithy form, what I already know but tend to forget or neglect: Do not steal. By presenting me with that challenge, almost in aphoristic style, formal norms serve me in those moments of human weakness and temptation which are so much a part of our sin-affected situation.[11]

In conclusion, we see that formal norms are absolute in character and motivational in function. They do not give us specific information to answer the practical moral question, "What ought I to do?" Formal norms presume that we know. Formal norms help us to answer the question, "Must I do this or avoid that?" Formal norms remind us of what is good or bad and encourage us to do good and avoid evil.

Material Norms

Formal norms are not the area of greatest controversy in contemporary theology, especially Catholic theology. Material norms are. Material norms relate to the sorts of actions we ought to perform. Material norms attempt to attach formal norms to concrete pieces of behavior—to speech, to killing, to making promises, to sexual conduct, etc. Thus we have material norms like these: entrusted se-

crets ought to be kept, do not speak falsely, do not kill, do not use artificial means of contraception.

Material norms lead us closer to answering the practical moral question, "What should I do?" Situations of conflict have forced moral theologians to look more closely at the meaning and limits of material norms. Consider these two examples which are typical of the kinds of moral dilemmas that have forced a great deal of rethinking about the meaning and limits of material norms. If a doctor tells the truth to her patient, she may harm the patient's psychic health. If the doctor speaks a falsehood, she may begin to damage the confidence the patient has in her and the doctor may begin to experience a loss of truthfulness in herself. How is the doctor to live with the material norm: Do not speak a falsehood? Or take the case of the married couple who have all the children they can reasonably care for. They cannot enlarge their family without compromising the well-being of their present children. At the same time, the couple feels that fairly regular sexual expression is necessary for the growth and development of their marriage. They do not feel that they can respond adequately to both values and follow the proscription of contraception in *Humanae Vitae*. What do they do?

Mixed Consequentialism—The Revisionist Theologians

I will report these representative examples of Catholic revisionist thinking on material norms in chronological order to show how the discussion has progressed.

1. *Peter Knauer.* Peter Knauer's work represents what may be considered the first step in a new direction for interpreting the meaning and limits of material norms. His major

article on moral norms appeared in various forms between 1965–1967.[12]

Peter Knauer makes his contribution to the discussion of material norms through his efforts to reinterpret the principle of double effect. The principle of double effect has been staple ethical fare for centuries in Catholic theology. It helps us through situations of conflict where two values are at stake at the same time and both cannot be preserved. For example, in the case of ectopic pregnancy the life of the mother and the life of the developing fetus are at stake. The principle of double effect helps us to determine whether causing or permitting harm to the mother or the fetus is morally evil. The traditional rendering of the principle of double effect, to put it briefly, assumes that there is a significant moral difference between intending evil and permitting evil as a side effect of a good action. The principle asserts that with a proportionate (commensurate) reason we may permit evil to occur but we may never directly intend to do evil even for a good reason.

Knauer's interpretation of the principle of double effect is this: "The principle of double effect means that to cause or permit an evil without commensurate reason is a morally bad act."[13] His major thesis which has implications for the meaning and limits of material norms reads like this:

> Whether there is a violation of a commandment (that is, whether an act is murder, lying, theft) can be ascertained only if it is established that the reason for the act in its existential entirety is not commensurate.[14]

The key to understanding Knauer's thesis hinges on his distinction between physical evil and moral evil, and on what constitutes a commensurate reason. We need to understand his meaning of each.

Physical evils are such things as sickness, error, destruction, ignorance, loss of reputation, death, or whatever harm we may experience.[15] We do not intend physical evils for themselves but only accept them on account of some associated good which we do want but cannot get apart from taking the physical evil that inevitably comes along with it. Moral evil, says Knauer, "consists in the last analysis in the permission or causing of a physical evil which is not justified by a commensurate reason."[16] Commensurate reason, then, determines to a great extent the moral content of our actions.

When is a reason a "commensurate reason"? And to what is a reason "commensurate"? Knauer is emphatic that a commensurate reason is not just any reason; nor is it simply a serious reason, a sincere reason, or even an important reason.[17] A reason is commensurate for Knauer when there is no long-run contradiction between the value intended and the means of achieving it. Or, to put it another way, a reason for acting is commensurate if causing or permitting some physical evil does not, in the long run, undermine the intended value but actually supports it.[18] Whether a reason for an action is commensurate or not depends on objective criteria and not merely good will.[19] The objective criteria are derived from the proper relationship of three elements: the action, the intention of the agent, and the circumstances in which the action takes place. Since the relationship of these elements cannot be determined in advance, it is not possible to give a catalogue of commensurate reasons for which the act would be regarded as permissible at all times and for which there would be no need for any further considerations.[20]

How does Knauer's thesis work in practice? The practical consequences of his thesis are well illustrated in this example which can serve as a summary of his position:

> Whether the removal of a limb is a health measure or a mutilation of the patient cannot be recognized in the concrete actuality which might be photographed. The reason why the surgeon removes the limb must be looked at. What value does the act seek to serve? It is done because of the health of the patient. But this by itself does not determine the morality of the act. A purely good intention in the psychological sense does not determine the moral goodness of an act. It must be established that this reason is a commensurate one. If, in the given circumstances, the act is the best possible solution of the problem in terms of the horizon given by the whole of reality, it may be said that the act is morally good. In a moral sense, what is then intended is not the taking of the limb, but the health of the patient.[21]

Knauer's analysis has important implications for the meaning and limits of material norms. Should we take material norms as statements of moral qualifications which can be universally applied to particular cases? Knauer says that our norms generally appear to be these kinds of universal statements and receive this kind of application. However, this way of regarding material norms obscures the distinction between physical and moral evil. According to Knauer's position, concrete material norms, especially negative ones, are prohibitions of what causes physical evil without a commensurate reason. For Knauer, "a moral judgment is naturally possible only when in a concrete act it is established whether the reason for the act is commensurate or not."[22] Material norms must not be read as identifying the physical act with the moral order. To prove that the act identified by the material norm is immoral, we must be able to show that this act does not serve the value at stake, but that in the long run it really subverts it. In other words, it must be shown that this particular act does not have a commensurate reason.[23]

2. *Bruno Schüller.* The next significant contribution to the discussion of material norms by a revisionist theologian comes from Bruno Schüller. He tries to find a middle ground between formal norms, which do not specify concretely what we ought to do, and letting the immediate situation alone determine what we ought to do. Schüller's main thesis is this:

> Any ethical norm whatsoever regarding our dealings and omissions in relation to other men or the environment can be only a particular application of that more universal norm, "The greater good is to be preferred."[24]

This thesis expresses Schüller's interpretation of material norms as particular applications of the universal, formal norm "The greater good is to be preferred." Richard McCormick has explained well the meaning of Schüller's "preference principle" which lies behind his interpretation of material norms when he writes:

> Stated negatively, it reads: put in a position where he will unavoidably cause evil, man must discover which is the worst evil and avoid it. Stated positively, this is its formulation: put

before two concurring but mutually exclusive values, man should discover which merits preference and act accordingly.[25]

In light of the preference principle, material norms light up certain values at stake in a situation of conflict. The preference principle limits the application of the material norm by insisting that the norm be followed except in those instances when another more important value is present which deserves preference. This means that there can be exceptions to material norms. Therefore, following in line with Knauer, Schüller would say that we can cause some harm (physical evil) when a greater value demands it.

On what foundation does Schüller rest his position? He explains his theoretical foundation this way:

> Human beings are not in a position to do everything for each other that would be required if everyone wanted to be called good in every sense of the word. The good things which constitute the welfare of a human being can come into conflict with each other, so that the only thing possible is to choose the more important ones.[26]

We only need to recall Knauer's example of the amputation to illustrate this. The injured person must allow his limb to be amputated in order to save his life. Traditionally, theology tried to work out a conflict of values according to the "order of charity" (*ordo caritatis*). This means that what we are to do according to what love requires is worked out by a correct choice of priorities among competing values. For Schüller this happens when we follow the preference principle which says we ought to avoid the greater evil and may do some evil only when necessary for a proportionally greater good.[27]

Schüller illustrates his position with the example of a justifiable exception to the prohibition of killing.[28] The material norm "Do not kill" says that life deserves preference before other co-present values. To make this norm exceptionless would be to say that there is no good thinkable which could conflict with a person's life and which would deserve preference. That traditional theology has made exceptions to the norm against killing in cases of self-defense, just war, and capital punishment shows that we have said there are other goods which deserve preference. While Schüller's position may not alter all traditional conclusions, it does show how all situations of conflict are at least discussable and that material norms are valuable aids to moral choice, even though they are limited ones.

3. *Josef Fuchs.* In 1971 Josef Fuchs wrote a significant article on the issue of "absolutes" in moral norms.[29] For Fuchs the meaning and limits of material norms rest on the distinction between premoral evil (Knauer's "physical evil") and moral evil.[30] Morality, in the strict sense of that term, occurs only in human actions which bear the deliberate decision of the moral agent. This means that the truly moral action is only the one that includes the intention of the moral agent. Particular actions, like driving a car, causing a wound, speaking, or even killing, are not accurately evaluated as moral or immoral apart from consideration of the intention of the moral agent. The most we can say of these actions by themselves is that they are "premoral." Fuchs gives this illustration:

> One may not say, therefore, that killing as a realization of a human evil may be morally good or morally bad; for killing as such, since it im-

plies nothing about the intention of the agent, cannot, purely as such, constitute a human act. On the other hand, "killing because of avarice" and "killing in self-defense" do imply something regarding the intention of the agent; the former cannot be morally good, the latter may be.[31]

Fuchs draws two conclusions which are fundamental to his understanding of the meaning and limits of material norms:

(1) An action cannot be judged morally in its materiality (killing, wounding, going to the moon) without reference to the intention of the agent; without this, we are not dealing with a human action, and only with respect to a human action may one say in a true sense whether it is morally good or bad. (2) The evil (in a premoral sense) effected by a human agent must not be intended as such, and must be justified in terms of the totality of the action by appropriate reasons.[32]

This position has significant implications for how we are to judge the morality of an action. Traditionally moralists claimed that certain actions (like contraception, sterilization, masturbation, direct killing of the innocent, divorce and remarriage) were intrinsically evil in themselves. This means that no intentions or circumstances could enter to purify them. The morality of actions was already determined before the person did them in whatever circumstances. To be able to declare an action "intrinsically morally evil" for Fuchs

. . . would presuppose that those who arrive at it could know or fore-

see adequately *all the possible combinations* of the action concerned with circumstances and intentions, with (premoral) values and non-values (*bona* and *mala "physica"*).[33]

The most we can say about an action apart from considering the intention and circumstances is that this action is good or evil in a premoral sense.

For (1) a moral judgment of an action may not be made in anticipation of the agent's intention, since it would not be the judgment of a "human" act. (2) A moral judgment is legitimately formed only under a *simultaneous* consideration of the three elements (action, circumstances, purpose), premoral in themselves; for the actualization of the three elements (taking money from another, who is very poor, to be able to give pleasure to a friend) is not a combination of three human actions that are morally judged on an individual basis, but a single human action.[34]

What does all this have to do with the meaning and limits of material norms? Fuchs says that material norms cannot be moral evaluations of actions unless they take into account intentions and circumstances. Without considering all three elements of a moral action, material norms describe actions expressing premoral good or evil. Therefore, there seems to be no possibility according to Fuchs for material norms to describe an action materially (killing) and say that it is always immoral.[35] Material norms light up premoral goods or evils and demand a proportionate reason to cause or permit a premoral evil.

An important implication for the meaning and limits of material norms comes from this position. On this basis, Fuchs concludes that, *theoretically* speaking, there can be no material norm that would be without exception, or "intrinsically evil" in the strict sense. This does not mean, however, that there is no *practical* worth to formulating material norms as universals.[36] Material norms that are practically absolute do point out a value or a non-value in a premoral sense. They indicate that a non-value may be caused or permitted only when urgent values are at stake which deserve preference. Also, certain material norms can be formulated "to which we cannot conceive of any kind of exception, e.g., cruel treatment of a child which is of no benefit to the child."[37] Furthermore, material norms can be stated as universals by a particular culture or society in a particular period of time and "suffice for ordinary use in practical living."[38] These time-conditioned formulations are open to revision as the times change and the conditions which gave rise to the norms change. Material norms for Fuchs, then, are limited, at least theoretically, and so are not without exception. However, in the practical order many material norms function as useful guides to moral behavior with the force of being exceptionless moral norms.

4. *Louis Janssens.* Louis Janssens has contributed what many consider one of the principal moral reflections of our times in his article, "Ontic Evil and Moral Evil."[39] Since Janssens' work is so significant for the contemporary discussion on moral norms, it deserves substantial consideration. This article makes a significant contribution to the discussion of material norms by beginning with a thorough analysis of the structure and the morality of the human act. Janssens does this by returning to St. Thomas, especially his analysis of the structure of the human act (*ST*. I–II, qq. 6–17) and the morality of the human act (*ST*.

I–II qq. 18–20). Janssens points out that in Thomas the starting point for understanding human action is the person, especially the end of the inner act of the will, or the intention (*ST*. I–II, q. 8, a. 2; cf. I–II, q. 18, a. 6).

> Thomas' view centers on the agent and that *ipso facto* the end of the agent is the fundamental element of the structure of the human act.[40]

Along with the intention, the human act also includes the means-to-an-end (the physical action, or the act-in-itself). The intention of the agent and the means-to-an-end form two structural elements of *one* composite action. To determine the morality of the human action, both of these elements must be taken together. The significance of this is that the physical action itself (the material event, or means-to-an-end) cannot be evaluated morally without considering the actor, especially the intention.[41] This is the position St. Thomas takes in his analysis of what determines the morality of an act (*ST*. I–II, q. 20, a. 3, ad 1). Janssens concludes:

> For this reason [St. Thomas] reacts sharply against those who are of the opinion that the material event of an act can be evaluated morally without consideration of the subject, of the inner act of the will or of the end. As he sees it, an exterior action considered as nothing but the material event (*secundum speciem naturae*) is an abstraction to which a moral evaluation cannot be applied. This object-event becomes a concrete *human* act only insofar as it is directed toward an end within the inner act of the will. Only this concrete totality has a moral meaning.[42]

On these grounds, actions that have the same material features can have different moral meaning depending on the intention which directs the action. For example, making a donation can be morally good when the intention is to bring relief to a person in need. But making a donation can be morally bad if directed by the intention to satisfy one's vanity and win praise.[43] So what is true about the structure of the human act is true about its morality: the formal element, the intention, determines the moral significance of the action.

After showing that the moral goodness of the inner act of the will is the formal element of the exterior act, Janssens shows that St. Thomas argued that "not any kind of exterior action, however, can become the material element of a morally good end."[44] Only an action which is adequately proportionate to the intention can (*ST.* I–II, q. 6, a. 2). But how do we determine what is adequately proportionate? Janssens answers:

> To give an act the character of moral goodness, it is therefore not enough that the end of the subject is morally good: the act is good only when tl exterior action (material element, means) is proportionate to the end (formal element) *according to reason,* when there is no contradiction of the means and the end in the whole of the act on the level of reason (*secundum rei veritatem*). Only then is the undivided and composite action morally good, because the means share in the moral goodness of the end within the totality of the act.[45]

The act of self-defense serves to illustrate this. In the case of self-defense, the use of violence (a means-to-an-end) which wounds or even kills the assailant is justifiable when it falls within the limits of what is necessary to save one's own life (the intention). Violence which exceeds the bounds necessary for self-defense is morally evil because this violence (the means-to-an-end) is not proportionate to the intention of self-defense. Therefore causing harm or even death (a means-to-an-end) can be justifiable if it is proportionate to the good intended (the end).[46]

In this example, we can appreciate Janssens' important distinction between "ontic evil" (Knauer's "physical evil" and Fuchs' "premoral evil") and moral evil. The distinction between them and the relation of ontic evil to moral evil are important for understanding Janssens' interpretation of the meaning and limits of material norms.

Ontic evil or, as he speaks of it in another place, "premoral disvalue"[47] is Janssens' way of accounting for the ambiguity of human actions. This ambiguity is the result of the limitations of being human. Ontic evil/premoral disvalue expresses the lack of perfection in anything whatsoever. These notions express limitation, the failure to reach the full actualization of human potential.[48] Ontic evils or premoral disvalues are what we experience as regrettable, harmful, detrimental to full human growth. These would be such things as suffering, injury, fatigue, ignorance, violence, death, etc. Ontic evils are inevitably present in human actions because of the unavoidable limitations that come with being human. As Janssens puts it, ontic evil is present in our actions "because we are *temporal* and *spatial,* live together *with others* in the same *material world,* are involved and act in a *common sinful situation.*"[49] This means that we are not able to realize the good without causing or admitting to some ontic evil, or premoral disvalue.

Ontic evil is not moral evil. If these were the

same, we could not act morally at all. Moral evil is causing or permitting ontic evil without a proportionate reason.[50] Janssens follows St. Thomas' analysis of the human act again to maintain that there can be no moral judgment of the means-to-an-end (the material element) unrelated to the intention (the end, or the formal element). The moral judgment is a judgment of the proportion of means to end. There is a proper proportion, and the action can be considered moral, when "no intrinsic contradiction between the means and the end may be found in the total act when the act is placed in the light of reason.[51] On this point, Janssens is in line with Knauer by maintaining the axiom of "due proportion" (Knauer's "commensurate reason") as the necessary requirement for judging the morality of the human act. This axiom requires that when we are not able to avoid causing or permitting premoral disvalue (or ontic evil) in our efforts to do good, we must cause or permit the least amount of disvalue possible.

We have already seen this axiom at work in the above example of self-defense. Janssens also makes an application of this axiom to a material norm of marital sexuality:

> According to *Gaudium et spes* the marriage act must be ordered to the conjugal love and to the human transmission of life, viz., to responsible parenthood. This must be the end of marital intercourse; each conjugal act must include a *debita proportio* to this end. Consequently, if the marriage partners engage in sexual intercourse during the fertile period and thereby most likely will conceive new life, the marital act may not be morally justifiable when they foresee that they will not have the means to provide the proper education for the child. The rhythm method, too, can be immoral if it is used to prevent the measure of responsible parenthood. But the use of contraceptives can be morally justified if these means do not obstruct the partners in the expression of conjugal love and if they keep birth control within the limits of responsible parenthood. Marital intercourse can be called neither moral nor immoral when it is the object of a judgment which considers it without due regard for its end. A moral evaluation is only possible if it is a study of the totality of the conjugal act, viz., when one considers whether or not the conjugal act (means) negates the requirements of love and responsible parenthood (end).[52]

According to this example, we make a judgment that an act is "morally evil" (and therefore "forbidden always and everywhere") too soon if we consider only the external, material act apart from considering the intention of the agent within the given set of circumstances. Therefore, to make a moral evaluation of an action, we must consider the intention of the moral agent and the proportionate relationship of the material action and the intention. If the action does not negate or undermine the basic value intended and if it excludes as much premoral disvalue as possible, then we can say that there is due proportion of means to end and this particular causing or permitting of ontic evil or premoral disvalue is not morally evil.[53] Only when we bring about or permit more ontic evil than necessary to accomplish a good intention is the action immoral.[54] In every situation in which we have to choose between several possibilities, we ought to do that which will contribute as much as possible to the well-being and development of persons and social groups and avoid as much as possible what harms or hinders this well-being.[55]

We can now understand Janssens' interpretation of the meaning and limits of material norms. Because actions must be considered in their entirety (material action, intention, and circumstances taken together), with all the parts in proper relationship, material norms prohibit causing or permitting ontic evils or premoral disvalues without a proportionate reason. As Janssens says:

> Briefly, concrete material norms invite us to bring about the ideal relations which lessen more and more effectively all forms of ontic evil which by their definition hamper the development of human beings and communities.[56]

Material norms are not yet moral judgments in the true sense. They would pronounce us guilty of immorality when we do more harm (ontic evil/premoral disvalue) than necessary to achieve good. Material norms do not solve our moral problems, but they do light up premoral values and disvalues and prepare us to exercise prudence. Material norms instruct us on important values (e.g., life, human integrity and dignity, truthfulness, private property) and warn us that we cannot do more harm than necessary in trying to achieve these values.[57]

5. *Richard A. McCormick.* Richard Mc-Cormick's annual "Moral Notes" in *Theological Studies* which reviews moral literature and comments on recent developments in moral theology have won him the esteem of moralists of every stripe. Since his opinions are so highly valued, his contribution to the discussion of the meaning and limits of material norms should not go unnoticed.

Like Knauer, Schüller, Fuchs, and Janssens, McCormick says that "proportionate reason" is decisive for determining right and wrong moral actions. McCormick's position, in summary, is that actions which cause non-moral evil (Knauer's "physical evil," Fuchs' "premoral evil," and Janssens' "ontic evil" or "premoral disvalue") are moral only if there is a truly proportionate reason which justifies the action. For example, taking life is wrong unless there is a proportionate reason to do so.

McCormick's greatest contribution to the discussion of norms is that he has borrowed selectively from Knauer, Schüller, Fuchs, Janssens, and others to flesh out in greater detail what constitutes a proportionate reason. McCormick, like his revisionist colleagues, does not maintain that any reason at all is a proportionate reason. Rather, he recognizes not only the decisiveness of the judgment of proportionality but also how difficult this judgment is to make. He wisely entitled the lecture in which he most thoroughly presented the criteria for a proportionate reason as *Ambiguity in Moral Choice.*[58] In this lecture he says:

> Proportionate reason means three things: (a) a value at least equal to that sacrificed is at stake; (b) there is no less harmful way of protecting the values here and now; (c) the manner of its protection here and now will not undermine it in the long run.[59]

Put negatively, these criteria read as follows:

> An action is disproportionate in any of the following instances: if a lesser value is preferred to a more impor-

tant one; if evil is unnecessarily caused in the protection of a greater good; if, in the circumstances, the manner of protecting the good will undermine it in the long run.[60]

McCormick has recently revised the third criterion in response to criticisms of his first effort. In a recent work, *Doing Evil To Achieve Good,* which he edited with Paul Ramsey, McCormick revises his third criterion by dropping the condition "in the long run." He explains his revision this way:

> Wrongfulness must be attributed to a lack of proportion. By that I mean that the value I am pursuing is being pursued in a way calculated in human judgment (not without pre-discursive elements) to undermine it. I would further explain (tentatively) the disproportion in terms of an association of basic goods whereby the manner of protecting or pursuing a good brings other values or goods into play and can be responsible for disproportion as a result. In other words, I would abandon the *long-term effects* explanation of teleology; but I see no reason for abandoning the teleology itself.[61]

The judgment of the proper proportionality in the circumstances depends a great deal on how we define "in the circumstances." McCormick has given some guidelines on how to define this. He does not want to define the circumstances too narrowly. Nor does he want to define them in terms of the quantitative good that can be saved in a conflict of values. McCormick's guidelines for defining "in the circumstances" include the following: (1) Weigh the social implications and after-effects of an action insofar as they can be foreseen. (2) Use the test of generalizability: What if everyone in similar circumstances did this? (3) Consider the cultural climate with its tendencies to favor certain biases. (4) Draw upon the wisdom of past experiences especially as this wisdom is embodied in norms that have served humankind well through conflicts in the past. (5) Consult broadly, seeking the experience and reflection of others in order to prevent the strong influence of self-interest from biasing perception and judgment. (6) Allow the full force of one's religious beliefs to be brought to bear on interpreting the meaning of the moral conflict and to enlighten options.[62] This is the kind of homework McCormick requires if we are to assess proportionate reason properly.

In light of this understanding of proportionate reason, we can understand McCormick's interpretation of material norms. These norms are constant reminders of values and disvalues. They do not let us forget that when we are faced with a non-moral evil, or a disvalue, we cannot simply settle for it as though it were a good. To say that something is a non-moral evil or a disvalue, like war, contraception, or sterilization, is to imply that we ought to strive to the point where causing or permitting such a disvalue is no longer required. This means that material norms point out the kind of conduct that ought to be avoided as far as possible. However, in the world of inevitable conflict of values, causing or permitting non-moral evil to happen may be permitted with a proportionate reason. It is precisely this lack of proportionate reason that makes acting contrary to a concrete material norm, or causing non-moral evil, morally wrong.[63]

What McCormick demands for a proper consideration of proportionality requires the moral person to be very much reliant on communal discernment. Weighing of values in conflict is not and should not be an individualistic soul-searching. "Deciding by myself" has no place in assessing proportionality for McCormick. The meaning and limits of moral norms for McCormick direct the moral person to more moral consultation and guidance than would ever be called for when the norms were interpreted to propose certain actions as intrinsically evil in themselves and never justified.

This ends our report of a representative sampling of revisionist literature on moral norms. This survey shows that for the revisionist theologians there can be exceptions to material norms when there is a proportionate reason. To say that there can be exceptions to material norms is really nothing new in Catholic thought. St. Thomas said as much. In his treatment of natural law (*ST.* I–II, q. 94) he distinguishes universal principles (formal norms) which are absolute from secondary or concrete precepts (material norms) which are not always applicable (*valent ut in pluribus, ST.* I–II, q. 94, a. 4). His treatment of prudence (*ST.* II–II, q. 51, a. 4) affirms the same thing when he emphasizes that the consideration that makes up this virtue requires us to examine each situation in light of higher principles and not only material norms.

To admit to exceptions in material norms is not to deny their validity or usefulness. These norms continue to be useful to light up important premoral values and disvalues and to warn us that we ought not to cause more harm than we need to in order to do the good. Josef Fuchs, Louis Janssens, and Richard McCormick[64] argue that, *theoretically* speaking, we cannot claim concrete material norms as exceptionless. However, we ought *practically* to hold some as such. They call these kinds of material norms "practical absolutes" or "vir-

tually exceptionless" moral norms. We need to take a brief look at what these are like.

Virtually Exceptionless Material Norms

The revisionist theologians make their theoretical and practical distinctions about the absoluteness of material norms on the basis that human actions are a mixture of premoral value and disvalue. There is probably no human action which does not have some mixture of good and bad. The moral choice in a love ethics ought to maximize premoral value and minimize premoral disvalue. So, to have an absolute material norm, we would have to be able to describe a physical action, apart from intention and circumstances, which causes so much premoral disvalue as to outweigh any conceivable good. To make such a claim for a physical action demands a foreknowledge of this action in all possible combinations of intentions and circumstances. The revisionist theologians claim that the limitations of human knowledge make such a vantage point theoretically impossible.

However, the revisionist theologians maintain that some material norms are practical absolutes, or virtually exceptionless. This means that while it is theoretically impossible to demonstrate them as absolute, these norms highlight values which, in the general course of events, will take precedence and, for all practical purposes, should be preferred. Some examples are in order. Josef Fuchs, as we have seen, cannot conceive of any kind of exception to the norm which would prohibit "cruel treatment of a child which is of no benefit to the child."[65] Richard McCormick speaks of "the direct killing of non-combatants in warfare"[66] as a practical absolute. Louis Janssens identifies "You shall render help to a person in extreme distress" and the prohibition of rape as two examples of virtually exceptionless norms.[67] Paul Ramsey includes rape along with "Never experiment medically on a human being without his informed consent," "Never punish a man whom one knows to be innocent of that for which he would be punished," and "No premarital intercourse" as being significantly closed to exceptions.[68] Thomas L. Beauchamp and James F. Childress place in the same category this norm, "Always obtain the informed consent of your competent patients except in emergency or low-risk situations."[69] As with Fuchs' "cruel treatment" and Ramsey's "pre-marital" (which for him is not the same as pre-ceremonial), there might be considerable debate about what constitutes an "emergency" or "low-risk" in the Beauchamp-Childress example.[70] Nevertheless, what these examples show is that some material norms can and should be regarded as virtually exceptionless.

What is the force of saying "virtually" exceptionless? For McCormick, "virtually" indicates that we cannot prove with the sharpness of a syllogistic click that no exception could ever occur. The conclusion that we ought to hold some material norms as "virtually" exceptionless is based on a prudential judgment that weighs the values at stake in light of past experience of human failure, inconsistency, and frailty, and in light of a certain agnosticism with regard to long-term effects. These norms light up values which, in the general course of events and for all practical purposes, ought to take precedence even though their preference in every instance cannot be absolutely demonstrated.[71]

For Donald Evans, who coined the expression "virtually exceptionless," the point of saying "virtually" is to avoid a "creeping legalism" which tries to extend the range of moral absolutes farther than can be justified.

Evans sees moral norms on a continuum. Some are open to extensive revision, some less open, and others are in varying degrees virtually exceptionless. "Virtually" respects the freedom and discretion of the moral agent, the ambiguity of moral action, the limitation of human knowing, and the limitations of any attempt to capture the experience of value in a pithy formula. The force of being "virtually" exceptionless also puts the burden of proof on those who would want to make an exception.[72]

For Albert DiIanni, the force of being "virtually" exceptionless means that while we cannot theoretically demonstrate their absoluteness, we ought to teach these norms and act *as if* they were absolute. To be virtually exceptionless for DiIanni means that there are no live options to these norms. Since their practical exceptions are so unimaginable, we ought to live with them and regard them in our moral education as being absolute.[73]

Notes

1. *The Moral Choice*, p. 220.
2. "Norms and Priorities in a Love Ethics," *Louvain Studies* 4 (Spring 1977): 207.
3. "The Question of Moral Norms," *American Ecclesiastical Review* 169 (June 1975): 385–386.
4. O'Connell, *Principles for a Catholic Morality*, pp. 160–162.
5. O'Connell, "The Question of Moral Norms," p. 386.
6. "Norms and Priorities in a Love Ethics," p. 208.
7. *Ibid.*, p. 216.
8. Traditionally, these kinds of actions are considered *secundum se* evils. This means that these actions carried their own absolute condemnation in their

very name (*mox nominata sunt mala*).
The very meaning of the name joins the
material action to a sinful intention (*ex
libidine*). The essence of *secundum se*
evil actions is to be immoral so that such
an action can never be made good by any
configuration of intention and circumstances. John Dedek has provided two
valuable historical studies which explore
this sense of moral absolutes in St.
Thomas and his predecessors. The first
study was "Moral Absolutes in the Predecessors of St. Thomas," *Theological
Studies* 38 (December 1977): 654–680.
The second was "Intrinsically Evil Acts:
An Historical Study of the Mind of St.
Thomas," *The Thomist* 43 (July 1979):
385–413. For another historical essay
with similar findings, see Franz Scholz,
"Problems on Norms Raised by Ethical
Borderline Situations: Beginnings of a
Solution in Thomas Aquinas and Bona-
venture," in *Readings in Moral Theology
No. 1*, pp. 158–183.

9. Richard A. McCormick has explained
these issues regarding synthetic terms
well in his "Moral Notes," *Theological
Studies* 37 (March 1976): 73–74; 39
(March 1978): 93.

10. O'Connell, "The Question of Moral
Norms," pp. 385–387; also *Principles for
a Catholic Morality*, pp. 161–162. Louis
Janssens, "Norms and Priorities in a
Love Ethics," p. 209.

11. *Principles for a Catholic Morality*, pp.
161–162.

12. "The Hermeneutic Function of the Principle of Double Effect," *Natural Law
Forum* 12 (1967): 132–162. I am following this version as it has been reproduced
in *Readings in Moral Theology No. 1*, pp.
1–39.

13. *Ibid.*, p. 10.
14. *Ibid.*, p. 21.
15. *Ibid.*, p. 2.
16. *Ibid.*

17. *Ibid.*, pp. 6, 27.
18. *Ibid.*, pp. 10–14, 27.
19. *Ibid.*, pp. 6, 14, 26.
20. *Ibid.*, pp. 32–33.
21. *Ibid.*, p. 22.
22. *Ibid.*, p. 26.
23. *Ibid.*, pp. 31–34.
24. "Zur Problematik allgemein verbindlicher ethischer Grundsätze," *Theologie
und Philosophie* 45 (1970): 4. I have accepted this translation found in "What
Ethical Principles Are Universally
Valid?" *Theology Digest* 19 (March
1971): 24. I will use the *Digest* version
for this summary review.

25. "Moral Notes," *Theological Studies* 32
(March 1971): 90.

26. "Various Types of Grounding for Ethical Norms," in *Readings in Moral Theology No. 1*, p. 190.

27. Schüller, "What Ethical Principles Are
Universally Valid?" p. 25.

28. *Ibid.*, pp. 26–27.

29. Josef Fuchs, "The Absoluteness of
Moral Terms," *Gregorianum* 52 (1971):
415–457. I will follow the reproduced
version in *Readings in Moral Theology
No. 1*, pp. 94–137.

30. *Ibid.*, p. 119.
31. *Ibid.*
32. *Ibid.*, p. 120.
33. *Ibid.*, p. 124.
34. *Ibid.*, p. 121.
35. *Ibid.*
36. *Ibid.*, p. 125.
37. *Ibid.*, p. 126.
38. *Ibid.*
39. *Louvain Studies* 4 (Fall 1972): 115–156. I
will follow the reprinted version in
Readings in Moral Theology No. 1, pp.
40–93.
40. *Ibid.*, p. 44.
41. *Ibid.*, p. 49.
42. *Ibid.*
43. *Ibid.*, p. 51.
44. *Ibid.*, p. 52.

45. *Ibid.*, p. 55.

46. *Ibid.*, pp. 56–58.

47. "Norms and Priorities in a Love Ethics," *Louvain Studies* 4 (Spring 1977): 207–238. Throughout this article, Janssens uses "premoral disvalue" in the same sense that he uses "ontic evil" in his earlier article, "Ontic Evil and Moral Evil."

48. "Ontic Evil and Moral Evil," in *Readings in Moral Theology No. 1*, p. 60.

49. *Ibid.*, p. 61.

50. *Ibid.*, pp. 67–68.

51. *Ibid.*, p. 71.

52. *Ibid.*, pp. 72–73.

53. *Ibid.*, p. 78.

54. *Ibid.*, p. 80.

55. "Norms and Priorities in a Love Ethics," pp. 213–214.

56. "Ontic Evil and Moral Evil," *Readings in Moral Theology No. 1*, p. 216.

57. *Ibid.*, p. 86. Also, "Norms and Priorities in a Love Ethics," p. 216.

58. Pere Marquette Lecture of 1973 at Marquette University (Milwaukee: Marquette University Press, 1973). This is reprinted as the first chapter in *Doing Evil To Achieve Good*, edited by Richard A. McCormick and Paul Ramsey (Chicago: Loyola University Press, 1978), pp. 7–53.

59. In the Marquette University edition, p. 93; in *Doing Evil*, p. 45.

60. In the Marquette University edition, p. 94; in *Doing Evil*, p. 45.

61. "A Commentary on the Commentaries," in *Doing Evil*, p. 265.

62. In the Marquette University edition, pp. 95–96; in *Doing Evil*, p. 46.

63. "Moral Norms and Their Meaning," *Lectureship*, edited by Mount Angel Abbey (St. Benedict, Oregon: Mount Angel Abbey, 1978), pp. 43–46.

64. For Fuchs, see "Absoluteness of Moral Terms," in *Readings in Moral Theology No. 1*, pp. 125–126; for Janssens, see "Norms and Priorities in a Love Ethics," pp. 217–218; for McCormick, see *Ambiguity in Moral Choice*, in the Marquette University edition, pp. 86, 87, 92; in *Doing Evil*, pp. 42–44.

65. "Absoluteness of Moral Terms," in *Readings in Moral Theology No. 1*, p. 126.

66. *Ambiguity in Moral Choice*, in Marquette University edition, pp. 86–93; in *Doing Evil*, pp. 42–44.

67. "Norms and Priorities in a Love Ethics," p. 217. However, just how Janssens sees the norm prohibiting rape to differ from a synthetic, formal norm is not readily evident.

68. "The Case of the Curious Exception," *Norm and Context in Christian Ethics*, edited by Outka and Ramsey, pp. 67–135.

69. *Principles of Biomedical Ethics* (New York: Oxford University Press, 1979), p. 43.

70. Donald Evans has made a good analysis of the significance of words with "elastic" meanings in norms such as these. See his study of Paul Ramsey in "Paul Ramsey on Exceptionless Moral Rules," *The American Journal of Jurisprudence* 16 (1971): 184–214, esp. 198 ff.

71. McCormick, *Ambiguity in Moral Choice* in the Marquette University edition, pp. 86–93; in *Doing Evil*, pp. 42–44.

72. Evans, "Paul Ramsey on Exceptionless Moral Rules," pp. 205–207. See also his article, "Love, Situations, and Rules," *Norm and Context in Christian Ethics*, pp. 367–414, esp. pp. 402–414.

73. DiIanni, "The Direct/Indirect Distinction in Morals," in *Readings in Moral Theology No. 1*, pp. 215–243, esp. 236–238.

40

The Absoluteness of Behavioral Moral Norms

Josef Fuchs, SJ

Christ's mission was not to establish a new moral order, new moral laws. Nor was it his primary intent to teach a moral doctrine corresponding to creation. The significance of his coming was rather to redeem sinful mankind, to transform man interiorly by grace, to make him one who believes and loves. Loving faith must and will bear fruit; it must express and verify itself in morally correct conduct, i.e., by doing what is right, thus giving witness to the truth by "doing the truth"—*testimonium veritati*. In the dynamism of faith and love, the Christian is concerned not only with living in faith and love, but also with carrying them out by a way of life proper to man as Christian. Indeed, faith, love and salvation do not depend upon the rectitude of the norms of living that are basic to one's life practice. Yet faith and love are not genuine if there is no effort to manifest through one's life practice the right mode of life, i.e., corresponding to the reality of human-Christian existence. Thus, in the dynamism of faith and love, the problem of the absoluteness of moral norms arises in this present age of uncertainty and revolution. Have we perhaps overstressed the absoluteness of our system of moral norms, and precisely for this reason failed to achieve the right life practice as an expression of our faith and love? Or are we perhaps at the point of renouncing the absoluteness of an inherited system of moral norms, and so running the risk of faith and love no longer manifesting themselves in the "right" day-to-day manner?

No small number of convinced Christians are allergic to "absolute" norms—not, indeed, to the possibility of "right", "objective", and therefore "absolutely" binding judgment in concrete instances, and consequently the possibility of moral imperatives too, but to "universally binding" and in *this* sense absolute norms of moral action. They make their judgment on experiential grounds, so that what was yesterday an absolute, i.e., presented as

---

This article is excerpted from Personal Responsibility and Christian Morality *(Washington, D.C.: Georgetown University Press, 1983) 115–152.*

always and without exception right, must today yield to other insights. They fear that the so-called absolutes, or universally valid norms characteristic of a static world-view, cannot be absolute for men of a dynamic world-view. They hold that the cultural fact of the discovery of moral norms in the past cannot be taken as a final conclusion, or rather, that man must always address himself anew to this fact, in order to examine the conclusions reached, to deepen and enlarge and adduce new experiences and evaluations. Their great concern is that abstract and therefore timeless and in *this* sense "absolute" norms do not perhaps take due account of the times; i.e., are not sufficiently realistic and responsive to the concrete mode of reality represented by (redeemed) creation; and that consequently they can obscure rather than illuminate the "objective" and in *this* sense "absolute" task of the present day. That this concern for relevant behavior on the part of the believing and loving Christian and for absolute fidelity to the order of (redeemed) creation in its concrete manifestations is genuinely "Catholic" is unquestionable.

Other convinced Catholics incline toward a view just as typically "Catholic". They fear that with the dissolution of so-called absolute ordinances and norms, in the sense of "universally valid" and "timeless" truths, truth itself will be lost. They think that if "absoluteness", understood as "immutability" and "universal validity" yields to the principle of change and historical conditioning, then faithfulness to reality, i.e., to (redeemed) creation, will no longer determine concrete action as the expression of faith and love, but will be replaced by a relativistic subjectivism. They presume that deviation from absoluteness (i.e., timelessness and immutability) might imply also a

swerving from absoluteness understood as objectivity oriented to the reality of the (redeemed) created order.

Basically, both tendencies share the same interest: the believing-loving Christian must concern himself with recognizing the absolutely valid, or that which always corresponds objectively to the concrete human (Christian) reality in a moral matter. For this is the Will of God based on creation and redemption—so that what is objectively right partakes somehow in the absoluteness of God. The problem is whether and in what degree the absolute—in the sense of the objective as applied to universal or universally valid norms—is conceivable or in any sense guaranteed. When we address ourselves to this question, we do so in the conviction that global solutions of the problem are not solutions; nuanced consideration is required. Neither the opinion that love should be the sole moral absolute nor the conception of natural moral law as an all-embracing set of invariable norms is satisfactory, although there is some truth in both these points of view. It will not escape the informed reader that the problematic thus presented is of importance not only for (Catholic) circles within the Church—particularly in the present climate of "uncertainty"—but also for dialogue with those non-Catholic Christians who are experiencing and dealing with the same problematic on a broad scale, and with all men concerned with genuine morality. For God will judge Christians, Jews and pagans alike according to their works (cf. Rom 2:9–11), the righteousness of which they can know fundamentally in their "hearts" (cf. Rom 2:15). Accordingly, the following considerations are limited to the shaping of life within the world, i.e., innerworldly actions, those relating man and his world.[1]

I. Absolute: Universally Valid or Objective?

Absoluteness in moral imperatives is directly opposed, obviously, to all arbitrary judgment and to all relativism, and thereby positively affirms the objectivity grounded in human reality itself. The real problem, we repeat, lies in determining to what degree the absolute, in the sense of the nonarbitrary but objective, is comprehensible and guaranteed in the case of universally valid norms. We are accustomed to having moral ordinances placed before us in the guise of norms purporting to be universally valid: in revelation (Holy Scripture), in the teaching of the Church, in the formulated tenets of the natural moral law, conscience finds itself confronted with moral imperatives in the form of moral norms. In what follows we shall consider what degree of the absolute character of norms is implied in each of the individual instances.

1. *Norms in Holy Scripture.* Moral imperatives in Holy Scripture are of the greatest interest, for God's world has absolute value, since he is The Absolute. And since he speaks, therefore, via human concepts and so in terms of universals, Christianity with good reason has been inclined to understand the moral precepts found in Holy Scripture as universal, ever valid and unchangeable norms and, in this sense, as "absolute". On the other hand, God's speaking in human mode signifies that the moral imperatives appearing in Holy Scripture should not be interpreted as direct divine "dictates". Thus we are inevitably faced not only with the question as to which moral imperatives are actually to be found in Holy Scripture, but also with the question by which hermeneutic rules they are to be understood

and evaluated.[2] There is no doubt that here moral theology will have to go to school to contemporary exegesis, to avoid lapsing into unauthorized good-will reading.

Holy Scripture was never meant to be a handbook on morality: consequently it may not be so used. Inasmuch as it speaks of God's ways with mankind, it must speak also of man's behavior—his religio-moral behavior—toward God. Indeed, since Scripture is concerned with the conversion and salvation of the sinner, and therefore with his personal transformation, statements regarding the religio-moral situation of man are central to the Bible. Nevertheless, it is not the particular moral imperatives which have this central position, but the fundamental imperative of fidelity and obedience to God, of the following of Christ, of life according to faith and baptism or, as with John, according to faith and love. But *these* moral-religious imperatives are transcendental—that is, they refer to the personal human being as a whole and not to specific moral conduct. And even though Holy Scripture speaks also of particular attitudes and values—goodness, mildness, mercy, justice, modesty—these are still not operative norms of behavior, since it has yet to be determined which actions are to be regarded as just, modest and kind. Certainly, Scripture knows operative norms of conduct as well—a few at least. The question is precisely with reference to these, insofar as the absoluteness of moral norms is the point at issue.

We shall limit ourselves to the New Testament. References there to concrete moral behavior, norms of activity, are relatively few; but these few are important. The critical question is: In what sense are they absolute—in the sense of objective, nonarbitrarily grounded imperatives or, more than that, universal norms admitting of no exception? The answer to this question is not altogether easy.

The Christian centuries have tried earnestly to understand the demands of the Sermon on the Mount (Mt 5–7). No Christian doubts their absolute validity, absolute to be understood in the sense of objective. The question is: absolute validity, as what—as universal norms, or as models for the behavior of the believing and loving citizens of God's kingdom who will be ready for such modes of conduct, perhaps, under certain conditions not individually specified by the Lord? The latter interpretation seems probable from the context and manner of expression. In recent years there has been renewed and heated discussion of the Lord's words about the indissolubility of marriage (Mt 19:3–10). Regarding the scope of these words, it is asked: Is it a question of a moral imperative or of something more? Is the moral imperative to be understood as a norm to be followed as universal practice or as an ideal? The discussion makes at least this much clear: The acceptance of an absolute in the sense of an objectively valid moral affirmation in Scripture does not necessarily involve recognizing it as an absolute in the sense of a universal norm.

It should be noted first of all that while Paul ascribes to the Lord definite sayings regarding moral behavior (indissolubility of marriage: 1 Cor 7:10 f.) and attributes others to his own personal understanding in the Holy Spirit (virginity: 1 Cor 7, 12, 25), he presupposes that most of the behavioral norms of which he speaks are valid. This is particularly to be inferred from the many ordinances in which he accepts the moral wisdom of the "good" men of his time, both Jew and Gentile; one thinks, among other things, of the tables of domestic rules and the catalogue of vices. On the one hand, this means that Paul does not present himself as a teacher of moral living, still less as a teacher of specifically Christian norms of conduct; what he does have to transmit is something quite different from a moral code. On the other hand, his having assumed a given morality can lead us to consider whether such a morality, at least in many of its regulations, is not historically and culturally conditioned. It could scarcely be supposed that the Stoic, Judaic and Diaspora-Judaic ethos which Paul represents was in all respects a timeless ethos. If it is self-evident to us today that the Pauline directives concerning woman's position in marriage, society and the Church (1 Cor 11:2–16; 14, 34–6; Eph 5:22–4; Col 3:18; 1 Tm 2:11–15) are to be regarded as conditioned by his times, reflecting Jewish tradition and the position of woman in the culture in which Paul and his contemporaries lived, we must indeed ask ourselves according to what criterion we decide that those directives which Paul seeks to validate, even theologically, are historically conditioned and thus not absolute (i.e. universal), and that they hold as absolute in the objective sense rather for the age whose ideas on the position of women they reflect. Consequently, such directives cannot be normative for a period in which the social position of women is essentially different. Holy Scripture itself gives us no criteria for such a judgment, but it comes from our knowledge of the difference in the social position of women in various ages together with our own insight into moral imperatives which arises out of various social situations. This same power of discernment will permit us perhaps to make a judgment—at least in principle—as to which suits the nature of women in society better, and hence is the moral ideal, the social position of women in Paul's cultural milieu or that of women in our cultural milieu—along with corresponding moral demands.

By analogy with the instance of woman's position in marriage, society and the Church, a further question inevitably arises: whether the possibility of similar considerations regarding other behavioral norms to be found in the Pauline corpus is to be absolutely excluded— on the theoretical level at least, especially since the criteria for such reflections are not provided us by Holy Scripture itself. For the affirmation that certain explicitly mentioned modes of conduct ban one from the kingdom of God, from companionship with Christ and from the life given by the Spirit remains true if these modes are to be judged negatively, in accordance with the moral evaluation proper to that age and accepted by Paul. Paul therefore did not teach such evaluation as thesis, but admitted it as hypothesis in his doctrinal statement on the Christian mystery of salvation. Thus it remains to be established whether in Paul's cultural milieu, because of the actual conviction of the morally high-ranking segment of society, every "honorable" Christian had to share this conviction exactly, or whether this conviction was the only objectively justified one and was not based on definite options.

(In Paul we have actually a model for "Christian" discovery of moral norms. With him such discovery derives neither from Christ alone nor from the Old Testament alone. It occurs within an existing culture and as a consequence of its established moral values. It draws from Jewish tradition and from Greek popular philosophy, just as it carries along the culture in which Christianity took root. This does not exclude the fact that Paul himself also reflects upon the values he found already present, as, for example, the social position of

women, and that, in particular cases, he himself independently—in the Holy Spirit—recommends practices like virginity or that he appeals to the word of the Lord.)

The foregoing considerations obviously do not permit us to conclude that the norms of behavior found in the New Testament are no longer valid today. Only, we must reflect whether the criterion of their possible absolute (i.e., universal) validity is Holy Scripture itself, whether it can be and is intended to be.[3] The moral behavioral norms in Scripture are directed to actual persons of a definite era and culture. Hence their character of absoluteness would not signify primarily universality, but objectivity; and the latter can denote either the objectively right evaluation in a particular culturally conditioned human situation or necessary conformity to the moral views of the morally elite in a given society.

2. Norms of the Ecclesial Community. Neither from Christ nor from Paul or John has the Church inherited a system of moral norms. On the other hand, the ecclesial community— how could it be otherwise?—always maintained definite moral norms and passed them on to later generations. But in this connection it may be no means be said that there was ever in the Church a definitive or in all respects universal code of precepts. Nevertheless, the Church community had "its" morality which, even if it did not derive purely from revelation, was regarded as being connected with or compatible with Christian belief. This morality— as being the morality of the Christian community—was "Christian" morality. Insofar as it had been handed down, it was a more or less codified morality, which just for this reason was lived in the one Church in different cultures and epochs. Naturally, this brief exposition is a simplification. But it enables us to understand how the Church, unlike Paul, begins not only to set forth dogmatically particular moral concepts—indissolubility of marriage (word of the Lord) and virginity (Paul's opinion, in the Holy Spirit)—but in principle the whole compass of the morality practiced by the Christian community, which Paul had not taught but rather "presupposed", as also did the Church after Paul with regard to many questions. While Paul, earlier, expressed himself *in obliquo* and hypothetically on moral questions, the Church slowly began to do this *in recto* and dogmatically. The Church teaches *in rebus fidei et morum* and indeed, as she repeatedly declared during Vatican Council II, also on moral questions about which she has had no explicit revelation. Now the question: If the Church addresses herself thematically and dogmatically to moral questions, have we then pronouncements that are true universals? Is the claim of absoluteness for the norms transmitted by the Church a claim of universal norms? Does the Church give us thereby a system of universal morally valid norms which God has not given us in Holy Scripture?

In general, then, unlike Paul, the Church "teaches" norms of moral conduct. Why, really? The answer often given runs: Because the Church has to teach the way to salvation and true morality is the way to salvation. This answer might be considered valid if taken *cum grano salis*. For ultimately there is the question whether marriage, for example, is to be understood and lived according to Congolese or Western European style; surely not an unimportant cultural and ethical question, but not in itself determinative of salvation. Still the matter admits of a different interpretation. The manner in which faith and love—which do determine salvation!—are expressed in daily life, by premarital abstinence or premari-

tal intercourse, for example, is not a matter of totally free choice. And since man must strive to incarnate his faith and love in the "true" way of human beings, the Church assists him by her "teaching". Clearly, this answer also does not entirely satisfy. In any case, it remains true that the materiality of culturally and ethically right mastery of the concrete reality of life—education, economy, technology, sexuality, etc.—is not directly concerned with salvation, or union with God; only faith and love, together with the effort to incarnate this materiality in the "true" way in the reality of life are thus concerned.

That the material mode of this incarnation can represent only a *secundarium,* already makes it reasonable that within certain limits moral pluralism might well be possible. If, for example, faith and love have to be expressed in the maintenance of the "right" social position of woman, then the concrete expressions in the Pauline conception and in the twentieth century Western European conception must (!) be regarded as necessarily differing from each other. Yet the Christian community is obliged to see to it that moral behavior as an expression of faith and love does not come down to fulfilling one's own wishes; it must not fail to manifest the unconditional character of faith and love by unconditionality in stating moral precepts. However, it could follow from what has been said that this quality of absoluteness does not represent primarily the universality of a norm, but an antithesis to arbitrary judgment; or, positively stated, orientation toward concrete human (total) reality, and, in this sense, objectivity, truth. This objectivity-truth is achieved, on the one hand, through right understanding of the revealed word of God, insofar as it contains morally significant affirmations; on the other hand, through the right moral understanding of man's concrete reality, in which connection, obviously, the light of revelation and the moral understanding of man are not to be viewed as two completely unrelated possibilities.

With respect to norms of moral behavior, the light of the Gospel does not manifest itself in formally expressed statements alone. Rather, there is also the possibility suggested by Vatican II in the Constitution on the Church in the Modern World, when reference is made to the necessity of judging contingent realities in the world of men in light of the Gospel.[4] Edward Schillebeeckx alludes to this statement;[5] nevertheless, he is of the opinion that the Christian, on the basis of his faith, can more easily assert negatively the incompatibility of a given social situation with his faith than discover positively how the situation might be changed. Karl Rahner has spoken, in the sense of Vatican II, of a moral faith-instinct.[6] Maurizio Flick and Zoltán Alszeghy have pursued in greater detail the question of the significance of the Gospel—which itself gives no directives—for moral judgment of contingent human realities.[7] They maintain that it is possible, especially for a believer, to draw "an objective picture of revealed reality" on the basis of the content of revelation. Inasmuch as the development of dogma has often been indebted to such an "objective picture," a great deal might be gained for the proper mastering of concrete human reality via such an "objective picture." However, they are also of the opinion that actual problems—those, for example, pertaining to development and progress—can find direct solutions neither in the Gospel and faith, nor in theology, but only in a Christian ideology, which, of course, must be approached in terms of the eventual possibility of a critique by the Gospel and theology (and their "objective picture of revealed real-

ity"). Only on this condition can a "political theology" venture an attempt to make the Gospel and faith effective for the reality of the world.[8] The "imperatives,"[9] known or determined by a "political theology," do not follow directly from faith and the Gospel, therefore, but only from an ethical interpretation ("political ethics"). And this ethics is "human" ethics; it is theological only to the extent that it has been projected by the believer as an imperative of a Christian theology which, in turn, depends in any case on an "objective picture of revealed reality."[10] It need scarcely be said that the imperatives of a Christian theology so projected are not absolutes in the sense of universalia. They represent the attempt to be as objectively relevant as possible to given realities through man's reflection in light of the Gospel, as described above; they are not to be arbitrary precepts, therefore, but the most objective possible, and in this reduced sense, absolutes.

The assistance of the Holy Spirit has been promised to the Church's endeavors. Inasmuch as the Church, to a far greater extent than Holy Scripture, has begun to address herself directly and dogmatically to moral questions, she becomes, in a much higher degree than the Scripture, concretely important because of the assistance of the Spirit of Christ. Some concepts of moral theology create the impression that the Holy Spirit slowly began to impart via the Church what he had not conveyed through Scripture—a vast collection of moral behavioral norms proclaimed for the whole world and for all time; *absoluta,* in the sense of universally valid norms. However, under this aspect, the Church is seen often in an all too spiritualized way; how very much the Spirit is merely "incarnated" in the Church is overlooked, in other words, how very human the Church is and remains despite the assistance of the Spirit. She arrives at norms of moral conduct only by way of a long process of learning to understand and to evaluate. And this comprehension and evaluation are accomplished not only by the hierarchy of the ecclesial community who, it may be, ultimately provide a decisive orientation, but by the Church as a whole, within the community of believers—where a special role often falls to the theologians.

It is not true that a moral question is submitted to the pastors of the Church, so that in solitary reflection they can reach an authoritative decision. Before there is a question of "decision" the "teaching" Church is in all instances a "learning" Church. The Spirit assists the whole process of teaching and leading in the Church—i.e., comprehending, discovering, evaluating, mutual listening, deciding.[11] He guarantees that error, which in human comprehension-discovery-evaluation-listening-deciding can never be absolutely excluded, will not become in the end an essential component of the Church. It stands to reason, then, that the same ecclesial community or a particular cultural group within it—pluralistic, therefore—will at times begin to experience and evaluate in a new and different way, regarding specific points. In this connection it is noteworthy that in the Church's two thousand years, seemingly no definitive doctrinal decision on moral questions has been made, at least insofar as these would be related to natural law, without being at the same time revealed. On the other hand, this is not to say that the nondefinitive authoritative guidelines of the Church are meaningless, as if one might ignore them, oblivious to the fact that they also come under the assistance of the Spirit of Christ abiding with the Church. Hence a certain presumption of truth must be granted them. Yet one may not see in such instances

any conclusive legislation or doctrinal definition of an ethical norm whose validity would be guaranteed by the Holy Spirit. Declarations by the Church *in rebus morum* can be understood in all cases as attempts to formulate "absolute"—i.e. nonarbitrary, but objective —imperatives, properly conformed to a concrete human reality and expressed in terms of a presumptively valid ecclesial orientation. If, on the contrary, such pronouncements had the assurance of infallibility, they could be set forth as universally valid norms, guaranteed to hold true always, everywhere and without exception. But even in such a case there would have to be a reservation; for it can be imagined and probably demonstrated, if need be, that a strict behavioral norm, stated as a universal, contains unexpressed conditions and qualifications which as such limit its universality.

The Church arrives at moral pronouncements—in the sphere of natural law morality, at least—via man's reflection on himself. But man—also a Christian and a member of the Church—is not a static being, whose nature is incapable of development. Thus, new questions will come up because of new experiences, insights and evaluations in a new light and a changed culture. Even the Christian is obliged to question in retrospect, to go back to the past in order to find out what was once believed in the Church—even authoritatively, perhaps—about the right way to embody faith and love concretely. And more than this, without losing contact with the Christian wisdom of the past, he must always be thinking out various questions that affect his life in this way or that at different times.[12] It cannot be that the Christian and ecclesial past (from which year to which year?) enjoyed the prerogative of finding the (nonrevealed) "truth" about moral behavior, while later Christians would have only the task of recording, confirming, applying the "truth" of the past—conclusive, absolute and universal in the strict sense—without advertence to really new problems never before reflected upon or resolved. Furthermore, it often happens that old problems presenting themselves in a new guise are, at bottom, new problems. Also, it is scarcely conceivable that all Church traditions or decisions concerning moral behavioral norms would be in the full sense timeless and unconditioned, i.e., absolute, completely explicit and not in some respect conditioned either by fixed ideas or value judgments or by man's limited understanding of himself.[13] For example, the Church's opposition in the past to religious freedom is understandable if religious freedom and indifferentism are equated conceptually. Moreover, it is today an historical fact that the sexual morality handed down in the Church came under the influence of certain nonChristian (Jewish and pagan) evaluations in the first Christian centuries and is conditioned by them. The Church is not a "spiritualized" reality, thinking, speaking and existing in a vacuum, unrelated to any culture, and under such conditions devising norms of moral conduct that are in the purest sense "universal." But if norms of conduct can include culturally and historically conditioned elements, only then is there a possibility that they can be expressed in a manner that will respond to concrete human reality; i.e., be objective and, in this sense, absolute. ("Can" means here that even in the moral judgment of a real situation, the Church could err.)

3. *The Natural Moral Law.* If Holy Scripture and the Church do not provide a system of universal moral norms, one expects this at least from the moral law of nature (natural moral law, natural moral order, order of creation, natural law). A well-defined concept of natural law underlies this expectation. Natural law is understood to be the summary of precepts which are based on the given and unvarying nature of man as such and which can be deduced from it. In his critical study, *The Natural Law Yesterday and Today,*[14] E. Chiavacci terms this concept "preceptive." According to this view, "immutable" nature points out to the man who "reads" and "understands" her what right behavior can and must be once and for all in the different areas of reality. A concept of this sort ends in a codifiable summation of the numerous precepts of natural law, which, because rooted in an unchangeable nature, are unvarying and universal. Thus it is maintained that all these precepts (norms) are to be applied in actual life situations—appropriately, to be sure, but unequivocally.

This notion of a static-universal system of norms is valid to the extent that it believes man is and always will be man (tautology!) and that he must always conduct himself rightly—that is, as man. But this quite accurate perception does not entail as a necessary consequence a static-universal system of moral norms. In the first place, the state of being man does not exclude that the human state may differ in different epochs and cultures, just as it is actualized in different individuals and life situations without placing man's nature in question. Against this assertion of the unchangeableness of human nature stands Aquinas' affirmation of its mutability.[15] The two positions are not in conflict if man, his component structures and even his ways of being human, together with their structures, are differentiated rather than divided. Only there must be no attempt to distinguish what precisely is changeable from what is unchangeable. For even that which essentially constitutes man, that which therefore belongs unalterably to his nature, as also his permanent structures, is basically mutable. Mutability belongs to man's immutable essence; irrevocably, man is man (tautology!). To be sure, a priori, some essential elements of man's nature can be identified: body-soul unity, personality, accountability, interpersonality; while one cannot say with equal a priori validity, respecting other components of existential man, whether they belong necessarily and unchangeably to human nature. But even these a priori and inalienable elements of man's nature subsist in it in variable modes, a fact which can be correspondingly significant for moral behavior.

Second, the question of mutability-immutability is connected with man's historicity.[16] History is possible only in virtue of the mutability of that which remains ever the same. Now man is an historical being, not only in terms of the successive variations of past, present and future, but above all, in the sense that man himself designs and brings to realization the plot-lines of his given existence and its progress into the future. He has to actualize what is sketched out for him as possibility. In the process of his self-realization he continually modifies his existence. In his spiritual and bodily aspects and his external relationships (environmental change), he becomes to an ever increasing degree a different person. Morality would have him live rightly the actual man, i.e., the man (humanity) of each actual moment, the present with the past enfolded within it and the projective future: that is, starting from each present reality he should "humanize" himself and his world. Whatever leads to our unfolding, in the fullest and best sense of the word, is good.[17]

Third, mutability and historicity are connected with the fact that man is person and nature in one. Person and nature can be placed counter to each other, so that nature expresses the intrapersonal given of man and his world, while person represents the I, possessing and shaping itself in terms of the given nature. However, one's personhood also is given and in this sense it is nature, indeed the determining element of one's humanness, and in this sense of human nature. The man consists above all in his being a person (i.e., possessing *ratio*). Nature is not understood as human, unless it is thought of as a personal nature. Thus, it is not enough to say nature (for example, sexuality) "belongs to" the human person.[18] For then it would be possible to understand nature (sexuality) as nonpersonal;[19] hence one could speak of the meaning of sexuality, rather than of the meaning of *human* sexuality, and make the consideration of this meaning (i.e., sexuality) a moral problem for the person reflecting upon his sexuality. The term "law of nature" is not merely open to misunderstanding; it frequently is responsible for it. It would be possible and perhaps more meaningful to speak of "person" as moral norm instead of "nature".[20] But then there would be the danger that "personhood" would be viewed too onesidedly; that is, with practically no consideration of nature, provided person and nature are to be thus differentiated. In any case, nature, considered infrapersonally, cannot be the norm of moral behavior. Rather, man is essentially person and has to understand himself therefore as person—"in a human nature"—and achieve self-realization according to this self-understanding. Self-realization entails that he himself must discover the available possibilities for his action and development, and determine on the basis of his present understanding of himself which of these possibilities are right, reasonable, human (in the full and positive sense of these words), and so contributive to human progress. In this way, he arrives simultaneously at the moral judgment of a concrete situation and the affirmation of moral norms.

In reality, this is tantamount to the traditional statement that the *lex naturalis* is a *lex interna* (or *indita*), not a *lex externa* (or *scripta*). The preceptive understanding of natural law as a summary of precepts conformable to nature is not quite in keeping with this traditional concept; for, thus, a *lex interna* becomes furtively a *lex externa,* resembling general positive or positively formulated laws. The *lex interna* signifies the possibility and duty of man (humanity) to discern, as he himself evaluates himself, what in concrete "human" action here is capable of being—inasmuch as man is essentially person-reason— and what can be affirmed propositionally in the problem area of "behavioral norms." Here we are obviously dealing with moral perceptions of an absolute nature, but it is equally obvious that absolute means at least primarily correspondence of behavior to personal human reality; objectivity, therefore, and not, or at least not primarily, universal validity.

4. *Conscience.* As explained according to traditional manuals, the function of conscience was the application of the moral law, or its norms, to the concrete case, a formulation founded on a "preceptive" understanding of the moral law, oriented to the specificity of positive law. The traditional statement naturally has some validity; in forming the dictates of conscience, we never begin at pure zero. We always bring to our actions existing orientations and norms. Yet conscience—as judgment of concrete action—is not only, and not on the deepest level, the application of general norms. Knowledge of the essential function of conscience casts light also on the essence and meaning of behavioral norms.[21]

The function of conscience is to help man, as agent, make his action authentic (i.e., self-realizing). Hence conscience ought to assist action toward objectivity, toward truth, in conformity with the concrete human reality. It is necessary above all that action be conformable to the evaluating judgment (of conscience) with respect to the given concrete moment and its options. For this judgment itself belongs, at the moment of action, to the concrete human reality; it is, so to speak, its final form, so that the agent is enabled to realize himself only by fidelity to this judgment (mediating truth to him, yet erring occasionally). Clearly, for this very reason, the agent must strive for objectivity in forming this judgment regarding the concrete reality—i.e., that *ratio,* which makes the judgment may be *recta ratio.* (The terms *ratio, recta ratio,* derive from Scholastic tradition. Here they signify, rather than specifically discursive thinking, an evaluative observing-understanding-judging, which can also occur "intuitively".) Now the behavioral norms of the moral law should also be *recta ratio;* only insofar as they are *recta ratio,* are they behavioral norms and can they, as such, objectively have a meaning for the function of conscience as *recta ratio* in action. The difference between judgment of conscience and norm of action consists basically in the fact that man with his evaluating *ratio* forms a moral judgment of his conduct *either* at the moment of action and in reference to it or in advance and not with reference to the actuality of the particular event as such. In terms of the concrete situation, then, it is clear that the norm of action cannot represent an exhaustive judgment of the actual reality, and that the actor must judge in light of his conscience to what degree a norm of conduct corresponds morally to a given situation.

As only the *ratio* (*recta ratio*) of conscience judges the reality ultimately and comprehensively in terms of the concrete element in it that is to be actualized, the *ratio* (*recta ratio*) of behavioral norms exercises merely an auxiliary function. As a consequence, the decisive aspect of such norms is that they are *recta ratio*, hence their objectivity; to the extent that they are objective, they are absolute. Of course, they can be behavioral norms only insofar as they are discernible in advance; therefore they are necessarily abstract and in some way generalized. Further consideration is called for on this point.

II. The Absoluteness of Human Behavioral Norms

The title of this section requires clarification. Our previous reflection on behavioral norms in Holy Scripture, Church teaching and natural law, should have made it evident that the affirmations in Scripture and in the teaching of the Church on absolute norms of behavior are not as definitive as might be supposed, particularly if the absoluteness denoted is to be primarily synonymous with universality. In addition to this, Christian behavioral norms, in their material content, are not distinctively Christian norms that would hold only for Christians, but "human" norms, i.e., corresponding to the (authentic) humanness of man, which we have traditionally called norms of the natural moral law, or moral law of nature.[22] These observations suggest the need for further reflection on the absoluteness of moral norms of behavior considered as *human* (related to natural law), and hence, insofar as they can be discerned by man himself, as *recta ratio*.

1. *The Human as Recta Ratio.* We shall continue to employ the traditional term *recta*

ratio. The human is in it, that which is humanly right. Whatever is not *recta ratio* is necessarily nonhuman, not worthy of man, antithetic to a steadily advancing "humanization". *Recta ratio* does not mean innate discernment or moral truth, "inscribed" somehow, somewhere. Hence it does not denote a norm of conduct "inscribed in our nature," at least not in the sense that one could read off a moral regulation from a natural reality. The "nature" upon which the moral law is inscribed is preeminently and formally nature as *ratio*, but only, of course, as *recta ratio*. From this viewpoint, the preferred expression would probably be that of Paul in Romans: the moral law is "engraved on the heart" (Rom 2:15).[23] Apart from this, realities of the natural order, *ratio* excepted, can neither provide a basis for, nor affirm, any moral laws. Considered positively, then, the task of *homo-ratio* in discovering or projecting behavioral norms consists in understanding man himself, his own total reality, together with his world, in order to assess the significance of the alternatives for action available to him and so arrive at a moral affirmation. There will be some a priori and hence self-evident affirmations: for example, that man has to act responsibly and in an interpersonal and social context. Others will presuppose experience; for instance, conduct as related to the life of another, or sexual behavior. In this regard some things will be immediately evident, e.g., that there should be respect for life (it may not be destroyed at will), that sexuality has to be viewed in relation to a particular culture, etc. Still other affirmations call for long and perhaps varied experience, until man understands the value of different possibilities for the realization of genuine humanness. How mankind and the Christian centuries as well have striven in the most diverse ways to come to an evaluative understanding of sexuality and marriage and their actualization!

2. *Criteria of Evaluation.* Do criteria for the evaluating *ratio* exist? A prime criterion is obviously correspondence of behavior—hence also of the behavioral norms to be discovered —to the meaning, in general, of being man and to the significance of particular givens— i.e., sexuality and marriage as *human* givens.[24] It is probable that penetration of meaning occurs far less frequently on a priori or metaphysical ground than has often been supposed. It implies varied experience on the part of man (humanity) and a long apprenticeship in unprejudiced weighting of these manifold experiences. And it is not only the "meaning" itself of experienced realities that constitutes a criterion for the evaluating *ratio,* but also practical knowledge of the outcomes and consequences which determined modes of conduct can have—and this under all kinds of presuppositions[25]—for example, in the economic sphere, in social life, or in the area of sexuality and marriage. Of itself, experience yields no norms of conduct; assessment of its outcome is required to enable us to perceive in which direction to seek or not to seek genuine human self-realization. A basic criterion for true penetration of human reality, as well as for a just appraisal of experience, is to be found in the interpersonality of the human person.[26] The conduct of individual persons in different areas of life has to be scrutinized in terms of its interpersonal significance and implications. No one is a self-enclosed individual; each one lives as a person in relation to persons. Humanness essentially involves interhuman relations. Technological and economic progress, for instance, cannot be assessed in the concrete as "human values" unless interpersonal and social aspects are fundamentally involved in the judgment.

To arrive at a behavioral norm regarding premarital intercourse or birth control, for example, a whole complex of factors obviously has to be considered. (It should not be necessary to add that this takes place in an explicit manner only in scientific reflection.) What must be determined is the significance of the action as value or nonvalue for the individual, for interpersonal relations and for human society, in connection, of course, with the total reality of man and his society and in view of his whole culture. Furthermore, the priority and urgency of the different values implied must be weighed.[27] By this procedure, man as assessor (the evaluating human society) arrives at a judgment, tentatively or with some measure of certitude, as to which mode of behavior might further man's self-realization and self-development. As soon as this judgment has been made, it is recognized as a moral norm by the ever present conviction reflected in it that this human action is bound absolutely to *recta ratio.* The fact is simultaneously asserted that the many values to be considered according to their priority and urgency, or nonvalues, do not, strictly speaking, belong as yet to the moral sphere—that is, they are not as yet moral precepts, but are pre-moral. Only the all-embracing view and total appraisal which, as such, determine the mode of action that is good for men, lead to a moral statement. This implies that one or other aspect of an action cannot of itself, and without regard for the remaining factors, determine the morality of an action.

3. *Relativism?* Facts—social, technological, economic, etc.—change. Man's experience, i.e., those of human societies, likewise change, on the basis of changing data. Evaluations also, the mind's grasp of human realities, and self-understanding can be altered. One thinks, for example, of the efforts toward an ex-

panded conception of marriage and sex in the milieu of the Catholic Church in the recent past. And in the process, man (that is, human society), oriented toward development and progress, also changes himself. All these manifold possible—and actual—alterations have to be brought into the moral judgment of human conduct. Such "new" aspects could call for action which, independent of such aspects, would be out of the question; or they might exclude a course of action which would be commanded under other circumstances. If the minimum family income set decades ago is linked to certain social and economic factors; if the institution of private property in our present economic, social and political situation must be viewed as differing in its concrete meaning from previous decades or the Middle Ages; if conceptual grasp and interpersonal and social experience in the realm of family and marriage necessarily co-determine behavior in this area, then on principle, corresponding changes regarding the "right" human behavior in other spheres of life cannot be ruled out. Under this aspect, behavior norms have, at least theoretically, a provisory character.

Changes in the data, differences in concepts and experiences—or even interpretations—occur not only in successive cultures, but also, in cases of actual pluralism,[28] within the same culture. This is readily understandable if heterogeneous economic, social or political situations admit, respectively, of different modes of behavior. But what if varying experiences and concepts and varying self-images of men in different societies or groups lead to different options and so to a diversity of statements on behavioral norms in relation to similar bodies of facts? One might point out, perhaps, that in many cases a given self-concept and a given viewpoint and form of a reality—e.g.,

marriage in, let us say, a certain African tribe —may not in themselves correspond in all respects to *recta ratio*. Then, of course, the question arises whether another form of marriage, presupposing another culture, may legitimately be imposed upon men belonging to an endemic culture—by missionaries, for instance[29]—provided the indigenous culture itself has not changed by a rather gradual process, and provided it admits of a "human" form of marriage. But might it not be assumed also that on the basis of dissimilar experiences, a heterogeneous self-concept and varying options and evaluations on the part of man (humanity) projecting himself into his future in human fashion—*secundum rectam rationem* —are entirely possible, and that these options and evaluations within the chosen system postulate varied forms of behavior? Who would expect human individuals, groups or societies to arrive at self-understanding and values exempt from all one-sidedness or merely from incompleteness? There *recta ratio* which is to guide our conduct has to allow for such conditionality, essentially connected with humanness; without it man de facto does not exist. Moreover, must it not be supposed that the behavioral norms encountered in a particular civilization or cultural area were formulated partly in consideration of just this civilization and culture, hence for them alone? And this despite the fact that definitive or generally valid norms of conduct were actually intended, simply because the possibility of other civilizations and cultures was not taken into consideration.

Is this relativism? If behavioral norms are to be operative, the entire pertinent reality (including the social factor) has to be taken into account and enter into the judgment. The a priori, hence universal, nonhistorical social ethics that stands opposed to this, that provides norms in advance for every social reality, sacrifices the indispensable objectivity and therefore validity of duly concrete solutions to an a priori universalism. The critical question, then, is not one of relativism but of objectivity, or the "truth" of the action which must be in conformity with the whole concrete reality of man (of society). Our previous consideration had to do with moral behavioral norms which men (humanity) "discover" as being appropriate to their actual civilization, experience, etc. We asked: Is this relativism? And now there is the correlative question: Is it not rather the necessary connection with concrete human reality to which human behavior must be adapted if it is to be objective, true, and so, "right," *secundum rectam rationem?* The demand to be this is absolute! Rightly does Chiavacci point out[30] that the objectivity of morality is not necessarily based on an unchangeable being (in other words, on a "preceptive" understanding of natural law), but on the indispensable correspondence of act to being.

III. The "Applicability" of Moral Norms

If the absoluteness of moral norms is constituted primarily by their objective effectiveness vis-a-vis the given reality and thus not preeminently by their universality or their universal validity, the question of the applicability of moral norms to reality in the concrete inevitably arises.

1. *The So-called Exceptions to the Norm.* A very small step in the direction of universal validity in applying moral norms brings home the realization that possibly these norms cannot be stated, as we once believed they had to be, so as to apply to all epochs or in all cultures or social groups, or in all conceivable individual cases. And so we have the problem of the exception to the moral norm.

According to press reports, a French bishop is supposed to have said at a conference of French bishops on *Humanae vitae* that, according to *Humanae vitae* the use of contraceptives is an *evil*, like killing; but killing in a morally justified war of defense and the use of contraceptives in certain cases of conflict would not be morally culpable (in no sense wicked). Have we not overlooked the distinction—crucial in this case—between evil and wickedness—that is, between evil in the *premoral* (physical, ontic) sense and evil in the *moral* sense (wickedness)? Objectively, there is no conflict of moral precepts, only a conflict of value judgments (*bona physica*) in the premoral sense.[31] Only the right—*secundum rectam rationem*—solution of this conflict makes the absence of conflict evident in the moral situation. Killing is a realization of an evil, but it is not always a moral evil. In this regard, there is also no moral norm applying to killing, but only such as designates unjust killing as immoral. If someone (with *Humanae vitae*) regards the use of contraceptives as a *malum*, but considers certain exceptions morally justifiable, he must understand that the *malum* of contraceptive use affirmed by him in this form lies in the premoral sphere ("it is evil") while only the objective unjustified realization of the evil belongs in the area of the moral ("it is wicked"). In general, whoever sets up negative norms, but regards exceptions as justified, by reason of overriding right, or warranted compromise, or for the sake of the lesser evil (or the greater good), shows by this that the *malum* repudiated by the norm is *not* (yet) to be understood as moral evil. Hence its realization to avoid another *malum* (or for the sake of a relatively higher *bonum*) can be justified morally on the ground mentioned previously.

If, on the contrary, one prefers to give this norm moral validity, its formulation in universal terms has to be restricted, and the "exception" is no longer an exception. The norm is objective only within the limits of the restriction.

2. *Moral and Premoral Evil*. The basic distinction between moral and premoral evil[32] should be carried still further in the interest of clarifying the significance of moral norms for concrete behavior. Morality, in the true (not transferred or analogous) sense is expressible only by a human action, by an action which originates in the deliberate and free decision of a human person. An action of this kind can be performed only with the intention of the agent. One may not say, therefore, that killing as a realization of a human evil may be morally good or morally bad; for killing as such, since it implies nothing about the purpose of the action, cannot, purely as such, constitute a human act. On the other hand, "killing because of avarice" and "killing in self-defense" do imply something regarding the purpose of the action; the former cannot be morally good, the latter may be.

Here we take up the question: when is human action, or when is man in his action (morally) good? Must not the answer be: when he intends and effects a human good (value), in the premoral sense—for example, life, health, joy, culture, etc. (for only this is *recta ratio*); but not when he has in view and effects a human nongood, an evil (nonvalue) in the premoral sense—for example, death, wounding, wrong, etc. What if he intends and effects good, but this necessarily involves effecting evil also? We answer: if the realization of the evil through the intended realization of good is justified as a proportionally related cause,[33] then in this case only good was intended. Man has almost always judged in this manner. A

surgical operation is a health measure, its purpose is to cure, but it is at the same time the cause of an evil, namely, wounding. This, however, appears to be justified in view of the desired cure and is capable of being incorporated in the one human act—a curative measure. The surgical operation is morally right, because the person acting desires and effects only a good—in the premoral sense—namely, restoration of health. If the surgeon were to do more than was required in performing this operation, that "more" would not be justified by the treatment indicated—that is, it would be taken up as an evil—in the premoral sense—into the surgeon's intention; it would be morally bad. The conclusion in definitive terms is: 1) an action cannot be judged morally in its materiality (killing, wounding, going to the moon), without reference to the intention of the agent; without this, we are not dealing with a human action, and only of a human action may one say in a true sense whether it is morally good or bad;[34] 2) the evil (in a premoral sense) effected by a human agent must not be intended as such, and must be justified in terms of the totality of the action by appropriate reasons.

These considerations are not without significance for the question of the application of norms to the concrete case. We have already seen this in connection with the so-called exception to the norm. The problem presents itself also in the form of the traditional doctrine, morality in a comprehensive sense, as applied to a concrete action, is determined not only by the morality of the act as such, but also by the morality of the circumstances and the purpose of action, with the reservation, however, that neither the purpose nor special circumstances can recind the negative morality of an action. This point has value only as a rule of thumb (although it has also the theoretical force that something morally has cannot become morally good in view of a good purpose). In theoretically precise reflection, one must, of course establish some additional points. For 1) a moral judgment of an action may not be made in anticipation of the agent's intention, since it would not be the judgment of a "human" act; 2) a moral judgment is legitimately formed under a simultaneous consideration of the three elements (action, circumstance, purpose), premoral in themselves; for the actualization of the three elements (taking money from another, who is very poor, to be able to give pleasure to a friend) is not a combination of three human actions that are morally judged on an individual basis, but a single human action. A surgical operation is not made up of several human actions (wounding, healing, for the purpose of restoring health), but is only one healing action, the moral quality of which is based on a synchronous view of the three—premoral—elements in conformity with the evaluating *recta ratio*. The same thing could be said about the transplant of an organ from a human living organism, about underground coal mining with its threat to health, about the moon-landing and the incalculable dangers involved, etc. But now the critical question: what value do our norms have with respect to the morality of the action as such, prior, that is, to consideration of the circumstances and intention? We answer: they cannot be moral norms unless circumstances and intention are taken into account. They can also be considered as moral norms only because we tacitly judge the action in the light of possible circumstances and intention. But since, theoretically, this is impossible, and since in practice these elements of an action are necessarily incomplete, we cannot rule out the possibility that in the practical application, an objectively based instance of conflict—the exceptional case—can show that the norm does not have, objectively, the range of validity previously supposed. The absoluteness of a norm depends more upon the objectivity of its relationship to reality than upon its universality.

"The end does not justify the means"—that is, the morally bad means. This tenet is, of course, correct. When and to the extent that it has been established that an action is morally bad, it may not be performed as a means toward attaining a good end. On the other hand, if there is a question only of evil in the premoral sense, such as death, wounding, dishonor, etc., the intention and the realization of a good can possibly justify the doing of an evil—e.g., the evil of a surgical operation in the interest of health, or a transplant. Needless to say: 1) the performing of the evil is not an isolated (human) action, but only an element of the one action. Therefore, a morally bad (human) action is not being used as a means to a good end. This point was often overlooked in the traditional statement of the principle of an act with a double effect. Thus, in cases in which, during the course of the action, the bad effect preceded the good, temporally or physically, opinion was always inclined toward prohibition, on the grounds that otherwise the good effect would be achieved through the realization of the bad effect (as means). Actually, many good Christians cannot understand why, in a situation where life is endangered, as, for instance, ectopic pregnancy or uterine diseases, the removal of the fetus was prohibited, while the removal of an organ from the mother, whose serious illness was anticipated because of the pregnancy, together with the fetus, was permitted; although in both cases, there was a liability involved with respect to the life of the fetus—a (premoral) value.[35] The theory failed to take into account that the evil involved is such, not on moral but on premoral grounds (like wounding, loss of honor, death, etc.), and that consequently its actualization occurs, not as a separate human act with its own morality and not, in this context, as an immoral means to a good end, but as a component of one action which is specified through the intention of the agent. Once more, moral norms are not likely to be fully expressed so long as intentions and circumstances are not taken into consideration, at least implicitly. They are objective, therefore, only when this qualification can be presupposed.

3. *"Intrinsece Malum"?* The question of the applicability of moral norms may arise in still another form known from tradition. If the absoluteness of the moral norms signifies objectivity more than universal validity, can behavioral moral norms be universal at all, in the sense of being applicable always, everywhere and without exception, so that the action encompassed by them could never be objectively justified? Traditionally, we are accustomed to speak of an *intrinsece malum*.

Viewed theoretically, there seems to be no possibility of behavioral norms of this kind for human action in the inner-worldly realm. The reason is that an action cannot be judged morally at all, considered purely in itself, but only together with all the circumstances and the intention. Consequently, a behavioral norm, universally valid in the full sense, would presuppose that those who arrive at it could know or foresee adequately all the possible combinations of the action concerned with circumstances and intentions, with (premoral) values and nonvalues (*bona* and *mala* "*physica*").[36] A priori, such knowledge is not easily attainable. An a priori affirmation would not come to be a moral judgment by way of the premoral. Add to this that the conception opposed to this does not take into consideration

the significance for an objective understanding of morality attached to, first, practical experience and induction, second, civilization and cultural differences, third, man's historicity and "creative" perceptions.

Despite all this, we often make statements connoting "universal validity." But "Thou shalt not kill" is obviously too broadly stated; it would be better to say, "Thou shalt not commit murder"—that is, "Thou shalt not kill unjustly." This last formulation is universal and exact. Nevertheless, a high price has been paid for this advantage over the formulation "Thou shalt not kill." For while "killing" expresses an unequivocal fact, "murder" does not, since it leaves undetermined when killing is lawful and when it is not. Accordingly, the inference is self-evident: a precise description of an action as a statement of fact would, theoretically, scarcely admit of a universal moral judgment in the strict sense. An operative universal moral norm contains a formal element not yet defined materially, "lawful," "in an authorized manner." Hence the attempt on the part of moral theology to discover which values, realizable in this world, can justify "killing" and which cannot. If it is believed that, in moral theology, the line between "lawful" and "unlawful" has to be drawn precisely, we have once again a definitive statement of fact and, within its limits, a universal moral judgment. But here we must pause for further reflection. How could one make a judgment that would take in *all* the human possibilities—even granting that one had succeeded in understanding rightly and judging rightly those possibilities that were foreseen? Today, actually, such reflection begins thus: might there not be at the present time and in the future a society in which—as distinguished from earlier societies—by reason of its social and cultural structures, capital punishment would not be an appropriate and therefore warranted means of administering justice? Further, is there meanwhile no life situation that might justify suicide, as, for example, the only means of preserving a state secret, a possibility which presumably is open to consideration, inasmuch as it was excluded indeed in the norm as stated in the past without, however, having been reflected upon at any time? "Killing" vs. "murder" was mentioned as only one example that might shed more light on the problem of the applicability of behavior norms stated as universals.

Theoretically, no other answer seems possible: one cannot easily formulate universal norms of behavior in the strict sense of *intrinsece malum*. Practically, however, norms properly formulated as universals have their worth, and indeed on several counts. 1) Such norms, insofar as they are based on true perception, indicate a value or a nonvalue in the premoral sense. But negative values are to be avoided; in particular, as evil they may never serve as purposes for human action, and only for adequate reasons may they be actualized concurrently with relatively higher or more urgent values. 2) There can be norms stated as universals, with precise delineations of action to which we cannot conceive of any kind of exception—e.g., cruel treatment of a child which is of no benefit to the child.[37] Despite misgivings on the level of theory, we get along very well with norms of this kind. 3) Norms can be stated as universals (in the case of a specific culture or society, particularly), corresponding to human and social situations that have been actually experienced. In these instances, Aquinas' opinion concerning so-called secondary principles of the natural law, including, therefore, "operative" behavioral norms, holds true by analogy: they can be applied in ordinary cases, "*valent ut in pluribus*."[38] And this for the reason that they are stated so as to suit conditions wont to occur in practice (and only for such);

they suffice for ordinary use in practical living. 4) The extent of the inapplicability of a norm to a concrete case (for which it was actually not intended), the degree to which specific norms of our society are stated with precise relevance to present-day conditions in our society, or to those of yesterday's society (from which our present one derives) and so are not relevant to ours; or are generalized and so apply to other societies and cultures as well—such difficulties can neither be presumed as free of doubt, nor may they be completely ignored. Where the first suspicion of one or other of the conditions mentioned above exists, a point of reference is at hand for a thorough examination, to determine the factor upon which the delimiting process should be objectively based.

The absence of a distinction—made only later on—between theoretical and practical possibility characterized not only the moral-theological discussion of the past on *intrinsece malum* and the universality of behavioral norms, but also, by way of consequence, the official ecclesiastical use of these expressions. Apart from this, the terms would have a better meaning if they could be aligned with the term "absolute" in the sense given it above. Every action that is objectively—*secundum rectam rationem*—not justified in the concrete human situation (according to Schillebeeckx, the sole norm and only adequate norm of conduct) is *intrinsece malum* and therefore absolutely to be avoided.[39]

IV. Norms as Authentic Orientation

To summarize: moral theology is concerned primarily with objectivity—its true *absolutum* —which consists in the *recta ratio* of a human-Christian actualization of the concrete reality. *Recta ratio* can be satisfactorily present only in a conscience situation. But human society requires and discovers—"creates"—norms stated as universals; the same is true of scientific moral theology. Nevertheless, universality in norms has certain limits, at least theoretically, because of the objectivity required of a true *absolutum*. What are the practical implications?

1. *Formal Principles and Material Norms of Action.* Undoubtedly, there are universal ethical statements in the strict sense. Nevertheless they always remain formal in a certain sense, at least insofar as they are not material norms of action, i.e., norms which indicate whether actions exactly described materially are ethically permissible or not. That our actions must be authentic self-realization or, what is the same, that we have to do the good and not the evil, is nothing other than the formal formulation of man's ethical self-understanding. This formal and hence absolutely universal formulation can be applied to different spheres of life without losing its formal character: the imperative to be just, chaste, and merciful thus materially states nothing about the materially determined actions which can express justice, chastity, and mercy. Likewise, the formal formulation of ethical self-understanding can express itself in transcendental norms, which thus do not describe the material content of actions: for example, that the Christian man has to realize himself as Christian, that he should live faith and love, baptism and the following of Christ in every action. They are universal. Categorial evaluations, on the other hand, may be influenced to a certain degree by determined experiences, by factual options in a given society, and by a specific self-understanding. Above all, this applies to the hierarchy of values—for example, in the area of marriage and family. This applies in the same way and even more to "operative" norms of action, which were treated above. In this case,

to defend as a theoretical possibility the regular universality of ethical statements—perhaps on the basis of an a priori metaphysical understanding of determined action—is to succumb to the utopia of rationalism.

2. *Moral-Theological Reflection.* Ethical or moral-theological reflection is always associated with moral experience. This, however, can never be a solipsistic experience. Its substance is always related to the moral consciousness of the community.[40] But this moral consciousness is shaped by manifold experiences and diverse influences. In the Christian community led by the Spirit, the human-Christian self-concept is always the matrix and potential corrective of moral understanding, even when the Christian message as such transmits behavioral norms that are scarcely "operative," definitive or universal. On the other hand, it cannot be denied that in the course of the centuries, Old Testament-Jewish concepts and the ethical opinions of non-Christian ideologies of various kinds exercised their influence. It is likewise undeniable that in the Christian communities of those centuries *errare humanum est* and that error in the moral sphere cannot therefore be excluded *a limine*.

If today, in Christian as well as non-Christian sectors, the universality of norms is being questioned on both theoretical and practical levels, with very obvious consequences, the fact still remains that men of today and also the Christian community of today are susceptible to error. There is equal a priori probability, however, that, in their reflections, they can achieve true insight. In this connection, where might the basis be found that would validate the right or necessity of questioning or rethinking, for without penetrating and common reflection in relation to this basis, will not a community run the risk of deviating from "its own" clear-sighted moral sense, which has developed within it and in virtue of its own particular reality? Theoretically speaking, three possibilities that could warrant doubt or rethinking come to mind. First, it can be shown that in the Christian past, faulty evaluations were made and false norms set. If such could be and were identified hitherto, similar identifications could in principle be made also today. Those erroneous evaluations and norms could have been objectively "false" for men of earlier times as well, although today we could probably show why the errors were scarcely avoidable or even not avoidable at all because of the state of knowledge—or awareness—at that time. Second, inasmuch as we ourselves formulate moral norms, such norms may well be imprecise or, the most likely eventuality, stated in too generalized a manner, either because there was only an implicit awareness of limits, or because limits were not adverted to at all. This helps to explain why, third, particular inherited moral statements can be related very accurately to a social situation, a culturally conditioned evaluation, a partially developed self-concept, and the like, rather than to a designated era of the past, whereas for us today those situations and evaluations are "past." In cases where we can prove this and where it is clear that a moral statement has its basis in precisely those givens that have since changed their bases, a moral reformulation is not only conceivable; it is called for.

3. *The Individual and His Conscience.* Undoubtedly, the question of the absoluteness of moral norms has considerable significance for the individual and the forming of his situation-conscience, in light of which (not then—directly—in light of the norms!) he acts. For since we never begin at zero to form our situation-conscience, but always include norms in our starting point, the question of absoluteness, i.e., universality, regarding the norms of the individual and his concrete behavior, becomes important. To repeat, we are not solipsists either in forming a situation conscience or in developing a moral sensibility, or in appropriating moral norms. Rather, despite the uniqueness of the individual, there is a human orientation to moral questions only in terms of a group, a community, a society, conceived as a whole. In his moral convictions and in forming his situation-conscience, the individual cannot simply detach himself from his roots in the moral convictions of the community; nor may he forget that he will find the (i.e., "his") right solution of many an individual moral problem only by relating to the moral perceptions and self-concept of his community. Specific problems usually occur in an integrated context and cannot easily find their distinctively appropriate solutions in another context. In the ecclesial community, it is to be noted further, moral traditions can also be co-determined, in that a Christian member's self-concept and ideal morality, springing from faith (even though the inferences may be partially underdeveloped), can contribute to the ratifying of a moral evaluation. On the other hand, doubts and reversed judgments occurring justifiably in a community can also, naturally, influence the mental attitude and formation of conscience taken by the individual according to his capacity and responsibility, when he decides to participate in the reflective evaluations of his community and follow the judgment of his adviser. Doubtless, much depends on a responsible discernment of spirits, perceptible through[41] and dependent upon a moral faith-instinct (K. Rahner) which, however, must not be equated with mere susceptibility to what has been traditionally handed down.

There is, of course, the theoretical possibility that the "curious exception" (Ramsey) may present itself, not only as a public phenomenon in the life of the community, but also independently in a justified individual case. For the actuality of this possibility, one should not only deal with the uniqueness of the individual and of the particular case—this would be very superficial—but with the basis which in itself is objective and demonstrable—perhaps along the lines of one of the possibilities mentioned above (under 2). Nevertheless, the individual case, granting the demonstrability of the objective basis, probably will be presented as a rule within the community in a similar and analogous manner and be carried through to a competent (not necessarily authoritative) judgment.

4. *The "Pedagogical" Value of Norms.* The moral task of the Christian is not to fulfill "norms" but to "humanize" (Christianize) each of man's concrete realities, understood as a divine call. Norms of moral behavior should help to bring this about rightly, "objectively". The true significance of these norms consists in this "pedagogical" service—not in a universal validity that could compromise objectivity. Accordingly, the function of the norms is then "only" pedagogical.[42] They are guides to right actualization—that is, they are not intended, being abstract, to be an easy solution, nor can they even, at least normally, designate with precision their own range of validity.[43] Yet, practically speaking, they are indispensably important, because no one who is incorporated in a community is without norms. The "pedagogical" service of norms reaches its highest intensity in cases where the individual (as a member of his community) is not entirely capable of finding his way.[44] To be sure, precisely in such instances norms are liable to be understood and lived as law or tabu because they do not easily manifest their proper limits.

Once again: the moral task proper to man is not to fulfill norms so that in the final analysis

life's reality would serve merely as material, so to speak, for actualizing moral values—that is, obeying norms. Inversely, the concrete reality of life itself—that is, its actualization—is the real task; hence the mandate to take up a given reality and to form it "creatively" and in a spirit of self-commitment, into something "worthy of man" (and therefore of his Creator and Redeemer).[45] The understanding of concrete reality itself could by itself enable the evaluating individual (Christian) to judge which "designs" of his shaping action are really "human" (Christian). By forming this judgment, he would simultaneously and at least implicitly recognize the norms, which he has probably carried over, just as the full meaning of the norms "carried over" reveals itself totally only in a comprehending evaluation of concrete human reality. Nevertheless, in the foreseeable future man will carry over, presumably, less numerous, less detailed and fewer behavioral norms known in advance to fulfill the work of performing responsibly the many tasks involved in shaping man's world. Rather, there will be, probably, fundamental principles, a deepened insight into human and Christian values and a heightened sense of responsibility.[46]

If moral behavioral norms have their "relative" significance for the human and Christian realization of man's world, a reflection on their absoluteness belongs to the task of a theoretical consideration of questions regarding Christian morality. Only theoretically neat attempts at solution, not apologetical efforts, can assist praxis effectively. Indeed, not only should these attempts at solution include a designation of limits, but also the indication of the limits of the designated limits. In other words, abstract discussion is not enough. There should be further reflection on how the theological analysis and its outcomes affect the daily life, not only of the "experts" but also of the "ordinary Christian". This latter provision is of very great importance, because moral judgments—concerning really contingent realities—do not require metaphysical proof, only a so-called moral certitude; with this we may be and should be content.

Notes

1. Blasphemy is not infrequently referred to as an "intrinsically" bad act. It should be noted, however, that blasphemy, if it is really such, means expressly a contradiction addressed to God, i.e. the real essence of immorality, and therefore different from any other innerworldly acts. An analogy would be an act directed against the salvation of one's nearest and dearest.

2. Cf. J. Blank, "New Testament Morality and Modern Moral Theology", *Concilium* vol. 5, no. 3, 6–12. Cf. also A. Grabner-Haider, "Zur Geschichtlichkeit der Moral (Biblische Bemerkungen)", *Catholica* 22 (1968), 262–70; W. Kerber, "Hermeneutik in der Moraltheologie", *Theol. u Phil.* 44 (1969), 42–66, especially 52–60.

3. So also H. Rotter, "Zum Erkenntnisproblem in der Moraltheologie", in J. B. Lotz (ed.) *Neue Erkenntnisprobleme in Philosophie und Theologie*, Freiburg 1968, 226–48. The reference here is to 238ff.

4. Cf. *Gaudium et spes*, n. 46.

5. E. Schillebeeckx, "The Magisterium and the World of Politics", *Concilium* vol. 6, no. 4, 12–21, especially 16.

6. K. Rahner, "Zum Problem der Manipulation", in *Schriften zur Theologie* VIII, 303ff.

7. M. Flick and Z. Alszeghy, *Metodologia per una teologia dello sviluppo*, Brescia 1970, 47–68, 91–9.

8. Loc. cit.; cf. *Diskussion zur "politischen Theologie"*, ed. H. Peukert, Mainz-Munich 1969.

9. K. Rahner distinguishes between norms and imperatives: *The Dynamic Elements in the Church*, London 1964, 13–41.

10. In his article " 'Politische Theologie' in der Diskussion", *St. d. Zt.* 184 (1969), 289–308, J. B. Metz rightly saw that political theology can lead to action only by way of political ethics (293–6). Yet it is not made clear why "political ethics", precisely as an "ethics of change" (in distinction from an "ethics of order"), is assigned specially to political theology as a "specifically Christian hermeneutics."

11. Cf. R. A. McCormick, "The Teaching Role of the Magisterium and of Theologians", in *Proceedings of Catholic Theological Society of America* 24 (1969), summarized by the author in *Theol. Studies* 30 (1969), 647f. On the action of the Spirit in the Church, cf. also K. Demmer, "Kirchliches Lehramt und Naturrecht", *Theol. u. Gl.* 59 (1969), 191–213; B. Schüller, "Bemerkungen zur authentischen Verkündigung des kirchlichen Lehramtes", *Theol. u. Phil.* 42 (1967), 534–51.

12. For the conditioned, not ahistorical, character of the moral pronouncements of the Church, cf. A. Auer, "Die Erfahrung der Geschichtlichkeit und die Krise der Moral", *Theol. Qu.* 149 (1969), 4–22; C. E. Curran, "Natural Law and the Teaching Authority of the Church", in *Christian Morality Today*, Notre Dame, Indiana 1966, 79–91; idem, "Absolute Norms and Medical Ethics", in idem (ed.), *Absolutes in Moral Theology?*, Washington D.C. 1968, 108–53, especially 127ff; L. Sartori, "La legge naturale e il magistero cristiano", in L. Rossi (ed.), *La legge naturale,* Bologna 1970, 219–44. According to Curran, changes in the moral teaching of the Church are to be

understood as development, not as contradictions of the past: "Natural Law . . .", 87.

13. Cf. E. Chiavacci, "La legge naturale ieri e oggi", in F. Festorazzi et al., *Nuove prospettive di morale coniugale*, Brescia 1969, 61–91. The reference here is to p. 75.

14. See note 13 above.

15. Chiavacci, loc. cit., 65ff, is of the opinion that Thomas, although he cites many "auctoritates" for other formulations also, basically does not consider detailed norms as natural law; and that this theory derives from other sources. Cf. also D. Mongillo, "L'elemento primario della legge naturale in s. Tommaso", in *La legge naturale* (see note 12 above), 101–23; D. Capone, "Ritomo a s. Tommaso per una visione personalistica in teologia morale", *Riv. di teol. mor.* 1 (1969), 85ff.

   On the whole problem of change with regard to moral questions, cf. J. Gründel, *Wandelbares und Unwandelbares in der Moraltheologie*, Düsseldorf 1967, especially 46–73.

16. Cf. A. Auer (see note 12 above); I. Lobo, "Geschichtlichkeit und Erneuerung der Moral", *Concilium* 3 (1967), 363–75; A. Grabner-Haider (see note 2 above); M. Sheehan, "History: The Context of Morality", in W. Dunphy (ed.), *The New Morality, Continuity and Discontinuity*, New York 1967, 37–54.

17. Cf. A. Auer, loc. cit. (see note 12 above), 12: "Gut ist immer nur, was der Wachstumsbewegung der menschlichen Person und der menschlichen Gemeinschaft dienlich ist. Aber das lässt sich eben nicht nur aus der Vergangenheit bestimmen; es bedarf auch der Hinwendung zur Zukunft"; J. Fuchs, "On the Theology of Human Progress", in *Human Values and Christian Morality*, Dublin 1970, 178–203, especially 185–90. From the moral psychologist's point of view, see I. Lepp, *La morale nouvelle*, Ital. ed: *La morale nuova*, Milan 1967, 78.

18. This terminology occurs in the encyclical *Humanae vitae*, n. 10.

19. Cf. C. E. Curran, "Absolute Norms . . ." (see note 12 above), 118f.

20. B. Quelquejeu's phrasing tends in this direction, see "Brèves notes à propos de 'Nature et Morale' ", *Supplément de La vie spirituelle* 81 (1967), 278–81; also L. Janssens, *Personne et Société*, Gembloux 1939, 199–243; idem, *Personalisme en Democratisering*, Brussels 1957, 93f; H. Mertens, "De persona humana ut norma moralitatis", *Coll. Mechl.* 44 (1969) 526–31.

21. This is not the place for an analysis of the phenomenon of conscience; only *one* fundamental aspect, conscience as judgment, is being considered.

22. Cf. J. Fuchs, "Gibt es eine spezifisch christliche Moral?", *St. d. Zt.* 185 (1970), 99–112; idem, "Human, Humanist and Christian Morality", *Human Values and Christian Morality*, Dublin 1970, 112–47; B. Schüller, "Zur theologischen Diskussion über die lex naturalis", *Theol. u. Phil.* 41 (1966), 481–503; idem, "Inwiewiet kann die Moraltheologie das Naturrecht entbehren", *Leb. Zeugnis*, March 1965, 41–65; A. Auer, "Nach dem Erscheinen der Enzyklika 'Humanae vitae'. Zehn Thesen über die Findung sittlicher Weisungen", *Theol. Qu.* 149 (1969), 75–85, especially 75–8; F. Böckle, "Was ist das Proprium einer christlichen Ethik?", *Z. f. ev. Ethik* 11 (1967), 148–59; K. Demmer, "Kirchliches Lehramt und Naturrecht" (see note 11 above), 200; R. A. McCormick, "Human Significance and Christian Significance", in G. H. Outka and P. Ramsey (eds.), *Norm and Context in Christian Ethics*, New York 1968, 233–61; J. McMahon, "What Does

Christianity Add to Atheistic Humanism?", *Cross Currents* 18 (Spring 1968), 129–50; J. M. Gustafson, *Christ and the Moral Life,* New York 1968, especially chapter VII.

23. J. Fuchs, *Human Values* . . . loc. cit. (see note 22 above), 140–47. In the encyclical *Humanae vitae,* n. 12 states: "leges in ipsa viri et mulieris *natura* inscriptae".

24. R. A. McCormick insists—probably against J. G. Milhaven (see note 25 below)—upon far-reaching effects and consequences of actions whose significance is known without experience: "Human Significance . . .", loc. cit. (see note 22 above), 219–31; published also in *Theol. Studies* 27 (1966), 228–41.

25. So, especially, J. G. Milhaven, "Toward an Epistemology of Ethics", in *Norm and Context* (see note 22 above), 219–31; published also in *Theol. Studies* 27 (1966), 228–41.

26. W. van der Marck, in *Toward a Christian Ethic: Renewal in Moral Theology,* Shannon (Ireland) 1969, advances (perhaps rather onesidedly) the thesis that the moral value of actions consists exclusively in their significance for the creation of positive interpersonal relations. This can be compared with the thesis of J. Fletcher and A. T. Robinson regarding love as the sole *absolutum;* also J. M. Gustafson, "Love Monism, How Does Love Reign?", in J. C. Bennett et al., *Storm over Ethics,* United Church Press 1967, 26–37.

27. Cf. B. Schuller, "Zur Problematik allgemein verbindlicher ethischer Grundsätze", *Theol. u. Phil.* 45 (1970), 1–23, especially 3f. English in *Theology Digest* 19 (Spring 1971), 23–28.

28. On the problem of morality in a pluralistic society, cf. R. Hofmann, "Das sittliche Minimum in der pluralen Gesellschaft", *Theol. Qu.* 149 (1969),

23–38; also A. Hertz, "Sitte, Sittlichkeit und Moral in der pluralistischen Gesellschaft", *Neue Ordno* 18 (1964), 187–96; W. Schöllgen, *Moralfragwürdig? Über gesellschaftlichen Pluralismus und Moral,* Hückeswagen 1967.

29. On the problem of "norms of morality and the christianization of nations", cf. E. Hillman, "The Development of Christian Marriage Structures", *Concilium* vol. 5, no. 6, 25–38; idem, "Pogamy Reconsidered", *Concilium* vol. 5, no. 4, 80–9.

30. Loc. cit. (see note 13 above), 81.

31. Cf. J. de Broglie, "Conflit de devoirs et contraception", *Doctor communis* 22 (1969), 154–75.

32. For this distinction, cf. W. van der Marck, *Toward a Christian Ethic* . . . (see note 26 above); P. Knauer, "The Hermeneutic Function of the Principle of Double Effect", *Natural Law Forum* 12 (1967), 132–62; B. Schüller, "Zur Problematik . . ." (see note 27 above).

33. Cf. P. Knauer, loc. cit.; the decisive question treated by Knauer is: what is a "proportionate" reason? C. J. van der Poel, "The Principles of Double Effect", in *Absolutes in Moral Theology?* (see note 12 above), 186–210. Van der Poel obviously depends on W. van der Marck, *Toward a Christian Ethic* . . . (see note 26 above), 65–74, and *Love and Fertility,* London 1965, 35–63. Cf. also C. E. Curran, "Absolute Norms . . ." (see note 12 above), 112–14.

34. Reference is made to this especially by W. van der Marck, C. van der Poel and P. Knauer (see note 33 above).

35. Cf. e.g., P. Knauer, loc. cit., 149: "In other words, a solution which includes both the death of the fetus and the removal of the uterus with consequent sterility is said to be better than that the fetus alone loses its life. Who can understand this?" Similarly, C. E. Curran,

"Absolute Norms . . .", loc. cit., 112; W. van der Marck, *Love and Fertility,* op. cit.

36. P. Knauer has a similar statement, "The Hermeneutic Function . . ." (see note 32 above), 138: "What is intrinsically an evil act is brought about when no commensurate reason can justify the permission or causing of the extrinsic evil, that is, any given premoral physical evil or injury." B. Schüller, "Zur Problematik . . ." (see note 27 above), consistent with his own approach, states (pp. 4 and 7): "These norms can only be unconditional and valid without exception when they command us to realize a good that can never compete with another more important and therefore preferable good. . . . Whatever we can aim at in our actions in relation to our fellowman is neither an absolute good nor an absolute evil for him." An "intrinsece malum" of a concrete norm of action would nevertheless be possible when the circumstance and purpose—putting aside all other circumstances and purposes—is already fixed in the formulation of the norm; for example, "one must never treat a child with severity out of cruelty", but "out of cruelty" is not only a description of action but also a statement of ethical value (or lack of value).

37. Cf. A. T. Robinson, *Christian Morality Today,* London 1964, 16.

38. Thomas Aquinas, *S.T.,* Ia–Iae, q. 94, a. 4.

39. So also J. Coventry, "Christian Conscience," *The Heythrop Journal* 7 (1966), 152f: also C. E. Curran, "Absolute Norms . . ." loc. cit. (see note 12 above), 169.

40. J. M. Gustafson insists strongly, and rightly so, on this: "Moral Discernment in Christian Life," *Norm and Context* (see note 22 above), 17–36.

41. Cf. Gustafson's significant title: "Moral Discernment in Christian Life" (see note 40 above).

42. By analogy with the Pauline concept of law as a "pedagogue" leading to Christ, R. Marlé, in his "Casuistique et morales modernes de situation," in E. Castelli (ed.), *Tecnica e casuistica,* Rome 1964, 111–20, writes of a pedagogical function of moral law with respect to the actual situation.

43. With Thomas Aquinas, J. de Finance, in his *Ethica generalis,* 2nd ed., Rome 1963, 186, points out that even an aggregation of norms, being abstract, can never produce a *concretum.*

44. In opposition to many psychologists, I. Lepp, from the standpoint of a moral psychologist, maintains that "closed morality" with its norms and also the "superego" with its controlling powers are extremely important for the individual as well as for society, so long as a breakthrough to an "open morality," as he calls it, has not yet occurred: loc. cit. (see note 17 above), 91 ff. In his article, "Massstäbe sittlichen Verhaltens. Zur Frage der Normfindung in der Moraltheologie," *Die Neue Ordnung* 23 (1969), 161–74, A. K. Ruff speaks (p. 164) of norms as having an irreplaceable "exoneration function."

45. Cf. the dynamic contribution of P. Antoine, "Situation présente de la morale," *Le Supplément,* no. 92, 23 (1970), 8–27; also J. M. Gustafson and J. Laney (eds.), *On Being Responsible: Issues in Personal Ethics,* Harper Forum Books; J. Rief, "Moralverkundigung angesichts der Krise der Moral," *Theol. pr. Qu.* 117 (1969), 124–38.

46. For positions on either extreme of this position, see P. Ramsey, "The Case of the Curious Exception," and J. Fletcher, "What's in a Rule. A Situationist's View," in *Norm and Context,* 325–49.

41

Catholic Ethics:
Has the Norm for
Rule-Making Changed?

John R. Connery, SJ

The above question is an inquiry into the norm underlying the traditional rules of Catholic ethics. Often referred to as "secondary rules," the latter are generally identified with the so-called Ten Commandments of the Old Testament (Ex 20:1–17), e.g., "Thou shalt not steal," "Thou shalt not commit adultery," etc. These rules have been interpreted and developed over the centuries through the combined efforts of the Fathers, theologians, and the official Church on the local and universal level. The rules of sexual morality, for instance, have been developed in reference to what Roman Catholics call the Sixth and Ninth Commandments, although numerous other passages from Scripture have played an important role in this development. Although these sources are accepted as "revelation," there is no doubt that the rules derived from them coincide with human experience and that reflection on this experience was an essential element in formulating them. In this respect, the experience not only of the Jews and Christians but also of neighboring cultures was influential.

When the question is raised about the norm for making rules, the concern seems to be about a "primary" rule or norm underlying all of these "secondary" rules, which will explain them. More concretely, the question would be: What makes an act morally good or morally bad? Or: Why are stealing, adultery, murder, etc. morally bad? One must be careful, however, when discussing this question not to assume that there was a chronological development of secondary rules from some basic primary rule or norm on which they depended. There is good evidence to show that the kind of inquiry we are speaking of was of much later vintage. In the Old Testament one finds little philosophizing about rules. To the Jews the rules were part of God's covenant with Israel; they were His law. No further explanation was needed. The early Christians in-

---

This article originally appeared in Theological Studies 42 *(June 1981): 232–250.*

herited much of this attitude toward the rules. We even find among them a certain suspicion of philosophy and philosophizing. A coherent, rational explanation of the basis of Christian rules began to develop only at the end of the first millennium.

This study will attempt initially to explain a new norm for making rules, commonly known as proportionalism, which some theologians are advocating today, and show how it differs from the traditional norm. Since some of the advocates of the new norm claim that it has its roots in St. Thomas, the study will examine this claim to see whether it can be verified. It will continue with an examination of the impact a change in the basic rule or norm of morality would have on secondary rules and on Church teaching regarding such rules. It will conclude with a critique of proportionalism.

Norms of Morality

Over the course of history many theories about primary rules, or what is often called the norm of morality, have been proposed and defended. The fundamental question comes to this: What makes an act morally good or bad? It is not possible or pertinent in this brief presentation to enumerate even in summary form all the responses that have been made to this question. Peter Knauer, S.J., who was the first in recent times to suggest a new approach to rule-making, reduces all these opinions to three categories.[1] They classify as morally good (1) that which leads man to his last end, (2) that which corresponds with human nature, and (3) that which is "simply good." This may be an oversimplification, but with a little explanation it will suffice for our purposes.

Those who identified moral good with that which leads man to his last end were never able to attract many followers, because it always seemed that a judgment that an act would lead man to his last end would depend on whether the act was already morally good. This presumes the existence of a prior norm of morality. The second opinion, which identified the morally good with that which corresponded with human nature, has been, and still is, more generally accepted. This norm has been proposed in different ways by different proponents, but all agree in making man's rational nature the basis of morality. Thomas Aquinas spoke of *recta ratio* as the norm, but this was also anchored in man's rational nature. Knauer objects that this norm does not distinguish adequately between physical and moral evil; in fact, it will really identify only physical or premoral evil.

Proportionalism

The third norm of which Knauer speaks is the norm under discussion in this article. The statement that it is "the simply good" is somewhat cryptic as it stands; its meaning is a little more nuanced. There is no doubt that if one could perform an act that was "simply good" in all its aspects, it would be a morally good act; it is presumed, of course, that it would be a human act, arising from deliberate consent. Unfortunately, it may be practically impossible to place an act which is simply good, at least if one has to consider all the effects of one's act. As human beings, it is our unfortunate lot that our acts are generally mixtures of good and evil, and since this is the case, they will not be simply good. To Knauer it is sufficient for a morally good act that only the good be intended and that any evil connected with the act be beyond the intention of the agent. He maintains that the evil in an act will be beyond the intention of the agent if there is a proportion between the evil and the good to be achieved.[2] Thus, even if the evil is a means to a good end, it will not be intended if it is proportionate to this good. Others do not give the same importance to intention. While they rule out intending an evil end, they see no moral significance in intending an evil means. Schüller, for instance, argues that there is no moral difference between permitting evil and intending evil as a means.[3] As long as there is a proportionate good to be achieved, whether it is achieved through an evil means or with concomitant evil effects is of no moral significance. What is of moral significance is that the good be proportionate, since that is what makes the difference between a morally good and morally bad act.

Because of the emphasis put on proportion, this norm is often referred to as proportionalism.[4] Frequently it has been put in terms of a proportionate reason (good) justifying the use of some evil means. This is probably because it is in this area that the chief problem lies; it is here that it comes into conflict with the tradition. But if it is to be a general norm, it must cover other possible combinations of good and evil, e.g., where the evil is an effect rather than a means.[5] Briefly, it would have to assess all the evil in an act, including the effects, and the proportionate reason would refer to all the good expected from a particular act. The moral judgment would depend on the balance. Prior to this balancing, the evil in the act would be premoral or ontic, as it is sometimes called. Similarly, the good in the act would be premoral or ontic. The act would be morally good if the ontic good outweighed the ontic

evil, morally evil if the ontic evil outbalanced the ontic good.

When the question is asked about changing the norm for rule-making, the meaning in the present context seems to be whether we are moving from a norm which related the moral goodness of an act to its conformity with man's rational nature to one which relates it to a proportionate reason, or a balance of good over evil. A clearer picture of the meaning of this change can perhaps be obtained from a consideration of the elements of the human act. Traditionally, these elements have been classified as the object, end, and circumstances of the act. If one followed the traditional norm, one would conclude that if all these elements were in accord with the demands of right reason, or man's rational nature, the act was morally good. If any of these elements was contrary to right reason, the act was morally bad. This was all epitomized in the axiom *bonum ex integra causa, malum ex quolibet defectu.*[6] Thus a bad end or intention could vitiate an act that might be good *ex objecto*. Similarly, an act could be morally bad *ex objecto* in spite of a good end or intention. The latter was frequently expressed in another axiom: the end does not justify the means (Rom 3:8). Ordinarily the comparison was made with secondary rules rather than with the basic norm of morality. Thus, if what you were doing was stealing (object), it would be wrong in spite of a good intention. It should also be mentioned that if the circumstance in question was an unintended effect, while it might vitiate the morality of the whole act if it were bad, it would not necessarily do so. More about this later.

If the basic rule were changed, the morality of an act would not be determined by comparing its various elements with the demands of man's rational nature. At most, this would tell you whether there was some premoral or ontic evil in any of the elements of the act. To make a moral judgment of the act, one would have to weigh all the good in the act against all the evil to see where the balance lay. Such weighing would include unintended good and evil effects, at least if they were foreseen. Ultimately, an act would be judged morally bad only if the bad outweighed the good. One could not say, according to this approach, that an act would be bad *ex quolibet defectu;* it would be morally bad only if the evil it contained outweighed the good it was expected to accomplish.

What this is saying is that a moral assessment cannot be made of any isolated aspect of the human act. It can be made only of the whole act on the basis of the balance of good and evil in its combined elements. There is indeed an underlying assumption that evil may never be intended as the end of the act; the intention must be directed at a good end. Granted that the intention is directed ultimately at the good in the act, the latter will be morally evil only if the good intended is not sufficient to offset the evil.

It should be obvious that the key to this kind of moral assessment is the proportionate reason; the good to be achieved must be proportionate to the evil involved. Knauer admits that it is impossible to do this kind of quantitative weighing when one is dealing with qualitatively different values.[7] It is like comparing apples and oranges. His position is that the reason for an act will not be proportionate if there is a contradiction between the act and the reason, or if in the last analysis what one does to achieve one's goal is self-defeating. He gives the example of traffic limitations. Generally, speed regulations should be such as to

facilitate traffic and prevent loss of life. But how does one weigh the value of life against the value of faster traffic? He seems to argue that you can make an evaluation only if you can reduce the issue to one factor, the loss of life. Slower traffic might reduce the loss of life from traffic accidents but might increase the loss of life from other causes, e.g., people would not be able to get to an emergency room on time. The best limit would be that which resulted in the lowest overall loss of life. Traffic regulations that are too severe in limiting traffic would actually be self-defeating.

He also gives the example of the student who wants to learn the greatest possible amount in the shortest time. The more time he spends at study, the more he learns. But if he goes beyond a certain limit, he will undermine his health and have to give up study altogether. What he actually does by his actions is defeat his whole purpose. So Knauer argues that one's acts will not be proportionate if ultimately they are self-defeating or contradictory to his goal.

Proportionalism in St. Thomas

Some of the proponents of proportionalism maintain that this is basically a Thomistic approach. If this is true, adopting it will not involve changing the traditional approach but recovering it. The most serious study on this point was made by Louis Janssens.[8] He develops his argument from Thomas' concept of the rational will as the basis of human acts. The will aims at good, which it pursues as an end. But not every good the will aims at will be a moral good. To be a moral good, it must correspond to reason. If it does not, it may still be a good in reference to some lesser appetite, but it will be morally vitiated because it is contrary to man's rational nature.

Janssens admits that according to Thomas there is an exterior aspect to the moral act as well as the will aspect, but he argues that in Thomas they are one act, and a moral judgment of the exterior act cannot be made apart from the interior act, and hence from the will of the agent. He gives the example of killing. If one viewed just the exterior act, one could not make a judgment on the morality of the act. The same exterior act, killing, may be moral or immoral according to the intention of the agent. If it is an expression of a will for justice, it is a good act. If it is an expression of anger, it is a bad act. Janssens then takes up a difficulty, what seems to be a contradiction in Thomas. In one place he says that the goodness or badness of an act is determined by the end, the object of the inner act of the will. In another he asserts that the morality of the external act depends on whether or not it is in keeping with reason. Is he not saying that the morality of the exterior act can be evaluated by itself and apart from the end of the inner act of the will? Janssens feels that this problem is solved by the distinction Thomas makes between the formal and material element in the moral act. The inner act of the will is the formal element in determining morality, since it is through the will that the exterior act becomes moral. So the moral species of the act depends formally on the end (of the inner act of the will) and only materially on the object of the exterior act. Janssens feels that this substantiates his understanding of Thomas, i.e., that it is the will of the end that is decisive in determining morality.

Janssens finds confirmation of this interpretation in several passages of the *Summa theologiae,* but his chief support comes from Thomas' article on self-defense. In that article Thomas says clearly that moral acts acquire their species from what is intended. His argument then is that since the intention in using violence against an unjust aggressor is self-defense, it is permissible even though injury or even the death of the aggressor might result. These would be *praeter intentionem.* According to Janssens, this treatment of self-defense shows that in Thomas it is the intention that determines the morality of the act. In support of this position he keeps quoting St. Thomas' statement: "finis dat speciem in moralibus."

In the article Thomas sets down another requirement for the liceity of self-defense which seems to support the proportionalist position. It is the requirement that the means (the violence) be proportioned to the *finis* of the act. If the violence used goes beyond the needs of self-defense, the act is wrong. St. Thomas does not say so explicitly, but the reason for this requirement seems to be related to the intention. The use of more violence than necessary would imply an intention beyond that of self-defense, e.g., vengeance or anger. The injury or killing would hardly remain *praeter intentionem* under these circumstances. To the proportionalist the requirement of a proportion between the means and the end seems to put Thomas in their camp.

According to Janssens, then, in St. Thomas it is the end that is the key to the morality of the human act. All that is required of the means is that it be proportioned to the end. If this is the correct interpretation, it seems to follow that Thomas was a proportionalist. Is this an accurate interpretation of Thomas' analysis of the moral act? I think there is serious reason to question it. There is no doubt that Thomas says an act can be human or moral only in so far as it proceeds from man's rational will.[9] It seems quite clear that a human act by definition must be the product of the will. Nor can one doubt that the end of the act (the object of the will) will give it a moral species.[10] But if one studies the treatise on the goodness and badness of human acts in Thomas, he will find that ordinarily there is more to the human act than just the act of the will; there is the exterior aspect of the act. Although this is all one act, if one is going to analyze its morality, one must consider the whole act, must consider the object and circumstances as well as the end. And Thomas says explicitly that an act receives its moral species from the object and circumstances as well as the end.[11] Therefore, when he says that the human act receives its moral species from its end, this is not to be understood in an exclusive sense. He is not denying that it can acquire its moral species from other sources.[12]

Actually, Thomas tells us that a moral act can have two moral species: one from the object, one from the end. He gives the well-known example of the man who steals to get money to commit adultery. His act includes two moral species, stealing and adultery, one from the object, the other from the end. It is true that Thomas considers him more an adulterer than a thief; in Thomas' language, he is formally an adulterer, materially a thief.[13] But this does not mean that he is not really a thief or that his only sin is adultery. His act contains a double malice, although the more basic problem is the sexual failure.

A proportionalist might argue that the above does not prove that Thomas was not a proportionalist. All it shows is that adultery is not a proportionate reason for stealing—which a proportionalist would admit. A pro-portionalist would have no problem with the immorality of the adultery, since it involved the intention of an evil end. So the proportionalist could admit a double malice in an act, one of which might be *ex objecto* in a sense, without abandoning his position.

But there is a difference between Thomas' analysis and that of a proportionalist. While both admit a double malice in an act, the proportionalist relates it all to the end of the act; the stealing is wrong because of the absence of a proportionate reason. Thomas would not agree. He asks specifically whether the goodness or badness of the exterior act depends on the goodness of the will.[14] In his response he presents with approval the Augustinian thesis that there are some things which cannot be justified by any good end or good will. He goes on to explain that moral evil in the external act can come from two sources: from the matter of the act (object and circumstances) or from the end. That which comes from the ordering of an act to the end depends on the will, but that which comes from the matter or circumstances comes from reason, and on this the goodness of the will depends. He then goes on to say that the badness of an act can come from any one defect, but that its goodness depends on the goodness of all its elements. So, for the goodness of the external act, a will which is good only by reason of the intention of the end is not sufficient. The external act can be bad either by reason of the intention or by reason of what is willed. According to Thomas, therefore, an act can be bad apart from a good intention, i.e., a proportionate reason. The stealing in the above example, then, is wrong apart from the intention.

In the preceding article Thomas touches on the same issue.[15] He asks whether the goodness or badness of an act is found primarily in the will. His answer is that moral good and evil are found primarily in the will. He then explains that goodness or badness can be found in the exterior act in two ways: by reason of the matter or circumstances, e.g., almsgiving, or by reason of the intention (end), e.g., almsgiving out of vainglory. The goodness or badness which the exterior act has by reason of its end is in the will first and redounds to the exterior act. That which it has by reason of the matter or circumstances does not come from the will but from its conformity with reason.

All of the above seems to make it clear that in Thomas there is moral goodness and badness in actions apart from the will or intention of the end. It is a simplification, then, to say that according to Thomas it is only the end that specifies the moral act. This is only part of the story. The moral act can be specified by its object and circumstances as well, and these specifications are independent of the intention of the end. He does not deny, of course, that some acts may be morally bad by reason of the intended end, but in his general analysis of the morality of human acts he asserts clearly that some acts have an objective morality that is independent of the end of the act.

We have already pointed out that Janssens finds confirmation of his interpretation of Thomas in the latter's article on self-defense.[16] The same is true of Knauer. There seems to be no question that Thomas' basic justification of killing in self-defense comes from the intention. It is definite also that he calls for a proportion between the violence used and the needs of self-defense. So one must ask: Does this make his explanation of the morality of self-defense proportionalistic? In saying that it is the intention that determines the moral species of the act of self-defense, Thomas

seems to be arguing along proportionalistic lines. It is less clear, though, that the other side of this statement, that what is *praeter intentionem* does not affect the morality of the act, reflects proportionalism. This should become more apparent as the discussion goes on.

Furthermore, there is some difference between the Thomistic requirement of proportion in self-defense and that of the proportionalist. Thomas calls for proportionate means, the proportionalist speaks more of a proportionate reason (end). Knauer makes the claim that these requirements mean the same thing. Whatever one may think of this claim, Thomas' interest in proportion is related to the means, and his concern is that excessive violence would be aimed at the death of the assailant rather than self-defense. This would invalidate his original justification, since the killing would no longer be *praeter intentionem*. The proportionalist is more concerned with the original justification of self-defense. Is it a proportionate reason for killing? Thomas is satisfied with the simple explanation that it is natural for a person to defend himself.[17] The proportionalist would look for some kind of proportion between the good and evil in the act of self-defense—between what is saved or defended and the damage done. For Thomas, such a comparison is unnecessary. The damage done is acceptable to him not because it is a lesser evil or because there is a proportionate reason for it. It is acceptable because it is *praeter intentionem;* it has no moral bearing on the act.[18]

Even if one could give a proportionalist interpretation to Thomas' treatment of self-defense, in view of his general analysis of the moral act there is no basis for universalizing this explanation. This is clear even in his treatment of other kinds of killing. It is clear, for instance, that he considers taking the life of an innocent person wrong *ex objecto*.[19] "Nullo modo" is his response to the question regarding its permissibility. There is no implication at all that it would be permissible for a proportionate reason. Explicit confirmation of this may be found in his treatise on baptism.[20] He is dealing with the question of doing a caesarean section on a dying mother to baptize the fetus. It was argued that this should be permissible even though it meant the death of the mother because the eternal life of the fetus was more important than the temporal life of the mother. This seems a clear case where a proportionalist would admit a proportionate reason for causing the death of the mother, even if it had to be considered a means to an end. But Thomas refuses to allow it. Quoting St. Paul (Rom 3:8) that one may not do evil that good may result, he says simply that one may not kill the mother to baptize the child. He does not deny that the eternal welfare of the child is more important than the physical welfare of the mother, but simply does not consider it a decisive factor. The decisive factor is that taking innocent human life is wrong apart from whatever reason one might have for doing it.

Proportionate reason does not even seem to play a part in St. Thomas' treatment of killing which is *praeter intentionem* (accidental killing).[21] In other words, he does not make any demand that it be balanced by a proportionate good. In q. 64, a. 8, he takes the position that one will not be responsible for such killing if what he is doing is licit and there is no neglect, that is, if the killing is not the result of neglect. Initially, the principle he was using called for some kind of necessity, but before the time of Thomas it was softened to a requirement of liceity.[22] As long as the act was licit, one would not be responsible for any death re-

sulting from it, presuming, of course, that it was *praeter intentionem*. It would be clearly wrong to intend such a death.

This is not the place to develop it, but I think a strong case can be made to show that the principle of double effect as formulated in the nineteenth century was more dependent on this article in St. Thomas than on the article on self-defense. What is missing in the article is any mention of proportionate reason. Thomas makes no demand for a proportionate reason to justify accidental killing. All that is required, apart from the demand that the killing be *praeter intentionem*, is that the act from which the killing results be licit and that there be no neglect. The liceity of the act from which the evil effect results is, of course, an important condition of the principle of double effect. The proportionate-reason requirement was added by J. P. Gury, S.J., when he formulated the principle in the nineteenth century.[23] There is good reason to believe, however, that this requirement was added not to balance the evil effect but rather to guarantee that it would remain *praeter intentionem*. As already seen, this condition was a requirement in Thomas and was basic to his justification of accidental killing. The requirement of proportionate reason, then, did not call for a careful comparison of values. All that was required, as Knauer rightly says, was that the proportionate reason be serious. This was enough to make sure that the intention would be directed at it rather than at the evil effect. The concern in accidental killing, therefore, is not primarily a balance of good over evil; it is rather the intention of the agent.

Putting everything together, it is hard to detect any convincing evidence of proportionalism in Thomas. It can hardly be argued, therefore, that those who are proposing this norm today are really recovering a Thomistic methodology. In stating that Thomas was not a proportionalist, however, I am not implying that he held that all moral evil is in the object, or that an act cannot receive its moral species from the end. What is meant is that he held that acts can receive their moral species from their objects and that therefore some acts can be morally bad *ex objecto* (since they can become morally bad *ex quolibet defectu*). This means that they are morally bad apart from the reason behind them. Not all objective evil, then, is ontic or premoral. While every act must come from the will, it can be morally wrong by reason of its object and apart from an ultimate good intention.

In answer, therefore, to the question whether the norm for rule-making has changed, we would have to say that a number of present-day theologians have adopted a new rule, proportionalism. This rule is often stated as follows: an act will be morally bad (1) if it has an evil end or (2) if it causes evil without a proportionate reason (or if it causes more evil than good, or if it causes more evil than it should). Apart from these two instances, any evil in an act will be only ontic or premoral; it will not be moral evil. As is clear, this approach differs from the traditional approach according to which an act can be morally evil *ex objecto,* that is, apart from the reason behind it.

The proportionalist also rejects the distinction between "direct" and "indirect" that has been traditional in Catholic ethics. The distinction is between intending some moral evil as a means or an end and permitting it. To the proportionalists this distinction has no moral significance unless one is thinking of intending evil as an end. As long as one has a proportionate reason, it is just as permissible to intend evil as a means as it is to permit it. In the tradition it was just as wrong to intend evil as a means as it was to intend it as an end. I will have more to say about this later.

Impact on Secondary Rules and Church Teaching

More important perhaps than the original question about a change in the basic norm of morality is the question regarding the impact such a change would have on secondary rules. How would it affect such rules as: "Thou shalt not steal," "Thou shalt not commit adultery," etc.? Perhaps the key change would be in the concept of the rules themselves. Traditionally, the understanding has been that these rules, as they are interpreted, deal with moral evil. A change in the basic norm would change this understanding. The rules would no longer deal with moral evil as such, but only with ontic or premoral evil. Such things as adultery, stealing, killing an innocent person are in themselves only ontic evil, so a rule prohibiting them can only be dealing with ontic evil. One violating these rules, then, would be causing only ontic evil. He would be guilty of moral evil only if he violated them without a proportionate reason. Every rule, therefore, would have to carry an implicit rider "unless there is a proportionate reason," and this rider would add the moral dimension to the rule.

For the proportionalist, then, secondary norms as they stand do not deal with moral evil. To give them moral force, one would have to rule out all possible proportionate reasons, and to do this, one would have to be able to foresee all possible combinations of object, circumstances, and effects both intended and unintended.[24] Since this is an impossibility, a secondary norm proscribing such acts as adultery, stealing, etc. as immoral is also an impossibility. Proportionalists hold that this is true even of Church moral teaching, especially since it is generally not infallible. Even the special guidance of the Holy Spirit will not give the Church the omniscient perspective necessary to set up unconditioned norms.

In fairness to the proportionalists, however, it must be admitted that they are speaking here on the level of theory. They are willing to admit that in practice norms do deal with moral evil. The fact that the human mind cannot foresee all possible combinations of object, end, etc. in which a norm might apply does not mean that it cannot foresee any such combinations. The human mind is not without all foresight. And where Church teaching is concerned, the guidance of the Holy Spirit may well give it more than ordinary foresight. Therefore, when the Church teaches that something is morally wrong, even a proportionalist would have to admit that it would apply to foreseeable circumstances. Actually, in the past, when controversy has arisen over the application of a particular norm, the Church has not hesitated to teach that the norm would apply in particular circumstances, e.g., abortion to save the life of the mother.

Consequently, a change in the norm of morality to proportionalism would demand that a conditional clause be an implicit part of every secondary rule dealing with evil.[25] A proportionate reason would allow one to violate the rule. Or perhaps it is preferable to say that a proportionate reason would exempt an act from the rule or law. All this sounds much more liberal than current thinking (according to the present norm) seems to allow; current thinking does not admit exceptions in certain rules. Whether it will really be more permissive will depend on what one considers a proportionate reason. One could be a proportionalist, for instance, and still deny

that a proportionate reason existed, e.g., for adultery, taking innocent human life, etc. In that case, although the rule in theory would still yield to a proportionate reason, in practice it would stand as it is and a violation would constitute moral evil, since there is no proportionate reason. So a change in the norm for rule-making would not necessarily bring about a practical change in the rules themselves. At most, such a change would provide a theoretical allowance for exceptions. One might be able to fantasize or conjure up cases where a proportionate reason might exist, but the rules would still bind in the ordinary case, and this could include cases where observance would cause considerable hardship. The practical problem with proportionalism is that some might want to make every difficult case an exception. But this would hardly be condoned by conscientious followers of proportionalism. I do not think they would subscribe to the principle that a rule obliges only when it is easy to observe it. On the other hand, the greater the difficulty, the more the pressure to find in the difficulty itself a proportionate reason.

Even if the Church were to adopt proportionalism as its basic norm, it would not necessarily change the secondary rules it teaches and has taught in the past. It might continue to condemn without exception adultery, abortion, etc. What would change is that instead of claiming that these acts are morally wrong in themselves, it would simply say that they are morally wrong because there is no proportionate reason to justify them. It could do this even though it held the theoretical position that a proportionate reason would justify them. It would be a mistake, therefore, to presume that a change in ecclesiastical metaethics would lead to a change in Church rules.

It might be well to make the point here that

the question of changing the norm for rule-making is not the same as allowing for exceptions to rules. There is a history of exception-making in the Church that goes back to Aquinas. One did not have to wait for proportionalism to provide for exceptions. Thomas himself advised that the more remote a rule might be from first principles, the greater the likelihood of exceptions.[26] He gives the familiar example of the duty to return a deposit. Ordinarily this is what one must do. There may be circumstances, however, in which this would not be a duty, and might even be morally wrong, e.g., to return a sword to someone who had suicidal or homicidal intentions. And the more detailed the rule, the greater the likelihood of exceptions, e.g., if the rule prescribed not only the return of the deposit but also a detailed procedure for doing so.

Thomas does not say that all rules will allow for exceptions. We have already seen how absolute was his condemnation of the killing of an innocent person. It may be enlightening to see how he deals with a possible exception to the precept against fornication.[27] The exception has to do with a man who will guarantee the education of the child that might result from his nonobservance of the law. Thomas' response is that rules are formulated on the basis of what ordinarily happens, not on the basis of a rare possibility. Presumably, then, it would oblige even in this case. But even if one wanted to maintain that Thomas would allow fornication where such a guarantee existed, it would not be on the basis of a proportionate reason. It would have to be because such an act would not be evil, since it would not be *contra bonum prolis*. It would not be a violation of the rule, and hence would not need a proportionate reason. Today, of course, one wonders how the good of the child could be provided for adequately outside of a marriage commitment. One also wonders whether it is only the good of the offspring that is at stake in fornication.

Critique of Proportionalism

To recapitulate in terms of means and end, it must be said that to the proportionalist a means has no independent morality of its own; its morality comes from its relation to the end of the act. Traditionally, an ethics of means has been strongly asserted. Traditionalists would certainly agree that there are means which receive their morality from the end of the act, e.g., violence, mutilations, etc. But this is not true of all means. Some means have a morality of their own and a good end will not justify them. All this has been summarized in the axiom "The end does not justify the means." Proportionalists will deny that their method is a violation of this axiom. They argue that the axiom has always applied to an immoral means and that they still hold it true in this sense.[28] I do not think this defense can be questioned, at least theoretically. In practice, however, the proportionalist deprives the axiom of real meaning. If there is no independent morality of means, that is, if the morality of the means always depends on the end, the axiom loses any meaning or force it might have had. The proportionalist has to admit that the end really justifies the means. If one were to give the axiom a proportionalist meaning, it would have to be expanded to read: the end does not justify a means which is immoral by reason of the end. In this sense it becomes a circular statement. A proportionalist may certainly continue to use such an axiom, but it serves no useful purpose. Many proportionalists today seem willing simply to say that it is permissible to do evil to achieve a good purpose.

Intending Evil

Although proportionalists allow one to intend evil as a means, they do not allow one to intend it as an end. One wonders whether this is a consistent position. Presumably, the reason one is allowed to intend evil as a means is that the evil is only ontic and a proportionate good may be achieved. But if this is true, one wonders why it would not be allowed to intend evil as an end as long as it was related to some proportionate good end (also intended). If the proportion between good and evil is the essential criterion of moral good and evil, why is it wrong to intend evil as an end in a situation in which it is balanced by a proportionate good? In itself, the evil end constitutes no more than ontic or premoral evil, just as the means. Or if it is wrong to intend evil in such a situation, why is it permissible to intend it as a means as long as it is balanced by some good end? In other words, if it is the proportion that is the primary criterion, why will it not justify the intention of evil as an end as well as the intention of evil as a means?

It seems, then, that in proportionalism the traditional distinction between intending and permitting loses any significance it might have had. As long as the evil in an act is balanced by the good, it does not matter whether it is permitted or intended, whether it is intended as a means or an end. So the proportionalist does not have to have special concern for evil which is intended. But freedom from the distinction between permitting and intending may not be an unmixed blessing. While the proportionalist may be less bound by intended evil, he will be more bound by permitted evil. Any evil in the act will have to be weighed. Permitted evil

will weigh into his moral judgment just as much as intended evil, and the fact that it is not intended will not be pertinent. He must face the problem, then, of assessing all the evil connected with a particular act, as well as all the good. We will pursue this difficulty later.

Ontic Evil

A more basic objection to proportionalism aims at the "demoralization" of all the good and evil that is found in human acts. In proportionalism such good and evil in themselves can only be ontic or premoral. A judgment of moral good or moral evil can be arrived at only by balancing this ontic good and evil. So it is not enough to judge that what one does goes against right reason to conclude that it is immoral. Before a moral judgment can be made, one must go a step further and compare it with the good to be sought as well as other goods and evils connected with it. The tradition has been that such things as adultery, killing an innocent person, stealing, etc. could be judged morally evil in themselves. They were contrary to right reason and could be judged morally wrong apart from a consideration of the reason behind them and/or the other goods or evils connected with them in a particular act. One could generally presume that such acts would produce more evil than good, but the moral judgment did not depend on this factor and one did not have to wait for an assessment of all the good and evil connected with the act to make it. On the same basis a rule could be formulated prohibiting such acts, and the understanding was that this rule dealt with moral evil. Proportionalism denies a moral dimension to such judgments and the rules derived from them and for a moral judgment requires a comparative assessment of all the good and evil in a particular act. This calls for such a radical revision of one's whole moral outlook that one is forced to question the validity of the system which demands it.

Weighing Good and Evil

The relativization of morality involved in proportionalism also imposes on the moral agent the extremely elusive task of weighing good and evil. Knauer, as pointed out earlier, calls attention to this problem and concedes the impossibility of weighing qualitatively different values. He suggests the possibility of reducing them to one factor and gives the example of traffic regulations. The criterion would be the number of deaths connected with a specific regulation. Certainly, there is a point where slower traffic would be self-defeating in this respect. Fewer deaths might occur from automobile accidents but the number might be less than the number of deaths caused by the delays the regulations caused. Admittedly, the latter number would be very difficult to calculate. But even if it were calculable, one wonders whether all the evil effects resulting from slower traffic could be reduced to this one category. What about the loss of revenue resulting from slower traffic? What about the loss of jobs? Some of these losses might be put in terms of resulting deaths, but surely not all of them. Realistically, one can seriously question whether the kind of reduction Knauer speaks of is a possibility.

Knauer also suggests the possibility of using long-term effectiveness as a criterion of proportionate reason. We have already cited the example of the student who studies day and night to learn as much as possible in the shortest time. Knauer argues rightly that this would be self-defeating, since eventually it would not

achieve the desired good. He is speaking, of course, in terms of proportionate means rather than proportionate reason or end. One can agree with him that if an evil means is not productive of good, it is not permissible to continue to use it. But can one argue that because it may be self-defeating over the long haul, it is not permissible to use it here and now when it is still effective? For instance, is it wrong for a student to study all night for an examination because if he did this every night he would undermine his health and not be able to study at all? Studying all night seems to be self-defeating only where the individual intends to make a practice of it. So one must at least make a distinction between a proportionate reason for a single act and one for a practice.

But even if a means were effective, and would continue to be effective in producing some good on a long-term basis, is this an adequate criterion of its morality, even from a proportionalist viewpoint? If one is a proportionalist, it seems that some comparison between the good and evil involved is still called for. Even if an evil means would effectively produce some good and continue to do so, it is possible that the good produced would not outweigh the evil. So one wonders whether Knauer's criterion really provides an escape from a comparison of values. As pointed out above, St. Thomas avoids this problem in his article on self-defense by focusing on the intention of the agent rather than a comparison of values. As long as the evil in the act is *praeter intentionem,* it does not affect the morality of the case. One does not have to weigh it against the good to be achieved to make a moral judgment about the legitimacy of self-defense.

The problem of weighing to which Knauer calls attention is accentuated when one considers the possibility of weighing a whole set of good and evil effects. What weight, for instance, does one give to evil effects that may be seen only as a remote possibility? What weight does one give to effects that may be a result of a concurrence of causes? Are all similar effects given the same weight whether they are certain or only a remote possibility, whether they are traceable to a particular act or the result of a concurrence of causes? If not, how does one estimate the different weights of such evil (and good) effects? On the surface, it seems to be a herculean task.

A proportionalist might argue that he is no worse off in this respect than a traditionalist applying the principle of double effect. The latter also has to consider proportionate reasons and must therefore weigh values. This may seem true, at least if one follows recent formulations of the principle. They call for a proportion between the good and bad effects of an act as a condition for its licit application. As already shown, however, the approach of the traditionalist to the proportionate reason differs from that of the proportionalist. The main concern of the traditionalist is that the evil in the act be *praeter intentionem*. The requirement that the good effect be *proportionate* to the evil effect is meant to guarantee the proper direction of the intention; it must be of some importance to provide this guarantee. But it is on the intention rather than the weighing of good and evil that the morality of the act depends. The weighing of values is of only secondary importance. In proportionalism, however, where the morality of the act depends basically on the proportion and therefore on the weighing, the weighing is of primary significance. So the seeming similarity between proportionalism and the traditional approach to double effect is somewhat deceptive.

Certainly, even a proportionalist will not be responsible for unforeseen effects if they are not overlooked through neglect. His judgment of the morality of a particular act may not represent objective reality in this case, but he will not be responsible for what through no fault of his own he failed to see. But he must take account of all foreseen effects in making his calculus. He cannot fall back on the distinction between permitting and intending, since he cannot make a moral judgment unless he weighs all the effects. The traditionalist must also consider unintended effects, but he is freed from the kind of analysis the proportionalist must make, since the more basic question is not whether the evil effects outweigh the good effects but whether they are intended. One who follows the traditional approach does not have to do the kind of impossible weighing proportionalism seems to demand.

To conclude briefly, I feel that the proportionalist, by shifting the basis for moral judgment to a comparative standard, makes moral decision-making more difficult than is healthy for moral life. While it may seem to simplify the moral enterprise by eliminating the distinction between permitting and intending evil, it imposes on the moral person a kind of calculus that will make moral assessment largely inaccessible, if not impossible. For reasons such as these, I do not feel that a shift to proportionalism is in the best interests of a healthy moral life.

Notes

1. "The Hermeneutic Function of the Principle of Double Effect," in Charles E. Curran and Richard A. McCormick, S.J., eds., *Readings in Moral Theology* 1 (New York: Paulist, 1979) 1–3.

2. Ibid. 5–6.

3. "The Double Effect in Catholic Thought: A Reevaluation," in Richard A. McCormick and Paul Ramsey, *Doing Evil to Achieve Good* (Chicago: Loyola University, 1978) 165–92.

4. In a previous article I identified proportionalism with consequentialism (see *TS* 34 [1973] 396–414). Richard A. McCormick, S.J., criticized this identification in his "Notes on Moral Theology" (*TS* 36 [1975] 93–99). Although from the standpoint of traditional morality, proportionalism and consequentialism present the same problem, denying the possibility of an independent morality deriving from the object of the act, it may be more accurate to say that proportionalism involves an assessment of all the good and evil in an act rather than just the consequences. Even when proportionalists speak of an act getting its morality from the *finis* or end (the intended consequence), they still call for a proportion between the means and end, and, presumably, other unintended consequences. Bruno Schüller has written a more extended critique of the above article in "Neuere Beiträge zum Thema 'Begründung sittlicher Normen,'" in *Theologische Berichte* 4 (Einsiedeln: Benziger, 1974) 164–80.

5. One gets the impression that those who follow proportionalism often short-cut the process of making a moral judgment of an act. They apply the proportionate-reason criterion only to the intended effect, the end of the act. If the intended good outweighs the evil means, they judge the act morally good. Little or no attention is given to other effects of the act. It is difficult to see how a system that makes the moral judgment depend on a balance of the good and evil in an act can overlook any good or evil that might in any way be connected with it.

Such failure runs the risk of making a false moral judgment. In a system, however, in which the moral judgment is closely bound to the intention, unintended effects play a less important role.

6. *Summa theologiae* 1–2, q. 18, a. 4, ad 3.

7. "The Hermeneutic Function," 11–12.

8. "Ontic Good and Evil," *Readings in Moral Theology* 1, 44–59.

9. *Summa theologiae* 1–2, q. 1, a. 1.

10. 1–2, q. 1, a. 3.

11. Ibid.

12. Thomas' special concern about the moral influence of the end of the act comes from the fact that it seems to be extrinsic to the act. One might want to argue that anything extrinsic to the act should not influence its morality. Thomas simply insists that the end is not totally outside the act. Far from excluding other aspects of the act as sources of morality, he is merely arguing that the end must also be included (1–2, q. 1, a. 3, ad 1).

13. 1–2, q. 18, a. 6.

14. 1–2, q. 20, a. 2.

15. 1–2, q. 20, a. 1.

16. 2–2, q. 64, a. 7.

17. That Thomas does not regard it merely as a matter of proportion seems to follow also from the way he responds to an objection about fornication or adultery. The objection is that if killing is allowed in self-defense, these acts should also be allowed, since they are less evil than killing. Thomas responds that even so they are not permitted, because they are not defensive acts. Actually, they are closer to surrender than self-defense. As such, they would encourage aggression rather than discourage it. It is true, of course, that the victim may save her life, but one might have to conclude that to Thomas it is not the saving of life as such that justifies what is done, but the prevention of aggression.

18. Thomas says nothing about any requirements of proportion between what is defended and the damage done. Later authors will discuss this issue. But there is no requirement that there be a life-for-life proportion. In other words, there is no requirement that the life of the person attacked be at stake to justify taking the life of the aggressor. All that is required is that it be some important value, even though less than life itself. These authors argue that if self-defense is permissible only when one's life is at stake, one is at a serious disadvantage when other goods are attacked. The subsequent loss of life to the aggressor results primarily from his own actions. If he wants to save his life, he can always stop the aggression. It is not quite accurate to say that he loses his right to life in these circumstances. He never had a right to life that would give him a right to attack others or protect him in such an attack. His right to life gives him a right to pursue his life by just means and protect himself against unjust attack. It is not a right to attack others unjustly. The obligation to respect his life is his own, not that of his victim. Similarly, the failure to respect life, his own as well as that of his victim, is his own.

19. 2–2, q. 64, a. 6.

20. 3, q. 68, a. 11, ad 3.

21. 2–2, q. 64, a. 8.

22. The principle was stated in the Council of Worms (868) c. 29 (Mansi, 15, 874).

23. *Compendium theologiae moralis* 1 (9th ed.; Paris, 1857) n. 9. Gury is not the first to mention proportionate reason, but he is the first to formulate the principle of double effect.

24. Josef Fuchs, S.J., "The Absoluteness of Moral Terms," *Readings in Moral Theology* 1, 116–32.

25. Proportionalists maintain that present norms are the product of a proportionalist refinement (see McCormick, "Notes on Moral Theology," *TS* 36 [1975] 98). They give the example of killing. Self-defense was considered a proportionate reason for killing, and so the latter was justified. Similarly, killing combatants in a just war and capital punishment were considered morally good because of a proportionate reason. Direct killing of an innocent person was considered morally bad because there was no proportionate reason to justify it. They argue that if we wish to be consistent, we must admit that a proportionate reason would at least theoretically justify such killing. In other words, if the norm is a proportionate reason, every secondary norm must yield to it.—It is quite true that in Thomas the moral judgment regarding killing depended on the intention of the agent, but as shown there is no clear evidence that any weighing of good and evil was basic to the judgment. And such acts as adultery, stealing, etc. were judged morally wrong apart from the intention of the agent. So there was no room for any kind of comparative assessment. To postulate some prior comparative assessment on which the moral judgment of adultery etc. depended is to assume what must be proved. Such a comparison is not necessary to show that something is contrary to *recta ratio*. And once the moral judgment is made, there is no place for such an assessment. A comparative assessment is possible only if one is dealing with ontic or premoral evil.

26. 1–2, q. 94, a. 4.

27. 2–2, q. 154, a. 2.

28. Fuchs, in *Readings in Moral Theology* 1, 116–32.

Part 6

MAKING MORAL CHOICES: "WHAT OUGHT I TO DO?"

part 6

Making Moral Choices: "What Ought I to Do?"

Introduction

"Making moral decisions is as common an experience as walking and as difficult to analyze. . . . Fortunately, most people manage both operations with some degree of success despite the lack of a descriptive rationale."[1] This moderate success, however, is no reason for not examining the process, the "how" of making moral choices. Each of us proceeds in some manner or other, usually unaware of how it is we are proceeding. Some simply follow rules or the directives of authorities. Others do what will seem to produce good results. Some are very logical in their approach, while others are more feeling and intuitive. If one decides too simplistically, important considerations can be left out. When this happens, our decisions run the risk of being less good, good only by accident, or downright bad. Careful consideration, then, of the processes that lead to moral decisions can contribute considerably to the quality of those choices.

Daniel Maguire lays out the various considerations that ought to go into a well-balanced judgment about the morality of an action. He discusses key questions one should ask to obtain an adequate factual understanding of the situation at hand, as well as sources of moral insight and tools for sorting out and weighing competing values. Lisa Cahill's article on homosexuality complements Maguire's by showing how the multiple sources of Christian ethics considered in Part 4 can work together to generate a Christian response to a concrete moral issue. Both selections provide helpful examples of how one reasons morally or humanely as a Christian.

But are moral reasoning and decision-making only a matter of careful logical analysis? William Spohn explores the role of the "reasoning heart" or "discernment" in discovering what one should do morally. He explains how symbols and affections shape a sense of the self which in turn influences one's moral choices. They also help interpret what is going on in the situation. For the Christian, the primary and normative source of these symbols and distinctive set of affections is the Christian narrative, the story of Jesus. James Gustafson further probes how Christian faith affects

---

[1] William C. Spohn, "The Reasoning Heart: An American Approach to Christian Discernment," *Theological Studies* 44 (March 1983): 30.

discernment. After examining what discernment is and is not, he discusses the various ways in which moral discernment can and ought to be different in Christian moral life. Neither Spohn nor Gustafson wishes to denigrate a reasoned approach to moral choices. Rather, they wish to highlight an oft neglected and legitimate complementary source of wisdom and approach to ethical reasoning. Both succeed in situating moral decision making in the larger context of the Christian story, maintaining the unity between who one is and what one does. In so doing, they make it less likely that this aspect of Christian moral life will be divorced from other essential aspects as was sometimes the case in the past.

42

Ethics: How to Do It

Daniel Maguire

Ethics is the art-science which seeks to bring sensitivity and method to the human task of discovering moral value. With that said it should be clearer what an ethicist (moralist, ethician) is. Two questions leap out of that definition: 1) What does an ethicist do that everyone else does not do, since everyone is involved in knowing moral values? 2) What does moral mean?

Answers: Nietzsche is right when he says that humans are valuing animals. Programmed though they may be, they are not as programmed as squirrels, but are rather "condemned to freedom," to some freedom at least. Human consciousness brings with it the noble onus of having to sort and pick amid competing and often conflicting values to determine which options are moral and which are not. Therefore, it is true to say that every person is an ethicist in pursuit of moral value. The special task of the professional ethicist is to attempt to bring sensitivity, reflection, and method to the way in which humans have learned to do, or stumbled into doing, ethics. The ethicist stops to think how moral judgments are and should be arrived at; most people do not so stop and so think. They should have something to learn from the ethicist who does.

The second question was: What does moral mean? Moral (as opposed to immoral) means that which is normatively human—in other words, that which humans ought to be. An example: most humans decide that sexual fulfillment ought not to be found in rape. A rapist is not what humans ought to be, which is to say that rape is immoral. When we call something immoral, we mean that it is incompatible with humanity. Conversely, that which is truly fulfilling of our humanity is moral.[1]

Some primitive peoples have a very suggestive punishment for incest. The incestuous couple are forced to eat with the hogs for a period of time. However indelicate the example, the symbolic dramatization of immorality is powerful. They have acted in a way that is piggish, counter-human, not human. That is what the judgment of *morality* is all about. (We prescind from whether this guilt rite does any injustice to the mores of the pigs.)

How, then, does one go about deciding whether one's judgment of humanness and

This article is excerpted from Death By Choice *(Garden City: Image Books, 1984) 65–96.*

533

moralness is right or wrong, especially in disputed matters where a lot of other humans disagree? Or, in other words, how do you do ethics?

The first step in ethics is to set up the moral object. Moral object is a technical term. It means an act with all of its attendant and meaning-giving circumstances. An action considered by itself aside from its circumstances has no moral dimension. Thus suppose one gentleman is putting a bullet into another gentleman's head. This raw fact, however impressive, does not give us a moral object that can be validly judged. Until we add the *circumstances,* we do not know whether this action is moral or immoral. Is it a killing emanating from robbery, self-defense, or caprice? When we know that, we will have the circumstances that allow moral judgment. We will have the moral object.

The moral object can be known through a series of reality-revealing questions. Each of these questions is important and it is ethical heresy to neglect any one of them. The bane of ethics is incompleteness, and incompleteness is the product of unasked questions. The goal of the doctrine of the moral object is to get as much of a grasp of the reality as possible because *morality is based on reality.* If you do not ask all the reality-revealing questions, your judgment will be based on only part of the reality and it will be right only by accident. Therefore, no moral judgment can be reached until all questions have been answered as fully as possible.

The Reality-Revealing Questions

The trouble with the questions to be set out here is that most of them are obvious, but, unfortunately, it is the obvious in ethics that is most often ignored. Hopefully the examples given throughout will illustrate this. The first question, then, is *what?* The question "what?" is really the beginning of ethics. And it is a beginning that most people resist. The implication, lest it be missed, is that people usually do not know *what* they are talking about. It is the way of humans to skim off an impression of reality and treat it as though it were the reality itself. Therefore, "what?" is a formidable question. It must be asked because the answer involves concrete facts and data which are loaded with moral meaning.

Let us test this first simple question on something like abortion. Some people argue that a woman has a clear-cut right to an abortion at any time for any purpose since she has a right over her body and the fetus is, in effect, an appendage of her body. I would suggest that anyone who would so argue does not know *what* he or she is talking about. Such an argument might be closer to reality if the woman alone were to be considered. Pregnancy, however, is not a condition of aloneness. Someone or something else is part of the *what* that we are talking about. And this someone or something is not just an appendage. Good ethics would ask *what* it is. Knowing what it is will not give the answer to the morality of abortion, but it will be a marvelous beginning. Look at some of the facts about fetuses and you might sense the unreality of considering the fetus as mere appendage.

What you have is a genetically unique reality. Around four or five weeks after conception, when a mother might just be beginning to think she is pregnant, the basic roots of all the organ systems of the embryo have been laid. A cardiovascular system has already begun forming. Primitive brain vessels are developing. By the eighth week, it is possible to get an EEG reaction. During the ninth and tenth weeks, the fetus is capable of reflex activities such as squinting and swallowing. All of this has happened before the mother feels fetal movements, "quickening," as it is called.

If you would judge the morality of abortion, know *what* you are aborting. There may indeed be some good and morally compelling reason why this "miraculous" ensemble of cells which is concertedly expanding toward infant and personal life might have to be squelched and rejected. The embryo or fetus is, after all, not the moral or legal peer of the woman.

The second reality-revealing question is *why?* This refers to the motivating reason or intention of the agent.[2] One person may be giving money to another person. The mere *what* is not very significant in this case. The morality could emerge from the *why*. If the money is being given to embarrass the recipient later by revealing the debt, the act takes on one moral meaning; if the money were being given out of compassion, the morality would be different. What we are speaking of here is the moral significance of motive.

In the example given above by Joseph Fletcher, saving money to educate a child and saving money for mean and miserly purposes changes the moral quality of the money saving. Becoming a lawyer to help the poor and becoming a lawyer to help the Mafia are two morally different realities and they are different because of the different motive, because of the different *why*.

Performing a craniotomy to save the mother is not the same as doing a craniotomy to eliminate a competing heir. A different *why* makes a different reality. If an abortion is motivated by a desire to spite the husband-father, it would have one moral meaning. If the abortion was performed due to a sudden critical development in the mother's health, the case is not the same. If a doctor injects a fatal dose into a patient's vein because the patient has repeatedly begged for release from agony, it is not the same as if the doctor is doing it because he finds the patient a cantankerous old buzzard who is a nuisance to treat.

What all of these examples illustrate is that *motive gives essential and constitutive meaning to human action.* We have not passed judgment on any of the above cases, for to do so would be to break the rule that no moral judgment should be made until all the reality-revealing questions have been asked. We are only saying that to exclude motive is to exclude reality to a substantial degree.

Good motive alone, of course, is not enough to justify an action morally. Poisoning a city's water supply would not be justified by the motive of easing population pressures. Likewise the noble motive of checking air pollution would scarcely justify a systematic plan to assassinate oil magnates.

An example of the inadequacy of good motive alone is easily found at the collective level of life where a one-rubric ethic of motive is regularly plied. Thus the avowed motive for the bombings of Hiroshima and Nagasaki, which terminated or maimed an enormous number of lives, was "to save American lives." Most sensitive persons have judged this good motive grossly insufficient to justify the holocausts in those two population centers. Similarly many of the things that nations do "to make the world safe for democracy" or "to promote the revolution of the proletariat" can hardly be sanctified by good intention alone. The American colonel who stood in the ashes of Ben Tre and proclaimed: "We had to destroy this village in order to save it," had good intentions. The survivors of Ben Tre could attest to the insufficiency of good motive alone.

The motive factor does not of itself give the moral answer to cases of abortion, suicide, or mercy killing, but it is intrinsic to that answer.

All terminations of life are not the same morally since they do not all have the same motive. It is *morally* and *really* absurd to equate the mercy killer with the robber killer and the rapist killer. There are real differences at many levels in these types of cases and certainly at the level of motive. Legal or moral judgment that does not recognize this is unreal.

The next reality-revealing, and thus morality-revealing question is *how?* What we are saying here is that the manner or style of an action contributes to the constitution of its morality in an integral way. Driving a car can be good, but *how* you drive can make it a moral crime. Sexual intercourse can be a morally fine action but if it is brought about by force or deceit, it will be morally defective at the circumstantial level of *how*. It could be defective for other reasons, too, which would be unearthed by other reality-revealing questions, but the point here is that *how* something is done is morally significant.

What you might be doing may be good; *why* you are doing it may be excellent; but the action may fail morally by *how* you do it. For example, if someone goes into the poverty-stricken inner core of his city to help the poor, they may pass the *what* and the *why* questions with flying colors and fail the *how* by acting with an air of superiority that offends. In this way, a good action could become insulting and therefore bad.

Again, this is not to say that if you do it nicely, it is good. It is simply to say that how you do it matters morally. The *how* question is closely related to the matter of *means*. The wrong means to the right end equals a wrong action. *How* matters. It is not a matter of indifference whether you use a sledgehammer or a pill to respond to someone's request to put them out of their misery. If it is determined that on every account the act is moral, the means chosen could make it immoral.[3]

Who? is also a critical question. Every who, i.e., every person is unique. They have their own unrepeatable story that is embodied in their personality and outlook, their own degree of sensitivity, their own conscience and their own superego, and, if the thesis holds that we are all neurotics, their own neurosis. To do ethics abstractly and ignore the who that you are dealing with is a tragedy. Perhaps this is what is behind Sartre's poignant observation that the greatest evil of which a person is capable is to treat as abstract that which is concrete. In making ethical judgments we can easily consider everything except the person involved. We can abstractly pass over the wisdom of the old adage that one person's meat may be another person's poison.

Note what is being said here: the subject—the *who*—constitutes part of the objective reality to be evaluated. Note what is not being said here: this does not mean that what Lola wants is good for Lola. It does not mean that an arbitrary subjectivism where everyone does their own normless thing is being suggested. It merely means that if you do not know the *who* with all their hopes, needs, and personal possibilities, you do not know what you are judging.

An abortion may seem morally indicated in the case of a rape victim who has a history of mental illness and who is clearly traumatized by the sexual assault. If, however, the girl is so constituted by training and disposition that she could not approve of an abortion, she could not morally decide for one. *A fortiori,* it could not be decided for her. Likewise, it is, I believe, immoral to draft into military service a thoroughly nonviolent man. The full reality of the *who,* as he is, for better or for worse, must be factored into the final moral judgment.

Does this mean that what is objectively moral for one person may be objectively immoral for another? The answer is yes.[4] An example from anthropology can illustrate this. It is reported that in the past, Eskimos would let their grandparents go off to freeze to death at a certain point because this was their way of keeping population within the limits of food supply.[5] The grandparents did this willingly. The story is told, however, of some missionaries who went to the Eskimos, discovered this practice, and condemned it roundly in terms of divine authority. The Eskimos were mightily impressed with the missionaries' veto of their long-standing custom. With their point made, the missionaries departed, promising to return in a few years to see if the faith was being kept alive. They returned and found that the group had died out, presumably enervated and finally killed off by the relative population pressure and lack of food.

The story, if true, shows the moral and real significance of several of our reality-revealing questions. Of the questions we have considered so far, the missionaries obviously did not know the *what* or the *who*. On the contrary, in the absence of viable alternatives, these Eskimo *whos* knew *what* they were about in practicing socially motivated geriatric suicide. The missionaries did not understand either the culture of these people or their ecological situation. As a result they did bad ethics and they killed, as bad ethics can often do. (They also failed to ask other reality-revealing questions we will list, concerning alternatives and effects.)

In the absence of alternatives, the Eskimo practice of benevolent suicide would appear to have been quite moral. The action of the missionaries was objectively immoral, although their intentions were the best, because they ignored the reality of the case for which they so confidently prescribed and because they did not explore alternatives.

Some of the other interrogatives essential for good ethics are *where?* and *when?* Very often these questions will not evoke morally relevant information. If someone shoots you on a Monday or a Tuesday, at home or away, it probably will not affect the moral substance of the act. But it might. Loading a gun is a constitutionally proper and typically American act, and it might also be quite moral. Loading one in a crowded bus might not be. The *where* would suddenly be quite significant. Having an abortion in a back-room abortion mill could render immoral what might have been a morally defensible act, all other things considered. The *where* could be decisive.

When could be most important in evaluating an abortion. An abortion around the fourth week of pregnancy is not the same as an abortion around the sixth month of pregnancy. The time factor affects what you are dealing with; it influences the chain of effects, and the alternatives open to you. So the *when* question in these cases brings a good deal of reality into focus. This is not to establish then that any abortion is moral, but to say that the age of the fetus is relevant. The more advanced the fetus, the more compelling the reasons needed to justify aborting that fetus, if one holds, as I do, that abortion might, at times, be justifiable. Only one who has no awareness of the empirical moorings of human ethics could say that the age (the *when*) of the fetus does not matter.

The final two questions used to set up the moral object and thus make moral judgment possible are: *What are the foreseeable effects?* and *What are the existent viable alternatives?* First to the effects. Effects or consequences are so important in ethics that there is a particular ethical leaning known as consequentialism, which argues in substance that actions are good or bad depending on their consequences. The consequentialist strain, if we may call it that, is good as far as it goes but it does not go far enough. There is more to life than effects and consequences; there is also more to ethics, since ethics is the art-science of human life. Thus to look *merely* at effects is to succumb to the lure of a simplistic one-rubric ethics.

There is no doubt that effects are a major factor in establishing moral meaning, in knowing whether acts are good or bad. If atomic testing in the atmosphere is immoral, and it clearly is, it is so because of effects. If reproduction or adoption of children by single persons is morally right, the moral judgment would emerge largely from an analysis of effects. If the Supreme Court ruling on abortion is right or wrong, it will be so because of its effects on American society. Thomas Aquinas justified the existence of prostitution in society because of the probable bad effects of its abolition. A war is judged as justifiable or unjustifiable largely on the basis of its effects.

With regard to the question on alternatives, it might be said that this last question is the most neglected of the questions. All of these questions are in pursuit of reality. And just as foreseeable effects pertain to the reality that must be judged, so too do alternatives. A realistic moral judgment looks at all the alternatives, or possible forms of reality, open to the agent. To do less is to divorce yourself from part of the real. It might be said by way of baleful comment on humankind, that in any situation involving a hundred alternatives, we see and act on about ten of them. It is the role of one's creative imagination to sense and seize upon alternatives and thus to expand the possibilities of life. Imagination is the transcending, expansive faculty of the human person, our highest faculty, I judge. Unfortunately, it is, in almost all of us, withered, like an arm that was tied to one's body at birth and hence is undeveloped because unexercised.

With the completion of these questions . . . what, why, how, who, where, when, what are the effects and the alternatives? . . . we have done what we can to set up the moral object. Now moral judgment can be made and we turn our discussion to some of the ways ethics uses to evaluate the moral object. The moral object constitutes what might be called, in lawyer's language, a fact sheet, a complete laying out of all the essential circumstances of the case. The first tool for the evaluation of this object that we will look at is moral principle. What are principles and how do they help you distinguish right from wrong?

Principles

Moral principles are the repositories of human ethical experience. More technically, they are propositions that express a value judgment about what befits or does not befit the behavior of human beings. Examples of principles are: do not kill; keep promises; tell the truth; pay your debts; do unto others as you would have them do unto you; act in such a way as to promote human harmony and community, etc. Principles obviously can be positive or negative in their formulation and they can be very generic (Do good and avoid evil) or rather specific (Thou shalt not commit adultery). The question is, what are they worth?

If there are principles for every moral situation, it would certainly simplify the work of ethics. All that one would have to do in situation x is find the appropriate principle and follow its guidance. Unfortunately for our love of ease and simplicity, ethics is not done by principle alone. Principles, however, do contain a distillation of moral insight and a proper understanding of them is required for moral acuteness.

Good Exceptions to Good Principles

It is part of the common wisdom to say that a person who has no principles is a knave and not to be trusted. But what of persons who are replete with principles which they wield unbendingly? Could they not be the kind of good persons who feature as the saints in the satirical definition of a martyr: a martyr is someone who has to live with a saint. To be without principles is to be evacuated of much moral wisdom; but not to know the limits of principles can be equally dehumanizing and cruel.

The precise task of ethics is to find the meaning of human, moral behavior. Principles are relevant generalizations about the normally valuable. They contain a lot of meaning. But human meaning is not entirely generalizable, because it derives from persons who are not entirely generalizable. Principles are fine . . . as far as they go. But they do not and cannot cover every case. Ethics is more than an enterprise of principle.

Let us take the principle "Thou shalt not kill." Where did we get this principle and what are its limits? This principle, like every principle, was born of an experience of value. Suppose we go back imaginatively to the first persons of our species. Suppose we tell *a story.*

Our story begins way back when evolution had just pushed people over the brink into what would later be called specifically human consciousness. These first newly evolved persons would look at themselves and at one another, and value experience would begin. They would readily sense that all life, whether it be in leaf, flower, bird, or beast, is marvelous, a kind of miracle of energy and organization. In looking at human life they would see its special powers transcending anything else. Here are creatures who can perceive not only what is but what can be and can bring it

about. They can find and create beauty. They can speak and sing and laugh and be merciful. They can and sometimes do transcend everything, even their own selves, in the phenomenon of benevolent love which can extend to supreme sacrifice. This kind of life, they might conclude, is outstandingly valuable. They might even reach for superlatives and call it sacred.

From this experience an ethical conclusion would follow naturally, to the effect that this kind of life should be treated as inviolable. Awe and love are the proper response to such life. Violation of such life is wrong.

At this point, our first humans have become ethicists. From their primal experience of human life as uniquely awe-inspiring and valuable, they drew forth a principle: Thou shalt not kill. They might, at this point, feel that their ethics was done. After all, they had had a primal value experience and they had formed a principle to guard the experienced value. That should do it. Human affairs would then be manageable by principle, at least as regards killing. Killing is something you do not do. So be it.

Sooner or later, however, as it always does in ethics, the context that spawned the principle begins to talk back to the principle and the deficiency of principle begins to show. Let us suppose that this happened to our first primitive group when one of their members, an older man weakened and slowed by the years, was coming home from the hunt with a load of venison. Another member of the group spies him while he is still a distance from the camp. And this other member has a little "value experience" of his own. He reasons: there are two ways to get venison. I could go off on the hunt, which is exhausting and often dangerous, or I could knock off this old fellow, which is clearly more efficient, and produces just as much venison.

But, alas, the best-laid plans of mice and primitive men often go astray. The old man, hobbled and all as he was by old age, carried a big stick and with this stick he bludgeoned his iniquitous marauder and killed him. And being an honest man he came home and reported his tragic deed.

"Murder" cry the others when they hear of it. "This contradicts our primal value experience of human life as sacred and it breaks the principle to which that experience gave birth." So now what!

Well, the tribal sages would convene and what later ethicists would call the exception-making or "unlessment" process would commence. Some of the sages would point out that if they had been in this situation and had realized what the assailant was about, they would have fought him off by every means even if it regretfully meant killing the assailant.

"Would that not make us as bad as the assailant?" others asked. These were the ones who believed that their established principle was an absolute. But the wiser sages would argue that it is one thing morally to kill for gain and another thing to kill in self-defense. The motive makes it a different reality meriting a different moral judgment, provided, of course, that there were no viable alternatives to killing and that the foreseeable effects were acceptable. With all these conditions met, killing in self-defense could be licit.

And so it was that ethics made the fateful step to the third level, the troublesome level of unlessment, where you say that this principle holds, unless . . . "But do not fret," the happy exceptionists told the absolutists. "This third level has only one entry. Your principle is almost intact." The absolutists grumbled about the breakdown of morals and the permissiveness of their new society, but the unlettered people generally thought and felt that

the self-defense clause was a great one and it became a matter of moral consensus.

All was well until one day the context talked back again. During a birth process, the baby was being presented in such a fashion that the midwife could not get it out. She was an experienced midwife and she explained to the people around what this meant. "During the absolutist days," she said, "I saw cases like this and both mother and baby died. But now that we have made one exception, couldn't we make another since this is such a good one. If we make the exception, we will have one death; if we do not, we will have two." After her speech, the midwife, being a practical sort who knew there was no time to wait for the academic types to unravel this, went in and performed a primitive act of feticide or infanticide and saved the mother.

This, of course, was not the end of the matter. The old absolutists shrieked: "We told you so! We told you when you made that first exception that you had entered on a slippery slope and that you would slide further into exceptions." "That first exception was like a wedge," one of them said; "now the wedge is being driven further and who knows where it shall end." "Why, it is like dominoes," exclaimed another staunch citizen. "The mistake was in tipping over the first one. On the long haul, the old absolute would do less harm than we are going to see done now." Cries of "the camel's nose under the tent" and "the crack in the dike" filled the assembly.

But then the mother who had been saved by the killing of her child came in and stood before them. The assembly hushed and became still as she bore quiet but eloquent witness to her great sadness that her child had to be killed lest she and it die together. "This was tragic," she said with deep feeling, "but I do not believe it was immoral. Morality like life would appear to be the art of the possible. We must seek to achieve as much value as we can but when values conflict as they did in this case, even death-dealing actions . . . though still utterly tragic . . . may be the best we can do in the service of the good."

Well, that little speech changed the mood of the assembly. Some of the male chauvinist elders huffed and puffed and saw the speech as suspect in its origins. They were supported by the lawyers, who pointed out that the woman was an "interested" witness and therefore biased. But, by and large, most people were glad that the woman was still alive to be with them and with her children. And they liked her distinction between the tragic and the immoral and they agreed that this case was tragic but not immoral. Another entry was put into the line of exceptions.

Eventually other exceptions followed. For example, some of the rogues in the community got to be so hardened in crime that the assembly regretfully instituted capital punishment as a way of coping with the spread of serious crime. Later, some mothers with an eye on the infanticide case, had their fetuses removed from their wombs because they were so ill that they did not think they could in any way survive the pregnancy. And further on, some mothers had their fetuses removed just because they found pregnancy such a bore, and so abortion for some became their manner of birth control. Some added other things to the exception list: duels in cases of honor, infanticide, euthanasia in its active and passive forms, killing off the mentally defective, killing people from supposedly defective races, and eventually almost any kind of killing. As time and reason made them more wise, however, it became clear to most that a lot of the exceptions were bad exceptions. And they realized too that no two exceptions were completely alike, and that therefore, in cases apparently identical, you might grant one exception and deny the other.

The self-defense doctrine, however, persistently expanded for cases in which other communities of humans attacked *en masse* and this came to be known as war and it became one of the most popular exceptions. Not even the old absolutists objected to this, though they still protested all the other exceptions. In fact, what developed as the exceptions multiplied is that different people got sensitive about different kinds of killing but very few were sensitive all the way across the line. Some people could swallow wars and slaughters like oysters in season, but would react with horror to the very prospect of an abortion or euthanasia. Others were out to liberalize all the abortion customs but saw war as wrong. And a lot of people were just confused.

People started to put stickers on their carts to show their views on life/death issues. (The wheel had now been invented, though it is a matter of no small note that men thought of killing long before they thought of the wheel.) Some carts would have inscriptions on one side saying: Life is sacred; stop the war! And, on the other side: Liberalize abortion laws! Other carts urged the people to support "our boys" who were away somewhere killing in the national interest, and, alternately, they would condemn all abortion. The people had good reason to be confused. And so they lived not so happily ever after.

At this point we can leave our fictionalized account of the beginnings of the human ethical drama with the quandaries thereof, and see what it teaches. First, it teaches that there are three levels of reality to be distinguished in discussions of moral principle. Graphically they appear as shown below.

The problem presented here is how to

1. Primal value experience				Life is sacred.					
2. Principle				Thou shalt not kill.					

unless

3. self-defense	war	capital punish-ment	feticide to save mother	abortion of con-venience	abortion after rape	suicide	passive eutha-nasia	active eutha-nasia	genocide, etc.

know whether the principle is a good principle and how to know whether the exception is a good exception. In general it can be said that the principle is a good principle if it is truly rooted in the experience of the value of persons and expresses that experience in a concrete way. Graphically, if you can draw a line from level 2 to level 1, then level 2 is legitimate, and a true moral principle.

What about the *unless* line? Of the unlesses or exceptions it can also be said that they can only be justified if they proceed from the primal experience of the value of human life and *if they express in exception form what the principle expresses in rule form.* An exception to the principle "Thou shalt not kill," if it is a good and moral exception, must be an expression of the appreciation of the sacredness of life. If killing in self-defense when there are no alternate modes of protection is a good exception—and all but absolute pacifists say it may be—it is because life is so sacred that this kind of action protects and enhances the very sacredness of life. Even though it involves killing and thus ending an individual's life, it promotes the over-all conditions of life. In our still barbaric state, the right of self-defense gives life the possibility to continue without being overwhelmed by evil.

Graphically, therefore, if you can draw a line from an exception listed on line 3 to the primal experience of line 1, it is a good exception. A bad exception exists when the line cannot be drawn. Such an exception is not rooted in the primal experience. On war and on capital punishment, people differ on whether such a line could be drawn, as they do on most of the other issues that could be listed on line 3. If euthanasia is justified, it is because it seems that sacred human life is such that voluntary moral dominion over its demise is befitting. In summary, therefore, the principle and the exception, if they are good, are good for the same reason—they express the concrete demands of the sacredness of human life in a specific situation.

Patently, this does not mean that the principle against killing is not a good principle just because it is open to exceptions. Rather, it is good as far as it goes, but it does not go all the way since individualized situations cannot be comprehended by generalized principles. It is perhaps best to say that practical moral principles have limited applicability. A very generic principle like "Do good and avoid evil" has unlimited applicability because it is "uncontaminated" by particularizing circumstantial content and because it is, in essence, an unapplied explanation of the terms good and bad. Good is that which should be done; bad is what should not be done.

As Thomas Aquinas says, in speaking of what I call practical moral principles: ". . . although there is some necessity in the common principles, the more we descend into particularities, the more frequently we encounter defects."[6] This means that the principle is good but not without what Aquinas calls "*de-*

fectus," deficiency, limit. There are cases where greater values than those contained in the principle supervene and prevail. Thus in the case of killing in self-defense, the value of self-preservation in the face of evil may prevail over the value of not killing.

Ethics is a conversation among competing values and the ethical choice seeks the most valuable option obtainable, although in so doing other values will be lost and left unrealized. My argument for positive action to induce death is based on the fact that in some cases a thorough study of the moral object shows that induced death may be more valuable than protracted living. In those cases, the good principle of maintaining life yields to the higher value that is found in inducing death.

This could also be explained by saying that when a principle proves deficient, it is because another principle proves applicable. Thus if an armed man intent on murder asks me where his intended victim is hiding and I deny him that truth by telling him an untruth, the truth-telling principle has yielded to the principle which contains more value here, i.e., the life-saving principle. Therefore, the truth-telling principle is good as far as it goes, until it meets a situation where another principle better expresses the value needs of that particular case. Ethical inquiry, therefore, is an exchange between the moral meaning found in the empirical context, and the moral meaning found in the several principles contending for application in this concrete case.

In conclusion regarding principles, it must be noted that principles are not all equally open to exceptions. Some have greater elasticity than others. The general norm in this regard is that the more generic a principle is, the less likely is it that the empirical context (where ethical meaning is also found) will talk back in the form of exceptions. Thus, "To

each his/her own" is generic enough to be rather free of exceptions.[7] The same is true for "Do good and avoid evil." Likewise, if a principle has so many circumstances larded into it that it comes to describe something outlandishly evil, it is likely that it will not have any exceptions. Thus the principle "Do not rape a girl who is suffering from mental illness" imports an action that is so ghastly in its meaning and consequences that the principle would appear to be absolute since no competing values could seem to outweigh the harm such an action portends. Some people argue, and I disagree, that the principle against ever doing anything positive to hasten the death of a terminally ill patient is in this category. To make this case, it would be necessary to show that the foreseeable consequence of any forms of mercy killing are so disastrous that they outweigh all possible contending values. It is my position that this case cannot be made.

Thus far, then, with principles. Whatever their limits, they are indispensable for the business of ethics.

Other Means for Evaluating the Moral Object

If there is one topic which reveals what an ethicist is and how he or she thinks, it is the discussion of principles. For that reason, I lingered a bit on that topic.[8] There are, however, other tools and faculties which are essential to good ethics. Each of these, in its own way, converges on the moral object and aids in the delicate task of weighing the values contained in that object.[9]

Alongside in-principled moral wisdom, we can place *reason* and *analysis,* an ethical process that is tedious and therefore neglected. Reason and analysis here means perspiring thought and research. Ethics must do its homework or be poor ethics. The reason for this attaches to what we said about the moral object. Morality is a dimension of reality and if you have not done your homework, you are probably settling for figments of the real. Thus reason must glean from the data and the debris of human experience in all of its empirical and conceptual complexity. If morality were merely a matter of deducing principles from a contemplation of our nature abstractly viewed and then deducing answers from those principles, ethics would be more simple and more sure. On the contrary, empirical facts have moral import and must be probed and picked apart analytically. If you are dealing with an irreversibly comatose patient, the empirical/medical fact of that person's condition must be part of your moral judgment. If a pregnant woman has cancer of the uterus, that empirical fact is morally significant. The hydrocephalic condition of an infant is relevant to the judgment on how to treat that child when it comes to ordinary and extraordinary means for preserving its health. If the prognosis is good, bad, or uncertain, that counts heavily in determining the moral meaning of the various options.[10] Good prescription (i.e., prescribing well what ought to be done or not done) derives in major part from good description, and reason and analysis, by discovering and comparing, reveal the telling facts.

Gemüt is another faculty for moral discovery. In general it is a good principle to beware of pedants bearing foreign words and telling you there is no word like it in the larders of one's own native tongue. But *Gemüt* is a word worth borrowing from German moralists. It is usually translated as sentiment or feeling. It is a rich word, however, and we will use it as denoting an affective perception of moral truth. More simply, in the phrasing of Pascal, the heart has reasons of which the mind knows nothing. *Gemüt* refers to what the heart knows.

It is, I judge, a palpable fact of life that very often the heart is wiser than the head when it comes to judging what is morally good. Of course, the heart can also be mean, self-serving and dead wrong. But ethics has all too often neglected the special contribution that our feelings and affections can make if we will pay them heed. Let me go to my favorite ethicist, Thomas Aquinas, for a word on this. Thomas did not neglect the role of affectivity and feeling in moral appreciation. He said there are two ways of coming to a correct moral judgment, by a perfect use of reason and study, or by having a kind of connatural instinctive feeling for the truth. By way of illustration, he says that one could know the moral truths about a virtue by learning what formal ethics has to say about it, or by the distinct route of a connatural feeling which grows out of a love for the value which the virtue imports.[11]

Henri Bergson in different language points to the same cognitive power of affective experience. "There is a genius of the will as there is a genius of the mind . . ." he writes.[12] This should not really be surprising if one reflects on the fact that knowledge is conscious awareness; it is an opening of the consciousness to reality. Awareness, however, is not just a phenomenon of the intellect; through emotion and feeling and affection we become aware and open to new aspects of reality. After all, the one subject thinks and feels and both thinking and feeling sensitize and open consciousness to reality.[13]

It should be noted here too that *Gemüt* is a product of nature more than of education, though it is, of course, affected and conditioned by education. Thus the *Gemüt* of the unlettered might be as reliable as the *Gemüt* of the learned. Very often in the history of the race, the *illuminati* of the land would have done well to attend to the wise *Gemüt* of the lowly.

For now, however, let this be the final word on *Gemüt*. Moral inquiry will go astray if it proceeds from either headless heart or heartless head. *Gemüt* is the *votum* of the heart. *Gemüt* may need to be corrected or overruled by reason, but it should always be heard.

Creative imagination is, I submit, the supreme faculty of moral persons. Philosophers have been challenged for centuries to distill the quintessential human quality that marks out human life as unique. Some have said that humans could be defined as the *animal rationale,* the animal capable of reason. Others have thought, quite ingeniously, that humanity's distinctive essence is better captured in the title *animal risibile,* the animal capable of amusement. I think that more basic than either of these would be the title *animal creativum,* the animal capable of creativity.

The root of our creativity is in other consciousness not only of the actual but of the possible. Other animals can know what is and react to it; humans can know what might be, and create it. Creativity is the high point of the human spirit.

As mentioned above in our treatment of viable alternatives, our creative imagination is an all too rarely exercised power. This is unfortunate for human life, and therefore for ethics. If humans do not respond creatively to their context of conflicting values and disvalues, their response will be less than fully human and therefore less than moral.

Group experience is another necessary ethical instructor. Even in matters that seem entirely personal and private, the sensitive moral thinker must glean from the experience of

other persons and groups of persons. Group experience has many *loci;* it is found in tradition, principles, customs, literature, and in analytical studies of the practices of other peoples. Good ethics, in other words, has good antennae. It listens.

Good ethics knows that morality is not a self-evident property of human situations. Morality is not like a color, so that as I see that an object is yellow, I also see that abortion is immoral. In our immaturity, it did seem that way, and getting disabused of this simplism is one of the pains of growth. Morality, rather, is a relational matter. It has less in common with physicists looking into their microscopes and more in common with detectives looking at hosts of clues and seeing how they hang together. When they see how the slipper and the key and the phone number all *relate,* they have achieved insight.[14] And when ethicists see how all the factors and values relate in the most humanly valuable way, they have achieved moral insight. Because of the enormous number of complexities, imponderables, and unpredictables involved in this, one must go to the various archives of human experience and see how the same or similar problems were met. It is so easy to embrace merely apparent value and miss true value. Group experience is a check on this.

On Knowing What Nobody Else Knows

In the persistent effort of humankind to practice reductionism in ethics, there is a popular tendency to reduce ethics to conscience. Much language about the absolute freedom of conscience is tinged with this reductionism. It would seem that nothing is needed except to be faithful to one's conscience and to respect people who are being faithful to theirs.

Beyond that, all discussion of ethics is in the category of pedantic trappings.

The problem with this is that conscience can be wrong. A formidable amount of harm is done by people who are acting in perfect obedience to their consciences. If someone were in conscience to decide that infant sacrifices were necessary to placate the reigning divinities, there would be little talk about freedom of conscience in the public and legal response to this plan. The role of subjective discernment, however vital and irreplaceable, is not a substitute for a systematic ethics which tries to illuminate what makes some consciences right and some wrong.

With that said, however, the question of the signal role of the judging subject, i.e., of the person in the situation, awaits us. The judgment of the concerned party (parties) is of singular significance in moral inquiry. There is something that the subject knows that no one else knows. The person involved in a moral decision has a role that is unique and untransferable. There is a contact with reality that the subject has which cannot be supplied by any ethical methodology or any moral principle. This has got to be disconcerting to any professional ethicist who wants to wrap it all up at the more manageable level of theory and principle. And maybe that is why this central fact of ethical life is more than a little neglected in formal ethics.

There are three basic reasons to stress the inalienable role of the discerning subject; first, only the experiencing subject has an immediate awareness of the concrete and unique realities of their case. Now, of course, we have to contend with the point of the old adage, *nemo iudex in suo casu,* no one is a judge in their own case. This means that you cannot expect the highest degree of objectivity from the man who is sliding into second base as to whether

he should be deemed safe. In judging our needs, the wish is often the father of the self-serving thought. On the other hand, this man who experiences his foot on the bag *before* he experiences the ball on his shoulder has knowledge that the umpire looking through the swirl of dust does not have, even though he may have to take this knowledge back to the dugout with him after being called "out." (He has every right to remind the umpire of the inalienable credentials of the discerning subject.) The ethicist judging through the swirl of competing principles and theories can also be wrong and may miss the true value of the situation, which only the person suffering the circumstances directly may appreciate.

Principle-ists (and by that I mean those who have an unwarranted confidence in the universalizability of principles) indulge in a game of simplism. The gain of the game is clear. If we stress the similarities and constancies of human affairs, ethics can become a kind of magisterium which absolves individuals of their unique role in evaluation—rather, it arrogates that role to itself. This also lends a greater sense of order in ethics, though surely a lesser sense of reality.

Moral judgment is a judgment of how persons relate to other persons and to things; but it is concrete persons and things who are related. It is in their concreteness that they are ultimately morally meaningful, however many constancies may be detected in the web of relationships. There is a uniqueness and unrepeatableness that is underestimated by the principle-ists. The principle-ist can be so impressed with what is normally good that he or she forgets what is good here and now. It has been said that generalization is the root of all error. That overstates the case but the overstatement sins by excess where the principle-ists sin by deficiency.

A second reason for the irreplaceability of the subject's role is that the truth in moral matters is often found by way of affectivity and intuitive feeling and by creative imagination. The discerning power of these faculties cannot be encapsulated in principle form. They comprise a task that only the subject can accomplish. Of these two faculties we have already spoken.

Thirdly, within the exclusive preserve of the subject there is what I choose to call the sense of profanation.[15] Most peoples consider it wrong to shoot captives by way of reprisal. Thus in the Second World War there was much publicity about German troops who reportedly would round up a number of civilians and shoot them in reprisal for a sniper shooting of a German soldier. Why is there such a general consensus that this is wrong? Some ethicists would say that the negative judgment springs from a calculus of the short- and long-term effects of such activity. This consequentialist calculus, it is said, would show that although there may seem to be short-term gains from such intimidating tactics, overall the act intensifies hatred and eventually evokes an even greater loss of life. That is true as far as it goes, but I believe there is something more to be said here. At this point the sense of profanation enters.

A story might illustrate this. It comes out of World War II and involves a German soldier in Holland who was on a firing squad which was assigned the task of shooting innocent hostages. Suddenly he stepped out of rank and refused to shoot them. His officer charged him with treason and lined him up with the hostages, whereupon he was promptly shot along with them by his erstwhile companions.[16] Knowing the territory as he did, this soldier could not have failed to foresee the results of his act. Yet he refused to kill the hostages and took the ultimate penalty of death in preference to doing so. In so doing he acted out Socrates' dictum that it is better to suffer injustice than to commit it. Why? How did this soldier come to this sudden and heroically self-sacrificing conclusion?

Does it seem realistic to say that he, even implicitly, conducted a calculus of the long-term results of this kind of activity? Or did he not look at the hostages huddled together, limp with terror, and realize that he was being ordered to commit a moral crime? Was it so much a reasoning process as it was a shrinking from moral horror that moved him? Was it a "conclusion" that he reached or a profound experience of evil that overwhelmed him and made him prefer death? Cardinal Newman once said that men will die for a dogma who will not stir for a conclusion. Dogma in that sense denotes an experience of the sacred. Did not the German soldier experience the sacredness of the innocent life lined up before him, and the horror of its violation? If an ethicist could have provided him later with a full consequentialist analysis of the correctness of his decision, would he not, most likely, have felt that this intellectual explanation, however accurate, was not, even in a seminal fashion, what pulled him from the ranks of the killers into the ranks of the condemned? It seems better to attribute this to a native deontological[17] sense of what ought not to be done. This reaction would seem to be more instinctive than rational, an eruption from the precordial depths of personal consciousness, where feeling and thought are even more intimately commingled and whence a cry of pain is likely to burst out in the face of profaning evil.

The reaction of moral shock is not a reaction born of syllogism or intellectual effort. It is analogous to the sense of the sacred, for it is its opposite. It is a sense of profanation of the sacred. It is an experience that is by its nature prior to ethical deliberation, which might or might not follow from it.

Of course, this sense of moral shock or of profanation of the sacred is not infallible. It could be contradicted by subsequent sensitive reasoning. It could also be the result of bias. Thus many of the so-called "right to life" people are racked with horror at the prospect of the destruction of fetal life, even in its early forms. Yet they have no sense of horror or moral shock at the plight of a woman who finds herself carrying a drastically brain-damaged fetus, or who already has more children than she can care for and finds herself pregnant. In fact, the fetal fixation of large parts of the "right to life" movement which limits the sense of profanation to the intrauterine world is morally suspect. The movement seems lacking in horror over the poverty, the economic cancer of arms race spending, sexist dominative patterns operating in the sexual encounter, racism and other social ills. Selective horror focused on the woman contemplating an abortion with no sensitivity to the causes that brought her to this moment is not really pro-life or anti-abortion.

It must be noted too that this sense can be muted by the savage environs in which our moral faculties take shape. Capital punishment was once a public and even festive event. There was very little sense of profanation in evidence. The sense of profanation, however, has grown, and now capital punishment is done privately if at all. The immorality of capital punishment can be argued in several ways —by stressing that it does not really deter as it is supposed to—that it is ultimately vindictive and primitive, etc. But I believe that if persons were forced to company with a person before and at the execution, the sense of profanation could be stimulated. This would be an in-structive experience different from but supportive of reasoned criticism of the institution of punitive killing.

Discerning subjects, we may conclude, have their work cut out for them. To make good moral decisions, we must be faithful to our total experience of life and a good part of that experience is highly personal. It expands within the multiple ways in which we react evaluatively to our moral context. A neglect of our basic perceptions will leave us open to an abstract and cold ethics that will eventually become cruel. At the same time, individuals cannot cut themselves off from the matrix of the historical human family with its accumulated wisdom and its principles and methods. The marriage of subjective discernment and shared theory was made in heaven.

Notes

1. The term "moral" can be the opposite of immoral or of amoral. As the opposite of amoral, it means that a subject is open to value judgment of an ethical sort. So, for example, to say that war is a moral matter means that war can be evaluated morally, not that this war is a good war. Moral as the opposite of immoral means good as opposed to bad. Thus this is or is not a moral war.

   The term human also can have two meanings; descriptive or normative. Thus, descriptively, it can be said that it is human to lie. That is, humans do it. Normatively, one could say, it is not human to lie, meaning humans ought not to do this. Normative language is ought language.

2. The words "motive," "intention," "why" are large and potentially ambiguous words. Historically, ethicians have made a host of distinctions within this

category. The favored Latin word was *finis* and distinctions were made between the *finis operantis*, the *finis operis*, the *finis qui*, the *finis cui*, etc. This was not useless quibbling; sensitivity to the nuances in critical categories is the glory of careful theory, however much it may tax the theorist. For an example of sensitivity to the meaning of *finis*, see Vitus de Broglie, S.J., *De Fine Ultimo Humanae Vitae* (Paris: Beauchesne et ses Fils. 1948). De Broglie opens with the acknowledgment: *"Finis, universim sumptus, non facile definitur."* For our purposes, when speaking of the *why* I am speaking of the *finis operantis*, the good desired by the actor, the motive. The question *what* can also admit of wide interpretation encompassing all of the other questions. I use it to evoke awareness of the basic facts of the case, usually the physical facts, but recognizing that the question could evoke a good deal more than that. Overlap can occur with other questions used in this presentation, but I believe that the congeries of questions as presented is calculated to enhance completeness.

3. Relevant here is the old adage from Scholastic philosophy: *Bonum ex integra causa malum ex quocumque defectu.* This means that the goodness of an act could perish due to a defect discovered in any of the aspects being discussed through the probing medium of these questions. Thus the what, the why, the when, the who, etc., could be morally praiseworthy, but the action fails at the one level of how, etc.

4. The word "objectively" is inserted here to show that we are not talking about subjective guilt. Subjectively, we might say that Hitler was morally innocent if he truly and utterly came to believe that the establishment of the Reich was necessary and good. Subjective guilt refers to the case of a person acting in bad faith. So, again, a criminal might be free of subjective guilt if he or she truly believes that the mob's way of life is a normal and acceptable way of life. By objective standards (and objective standards are the goal of ethics) we would judge both Hitler and the mobster to be wrong.

5. Margaret Mead alludes to this saying, however, that it was the "grandmothers" who were so allowed to depart. See "The Cultural Shaping of the Ethical Situation" in Vaux, op. cit., p. 5.

6. ". . . *etsi in communibus sit aliqua necessitas, quanto magis ad propria descenditur, tanto magis invenitur defectus"* (*Summa Theologica* I II q. 94, a. 4). Thomas says (*ibid.* and a. 5) that principles are applicable most of the time (*"in pluribus"*); in particular cases (*"in aliquo particulari et in paucioribus"*) they may not apply. Thus he says that it is a good principle to give things back to their owner when these things are held in trust. But if the owner manifests the ethically significant circumstance of doing serious harm with the object held, then the principle can be seen as non-applicable and the object should be retained. In this case values more important than the principle take precedence. Thomas by no means saw principles as the all-embracing derivatives of a nature statically conceived. Thus he says "The Nature of man is mutable" (II II q. 57, a. 2, ad 1). Unlike the divine nature, our nature is variable (Supp. 42, 1, ad 3; 65, 2, ad 1; *De Malo*, 2, 4, ad 13). On the position of St. Thomas regarding exceptions to moral principles, see John C. Milhaven, "Moral Absolutes and Thomas Aquinas," in Curran, *Absolutes in Moral Theology?*, pp. 154-85.

7. Eminent domain might be considered an exception to this principle since when

the common good prevails, each one may lose their right to what they have legitimately considered their own. Also emergency hunger may justify taking what is someone else's if it is needed to stay alive.

8. There is, I believe, another area that is highly revelatory of the heart of one's ethical method . . . sin. A full discussion of the theory of what sin does or does not mean—which would not be in place within the purposes and confines of this volume—shows forth almost every presupposition in one's theory.

9. The term value is highly generic and not every value is a specifically moral value. There may be esthetic or economic or military values which, considered in themselves, do not admit of moral valuation. They do admit of moral evaluation when put into their full circumstantial human situation since morality is a dimension of all human activity. Here we are using the term value in a broad sense of that which is good for people. Thus it includes health, relief from pain, peace of mind, peace of conscience, good medicine, community, friendship, etc. In a moral analysis it usually becomes clear that any choice locks out some values and embraces others. To make the most valuable selection in a way that, overall, befits persons as persons, is the work of ethics.

10. The terms reason and analysis, of course, admit of a rich development in ethics. For a discussion of the profound significance of reason as a moral category in Thomistic thought, see Joseph Pieper, *The Four Cardinal Virtues* (New York: Harcourt, Brace & World, 1965), pp. 155–58 et passim.

11. "*Sicut de his quae ad castitatem pertinent per rationis inquisitionem recte iudicat ille qui didicit scientiam moralem: sed per quandam connaturalitatem ad ipsa recte iudicat de eis ille qui habet habitum castitatis*" (II II q. 45, a. 2). Connaturality for Thomas comes about *per caritatem,* through love.

12. *The Two Sources of Morality and Religion* (Garden City: Anchor Books, Doubleday & Company, Inc., 1956), p. 58.

13. Theologian John Macquarrie puts it this way: "Being, then, gets disclosed in existing. But existing is not just beholding or contemplating or perceiving, for it is also concern and involvement and participation. Feeling is always a constituent factor in existing . . . We are, however, disclosed to ourselves, and being is discussed, in affection and volition as well as in cognition, or perhaps better expressed, all affective and connotative experience has its own understanding." *Principles of Christian Theology* (New York: Charles Scribner's Sons, 1966), pp. 87–88.

14. For this comparison I borrowed from Bernard J. F. Lonergan, *Insight* (New York: Philosophical Library, Longmans, 1957), p. ix.

15. This sense may fit within a treatment of what I call *Gemüt,* but it deserves special mention here in this discussion of the unique credentials of the discerning subject. This sense also can be a collective experience.

16. This story is recounted by J. Glenn Gray in *The Warriors: Reflections on Men in Battle* (New York, Evanston, and London: Harper Torchbook, Harper & Row, Publishers, 1959), pp. 185–86. This book is a neglected classic.

17. This ethical term derives from the Greek word meaning *ought.*

43

Moral Methodology:
A Case Study

Lisa Sowle Cahill

Christian ethics is made increasingly problematic in an era of ecumenical revision
and expansion of traditional theological perspectives. The conclusion now appears unavoidable that those accepted approaches to
moral issues which lack interrelated references
to Scripture, tradition, and both actual and
ideal human experience, are inadequate to the
breadth of the Christian religious experience
and its theology. Our dilemma is complicated
by the fact that contributions from these
sources are often unclear, in tension with one
another, or both. This paper will exemplify
one way in which the multiple sources of
Christian ethics might work together to generate an adequate Christian response to a concrete problem, homosexuality.

*for whom? language sets
agenda*

Narrow Approaches

In recent years, several theologians and
denominational bodies have attempted to develop a "Christian" perspective on this issue.

Too frequently, however, the foundations of
Christian moral insight are circumscribed narrowly, excluding or minimizing the authority
of other sources. An adequate approach
would correlate several interdependent reference points, and would attempt an appropriate and critical hermeneutic of each in
relation to all. For some, Scriptural texts such
as the story of Sodom and Gomorrah (Gn
19:1–28) are taken to be definitive and clear
sources of moral rules which can be trans-
posed from the biblical to the contemporary
setting, and which are normative for all Christians. Little, if any, attention is given to histor-
ical-critical scholarship which might explicate
original contexts or subsequent interpretative
appropriation by the Jewish and Christian traditions. For example, it is not remarked that
the destruction of Sodom and Gomorrah has
been interpreted recently as *primarily* a condemnation of inhospitality rather than homosexuality (D. Sherwin Bailey, *Homosexuality
and the Western Christian Tradition*, New
York: Longmans, 1965, pp. 1–28).

This article originally appeared in Chicago Studies *19 (Summer 1980): 171–187.*

Others, such as Norman Pittenger, in *Making Sexuality Human* (Philadelphia: Pilgrim, 1970) also appeal to a more general norm or ideal, "love," claiming that it has a biblical basis. Any genuinely self-offering love which respects the dignity of the beloved, whatever its sexual expression, is said to be a participation in the love of God. The various New Testament meanings of love remain undifferentiated. "Love" connotes sincere and honest interpersonal relationship, and is given little more specific content. The "loving" act is the good act.

In 1973, the trustees of the American Psychological Association voted to remove homosexuality from the list of psychiatric illnesses. Alan Bell, a psychologist, comments that "homosexuality . . . is a sexual variation well within the normal range of psychological functioning" (Homosexuality: An Overview," in *Male and Female: Christian Approaches to Sexuality,* ed. Ruth T. Barnhouse and Urban T. Holmes, III, New York: Seabury, 1976, p. 141). Implicit in such statements, and particularly in their assimilation by normative ethics, is the assumption that the morally commendable human act is the "healthy" human act. Further, what is healthy or sick can be determined by the empirical sciences. In the end, empirical, descriptive studies define the truly human, and conformity to that definition constitutes the moral "ought."

In the *Declaration on Certain Questions Concerning Sexual Ethics,* issued in 1975 by the Vatican's Sacred Congregation for the Doctrine of the Faith, we find an appeal to "natural law," a traditional basis of Roman Catholic ethics. "According to the objective moral order, homosexual relations are acts which lack an essential and indispensable finality," i.e., procreation (paragraph 5). The explicit presupposition of this analysis is that persons have a "nature" or certain essential characteristics, which they share universally, which are knowable by reason, which ought never to be violated in moral activity, and which conduce to specific and unchanging moral norms. In this instance, the law of nature demands that all sexual acts be open to the possibility of procreation, as well as expressive of the love of spouses. Scriptural texts are cited in a footnote, but they are a secondary rather than a primary consideration, adduced in support of a conclusion arrived at on other grounds.

Although the foundation of its argument is the law of nature, the *Declaration* bolsters its case with an appeal to Christian tradition, identified as "the constant teaching of the Magisterium" and "the moral sense of the Christian people" (paragraph 8). This insistence that present ethical judgments must maintain continuity with moral teaching of the Church presupposes that the Christian community in the past has articulated authentically and for all Christians the *concrete* significance of life in Christ.

Each of these evaluations appeals to one possible source of normative Christian ethical reflection, whether it be Scriptural texts, broad Scriptural themes, empirical evidence, essential human characteristics, or the experience of the faith community, authoritatively articulated. An adequate Christian ethics ought attend to all of these sources, attempting to achieve their balance within a community of interpretation.

Integrated Approaches

These sources may be considered to exist in two broader categories and four more specific ones. The category "revelation" might be said to include within it *Scripture* and *tradition*. Within "human experience," are comprehended *descriptive* accounts of experience, such as those provided by the empirical sciences, and *normative* accounts, such as that proposed by natural law ethics. By "Scripture," is meant that body of texts (the "canon") which functions authoritatively in the Christian community as it defines and preserves its identity as faithful to Jesus Christ. To say this much is to already and inevitably enter the "hermeneutical circle" within which the Scriptures form the Church which interprets the Scriptures. Thus we arrive at the source with which, in another sense, we began, tradition. As the historical self-identity of the community which preserves and is preserved by Christ's presence within it, tradition is not really a distinct source, but a context for interpreting the others.

Descriptive accounts of human experience begin not with the explicit Word of God, or the presence of His Spirit within the Church, but with the existence of the creature in the historical process. A salient example in contemporary ethics is the findings of the empirical sciences, such as psychology, sociology, anthropology, and physiology. They enlighten our perception of what is in fact the case in actual experience. To such descriptions of what "is," can be juxtaposed and contrasted normative accounts of what "ought" to be. Descriptive accounts, even ones based on empirical investigation, are not always "value-free." Nonetheless, it seems a legitimate distinction can be made between accounts whose primary objective and function is to elucidate the historical reality of humankind, and those whose objective is to formulate an ideal by which to evaluate historical actuality. Some concept of "the normatively human," or the essentially, authentically or genuinely human, is necessary in order to transcend the particularities, intricacies, ambiguities, and distortions of concrete human existence.

Scripture and Homosexuality

The most obvious starting-point for Christian ethics, then, *as* Christian, is that body of literature which commemorates events of foundational significance for communal faith and practice. Importantly for ethics, the Scriptures provide images and symbols by which the moral orientation of the Christian is formed, as well as insight into what sorts of specific conduct are consistent with Christian character.

To use Scripture as a resource for any normative moral judgment would seem to entail appreciation of at least three of its dimensions. These are specific texts on the issue at hand, if any; specific texts on related issues; and general biblical themes or patterns. We might begin by recalling those familiar biblical texts which apparently yield clear prohibitions of homosexual acts, and even the homosexual condition. The compendia of laws in Leviticus and Deuteronomy outline the requirements of cultic and ritual purity essential to the integrity of the Chosen People. The Hebrews are enjoined to avoid the "abominable customs" of pagan nations (Lv 18:3, 18:24, 18:30). Twice it is repeated that "You shall not lie with a male as with a woman; it is an abomination" (Lv 18:22 and 20:13). Although it is undeniable that, in these texts, homosexual acts are condemned as sinful, the attention of the author in each case seems to be directed elsewhere. First and foremost, the People of Yahweh are to resist idolatry and the temple cults of pagan religions, e.g., male prostitutes (Dt 23:18). These considerations may influence the way in which the central message of the text is interpreted; they inhibit any facile transposition of ostensible negative moral norms to other social and historical settings.

A similar situation emerges as the ethicist turns to the New Testament. St. Paul is the only author to mention homosexuality explicitly, and includes it in lists of sins attributed to those who will be excluded from the Kingdom of God (1 Cor 6:9, Rom 1:26–27). Since Paul appropriated similar lists of sins from Jewish preaching of the time, they function as a rhetorical device in his letter, rather than as a moral discourse. It is nonetheless significant that they were preserved by Paul, and eventually by the Christian community in the canonical collection, but whether this incorporation is decisive for *ethics* in the light of the author's somewhat different concerns is problematic. Paul's Epistle to the Romans contains the only extended reference to homosexuality in the Bible. There it is portrayed as a consequence of abandoning God for idols. The sovereignty of the Creator and the futility of rebellion against the order he has made dominate the passage (1:20, 25). Violations of natural interrelationships among creatures and their Creator amount to forms of idolatry; perversions of appropriate relationships of maleness and femaleness are both the representation and the consequence of such disorder. Since idolatry is central, Paul does not embark on a discussion of sexuality in general, or even specify circumstances which would count as committing the sin mentioned. Paul's moral repugnance to homosexual acts was no doubt thoroughgoing, but a full response to this fact awaits the complementarity of other ethical insights, both biblical and nonbiblical.

Related Texts

The meaning of texts referring specifically to homosexual acts is enhanced when they are situated among texts on related issues, e.g., marriage, adultery, fornication, procreation. Many such texts coalesce with those negatively evaluating homosexual acts by indicating a positive heterosexual, marital, and procreative norm for sexual love. Perhaps the most paradigmatic are the Genesis narratives of the creation of humanity. In all three creation accounts (chs. 1, 2, 5) humanity is constituted male and female, so that sexual differentiation is definitive of humanity from the beginning. Gn 1:27 and 5:2 associate the duality of the sexes with the "image" and "likeness" of God in the creature; "So God created man in his own image, in the image of God he created him; male and female he created them" (Gn 1:27). In chapter 2, a union of two like but distinct beings is accomplished, when they "become one flesh" (v. 24). Neither man nor woman alone is complete humanity; only their duality, complementarity, and union give human nature its fullness. That the sexuality of the man and woman is part of their very creation suggests that the relation between the sexes is a profound part of human reality.

The union of Adam and Eve is succeeded by the mothers and fathers of the Judaeo-Christian religious tradition, Abraham and Sarah, Isaac and Rebecca, Jacob and Rachel (along with Leah and two handmaidens), Moses and Zipporah. The covenantal commands of God forbid adultery (Ex 20:14, 17; Dt 5:18, 21), and enjoin filial respect for parents (Ex 20:12, Dt 5:16). In fact, the entire system of Hebrew law presupposes and institutionalizes the family and procreation.

The New Testament offers a similar picture. Jesus does not mention homosexuality, nor any sexual sins save that of adultery. It is possible, however, to distill an affirmative view of marriage and family from his teachings and deeds. Familial relationships are presupposed by many parables, e.g., wedding feasts (Mt 22:1–14; Lk 14:7–11), the bridegroom (Mk

2:19–20; Mt 5:14–17, 25:1–13; Lk 5:27–32); a wedding celebration is also the setting for a miracle story in Cana (Jn 2:1–11). More normatively, Jesus teaches his disciples to consider God as in the relationship of a parent to them (Mt 6:9–15; Lk 11:2–4), and compares God's forgiving love to that of a father for his prodigal son (Lk 15:11–32). Nonetheless, marital or familial status is not definitive of one's standing in the Kingdom of God (Mk 3:1–35, 12:25, Lk 18:29; cf. 1 Cor 7, Lk 14:26, Jn 4:1–42). The demands of discipleship take precedence over all human relations and loyalties.

Jesus's ethical teachings in general, e.g., on divorce (Mt 5:31–32, 19:9; Mk 10:11–12; Lk 16:18; 1 Cor 7:10–11), proclaim and enjoin those ideals of human conduct and relationship which are most consistent with God's intention in the creation, and with existence in the Kingdom. In challenging the Hebrew practice of divorce, Jesus appeals to the Genesis accounts of the equality and union of male and female (Mt 19:4–6, Mk 10:6–9). Herein the ideal is established. Exceptions to the permanence of this bond are not what God intended, but are allowances made only for "hardness of heart" (Mt 19:8, Mk 10:5). Also those who decide not to marry at all are considered to be exceptions to the norm, marriage. Jesus focuses on the ideal to which persons ought aspire in their conduct, rather than the casuistry of exceptions, even justifiable ones. Certainly it is a distortion of Jesus's own perspective to interpret his teachings as in themselves laws which exclude any exceptions they do not contain. The primary concern in the teaching of Jesus is not the definition of ethical criteria for inclusion in the Kingdom. Rather, he portrays God's relationship to us as merciful acceptance, and expects persons to respond with gratitude to God and reconcilia-

tion with even those among their fellows who are most antipathetic.

On the one sexual offense which Jesus mentions, his position is unambiguous. He presses behind adulterous actions to condemn with equal force even the lust which instigates them (Mt 5:27–28). Nevertheless, his attitude toward those who offend the norm is one of compassion and forgiveness, e.g., toward the woman about to be stoned for adultery (Jn 8:2–11), and the Samaritan woman at the well who has had five husbands (Jn 4:1–42).

The letters of St. Paul provide a general perspective on sexuality, which, by contrast, appears quite negative (1 Cor 7:25–40). He advises Christians who are not already married to stay single, unless they require a spouse as a sexual outlet. Once married, husband and wife should love one another devotedly, but the one who remains a virgin has made the better choice. Since Paul, along with other early Christians, may have expected the end of the world and the return of the Lord in the relatively near future, he advises Christians to prepare, rather than to undertake any changes in their station in life. His central message, in the light of the eschaton, is simply that that which distracts one from single-hearted devotion to God is to be avoided. At the same time, he does compare the relation of Christ to his Church to marriage, and exhorts spouses to love one another faithfully (Eph 5:21–33).

Both Testaments also portray nonmarital love, including friendships between persons of the same sex. Yet these are colored by no clear sexual connotations. Between David and Jonathan (whose love is passionate, even sensual), Naomi and Ruth, Mary and her cousin Elizabeth, Jesus and Lazarus, Jesus and John, is the goodness of love between friends of the same sex, but no model of sexual relations between them. In the end, Scripture grounds via specific texts not only a negative appraisal of homosexuality, but a positive view of heterosexuality as normative for human love which has a sexual expression.

General Biblical Themes

Texts referring to sexuality need to be elucidated further by the larger biblical themes or patterns by which they are surrounded. Especially important for Christian ethics is the model of Jesus Christ which is presented in the Bible. Indeed, it is the self-disclosure of God in Christ that illumines the entire horizon of Christian existence. The Christian person is formed within a community rooted in a Scriptural self-understanding and defined by certain common ideals, purposes, and symbols, e.g., Creation, Cross, Kingdom of God.

The qualities which ought to inform Christian character coalesce in Jesus. The focal events of his life for the Christian community are Cross and Resurrection. Christians know the reality of suffering to be the mark of sin, guilt, judgment, and to an equal degree, of obedience to the will of the Father. Reconciliation and exaltation are the converse of repentance and Cross. Jesus Christ, then, is a model not only of forgiveness, inclusive acceptance, reconciliation, and liberation, but also of suffering, guilt, judgment, sacrifice, fidelity, and service. His death on the cross, for example, reminds us of our universal sinfulness and the "brokenness" of creation. Since all of their descendents share in the sin of Adam and Eve, we are well advised to "Let him who is without sin among you be the first to throw a stone . . ." (Jn 8:7). The death of Jesus is for all persons, now redeemed, but first of all sinners, homosexuals no more and no less than anyone else.

Jesus associates with those whom the people of his time considered outcasts. Forgiveness is mediated to all in Jesus, even those whom "the righteous" condemn and shun. Fidelity to the Father in Jesus entails a responsibility to love others as Jesus loved, in conformity to the final paradigm of self-sacrifice, and in anticipation of the Kingdom which begins now. To the extent that homosexual love is characterized by fidelity and service, by sacrifice and liberation, by repentance and reconciliation, it follows Jesus' teaching and example. The larger community also must include homosexuals in their attitudes of love, forgiveness, and reconciliation, as well as judgment. Although these themes and their applications could be multiplied, it will suffice to take note of the fact that, while Scripture specifically affirms a heterosexual norm, and prohibits homosexual acts, it also affirms qualities of relationship which can be achieved by homosexuals. This positive view of the potential quality of homosexual love stands in tension with the negative implications of the specific texts on homosexuality and marriage. Is it adequate to the biblical witness to permit the larger biblical context to relativize all specific condemnations of homosexuality to the point of moral irrelevance? A final ambiguity on the issue of homosexuality in the Bible leads to the question whether Scripture is a sufficient as well as a necessary and primary source of Christian ethics. Does the community of interpretation for which Scripture is authoritative also assimilate appropriately other sources of insight within its perspective?

The Role of Experience

Paralyzed by complications and uncertainties in the hermeneutics of its primary source, particularly when that source is understood as a "text," contemporary Christian ethics often leans on the empirical sciences for assistance in the interpretation of human moral behaviour, in particular, of sexual behaviour.

Such evidence seems especially persuasive when it can be buttressed empirically, e.g., by sociology, psychology, anthropology, and studies of human sexual response, acts, and patterns of relationship (e.g., the pioneering work of Alfred Kinsey, and William Masters and Virginia Johnson). Such studies, too, seem to confirm heterosexuality, monogamy, and parenthood as prevalent cross-cultural standards. However, they by no means are such without exception. Other forms of sexual relationship are reported with some frequency, and in many instances do not appear to be psychologically damaging or to render persons unable to function in society. Although sometimes homosexuality is associated with neurosis, same-sex preference as such is not in principle incompatible with psychological health, or with the capacity to enter into loving and faithful relationships. One particularly valuable contribution of psychology to ethics is the distinction between a homosexual *orientation,* or "constitutional" homosexuality, in which the person may be confirmed in a sexual orientation by little-understood factors largely if not wholly beyond his or her control; and homosexual *acts* of genital intimacy, performable either by a confirmed homosexual, or by someone having, in general, a heterosexual preference.

Although the empirical sciences are the most notable among those descriptive analyses of experience which have become influential upon formal ethical reflection, there are other varieties. It is worthwhile to note among these what might be termed the "personal story," which describes the experience of an agent involved in the sort of conduct under scrutiny. Such a story is often offered as a morally persuasive "voice" for a class of persons, or for a generalizable dimension of experience. Verification then becomes consensual rather than empirical.

Descriptive assessments of morality in our own day are scarcely less problematic in their relation to Christian ethics than are biblical prohibitions addressed to foreign cultures and eras. Does normative morality depend on statistical frequency or on psychological and physical "health"? In most such studies, the underlying definition of human "health" is analogous to that pertaining to plant and animal life: the successful self-preservation and self-maintenance of an organism in its environment. Christian norms such as suffering, self-sacrifice, and self-denial for others at the very least challenge this definition.

Natural Law Tradition

A third alternative for the ethicist is to attempt to define or appropriate some concept of "the normatively human" or human nature, and thus to avoid the reduction of normative moral evaluation to descriptive or empirical analysis. The discovery of a methodology for deriving such a concept is an obvious barrier to this project, if it is not possible to derive it through empirical investigation. The Roman Catholic tradition of theological ethics nominates a candidate method, with attendant successes and shortcomings. This tradition has been committed to an objective moral order, under the providence of its Creator, which humans know and to which they conform by the powers of intellect and will. The essential human qualities, which reason discovers by abstracting from experience, and which choice ought to ratify, are not in any specific way epistemologically dependent on empirical verification, although it is expected that they will in general be confirmed by it. The "natural law" teaching that sex (in particular, sexual intercourse) is above all unitive and procreative is claimed to be consistent with biblical perspectives and with concrete experience.

The more egregious and notorious problems in this method arise at the level of the specific conclusions whose consistency with and, indeed, entailment by the heterosexual and procreative norm is asserted. The prospect of disagreement among those both within and without Christianity has not made the magisterium reluctant to articulate absolute prohibitions not only of adultery, prostitution, sexual promiscuity, but also all homosexual acts, premarital sex, and artificial contraception. To the Church's insistence that the presence of the Holy Spirit preserves its voice from falsehood, and obligates it to dispel the obfuscation of sin, error and ignorance, it has been observed forcefully enough that even "authentic" teaching of the Church is articulated within the historical process and is subject to the contingencies and limitations that that process implies. A specific definition of "human nature" proposed with excessive certainty, abstraction, rationalism, rigidity, and authoritarianism exposes the intrinsic liabilities of the method by which it is derived more readily than would a more cautious or provisional proposal.

This brief investigation of the third source concludes with an insistence on the importance of deriving some working definition of the essentially human in the light of which the actually human may be considered. The commitment to this task is the indispensable contribution of natural law ethics. At the same time, it is necessary to consider whether carefully nuanced conclusions about exceptions to norms grounded in conceptions of the genuinely human are not only possible but advisable. As Aquinas had the good sense to remark, one doesn't really want to quarrel

with the more general natural law principles, but as one gets down to specifics, there is increasing room for error (*Summa Theologica,* I-II, Q. 94, a.4. Considerable discussion has swirled around precisely what Thomas meant in so saying).

The Community

Obviously enough, Scriptural images, scientific research, and insights into essential humanity are not discrete data with clear and distinct meanings apart from their ongoing relevance to the community within which they are discovered or received and understood. This community itself is the "tradition" of Christian faith and practice. In its function as an authoritative source for ethics, tradition is sometimes conceived as a series of propositions or even catalogues of sins transmitted from the past. Although tradition includes the articulation of specific moral directives for the life of the community, it is not limited to them. Specific criteria for what counts as "tradition" might include antiquity, widespread usage, consensus of the faithful, and authoritative definition. Tradition generally might be understood as the "story" of a people, for whom the Scriptures are formative, and whose historical self-understanding continues to form and inform present and future. (Stanley Hauerwas has eloquently developed the importance for ethics of "story," "vision," and "character.")

The question which expresses best the relevance of tradition for ethics is whether the purposes, decisions, actions and relations of Christian persons are shaped by the story of the Christian people. Normative moral rules are subsequent and secondary; they delineate with varying degrees of specificity and reliability those sorts of conduct coherent with that story. The consistent positive contribution of the Christian tradition on sexuality is that "normative" human sexuality is heterosexual, marital, and has an intrinsic relation to procreation, love and commitment. Hence the traditional condemnation of homosexual acts as not truly expressive of the meaning of human and Christian sexuality and even in contradiction to it. However, the sticky task of Christian ethics is determining when, why, and how to make exceptions to norms.

Summary

It becomes increasingly apparent that the sources of Christian ethics are several, and that their interrelationship in normative evaluations is exceedingly complex. The evaluation of homosexuality and homosexual acts is a case in point. It may be valid indeed to develop a negative rule about homosexuality within the Christian tradition, but not as a straightforward conclusion from Scripture or any other single source. The Christian ethicist is pressed to the nigh insuperable task of maintaining a "balance" among the dialectical reference points mentioned. 1) *Scripture:* a) *Specific Scriptural texts on the precise question.* Homosexual acts are unqualifiedly condemned, though in the context of discussions of other issues. b) *Specific Scriptural texts on related questions.* These yield a norm of heterosexual marital commitment. c) *Overarching Scriptural themes or patterns.* The lives of all Christians as individuals and in community are characterized by brokenness, self-sacrifice, forgiveness, and reconciliation, the paradigm of which is Jesus Christ. 2) *Descriptive accounts of human experience.* Empirical evidence points to the conclusion that

homosexuals are a sexual minority, but can be psychologically and socially healthy, and can engage in loving relationships, whether or not these have a genital expression. 3) *Normative accounts of human experience (the normatively or essentially human).* The most authentically human expressions of genital sexuality respect the procreative and male-female unitive purpose of sexual acts. 4) *The tradition of the Christian community.* In the broad sense, tradition enjoins conformity to Jesus Christ. While homosexual persons are (in theory) not condemned, genital expression of relationships of love have been excluded for them.

Although my use of both biblical and non-biblical sources is not beyond equivocation, I would suggest that these are the sorts of considerations to which normative ethics ought attend. What, if anything, can be concluded from these sources? In the case of homosexuality, their complexity will be respected only by the proposal of a nuanced judgment, rather than a simple condemnation of homosexual acts as seriously sinful in all circumstances or blanket approval of all "loving" sexual acts. In my assessment, these sources together point unavoidably toward a heterosexual norm for human sexuality. This norm does not necessarily exclude exceptional applications, in cases where human and Christian values even more important than those protected by the norm are at stake, and where their realization cannot be accomplished without overriding the specific sexual norm. Descriptive or empirical accounts of human experience may be particularly helpful precisely at this point. They can serve to elucidate the situation in which the norm is to be applied, clarify the human options actually open to the persons involved, and question proposed applications of the norm which do not consider appropriately the "facts" of such a situation.

Orientation and Acts

The most important contribution of empirical research on the phenomenon of homosexuality is the distinction between orientation and acts. It is important to permit this distinction to influence applications of the heterosexual norm, even while continuing to uphold the norm itself. I would argue that heterosexuality *per se* is to be preferred to homosexuality. However, a normative judgment that the homosexual orientation is a less than fully human and Christian form of sexual preference does not necessarily entail a corollary prohibition of those genital acts through which confirmed homosexuals express and strengthen a committed relationship. It is essential to distinguish carefully between 1) normative evaluations of homosexuality, as a general sexual orientation, 2) evaluations of the concrete justifiability of homosexual acts in specific circumstances, and 3) the moral character and potential of homosexual persons. Far from branding all constitutional homosexuals as "sinners" in the specific sense, Christian ethics accepts the fact of homosexuality or heterosexuality as beyond the control of most individuals. Certainly homosexual persons (sexually active or celibate) are not inhibited by their sexuality from realizing in their character morally commendable qualities, or qualities consistent with their faith in Jesus Christ and life within his community. The cultivation of love, self-sacrifice, fidelity, and service are even more important for Christian moral agents than avoidance of the specific sorts of conduct which are *in general* not expressive of those virtues.

Given the heterosexual norm thus far delineated, a distinctively *Christian* perspective on homosexuality might perceive in it the suffering, tragedy, and irreconcilable conflict which are part of historical existence after the fact of sin, as part of the "brokenness" in which all creation shares. Although all human experience confirms the presence of evil and suffering within it, the faith community interprets this with the image of the Cross. With the corollary image, Resurrection, the Christian community expresses its distinctive confidence that evil, tragedy, and absurdity, are not the final word. The human situation, considered in the light of these central images together, is seen to be imbued not only by guilt, suffering, ambiguity, but also by mercy, forgiveness, reconciliation, redemption.

In view of these observations, two inadequate approaches to homosexuality can be discerned, as well as, hopefully, a more positive one. In one sort of evaluation, normative theological ethics relies too one-sidedly on empirical studies which verify that the homosexual is psychologically and socially healthy. The ethicist then proceeds to the conclusion that the homosexual orientation is humanly and morally normative, and that homosexual acts are in no way morally questionable. The positive contribution of this approach is its affirmation of the homosexual person in his or her concrete reality. However, from a Christian viewpoint, this can also be understood as an attempt to deny the disconcerting reality of suffering and ambiguity concretized in the situation of the homosexual. This is to explain away the tragic dimension of our existence in history precisely when and *because* it thrusts itself painfully upon our experience. Such a solution also betrays frequently a confusion between affirming homosexual persons as persons, affirming the justifiability of homosexual acts in exceptional instances, and affirming homosexuality as an orientation. To see the orientation as non-normative, and as in a real sense "suffering," is not to offer a negative moral judgment on homosexual persons, on their potential for praiseworthy relationships, nor necessarily on homosexual acts.

In another sort of evaluation, the association of the phenomenon of homosexuality with the brokenness of the creation, or with the "Sin" in which all persons and institutions share, is simplistically or uncritically identified with personal "sin," the sin of the homosexual person. If the orientation is evidence of the effects of Sin, then, it is inferred, genital acts expressing that orientation must be "sins." Some go even further, in insisting that the homosexual person, regardless of the level of his or her sexual activity, must be a "sinner." This evaluation falls short because of its imputation of guilt to individuals for a condition for which their responsibility is far from clear, or at a lesser level, for acts which, given that condition, are the concretely possible expressions of important human and Christian virtues or values.

A Judgement

A Christian perspective on homosexuality, then, would recognize suffering as such, but would interpret it by Cross and Resurrection. Both sacrifice and liberation are *positive* concepts, calling for embodiment in Christian life and action. Christian ethics focuses on character, formed by the biblical and communal vision, and enhanced by Christ-like qualities. Acts are not irrelevant to the development of character. The relation of specific sorts of acts to character is determined by consideration of the four sources mentioned, in combination or balance (tradition always forming the context for the interpretation of others, and Scripture always forming the tradition). In this case, those sources evidently conduce to the judgment that those sexual relations and acts which best embody the Christian vision are heterosexual and procreative acts within a permanent commitment. Even in this sort of specific assessment, the proper focus of Christian ethics, is character and moral values or characteristics (for example, honesty, fidelity, love, service, self-denial), rather than on physical values and material acts (for example, acts of genital sexuality). The latter are good or evil precisely because of their relation to the former, as generally accomplished their realization and enhancement, or as generally excluding and inhibiting them. If because of conflictual situations, the material acts usually conducive to and expressive of moral values do *not* actualize them or in fact inhibit them, then these acts are not to be commended in the situation. The less-than-ideal ("broken") situation can and must be "redeemed" through fidelity to the higher religious and moral values, even if unavoidably embodied in less-than-ideal material decisions and acts. In the concrete situation this is the best alternative and therefore a positive and morally commendable one, which should be appreciated in the light of the Christian values, qualities, and ideals which it positively achieves. This amounts to a suggestion that while heterosexual marriage is the normative context for sexual acts for the Christian, it is possible to judge sexual acts in other contexts as *non-normative but objectively justifiable in the exceptional situation,* including that of the confirmed homosexual.

Conclusion

There lately has been considerable discussion in Roman Catholic ethics over the viability of absolute moral norms and the concept of "intrinsic evil." This includes the distinction between moral and premoral evil. (See C. Curran and R. McCormick, eds., *Readings in Moral Theology No. 1: Moral Norms and the Catholic Tradition,* New York: Paulist, 1979; and R. McCormick, *Ambiguity in Moral Choice,* Milwaukee: Marquette Univ. Theology Dept., 1973.) I accept the distinction between moral and premoral or "ontic" evil, and see it as relevant to this problem. Another way to state my conclusion would be to say that genital homosexual acts are "evil" in that they are to be avoided generally. However, they are "premoral" evils in that their sheer presence does not *necessarily* make the total act or relation of which they are a part "morally" evil or sinful. The total act is not sinful if there is sufficient reason in *this* case for causing "premoral" or "ontic" evil. Killing in self-defense is analogous. Still, I consider the justifiability of any conclusions drawn within Christian ethics to be dependent on their consistency with Scripture, tradition, and the empirical sciences, as well as with natural moral reason.

This essay represents a tentative attempt to explore the problem of homosexuality from a perspective which considers several dimensions of theological ethics as it takes place within a faith community. I have highlighted four reference points (Scripture, tradition, descriptive, and normative accounts of experience), and suggested the necessary relevance of all to any issue which the Christian ethicist might address. Although a "balance" of sources is recommended, the question of priority in cases of conflict is unavoidable. On the issue of immediate concern, I have tried to account for discrepancies among the sources by articulating a norm which contemplates exceptions, i.e., a nuanced position rather than an unequivocal "yes" or "no." To assume that these sources can somehow be combined in a coherent position, however, is already to make a commitment in faith to the proposition that "revelation" and "human experience" are complementary realities rather than radically conflictual ones.

44

The Reasoning Heart:
An American
Approach to
Christian Discernment

William C. Spohn, SJ

Making moral decisions is as common an experience as walking and as difficult to analyze. Physiologists despair of providing a full description of the interplay of nerve, muscle, tendon, and bone that comprises walking. Moral philosophers rarely attempt to delineate the processes which lead to moral decisions. Fortunately, most people manage both operations with some degree of success despite the lack of a descriptive rationale. However, rapid cultural change and social instability can confuse moral decision-making just as a slight malfunction of the inner ear can ruin a person's balance. In such periods of confusion greater attention needs to be given to examining the actual practice of moral agents.

"Discernment" plays a central role in making moral decisions. It is the skill of moral evaluation in the concrete. It employs symbolic and affective criteria to accomplish this evaluation. When taken in a religious context, discernment connotes a graced ability to detect what is the appropriate response to the invitation of God. It goes beyond the question "Is this action morally right?" to the more personal question of appropriateness: "Is this action consistent with who I am and want to become? What sort of person does this type of action?" Abstractions are less helpful here than the resources of memory and imagination.[1]

Moral philosophers and theologians do not usually consider the processes of discernment, the use of symbols and affectivity to find the personally fitting course of action. They concentrate on justification of decisions rather than on their initial formulation. It is doubtless important to give publicly intelligible reasons for what we have decided; but it would

---

This article originally appeared in Theological Studies *44 (March 1983): 30–52.*

be misleading to imply that we must make our decisions in the same logical way that we justify them. Moral theologians have often used the practical syllogism in framing their arguments: moral principle was applied to relevant case to yield a moral conclusion about action. However, do we actually *make* our decisions by the practical syllogism? An exclusively rational moral agent might do so, but ordinary mortals perceive and evaluate their situation in a more complex fashion.

In this discussion I will refer to this neglected aspect of moral experience by the term "the reasoning heart." If Pascal was correct in assigning the heart its own distinctive reasons, then we should determine the moral capacities of memory and imagination. The "heart" refers to the agent as engaged, as a being of vision and feeling. In biblical morality it is the seat of affectivity and virtuous qualities. The heart refers to the moral agent in his or her particularity, as a definite character with a specific sense of identity and set of dispositions. Discernment is precisely this reasoning of the heart.

Discernment should not be set in opposition to the "reasoning head," to abstract reasoning with general moral principles. We need not be as pessimistic as Pascal that reason is oblivious to the reasons of the heart. The concrete judgments of discernment complement these general moral considerations. Discernment operates within the boundaries set by general principles of justice, honesty, and the like. Discernment attends to the particular situation, illuminating its meaning for this agent and indicating what response is appropriate. It makes *judgments of affectivity* which are based upon central convictions of the person's character. These are open to their own kind of scrutiny. It is a different scrutiny from the formal logic which tests out the general

judgments of morality which we will call *judgments of rationality*. Just because discernment is personal does not imply that it is private: the aesthetic judgments of affectivity are accountable to symbolic and affective criteria which are derived from public traditions.

Situation ethics and intuitionism make the mistake of opposing concrete judgments of affectivity to general norms of morality. Judgments of rationality are necessary in morality to set the boundary conditions for action and to provide reasons for conduct which are publicly intelligible. Training in sound moral reasoning can help the agent detect logical and unwarranted exceptions to norms. However, another set of skills is necessary to become a discerning person. This article will argue that discernment can be scrutinized by attending to the central symbols which shape self-understanding and to the dominant affective convictions which dispose the self to action. The Christian tradition offers certain normative symbols and patterns to affectivity which can serve as criteria for Christian discernment. These symbols and affections are correlated with the fundamental religious convictions about God and Jesus Christ. Therefore, while discernment is a personal skill like prudence, it need not be strictly private but should also be accountable to the public convictions of the Christian tradition.[2]

Karl Rahner has provided one of the most widely accepted accounts of Christian discernment. He analyzes the Spiritual Exercises of Ignatius of Loyola to determine how concrete courses of action can have a religious significance, an indication of divine calling. In subsequent applications Rahner suggests that Christian discernment may be at the core of the assent of faith and should become central to the pastoral task of moral theology. He proposes training the laity in an "existential ethics" which can perceive God's invitations in the concrete situations of politics and economy in order to supplement the traditional "essential ethics" of natural law.[3]

However, Rahner has not given sufficient attention to the role of religious symbols and affectivity in guiding sound discernment. This article will argue that a more adequate account of Christian discernment may be derived from American theologians, particularly Jonathan Edwards and H. Richard Niebuhr. They provide a richer analysis of the moral agent, extend discernment to a critical reading of the signs of the times, and also incorporate biblical material into the act of discernment more adequately than does Rahner. All three theologians suppose that God is active in history and enters the experience of men and women. God's intentions for the world and individuals are not only to be found in the general structures of creation and universal moral principles. For the Christian the moral question "What ought I to do?" needs to be preceded by a more fundamental question: "What is God enabling and requiring me to do?" To answer the question, the Christian must always engage in serious discernment.[4]

Symbolic Criteria for Discernment

The first criteria for discernment are the symbols which guide its evaluation of the concrete situation. Judgments of affectivity, the conclusions of the reasoning heart, are felt to be appropriate both to who I am and what I am responding to. Karl Rahner tests possible responses against a basic sense of the self. Niebuhr clarifies this by analyzing the basic symbols which shape the individual's self-understanding and the symbols the agent uses to interpret the situation. While Rahner analyzes

the moment of individual consciousness to discover the structure of discernment, Niebuhr brings the history of the person to bear on the process, thus utilizing the symbolic resources of imagination, memory, and the Christian tradition.

Rahner notes that traditional spirituality recognized that Christians can receive particular calls from God, vocations which are not simply the application of general moral norms and values. These are not only calls to a particular state in life, such as marriage or ordination, but also to specific courses of action. Traditional moral theology had difficulty in explaining the serious sense of obligation which accompanied these vocations. How could one person be obliged to do something when another individual faced with the same choice would experience no moral obligation at all?

In these vocation experiences the will of God is not discovered by appealing to general moral principles. In fact, these material norms of "essential ethics" are presupposed. An "existential ethics" which will examine the formal structure of vocation experiences to test their authenticity must complement essential ethics.

Most people come to serious decisions in a manner that is quite similar to the ordinary process of discernment in the Spiritual Exercises.

> In such decisions a man thinks things over for a long time. Consequently in every case he will probably make his decisions through a fundamental global awareness of himself actually present and making itself felt in him during this space of time, and through a feeling of the harmony or disharmony of the object of choice with this fundamental

feeling he has about himself. He will not only nor ultimately make his decision by a rational analysis but by whether he feels that something "suits him" or not. And this feeling will be judged by whether the matter pleases, delights, brings peace and satisfaction.[5]

Rahner has outlined the formal structure of the experience of discernment; the options facing the person are tested against the global awareness of the self. The criteria used are not logical but aesthetic, because peace, radical satisfaction, and delight are the signs which determine which option harmonizes with the sense of self. The right option is not only morally correct; it also is the most appropriate one, the one most consistent with the kind of person the agent is and aspires to become.

Rahner fails to explain how each person has this "fundamental sense of self" that is unique. Instead, he focuses on a certain kind of religious experience. This is the experience of radical receptivity to God, a nonconceptual awareness of God, who is the goal of human reaching out to infinity. This orientation to God as mystery constitutes for Rahner the core of every human person. The test of discernment is precisely this "experience of transcendence as such."[6] If a proposed course of action harmonizes with this central religious attitude, then it is recognized as the will of God for the person. The end will indicate what is the most appropriate means. Here the end is God Himself, who is present in the person's longing and hope. The most apt means to the end are determined by a judgment of affectivity. The means will harmonize with this radical longing for God, while inappropriate courses of action will stifle and obscure this reaching out to God.[7] This process

of discerning the means presumes that the end is actually present, that conversion has occurred to the extent that God is the final value of the person's life. Only such a person would have been able to make the Spiritual Exercises.

This sense of self is difficult to locate in our consciousness. The awareness of self which accompanies our every thought cannot itself be expressed conceptually. When we focus on who we are, our cognitive description never measures up to the full reality. Hence Rahner describes this as an "unthematic" awareness, since it cannot be adequately thematized or comprehended directly.[8] It remains a sense, an awareness that is concomitant to all our conscious experiences. Can such an elusive sense serve the role of criterion in practical discernment?

American theologians have also employed the self as a basic norm in moral reflection, but they have a richer notion of the self than Rahner. He focuses on radical freedom and "transcendence" as the core of the self, while their description points to the unique history which has formed the individual. That history is present to the discerning person through memories and symbols which form his or her identity. The pattern of God's previous action in the person's life can therefore become a more central part of discerning the immediate situation. Rahner concentrates on the moment of discernment, like one freezing a moving picture to examine a single frame of film. Considering the personal history and social context of the person would be like viewing the film progressively up to this moment, thereby providing a richer framework for discernment. What is needed is a fuller phenomenology of moral character than Rahner offers, a description which sees the self emerging as an identity in a specific history and social context.

H. Richard Niebuhr and other American thinkers have developed a theory of the self which shows the importance of symbols in shaping personal identity. First we will examine how symbols from the Christian tradition shape the self and then we will consider how these symbols aid in discerning the signs of the times, God's call in the larger social world.

In *The Responsible Self* Niebuhr argues that the self-understanding of the moral agent is prior to questions of action.[9] Whatever answer I give to the moral question, "What ought I to do?" will be profoundly affected by my answer to the question of identity, "Who am I?" Identity rests more on images and metaphors of the self than on definite ideas. They provide pictures through which the unique character of the self can be glimpsed and they organize habitual ways of responding to the world. For example, if I feel myself to be a victim, I am likely to inject weariness and fear into even innocent relationships. My defensiveness may be all the more powerful if this image of being a victim remains unconscious. My spontaneous reactions will be defensive or even hostile, leading me to actions which are more appropriate to my fear of being violated again than to the actual situation, which may contain nothing objectively threatening. Discernment will be operating but it will be neurotic discernment, skewed by my inadequate self-image. Until this level of self-understanding is altered, it will distort my perception and evaluation of the world around me.

Christian conversion involves moral transformation precisely because it challenges the central images of the self. *Metanoia* means rethinking my personal history through a new set of images which the community proposes as normative. If I have previously conceived of myself as victim, I no longer can remember the past as a series of undeserved injuries and fear

a future which will contain more of the same. Viewing myself as one who has been forgiven and empowered to forgive others, I need to reinterpret that history of injuries. Because I now believe that the cross and resurrection of Jesus will be part of my own experience, my attitude towards injury cannot be simply resentment and wariness. The events are not changed, but their meaning must be if I am to be a Christian. If the God I now believe in brought life precisely where death had seemed invincible in the experience of Christ, then I am enabled to look for life in the most threatening memories of my own past. Reinterpreted in light of the normative images of faith, my past can issue in compassion for the suffering and a new capacity for service.[10]

Most systems of ethics are incapable of describing the change of personal identity which Christian faith requires. They do not consider the moral agent in his or her particularity, but rather focus on certain aspects of the agent which are shared in common with other moral agents. Whether that common aspect be a general human nature, rationality, or logical discourse, it prescinds from the particular identity of the person. These generalizable features of the moral agent are necessary to provide the foundations of judgments of rationality in ethics—moral principles and general theories of virtue. However, they are incapable of grounding judgments of affectivity, which are the bases of discernment. A Christian ethics which only addresses judgments of rationality will consequently shed little light on the transformation of the particular person. Because human nature and rationality presumably remain the same after religious conversion, the moral life can seem largely unaffected by coming to faith.

American philosophy, with its characteristic stress on experience, offers a more promising approach to the particularity of the moral agent. Particular events become intelligible when they are located as parts in an intelligible whole. Particular persons derive their uniqueness from the contexts in which they view themselves and from the history of their own choices. For George Herbert Mead, the self is not understood substantially but interactionally. Niebuhr developed Mead's notion that the self comes into being through interaction with others. "[The] self is a being which comes to knowledge of itself in the presence of other selves . . . its very nature is that of a being which lives in response to other selves."[11] The self does not have its meaning because it is an instance of human nature; the meaning of this particular self emerges through dialog with others. Therefore a new "root metaphor" is necessary for moral philosophy: the self-as-responder is more adequate to the interactional development of the self than previous root metaphors. These have been self-as-maker, which likens the moral life to a constructive quest for human happiness, and self-as-citizen, which portrays the moral life as a life of obedience to universal laws.[12]

The truly responsible self is not merely reactive; rather, it functions like the good conversationalist who seeks to further the dialog with others. Such a person attempts to make sense out of the previous remarks and to contribute something which makes further response possible. The bore, on the other hand, derails the conversation by using others as sounding boards for self-centered monolog. As the responsible self interacts with the larger community, it makes commitments which provide it with a sense of integrity. Josiah Royce has written that personal individuality is not a given commodity but only gradually arises as the self becomes committed to causes beyond itself.[13] Authentic Christian commit-

ment rests on loyalty to the cause of Christ, which is universal reconciliation.

Defensiveness is a major threat to the responsible life. The very community which initially forms the self can become a parochial allegiance, setting itself over against other groups as rivals. Accountability is then limited only to the local social context as defensiveness takes the place of identification with others who are different. This constricted loyalty yields a faith which must inevitably conflict with faith in the one sovereign Lord of all humankind. The Church itself can generate this sort of parochialism, in contrast to genuine faith in Christ. Loyalty to the Church community can be Christian only if it is loyalty to a more universal community. "And even when I find that I can be responsible in the church only as I respond to Jesus Christ, I discover in him one who points beyond himself to the cause to which he is faithful and in faithfulness to which he is faithful to his companions—not the companions encountered in the church, but in the world to which the Creator is faithful, which the Creator has made his cause."[14] The responsible Christian is therefore accountable not only to the community of faith but also to the universal community and to its Lord. The universal frame of reference is the whole within which the individual finds meaning as a part.

Discernment seeks to be responsible to social contexts by aid of the images with which they shape our self-understanding. Our sense of self is defined in large part by images of being parent, citizen, colleague, friend, committee member, theologian, and the like. Niebuhr argues that a coherent sense of self depends on an ultimate loyalty which structures all the lesser loyalties: faith in one God who acts in all the events that happen to us. Christian discernment seeks to be accountable to this Lord through understanding itself in the normative symbols of revelation. And the primary "symbolic form" for understanding how to respond to God is the person of Jesus Christ.

The sense of self which guides discernment is more than a present awareness. It has been shaped over time through suffering and decision. Therefore it can only be captured in a timeful symbol, one which can display the evolving identity of the self. To appreciate this historical uniqueness, we need to move from self-image to story. The fuller answer to the question "Who am I?" must be an autobiography, a narrative which can portray the character that emerges in time. In this aspect as well as in self-images, the Christian tradition provides a normative account, namely, the story of Jesus as located within the larger story of Israel. Biblical narratives function as paradigms in discernment because they reveal challenges in the present which are analogous to those of the past.

Biblical narratives can uncover the conflict of loyalties between our old way of life and the life of faith; at the same time they encourage us on the path of this costly grace. Dorothy Day, founder of the Catholic Worker movement, wrote of the costliness of her own decision to become a Christian. She was living with a man whom she deeply loved and who was the father of her only child. However, he could not stomach institutional religion and so had insisted that she would have to choose between him and the Church. She wrote: "God always gives us a chance to show our preference for Him. With Abraham it was to sacrifice his only son. With me it was to give up my married life with Forster. You do these things blindly, not because it is your natural inclination . . . but because you wish to live in conformity with the will of God."[15]

The story of Abraham could guide her discernment because it was characteristic of the believer before God and also characteristic of the God who calls to faith today. Character cannot be portrayed through abstraction; it is glimpsed through the surprising twists and turns of the plot of a narrative. Dorothy Day could grasp more than some analogous elements between her situation and that of Abraham. She could also discern the presence of the God of Abraham, who continues to act in character. The path from quandary to resolution which shaped the faith of Abraham could be revelatory for her because it disclosed God's call and promised His faithfulness.

Stories move from one scene to another and convey the hearer from here to there. They capture the self-in-time and point towards the particular path for the self to take. Sallie McFague writes that human experience itself has a narrative quality which these paradigmatic stories of faith support. "We love stories, then, because our lives are stories and we recognize in the attempts of others to move, temporally and painfully, our own story. We recognize in the stories of others' experiences of coming to belief our own agonizing journey and we rejoice in the companionship of those on the way."[16] Our lives are stories because they have a dramatic unity that moves through time, a plot which reveals and shapes our particular character. That same dramatic unity intimates what should come next, a future coherent with what has gone before.

The story of Jesus makes a normative claim upon Christian discernment. It is not just any story, but one which claims our lives by asserting that it must be the truth of those lives. This is the story which reveals in a definitive way God's intentions for the world and for us. Christian conversion occurs when we let the story of Jesus become our story, as we let the particular shape of our lives be conformed to the particular shape of Jesus' life. The confession of faith appropriately takes a narrative form for Israel and for Christians: it is a self-involving confession to take the same journey ourselves.

Stanley Hauerwas writes that Peter's confession in Mark 8 is called into question by his subsequent reluctance to take the journey which will lead to the cross. "Jesus thus rebukes Peter, who had learned the name but not the story that determines the meaning of the name."[17] Peter projected his own worldly story of ambition and success onto the title of "the Christ." Jesus counters with the story of the cross which awaits him, and that story must change Peter. "A story that claims to be the truth of our existence requires that our lives, like the lives of the disciples, be changed by following him."[18]

The narrative of the Gospel embodies a whole way of life that is inseparable from the character of its central figure. Peter, like all of us, wanted to separate his relationship with Jesus from the threatening demands of that way of life. He wanted faith without discipleship. The Gospel narrative itself is best understood from the destiny to which it inexorably led: the cross and resurrection of Jesus. It is normative for the character of individuals and for the Church, which is the "organized form of Jesus' story."[19] The canonical Scriptures have authority for those who join this community. This does not mean that the biblical narrative is the sole source of moral wisdom but that the cross and resurrection of Christ must test moral insight from any sources. The truth of the narrative itself is manifest in the lives of the people that it forms; it cannot be established without some lived participation.[20]

Discernment operates by fitting the part into a whole which illuminates the significance of the part. The sense of self of the individual gains intelligibility when its social and historical contexts provide this illumination as larger wholes. The present moment fits within the story which forms the individual's character, and that story must be appropriate to the normative context of the story of Jesus for the believer. This normative context can guide discernment by suggesting the response which best "fits in." Niebuhr describes this aesthetic logic which attempts to locate particular actions in a larger meaningful pattern.

> We seek to have them fit into the whole as a sentence fits into a paragraph in a book, a note into a chord in a movement in a symphony, as the act of eating a common meal fits into the lifelong companionship of a family, as the decision of a statesman fits into the ongoing movement of his nation's life with other nations, or as the discovery of a scientific artifact fits into the history of science.[21]

The personal history of the individual and of the believing community, therefore, can shape the process of discernment so that this sense of self can be a trustworthy criterion for decision. The self as an emerging character in time and society is a more adequate criterion for serious decisions than any religious experience which prescinds from the story of the individual or of the believing community.[22]

The second major way in which symbols guide the reasoning heart of discernment is through interpreting events to unearth their religious significance. After considering the general pattern of symbolic interpretation of events, we will apply this reflection to the specific situation of the nuclear threat.

Discernment seeks the disclosure of the whole in the part. This movement complements that in which the individual part is illuminated by its context. As David Tracy notes, the claim which religion makes to truth is a disclosure of the whole, a revelatory model of meaning. "Unlike the classics of art, morality, science and politics, explicitly religious classic expressions will involve a claim to truth as the event of a disclosure-concealment of the whole of reality *by the power of the whole*—as, in some sense, a radical and finally gracious mystery."[23] Symbols are the appropriate vehicles of disclosure. They are the prisms which refract experience in novel ways for the imagination.

Religious discernment uses symbols to seek the disclosure of the gracious mystery of God in social events as well as personal ones. It seeks to discover more than God's call as a specific invitation to action. In the public realm it searches for the action of God challenging and redeeming in all events. The symbols and stories of Scripture function as paradigms for reading the signs of the times for the disclosure of God's action.

This disclosure of the whole in the part comes to the participant in faith, to the reasoning heart which looks for revelation and is willing to be instructed by it.[24] At first glance it seems that when we move from the question "Who am I?" to the question "What is going on?" we have left the standpoint of the participant for the standpoint of the objective observer. However, to answer that second question we necessarily refer to events, and there can be no single objective description of events which exhausts their meaning. To understand events, realities which occur in our

experience, we need to complement the reasoning head with the reasoning heart. The discerning heart reasons by evaluating events from different angles and trying to fit them into different contexts.

Events cannot be dissected to find their causes. Their meaning is not readily available for public inspection, like the ingredients listed on the label of a can. For example, the events of Paul's ministry disclosed only a pattern of failure to his Gnostic opponents in Corinth. In the Second Letter to the Corinthians Paul interprets them in an entirely different context which discloses new meaning (1:8–10):

> Brothers, we do not wish to leave you in the dark about the trouble we had in Asia: we were crushed beyond our strength, even to the point of despairing of life. We were left to feel like men condemned to death, so that we might trust not in ourselves but in God who raises from the dead. He rescued us from the danger of death and will continue to do so.[25]

Paul reverses the very charges of his detractors: his sufferings are rather the actual credentials for his ministry than proof of its failure. "Therefore I am content with weakness, with mistreatment, with distress, with persecutions and difficulties for the sake of Christ; for when I am powerless, it is then that I am strong" (12:10). When interpreted in the light of Christ's death and resurrection, these same facts come to bear a very different meaning. God's action is disclosed and that calls for an appropriate response.

In the middle of the Second World War, Niebuhr performed one of these symbolic interpretations of public events. He tried to interpret, or make sense out of, the suffering of innocent victims of war by asking the question "What is God doing in the war?" He employed the biblical symbols of divine judgment and the crucifixion in this interpretation. From viewing the war through these new lenses, he concluded that God was on neither side in the war and was judging all parties for their self-interest and self-righteousness. The scandal of innocent suffering of millions who were caught between the great armies could be meaningful only when seen in the context of Jesus Christ's vicarious suffering.[26]

Niebuhr's question offended nearly as many of his readers as did his answers. "What is God doing in the war?" grated on the sensibilities of those who protested that the benevolent Father of all could only grieve over human sinfulness in war. Niebuhr insisted that God must be doing something in every event, even in the most tragic. Either we are monotheists who are disposed to look for the presence of the one sovereign Lord in every deed and suffering, or we will be polytheists who assign portions of reality to another deity. Nevertheless, God is not the Great Manipulator of the universe who predetermines every action. Jesus believed that "the will of God is what God does in all that nature and man do. . . . The Universal One whom he calls Father is Lord of heaven and earth. His action is more like that of the great wise leader who uses even the meannesses of his subjects to promote the general welfare."[27] To be truly responsible in faith, Christians need to imitate Jesus in seeking out the hidden divine intention by locating even destructive events in the context of God's creating, redeeming, and judging activity.

What if we ask this strange question today: "What is *God* doing in the global buildup of armaments and the threat of nuclear annihilation?" If we restrict our discussion to the judgments of rationality employed in just-war reasoning, this fundamental question cannot even be raised. Using certain biblical symbols as lenses, we can attempt to discover an appropriate response to the signs of the times. The black civil-rights movement and Latin American liberation theology encourage this interpretation. Both movements read the situation of oppression through the lens of the Exodus symbol, and this has given direction in faith to millions in their struggle for justice.

Which symbols should we use? Scripture contains a wide range of symbolic events; hence selecting the appropriate ones must be done critically. The reasoning head must establish some general criteria for using biblical symbols. Since judgments of affectivity presuppose moral judgments of rationality as outer limits of action, this symbolic interpretation should be consonant with sound moral reasoning. The appropriate symbols must be central to the overall message of the canon. They should correlate with an image of God which coheres with the full teaching of the Scriptures. If taken from the Old Testament, these symbols must be consistent with the fundamental event of God's definitive revelation in Jesus Christ. The Exodus from Egypt is central to Israel's faith consciousness, correlates with the basic image of God as Redeemer, and foreshadows the cross and resurrection. Whether it leads to morally sound judgments must be determined from the particular application.

On the other hand, an inadequate symbol will function as "an evil imagination of the heart" which will disclose only a self-serving meaning and distort the truth of who we are and what we are doing.[28] The Dutch Calvinists of South Africa are accustomed to justify apartheid by appealing to their national election and the canonically minor symbol of "taking the Land" from the Canaanites. This symbol also fails the test of adequacy to the New Testament and leads to conclusions that violate ordinary moral standards.

One set of biblical symbols already operates in some thinking on the nuclear issue: that of crusade and martyrdom. An alternative symbol, which may yield a more illuminating significance for faith, is that of Israel's exile in Babylon.

Part of the legacy of the Cold War which affects the nuclear issue are the images of martyrdom and crusade which shaped Cold War rhetoric. The communist challenge was not fundamentally ideological but religious. An atheistic and monolithic totalitarian state threatened our way of life and religious liberty. This interpretation pointed to two responses. Passively, one would prefer to endure martyrdom rather than give up the Christian faith. This symbol proved to be helpful as it guided the resistance of Christians to religious persecution in Eastern Europe and China. In a more active mode this vision employed the image of the crusade to marshal defenses. War becomes holy when waged for God's cause; the rhetoric of John Foster Dulles and others underlined the godless character of communism to prepare an arsenal of nuclear and conventional weaponry.

Despite some attempts to justify the crusade symbol from the Old Testament, it appears to be an evil imagination of the heart. Roland H. Bainton traces the crusade mentality back to the holy war of Judges and Deuteronomy. It renders an image of a God who delights in battle and exterminates the enemy without distinction of guilt or innocence. When Europe was threatened by the forces of Islam, the crusaders tended to ignore the restraints on knightly warfare. Bainton describes how the Allied cause in the Second World War was corrupted by becoming a crusade:

> The enemy being beyond the pale, the code of humanity collapses. . . . Those who have fought in a frenzy of righteousness against the enemies of God—or of the democratic way of life—are disposed to demand unconditional surrender, thus prolonging resistance by their refusal to state terms. The crusader is severely tempted to arbitrariness in the final settlement, for the mood of holiness leads to the punishment of war criminals by the victors under the fictitious trappings of impartial justice.[29]

A truly evil imagination of the heart occurs when we merge the symbols of martyrdom and godly crusade in the nuclear era. Then it appears better to destroy the infidel even at the cost of our own lives. However, martyrdom which takes the whole world into its blessed sacrifice becomes demonic. Martyrdom connotes self-sacrifice, not the wilful sacrifice of countless others. Murder-suicide would be a more truthful symbol for nuclear vengeance.

What would be a more adequate symbol for interpreting the nuclear threat? It would have to be more appropriate to the contemporary situation than to Cold War realities. It would also have to indicate a more authentic faith response than crusade or martyrdom. The exile of the Israelites in Babylon may help to revision the nuclear issue. After being conquered by the Babylonians and subjected to mass deportation, Israel faced a profound crisis of faith. If Marduk, the deity of their conquerors, had prevailed over Yahweh, then perhaps the God of Abraham was only a minor deity. The seventy years of exile deepened this crisis. Since all the promises had come to nothing—the Temple, the Davidic monarchy, the Land—could this mean that the covenant was null and void?

Ironically, Israel broke through to a new kind of faith during the Exile. The prophets returned to their deepest faith memories to recognize that the Exile was a second Exodus, disclosing a purified image of God. Yahweh was not the warrior king who fought on the side of the righteous, nor the god of royal civil religion who propped up a specific way of life. In Babylon, Israel came to realize for the first time that Yahweh alone was God and sovereign over all the nations. God would still be God even if Israel were dominated by foreign enemies. Yahweh would deliver His people in His own time and re-establish the covenant with a newly repentant people.

Looking at our contemporary situation through the lens of the Exile discloses some common features, even though it does not dictate a single strategy of response. It can uncover at the root of our national defensiveness a fear of being dominated by communism, a fear which is nearly ultimate. God's cause is not identical with any nation's aspirations, and the loss of our wealth and freedom would not mean the end of God. Perhaps such a loss would enable us to discover the true God we had not known before. On the other hand, any nation which would willingly devastate God's creation rather than endure an exile thereby indicates that its ultimate allegiance is to a life of national affluence. If a symbolic discernment of national values issues in a call to repentance, that does not settle all the moral questions. Moral analysis through judgments of rationality and reformulation of policy through political prudence must complement a symbolic reinterpretation. Failure to attend to these dominant symbols can only

escalate the danger that evil imaginations of the heart will guide our political strategy and moral debates.

Discernment remains a personal search for the action of God in one's own history and in the events of the world. Although its conclusions are not morally generalizable as judgments of rationality are, the reasoning heart of the Christian finds normative guidance in the symbols and story of revelation.

Affective Criteria for Discernment

Christian discernment has a second set of criteria for discovering an adequate response to God: a specific set of affections which flow from the story of Jesus. These affections complement the symbols which seek the disclosure of God's intentions in events. They set a normative matrix which guides the *manner* of action, because the morality of an action is established by both what we do and how we do it. How we act should be appropriate to the distinctive values displayed in the biblical narrative. These affections are not transitory feelings or unfathomable moods; they are deep convictions of the reasoning heart which dispose the moral agent to act in definite ways. Religious affections are virtues, since they are habits which dispose the agent to moral action with ease and delight; this traditional Puritan term emphasizes their felt quality in experience. Roman Catholic moral theology has followed Thomas Aquinas in giving the virtues a considerable role in moral decision-making. However, the narrative of the gospel did not enter into his definition of the virtues—that rested on an assumed common human nature, even though these natural virtues were elevated by the gift of charity. An American approach to discernment makes a more integral connection between the affections (or virtues) of the Christian life and the biblical narrative. The story of Israel and of Jesus can thereby provide both symbols and a distinctive set of affections as criteria for discernment.

Karl Rahner's account of discernment discounts any role for a distinctive set of affections for two reasons. First, Rahner has no developed theory of human affectivity. Because the core of the person is self-defining freedom before God, felt dispositions are only the raw material on which freedom operates. Their moral significance arises only when they are caught up in the movement of human transcendence; he does not discuss their positive role in disposing the moral agent to evaluate and act.[30]

In addition, Rahner assigns the Gospels a minimal role in shaping the content of Christian ethics. He distinguishes a formal from a material dimension in the following of Christ, which reduces the contribution that Scripture can make to morality. The formal dimension is the same for all: a radical surrender to God made by explicit believers as well as those who are affected by grace "anonymously." "Once a man has reached Jesus, then it contains this simple message: just to be prepared to make the final act of hope and self-surrender to the incomprehensible mystery."[31] Formally, this self-surrender corresponds to the self-emptying of Jesus in the Incarnation and the cross. However, the actual conduct of the moral life, the material dimension, cannot be a copy of the life of Jesus. "The continuation of the life of Jesus that is new and different for each of us must be discovered by each individual in the way that is valid for him."[32] The love command does not refer to the specific historical example of Jesus; love resists definition, because it demands the person totally, not only in particular actions.[33]

When the natural law is the principle for interpreting the gospel, a certain leveling effect may inevitably occur. To maintain a moral system that is intelligible to those outside the Christian tradition, that tradition's distinctive contributions to reformulating moral standards and values is downplayed. In discernment a person asks not only about the morality of the action ("Is it right or wrong?") but also about the appropriateness of the action ("What kind of person does this sort of thing? Is it consistent with the person I am or want to be?"). To answer these questions, the Christian must turn to the central personal qualities which the biblical narrative exemplifies.

The American theological tradition has its roots in the Puritan experiment and in its ablest spokesman, Jonathan Edwards. In defending the conversion phenomena of the seventeenth-century Great Awakening, Edwards argued that sound religious affections are the true test of religious experience. His thesis was that "true religion, in great part, consists in holy affections."[34] In his masterpiece, *Religious Affections*, this Puritan pastor analyzed Christian conversion and growth as primarily a change of heart centering on the affections, the "springs that set men agoing, in all the affairs of life."[35] He provides twelve signs, culminating in consistent moral practice, by which the individual can gauge whether this change of heart has in fact occurred. Underlying them all as the primary gift of true conversion is a new capacity to appreciate the loveliness of God for its own sake. This same gift enables the convert to appreciate the credibility of sound doctrine and relish the goodness of proper conduct.

Authentic conversion produces a character which bears some resemblance to the character of Jesus depicted in the Gospels. The Holy Spirit gradually develops a specific set or constellation of affections in the Christian. These affections are the main dispositions which shape the person's character. This configuration of affections has a specific historical referent. Edwards held that one of the distinguishing signs of Christian affections is that "they naturally beget and promote such a spirit of love, meekness, quietness, forgiveness and mercy, as appeared in Christ."[36] Just as Paul could specify the fruits of the Spirit which he expected the Galatians to manifest, Edwards presumed that certain common traits would emerge in the diverse personalities of Christians. These affections correlate with the dispositions manifest by God and Christ in the work of redemption. "There is grace in Christians answering to grace in Christ, such an answerableness as there is between the wax and the seal; there is character for character: such kinds of graces, such a spirit and temper, the same things that belong to Christ's character, belong to theirs."[37]

While this is an ethics of the imitation of Christ, it is not primarily concerned with reproducing the external aspects of his life and work. Rather, those dispositions which were the main ingredients of the character of the Redeemer shape the character of the redeemed. As they grow in sanctification, mature Christians should come to prefer spontaneously the conduct which is consistent with the goodness of Christ.[38]

Why should there be a *specific* set of affections which characterize the Christian? Our affections are constituted by the objects toward which they tend. Because our faith holds certain things to be true about God and the world, affections which correspond to these convictions are evoked in our hearts. "The particularity of Christian affections has to do with the objects towards which they are directed," Don Saliers writes. "They are given their particular character by virtue of the stories, concepts and practices which belong

to Christianity. . . . To believe that God redeems, judges, and shows compassion for the contrite, involves a distinctive set of affections."[39] Dispositions and beliefs are mutually interdependent, because the belief shapes the affection and the affection enlivens and illumines the belief. Could one know the meaning of God's mercy without personally experiencing forgiveness? On the other hand, the forgiven person needs to know the necessity of repentance and the possibility of hope if it is to be genuine Christian forgiveness. We move from one pole to the other: we can examine affections to see what their objects are, and we can examine the convictions of belief to determine what the appropriate affections should be.[40]

Because of this interdependence of affection and faith convictions, narrative and doxology are the most common ways in which the biblical authors confess their faith. Both literary forms involve the listener or speaker insofar as they evoke the affective response which is integral to their cognitive content. They also challenge the hearer to become a participant, to act in correspondence with the movement of the story of the confession. So the prophet praises Yahweh in Isaiah 40 with images which also pointedly address the despairing exiles in Babylon: "The Lord is the eternal God, creator of the ends of the earth. He does not faint nor grow weary. . . . He gives strength to the fainting; for the weak he makes vigor abound . . . they that hope in the Lord will renew their strength, they will soar as with eagles' wings; they will run and not grow weary, walk and not grow faint" (40:28–31). In doxology the memory of the faith community becomes a paradigm for action and for affection. The Psalms, for instance, repeatedly recall God's action in the Exodus to evoke the particular form of trust which correlates with the image of God as redeemer of the enslaved. Confession of faith involves the whole person, as the reasoning heart illumines the path from conviction to action through engaging the appropriate affections.

The biblical narratives enter into the definition of Christian affections because they embody the meaning of the affections metaphorically. Hauerwas writes that all virtues are narrative-dependent because their meaning is inseparable from a way of life. Only the story of an individual or a people can display how the qualities it endorses should become realized in our lives. Christian virtues are distinctive because the narrative on which they depend is the story of Jesus Christ.[41] Christian convictions do not merely provide additional motivation to enact natural virtuous dispositions; they also redefine these dispositions. "The singular feature of Christian rejoicing is that it occurs even in the midst of suffering, pain, and tribulation—even in the midst of grief. . . . The language which describes the world as God's creation and the arena of divine mercy is related *internally* to the ability to rejoice in all circumstances—even in the midst of suffering."[42]

Although this configuration of specific Christian dispositions is inseparable from the story of Jesus, some summary of them is possible. James Gustafson refers to these dispositions as "senses of the heart" which are the main threads in the fabric of Christian life: a sense of radical dependence, of gratitude, repentance, obligation, possibility, and direction. These dispositions are mutually sustaining and interdependent: repentance which lacks a sense of possibility and hope would not be faithful to the biblical witness. Together they provide the Christian with a set of reasons for being moral and serve as intentions to act in specific ways. Hence they ground a

"moral life of a qualitatively different sort."[43] Gustafson bases these reasons for being moral on the particular images of God which are displayed in biblical revelation and confirmed in the present experience of believers.

These distinctive Christian affections can serve to discern appropriate action in two ways. First, they set an affective matrix against which options are gauged to see if they are harmonious or not. This affective matrix corresponds to the qualities manifest in the Gospel story. The Christian "tests the spirits to see if among all the forces that move within him, his societies, the human mind itself, there is a uniting, a knowing, a whole-making spirit, a Holy Spirit. And he can do so only with the aid of the image, the symbol of Christ. 'Is there a Christ-like spirit there?' "[44] Niebuhr has brought together here the central resources of the reasoning heart in discernment: symbol and affectivity as they mutually define each other and form an aesthetic test of action.

As the Christian affections become deeply rooted in the character through practice responsive to God's call, they can intuitively suggest appropriate behavior. Edwards noted that mature Christians often come to decisions without "a long chain of reasoning," by means of a certain discerning taste. Just as a well-trained palate detects what is missing in a sauce, so the relish for the divine beauty can inform a mature Christian how to act.

> Yea its holy taste and appetite leads it to think of that which is truly lovely, and naturally suggests the idea of its proper object . . . whereby, in the lively exercise of grace, [a holy person] easily distinguishes good and evil, and knows at once, what is a suitable amiable behavior towards God, and towards

man, in this case and the other; and judges what is right, as it were spontaneously, and of himself, without a particular deduction, by any other arguments than the beauty that is seen and goodness that is tasted.[45]

Edwards recognizes how dispositions guide moral intuition, the knowledge by "connaturality" familiar to Catholic moral theology.[46] Yet Edwards is no intuitionist: these intuitions must be conformable to both the rules and the dispositions presented in the gospel. In our terms, judgments of affectivity complement without contravening the judgments of rationality in moral reflection.[47]

Rahner also uses affectivity as a criterion for discernment but makes it only formally dependent upon the biblical narrative. In commenting on Loyola's Exercises he notes a sense of radical peace and openness to God which tests the authenticity of possible inspirations. However, he centers almost exclusively on surrender to the absolute mystery of God as the affective touchstone.[48] Because they attend to the diverse images of God and the particularities of the story of Jesus, American theologians are able to make a richer purchase of biblical material for an affective matrix for discernment. If there is any formal pattern running through biblical ethics, it finds expression in the new commandment of Jesus in Jn 13:34: "Love one another just as I have loved you." This formal principle refers the believer immediately back to the "material," the memory of the actual ways in which Jesus Christ loved. These memories have some correspondence in the experience of the Christian, and they can set a diverse matrix for affective testing of discernment. In sum, Christians are called to be human in a specific way, not through copying an ancient portrait

but in having different reasons of the heart for being moral.

Christian discernment brings to light rich elements in moral decision-making. Judgments of affectivity legitimately ground some moral decisions through the discriminating functions of memory and imagination. These judgments are evaluated not by formal logic but by aesthetic criteria: by the sense of self, the evaluation of events through biblical symbols, and the correlation between certain ways of acting and the configuration of Christian affections. Because these criteria are normative within the public tradition of the Christian community, discernment is not finally accountable only to itself. The classic authors of Christian spirituality such as Jonathan Edwards and Ignatius Loyola have long realized the importance of discernment in Christian practice. Contemporary American theologians have a significant contribution to make to Catholic moral theology in critically integrating discernment into Christian ethics.

These same theologians can broaden the common Roman Catholic notion of discernment. Not only can we look for God's gracious disclosure in specific invitations but also in integrating our own histories and reading the signs of the times. Their rationale presents the hope that those who find God in some things may eventually be led to find God in all things.

Notes

1. " 'Discernment' seems to be appropriate for pointing to the ability to distinguish the important from the unimportant information and the insightful interpretations from the uninsightful. It refers to the ability to perceive relationships between aspects of the information that

enables one to see how it all fits together, or how it cannot fit together. It refers to the ability to suggest inferences that can be drawn from the information, and thus to an imaginative capacity" (James M. Gustafson, *Theology and Christian Ethics* [Philadelphia: Pilgrim, 1974] 104).

2. See Louise M. Des Marais, *Signs of Glory: Making Christian Choices* (Denville, N.J.: Dimension, 1975).

3. Cf. Karl Rahner, *The Dynamic Element in the Church* (New York: Herder and Herder, 1964) chap. 3, "The Logic of Concrete Individual Knowledge in Ignatius Loyola"; *The Spiritual Exercises of St. Ignatius* (tr. Louis J. Puhl; Westminster, Md.: Newman, 1963); Karl Rahner, "On the Question of a Formal Existential Ethics," *Theological Investigations* (hereafter *TI*) 2 (Baltimore: Helicon, 1963).

4. "Theologically, it might be said that God is enabling men to discern what God is enabling men to do; but the locus for discernment is in the self as it relates beliefs about the God in whom it trusts to the situation in which it acts" (Gustafson, *Theology* 115).

5. Rahner, *Dynamic Element* 166.

6. Ibid. 139. Accordingly, "the operative principle of choice will be God, or, more precisely, that concrete, unique, intrinsic orientation to God which constitutes the innermost essence of man, emerging actually into awareness in operation and active accomplishment . . ." (ibid. 160).

7. "For the freely accepted transcendent experience of the Spirit is only possible here and now through concentration upon one distinct object of choice among others. This means that this object does not in any way lessen or distort the experience of the Spirit but rather provides a concrete and practical means of expression for it" (Rahner, "Experi-

ence of the Spirit and Existential Commitment," *TI* 16, 32).

8. Karl Rahner, *Foundations of Christian Faith* (New York: Seabury, 1978) chap. 1.

9. H. Richard Niebuhr, *The Responsible Self* (New York: Harper & Row, 1963) 48.

10. For an account of the conversion of affections and the reinterpretation of past experience that results, see Paul V. Robb, S.J. "Conversion as a Human Experience," *Studies in the Spirituality of Jesuits* 14/3 (1982).

11. Niebuhr, *Responsible Self* 71.

12. "Responder" is a synecdochic analogy, because it takes a special part of experience to envision the whole. Although it is more comprehensive than the other two images, it does not for that reason rule out moral reflection on goals and norms; its claim is to greater, not exclusive, adequacy. "Yet the understanding of ourselves as responsive beings . . . is a fruitful conception, which brings into view aspects of our self-defining conduct that are obscured when the older images are exclusively employed" (ibid. 57).

13. "Yet their loyalty gives them a business. It unifies their activities. It makes each of these loyal beings an individual self—a life unified by a purpose" (Josiah Royce, *The Philosophy of Loyalty* [New York: Macmillan, 1909] 170).

14. Niebuhr, *Responsible Self* 86.

15. Dorothy Day, *The Long Loneliness* (New York: Harper, 1952) 256.

16. Sallie McFague, *Speaking in Parables* (Philadelphia: Fortress, 1975) 138–39.

17. Stanley Hauerwas, *A Community of Character* (Notre Dame: Univ. of Notre Dame, 1981) 48.

18. Ibid. 47.

19. Ibid. 50.

20. "I would only add that scripture creates more than a world; it shapes a commu-

nity which is the bearer of that world. Without that community, claims about the moral authority of scripture—or rather the very idea of scripture itself—make no sense. Furthermore, I shall argue that claims about the authority of scripture make sense only in that the world and the community it creates are in fact true to the character of God" (ibid. 55).

21. Niebuhr, *Responsible Self* 97.

22. Although Rahner appreciates the gradual self-definition which occurs over time, he does not develop any account of moral character as it bears on present experience.

23. David Tracy, *The Analogical Imagination* (New York: Crossroad, 1981) 163. "In an analogous fashion, religion, like art, discloses new resources of meaning and truth to anyone willing to risk allowing that disclosure to 'happen' " (ibid. 67).

24. "What concerns us at this point is not the fact that the revelatory moment shines by its own light and is intelligible in itself but rather that it illuminates other events and enables us to understand them. Whatever else revelation means it does mean an event in our history which brings rationality and wholeness into the confused joys and sorrows of personal existence and allows us to discern order in the brawl of communal histories. Such revelation is no substitute for reason; the illumination it supplies does not excuse the mind from labor; but it does give to that mind the impulsion and the first principles it requires if it is to be able to do its proper work" (H. Richard Niebuhr, *The Meaning of Revelation* [New York: Macmillan, 1941] 80). Much of what is contained in this article on the reasoning heart is derivative from this masterly work.

25. This and subsequent scriptural texts are from *The New American Bible* (Nashville: Thomas Nelson, 1971).

26. H. Richard Niebuhr, "War as the Judgment of God," *Christian Century* 59 (1942) 630–33; "War as Crucifixion," ibid. 60 (1943) 513–15.

27. Niebuhr, *Responsible Self* 164–65.

28. "Evil imaginations in this realm are shown to be evil by their consequences to selves and communities just as erroneous concepts and hypotheses in external knowledge are shown to be fallacious by their results" (Niebuhr, *Meaning of Revelation* 73).

29. Roland H. Bainton, *Christian Attitudes toward War and Peace* (Nashville: Abingdon, 1960) 243.

30. "If one were able to develop a theology and philosophy of freedom, it would become clear that freedom constitutes the very essence of emotion in comparison with which all other emotional factors would appear derivative, being mere conditions of possibility, a sign of the finite and passive character of created freedom and in the end analysable in terms of freedom" (Rahner, *TI* 16 [New York: Seabury, 1979] 64).

31. Karl Rahner, *TI* 16, 18.

32. Karl Rahner, *Spiritual Exercises* (New York: Herder and Herder, 1965) 119. Rahner's formal language about discernment does not do full justice to the practice of the Exercises. The retreatant only makes the "election," or serious life choice, after a lengthy period of meditating on the events of Jesus' life. He or she enters imaginatively into these scenes and uses the senses to appreciate them for days and even weeks. This constitutes a "school of the affections" which sets an aesthetic context to evaluate the decisions to be faced. Even more astonishing is the fact that in the eighty-six

pages of the chapter of *Dynamic Element* on Ignatian discernment the name of Jesus Christ occurs only four times, and even these are only passing references. This appears a significant omission in analyzing Christian discernment as well as the Spiritual Exercises.

33. See Karl Rahner, "The 'Commandment' of Love in Relation to the Other Commandments," *TI 5* (Baltimore: Helicon, 1966) 456.

34. Jonathan Edwards, *Religious Affections,* in John E. Smith, ed., *The Works of Jonathan Edwards 2* (New Haven: Yale Univ., 1959) 95.

35. Ibid. 101.

36. Ibid. 345.

37. Ibid. 347.

38. "That which men love, they desire to have and to be united to, and possessed of. That beauty which men delight in, they desire to be adorned with. Those acts which men delight in, they necessarily incline to do" (ibid. 394). Edwards' Christian ethics is a sustained response to the British "moral sense" philosophers, particularly Hutcheson and Shaftesbury. Against their position, he insisted that only the gift of the Holy Spirit could enable such a moral sense to function consistently and through trials. See Norman Fiering, *Jonathan Edwards' Moral Thought and Its British Context* (Chapel Hill: Univ. of North Carolina, 1981).

39. Don E. Saliers, *The Soul in Paraphrase* (New York: Seabury, 1980) 12, 19. "The essential feature of the order among Christian emotions is that they take God and God's acts as their object and ground" (ibid. 12).

40. The object and its appropriate affection are so interrelated that the convictions of faith are not mere speculative knowledge but are "sensible knowledge." "That sort of knowledge by which a man has a sensible perception of amiableness and loathsomeness, or of sweetness and nauseousness, is not just the same sort of knowledge with that, by which he knows what a triangle is and what a square is. The one is mere speculative knowledge; the other sensible knowledge, in which more than the mere intellect is concerned; the heart is the proper subject of it, or the soul as a being that not only beholds, but has inclination, and is pleased or displeased. And yet there is the nature of instruction in it; as he that has perceived the sweet taste of honey, knows much more about it, than he who has only looked upon and felt it" (Edwards, *Religious Affections* 272). Sensible knowledge is one form of judgments of affectivity. Note the resemblance to Newman's distinction between real and notional assent: John Henry Newman, *A Grammar of Assent* (New York: Doubleday, 1955) chap. 4.

41. Hauerwas argues that no universal account of human virtue can be given since the virtues are distinctively ordered and defined by the traditions which form them. While I agree with the penetration of virtue by a narrative tradition, I believe that some general descriptions of specific virtues can have cross-cultural intelligibility. Judgments of rationality are possible about virtues, even if they fall short of the description of character necessary to embody these skills. See Hauerwas, *Truthfulness and Tragedy* (Notre Dame: Univ. of Notre Dame, 1977) chaps. 3 and 4.

42. Saliers, *Soul in Paraphrase* 66.

43. James M. Gustafson, *Can Ethics Be Christian?* (Chicago: Univ. of Chicago, 1975) 92. "How one lives morally is related to these senses, and their accom-

panying tendencies in a moral direction, not only in terms of what persons and communities do, but also in terms of their perspectives on life, their perceptions of what is morally significant about events, their deliberations and their motivations" (ibid. 94). See also Gustafson, *Ethics from a Theocentric Perspective* 1 (Chicago: Univ. of Chicago, 1981) 197–204.

44. Niebuhr, *Responsible Self* 155.
45. Edwards, *Religious Affections* 282. Edwards' admission of this spontaneous awareness of what is to be done is surprising, given his consistent suspicion of "enthusiasm" or direct divine inspiration of particular content.
46. "Any singular moral judgment is a judgment by way of inclination and it will be a good one if I am inclined to what is my true good" (Ralph McInerny, "Maritain and Poetic Knowledge," *Renascence* 34 [1982] 207). The proviso is crucial, because the vicious person will have knowledge which is affectively connatural to the vicious principles that dominate his or her character.
47. See Edwards, *Religious Affections* 387, on the necessary convergence between the affections and the moral standards of the gospel.
48. Rahner, *Dynamic Element* 154. Although he analyzes with his usual care the words of Ignatius to describe the affections of that "consolation" which is the sign of the Spirit, he fails to attend to the fuller matrix of affective criteria which the previous meditations on the life of Christ have established. Not only the goals of one's aspirations need to be in harmony with these dispositions, but also the means which one proposes to use to attain these goals. Since we rarely reach our goals, our lives become morally stamped by the means we live with. The means need to justify our ends.

45

Moral Discernment in the Christian Life

James M. Gustafson

I. The Notion of Discernment

The practical moral question is asked in various ways. Sometimes it is, "What ought we to do?" Or, if one chooses to relax the imperative and accentuate the indicative, it is, "What are we to do?" When such ways of asking the question are scrutinized, it becomes clear that the words "ought" and "are" carry a heavy load of freight. There is not only the relative moral weight or authority implied by each, the degree of obligation that each suggests, but also an unexplored process of moral judgment-making. Indeed, the polemics out of which this book emerges have attended primarily to those processes. Most of the polemics in Christian ethics have been about *how Christians ought to make judgments*. They ought to use rules in a highly rational way, or they ought to exercise their graced imaginations, or they ought to obey the tradition of the Church, or they ought to respond to the situation of which they are a part. Not enough work has yet been done by either philosophers or theologians on just how people actually do make moral judgments, though the variously propagated "oughts" claim some validation on the basis that each is correlated with what people actually do.

I wish to suggest that the practical moral question of what we ought or are *to do* be held in abeyance in its strongest existential moral sense; and that it would be fruitful to look more carefully at how we *discern* what we ought to do, or are to do. Moral agents exercise some discrimination in making judgments, and it is this exercise of discrimination that I wish to explore. Such exploration is not done on the basis of a sampling of opinion; I have not approached a cross-section of men, not even a cross-section of Christians, with a schedule of questions to find out how they actually discern what to do. Nor does this exploration lead to a full-blown theory of the relations of motives, affections, rationality, and other aspects of moral selfhood as these

This article is excerpted from Gene Outka and Paul Ramsey, eds. Norm and Context in Christian Ethics *(New York: Scribners, 1968) 17–36.*

have engaged the attention of moral philosophers in the past. I am not proposing that what seems to me to be involved in moral discernment is something that can be packaged, delivered, and taught to people who wish to become more moral. Nor am I suggesting the absence of wide variations in the ways in which people discern what they are to do; obviously some men are more emotive in their responses, some more intuitive, some more rational.

My intention is more limited. It is based on the following rudimentary observations. Persons of moral seriousness do exercise discrimination in making judgments. They discern what they are or ought to do. Discrimination, or discernment, takes place not only in moral experiences but in other areas of human experience as well, such as esthetic experience. Common speech uses the adjective "discerning" with reference to persons who seem to be more perceptive, wiser, more discriminating than others are in judging, whether the object judged is a performance of a symphony, a person and his behavior, a political situation, or a novel. Thus by exploring the uses of the word "discern," we might be able to see what goes into moral judgments, and particularly into moral judgments that seem to have a quality of excellence.

In one usage, to discern something is simply to see that it is there; indeed, this kind of visual use of the word is the least qualitative, or value-laden. When I am driving in a fog, I might say to my companion, "I dimly discern the white line that divides the lanes." I do not see it with unusual accuracy; I am not making a qualitative judgment about what I see; I am using the word simply to indicate that I can see the line. Perhaps more commonly we use the verb "discern" to indicate a particular accuracy in perception or observation. Often we

use it when we can locate a detail that misses the perception of others. Often we use it when some subtle shading or coloring registers on us. In accord with such use, we might call a person "discerning" who has an unusual capacity to isolate significant detail, to perceive subtleties, to be penetrating and accurate in his observations. While in one sense, to discern something is simply to notice it, to see it, in another sense we reserve the word for a quality of perception, of discrimination, of observation and judgment.

It is this quality of perception, discrimination, observation and judgment that is involved when we speak of a "discerning person" or of "discerning comments" in various realms of discourse. As one who has to read hundreds of letters of recommendations for admission to graduate school, and who has to live with admissions based upon such letters, I have come to regard certain persons who write letters regularly as being "discerning." I do not mean that they give the most detailed descriptions of the candidates, nor that they simply notice the most obvious things about them. I mean that they seem to be able to get at salient characteristics of the students that have great importance in assisting me to make my judgment about them. There is an accuracy to their descriptions and their judgments that is borne out over time; they have an eye for pertinent characteristics (pertinent to what it takes, for example, to be a good graduate student). They enable me to have some understanding of the student; I can begin to draw my own "portrait" of him. This is more than a picture of a man of twenty-four who achieved a high academic record at Princeton University, and is interested in further study of ethics. By the letter writer's discernment of the qualities of mind, spirit, and character of the man, I can grasp some of his significant features, what his strengths and weaknesses are. I rely on the discerning letters of discerning men to help me make my judgment of what I ought to do with reference to the admission of a student to graduate school.

The same sort of process occurs in other areas of experience. Good literary critics are the most "discerning" ones. The difference between the good schoolboy type of writer on literature, who does all his homework (research) and writes up accurate summaries of what he has read, and the writer who moves the discussion to another stage is one of a quality of discernment. The discerning critic helps the reader to "see" things in the literature that he might not see on his own; he helps the reader to perceive some of the subtlety of the writer's words, characters, or plots; he helps him to understand what the writer's intention is in the way in which he concretely organizes his details. The same would be involved in distinctions between types of people who go to art museums. There are the clods who pace through the rooms with nothing registering upon their consciousnesses other than the fact that at the museum they saw works by Rembrandt and Picasso, about whom everyone who reads the newspapers knows something. At the other extreme are the discerning students, who not only are open to the impressions that a painting makes upon them, but sense the significance of detail, of the arrangement of color patterns, of lines, and all other aspects of the work. The discerning observer can not only say, "I don't like that one," but he can give some reasons for his judgment that express more than his feelings, that have some objectivity to him.

By reading the works of discerning critics of art and literature my own capacities for making judgments are deepened and broadened. I begin to "see" what is involved in accurate observation so that my own perceptions of the text or the painting are altered. I learn to be more discriminating in my own judgments. Presumably my judgments will be "better," at least to the extent of being more informed. I will be less likely to miss salient points I had missed before; I will become more "sensitive" to nuances, to details and their suggestive meanings, to the structure and wholeness of the piece at hand.

What seems to be involved in the quality of discernment toward which the foregoing paragraphs point? This question might best be answered by indicating what seems not to be involved, indeed, what is excluded. First, a person who has a scheme for analysis that he woodenly and mechanically imposes on whatever he observes would probably not be called a "discerning" person. The tourist who visits art museums with one checklist of things that he ought to look at, and another of the things he ought to look for in what he looks at, would hardly at that stage of his life receive the appellation "discerning." Checklists and wooden schemes of analysis cannot attend to the subtle nuances that are involved in refined discriminations; they seem to stress the more universal elements found in all objects of a given class, rather than the particularities to be appreciated in a single representative of what might be a class. Although they may help the novice to avoid gross errors, such schemes seem to be "external," that is, imposed from the outside on both the observer and that which he observes. They do not in themselves have or require the qualities of empathy, appreciation, imagination, and sensitivity that seem to be involved in discerning perception and judgment.

Thus, also, in moral experience, someone might suggest that in making a judgment the agent ought to keep in mind a scheme that includes the following six things: the potential consequences, the variety of his motives, the moral maxims accepted by his community, the empirical data about the situation as he defines it, the love of God, and the moral order of the universe as understood by reason. A person who has to make a moral judgment might run his dilemma through such a scheme with several possible results. He might be more confused after than before. He might try to "add up" all these considerations and find that their sum is far from a judgment. Or he might find that the scheme usefully points him in a direction, and then simply follow the direction. But the critic would probably say that each of these ways of making a judgment is wooden, mechanical, external, and certainly not discerning.

Second, the person who has formulated a set of first principles, has refined his understanding of deductive logic so that he can move from the universal to the particular, and has consequently determined on a rational basis what conduct is right and good, might not be viewed as a man of moral discernment. He might be called a man of intellectual discernment on the grounds of his virtuosity in formulating the universal principles and by the authority of his deductive logic. But since moral judgments involve more than the arrangement of ideas to each other in a logical and orderly way, in actual practice such a person might not demonstrate the perceptiveness that helps one to be aware of the complexity of the details of a particular instance. Indeed, if he assumes that his intellectual virtuosity is sufficient for making a moral judgment, he has to classify the case at hand, that is, attend less to its unique elements and accentuate those it has in common with others, in order to proceed. Intellectual clarity and the use of critical reflection are involved in moral discernment, just as they are involved in discerning criticisms or discerning descriptions in response to works of art, but in themselves they are not sufficient to exhaust what we normally include in the notion of discernment.

Third, the person who is skilled in accumulating the relevant information pertaining to a subject is not necessarily a discerning judge. All teachers know instances of students who are admirably exhaustive in their bibliographical preparation, are assiduous in reading with comprehension the important treatises on the subject, and are even orderly in arranging this material and reasonably clear in writing it up, but who are not really discerning students of the subject. "Discernment" seems to be appropriate for pointing to the ability to distinguish the important from the unimportant information and the insightful interpretations from the uninsightful. It refers to the ability to perceive relationships between aspects of the information that enable one to see how it all fits together, or how it cannot fit together. It refers to the ability to suggest inferences that can be drawn from the information, and thus to an imaginative capacity. One can find sociological studies, for example, that seem to be exhaustive in the accumulation of the data pertinent to the topic under research but are of limited value because the researcher lacked discriminating judgment and imagination. So it is in the sphere of moral judgments. Accurate accumulation of relevant information about a matter that is the object of moral judgment is indispensable, but such accumulation in itself does not constitute a discerning moral decision. The raw data for making judgments might be gathered, but the act of judgment itself involves more capacities than are required simply to pull relevant information together. Or, one can find biographies that are encyclopedic accumulations of objective data about the man involved, but do not enable the reader to penetrate in any way into the "character" of the subject, that do not give a coherent "picture" of the man so that he can be understood and not just known about.

Fourth, one might find persons who are articulate in giving their emotive and expressive reactions to a subject. By feeling deeply about something they are able to give an immediate reaction to its presence. But the reaction may be much more the expression of their indignation or their inordinate admiration than a discerning account of what was worthy of approval or disapproval, what was good or bad in the subject. The first hearing of music from India, for example, might evoke a judgment that it is unbearable, or that it is fascinating. Neither would be considered a discerning judgment, for neither would give reasons for the reaction. Whether it is the rhythm that either fascinates or repels, or the tonal qualities of the sitar, or the absence of Western style of harmony, would be matters that would be developed in a discerning judgment. Similarly in moral matters, the expressive ejaculation of approval or disapproval in itself is not a discerning moral judgment. Nor would response in action that was based only on the depth of one's sense of indignation or love necessarily be a discerning response. Some disinterestedness, some accuracy of knowledge, some reflective awareness of what the situation entailed beyond what is immediately present would be ingredients of a more discerning response. Some thoughtful discrimination between the values that compete for actualization, between the possible consequences of possible courses of action, would be likely to occur if the judgment were to be called "discerning."

Fifth, stubborn allegiance to a given basis for making a judgment hardly makes for discerning judgment. Moralistic critics of literature provide interesting examples here. All literature that uses profanity, that talks about sexual relations in four-letter words, or that details the accounts of homosexual or heterosexual relations has often been condemned as "bad." And the use of the word "bad" has seemed indiscriminately to include both moral and nonmoral (e.g., literary) values. The critic who makes such judgments may have a palpable consistency that gives him the appearance of integrity, of being a man who is clear about his principles of judgment. But such stubborn allegiance to such principles hardly enables him to have an appreciation for the varieties of values that might be present in a book, for the significance of the concrete and the detailed, for the cumulative effect of the character portrayals or the plot development. Discernment seems to require some sensitivity and flexibility, some pluralism of consideration that is *a priori* ruled out by dedicated allegiance to single principles of interpretation or criticism. Similarly, in moral experience, the person who has a highly visible integrity based upon stubborn dedication to one or two principles, values, or rules, is not likely to be discriminating in a complicated situation. His responses may be predictable, but they are not thereby discerning.

These remarks about what seems not to be part of "discerning" judgments all pertain to a quality of excellence in discrimination. By indicating what the discerning person (in a qualitative sense) may not be and do, perhaps we can get at the elements of a discernment both in a more descriptive sense of Everyman as a moral discerner, and in a more normative sense of what excellence in discernment is. Some of the same elements are involved in the discernment of the morally flat-footed clod and the moral virtuoso. When these can be enumerated, perhaps one can see what combinations and accents among them make for excellence.

Discernment of what one ought to do, even among the clods, no doubt involves a perception of what is morally fitting in the place and time of action. What is fitting is decided differently by different people: some attack a problem in a disinterested manner, with great objectivity involved in their collection of appropriate information, their use of generalized prescriptive principles or articulated values, and their careful assessments of possible consequences of alternative courses of action. Others are more passionate; they feel deeply about what the actual situation is, they trust their built-in compasses to guide them, and they express their courage and initiative in taking the risks involved in action. What is fitting is discerned with reference to some of the same things and some different things, and different valences are existentially placed on different things by different people. Some are more determined by emotions, and value their moral sensitivities highly; others distrust emotions, and value their moral reflection highly. But perhaps some of the same things are present in both flat-footed and virtuoso performances in each style.

What are the common elements in all moral discernment? Perhaps several. There is a "reading" of what actually is the case at hand. Sometimes this reading is simply a visual image of an event that evokes decision and action. Sometimes it is a highly researched reading. Sometimes it is checked against other readings; sometimes it is idiosyncratic. Sometimes there is a depth of interpretation: some will want to know how the case got to be what it is, what are the relations of various elements to each other, who among the participants is most important or has more at stake, what the pliable factors are, what patterns and structures are there, and how it differs from similar cases. Sometimes there is no desire to interpret

in a sophisticated way; sometimes there is no time to do so. The reading is from a perspective; this is important. Because the perspectives of moral participants differ, some see certain aspects to which others are blind; different persons accent the importance of different aspects; and in some persons there is simply suppression of factual matters that are abrasive to the moral predispositions. We have seen the importance of perspectives in "factual" judgments in the arguments about what really is the case in Vietnam. Sometimes the case is read more complexly because the moral discerner understands the situation and its participants to be part of an extensive pattern of relationships to other situations and other persons; sometimes it is read more simply because the time and space box in which it is seen is limited. Even different "situationists" differ on what the situation is. But for clod and virtuoso alike moral discernment involves such a reading of the case, an assessment of pertinent facts.

It is persons who discern; and persons have histories that affect their discernment. Some have never been seriously challenged to examine the bases of their judgments; others are highly self-critical and introspective. Some have developed characters on the basis of critical evaluations of past experiences and of the exercise of their initiative in becoming what they are throughout their personal moral histories. Others have more or less bounced morally through life, accumulating the effects of one occasion or episode after the other without a sense of self-direction. Some have acute senses of justice and injustice by virtue of having been the victims of oppression, or by virtue of being members of groups that have histories of being oppressed. Others are blithely confident about the goodness of men and the world because the world and men have been blithely supportive to them. Some are committed to getting all that they can out of life for themselves, and will discern what they ought to do in the light of that commitment; others are committed to loving the neighbor and meeting his needs because they have a religious loyalty that makes them believe this is how life ought to be lived. Several things have thus been suggested about the persons who discern: they are persons of persistent moral dispositions, or the absence thereof, and some have different persistent dispositions from others. They are persons of certain moral sensitivities or sensibilities, or the absence thereof, and some have different "feelings" from others. They are persons of certain commitments or the absence thereof, and some have different commitments from others. Moral discernment in a particular occasion is determined in part by these aspects of the self. These other-than-rational aspects of selfhood partially determine perspective, partially determine what is seen and accented, partially determine what is judged to be right and wrong, and thus what one will do.

Most persons who make moral judgments live by some beliefs, rules, and moral principles that enter into their discernment. They are members of communities that have rules of conduct and some power of sanction in enforcing them. Thus, most people decide not to steal something from a store when they go shopping, for there are rules against this, and potential disruptive consequences if they should be caught stealing. Most people discern that they ought to assist someone who is suffering not merely because the observation of the suffering of others makes them feel bad, but because the "golden rule" or the principle of meeting the neighbor's need readily applies. There are not only principles, rules, and values to which men are committed that partially determine their moral discernment; there is also usually some rational reflection about how these function at least in the instances where the normal habituated responses seem not to apply readily. Both the moral clod and the virtuoso are likely to be able to give some principles that will justify their judgments, and are likely to be willing to show that they arrived at the judgment on the basis of some rational discrimination. Some men will give intellectually sophisticated justifications, indicating their reasons for selecting some principles and not others as applicable to the case at hand, and defending the principles that are applicable. Others might simply appeal to the generalized expectations of a given society of which they are a part, or appeal to the authority of an institution, such as the Church, which has taught them the principles by which they live, and supports them in their use of those principles.

Many other elements could be adumbrated either as extensions of those described, or in addition to them. At the minimum, however, discernment involves a reading of the case at hand, an expression of what constitutes the character and perspective of the person, and some appeals to reason and principles both to help one discern and to defend what one discerns. Excellence in moral discernment perhaps involves various combinations of these. There is a discriminating and accurate reading of the situation, and an understanding of the relations of elements of the situation to each other, and of its relations to other situations. There is a stipulation of the more and less important factors, and empathy for its "inner" character as well as a description of its external character. There is a refined moral sensitivity that registers subtle nuances not only of fact but of value, that is not just emotion or sentiment, but appears to contribute to the perception of what one ought to do. Moral sensitivity seems to contribute in the "discerning" moral man an intuitive element that leads to accuracy in moral aim, judiciousness in evaluation, and compelling authenticity in deed. Just as discerning critics of art know much about art, so the discerning moral man often knows much about morality. He can think clearly about potential consequences and applicable principles; he knows something of the range of values that might compete with or support each other, and he can discriminate between alternative courses of action. He is likely to have a clear head, to be able to argue with himself and others before a judgment is made, and give good reasons for it afterward.

The discerning act of moral discernment is impossible to program, and difficult to describe. It involves perceptivity, discrimination, subtlety, sensitivity, clarity, rationality, and accuracy. And while some men seem to have it as a "gift of the gods," others achieve it by experience and training, by learning and acting. It is probably more akin to the combination of elements that go into good literary criticism and good literary creativity than it is to the combination of elements that make a good mathematician or logician; it is both rational and affective. How we discern what we ought to do, whether we be morally flat-footed clods or moral virtuosos, is a complex process indeed.

II. Moral Discernment in the Christian Life

The human processes of discernment are no different among Christians than they are among other men. There are the moral clods and the moral virtuosos among Christians; nothing can guarantee that because a man has

faith in God whom he believes to have been disclosed in Jesus Christ he will be a man of excellence in moral discernment. Nor does the morally discerning Christian have different faculties or capacities that other men are deprived of because they happen not to be Christians. No special affective capacities, logic, or rational clarity can be claimed by Christians as possessions they have by virtue of their faith. Whatever the gifts of grace are, they function in and through the human capacities of discernment that are probably fairly evenly distributed throughout all mankind. Whatever "newness" there is in the Christian life is not a replacement of insufficient moral sensitivity with more sufficient, insufficient rational clarity with more sufficient. All this, however, is not to say that moral discernment in the Christian life ought not to be different, cannot be different, and sometimes is not different. Just what some of these differences ought to be, can be, and are is the subject matter of the remainder of this chapter.

There is a text from St. Paul's Letter to the Romans that makes a good starting point for discussion of this subject.

> I implore you by God's mercy to offer your very selves to him: a living sacrifice, dedicated and fit for his acceptance, the worship offered by mind and heart. Adapt yourselves no longer to the pattern of this present world, but let your minds be remade and your whole nature be transformed. Then you will be able to discern the will of God, and to know what is good, acceptable, and perfect.
> *Romans 12:1-2* (NEW ENGLISH BIBLE)

Although this passage will not be exegeted in detail, it is suggestive not only of substantive themes of morality in the Christian life, but also of what changes might be registered in moral discernment. I shall use it at least as a starting point for further discussion.

We might characterize the Christian's obligation to answer the practical moral question, "What ought or are we to do?" in the following way. *Man is to discern what God enables and requires him to do.* Full explication of this sentence would require a book-length exposition of Christian ethics; here I merely suggest various lines that such exposition would take.

What is said about discerning what God enables and requires man to do is not presumed to be a description of how any one Christian does this, or how some "mean" or average Christian constructed out of a sample of all Christians does it. It is clearly said in a mode that suggests that something like it is appropriate normatively, and possible actually.

Christians have a particular stance, or perspective. They stand in a particular relationship which in turn affects their self-understandings, their perceptions and interpretations of the world, and they have certain norms by which they discriminate what is right and good. In St. Paul's language, they are a people who have offered themselves up to God; they are living sacrifices dedicated and fit for His acceptance; mind and heart are offered to God in devotion and in praise. This language suggests that something more is involved than the claim that Christians are people who hold certain ideas or propositions to be meaningful or true. It suggests that Christians are not people who are distinguished from others simply by their belief in a set of propositions about God, and by inferences they draw from those propositions about what man is and what his relationship to God and other men also is. Mind and heart are

offered to God; their "very selves" are given to him. A particular relationship of man's personal existence to God is implored by the apostle. It is not only belief that certain things are worthy of acceptance intellectually, but conviction and trust that it is appropriate to rely upon God and to give oneself in this reliance and its consequent service. Christians are, by virtue of this faith, in a particular position; they have by virtue of this faith a particular perspective. Just as my sons are different from my neighbor's sons partly because of their filial relations to me that are different from the filial relations other sons have to their own fathers, so Christians are different because of the relationship in which they exist to God in whom they believe and trust. Just as the understandings which my sons have of themselves are partially determined by the relationship in which they exist to me, so Christians' understandings of themselves are partially determined by the relationship in which they exist to God. Just as the perspectives my sons have on the world of which they are a part is partially determined by their relationship to me, so also are the Christians' by their relationship to God. Just as my sons "see" and interpret life around them partially under this perspective determined by their relation to me, so Christians interpret the world around them from the perspective of their faith in God.

Thus one impact of Christian faith as it affects moral discernment involves the self-understanding that it evokes and directs. If I dedicate myself to be fit for the acceptance of God in whom I believe, I will consciously intend to live in such a way that my words and deeds are worthy of Him. If I frequently offer my mind and heart to Him worshipfully, I will be renewed in this self-understanding as one who depends upon Him, who is grateful to

Him, who seeks to be consistent with what He gives and requires of me. The situation is parallel in structure to the self-understandings of others who have offered themselves, so to speak, to other objects of commitment. The devotee of the *Playboy* way of life has a self-understanding that is determined in part by his devotion to the symbols of that way of life, to the values that are pointed to by these symbols. He will see himself to be "sophisticated" and "cool"; he will value highly the gratification of his desires for a maximum of pleasure; he will intend to live in a way that is consistent with his self-understanding, which in turn is evoked and directed by *Playboy*. To put it simply, Christians will answer the question, "Who am I?" differently by virtue of their faith.

Just as one's interpretation of oneself is altered by Christian faith, so one's interpretation of the world around him is altered. Interpretations are informed by perspectives; indeed what one discerns to be important in his perception of the world around him is informed by his perspective. As I have indicated elsewhere,[1] the notion of perspective in matters of moral assessment is analogous to its use in matters of visual experience. Some things are seen clearly and some are shadowed by the perspective of the observer. Some are accented and others are diminished in the impressions that they register. Perspective and self-understanding both make one more sensitive to some things and less sensitive to others. The national leader whose obligation is clearly and primarily to the self-interest of his nation is likely to "read the situation" of Vietnam, or some other one, differently from the person who views his obligation to be primarily to a universal God of love who wills the well-being of all men. The former understands himself to be one who exercises power for the

sake of the interests of the nation; the latter understands himself to be one who is the servant of Jesus Christ. (I shall not deal here with the nest of issues that are involved in such a case as one who in a position of political judgment seeks to exercise his power as both a member of a nation and a Christian. The two "selves" are not necessarily either in irresolvable conflict or in perfect harmony.) Certain "facts" have greater importance from one perspective than from the other. Both might observe the same human suffering, but interpret its significance differently because one is viewing things from the perspective of national interest and the other from the perspective of redeeming love. The significance of what is going on is determined by the perspectives of those who see it and participate in it.

Surely H. Richard Niebuhr was getting at this when he suggested that "interpretation" is part of "responsibility." Interpretation is "in the light of" some things that are particular and thus partially constitute the perspective of the interpreter. Thus Christians interpret what is going on in the light of their beliefs about God, and what men and the world are and are to be before Him. Differences of opinion among Christians in their moral discernment are not only affected by differences in the data that they might have available, but also by differences in their understanding of what the "light" of the gospel is, and what it illuminates about the world and the self. (It is not our task in this chapter to enter into that technical theological realm where these differences of the latter sort are to be adjudicated.) In spite of differences, there are certain common elements. Christian affirmations about the goodness of God and the goodness of the world He created, the reign of God in the preservation of that which He created, the willful unfaith and disobedience of men, the redemptive purpose of God to reconcile the world to Himself, the hope of a consummation of all things in the coming Kingdom of God, the judgment of God on human disorder, and other affirmations, are part of the "light" that Christians bring to bear upon their interpretation of the world. At another level there are things believed about man: men are created to live together in order and in love, they are to seek each other's good, their lives are to be sustained and not oppressed or destroyed, they are to live in gratitude to God and to others for life and loving care, they are to respect each other, etc. Such assertions are related both to the gospel and to normal human experience; they become "lights" that help Christians understand both what is to be affirmed in the world and what is to be sought for the world.

The perspective of the Christian affects what he values; it gives direction to the moral ends that he seeks, to the longings and desires that he has, to the preferences that he articulates in word and deed. Valuations and preferences are by no means always the result of a conscious reflective process in which certain "values" are defined, judged, and determined to be worthy of acceptance, then in turn applied in rational discrimination to the interpretation of the world in which men live. Christians do not always first engage in a process of defining "love," which by tradition and experience they value highly, and then use this definition to engage in a rational process of interpretation of events in the world in the light of love. (It is clearly the task of the person whose vocation is theological and ethical thinking in the Christian community to engage in such deliberate, careful thinking, more than it is the task of every Christian.) Rather, Christians may have perspectives that are formed in their faith and belief in a God of love, who has demonstrated His love for man in creation, and in His forgiveness and renewal of life, who enables men to love one another as they have been loved, and who wills that men should love each other. This "loving" perspective is likely to color the things that Christians value and approve of in their perception, interpretation, and choices in the world. That which restores and brings life and joy is to be preferred to that which destroys and brings death and suffering and pain, for example. Not only in his rational discriminations, but in his moral sensitivities, the Christian is likely to be sensitive to oppression and injustice, to physical and mental suffering. Christians are likely to interpret not only what is the case, but what ought to be the case in the light of valuations that are determined by the perspective or posture of their faith.

The process of interpretation that is part of discernment is, as I have suggested, an expression of fundamental dispositions that are shaped in part by the faith and trust Christians have as they offer themselves up to God. Their sensibilities are colored by their faith and its perspective. But it is also, as has been suggested, a matter of using articulated and expressed beliefs. Both are part of the moral discernment of Christians. If Christians are to discern what God enables and requires them to do, they are involved in rational discrimination as well as sensible response. Just as I am more likely to do what is acceptable to my sons if I *know* what their needs and desires are, so I am more likely to do what is acceptable to God if I have some knowledge about what God seems to require and enable. Part of my response to my sons' needs is a matter of understanding based upon the human relationship that has been formed between us, with all the nuances of feeling and affection, of intuitive insight and perception. Part of it is a matter of thinking clearly and rationally about what they need in the light of who they are, the resources available to meet their needs, the ways in which they may not understand their needs any more clearly than I do, and the kind of order of life it takes for us to live together with some harmony and joy.

It is under this latter aspect of stipulated convictions and rational reflection that moral discernment in the Christian life uses dogma, moral principles formed in Scripture and the tradition, moral rules of the Christian community, and refined moral argumentation. If I am to discern what God enables and requires, I must be able to say some things about God. Thus the understanding and formed convictions that Christians have about God are important for the way in which they discern things morally, and what they actually discern to be morally appropriate. Variations are many, and changes both within the tradition and in the beliefs of an individual man occur through time. Some aspects of Christian belief are stressed on one occasion, others on another, and elements of belief are combined and recombined in particular times and places so that different themes are accented and muted. Sometimes we recall more cogently God as the awesome judge of human evil, sometimes God the redeemer of the world, sometimes God the restrainer of men who wills that order persist, sometimes God the just and merciful who wills a disruption of an unjust order.

Moral discernment, then, has reference to belief. It is the moral agent who discerns with reference to belief what he judges God to be enabling and requiring. This statement is important, for it precludes saying that Christians are "immediately sensitive" to what God is doing in the world (Lehmann), or that they

hear in a clear and direct way what the command of God is to them (Barth). Discernment is a human act made with reference to human statements about God as these statements are forged from Scripture and from the theological tradition. Theologically, it might be said that God is enabling men to discern what God is enabling men to do; but the locus for the discernment is in the self as it relates beliefs about the God in whom it trusts to the situations in which it acts.

Moral rules and principles also play a part in the rational reflection that is part of discerning what one ought to do. Not all of them are rooted particularly in the Christian tradition, but certainly there are some that have historical origins in the Christian faith, and particular authority for Christians. Rules can be understood as having a social function and generally a social sanction in morality. They are determinations of what is definitely required and what is definitely prohibited in the community. As such they are ready and authoritative references for the man who is to discern what he ought to do in normal instances. He discerns clearly and quickly that the situation in which he is to act is one in which his behavior ought to be conformed to those rules that regulate the life of the community. Others before him have faced situations comparable to his own, and have interpreted them in such a way that it is clear that Christians ought to do very specific things on such occasions. There need be no ambiguity in discernment. Just as one need not engage in a unique process of discernment to judge that he ought to obey the traffic signals, so one need not engage in a unique process to judge that as a Christian he has the duty to respect another person as a human being. Elaborate reasons can be given for traffic rules and for the obligations that drivers and pedestrians have to obey them, but members of the civil community do not require that such reasons be given on each occasion. Elaborate theological and ethical reasons can be given for the rule that Christians must treat other persons with respect as human beings, but both because such a rule can be readily internalized and because its authority is clear and unambiguous, they can discern readily prohibited limits and required actions that are enabled and demanded of them. This is not to say that there are not situations in which reflection and interpretation is not required pertaining to how the rules apply. But it is to say that often rules have immediate applicability, and even when they do not seem to apply readily, the agent can begin with the rule (and not a series of arguments for its validity) in his discerning. For example, in the realm of sexual behavior, there has been a commonly accepted rule, "Thou shalt not commit adultery." Reasons can be given for the authority of that rule, but the rule has relative autonomy by virtue of its long usage within the Christian community so that its members do not have to face every human relationship with a man or woman who is not their marriage partner as one that offers the moral possibility of adultery. Indeed, if for various reasons a relationship suggests that adultery might be committed, Christians begin with the rule. The weight of evidence and reflection clearly has to be such as to invalidate the application of the rule in that particular instance. Exceptions to such rules are not made lightly, and the existence of exceptions is hardly evidence for the invalidity of the rule.

Moral principles function in a similar way, though perhaps they can be distinguished in some instance from rules by the absence of social sanction. Nor are they so determined by what sociologists and anthropologists have called one's status and roles in the community.

In different human situations moral principles function differently. Certainly such a principle as the commandment to love the neighbor as the self would be part of the "light" that Christians would bring to bear upon their interpretation of the general situation and also be part of their intention in acting within it. It would function to set the direction of their activity: what they do ought to be in accord with what love requires. To discern what the principle seems to enable and require places an obligation on Christians to interpret what love seems to mean, and how this meaning is applicable in the particular occasion. Moral reflection on such a general principle requires a great degree of sophistication on some occasions; on others its requirements seem to be self-evident. When sophistication is required, the Christian is involved in the process in which the situation must be defined (its proper time and space limits determined, its complex of relationships delineated, its data formulated and organized); in which other principles bearing on the case that might not be easily harmonized with the love commandment have to be stipulated and recalled, other theological reference-points that love remembered, other values than love designated, and the use of "love" itself carefully delineated so that it has some particularity and does not cover everything. He is involved in a process in which analogies from Scripture or from the moral experience of the community are rehearsed and brought to bear; in which moral sensibilities are recognized, judged, and affirmed or qualified by reflection; and in which finally a judgment is made about what God is enabling and requiring. This reflection will illumine the discernment of God's will; it will never have clear and unambiguous authority so that the reflecting man will equate his serious judgment with God's will itself. Indeed, careful reflection is necessary in discernment because of the partialities of men, and the tendency to discern what is fit and acceptable for one's own gratification or the gratification of one's own group rather than fit and acceptable to God. Reflection is necessary because Christians, like others, tend to be conformed to the expectations of their own desires and to the ethos of the time in which they live, rather than remembering that they are not to be conformed to this world.

Moral discernment always takes place within communities; the moral discernment of Christians takes place within the Christian community. The community is in part the present gathering of Christians, in a congregation or some other group, that engages in the moral discourse that informs the conscientiousness of its members through participation in moral deliberation.[2] Through moral discourse in the Christian community, both the minds and hearts of men can be trained to discernment; their capacities to make discerning moral judgments can be deepened, broadened, and extended. Such training is not an automatic accrual from hearing sermons or receiving the sacraments; if the Holy Spirit is at work in the community to make men better discerners of God's will he is present in and through the moral deliberations that occur, as well as the preached word and the bread and wine.

But the community is not only the present gathering at this time and place. Those presently gathered are part of a historical community that has lived the moral life as Christians in the past, that has reflected upon situations comparable to the present ones with references to the same gospel, and the same intention to discern God's will. This does not mean that an answer from the fourth century is the answer to the twentieth century, but it does mean that in present reflection the community

does not have to begin *de novo* as if God's will for present and future had no consistency with God's will for the past. Certain values, or principles, or points for consideration that were arranged in one combination with reference to a past situation might be rearranged and added to with reference to a present situation to the illumination and accuracy of the present community. John Noonan's *Contraception*,[3] the greatest book yet published on the history of an issue in Christian ethics, makes this point clear. Moral discernment is in continuity with the past, not discontinuity; it learns from, and is thus informed and directed without being determined by, the past. (The current celebration of the openness toward the future is proper insofar as it recognizes that the God whose will one seeks to discern for the future is the God who has willed in the past. Much of this celebration refers primarily to human *attitude* in any case, and as such is insufficient to determine what men ought to be doing in particular instances. Attitude alone does not determine act. To be open to the future is not to discern what one ought to do in it.)

Perhaps all that has been said about moral discernment is only another way of talking about the virtue of prudence. Prudence is the virtue that is both intellectual and moral; it involves reason, sensibilities, and the will. It is a virtue: it is a lasting disposition of the self that comes into being not in the moment by some inspiration of the Spirit or by some visceral response to a narrowly defined situation, but by experience, training, reflection, and action. It does not exist independent from law, although it is the capacity to perceive what law might require in a particular case, and to perceive what might be required that is more than the law demands. It is open to the concrete situation, but not in such a way that the past is ignored, as if similar situations have never occurred before. It is an exercise of character that has been formed; the formation of character is important in the whole of the moral life of which a particular discernment is but a moment in time. It is formed and informed by love, trust, hope, and other gifts of the Spirit. But it is never simply an attitude; it is a capacity to discern that uses reason and intellectual discrimination.

Prudence in the Christian life refers to the fitting judgment, response, and act. But the fitting in turn refers to what God is enabling and requiring, not just what seems to be pleasing to men. Thus the exercise of prudence, of discernment, in the Christian life is intricate and complex; it can never be programed for all men, for some are gifted in different ways from others, and some have different roles from others. Its exercise is not only in moral discrimination; it is itself offered to God in praise and devotion, in reliance upon the grace of God to empower and inform it. But it is human; man is the exerciser of prudence in reliance upon God, and in discernment of God's will.

At best, however, the Christian who is morally discerning, who has the capacity to be perceptive, discriminating, accurate, and sensitive, probably has to modify his acceptance of the words of St. Paul. He said with assurance, "Then you *will* be able to discern the will of God." I suspect that more modest claims would be more precise. By offering oneself up to God, and by formation in prudence informed by love and faith and hope, "Then you *might* discern the will of God."

Notes

1. In the last chapter of *Christ and the Moral Life* (New York: Harper & Row, 1968).
2. I have developed this theme in several other places, most concisely in "The Church: A Community of Moral Discourse," *The Crane Review,* Vol. 7, pp. 75–85, and in "The Voluntary Church: A Moral Appraisal," *Voluntary Associations,* ed. D. B. Robertson (Richmond, Va.: John Knox Press, 1966), especially pp. 313–322.
3. John T. Noonan, Jr., *Contraception* (Cambridge, Mass.: Harvard University Press, 1966).